A Handbook For Travellers In Switzerland And The Alps Of Savoy And Piedmont

A

HANDBOOK

FOR

TRAVELLERS IN SWITZERLAND, SAVOY, AND PIEDMONT.

The Editor of the HANDBOOK for SWITZERLAND, PIEDMONT, and SAVOY, is very solicitous to be favoured with corrections of any mistakes and omissions which may be discovered by persons who have made use of the book. Those communications especially will be welcomed which are founded upon personal knowledge, and accompanied by the name of the writer to authenticate them. Travellers willing to make such communications are requested to have the kindness to address them to the Editor of the HANDBOOK, care of Mr. Murray, Albemarle Street.

CAUTION TO TRAVELLERS.—By a recent Act of Parliament, the introduction into England of *foreign pirated Editions* of the works of British authors, in which the copyright subsists, is *totally prohibited.* Travellers will therefore bear in mind that even a single copy is contraband, and is liable to seizure at the English Custom-house.

CAUTION TO INNKEEPERS AND OTHERS.—The Editor of the Handbooks has learned from various quarters that a person or persons have of late been extorting money from innkeepers, tradespeople, artists, and others, on the Continent, under pretext of procuring recommendations and favourable notices of them and their establishments in the Handbooks for Travellers. The Editor therefore thinks proper to warn all whom it may concern, that recommendations in the Handbooks are not to be obtained by purchase, and that the persons alluded to are not only unauthorised by him, but are totally unknown to him. All those, therefore, who put confidence in such promises, may rest assured that they will be defrauded of their money without attaining their object.—1851.

₊ No attention can be paid to letters from Hotel-keepers in praise of their own inns ; and the postage of them is so onerous, that they cannot be received.

LONDON : PRINTED BY WILLIAM CLOWES & SONS, STAMFORD STREET, AND CHARING CROSS.

A

HANDBOOK

FOR

TRAVELLERS IN SWITZERLAND,

AND THE

ALPS OF SAVOY AND PIEDMONT.

Eighth Edition,

CORRECTED AND AUGMENTED; WITH TRAVELLING MAPS.

LONDON:

JOHN MURRAY, ALBEMARLE STREET;

PARIS: A. & W. GALIGNANI & CO.; STASSIN & XAVIER.

1858.

THE ENGLISH EDITIONS OF MURRAY'S HANDBOOKS MAY BE OBTAINED OF THE
FOLLOWING AGENTS :—

Germany, Holland, and Belgium.

AIX-LA-CHAPELLE }	I. A. MAYER.	KISSINGEN	C. JÜGEL.
AMSTERDAM .	J. MULLER.—W. KIR-BERGER.—VAN BAK-KENESS.	LEIPZIG .	F. FLEISCHER.—WEIGEL.
		LUXEMBOURG	BÜCK.
		MANNHEIM .	ARTARIA & FONTAINE.
ANTWERP .	MAX. KORNICKER.	MAYENCE .	VON ZABERN.
BADEN-BADEN	D. R. MARX.	MUNICH .	LITERARISCH - ARTISTI-SCHE ANSTALT—
BERLIN .	A. DUNCKER.		I. PALM.
BRUSSELS .	MUQUARDT. — KIESSLING & CO.—FROMENT.	NÜRNBERG .	SCHRAG.
		PEST .	HARTLEBEN.—G. HECKENAST.
CARLSRUHE .	A. BIELEFELD.		
COBLENTZ .	BAEDEKER.	PRAGUE .	CALVE.
COLOGNE .	A. BAEDEKER.—EISEN.	ROTTERDAM .	PETRI.—KRAMERS.
DRESDEN .	ARNOLD.	STUTTGART .	P. NEFF.
FRANKFORT .	C. JÜGEL.	TRIESTE .	MUNSTER.
GRATZ .	DAMIAN & SORGE.	VIENNA .	C. GEROLD.—BRAUMÜLLER.—STERNICKEL.
THE HAGUE .	VAN STOCKUM.		
HAMBURG .	PERTHES, BESSER & MAUKE.		
HEIDELBERG .	MOHR.	WIESBADEN .	C. JÜGEL.—C.W. KREIDEL.

Switzerland.

BASLE .	SCHWEIGHAUSER.—NEU-KIRCH.	LAUSANNE .	HIGNOU & CO.—WEBER.
		LUCERNE .	F. KAISER.
BERN .	DALP, HUBER, & CO.	SCHAFFHAUSEN	HURTER.
COIRE .	GRUBENMANN.	SOLEURE .	JENT.
CONSTANCE .	MECK.	ZÜRICH .	H. FÜSSLI & CO.—MEYER & ZELLER.
ST. GALLEN .	HUBER.		H. F. LEUTHOLD, POST-STRASSE.
GENEVA .	KESSMANN.—MONROE.—DESROGIS. — CHERBU-LIEZ.—GEX.		

Italy.

BOLOGNA .	M. RUSCONI.	PARMA .	J. ZANGHIERI.
FLORENCE .	GOODBAN.	PISA .	NISTRI.—JOS. VANNUCCHI.
GENOA .	ANTOINE BEUF.	PERUGIA .	VINCENZ. BARTELLI.
LEGHORN .	MAZZAJOLI.	ROME .	GALLARINI.—SPITHÖVER—PIALE.—CUCCIONI.
LUCCA .	F. BARON.		
MANTUA .	NEGRETTI.	SIENA .	ONORATO TORRI.
MILAN .	ARTARIA & SON.—DUMOLARD FRÈRES.—MOLINARI.—SANGNER.—P. & J. VALLARDI.	TRIESTE .	HERMAN F. MÜNSTER.—
		TURIN .	GIANNINI & FIORE.—MAGGI.—MARIETTI. —BOCCA FRÈRES.
MODENA .	VINCENZI & ROSSI.		
NAPLES .	DETKEN.	VENICE .	HERMAN F. MÜNSTER.
NICE .	VISCONTI.—GIRAUD.	VERONA .	H. F. MÜNSTER.
PALERMO .	CHARLES BEUF.		

France.

AMIENS .	CARON.	NANCY .	GONET.
ANGERS .	BARASSE'.	NANTES .	GUE'RAUD.—FOREST AINE'.
AVRANCHES .	ANFRAY.		
BAYONNE .	JAYMEBON.	ORLEANS .	GATINEAU.—PESTY.
BORDEAUX .	CHAUMAS.	PARIS .	GALIGNANI.—STASSIN ET XAVIER.
BOULOGNE .	WATEL.—MERRIDEW.		
BREST .	HEBERT.	PAU .	AUG. BASSY.—LAFON.
CAEN .	VILLENEUVE.	PERPIGNAN .	JULIA FRERES.
CALAIS .	RIGAUX CAUX.	REIMS .	BRISSART BINET.
DIEPPE .	MARAIS.	ROCHEFORT .	BOUCARD.
DINANT .	COSTE.	ROUEN .	LEBRUMENT.
DOUAI .	JACQUART.—LEMÂLE.	ST. ETIENNE .	DELARUE.
DUNKERQUE .	LEYSCHOCHART.	ST. MALO .	HUE.
GRENOBLE .	VELLOT ET COMP.	ST. QUENTIN .	DOLOY.
HAVRE .	COCHARD.—BOURDIGNON.—FOUCHER.	STRASBOURG .	TREUTTEL ET WURTZ.—GRUCKER.
LILLE .	VAN/CKERE.—BE'GHIN.	TOULON .	MONGE ET VILLAMUS.
LYONS .	GIBERTON & BRUN.—AYNE' FILS.	TOULOUSE .	H. LEBON.—GIMET.
		TOURS .	COUSTURIER.
MARSEILLES .	MADAME CAMOIN.	TROYES .	LALOY.
METZ .	WARION.		
MONTPELLIER .	LEVALLE.		

Spain.

MADRID .	MONIER.	GIBRALTAR .	ROWSWELL.

Russia.

ST. PETERS-BURGH }	ISSAKOFF.—N. ISSAKOFF.—BELLIZARD.	MOSCOW .	W. GAUTIER.
		ODESSA .	VILLIETTY.

Malta.	Ionian Islands.	Constantinople.	Greece.
MUIR.	CORFU. . J. W. TAYLOR.	WICK.	ATHENS. . A. NAST.

PREFACE.

FOR a very long time Switzerland was the only country in Europe which possessed a *Guide-book* worthy of the name. The excellent work of Ebel, here alluded to, indeed deserved the highest praise; and it is upon the foundation of the materials collected by him that the original edition of this work was constructed. In the subsequent editions, however, many alterations have been made; and there has been incorporated a vast quantity of additional information, derived from the editor's personal experience, from the communications of travellers, and from books; so that at present there are not many traces of the original work of Ebel. So many tourists now explore the Higher Alps, that new Routes over several high and difficult passes have been included in the later editions.

In the later Editions an Index has been prepared for the Swiss Handbook, independent of the Section relating to Savoy and Piedmont; and as each is furnished with a map, the two parts may be bound up separately for convenience, without injuring the completeness of either.

Works of Reference on Switzerland, Savoy, and Piedmont:—
Brockedon—Passes of the Alps, 2 vols. 4to.
Latrobe, C. J.—Alpenstock and Pedestrian, 8vo.
Saussure—Voyages dans les Alpes.
Forbes, Professor—Travels in the Alps of Savoy, royal 8vo. Norway.
——— Tour of Mont Blanc and Monte Rosa.
Forbes, Sir John—A Physician's Holiday, post 8vo., 1853.
History of Switzerland, by the U. K. S., 1 vol.
Müller's History of Switzerland to 1842. 14 vols.
Töpffer—Voyages en Zigzag.
Wills' Excursions in the Higher Alps.

SWITZERLAND.

INTRODUCTORY INFORMATION.

CONTENTS.

SWITZERLAND.

CONTENTS OF SECTION I.

LIST OF ROUTES.

⁎ The names of many places are necessarily repeated in several Routes; but to facilitate reference, they are printed in *Italics* only in those Routes under which they are fully described.

SECTION II.

THE ALPS OF SAVOY AND PIEDMONT.

PRELIMINARY INFORMATION.—Page 271.

SKELETON TOURS.—Page 276.

a 3

INTRODUCTORY INFORMATION.

§ 1. Passports and Custom-houses.

An Englishman must now provide himself with a Foreign-Office Passport, which can be procured (fee 2s.) at the Foreign Office by leaving or sending a letter of recommendation from any M.P. or London banker, magistrate, clergyman, solicitor, or surgeon, and calling or sending the next day for the passport. Several persons, members of one family, may be included in the same passport. The Austrian ambassador's visa is given gratis (Chandos House, Cavendish Square), and should be procured, otherwise the traveller will be absolutely unable to cross the Alps into Lombardy, &c. If the traveller proceeds through France, the French visa (office, 36, King William Street, City; fee 4s. 3d.) *must* be obtained; and if through Belgium, the Belgian (office, 52, Gracechurch Street; fee, 2s. 6d.). Neither in the Sardinian dominions, nor in Prussia, nor apparently in any of the German States upon the Rhine, nor apparently on returning by the Rhine through Belgium, is any visa required to a Foreign-Office Passport. The rule in France is, that if a traveller has left France 10 days he requires a fresh visa to re-enter it; and this rule is now always enforced. But in all matters relating to passports, much probably depends upon the caprice of the individual gendarme. The French visa in Switzerland can only be procured at the office of the Consul at Berne (fee 5 fr.). No visas are required by Switzerland, but a passport is asked for at Geneva.

The traveller should take care to procure all the visas he is even likely to want before he leaves London, as he thereby saves himself much trouble and annoyance. Those who have not time or a servant at their disposal should forward their letters of recommendation to Lee, 440, Strand, who for a small charge will procure the passports and visas, and will also mount the passport in a case, which some travellers prefer. For further information see *Handbook for the Continent*, or *Handbook for France*.

Custom-houses.—The Swiss now levy import-dues only on a few bulky articles, and no examination of passengers' luggage is made on entering or leaving the country. Examinations are made on entering the Sardinian dominions, Austria, or the German States.

§ 2. Routes to Switzerland—Skeleton Tours.

There are now several good routes by which Switzerland may be reached from London :—

  a. By Basle.
  b. By Friedrichshafen.
  c. By Neuchâtel.
  d. By Geneva.

a. BASLE may be reached —

    London to Paris 12½ hours; Paris to Basle (railway by Strasbourg or Troyes) 15 hours.

    London to Cologne (railway and steamer) 22 hours; Cologne to Mayence (steamer) 14 hours; Mayence to Basle (railway) 11 hours.

A cheaper but slower route is by Rotterdam and the Rhine.

From Basle the traveller may go—

    To Lucerne (railway).

    To Berne (railway).

    To Geneva by Bienne, Yverdun, Lausanne, &c. (railways and steamers).

    To Schaffhausen (railway and diligence).

b. FRIEDRICHSHAFEN may be reached—

    London to Cologne 22 hours; Cologne to Mayence 14 hours; Mayence to Friedrichshafen 12 hours. This is a very pleasant way of entering Switzerland. From Friedrichshafen the traveller may go to Zürich by Romanshorn (steamer and railway).

c. NEUCHATEL may be reached—

    London to Paris 12½ hours; Paris to Besançon (railway) 10 hours ; Besançon to Neuchâtel (diligence—railway in progress, by Salins) 13 hours.

d. GENEVA may be reached—

    London to Paris 12½ hours; Paris to Geneva by Macon (railway), 15 hours.

a or *b* will be adopted by those who wish to visit first Lucerne or the Bernese Oberland ; *d* by those who aim at Chamouni and Zermatt.

For the guidance of travellers, skeleton tours are here given, adapted to the convenience and taste of persons of different degrees of bodily strength, and using different modes of conveyance.

The two first tours are tolerably complete; other tours are framed so as to show what may be done within a given time ; but no sounder advice can be given to those who desire real and thorough enjoyment in travelling than carefully to abstain from doing all that can be done in the time at their disposal. The grandest scenes of nature cannot be fully apprehended at a glance, and the impression which will be retained of sublime objects seen repeatedly, and under varying conditions of weather and light, will be far more prized than the crowd of imperfect images that can alone be carried away by a weary traveller in the course of an always hurried advance from one place to another.

Each traveller must, however, decide for himself the spots in which he may choose to halt, and the following outlines may conveniently be used for any portion of the alpine chain which it is desired to explore. The difficult passes are not included, as those who are able to cross them must know Switzerland tolerably well.

A.—CARRIAGE TOUR FOR PERSONS WHO DO NOT RIDE: about six weeks of leisure travelling. Those portions which cannot be traversed in an English carriage are marked as Char-road. A few easy excursions, which may be accomplished in a *chaise à porteur*, are given in italics.

Basle.	Weissenstein.
Münsterthal.	Lucerne.
Bienne.	Weggis, by steamer.

Ascend Righi, and return.
Fluëlen, by steamer.
Drive to Altorf, and return.
Lucerne, by steamer.
Thun, by Entlebuch.
Interlaken, by steamer.
Lauterbrunnen, and thence to Grindelwald, by char; returning to Interlaken.
Brienz, by steamer.
Reichenbach, by char.
Visit Giesbach, and return to Interlaken.
Thun.
Bern.
Freyburg.
Lausanne.
Geneva.
Sallenches.
Chamouni, by char.
Montanvert.
Flegère.
Return to Geneva.
Vevay, by steamer.
Chillon. (Hôtel Byron.)
Bex. (Making an excursion by char to Sepey, in the Val des Ormonds,

and returning to the high road at Aigle.
Sierre, by Martigny and Sion.
Excursion by char to the Baths of Leuk, and return to high road.
Brieg.
Domo d' Ossola, by Simplon.
Baveno.
Borromean Islands.
Luino, by boat.
Lugano.
Boat to Porlezza; thence by char to Menaggio, and by boat to Varenna or Bellagio.
Chiavenna.
Andeer, by Splügen.
Coire.
Sargans, visiting on the way the Baths of Pfeffers.
Wallenstadt.
Wesen.
Carriage to Rapperschwyl, and steamer on Lake of Zürich.
Schaffhausen.
Constance.
Friedrichshafen, by steamer.

B.—The foregoing Route may be varied by going at first from Basle to Zürich by Railway.

Horgen, Zug, and Immensee.
Ascend the Righi and descend to Weggis.
Fluëlen, by steamer.
Lucerne.
Sarnen, &c., *by the Brunig* to Reichenbach, Brientz, and Giesbach.

Interlaken.
Lauterbrunnen and Grindelwald, returning to
Interlaken.
(Thun, &c., as in preceding route.)

C.—ROUTE FOR MODERATE PEDESTRIANS, OR FOR LADIES ABLE TO RIDE, including most of the remarkable scenery of the Central Alps. Three months. It is assumed that wherever there is a good carriage-road it should be used. Excursions rather too difficult and fatiguing for ladies are given in italics.

Basle to Lucerne, by Railway; or by Schaffhausen and Zürich.
Ascend the Rigi from Weggis.
Descend to Arth.
Return to Lucerne.
By Stanz to Engelberg.
By Surenen Pass to Altdorf.

By Andermatt to Hospital.
Pass of the Furca to the Grimsel.
Excursion to the Lower Glacier of the Aar.
Baths of Reichenbach.
Pass of the Scheideck.
Faulhorn.

Grindelwald.
Excursion to the Lower Glacier of Grindelwald.
Wengern Alp to Lauterbrunnen.
Interlaken.
Excursion to the Giesbach, and return.
Thun.
Saanen, by the Simmenthal.
Vevey, by the Dent de Jaman.
Chillon, &c.
Lausanne.
Geneva.
Excursion to the Salève.
Sallenches.
Chamouni.
Montanvert.
Breven.
Jardin.
Martigny.
Orsières.
Cormayeur, by Col de Ferret.
Ascent of the Cramont.
Aosta.
Excursion to the Hospice of the St. Bernard, and return.
Châtillon.
St. Jean de Gressonay, by Brussone.
Mollia, by Riva and the Col di Val Dobbia.
Varallo.
Orta.
Excursion to the Monterone, and descend to Baveno.
Ponte Grande in the Val Anzasca, by Vogogna.
Macugnaga.
* Saas, by the Monte Moro.
St. Niklaus.
Zermatt.
Riffelberg.
Ascent to Schwarze See and *Hörnli.*

Visp, in the valley of the Rhone.
Viesch.
Ascend the Aeggischhorn.
Brieg.
Domo d'Ossola, by Simplon.
Baveno.
Borromean Isles.
Luino.
Lugano.
Excursion to Monte Salvatore.
By Porlezza and Menaggio to Bellagio, on the Lake of Como.
Varenna.
Lecco, by the Val Sassina.
Como, by the Erba.
Colico, by steamer.
Chiavenna.
Andeer, by Splügen.
Coire, by Via Mala.
Ragatz, by Pfeffers.
Wesen, by Wallenstadt.
Stachelberg.
Altdorf, by Klausen Pass.
Schwytz.
Glarus, by Muotta Thal.
St. Gall.
Rorschach.
Friedrichshafen.

   * Those who fear to undertake the Pass of the Moro are advised to return from Macugnaga to Vogogna, thence to proceed by Domo d'Ossola and the Simplon to Brieg and Visp. From Visp the valleys of Zermatt and Saas may be visited, returning to Visp; whence an excursion may be made to the Baths of Leuk and the Gemmi Pass. From Leuk by Viesch to Obergestelen; thence by the Nüfenen Pass to Airolo and Bellinzona; the steamer to Baveno on the Lago Maggiore is taken at Magadino.

D.—TOUR OF FOURTEEN OR SIXTEEN DAYS, hard travelling and fine weather.

Days.		Days.	
1	Schaffhausen. Rhine Fall. Zürich. Or	2	Rigi.
1	Friedrichshafen. Romanshorn. Zug. Or	3	Altorf. Andermatt.
1	Basle. Lucerne	4	Grimsel.
		5	Reichenbach.
		6	Grindelwald.
		7	Lauterbrunnen to Frütigen.
		8	Gemmi to Leukerbad.

Days.
9 Martigny.
10
11 } Chamouni.
12
13 Geneva.
14 Lausanne.

Days.
15 Bern.
16 Basle.

3, 4, and 5 may be shortened to one day by crossing the Brünig to Meyringen.

E.—TO AVOID THE VALAIS.

Basle.
Lucerne.
Andermatt.
Grimsel.
Brieg, by the Obergestelen.
Zermatt.
Aosta, by the St. Theodule.

Thence keeping on the S. side of the Alps across the St. Bernard,

or round Mont Blanc to Chamouni. Or,

Basle.
Lucerne.
Brientz, by the Brünig.
Kandersteg.
Visp, by the Gemmi.
Zermatt, &c.

F.—TWENTY-NINE DAYS IN SWITZERLAND, ON FOOT, during August and September, 1850.—R. W. T.

Aug.

8 { Schaffhausen.
   Rhinefalls.
   Diligence to Zürich.

9 { Town of Zürich.
   Steam to Rapperschwyl.
   Walked to Schmerikon.

10 { Walked to Wesen.
   Steam to Wallenstadt.
   Walked to Ragatz.

11 { Baths of Pfäffers ; thence over mountain to Untere-Zollbrücke, and on to Côire.

12 { Diligence to Tusis.
   Walked through Via Mala to Splügen, and over Splügen pass to Campo Dolcino, where indifferent accommodation.

13 { Walked to Chiavenna, where we were stopped on account of passports.

14 { Diligence back over the Splügen, and ditto over the Bernardin to Bellinzona.

15 { Wet day ; walked about town and neighbourhood.

16 { Walked over M. Cenere to Lugano.
   Steam to Capo Lago and back.
   Char to Magadino.

17 { Steam to Baveno.
   Walked over the Monterone, to Orta, on the Lago d'Orta.
   Char to Arona.
   Ascended statue of St. Carlo.

Aug.

18 { Walked to Stresa.
   Boat to Borromean Isles and Pallanza.
   Steam to Magadino, and diligence to Bellinzona.

19 { Midnight diligence to Faido by 7 A.M.
   Walked over the St. Gothard to Andermatt.

20 { Walked to Flüelen.
   1 P.M. Steamer to Weggis.
   Walked up Rigi to sleep.

21 { Sunrise on Rigi.
   Descended to Weggis.
   Steam (10 A.M.) to Lucerne ; saw town, and the Swiss monument.
   Walked to Winkel ; boat to Gestad.
   Walked to Sachslen.

22 { Walked over the Brünig to Meyringen, and on to Guttanen.

23 { Walked to Hospice of Grimsel, breakfasting at Handek.
   Descended to Rhone Glacier, and returned to Guttanen.

24 { Walked to Rosenlaui, turning off at Reichenbach.

25 { Walked on Rosenlaui Glacier, and over the Scheidegg to Grindelwald, visiting the Upper Glacier : thence ascended the Wengern Alp, to sleep at the "Jungfrau Gasthaus."

Aug.

26 { Descended to Lauterbrunnen; saw the Staubbach: thence on to Interlaken, and walked about shores of Lake Brienz.

27 { Walked to Neuhaus on Lake of Thun.
Row-boat to Spiez.
Walked to Kandersteg.

28 { Walked over Gemmi to Leukerbad ; visited the baths : walked to and ascended the ladders.

29 { Walked by direct path to Sion ; saw castles there ; and diligence to Martigny.

30 { Walked over Tête Noire to Chamouni.

31 { Walked to the Jardin and back (did not find it fatiguing).

Sept.

1 { Walked up Breven by footpath, 3½ hours, including ¼ hr.'s rest at Planpra.
Returned to Chamouni.
Walked to Servoz.
Char to St. Martin.

2 { Char to Geneva.
Saw town, and walked to the confluence of Arve and Rhone.

Sept.

3 { Steamer to Villeneuve.
Walked to Castle of Chillon, and on to châlets of Avants to sleep.

4 { Walked over the Jaman to Bulle.
Char to Freyburg.

{ Walked about town of Freyburg, and over 2 bridges.

5 { Char to Berne.
Saw the town.
Evening diligence to Basle.

Our proposed route from Chiavenna was to have slept same night at Colico ; then,

1st day, Lake of Como, and sleep at Como.

2nd day, Milan by railway, and back.

3rd day, Steam to Menaggio, and walk to Lugano.

4th day, Lake of Lugano, and walk to Luino.

5th day, Steam down Lago Maggiore, back to Bellinzona.

But Orta and its *lake* are well worth visiting ; also the Monterone.

§ 3. MONEY.

The coinage of Switzerland, by a decree of the Diet of 1850, has been reduced to conformity with that of France. The current money is francs and centimes, and accounts are now kept in these, the old Swiss batz being no longer a legal tender. This new and uniform coinage for the whole of Switzerland is distinguished by the word HELVETIA on the obverse, and is amongst the best in Europe.

The silver coins consist of pieces of 5 francs, 2 francs, 1 franc, and ¼ franc (50 centimes). The small coins consist of pieces of 5, 10, and 20 centimes, struck in base metal, and easier to carry than French or English copper. Centimes are sometimes called rappen. The old batz was worth 15 centimes. The old or Swiss franc was a French franc and a half.

Previously to this salutary change there was hardly a country in Europe which had so complicated a currency as Switzerland. Almost every canton had a coinage of its own, and those coins that were current in one canton would not pass in the next ; and as a change is contemplated in England, it may be interesting to know that, within six months after the new system was introduced, all trace of the old denominations was gone, except that the expression "franc de France," instead of "franc," was common. In remote districts the children begging screamed for centimes as if they had never heard of any other coin.

French Napoleons and francs, current all over Switzerland, are the best money the traveller can take with him ; but English sovereigns and bank-notes are taken at inns throughout Switzerland and on the Italian lakes, at a value of 25 francs.

A very safe method of taking money is by circular notes issued by Coutts & Co., Herries & Co., the London and Westminster Bank, and other banks, payable at all the large towns in Europe. They may be procured for any sum from 10*l.*·upwards.

On the lake of Como and in *Austrian Lombardy* zwanzigers or lire, value 8½*d.*, or 87 French centimes, are the current coin. A lira is divided into 100 centesimi : 23 zwanzigers are 20 francs.

In the *Sardinian* territories the coinage is the same as in France.

§ 4. MEASURES.—DISTANCES.—ELECTRIC TELEGRAPH SYSTEM.

In 1848 by the New Federal Constitution it was decreed that the *Swiss foot* should consist of 30 centimètres, or $\frac{3}{10}$ths of a French mètre :—that 16,000 of these feet should go to a *Swiss league* = 2 Eng. miles, 7 furlongs, 190 yards = 2·983 Eng. miles :—4800 mètres, or 23$\frac{1}{4}$ Swiss leagues, to a degree. A Swiss post is 3 Swiss leagues = 9 Eng. miles, nearly.

Upon this authentic basis the measurement of distances on the roads of Switzerland has been commenced, and league-posts have been partially erected.

An *official Post Office Directory* (Kursanzeiger ; Indicateur des Services Suisses) of the public conveyances, *Distances*, &c., between the principal towns of Switzerland has been published at Bern. See also the *New Post Map* of Switzerland published under direction of General Dufour, Winterthur.

1 mètre . . .	=	3·281 Eng. feet	= 3 feet 3 inches, nearly.
1 kilomètre . .	=	0·621 Eng. mile	= 3-5ths or ·5-8ths of a mile, nearly.
1 French foot .	=	1·066 Eng. foot	= 1 foot 1 inch, nearly.
1 French league	=	2·422 Eng. miles	= 2½ miles, nearly.
1 Swiss league .	=	2·983 Eng. miles	= 3 miles, nearly.
Old Swiss stunde	=	3·28 Eng. miles	= 3¼ miles, nearly.
1 Swiss arpent .	=	0·89 Eng. acres	= 9-10ths of an acre, nearly.
1 Swiss pound .	=	1·102 lb. avoird.	= ½ Fr. kilog. = 1 lb. 1 oz. nearly.
1 Piedmont mile	=	1·503 Eng. mile	= 1½ mile and 57 yards.
1 German mile .	=	4·6 Eng. miles	= 4½ miles, nearly.

Table of KILOMETRES reduced to English miles, &c.

Kilom.	Eng. Miles.	Fur-longs.	Yds.	Ft.	In.	Kilom.	Eng. Miles.	Fur-longs.	Yds.	Ft.	In.
1	0	4	213	1	11	8	4	7	169	0	4
2	1	1	207	0	10	9	5	4	162	2	3
3	1	6	200	2	9	10	6	1	156	1	2
4	2	3	194	1	8	20	12	3	92	2	4
5	3	0	188	0	7	30	18	5	29	0	6
6	3	5	181	2	6	40	24	6	185	1	8
7	4	2	175	1	5	50	31	0	121	2	10

To convert approximately French feet, in which the heights of mountains are usually given on the maps, into English feet, add 1-15th.

The distances in this work have been reduced to English miles, which are always to be understood wherever the word *mile* alone is used.

To calculate the distance along the mountain-paths is almost hopeless. In this work, therefore, the distances along the mountain-paths have been reckoned as the natives reckon them, in *hours*, meaning thereby the distance which a mule or a loaded man usually travels in an hour; and this is to be understood whenever the word *hour* alone is used.

The hour of course varies according to the nature of the ground. In very steep ascents it does not exceed 2 miles, in lesser acclivities $2\frac{1}{2}$ miles; but on the mountains it is *never more* than $2\frac{1}{2}$ miles. It has been ascertained by an experienced Alpine traveller that to clear 2 miles an hour up a steep mountain requires *very* good walking. An active walker will gain 5 or 10 minutes an hour on mules during an ascent, and still more on the descent; but persons not accustomed to exertion, or unused to mountain work, will find difficulty in keeping up with the mules when the ascent is very steep. The mules are nearly as long on the descent as on the ascent.

The sudden and almost simultaneous establishment of the *electric telegraph* along all the great high roads of the country was very remarkable. There is now scarcely a second-rate town or village that is not thus connected; and from any of them a message not exceeding 20 words can be sent for the *small charge* of *one franc* to any part of Switzerland. Luxurious or anxious travellers can thus, before starting in the morning, secure quarters for the night, or even order their dinner beforehand. The mode of arranging the wire is excessively primitive and economical, but seems to be effectual. It is stated that the insulation of the wires is not affected by their being covered with snow, and in many instances they are in contact with the foliage of trees.—It is singular and striking to see the telegraphic wires stretched from rock to rock along the pathless shores of the lake of Lucerne, and surmounting the steep ascent and gloomy solitudes of the Gries and other Alpine Passes. The central office of the Telegraph is at Berne.

§ 5. MODES OF TRAVELLING IN SWITZERLAND.—POSTING.

The means of travelling in Switzerland have been greatly improved and increased within the last 30 years. The high roads are excellent, and those over the Alps stupendous in addition. Where railways are not made, diligences run; and since 1823, when the first experiment with steam was made on the Lake of Geneva, every one of the large lakes is navigated by steamboats.

Posting is much more commonly resorted to by travellers in Switzerland since the Federal Government adopted in 1852 a general and uniform system of Posting (Extrapost), which has been introduced into all parts of the country, and all the great roads are now supplied with post-horses, except where the railways have been completed. There is still however difficulty in posting into Italy and in Savoy. Full information respecting the posting system may be obtained from the Official Swiss Post Book (*Tarif Suisse de la Poste aux Chevaux*), or the smaller *Extra Post Tarif*, which every traveller ought to procure on entering Switzerland.

Horses are charged 4 fr. each per post of 9 miles. *Postboy's* pay, according to tariff, is 1 fr. 50 c. for 1 or 2 horses; 2 fr. for 3 horses; 2 fr. 50 c. for 4 horses per post; but if he behaves well it is usual to give him 4 fr. or the price of a horse : price for *Carriage*, when furnished, 2 fr. per post.

The horses and harness are generally good; the postboys tolerably skilful, but they get over the ground very slowly. The *regulation pace* is a post in 1 hour 30 min., or 6 miles an hour, and is not often exceeded. Upon certain stages up hill the tariff compels you to take an extra horse, or leader (*renfort*), or to pay for it if not taken, sometimes with very little apparent reason. There is very little trouble in posting; the prices are fixed, and the postboy's pay is included.

Since the extension of railways, it has become very unusual to bring a carriage from England, and such a thing as a regular travelling-carriage is seldom seen in Switzerland. Those who wish to be luxurious, and do not mind the expense and in many instances the inconvenience of having a carriage attached to them, may hire a carriage on the confines of Switzerland for the journey.

In hiring a Swiss carriage for the journey let the traveller ascertain, before he concludes the bargain, under what class the vehicle would be ranged by the posting laws, and what number of horses will be required to draw it.

It is a great convenience in Switzerland for a solitary traveller that he may post in a car with *one horse*, the charges being per post—

For 1 horse	.	.	. 4 fr.
„ car	.	.	. 2 fr.
„ postboy	.	.	. 1 fr. 50 c.

but an extra trinkgeld is expected.

Tolls for the roads and bridges are abolished throughout Switzerland, and the owners indemnified.

TARIF FOR POSTING.

Distances in Posts.	CHARGE FOR HORSES.										
	1 Horse.		2 Horses.		3 Horses.		4 Horses.		5 Horses.		6 Horses.
	Fr.	Ct.	Fr.	Ct.	Fr.	Ct.	Fr.	Ct.	Fr.	Ct.	Fr.	Ct.
$\frac{1}{2}$	2	—	4	—	6	—	8	—	10	—	12	—
$\frac{5}{8}$	2	50	5	—	7	50	10	—	12	50	15	—
$\frac{3}{4}$	3	—	6	—	9	—	12	—	15	—	18	—
$\frac{7}{8}$	3	50	7	—	10	50	14	—	17	50	21	—
1	4	—	8	—	12	—	16	—	20	—	24	—
$1\frac{1}{8}$	4	50	9	—	13	50	18	—	22	50	27	—
$1\frac{1}{4}$	5	—	10	—	15	—	20	—	25	—	30	—
$1\frac{3}{8}$	5	50	11	—	16	50	22	—	27	50	33	—
$1\frac{1}{2}$	6	—	12	—	18	—	24	—	30	—	36	—
$1\frac{5}{8}$	6	50	13	—	19	50	26	—	32	50	39	—
$1\frac{3}{4}$	7	—	14	—	21	—	28	—	35	—	42	—
$1\frac{7}{8}$	7	50	15	—	22	50	30	—	37	50	45	—
2	8	—	16	—	24	—	32	—	40	—	48	—
$2\frac{1}{8}$	8	50	17	—	25	50	34	—	42	50	51	—
$2\frac{1}{4}$	9	—	18	—	27	—	36	—	45	—	54	—
$2\frac{3}{8}$	9	50	19	—	28	50	38	—	47	50	57	—
$2\frac{1}{2}$	10	—	20	—	30	—	40	—	50	—	60	—
$2\frac{5}{8}$	10	50	21	—	31	50	42	—	52	50	63	—
$2\frac{3}{4}$	11	—	22	—	33	—	44	—	55	—	66	—
$2\frac{7}{8}$	11	50	23	—	34	50	46	—	57	50	69	—
3	12	—	24	—	36	—	48	—	60	—	72	—

§ 6. DILIGENCES—LUGGAGE.

Well-appointed *Diligences*, though not very fast, running at convenient hours and very moderate fares, now traverse almost every road in Switzerland daily. The result is, that by far the greater number of persons travel by them in preference to the voiturier's carriage, whose prices are also kept down by the competition of the diligences. The only objection is, that, except from the coupé, very little of the beauty of the country is seen by those who travel by them.

They belong to the Federal Government, are managed by persons officially appointed, and are attached to the post-office, as in Germany, conformably with an enactment of the new Swiss Constitution of 1848. A list of diligences, &c. (Kursanzeiger, Indicateur des Services Suisses), is to be bought at the offices for a few sous. The places are numbered, and all baggage exceeding a certain fixed weight is charged extra, and often greatly increases the expense of this mode of conveyance, which is one reason among many why travellers should reduce their baggage to the smallest possible compass. The public conveyances are now quite as well organised as in Germany.

TARIF FOR POSTING.

POSTBOY'S DRINKMONEY.			CHARGE FOR POST CARRIAGES.		
For a Carriage with 1 horse or 2 horses.	For a Carriage with 3 horses.	For a Carriage with 4 or more horses.	For a Carriage with 1 horse or 2 horses.	For a Carriage with 3 horses.	For a Carriage with 4 horses or 6 horses.
Fr. Ct.	Fr. Ct.	Fr. Ct.	Fr. Ct.	Fr. Ct.	Fr. Ct.
— 75	1 —	1 25	1 —	1 50	2 —
— 95	1 25	1 55	1 30	1 90	2 50
1 15	1 50	1 85	1 50	2 30	3 —
1 35	1 75	2 20	1 80	2 70	3 50
1 50	2 —	2 50	2 —	3 —	4 —
1 70	2 25	2 80	2 30	2 40	4 50
1 ·90	2 50	3 15	2 50	3 80	5 —
2 05	2 75	3 45	2 80	4 20	5 50
2 25	3 —	3 75	3 —	4 50	6 —
2 45	3 25	4 05	3 30	4 90	6 50
2 65	3 50	4 35	3 50	5 20	7 —
2 85	3 75	4 70	3 80	5 70	7 50
3 —	4 —	5 —	4 —	6 —	8 —
3 20	4 25	5 30	4 30	6 40	8 50
3 40	4 50	5 60	4 50	6 80	9 —
3 55	4 75	5 95	4 80	7 20	9 50
3 75	5 —	6 25	5 —	7 50	10 —
3 90	·5 25	6 55	5 · 30	7 90	10 50
4 15	5 50	6 85	5 50	8 30	11 —
4 35	5 75	7 20	5 80	8 70	11 50
·4 50	6 —	7 50	6 —	9 —	12 —

The conductors, especially with a small additional fee, are generally civil ; the clerks, &c., at the diligence offices are occasionally insolent and disobliging. The diligences, as in France, are horsed with the post-horses, and go from the same offices, so that there is no remedy in the case of annoyance or incivility except to take a voiturier.

There is a very convenient plan adopted as to places. The diligence offices will book any number of passengers up to a certain hour. When the time for starting arrives, all the luggage and as many passengers as the vehicle will hold are put into the diligence, which is far superior to the French diligence, and the rest of the passengers are sent by other carriages, called "supplements," or "beiwagen," of which there are often 3 or 4. It is the fashion to object to *supplements;* but if there is a party of 4 or 5, they can generally get a supplement to themselves, and travel very comfortably, except that the supplement is usually changed at every stage. Unless at the place from which the diligence starts, it is useless to take places for the coupé, for at the intermediate stations the coupé is often found full, and the traveller proceeds in a supplement. The pace along level ground never exceeds 6 miles an hour ; at the smallest symptom of a hill this falls to a walk : down hill they occasionally go rather faster ; and to those who have not become hardened by use it is rather a nervous thing to see the heavy diligence turn round the corners of the zigzags in the face of precipices, with the reins of the 5 horses flying loose, and the horses apparently under no control. The horses however know the road, and, except in snow, an accident is seldom heard of.

The conductor's fee and the postilion's trinkgeld are included in the fare.

Travellers in Switzerland will frequently be glad to avail themselves of the public conveyances to forward their *luggage* from one place to another, while they are making pedestrian excursions among the mountains. In such cases, they have only to book their packages at the coach-office, after carefully addressing them, and, in some cases, entering a specification of their value in a printed form. They will then receive a receipt, and the article will be forwarded and taken care of until claimed.

In making application for packages so consigned, as well as for letters at the post-office, the Englishman should present his name on a printed card, as our pronunciation is frequently unintelligible to foreigners, and without this precaution the applicant may be told that his luggage has not arrived, when in reality it is all the while lying in the depôt. The traveller may also request to look over the packages in search of his own.

§ 7. VOITURIER OR LOHNKUTSCHER—CHARS-À-BANC.

The excellently organised systems of posting and public conveyances introduced since 1849, which place Switzerland on a par with any country of the continent—render travellers in a great degree independent of the voiturier, or lohnkutscher, or vetturino—whom formerly they were obliged to engage as soon as they crossed the Swiss frontier.

The towns of Basle, Schaffhausen, Zürich, Bern, Thun, Vevay, Lausanne, and Geneva are the head-quarters of the voituriers; at all of them there are many persons who keep job-horses for hire, and will either conduct the traveller themselves, or send coachmen in their employ. *Return* horses and carriages are sometimes to be met with, and the traveller may save some expense by availing himself of them.

Before making an engagement, it is prudent to consult the landlord of the inn, or some other respectable inhabitant, to recommend a person of approved character to be employed. As there are many very roguish voituriers, ready to take advantage of the traveller on all occasions, such a recommendation will be a guarantee, to a certain extent, for good behaviour. The landlord should be referred to apart, not in presence of the coachman, nor, indeed, with his cognizance. Besides ascertaining that the voiturier is a respectable man, that his horses are good, and his carriage (when a carriage is also required) is clean and stout, it is desirable in many cases that he should speak French as well as German, and, in all, that he be acquainted with the roads to be traversed. If the carriage is hired for a complete tour, the engagement should, in the first instance, not be made for any specific time, at least not for a long period, until man and horses have been tried and have given satisfaction. It is better to take him on from day to day, holding out the prospect of his being continued if he behaves well.

The usual charge per diem is 15 francs, and 1 franc trinkgeld or bonne-main, for a one-horse vehicle; 25 francs, and 2 francs trinkgeld, for a pair-horse vehicle; and so on. In the height of the season it is from 3 to 5 francs a-day more, and over the great passes it is higher still.

If the carriage is discharged at a distance from home, back-fare will be demanded.

For this consideration the coachman keeps himself and his horses, supplying fresh ones if his own fall ill or lame; he ought also to pay all tolls, and the charge for leaders (vorspann) to drag the carriage up steep ascents. These two last conditions, however, are not always acceded to, and these charges often fall upon the master.

It is advisable, before setting out on a long tour, to have an agreement in writing drawn up.

It is, however, now become unusual to engage a voiturier except for a particular journey of two or three days. Without troubling the traveller with the complications of back-fares, &c., the rate may be reckoned in the season for a good carriage and pair at about 40 fr. a-day over the more level parts, and 60 fr. a-day over the great passes, all charges, back-fare, vorspann, bonnemain, &c., included. A return voiturier will take one-half or two-thirds of these prices.

The usual rate of travelling is from 10 to 15 leagues, 32 to 46 miles a-day, proceeding at the rate of about 5 miles an hour. Whilst on the road the voiturier goes as fast as the diligence or post-horses, but it is necessary to halt in the middle of the day, about two hours, to rest the horses; and the distances which one pair of horses will achieve by means of walking up the smallest ascents, and using the break skilfully on all descents, are incredible.

Throughout Switzerland, *one-horse calèches*, or chaises, *einspänner*, are becoming common, instead of chars-à-banc, and may be hired at every inn. They hold comfortably 2 or 3 persons, and are furnished with a hood affording shelter from rain, while not shutting out the view. In front there is a board for the driver. They go at a rate of 5 or 6 m. an hour, except on very hilly roads. The fare is about 1 franc an English mile; and the driver receives 1 fr. trinkgeld for 8 or 10 miles. The luggage may be attached behind on springs.

The char-à-banc, the national carriage of French Switzerland, is nearly obsolete. It may be described as the body of a gig, or a bench, as its name implies, placed sideways upon four wheels, surrounded by leather curtains made to draw, whence it has been compared to a four-post bedstead on wheels. It is a very strong and light vehicle, capable of carrying two persons, or three at a pinch, and will go on roads where no other species of carriage could venture. It is convenient, from being so low that one can jump in or alight without stopping the horse, while it is going on; but it is very jolting.

§ 8. RAILWAYS.

Down to the year 1855 the only railway in Switzerland was a short line from Zürich to Baden, a village in the neighbourhood. The reason of this was not, as generally supposed, the extreme natural difficulties of the country, Switzerland being in fact, with the exception of the passes through the central mountains of the Alps and the Jura, not a very difficult country. The lowlands, or parts round Berne, Aarau, Neuchâtel, Lausanne, &c., are not worse than many parts of the south of England ; and by means of the valleys of the Rhine and the Rhone, railways can penetrate deep into the Alps with remarkable ease. The real difficulty consisted in the extraordinary and incredible jealousies between not only the different cantons, but the different communes or parishes, and the legal difficulties in obtaining the land.

A change of government, however, having taken place in 1848, a system of railways was planned by the Department of Public Works, and has been partially carried into execution, many of the lines being executed by English engineers and with English capital.

1. *The Central Swiss Railway*, from Basle through the Unter-Hauenstein to Olten, and thence to Berne, with branches to Soleure and Bienne, Lucerne and Zürich, open.

2. *The North-Eastern Railway*, from Romanshorn on the lake of Constance to Zürich, and thence to Olten on the Central Railway, open ; with a branch to Waldshut.

3. *The Rheinfall Railway*, from Schaffhausen to Winterthur and Zürich, open.

4. *The South-Eastern*, or *United Swiss*, from Coire (with hopes of a tunnel through the Alps at some future time) to Rorschach on the lake of Constance, open ; with a branch from Sargans, along the side of the lake of Wallenstadt, to Rapperschwyl, on the lake of Zürich. This line has been executed by Mr. Pickering, an English engineer. The neighbouring districts have been minutely surveyed in order to ascertain the best place for the tunnel through the Alps ; and it seems probable that the Lukmanier pass will be selected, which will require a tunnel 15 miles long. No pass has been discovered less than 6200 feet high ; and independently of the difficulty of surmounting that height, instead of tunnelling the ridge, the railway would be then impassable on account of the snow during many months of the year. Places have been found in which a shorter tunnel would be sufficient, but at such a depth that no shafts could be obtained, the advantage of this pass being that many shafts can be sunk at an average depth of 200 yards. By means of the proposed tunnel, the summit level would be about 5000 feet.

5. *The St. Gall and Appenzell Railway*, from Rorschach, through St. Gall and Winterthur, to Zürich. This is now *open*.

6. *The Western Railway*, from *Yverdun, on the lake of Neuchâtel, to Morges and Lausanne*, and thence to *Geneva, open*. A branch of this railway from Villeneuve, on the lake of Geneva, up the valley of the Rhone towards the Simplon, is open to Bex.

7. *The Glatthal Railway*, connecting Zürich with the manufacturing villages in the neighbourhood, will be carried to Sargans.

8. *The Baden Railway* has been continued from *Basle to Waldshut*, and will be carried on to Schaffhausen.

9. Railways are also open from Lyons and Macon to Geneva.

The earthworks on the South-Eastern line were made, under English engineers and foremen, by Piedmontese navvies, the Swiss not being found suitable for the work. These Piedmontese are said to be powerful men, and to work as hard, though not so skilfully, as the English navvy, living at the same time upon very poor food, and saving the greatest part of their wages.

The luggage arrangements on the Swiss railways are if possible more inconvenient than on the French or German railways; and there is a system of extortion for conveyance to and from the stations which the traveller should be on his guard against.

§ 9. GUIDES—PORTERS.

Guides by profession are to be met with in most parts of Switzerland; those of Chamouni (in Savoy) are deservedly renowned. They abound at Interlaken, Thun, Lucerne, and all the other starting-points from which pedestrian excursions are begun. Here, again, the traveller had better trust to the innkeeper to recommend a fit person; but it is advisable not to hire one for a length of time beforehand. He ought not to be too far advanced in years. Guides may be considered in two capacities, *General* or *Local*.

General Guides are to be found at Zürich, Lucerne, Berne, &c., and at the entrance to the mountainous country; and it is by no means a bad plan for an inexperienced traveller or party to engage one of them for the tour. He makes himself useful, not only in pointing out the way, but in acting as interpreter to those unacquainted with the language of the country, and also in relieving the traveller of the weight of his knapsack or travelling-bag, and in fact acts as *courier*, but at a far cheaper rate, and generally with more honesty. He will have a general knowledge of the routes, inns, &c., over a large extent, and would probably be a good local guide to his own peculiar district; but

Local Guides are as a general rule indispensable in ascending very lofty mountains, in exploring glaciers, and in crossing the minor passes of the Alps, not traversed by highroads, but by mere bridle or foot paths, rarely used, and in many places not distinctly marked, or confounded with innumerable tracks of cattle, Nevertheless, travellers having a good knowledge of German, in addition to some experience of mountain journeys, and provided with a good map, may cross some of these passes alone with impunity; but there are others, such as the Bonhomme, Mont Cervin, Monte Moro, &c., which no one would be justified in attempting without a guide. When snow is threatening to fall, or after a snow-storm has covered the path and obliterated the footsteps of preceding travellers, a guide may be required in situations where, under ordinary circumstances, his presence might be dispensed with. Of course, in clear weather, and over passes not crossing snow or glaciers, a guide is no more needed than he would be in any strange country, except that on the high mountains there is no one of whom to inquire the way, and that a mistake of the path might involve the disagreeable necessity of sleeping out on the mountain. A traveller of some experience is of opinion that upon an average, without a guide, 1 mile in 10 will be lost in mistakes of the way, even by practised mountaineers. No one, however, without at least a year's experience, should be foolish enough to trust himself over ice or snow without a guide. It is entirely a new world; and when the slightest check occurs, an inexperienced person is utterly at a loss. He does not know what ice will bear him, where the crevasses run, where avalanches fall, or where the safe track is likely to be; and with the best ordinary judgment, is quite as likely to run into danger as to avoid it. One golden rule to those who take no guide is, always to leave two or three good hours of daylight as a margin beyond the utmost time which the route is calculated to occupy. Another excellent rule is, *never* take a short cut upon your own judgment. It is frequently wrong to cut off the most apparent zigzag; but the villagers will often, for a few sous, show wonderfully short cuts.

In the eastern parts of Switzerland, where there are *no* professional guides, the traveller is often obliged to place himself in the hands of some peasant or cowherd, whose sole knowledge of a pass lies, perhaps, in his having crossed it once or twice, perhaps, many years before. This demands additional caution.

The established rate of hire is 6 F. francs a-day, and in the Oberland 1 fr. bonnemain; but, in addition to this, there will be a claim for money to return, if dismissed at a distance from home, unless the employer find him a fresh master to take back. For this sum the guide provides for himself, and is expected to discharge all the duties of a domestic towards his employer.

The guides at Chamouni form a corporation, and are subject to a number of stringent rules as to their employment, of which travellers and the best guides complain much. A monopoly has also been established in the Oberland, and in some other parts of Switzerland. In the Lower Valais it is a punishable offence for any one, not a professed guide, to carry a traveller's luggage ! !

For the most part, the guides may be said to be obliging, intelligent, and hard-working men. Few who have employed them cannot bear testimony to their coolness, intrepidity, and tact, in moments of danger—in the difficult pass, in the midst of the snow-storm, or among the gaping clefts of the glaciers. It is in such situations that their knowledge of the mountains, their experience of the weather, their strong arm and steady foot, are fully appreciated. The traveller should always follow the guide in crossing glaciers, and, in going over tracts covered with snow, should allow him to choose what his experience teaches to be the safest path.

A little civility and familiarity on the part of the employer—the offer of a cigar from the traveller's own case, or a glass of brandy from his private flask—will rarely be thrown away; on the contrary, it is likely to produce assiduity and communicativeness on the part of the guide. Many of them are fine and athletic men, and to carry for 8 or 10 hours a-day, and for a distance of 25 or 30 m., a load of 30 or 40 lbs. weight is made light of by them.

Some travellers content themselves with a mere porter to carry their baggage for them. Such a man is paid less than the professional guides; 3 or 4 fr. a-day will suffice for him. Those who travel in chars or on horseback will find that the driver, or the man who accompanies the horse, will render unnecessary the employment of any other person in that capacity. At Chamouni, however, the guides must be hired distinct from the mules. When the travelling party includes ladies unaccustomed to mountain-work, a guide is required to attend on each, to lead down the horses where the path is steep, and to lend their arms to the fair travellers when the exigencies of the case require them to dismount and proceed on foot.

In making purchases, as in the choice of inns, travellers should be cautious of following blindly the advice of the guide, who too often regards the percentage offered to him more than the interest of his employer.

§ 10. HORSES AND MULES.—CHAISES-À-PORTEURS.

Previous to 1800, or even later, until Napoleon commenced the magnificent carriage-roads over the Alps, which will assist in immortalising his name, the only mode of conveying either passengers or goods across them was on the back of men, or of horses or mules. Even now, upon all the minor passes, the entire traffic is carried on by the same means. In other instances, where the beauties of scenery attract an influx of strangers, mules are kept for their conveyance, even where they are not required for the transport of merchandise.

The customary hire of a horse or mule throughout Switzerland, generally fixed by a printed tariff, amounts to 9 fr. a-day, and 1 fr. or 2 fr. to the man who takes care of it; at Chamouni it is 6 fr., but there a guide must also be taken. Back-fare must be paid if the animals are dismissed at a distance from home, and at so late an hour of the day that they cannot return before night.

The ponies that are used in the Bernese Oberland, on the Rigi, and in other parts of Switzerland, are clever animals, that will carry you up and down ascents perfectly impracticable to horses unused to the mountains; but they are perhaps excelled by the mules of Chamouni and other parts of Savoy. Their sagacity, strength, and sureness of foot are really wonderful. The paths which they ascend or descend with ease are steeper than any staircase, sometimes with ledges of rock, 2 or 3 ft. high, instead of steps. Sometimes they are covered with broken fragments, between which the beasts must pick their way, at the risk of breaking their legs; at others they traverse a narrow ledge of the mountain, with an abyss on one side and a wall of rock on the other. In such dangerous passes the caution of the animal is very remarkable; he needs no rein to guide him, but will pick his own way, and find out the best path far better than his rider can direct him; and, in such circumstances, it is safer to let the reins hang loose, and trust entirely to his sagacity, than to perplex him by checking him with the curb, at a moment when, by confusing the animal, there will be risk of his losing his footing, and perhaps tumbling headlong. The rider who mounts a mule or mountain-horse must give up his preconceived notions of riding, and let the reins hang absolutely loose, otherwise he is in danger. There are very few instances of accidents from the falling of the animals; the only instance within the writer's knowledge happened to a gentleman who was a great horseman, and no doubt attempted to interfere with his mule. Those who are incredulous on this point should recollect that the horses constantly traverse the same paths in perfect safety with heavy loads on their backs, and no man near enough to interfere with them. Descending the passes on horseback is very disagreeable, and sometimes dangerous, and the rider should always dismount when requested to do so by the guide. In fact, those who can walk at all should, if they have not too much luggage, only hire the horses to the head of the pass, as they will be of very little use on the descent. Each saddle has a flap or pillion attached, on which a knapsack or carpet-bag not weighing more than about 30 lbs. may be carried. A portmanteau requires an extra mule. Side-saddles are now to be found wherever there are inns and regular mules or horses.

A tariff of the prices to be paid for horses in most places is in the *Indicateur, p.* 108.

Those who are unable or too infirm to ride or walk may be carried over the mountains in a " chaise-à-porteur " (Germ. Tragsessel; It. Portantina), which is nothing more than an arm-chair carried upon poles by two bearers in the manner of a sedan. Two extra bearers must be taken to relieve by turns, and each man expects 6 fr. a-day, and 3 fr. for each day of return. This is said to be a very uncomfortable mode of locomotion.

§ 11. SWISS INNS.

Switzerland is well provided with inns ; and those of the large towns, such as the Trois Couronnes, at Vevay ; Baur, at Zürich ; Gibbon, at Lausanne ; Schweizer Hof, at Lucerne ; the Ecu, Bergues, and Couronne, at Geneva ; the Bellevue, at Thun—yield, in extent and good management, to no hotels in Great Britain, France, or Germany. The great annual influx of strangers into the country is of the same importance to Switzerland that some additional branch of industry or commerce would be, and renders the profession of host most lucrative. Many of the Swiss innkeepers are very wealthy ; in a great part of the country they appear to be the only wealthy inhabitants. It is not uncommon to find an individual in this capacity who is magistrate, and it has happened that they are persons of such influence in their canton or commune that it is difficult to obtain redress against them for an injury or act of insolence, owing either to the interest they possess with the courts, or to their being absolutely themselves the justices. As a general rule, however, they are very respectable men, and no difficulties with them arise.

The approach to one of the first-rate hotels in the large towns, in the height of summer, exhibits rather a characteristic spectacle. The street before it is usually filled with several rows of vehicles of all sorts, from the dirty and rickety calèche of the German voiturier, to the neat chariot of the English peer, and the less elegant, but equally imposing, equipage of the Russian prince. Before the doorway is invariably grouped a crowd of loitering guides, servants, and couriers, of all nations and languages, and two or three knots of postilions and coachmen on the look-out for employment.

Couriers, voituriers, guides, and boatmen are apt sometimes to sell their employers to the innkeepers for a gratuity, so that travellers should not always implicitly follow the recommendations of such persons regarding inns ; and it is believed that the list of inns, drawn up with much care, and given in this book, has rendered the traveller of late years more independent of their recommendations. The innkeepers were formerly very much at the mercy of this class of persons, who invariably fare sumptuously and certainly not at their own expense ; and it not unfrequently happens that the attendance which ought to be bestowed on the master is showered upon his menials. The inns recommended here are from the best information that the editor can procure, but it is obvious that the information must be, with very few exceptions, eight or nine months old at the latest, and that in many instances it must be much older, and in the interval the landlord may have been changed, or may have become more careful from adversity, or careless from prosperity, and the inn may be completely altered. In the following pages the inns which are believed by the editor to be best in any town are mentioned first.

It may be laid down as a general rule, that the wants, tastes, and habits of the English are more carefully and successfully studied in the Swiss inns than even in those of Germany. At most of the large inns, in addition to the 1 o'clock dinner, there is a *late table-d'hôte* dinner at 4 or 5 o'clock, expressly for the English; and tea may always be had tolerably good. Several wealthy innkeepers have even gone so far as to build *English chapels* for their guests, as an inducement to English travellers to pass the Sunday with them. Cleanliness is to be met with almost everywhere, until you reach the S. slopes of the Alps and the approach to Italy. In canton Bern, in particular, the inns, even in the small and remote villages, are patterns of neatness, such as even fastidious travellers may be contented with. Still in many instances, even in first-class inns, the houses are deficient in proper drainage and ventilation, and the passages and staircases are unwholesome and offensive from bad smells. Care should be taken to impress on the landlords how disgusting and intolerable to English ideas such a nuisance is. The hotels Baur at Zürich, Ecu at Geneva, and Trois Couronnes at Vevay, are creditable exceptions, free from this reproach of filthiness and bad odours.

The practice is now general of the waiter rushing into your room before you and lighting the *wax* candles without consulting you. If a traveller proposes sitting up some hours, he may not object to this; but it is very different when, at 10 or 11 o'clock, you retire to bed, *to sleep*, and the infliction of a charge for wax candles, under such circumstances, can be looked on only as an imposition.

The following *list of usual Charges* will serve to guide travellers, and may protect them from extortion and imposition on the part of those innkeepers or couriers who may be disposed to take advantage of them.

List of Charges of the first-class Swiss Hotels.

	Fr. fr.	c.
Tea or coffee, morning or evening, with bread, butter, and honey (eggs and meat charged separately)	1	50
Ditto in private, each person charged extra	0	50
Déjeûner à la fourchette (table d'hôte)	2	50
Table d'hôte at 1, with vin ordinaire	3	50
Ditto ditto, at 5	4	0
Dinner in private (commandé à l'avance dans la salle à manger)	5	0
Servants, dinner or supper, 1 fr. 50 c.; breakfast or tea, 1 fr.		
Bougie	1	0
Demi-bougie	0	50
Lampe de nuit	0	50
Bain de pied, chaud ou froid (*exorbitant*)	0	50
Servants (service de l'hôtel), par jour par personne	1	0
From large families, who make some stay, so much is not expected.		

The charges for *Rooms* vary according to their situation on the lower floors, and the views they command ; but the best suite of apartments, in first-rate inns, ought not to exceed 4 fr. a-day for a sitting-room or salon, and 3 fr. for each bed. The *Salles-à-manger* in the larger Swiss inns are handsome, clean, and airy apartments. Smoking is not allowed in them, and in consequence of this, and of a higher charge being made for meals in private rooms, many more persons take breakfast, tea, and supper than in the German inns, and the society is more select than in France or Germany, and may be enjoyed in comfort, the guests being almost exclusively tourists.

A party of 3 or 4 persons staying a week or more, even in a first-rate hotel, ought not to pay more than 8 fr. each, board and lodging, including servants, per diem. At Interlaken the charge for good board and lodging is not more than 6 fr. a-day; and at some of the baths near Bex not more than 4½ fr. a-day for those who remain some weeks. At some of the small inns in remote valleys the charges are absurdly low.

English travellers halting at an *Inn* about mid-day to rest their horses, if there be no table-d'hôte at 12 or 1, should order a déjeûner à la fourchette (gabel frühstuck), for which they will be charged 1½ or 2 fr. per head. If they order *dinner*, they will be charged 3 or 4 fr. for the very same food. Similarly, when arriving at an inn in the evening, tea, with côtelettes de mouton, or bifteck aux pommes de terre, will replace dinner satisfactorily and economically. One fr. a-day is usually given to the servants, and is almost always added in the bill. This includes all the servants except the porter, who expects something extra.

French is almost invariably spoken at the inns, even in the German cantons, except in remote parts, as in the side valleys of the Grisons. Nevertheless, the German language is a very valuable acquisition to the traveller. English is spoken in the large hotels.

Swiss inns have, in general, the reputation of being expensive, and the innkeepers of being extortionate ; of late years, however, great improvement has taken place. A recent journey through the greater part of the country has scarcely afforded an instance of either ; but, where such cases have occurred, notice has been taken of them in the following pages. At minor and remote inns, manoeuvres are sometimes resorted to for the purpose of detaining the guests.

It is often supposed, and perhaps correctly, that two sets of charges are made—one for natives, or Germans, and another for the English ; on the principle that the latter have both longer purses and more numerous wants, and are more difficult to serve.

The *average daily expense* of living at the best inns in Switzerland will vary between 8 Fr. fr. and 10 fr. a-day, excluding all charge for conveyances, horses, and guides. Those who consult economy will, instead of going to inferior inns in large towns, avoid them, and sleep in villages whenever it is practicable. The German students, who understand the art of travelling economically, always proceed in a party, and usually send on one of their number a-head, to their intended night-quarters, to make terms with the innkeeper, and do not spend more than 5 or 7 frs. a-day. There is this advantage in travelling with a party, that numbers are more welcomed at an inn and better attended to than a solitary individual ; on the other hand, when inns are full, few stand a better chance than many ;

and travellers with ladies are allotted better rooms than single men.   All arrangements for the hire of carriages, horses, or guides, should be concluded over-night : he that waits till the morning will generally find either the conveyances engaged by others, or the price demanded for them increased, and, at all events, his departure delayed.

Among the mountains, the traveller may obtain, in perfection, the small alpine *Trout*, which are of great excellence ; sometimes, also, chamois venison, which, by the way, is far inferior to park venison ; wild strawberries are very abundant, and, with a copious admixture of delicious cream,—the staple commodity of the Alps,—are by no means to be despised.

Those who enter a Swiss inn, tired, hot, and thirsty, after a long walk or dusty ride, may ask for a bottle of "limonade gazeuse," under which name they will recognise a drink nearly resembling ginger-beer, but with more acidity, and, when good, very refreshing.   It supplies here the place of hock and Seltzer-water on the Rhine.

Swiss wines are generally considered execrable.   The best are those of Neuchâtel and Vaud ; such as they are procured at inns, they merit no great praise.   A sweet Sardinian wine (vino d'Asti) is common, and very good.

§ 12.—DIRECTIONS FOR TRAVELLERS, AND REQUISITES FOR A JOURNEY IN SWITZERLAND—MAPS.

The *best season* for travelling among the Alps is the months of July, August, and September, in which may, perhaps, be included the last half of June.   The higher Alpine passes are scarcely clear of snow before the second week of June ; and before the middle of October, snow almost invariably falls on the high Alps : and though the weather is often still serene, the nights draw in so fast as to curtail, inconveniently, the day's journey.   During the long days of July and August one may get over a great deal of ground.   In September the days are not too hot for hard walking, and there seems to be the best chance of fine weather.   On an average there is one season in four fine, two tolerable, and one bad.   Those who have not seen Switzerland in set fine weather do not know what Switzerland is.

Saussure recommends those who are inexperienced in Alpine travelling to accustom themselves for some time before they set out to look down from heights and over precipices : few persons, however, complain of vertigo in Switzerland, as there is generally something below to break the apparent depth.

The first expeditions up mountains produce intense thirst, and the traveller should be cautioned against indulging in cold water or cold milk when heated ; the guides and natives accustomed to mountain travelling never drink before resting ; exercise afterwards will render the draught harmless.

It is tiresome and unprofitable in the extreme to walk along a high road over a flat and monotonous country, where there is a carriage-road and conveyances are to be had : here it is best to ride ; the cost of a conveyance is counterbalanced by the economy of time.

After the middle of June, when the season for travelling in Switzerland begins, little danger is to be feared from *avalanches*, except immediately after snow-storms, which occur among the high Alps even in the height of summer.

In traversing *Swiss lakes*, implicit reliance should be placed on the advice of the boatmen, and no attempt should be made to induce them to launch their boats when they foresee danger. (See Rte. 18.)

In a few spots on the Italian side, and perhaps in some spots on the north side of the Alps, there is malaria in the districts about the embouchures of rivers where they empty themselves into lakes, and travellers should avoid sleeping in such districts.

For many years Keller's was the only map of Switzerland, and is still the clearest and most portable (3rd edit. Zürich, best; English and French copies inferior). Since the government surveys have been made more accurate maps have been published. *Leuthold's* (Zürich, 1857), 10 fr., is on the whole the best: for those who are content with less complete and more portable maps there are Leuthold's at 7 fr. and 3 fr. *Gross* (Zürich) has published a good map. *Ziegler* (St. Gall) has published good but not very clear maps at 8 fr. and 2 fr.; and a geological map under Studer and Escher at 22 fr. There are spurious and inferior editions of many of these maps published in France or Germany, against which the purchaser must be on his guard.

The Government Map of Switzerland—scale $\frac{1}{100000}$, or 2-3rds of an inch to the mile, published under the direction of General Dufour, and sold by all the principal booksellers, and analogous to the English Ordnance Maps, is by far the best. It will be comprised in 25 sheets, of which 15 have appeared, each sheet containing about 30 miles square, and costing from 2 to 6 fr. This map contains not only every road and every path of importance, but even every single house and barn, but is of course too large for pedestrians. The execution of these maps is admirable: the mountains engraved are absolutely portraits.

Studer and Escher's geological maps are elaborate works, the result of immense labour. Studer has also published an excellent map of the country round Monte Rosa (Wagner, Bern), smaller but more correct than Schlagentweit's.

See also Introd. to Savoy and Piedmont.

Requisites for Travelling.—The following hints are principally addressed to those who intend to make *pedestrian* journeys.

To travel *on foot* is the best mode of *seeing* Switzerland; and it saves a world of trouble to have no other baggage than a knapsack; one containing 3 or 4 shirts, socks, drawers, slippers, alpaca coat, thin waistcoat and trowsers, dressing materials, &c., need not exceed 12 or 14 lbs. English mackintoshes are much the best, but a waterproof is not of much use to a pedestrian, as it is too hot. A good umbrella, with the point cut off, is more useful, and will keep off the sun; when not in use it is stuck through the knapsack after the Swiss fashion.

The *shoes* or half-boots ought to be double-soled, provided with hobnails, such as are worn in shooting in England, and without iron heels, which are dangerous, and liable to slip in walking over rocks; three rows of nails are better, and Swiss nails are better than English, which are often too hard and slippery: the weight of a shoe of this kind is counterbalanced by the effectual protection afforded to the feet against sharp rocks and loose stones, which cause contusions, and are a great source of fatigue and pain; they should be so large as not to pinch any part of the foot. The experienced pedestrian never commences a journey with new boots, but with a pair that have already conformed to the shape of the feet. Thick knit worsted socks, or cotton stockings with worsted feet, ought invariably to be worn. It is advisable to travel in cloth trowsers, not in linen, which afford no protection against rain or changes of temperature in mountain regions. The clothes, if woollen, can hardly be too thin or light. In the months when Englishmen travel it is seldom cold, and often tremendously hot. No one who has not ascended a mountain or a pass in the sun can form an idea of the intense heat he will be subject to.

Portmanteaus are better in England than anywhere else, but should not be too large. A carpet-bag or knapsack should always be taken, as a portmanteau requires a luggage-mule or a porter, whilst a carpet-bag will go behind the saddle, and the portmanteau may be sent round by the high road.

Knapsacks are of two sorts: mackintosh with stiff sides, and intended to carry a complete equipment, in which case they should be tolerably large; and mackintosh or oilskin without a frame or stiffening, so as to pack in a portmanteau, but large enough to carry a supply of clothes for a day or two.

A *flask* is generally carried; but spirits during violent exertion, and especially at great heights, are to be avoided: wine diluted plentifully with water is delicious at great heights. Many persons find relief from the intense thirst by keeping a pebble in the mouth.

A *telescope* is not of much use, as the view is seldom minute. A racing glass (single) is better, but either of them is heavy to carry.

Lee, 440, West Strand, London, bookseller and stationer, furnishes many requisites for travellers, including a very portable writing-case.

A stout leather or canvas bag, to hold silver crown-pieces and dollars; cards or pieces of parchment, or, better still, adhesive labels, for writing directions for the baggage (the managers of public conveyances abroad often *insist* upon each package being addressed, before they will take charge of it); and one or two leather straps, to keep together books, coats, shawls, &c., or small parcels, will be found very useful.

The *alpenstock* is an almost indispensable companion upon mountain journeys, and may be procured everywhere in Switzerland for about a franc. It is a stout pole, about 6 ft. long, with an iron spike at one end. The pedestrian who knows how to use it appreciates its value as a staff and leaping-pole, but chiefly as a support in *descending* the mountains; it then becomes, as it were, a third leg. It enables one to transfer a part of the weight of the body from the legs to the arms, which is a great relief in descending long and steep hills. By the aid of it also travellers in the high Alps are enabled to slide down the ice with great ease after some practice, checking the velocity of their course, when it becomes too great, by leaning back, and driving the point deeper. In crossing glaciers, it is indispensable, to feel the strength of the ice, and ascertain whether it be free from crevasses and able to bear the weight. The alpenstock is usually of fir, but the best are of ash or lime, and sufficiently strong to bear the weight of a man seated on the middle while the ends rest on 2 supports. The best in Switzerland are on the Rigi, but the common alpenstocks are not to be trusted on high excursions. The chamois-horn often appended is inconvenient if not dangerous, and should be removed.

b 3

On high glacier excursions, where the glare of the snow is expected, black spectacles or a blue gauze veil or handkerchief must be worn. Further requisites for such an expedition are—ropes to attach travellers and their guides together, so that, in case one fall or slip into a crevasse, his descent may be arrested by the others ; a ladder, to cross those crevasses which are too broad to leap over ; and a hatchet, to cut steps or resting-places for the feet in the ice. Spikes for the feet are never used : 2 or 3 fresh nails with good heads are preferred.

These preparations are quite unnecessary for a mere visit to the lower part of the glaciers of Chamouni or Grindelwald, and are required only when a journey over them of many hours', or of one or two days' duration, is meditated.

Precautions for Health.—Nothing is more conducive to health than the combination of exercise, pure air, and wholesome enjoyment which is found by a pedestrian in the Alps. A few simple rules should, however, be observed :—

If not already in training, be content to make very short journeys at first. After a fortnight's practice you may undertake whatever you please.

Immediately on your arrival, after a day's walk, wash extensively with cold water and change your linen before sitting down to rest or eat. When you have only a knapsack you should keep one set of linen for the evening exclusively.

After a moderate walk ordinary diet with wine and beer is unobjectionable ; but when fatigued by unusual exertion there is nothing so useful as tea. After it you will sleep soundly when otherwise you would have been disturbed and feverish.

§ 13. OBJECTS MOST DESERVING OF NOTICE IN SWITZERLAND—THE COUNTRY AND PEOPLE—BATHS.

In order to travel with advantage in a country previously unknown, something more seems necessary than a mere detail of certain lines of road, and an enumeration of towns, villages, mountains, &c. The following section has been prepared with a view to furnish such preliminary information as may enable the tourist to turn his time to the best account ; to decide where to dwell, and where to pass quickly. The task is difficult : let this serve as an excuse for its imperfect execution.

Switzerland owes the sublimity and diversified beauty of its scenery, which it possesses in a greater degree perhaps than any other country of the globe, to the presence of the Alps—the loftiest mountains of Europe, the dorsal ridge or backbone, as it were, of the Continent. These run through the land, and occupy, with their main trunk, or minor spurs and offsets, nearly its whole surface. They attain the greatest height along the S. and E. frontier-line of Switzerland, but as they extend N., subsiding and gradually opening out to allow a passage to the Rhine and the Rhone, and their tributaries, they are met by the minor chain of the *Jura*, which forms the N.W. boundary of Switzerland. It is from the apex of this advanced guard, as it were, of the Alps, or from one of the intermediate outlying hills, that the traveller, on entering the country, obtains the first view of the great central chain. From the brow of the hill, at the further extremity of a landscape composed of undulating country—woods, hills, villages, lakes, and silvery, winding rivers—sufficient of itself to rivet the attention, he will discover what, if he has not before enjoyed the glorious spectacle of a snowy mountain, he will probably take for a border of fleecy cloud floating along the horizon. The eye, unaccustomed to objects of such magnitude, fails at first to convey to the mind the notion, that these clearly defined white masses are mountains 60 or 70 m. off. Distance and the intervening atmosphere have no effect in diminishing the intense white of the snow; it glitters as pure and unsullied as if it had just fallen close at hand.

There are many points of view whence the semicircular array of Alpine peaks, presented at once to the eye, extends for more than 120 m., from the Mont Blanc to the Titlis, and comprises between 200 and 300 distinct summits, capped with snow, or bristling with bare rocks, having their interstices filled with perpetual glaciers.

It was such a prospect that inspired those remarkable lines of Byron:—

> " Above me are the Alps,
> The palaces of Nature, whose vast walls
> Have pinnacled in clouds their snowy scalps,
> And throned Eternity in icy halls
> Of cold sublimity, where forms and falls
> The Avalanche—the thunderbolt of snow !
> All that expands the spirit, yet appals,
> Gather around the summits, as to show
> How earth may soar to heaven, yet leave vain man below."

List of Heights commanding such Alpine panoramas.

The Dôle, above St. Cergues, near Geneva ;
The Chaumont, above Neuchâtel ;
The Weissenstein, above Soleure ;
The Hauenstein, on the road from Basle to Soleure and Lucerne ;
The Albis, between Zürich and Zug ;
Monte Salvatore, rising amid the intricacies of the Lago Lugano ;
The Kamor, near Gais, in St. Gall ;
The Rigi, between the lakes of Zug and Lucerne ;
The Faulhorn, adjoining the Bernese Alps ;
The Rothhorn, above Brienz ;
Monte Monterone, between Lago Maggiore and Lago d'Orta.
Becca de Nona, above Aosta.

Of these the Rigi is probably the finest, as it is certainly one of the most accessible ; some give the preference to the Faulhorn, from its proximity to the great chain, and the High Alps rising close at hand are seen from it to great advantage. The passion for climbing mountains, so ardent in a young traveller, often cools; and many who have surmounted the Rigi, the Faulhorn, or Rothhorn, and the Dôle, consider any further ascents a waste of time and labour. Others, however, after having overcome the fatigue of the first 10 or 12 days, begin to feel a desire to ascend more and more difficult heights and passes ; and this desire not unfrequently becomes quite a passion.

For a *near view* of Alpine scenery, amidst the recesses of the mountains, the spots which afford a concentration of the most grand and sublime objects are the valleys of the Bernese Oberland, those which descend from Monte Rosa, especially the valleys of Zermatt and Macugnaga, and those around the base of Mont Blanc, including, of course, Chamouni. It is in these three districts that the combination of fine forms and great elevation in the mountains—of vast extent of glaciers and snow-fields, with the accompaniments of the roar of the avalanche and the rush of the falling torrent—are most remarkable. Here, in particular, the glaciers, the most characteristic feature of this country, are seen to greatest advantage, not only those fantastically fractured masses of iceberg which descend into the low grounds, but those vast fields of ice called Mers de Glace. To the neighbourhoods of Mont Blanc and Monte Rosa must be given the preference in point of sublimity ; and the traveller will, for this reason, do well in reserving them for the termination of his tour, and the crowning acts of his journey.

Amongst the remarkable points from whence a near view of grand Alpine scenery may be obtained without danger or serious difficulty, the following may be selected :—

The Gorner Grat, above Zermatt ;
The Cramont, near Cormayeur, on the S. side of Mont Blanc ;
The Breven, near Chamouni, on the N. side of Mont Blanc ;
The Aeggischhorn, near Viesch, in the Upper Valais ;
The Sidelhorn, near the Grimsel ;
The Torrenthorn, above the Baths of Leuk ;
The Arpitetta Alp, in the Einfisch Thal.

Of accessible *Glaciers* the most remarkable are those of Chamouni and of Grindelwald. That of Rosenlaui is celebrated for its extreme purity, and the dark blue colour of its chasms.

An interesting account of excursions and ascents in some of the wildest and grandest parts of the Bernese and Valais Alps is given by Gottlob Studer in a small work entitled ' Topographische Mittheilungen aus dem Alpengebirge.' The first part, accompanied by six panoramic sketches, was published by Huber (Bern and St. Gall) in 1843. Desor's ' Excursions et Séjours dans les Glaciers,' &c., and the sequel, ' Nouvelles Excursions et Séjours,' &c., Neufchâtel, 1844 and 1845, contain also some interesting excursions, but the descriptions are not free from occasional inaccuracy and exaggeration.

The very best *delineations of Swiss scenery, glaciers, passes, travelling incidents, &c.,* are given in the large lithographic views of Mr. George Barnard.* They combine in a high degree picturesqueness with truth. They are far superior to the views which are to be found in the Swiss print-shops.

The earlier attempts at applying photography to represent the glaciers and snow regions of the Alps were not successful, but of late admirable likenesses have been obtained, particularly by Bisson of Paris. Some fine specimens have been exhibited in London and Paris, and may now be purchased in both cities.

Lakes.—Madame de Staël has somewhere remarked, on the proximity of lakes to mountains, that Nature seems to have placed them in the midst

* Published by Maclean, Haymarket, London.

—

of her grandest scenes, at the foot of the Alps, in order to serve as mirrors to them, and to multiply their enchanting forms. Lakes are very numerous in Switzerland, and they certainly add a principal charm to its scenery. It is difficult to classify them according to their respective merits, as almost every one has some peculiarity which characterises it and renders it worthy of attention. The most remarkable are, the Lake of Lucerne, which exhibits in perfection savage grandeur and sublimity; Wallenstadt, Thun, and Brienz, all thoroughly Swiss; the Lake of Geneva, or Lac Leman, distinguished for its great extent, and for the diversified character it presents, being at one end rugged and sublime, at the other soft and smiling: it occupies an intermediate rank between the Swiss and Italian Lakes. These last, that is to say, Maggiore, Lugano, and Como, may be included in the tour of Switzerland, either from portions of them being actually situated within its territory, or from their vicinity to it. Their character is rather smiling than frowning; they are blessed with a southern climate, in addition to their own attractions; their thickets are groves of orange, olive, myrtle, and pomegranate; and their habitations are villas and palaces. Along with the lakes named above must be mentioned the little Lake of Orta, which, though situated in Piedmont, lies so close to the Simplon, and possesses such high claims to notice from its surpassing beauty, that no traveller, approaching that corner of Switzerland to which it is a neighbour, should omit to visit it.

The attempt to fix an order of precedence for the *Swiss Waterfalls* is not likely to meet with general approval, because much of the interest connected with them depends on the seasons and the weather, as well as on the taste and temper of the spectator. A fine waterfall is, indeed, a magnificent spectacle; but it will be appreciated, not merely by its own merits, but, to use a mercantile phrase, according to the abundance of the supply. Now, in Switzerland, waterfalls are as numerous as blackberries. The traveller, after a week or fortnight's journey, is *pestered* by them, and will hardly turn his head aside to look at a fall which, if it were in Great Britain, would make the fortune of an English watering-place, and attract visitors half-way across our island to behold it. The fact seems to be that there is a certain monotony and similarity in all falls of water; and after the curiosity has once been satiated by the sight of three or four, it is tiresome to go out of one's way to visit another, unless it be much finer, and have a distinctive character from any seen before. Thus, then, there is utility even in an attempt to classify these natural objects.

1. The Fall of the Rhine, at Schaffhausen, deserves the first rank, from the volume of water; but it is rather a cataract than a cascade—it wants height.

2. Fall of the Aar, at Handek, combines a graceful shoot with great elevation; an abounding river, and a grand situation. It may be said to attain almost to perfection—(Terni being a perfect waterfall).

3. Fall of the Tosa, in the Val Formazza: remarkable less for its form than for the vast volume of water, but in this respect very fine indeed, and well worth a visit.

4. The Staubbach, or Dust Fall: a thread or scarf of water, so thin that it is dispersed into spray before it reaches the ground; beautiful, however, from its height and graceful wavings.

5. The Giesbach, on the lake of Brienz.

6. The Fall of the Sallenche, near Martigny.
7. Reichenbach Falls, near Meyringen.
8. The Fall of Pianazzo, or of the Medessimo, on the Splügen.
9. Turtman Fall, near the Simplon road.
10. Cascade du Dard, Chamouni.

Other falls, too numerous to mention, are not placed (to use the language of the race-course) ; though, in any other country but Switzerland or Norway, they would deserve especial notice.

The design of this enumeration is to spare the traveller a long walk, or a day's journey, to see a fall, probably inferior to others which he has already seen.

The principal and most interesting of the *Swiss Alpine Passes* (see § 14) are the Simplon, the St. Gothard, the Splügen, and the Bernardino, regarding at once their scenery, and the magnificent and skilfully constructed carriage-roads which have been made over them. Of passes not traversed by carriage-roads, keeping below the ice, and practicable for mules, the most striking are those of the Bonhomme, La Seigne, Tête Noire, and Col de Balme, leading to Chamouni ; the Grimsel, Furca, and Gries, branching off at the head of the valley of the Rhône ; the Scheideck and Wengen Alp, in the Bernese Oberland ; the Gemmi, one of the most singular of all the passes ; and the Great St. Bernard, chiefly visited on account of its celebrated Hospice. Of passes crossing the ice, the most remarkable are the Strahleck from the Grimsel, Tschingel from Lauterbrunnen, Monte Moro and St. Theodule from Zermatt, and the Col du Géant beside Mont Blanc.

Alpine Gorges.—Especially deserving of notice are some of the avenues leading up to these passes ; in many instances mere cracks or fissures, cleaving the mountains to the depth of several thousand feet.

None of these defiles at all approach the *Ravine of the Via Mala*, one of the most sublime and terrific scenes any where among the Alps. The gorge of the Schöllenen, on the St. Gothard ; that of Gondo, on the Simplon ; and that extraordinary glen, in whose depths the *Baths of Pfeffers* are sunk—one of the most wonderful scenes in Switzerland—also deserve mention ; as also the *valley of Leuk*.

The most beautiful *Swiss Valleys* are those of Hasli, near Meyringen ; the Simmenthal ; the Vale of Sarnen ; the Kanderthal ; the Vallée de Gruyères, and Ormonds, or Pays d'en Haut Romand—all distinguished for their quiet pastoral character, and the softness and luxuriance of their verdure—" The rock-embosomed lawns, and snow-fed streams," spoken of by Shelley. And here it may be remarked that the traveller in Switzerland must not suppose that beauty of scenery is confined to the High Alps : the intermediate undulating country between the Alps and Jura, which, though still greatly elevated above the sea, may be called the Lowlands, in reference to the Highlands of Switzerland, abounds in peculiar and unobtrusive beauties—hills tufted with woods, among which picturesque masses of bare rock project at intervals, slopes bursting with rills, and meadows which, by the aid of copious irrigation, yield three crops of grass a-year, presenting at all seasons a carpet of the liveliest verdure, and of a texture like velvet, equal to that of the best kept English lawns ;—such are the beauties of these lowland scenes. The frequent hedge-rows, the gardens before the cottages, and the neatness of the dwellings—the irregular, winding roads, free from the straight monotony and everlasting avenues of France and Germany—remind one frequently of England. There are, besides, among the Jura, many scenes of great grandeur; such especially is presented by the Val Moutiers, or Münster Thal, between Basle and Bienne; the pass of Klus, at the foot of the Ober-Hauenstein; and the Lac de Joux.

Switzerland covers 14,000 square miles, and in 1850 there were 2,420,000 Inhab.; 1,420,000 Prot., 970,000 Cath.: 1,670,000 speak German, 474,000 French, 176,000 Italian dialects.

With regard to the natural beauties of Switzerland, there can be but one sentiment of admiration. On the subject of the *moral condition of the Swiss*, and of their character as a nation, there is much variety of opinion. The Swiss with whom the traveller comes into contact, especially the German portion of them, are often sullen, obstinate, and disagreeable, and he is annoyed by the constant mendicancy of the women and children, even in remote districts, and on the part of those who are not, apparently, worse off than their neighbours. This disposes the traveller to dislike and to take very little interest in the people amongst whom he is travelling; he has also heard much of their timeserving, their love of money, and their readiness to fight for any paymaster in former times, and he at once dismisses them from his thoughts, and regards them pretty much as Childe Harold regarded the Portuguese. It may be doubted, however, whether an ordinary traveller is competent to form an opinion of the whole nation from those classes with which he is thrown into contact, and which have been taught to make him their prey. And, whatever may be the case as to the Swiss individually, yet, looked at as a nation, they are in many respects deserving of admiration, and, at the present moment, of interest, as being the only nation in continental Europe where practical liberty is enjoyed, and where the madness of 1848 did not rage, and has not produced disastrous results. Mr. Grote, the historian of Greece, in the preface to his admirable Letters on Switzerland says, " The inhabitants of the twenty-two cantons are interesting on every ground to the general intelligent public of Europe. But to one whose studies lie in the contemplation and interpretation of historical phenomena they are especially instructive; partly from the many specialities and differences of race, language, religion, civilization, wealth, habits, &c., which distinguish one part of the population from another, comprising between the Rhine and the Alps a miniature of all Europe, and exhibiting the fifteenth century in immediate juxta-position with the nineteenth; partly from the free and unrepressed action of the people, which brings out such distinctive attributes in full relief and contrast. To myself in particular they present an additional ground of interest from a certain political analogy (nowhere else to be found in Europe) with those who prominently occupy my thoughts, and on the history of whom I am engaged—the ancient Greeks."

We are so accustomed to look upon Switzerland as " the land of liberty," that the generality of travellers will take the thing for granted; and it is only after diving to a certain depth in Swiss annals, that the question arises, what was the nature of this freedom, and how far was it calculated to foster nobility of sentiment and public spirit among the people? Was the abolition of the Austrian dominion succeeded by a more equitable government, extending to all the same privileges, and dividing among all alike the public burden? Was political equality accompanied by religious tolerance and harmony? Did the democratic principle produce fruit in the disinterestedness and patriotism of the children of the land? To all these inquiries there remains but one answer—a negative. The cow-herds of Uri, Schwytz, and Unterwalden, who had so nobly, and with so much moderation, emancipated themselves from a foreign yoke, in process of time became themselves the rulers of subject states, and, so far from extending to them the liberty they had so dearly purchased, and which they so highly valued, they kept their subjects in the most abject state of villenage; so that, down to the end of the last century, the vassals of no despotic monarch in Europe exhibited a picture of equal political debasement. The effects of this tyrannical rule were equally injurious to the governors and the governed, and the marks of it may be traced in many parts of Switzerland, even down to the present day, in the degraded condition of the people, morally as well as physically. It will be discovered from Swiss history that ambition, and a thirst for territorial rule, are inherent in republics as well as in monarchies, as we may learn from the encroachments and aggrandizing spirit of canton Bern. She retained, as tributary to her, for two centuries and a half, the district called Pays de Vaud, deriving from it an annual revenue of 1,200,000 francs, and yet denying to the inhabitants all share of political rights. Geneva, a weaker state, after throwing off the yoke of the Dukes of Savoy, with difficulty escaped the wiles of the Bernese government, which would have plunged her into a slavery not more tolerable than that from which she had just escaped.

Religious dissensions were a source of a long series of troubles to the Confederation, dividing it into two opposite parties, which not only were arrayed against each other in the field of battle, but also interfered with the internal peace of the individual cantons. Although by the laws the two parties in religion were allowed equal freedom of worship, the enjoyment of this privilege was embittered to either party, in the state where the other faith was predominant: it was, in fact, but a nominal tolerance.

Down to the times of the French revolution, the common people of Switzerland, except in one or two of the cantons, had no more share in the constitutional privileges, which all Swiss were supposed to possess as their birthright, than the subjects of the despotic monarchies of Austria or Prussia. The government was vested in the hands of aristocratic oligarchies, as exclusive, and as proud of birth, blood, and descent, as the most ancient nobility in Europe. The burgher patricians of the great towns managed, by gradual encroachments, to deprive the lower orders of the exercise of their rights, and gradually monopolised all places and offices for themselves and their children; and even in some of the small cantons, where the constitution had been for ages in theory a pure democracy, every male above the age of 20 having a vote, the result not unfrequently was, that the same persons, and their children after them, were always elected to the offices of trust and power.

The twenty-two cantons of which Switzerland is now composed were first united in 1814, when the old aristocracies were generally restored.

Each canton had a vote in the annual diet, and whilst the diet was not sitting, by a most extraordinary arrangement, Berne, Lucerne, and Zürich, were alternately the Vorort, or presiding canton, and had the supreme government. In 1830 many of the cantons made great changes in their government, and the power of the old aristocracies was much reduced ; the larger cantons becoming somewhat democratic in tendency, after the French model, and wishing to introduce great changes. The old mountain-cantons, however, Lucerne, Fribourg, Valais, Schwyr, Uri, Zug, and Unterwalden, were perfectly contented with their forms of government. From their geographical position it was impossible for them ever to become rich or commercial, and they probably perceived that the changes would do them no good, and would no doubt increase their taxation, and they wished to be let alone—a feeling in which most Englishmen will sympathise. It must, however, be added that these cantons are all catholic, and entirely subjected to their priests ; generally very poor, and with a tendency to oppress their protestant fellow-citizens. In pursuance of their views they, in 1841, formed a league, or Sonderbund, to oppose by force, if necessary, the suppression of certain convents, and to maintain the jesuits. It was clear that whether their objects were right or wrong such a combination could not be permitted, and it was accordingly put down in 1847 by force, not without bloodshed. Since that time nearly all the cantons who had not altered their constitutions have done so, and at present in the majority of the cantons, particularly in the large protestant cantons, democratic principles, somewhat after the French model, have prevailed ; and in the Diet the democratic, or radical party as it is called, has had the majority. Whatever may be thought of their principles, and although there are to be found amongst them many men full of the wild designs and vague aspirations common on the Continent, it must be admitted that hitherto they have behaved with moderation, and have effected many excellent changes, though with a great increase of taxation. The electric telegraph has been established, railways introduced ; the coinage instead of being the worst has been made the best in Europe ; diligences and posting established ; tolls on roads abolished ; custom-house duties imposed on bulky articles only, so that passengers' luggage is not examined ; and a large sum is devoted every year to the making and maintaining the roads. These are not small improvements in seven or eight years, and it does not appear that any oppression has been exercised, unless the suppression of some convents, and the expulsion of the jesuits, can be looked upon in that view. Up to the present time the Diet has acted with great prudence ; internally, where it has to contend with the jealousies of the cantons and the intolerance of the two religions— the discontent of the old cantons and the violence of the extreme democrats ; and externally, where it has a difficult task between the great governments of France and Austria. The history of Switzerland up to 1840 is very well related in the History of Switzerland published by the Useful Knowledge Society ; and a voluminous history (French and German) up to 1842 has been compiled by Müller. From that time, with the exception of Mr. Grote's Letters, which only relate to four or five years, there seems to be no compilation giving the general history of the country.

The traveller at all events should be slow to find fault with the Swiss government. There are no passports, no custom-houses, no tolls, no gendarmes; none of those ridiculous restrictions to prevent people from incurring danger which are so annoying in France and Germany; and no interference whatever with individual absolute freedom (with the exception of some vexatious regulations as to guides lately introduced), whilst there are nearly everywhere good inns, good roads, and tolerable means of locomotion.

The *Towns* of Switzerland exhibit many interesting marks of antiquity: their buildings are frequently found unchanged since a very early period; and in Lucerne, Freyburg, Basle, Bellinzona, and in several other instances, the feudal fortifications, with battlements and watch-towers, remain perfectly preserved. One characteristic and very pleasant feature are the *Fountains*, the never-failing ornament of every Swiss town and village. They usually consist of a Gothic ornamented pillar, surmounted by the figure of a man, usually some hero of Swiss history, either Tell, the dauntless crossbowman, or Winkelried, with his "sheaf of spears." Sometimes the figures of animals are substituted for the human form.

The Swiss, as compared with other nations on the Continent, have a respect for antiquity which we in England should consider decidedly an aristocratic feeling. The old heroes of the country are held in great veneration, and there is no feeling of hatred for the former noble families. Each canton also puts up its coat-of-arms in every place where heraldic display would be at all admissible.

A singular custom, connected with education, prevails in some parts of Switzerland, which deserves notice here, from the influence which it exercises over society. In many of the large towns, children of the same age and sex are associated together by their parents in little knots and clubs, called *Sociétés de Dimanche*. The parents seek out for their children an eligible set of companions when they are still quite young. The parties so formed amount to twelve or fifteen in number, and the variation of age between them is not more than two or three years. All the members meet in turn on Sunday evenings, at the houses of their parents, while children, to play together and partake of tea, cakes, and sweetmeats, attended by their bonnes or nurses; when grown up, to pass the evening in other occupations and amusements suited to their age. At these meetings not even brothers or sisters are present, except they are members of the society. From thus being constantly thrown together on all occasions, a strict friendship grows up among the members of each brotherhood or sisterhood, which generally lasts through life, even after the parties are settled and dispersed about the world. The females, even when grown up, distinguish their companions by such endearing terms as "ma mignonne," "mon cœur," "mon ange," &c. This practice renders Swiss society very exclusive, and few strangers, however well introduced, penetrate below the surface. When a young woman marries, her husband is admitted into the society to which she belongs, and thus the wife determines the caste of the husband.

Costumes have now disappeared from many cantons: they are, however, worn much in the Oberland of Berne, and the women in many cantons have peculiar head-dresses. The men never wear a costume, and are usually attired in brown undyed homespun cloth.

Ranz de Vaches.—It is not uncommon to find the Ranz de Vaches spoken of, by persons unacquainted with Switzerland and the Alps, as a single air, whereas they are a class of melodies prevailing among and peculiar to the Alpine valleys. Almost every valley has an air of its own, but the original air is said to be that of Appenzell. Their effect in producing home-sickness in the heart of the Swiss mountaineer, when heard in a distant land, and the prohibition of this music in the Swiss regiments in the service of France, on account of the number of desertions occasioned by it, are stories often repeated, and probably founded on fact.

These national melodies are particularly wild in their character, yet full of melody ; the choruses consist of a few remarkable shrill notes, uttered with a peculiar falsetto intonation in the throat. They originate in the practice of the shepherds on the Alps, of communicating with one another at the distance of a mile or more, by pitching the voice high. The name Ranz de Vaches (Germ. Kuhreihen), literally *cow-rows*, is obviously derived from the order in which the cows march home at milking-time, in obedience to the shepherd's call, communicated by the voice, or through the *Alp-horn*, a simple tube of wood, wound round with bark, five or six feet long, admitting of but slight modulation, yet very melodious when caught up and prolonged by the mountain echoes. In some of the remoter pastoral districts of Switzerland, from which the ancient simplicity of manners is not altogether banished, the Alp-horn supplies, on the higher pastures, where no church is near, the place of the vesper-bell. The cow-herd, posted on the highest peak, as soon as the sun has set, pours forth the first four or five notes of the Psalm, " Praise God the Lord ;" the same notes are repeated from distant Alps, and all within hearing, uncovering their heads and bending their knees, repeat their evening orison, after which the cattle are penned in their stalls, and the shepherds betake themselves to rest.

A word may be said on *Swiss Husbandry* to draw the attention of such persons as take an interest in the subject, to one or two practices peculiar to the country. The system of irrigating the meadows is carried to a very great extent and perfection ; the mountain-torrents are turned over the fields by means of trenches and sluices, and not unfrequently, when the ground is much inclined, the stream is conducted to the spot where it is required through troughs hollowed out of the stem of fir-trees. The trenches sometimes extend for miles. The drainings of dunghills, cow-houses, and pigsties are not allowed to run to waste, but are carefully collected in a vat by the farmer, and at the fit moment carried out in carts to the fields, and ladled over them, very much to their benefit, and to the equal disgust of the olfactory nerves of all who pass ; the air, far and near, being filled with this truly Swiss fragrance. The industry of the people and their struggles for subsistence, in some of the high valleys, are truly wonderful. The grain-crops are wretched, but the grass is sweet and good. (See § 15.) In the best and lowest pasturages they get three crops a-year. The cattle feed on the high mountains during the summer, and are supported in châlets by the hay of the valley during the long winter. An Englishman accustomed to buy everything, can hardly realise the domestic economy of a Swiss peasant. He has his patches of wheat, of potatoes, of barley, of hemp, of flax, and, if possible, of vines ; his own cows, his own goats, his own sheep. On the produce of his own land and flocks he feeds ; his clothes are of homespun, from the wool of his sheep ;

his linen and the dresses of the women of his family are made from his own flax or hemp, frequently woven by the women of his own family. The timber he requires for his house or for firing is supplied from the land of the commune or parish, either for nothing or for a very small sum. What little money he requires is derived from the sale of cheese. The interior economy of a Swiss village is very interesting: it is only by ingenious contrivances for saving labour and by amazing industry that it is possible for the inhabitants to maintain themselves in such a climate.

The Swiss mountaineers are skilful marksmen with the rifle, and, like their neighbours the Tyrolese, meet constantly to practise and engage in trials of skill. There are clubs or societies in almost every valley and parish, and constant matches between them; besides which, in most of the cantons, and every year, a *grand Federal Rifle Match* is held near one or other of the large towns, at which all the best shots from the whole of Switzerland meet to contend for a prize. An accomplished English nobleman (Lord Vernon) gained the *first* prize at the Federal Match held at Basle, 1849.

There is *no regular army* in Switzerland, nor, with the exception of a few superior officers, is there any one who makes the army his exclusive profession. Every Swiss able-bodied man is however a soldier, and up to a certain age is called out for some weeks in the year to be drilled. This duty does not seem to be unpopular; and large bodies of soldierlike men are occasionally met with, going to or returning from their annual drill. The number of men regularly drilled and liable to be called out at any time is 64,000, and there is a reserve of 60,000 more; but the whole male population between 18 and 44, amounting to 340,000 men, are supposed to be available on an emergency. There are some crack corps, admission to which is obtained by exhibiting incredible skill with the rifle. The Swiss are by no means indisposed for fighting in their domestic disputes, and the contests between the different parties have been sanguinary and well contested.

Annual *contests in wrestling* also (called *Schwing Feste*) are held in different parts of Switzerland. The cantons which distinguish themselves for skill in this and other athletic exercises are Bern, Appenzell, and Unterwalden.

In the mountains everything is carried on men's and women's backs. Children of nine or ten are seen with a little wooden frame on their backs; as they grow older the size of the frame increases, and the weights which the men carry are surprising: 70 or 80 lbs. for 4 or 5 hours over the mountains. A man will carry 45 lbs. from Meyringen to Guttanen, 3 hours up a mountain-path, for 2 francs, or up the Rigi for 4½ francs.

Baths and Kurs.—In the course of this work baths will constantly be mentioned. There are many mineral springs in Switzerland, much resorted to by the Swiss themselves and by foreigners, but treated with utter neglect by the English, not one in a thousand of whom ever goes through a course of these baths. The arrangements are generally very rough; and there is an empiric course, or "kur," prescribed for each, from which benefit is supposed to be derived. There are other "kurs" in which faith is placed by foreigners. At Gais and other places the patient is put upon a diet of the milk left after cheese has been made: this is called "cure au petit lait." Near Vevay the grape "kur" is popular. The white sorts only are used, and of these from six to seven pounds are not unfrequently consumed in one day. The grapes are only eaten in the morning and forenoon, the other diet being chiefly animal, neither vegetables, milk, coffee, nor wine, being allowed. The grapes are supposed to improve the quality of the blood, and to act on the liver and mucous membranes. It might be imagined that the appetite would be palled by so large a quantity of grapes, but, on the contrary, it is said to be keenly excited : the " kur " is followed during a fortnight or three weeks under medical surveillance.

§ 14. ALPINE PASSES.

No part of the Alps is more interesting, either in a picturesque or in an historical point of view, than the passable gaps or notches in the ridge of the great chain, and the minor mountain buttresses branching from it, whereby alone this colossal wall of mountains may be scaled, and a direct passage and communication maintained between northern and southern Europe, as well as between one valley and another. It has been through these depressions that the great tide of population has poured since the earliest times ; from these outlets have issued the barbarian swarms which so often desolated, and at last annihilated, the Roman Empire. There are more than 50 of these passes over the Swiss portion of the Alpine chain alone, or immediately communicating with the Swiss frontier.* A list of the principal passes is given in § 13.

In seeking a passage over the Alps, the most obvious course was to find out the valleys which penetrate farthest into the great chain, following the course of the rivers to their sources, and then to take the lowest traversable part in order to descend the opposite side. The variety and sudden transition presented by such a route are highly interesting. In the course of one day's journey the traveller passes from the climate of summer to winter, through spring. The alteration in the productions keeps pace with that of the temperature. Leaving behind him stubble-fields, whence the corn has been removed and housed, he comes to fields yet yellow and waving in the ear ; a few miles farther and the crop is still green ; yet higher, and corn refuses to grow. Before quitting the region of corn he enters one of dark, apparently interminable forests of pine and larch, clothing the mountain-sides in a sober vestment. Above this the haymakers are collecting the short grass, the only produce which the ground will yield. Yet the stranger must not suppose that all is barrenness even at this elevation. It seems as though nature were determined to make one last effort at the confines of the region of vegetation. From beneath the snow-bed, and on the very verge of the glacier, the profusion of flowers, their great variety, and surpassing beauty, are exceedingly surprising. Some of the greatest ornaments of our gardens, here born to blush unseen,—gentians, violets, anemones, and blue-bells, intermixed with bushes of the red rhododendron, the loveliest production of the Alps, scattered over the velvet turf, give it the appearance of a carpet of richest pattern. The insect world is not less abundant and varied,—thousands of winged creatures are seen hovering over the flowers, enjoying their short

* Mr. Brockedon has admirably illustrated them, both with his pencil and pen, in his beautiful work entitled ' The Passes of the Alps,' 2 vols. 4to.

existence, for the summer at these elevations lasts but for 3 or 4 weeks : the rapid progress of vegetation to maturity is equalled by the rapidity of its decay, and in 8 or 10 days flowers and butterflies have passed away. Above this region of spring, with its gush of springs, its young herbage and vivid greensward, its hum of insects just burst forth, and its natural flower-beds glittering with rain-drops, that of winter in Lapland or Siberia succeeds. The traveller may form an idea of the height he has reached by observing the vegetation. Vines disappear at 2000 feet, generally sooner ; oak-trees and wheat at 3000 feet ; beeches and barley at 4000 feet ; pines and firs at 6000 feet. Above 9000 feet flowering plants are very rare, but up to 11,000 feet they are found in sunny crevices. Above 11,000 feet a few blackened lichens alone preserve the semblance of vegetable life. It will of course be understood that in favourable situations these limits will be exceeded ; in unfavourable situations they will not be reached. At the summit of a high pass and amongst the glaciers the rarefied air is icy cold, and exercise and quick motion are necessary to keep up the circulation of the blood. The agreeable murmur of falling water, which has accompanied the traveller hitherto incessantly, here ceases,—all is solitude and silence, interrupted only by the shrill whistle of the marmot, or the hoarse cawing of an ill-omened raven. The ptarmigan starts up from among heaps of unmelted snow at the traveller's approach, and the lämmergeyer (the condor of the Alps), disturbed in his repast on the carcass of a sheep or cow, is seen soaring upwards in a succession of corkscrew sweeps till he gains the ridge of the Alps, and then disappears.

Such are the remarkable gradations which the stranger encounters in the course of a few hours, on a single pass of the Alps ; but the most striking change of all is that from the region of snow and ice on the top of the mountain, to the sunny clime and rich vegetation of Italy, which await the traveller at the S. foot of the Alps. (See Rte. 59.)

The works of Nature, however, will not entirely occupy the attention and wonder of the wanderer in such a pass ; at least a share will be demanded for admiration of the works of man. The great highways, passable for carriages, over the high Alps, are, indeed, most surprising monuments of human skill and enterprise in surmounting what would appear, at first sight, to be intended by Nature as insurmountable. These proud constructions of art thread the valleys, cross the débris of rivers on long causeways, skirt the edge of the precipice, with walls of rock tottering over them, and torrents thundering below. Where the steep and hard surface of the cliff has not left an inch of space for a goat to climb along, they are conducted upon high terraces of solid masonry, or through a notch blasted by gunpowder in the wall of rock. In many instances a projecting buttress of the mountain has blocked up all passage for ages, saying " thus far and no farther :" the skill of the modern engineer has pierced through this a tunnel or gallery ; and the difficulty is vanquished, without the least change in the level of the road.

Sometimes an impediment is eluded by throwing bridges over a dizzy gorge, and shifting the road from side to side, frequently two or three times within the space of half a mile. Often the road reaches a spot down which the winter avalanches take their habitual course every year, sweeping everything before them, and which, even in summer, appears reeking and dripping with the lingering fragments of snow which it has left behind. Will not so irresistible an antagonist arrest the course of this frail undertaking of man? Not even the avalanche;—in such a situation the road either buries itself in subterranean galleries, driven through the mountain, or is sheltered by massive arcades of masonry, sometimes half a mile or three-quarters of a mile long. Over these the avalanche glides harmlessly, and is turned into the depths below.

Every opportunity is seized of gaining, by easy ascents, a higher level for the road; at length comes the main ascent, the central ridge, to be surmounted only by hard climbing. This is overcome by a succession of zigzag terraces, called *tourniquets* or *giravolte*, connected together by wide curves, to allow carriages to turn easily and rapidly. So skilful is their construction, with such easy bends and so gradual a slope, that in many Alpine roads the postilions, *with horses accustomed to the road*, trot down at a rapid pace. Sometimes as many as 50 of these zigzags succeed one another without interruption; and the traveller, as he passes backwards and forwards, hovering over the valley, is as though suspended to a pendulum, and swinging to and fro. The road itself has a most singular appearance, twisted about like an uncoiled rope or a riband unwound.

The travelling-carriage descends sometimes rapidly and without interruption for hours. A drag of tempered iron is quickly worn down, in that time, as thin as the blade of a knife, so great is the friction; and it is usual to substitute for the iron drag a wooden sabot, formed of the section of a fir-tree, with a groove cut in the centre to admit the wheel.

The winter's snow usually falls upon the Alpine passes more than 5000 ft. high about the second week in October (sometimes earlier), and continues till the first or second week in June. Yet even after this, the passage across the neck or Col, as it is called, is not stopped, except for a few days, until the snow can be cleared away. In some of the minor passes, indeed, traversed by a mere rough footpath or bridle-path, the traffic is much increased after the fall of the snow, which, by filling up depressions and smoothing the way, permits the transport of heavy merchandise on sledges, which move easily over the surface as soon as it is hardened.

Along the lines of the great carriage-roads strong houses are erected at intervals, called *Maisons de Refuge*, *Case di Ricovero*, occupied by persons called Cantonniers, who are employed in mending the road and keeping it free from snow in winter, and are also paid to assist travellers in danger during snow-storms.

As near as possible to the summit of the pass a *Hospice* is generally erected, usually occupied by a band of charitable monks, as in the case of the Great St. Bernard, the Simplon, Cenis, St. Gothard, &c. The direction of the road across the summit of the ridge is marked by a line of tall poles, which project above the snow, and, from being painted black, are easily recognised. Bells are rung in tempestuous weather, when the tourmente is raging and the mist and falling snow hide the landmarks, that the sound may aid when the sight fails.

The morning after a fall of snow labourers and peasants are assembled from all sides to shovel it off from the road. Where it is not very deep, it is cleared away by a snow-plough drawn by 6 or 8 oxen. As the winter advances and fresh falls occur, the snow accumulates, and the road near the summit of a pass presents the singular aspect of a path or lane cut between walls of snow sometimes 10 or 20 ft. high. Carriages are taken off their wheels and fastened upon sledges; ropes are attached to the roof, which are held by 6 or 8 sturdy guides running along on each side, to prevent the vehicle upsetting and rolling over the slippery ice down a precipice. In this manner very high passes are crossed in the depth of winter with little risk. The spring is a season during which far greater danger is to be apprehended, from the avalanches which then fall.

The Swiss are essentially a road-making nation, and had good roads when those of continental Europe generally were still execrable. They bestow an amount of care and expense in avoiding hills and steep declivities which should make an Englishman ashamed of the state of things in the hilly parts of England. It is, however, strange that, after having spent enormous time and money in making a road level and good enough for a mail-coach at 11 miles an hour, they should persist in crawling along at 5 or 6 miles an hour.

§ 15. CHÂLETS AND PASTURAGES.

From the mountainous nature of Switzerland and its high elevation, the greater part of the surface, more than 1800 ft. above the sea, which is not bare rock, is pasture-land. The wealth of the people, like that of the patriarchs of old, in a great measure lies in cattle and their produce, on which account the pastoral life of the Swiss deserves some attention. The bright verdure of the meadows which clothe the valleys of Switzerland is one of the distinguishing features of the country; and the music of the cow-bells, borne along by the evening breeze, is one of the sweetest sounds that greet the traveller's ear.

The Alps, or mountain-pasturages (for that is the meaning of the word Alp in Switzerland and Tyrol) are usually the property of the commune; in fact common land, on which the inhabitants of the neighbouring town or village have the right of pasturing a certain number of cattle, the regulations as to which are often very curious.

" In the spring, as soon as the snow has disappeared, and the young grass sprouts up, the cattle are sent from the villages up to the first and lower pastures. Should a certain portion of these be exhausted, they change their quarters to another part of the mountain. Here they stay till about the 10th or 12th of June, when the cattle are driven to the middle ranges of pastures. That portion of the herds intended for a summer campaign on the highest Alps remain here till the beginning of July, and on the 4th of that month generally ascend to them; return to the middle range of pastures about 7 or 8 weeks afterwards, spend there about 14 days or 3 weeks, to eat the aftergrass; and finally return into the valleys about the 10th or 11th of October, where they remain in the vicinity of the villages till driven by the snow and tempests of winter into the stables.

" That portion of the cattle, on the other hand, which is not destined to pass the summer on the higher Alps, and are necessary for the supply of the village with milk and butter, descend from the middle pastures on the 4th of July into the valley, and consume the grass upon the pasturage belonging to the commune, till the winter drives them under shelter. The very highest Alpine pasturages are never occupied more than 3 or 4 weeks at the furthest."—*Latrobe.* The tourist in the higher Alps continually meets the flocks and herds migrating from one pasture to another, or to the valley below.

Sometimes the owners of the cattle repair in person to the Alps, and pass the summer among them along with their families, superintending the herdsmen, and assisting in the manufacture of cheese ; and in some parts there are whole villages only inhabited temporarily ; but in general only a sufficient number of men to attend to the herds and to make the cheeses remain with the cattle, in which case the cows or goats belonging to each owner are tried twice a-year, *i. e.* the amount of cheese produced in a day or two by each is ascertained ; then at the end of the season the cheese made is divided among the owners in the proportions indicated by the trial. The best cheeses are made upon pastures 3000 ft. above the sea-level, in the vales of Simmen and Saanen (Gruyère) and in the Emmenthal. The best cows there yield, in summer, between 20 lbs. and 40 lbs. of milk daily, and each cow produces, by the end of the season of 4 months, on an average, 2 cwt. of cheese.

The life of the cowherd (Fr. *Vacher*, Germ. *Senner*) is by no means such an existence of pleasure as romances in general, and that of Rousseau in particular, have represented it. His labours are dirty, arduous, and constant; he has to collect 80 or 90 cows twice a-day to be milked, to look after stragglers, to make the cheese, and keep all the utensils employed in the process in the most perfect state of cleanliness. In some parts the herdsmen live for many months almost entirely on milk and cheese, not eating 10 lbs. of bread or potatoes in the time. The cattle are frequently enticed home at milking time by the offer of salt, which they relish highly, and which is considered very wholesome for them. The allowance for a cow is 4 or 5 lbs. in a quarter of a year.

The *Châlet* (Germ. Sennhütte) in which the herdsman resides is literally a log-hut, formed of trunks of pines, notched at the extremities so as to fit into one another at the angles of the building, where they cross : it has a low flat roof, weighted with stones to keep fast the shingle-roof and prevent its being blown away by the wind. A building of this kind is rarely air-tight or water-tight. The interior is usually blackened with smoke and very dirty, boasting of scarcely any furniture, except, perhaps, a table and rude bench, and the apparatus of the dairy, including a huge kettle for heating the milk. A truss of straw, in the loft above, serves the inmates for a bed. The ground around the hut on the outside is usually poached by the feet of the cattle, and the heaps of mud and dung render it difficult to approach the door.

There is another kind of *châlet*, a mere shed or barn, in which the hay is housed until the winter, when it is conveyed over the snow in sledges down to the villages below. A pastoral Swiss valley is usually speckled over with huts of this kind, giving it the appearance, to a stranger, of being much more populous than it is in reality : in the Simmenthal alone there are, it is said, 10,000 châlets. This large number of châlets is necessary, because everything—goats, sheep, cattle, horses, and food—must be put under cover for some months during the snow.

The herdsmen shift their habitations from the lower to the upper pasturages, as their cattle ascend and descend the Alps, at different seasons, and they sometimes have 2 or 3 places of temporary abode. The weary traveller in search of repose or refreshment, after a long day's journey, is often disappointed, on approaching what he conceives to be a human habitation, to find either that it is a mere hay-barn, or else a deserted châlet; and thereby learns, with much mortification, that he has still some tedious miles to trudge before he can reach the first permanently occupied dwelling. What an agreeable contrast to reach a well-appointed châlet of the better sort, where delicious milk, cooled in the mountain stream, fresh butter, bread, and cheese, are spread out on a clean napkin before the hungry and tired stranger!

§ 16. GLACIERS* (GERM. GLETSCHER: ITAL. GHIACCIAIA).

The Glaciers are one of the most sublime features of the Alps, and one of the most wonderful phenomena of nature. A glacier may be described as a stream of ice, descending into the valleys of high mountain chains, fed by the snow which occupies their tops and fills the hollows and clefts between their peaks and ridges; what it loses at its lower end by the increased temperature is supplied by the descent of new masses from the upper regions. The snow which falls upon the summits and plateaux of the high Alps is at first a dry and loose powder. The action of the sun gradually converts this into a granular mass, as the portion which is melted during the heat of the day is recrystallised in irregular roundish grains. In this state the entire mass appears white and opaque, but the separate grains are transparent. In the course of successive years, in consequence of repeated thawings and freezings, the whole becomes consolidated into a seemingly solid mass of ice; but when closely examined this mass of glacier ice is found to be penetrated by innumerable fissures, and consists in fact of separate granules closely compressed and cemented together, and for this reason a glacier is not slippery like ordinary ice. It is, however, now asserted that this granular texture only prevails near the surface, and that deep glacier ice is close and solid. The inhabitants of the Alps have distinct terms for these modifications of the snowy covering of the high Alps. The upper granular and unconsolidated part they call *Firn*, or *Névé* in French, and apply the term *Glacier* (Gletscher) to the lower limbs of more solid ice, which stretch down into the valleys. The Firn, or Névé, is a region of complete desolation; no animal intrudes upon it save a chance insect, and only the scantiest lichens appear on the rocks around it. The firn occurs only at a height where the snow which falls in the winter does not entirely disappear in the course of the following year; while that which falls on the lower glacier is almost always melted in the course of the following summer, and never combines with the ice. Hugi maintains that the point at which firn changes to glacier is invariable among the Alps; and his investigations fix it at an elevation of about 7800 ft. above the sea-level.†

* The best information respecting glaciers is to be found in Professor Forbes' 'Travels in the Alps,' already alluded to, and in Agassiz's 'Etudes sur les Glaciers. Local names for glaciers— in Tyrol, Firn; in Carinthia, Käs; in the Grisons, Wader or Vedreg; in part of Italy, Vedretto; in the Vallais, Biegno; in Piedmont, Ruize; in the Pyrenees, Serneille.

† A serious error is conveyed by the common expression, "the line of perpetual snow," or, "where snow never melts." There is no spot on the Alps, nor on any other snow-clad mountains, where snow does not melt under the influence of a summer sun at mid-day. It melts even on the top of Mont Blanc; but there, and on the summits of the other high Alps, the duration of the sun's heat is so short, that very little is melted during the year, and, for the same reason, there is very little moisture in the air, and, consequently, very little snow can fall: so

Escher has computed the number of glaciers among the Swiss Alps at 600, and the extent of surface occupied by them at 1000 square miles : this, however, must be but a vague estimate. They vary from a few square yards to acres and miles in extent, covering, in some instances, whole districts, filling up entirely the elevated hollows and basins between the peaks and ridges of the Alps, and sending forth arms and branches into the inhabited valleys, below the region of forests, and as far down as the level at which corn will grow.

It is such offsets of the glacier as these that are presented to the view of the traveller from the villages of Chamouni, Zermatt, and Grindelwald. These, however, are, as it were, but the skirts and fringes of that vast everlasting drapery of ice which clothes all the upper region of the Alps. These fields or tracts of uninterrupted glacier have been called " Seas of Ice " (Mers de Glace, Eismeeren), and there are three such among the Swiss and Savoyard Alps, which merit especial mention ; that around Mont Blanc, that around the Monte Rosa and the Cervin, and that of the Bernese Oberland, around the Finster-Aar-Horn. The last sends out no less than 13 branches ; its extent has been estimated at 125 square m., and it is supposed to be the largest in Europe.

The greatest thickness of the glaciers has been commonly estimated at between 600 and 800 ft. Hugi rarely met with any thicker than 150 ft. ; he calculates the average depth at between 60 and 100 ft., and the greatest thickness of the Mer de Glace, on the N. flank of Mont Blanc, is estimated by Forbes at 350 ft. deep. Saussure had calculated it at 600 ft. Agassiz assures us that there are holes in the Aar glacier 780 ft. deep.

Notwithstanding their great extent and solidity, the glaciers are undergoing a perpetual process of renovation and destruction. The lower portions descending into the valleys are gradually dissolved by the increased temperature which prevails at so low a level. The summer sun, aided by particular winds, acts upon the surface, so that, in the middle of the day, it abounds in pools, and is traversed by rills of water. The constant evaporation, from every part exposed to the air, produces great diminution in the upper beds ; the temperature of the earth, also, which is at all seasons greater than that of ice, melts yearly a small portion of its lower surface, reducing the bulk and height of the glacier, which, towards the end of summer, is many feet lowered and shrunken. The vacancy thus caused is entirely filled up from above by the winter's snow falling upon the mountain-tops, and on the whole upper region of the high Alps, which flows into the higher valleys, pressed down by its own weight. Henceforth the ice-stream, like the river, moves onward steadily by day and night, and even in the winter, though its progress is slower,

> " The glacier's cold and restless mass
> Moves onward day by day."—*Byron*.

It is also sensibly retarded by hard frost, and accelerated by thaw. The

that on the whole, and in a series of years, the quantity which falls is about equal to the quantity which is melted. What is called "*the snow line*" does not depend on elevation alone, and can be taken only as a very general test of it. Independent of its variation, according to the degree of latitude in which the mountain is situated, it varies on the two sides of the same mountain, being higher on the S. side than the N. The snow will likewise rest longer, and extend lower down, upon a mountain of granite than upon one of limestone, in proportion as the two rocks are good or bad conductors of heat, and this is the case even in contiguous mountains, members of the same chain.

snow which has fallen in the winter on the lower part of the glacier melts in the spring, as it would on land; and, on cold nights, the small pools of water on the glacier freeze, and thaw again under the sun's rays.

The cause of the movement of glaciers has been much discussed and variously explained. De Saussure supposed that it proceeds from their weight alone, and that they slide down the inclined surface of the valleys, aided by the ice melting below, in contact with the earth. Others have thought that the descent was caused by dilatation of the glacier, in consequence of the water that penetrates the mass of ice, alternately thawing and freezing. The third, and apparently the correct theory of their motion, the result of patient and acute study of glacier phenomena, is that of Professor Forbes, who asserts that "a glacier is an imperfect fluid, or viscous body, which is urged down slopes of a certain inclination by the mutual pressure of its parts;" nearly in the same manner as lava descends from the mouth of a volcano, or honey would flow from a jar overset. Professor Forbes elsewhere explains that "a glacier is not coherent ice (like the ice of a river), but a granular compound of ice and water, possessing, under certain circumstances, especially when much saturated with water, a rude flexibility, sensible even to the hand." This viscous character of the glacier alone will account for its passing through straits formed by projecting rocks, which contract the width of its bed sometimes to one-half of its expanse in the upper part of a valley, and around promontories which intrude to turn it out of its course. Professors Faraday, Tyndall, and Huxley, take exception to the word "viscous," maintaining that ice is "plastic," and that the changes in the form of masses of ice are occasioned by the fracture and subsequent freezing together of the component parts (Proc. of Roy. Inst., 1850 and 1857). The centre of the ice-stream moves quicker than the sides, and, in fact, drags them after it, as would be the case with any other semi-fluid.

The surface of the mountain, which forms the bed of a glacier, however hard, is subjected to an extraordinary process of grinding and polishing from the vast masses of ice constantly passing over it. The harder fragments, such as granite and quartz, interposed between the ice and the rock, act like diamonds on glass, and scratch deep and long grooves on the surface. The seat of ancient glaciers, which have now entirely disappeared, may still be discovered by the furrows left behind them on the rocks. These furrows and polished surfaces (roches montonnées) are very remarkable above Guttanen on the Grimsel road. The motion of a glacier may be admirably observed at the Rosenlaui glacier. The foot of the glacier there, being on a surface of rock, marks its advance or retrogression daily by the heaps of rubbish it pushes forwards, whilst on the rocks above may be seen the moraine of the glacier in former years when it was larger.

The nature of the upper surface of the ice depends partly upon that of the ground on which it rests: where it is even, or nearly so, the ice is smooth and level; but whenever the supporting surface becomes slanting or uneven, the glacier begins to split and gape in all directions. As it approaches a steeper declivity or precipice, or where, as in the lower glacier of Grindelwald, it passes through a narrow passage, the layers of ice are displaced, upheaved, and squeezed one above another; they rise in toppling crags, obelisks, and towers of the most fantastic shapes, varying in height from 20 to 80 ft. Being unequally melted by the wind and sun, they are continually tottering to their fall, either by their own weight, or the pressure of other masses, and, tumbling headlong, are shivered to atoms with a roar like thunder. After the difficulties are passed, these aiguilles and obelisks of ice, being pressed together at the bottom of the descent, close up again, and, as soon as the surface of the mountain below them is level, assume a nearly level and compact character on their own surface. The glaciers assume this fractured character generally near their lower extremity, when they begin to bend down towards the valley.

The *Crevasses*, or fissures, which traverse the upper portion of the glacier, before it becomes entirely fractured and disruptured, run in a transverse direction, never extending quite across the ice-field, but narrowing out at the extremities, so that when they gape too wide to leap across, they may always be turned by following them to their termination. These rents and fissures are the chief source of danger to those who cross the glaciers; sometimes, from their numbers, monotonous sameness of appearance, and perplexing confusion, by which the traveller is nearly bewildered, and even the most experienced guides are frequently at fault and lose their way, and have the greatest difficulty in extricating themselves from their intricacies. Sometimes the crevasses are concealed by a treacherous coating of snow; and many a bold chamois-hunter has found a grave in their recesses. Ebel mentions an instance of a shepherd, in 1787, who, in driving his flock over the ice to a high pasturage, had the misfortune to tumble into one of these clefts. He fell in the vicinity of a torrent which flowed under the glacier, and, by following its bed under the vault of ice, succeeded in reaching the foot of the glacier with a broken arm. The man's name was Christian Boven: he was living in 1849, and acted as guide to the upper glacier of Grindelwald. More melancholy was the fate of M. Mouron, a clergyman of Vevay: he was engaged in making some scientific researches upon the glacier, and was in the act of leaning over to examine a singular well-shaped aperture in the ice, when the staff on which he rested gave way; he was precipitated to the bottom, and his lifeless and mangled body was recovered from the depths of the glacier a few days after.

These crevasses, though chiefly formed mechanically by the movement of the glacier, and the unequal pressure of its different parts, are greatly influenced by the action of the sun and wind. The S.E. wind, in Uri and among the Bernese Alps, is very instrumental in causing the glacier to split, and the loud reports thus occasioned, called by the herdsmen the growlings (brullen) of the glacier, are regarded as a sign of bad weather. The traveller who ventures to cross any of the larger glaciers may, at times, both hear and see the fissures widening around him. The crevasses exhibit in perfection the beautiful *azure blue* colour of the glacier; the cause of which has not been satisfactorily accounted for. It is the same tint of ultramarine which the Rhône exhibits at Geneva, after leaving all its impurities behind it in the lake; and the writer has even observed the same beautiful tint in footmarks and holes made in fresh-fallen snow, not more than a foot deep, among the high Alps on the borders of Tyrol.

The traveller who has only *read* of glaciers is often disappointed at the first sight of them, by the appearance of their surface, which is rough-tossed about in hillocks and gullies, and, except when covered with fresh, fallen snow, or at very great heights, has none of the purity which might be expected from fields of ice. On the contrary, it usually exhibits a surface of dirty white, soiled with mud, and often covered with stones and gravel. Such beds of stone, dirt, and rubbish are common to most glaciers, and are called *Moraines*, running along the glacier in parallel lines at the sides (called *lateral* Moraines, German *Gandecken*); or in the middle (*medial* Moraines, in German *Guffer*), and *terminal* or end Moraines. They are formed in the following manner:—The edges of the glacier, at its upper extremity, receive the fragments of rock detached from the mountains around by the destructive agency of moisture and frost; but as the glacier itself is constantly descending, this fallen rubbish goes along with it, increased from behind by the débris of each succeeding winter, so that it forms a nearly uninterrupted line from the top of the ice-field to the bottom, thus forming a lateral moraine. Wherever the glacier from one valley meets that of another, the moraines from the two unite and form one, running down the centre of the united glacier instead of along its margin, as before, thus forming a medial moraine. Such a confluence of moraines is well seen on the glacier of the Aar (Route 28); and upon the great glaciers descending from Monte Rosa (Route 106) six or eight may be seen running side by side, each traceable to its origin by the nature of the rocks composing it.

" The moraines remain upon the surface of the glacier, and, unless after a very long or very uneven course, they are not dissipated or ingulfed. On the contrary, the largest stones attain a conspicuous pre-eminence; the heaviest moraine, far from indenting the surface of the ice, or sinking amongst its substance, rides upon an icy ridge as an excrescence, which gives to it the character of a colossal back-bone of the glacier, or sometimes appears like a noble causeway, fit, indeed, for giants, stretching away for leagues over monotonous ice, with a breadth of some hundreds of feet, and raised from 50 to 80 ft. above its general level. Almost every stone, however, rests upon ice; the mound is not a mound of débris, as it might at first sight appear."—*Forbes.*

The *terminal moraines* are heaped up often to a height of 80 or 100 ft., and sometimes much higher: the moraines in the Allée Blanche and on the glacier of Blettière at Chamouni must be 500 or 600 ft. high. Not unfrequently there are 3 or 4 such ridges, one behind the other, like so many lines of intrenchment. The broken stones, sand, and mud, mixed with shattered fragments of ice, of which they are composed, have an unsightly appearance, being perfectly barren of vegetation; but each heap is, as it were, a geological cabinet, containing specimens of all the neighbouring mountains. The glacier, indeed, has a natural tendency to purge itself from impurities, and whatever happens to fall upon it is gradually discharged in this manner. It likewise exerts great mechanical force, and, like a vast millstone, grinds down not only the rock which composes its channel, but all the fragments interposed between it and the rock; forming, in the end, a sort of stone-meal. The extent of the moraine depends on the character of the strata of the mountains around the glacier: where they are of granite, or other hard rock, not easily decomposed by the weather, the moraine is of small extent; and it is largest where the boundary rocks are of brittle limestone and fissile slate. The researches of Swiss naturalists (Agassiz and Charpentier) have discovered extensive moraines, not only in the lower part of the Valais, but even on the shores of the Lake Leman, at a height of not more than 200 or 300 ft. above it; indicating that, during some anterior condition of our planet, the valley of the Rhône was occupied by glaciers, in situations at present 40 or 50 m. distant from the nearest existing ice-field, and 3000 or 4000 ft. below it. The existence of boulder-stones, so common on the Jura and elsewhere, is now generally attributed to glaciers, the boulders having been either carried on the surface of glaciers to their present position, or floated there on icebergs broken off from glaciers.

A singular circumstance occurs when a single large mass of rock has fallen upon the glacier; the shade and protection from the sun's rays afforded by the stone prevents the ice on which it rests from melting, and, while the surface around is gradually lowered, it remains supported on a pedestal or table, like a mushroom on a stalk, often attaining a height of several feet; at length the stone falls off the pillar and the process recommences. The glaciers of the Aar furnish fine examples of these *tables des glaciers*, as they are called. The surface of the glacier has been ascertained to lose 3 ft. of surface by melting in as many weeks. An exactly opposite phenomenon occurs when a small stone, not more than an inch thick, or a leaf, rests upon the ice. As it absorbs the sun's rays with greater rapidity than ice, not merely its surface but its entire substance is warmed through, and instead of protecting it melts the ice below it, and gradually sinks, forming a hole to a considerable depth, and generally a pool of water, of which the traveller is often glad to avail himself: these little pools are generally frozen over at night.

The occurrence of Red Snow, which at one time was treated with incredulity, is common among the High Alps, and is produced either by minute insects and their eggs, or by a species of fungus, called Palmella Nivalis, or Protococcus, a true vegetable, which plants itself on the surface of the snow, takes root, germinates, produces seed, and dies. In the state of germination it imparts a pale carmine tint to the snow: this increases, as the plant comes to maturity, to a deep crimson blush, which gradually fades, and, as the plant decays, becomes a black dust or mould. By collecting some of the coloured snow in a bottle, and pouring it on a sheet of paper, the form of the plant may be discovered with a microscope, as soon as the water has evaporated.

It has been already observed that the vacancy caused by the melting of the lower portion of the glacier is filled up by the winter snow from above. But, as may be supposed, it often happens, after mild winters and warm summers, that the supply is not equal to the void, and *vice versâ*: after severe winters and rainy summers, the glacier is overloaded, as it were · indeed, it is scarcely possible that an exact equilibrium of supply and consumption should be preserved, and there is no doubt that glaciers are subject both to temporary and to secular variation. The glaciers throughout the Alps appear to have made a general movement in advance between the years 1817 and 1822, in consequence of the coldness of the six preceding summers. The glaciers of Bossons and des Bois, in the valley of Chamouni, and that of Grindelwald, in the Bernese Alps, extended so far in width as well as length, as to overthrow large trees of the growth of many centuries. Afterwards they began to retreat, and soon regained their original limits. Instances have occurred of the sudden advance of a glacier, as in the Gadmenthal (Route 32), where a road has been destroyed by this cause, and even of the formation of new glaciers within the memory of man, as in the Upper Engadine (?), and at the base of the Titlis : but these have been followed by a similar retrocession, and the newly formed ice-fields are rarely permanent. It is certain that, at present, both the Mer de Glace, under Mont Blanc, and the Grindelwald Glacier, appear to have shrunk, and sunk considerably below the level they once attained ; but this may be merely temporary, or even only their dimensions in summer, when most reduced. Prof. Forbes state that in 1845 the glacier of Findelen, near Zermatt, was retreating ; since that time it has advanced, destroying fields and châlets ; and Sir C. Lyell has informed the Editor that it advanced in 1857, notwithstanding the unusual heat of that summer.

Professors Agassiz, Forbes, and Hugi have made some interesting experiments and observations upon the movement and rate of progress of the glaciers. In 1829 Hugi noted the position of numerous loose blocks lying on the surface of the lower glacier of the Aar, relatively to the fixed rocks at its sides. He also measured the glacier and erected signal-posts on it. In 1836 he found everything altered ; many of the loose blocks had moved off and entirely disappeared, along with the ice that supported them. A hut, which he had hastily erected, to shelter himself and his companions, had advanced 2184 ft. A mass of granite, containing 26,000 cubic ft., originally buried under the snow of the firn, which had become converted into glacier, had not only been raised to the surface, but was elevated above it, in the air, upon two pedestals, or pillars, of ice ; so that a large party might have found shelter under it. A signal-post, stuck into a mass of granite, had not only made as great an advance as the hut, but the distance between it and the hut had been increased 760 ft. by the expansion of the glacier. In 1839 M. Agassiz found that Hugi's cabin had advanced 4400 ft. from the position it originally occupied, when first built in 1827 ; and in 1840 it was 200 ft. lower. Hugi's observations on the Aar glacier give as its rate of motion 240 ft. per annum. Professor Forbes' more recent and precise experiments have ascertained the daily motion of the ice on the Mer de Glace, have proved that it proceeds regularly, and not by fits and starts, but accelerated in speed by thaws and retarded by frosts, and that the motion is different in different parts of the glacier. The advance of the ice-field of the Mer de Glace is calculated at between 600 and 700 ft. yearly, or nearly 2 ft. a day ; so that the traveller, whilst walking over the glacier, is insensibly descending to the valley below.

It is highly interesting to consider how important a service the glaciers perform in the economy of nature. These dead and chilly fields of ice, which prolong the reign of winter throughout the year, are, in reality, the source of life and the springs of vegetation. They are the locked-up reservoirs, the sealed fountains, from which the vast rivers traversing the great continents of our globe are sustained. The summer heat, which dries up other sources of water, first opens out their bountiful supplies. When the rivers of the plain begin to shrink and dwindle within their parched beds, the torrents of the Alps, fed by melting snow and glaciers, rush down from the mountains and supply the deficiency; and, at that season (July and August), the rivers and lakes of Switzerland are fullest.

During the whole summer, the traveller who crosses the glaciers hears the torrents rustling and running below him at the bottom of the azure clefts. These plenteous rills gushing forth in their sub-glacial beds, are generally all collected in one stream, at the foot of the glacier, which, in consequence, is eaten away into a vast dome-shaped arch, sometimes 100 ft. high, gradually increasing until the constant thaw weakens its support, and it gives way and falls in with a crash. Such caverns of ice are seen in great perfection, in some years, at the source of the Arveyron, in the valley of Chamouni, and in the glaciers of Grindelwald. The streams issuing from glaciers are distinguished by their turbid dirty-white or milky colour. The waters collected by the melting of the ice from all parts of the surface of a glacier often accumulate into torrents, which, at length, precipitate themselves into a hole or fissure in its surface in the form of a cascade.

The following striking passage from Professor Forbes's ' Alps,' p. 386, will form a good conclusion to this account of glaciers :—" Poets and philosophers have delighted to compare the course of human life to that of a river ; perhaps a still apter simile might be found in the history of a glacier. Heaven-descended in its origin, it yet takes its mould and conformation from the hidden womb of the mountains which brought it forth. At first soft and ductile, it acquires a character and firmness of its own, as an inevitable destiny urges it on its onward career. Jostled and constrained by the crosses and inequalities of its prescribed path, hedged in by impassable barriers which fix limits to its movements, it yields groaning to its fate, and still travels forward seamed with the scars of many a conflict with opposing obstacles. All this while, although wasting, it is renewed by an unseen power,—it evaporates, but is not consumed. On its surface it bears the spoils which, during the progress of existence, it has made its own ; often weighty burdens devoid of beauty or value, at times precious masses, sparkling with gems or with ore. Having at length attained its greatest width and extension, commanding admiration by its beauty and power, waste predominates over supply, the vital springs begin to fail ; it stoops into an attitude of decrepitude—it drops the burdens, one by one, which it had borne so proudly aloft—its dissolution is inevitable. But as it is resolved into its elements, it takes all at once a new, and livelier, and disembarrassed form : from the wreck of its members it arises 'another, yet the same '—a noble, full-bodied, arrowy stream, which leaps rejoicing over the obstacles which before had stayed its progress, and hastens through fertile valleys towards a freer existence, and a final union in the ocean with the boundless and the infinite."

§ 17. AVALANCHES—SNOW-STORMS—FLOODS.

"The avalanche—the thunderbolt of snow."—*Byron.*

Avalanches (Germ. Lawinen) are those accumulations of snow which precipitate themselves from the mountains, either by their own weight or by the loosening effects of the sun's heat, into the valleys below, sweeping everything before them, and causing, at times, great destruction of life and property. The fearful crash which accompanies their descent is often heard at a distance of several leagues.

The natives of the Alps distinguish between several different kinds of avalanches. The *staub-lawinen* (dust avalanches) are formed of loose fresh-fallen snow, heaped up by the wind early in the winter, before it has begun to melt or combine together. Such a mass, when it reaches the edge of a cliff or declivity, tumbles from point to point, increasing in quantity as well as in impetus every instant, and spreading itself over a wide extent of surface. It descends with prodigious rapidity, and has been known to rush down a distance of 10 m. from the point whence it was first detached; not only descending one side of a valley, but also ascending the opposite hill by the velocity acquired in its fall, overwhelming and laying prostrate a whole forest of firs in its descent, and breaking down another forest, up the opposite side, so as to lay the heads of the trees up the hill in its ascent. *Slide-avalanches* (Schleich-lawine or Schlipfe) slip down from inclined surfaces often without disturbance of the surface, and it is only when they begin to roll over and bound that they become schlag or grund-lawinen.

Another kind of avalanche, the *Grund-lawinen*, occurs in spring, during the months of April and May, when the sun becomes powerful, and the snow thaws rapidly under its influence. They fall constantly from different parts of the mountains, at different hours in the day, accordingly as each part is reached by the sun: from the E. side between 10 and 12, from the S. side between 12 and 2, and later in the day from the W. and N. This species is more dangerous in its effects, from the snow being clammy and adhesive, as well as hard and compact. Any object buried by it can only be dug out by the most arduous labour. Men or cattle overwhelmed by the staub-lawine can extricate themselves by their own exertions; or, at any rate, from the snow being less compact, may breathe for some hours through the interstices. In the case of the grund-lawine, the sufferers are usually either crushed or suffocated, and are, at any rate, so entangled that they can only be rescued by the aid of others. Such avalanches falling upon a mountain-stream, in a narrow gorge, are often hollowed out from beneath by the action of the water, until it has forced a passage under them; and they have then been left standing for the whole summer, serving as a bridge, over which men and cattle might pass.

The avalanches have usually a fixed time for descending, and an habitual channel down which they slide, which may be known by its being worn perfectly smooth, sometimes even appearing polished, and by the heap of débris at its base. The peasants, in some situations, await with impatience the fall of the regular avalanches, as a symptom of the spring having fairly set in, and of the danger being over.

Danger arises from avalanches either by their falling unexpectedly, while persons are traversing spots known to be exposed to them, or else (and this is the more fearful source of catastrophes) when an unusual accumulation of snow is raised by the wind, or when the severity of the season causes the avalanche to desert its usual bed, and the whole mass descends upon cultivated spots, houses, or even villages. There are certain valleys among the Alps in which scarcely any spot is totally exempt from the possible occurrence of such a calamity, though some are naturally more exposed than others. The Val Bedretto, in canton Tessin, the Meyenthal, in canton Uri, and many others, are thus dreadfully exposed. To guard as much as possible against accidents, very large and massive dykes of masonry, like the projecting bastions of a fortification, are, in such situations, built against the hill-side, behind churches, houses, and other buildings, with an angle pointing upwards, in order to break and turn aside the snow. In some valleys great care is bestowed on the preservation of the forests clothing their sides, as the best protection of the district below them from such calamities. These may truly be regarded as sacred groves; and no one is allowed to cut down timber within them, under pain of a legal penalty. Yet they not unfrequently show the inefficiency even of such protection against so fearful an engine of destruction. Whole forests are at times cut over and laid prostrate by the avalanche. The tallest stems, fit to make masts for a first-rate man-of-war, are snapped asunder like a bit of wax, and the barkless and branchless stumps and relics of the forest remain for years like a stubble-field to tell of what has happened.

A mournful catalogue of catastrophes, which have occurred in Switzerland, since the records of history, from avalanches, might be made out if necessary; but it will suffice to mention one or two instances.

In 1720 an avalanche killed, in Ober-Gestelen (Vallais), 84 men and 400 head of cattle, and destroyed 120 houses. The same year 40 individuals perished at Brieg, and 23 on the Great St. Bernard, from a similar cause.

In 1749 the village of Ruaras, in the Tavetsch Thal, was carried away by an avalanche; 100 men were overwhelmed by it, 60 of whom were dug out alive; and several of the houses, though removed to some distance from the original site, were so little shaken that persons sleeping within them were not awakened.

In 1800, after a snow-storm of three days' continuance, an enormous avalanche detached itself from the top of the precipice of Klucas, above Trons, in the valley of the Vorder Rhein; it crossed the valley and destroyed a wood and some châlets on the opposite pasture of Zenim; recoiling, with the force it had acquired, to the side from which it had come, it did fresh mischief there, and so rebounding to and fro, at the fourth rush reached Trons, and buried many of its houses to the roof in snow.

In 1827 the greater part of the village of Biel, in the Upper Valais, was crushed beneath a tremendous avalanche, which ran down a ravine, nearly two leagues long, before it reached the village.

One of the most remarkable phenomena attending the avalanche is the blast of air which accompanies it, and which, like what is called the wind of a cannon-ball, extends its destructive influence to a considerable distance on each side of the actual line taken by the falling mass. It has all the effect of a blast of gunpowder: sometimes forest trees, growing near the sides of the channel down which the snow passes, are uprooted and laid prostrate, without having been touched by it. In this way the village of Randa, in the Visp-Thal, lost many of its houses by the blast of a mass of glacier, which fell in 1720. The E. spire of the convent of Dissentis was thrown down by the gust of an avalanche which fell more than a quarter of a mile off.

Travellers visiting the Alps between the months of June and October are little exposed to danger from avalanches, except immediately after a snow-storm; and, when compelled to start at such times, they should pay implicit obedience to the advice of the guides. It is a common saying, that there is risk of avalanches as long as the burden of snow continues on the boughs of the fir-trees, and while the naturally sharp angles of the distant mountains continue to look rounded.

It is different with those who travel from necessity in the spring, and before the annual avalanches have fallen. Muleteers, carriers, and such persons, use great caution in traversing exposed parts of the road, and with these they are well acquainted. They proceed in parties, in single file, at a little distance from one another, in order that if the snow should sweep one off, the others may be ready to render assistance. They proceed as fast as possible, carefully avoiding any noise, even speaking, and, it is said, will sometimes muffle the mules' bells, lest the slightest vibration communicated to the air should disengage the nicely-poised mass of snow above their heads. These manœuvres are probably adopted to astonish travellers merely, for it is obvious that the lightest summer breeze must produce more effect than the loudest voice.

The avalanches, seen and heard by summer tourists on the sides of Mont Blanc and the Jungfrau, are of a different kind from those described above, being caused only by the rupture of a portion of the glaciers, which give way under the influence of a mid-day sun, and of certain winds, during the summer and autumn, when other avalanches, generally speaking, have ceased to fall. They differ, also, in this respect, that, for the most part, they do no harm, since they fall on uncultivable and uninhabited spots. It is more by the roar which accompanies them, which, awakening the echoes of the Alps, sounds very like thunder, than by the appearance which they present, which is simply that of a waterfall, that they realise what is usually expected of avalanches. Still they are worth seeing, and will much enhance the interest of a visit to the Wengern Alp, the Cramont (on the S. side of Mont Blanc), or the borders of the Mer de Glace ; especially if the spectator will bear in mind the immense distance at which he is placed from the objects which he sees and hears, and will consider that, at each roar, whole tons of solid ice are broken off from the parent glacier, and in tumbling many hundred feet perhaps, are shattered to atoms and ground to powder.

The *Snow-storms, Tourmentes,* or *Guxen,* which occur on the Alps, are much dreaded by the chamois-hunter, the shepherd, and those most accustomed to traverse the High Alps ; how much more formidable must they be to the inexperienced traveller! They consist of furious and tempestuous winds, somewhat of the nature of a whirlwind, which occur on the exposed promontories, the summit-ridges, and elevated gorges of the Alps, either accompanied by snow, or filling the air with that recently fallen, while the flakes are still dry, tossing them about like powder or dust. In an instant the atmosphere is filled with snow; earth, sky, mountain, abyss, and landmark of every kind, are obliterated from view, as though a curtain were let down on all sides of the wanderer. All traces of path, or of the footsteps of preceding travellers, are at once effaced, and the poles planted to mark the direction of the road are frequently overturned. In some places the gusts sweep the rock bare of snow, heaping it up in others, perhaps across the path, to a height of 20 ft. or more, barring all passage, and driving the wayfarer to despair. At every step he fears to plunge into an abyss, or sink overhead in the snow. Large parties of men and animals have been overwhelmed by the snow-wreaths on the St. Gothard, where they sometimes attain a height of 40 or 50 ft. These tempests are accompanied almost every year by loss of life; and, though of less frequent occurrence in summer than in winter and spring, are one reason why it is dangerous for inexperienced travellers to attempt to cross remote and elevated passes without a guide.

The guides and persons residing on the mountain-passes, from the appearance of the sky, and other weather-signs known to them, can generally foresee the occurrence of tourmentes, and can tell when the fall of avalanches is to be apprehended.

Floods.—In most of the Swiss valleys traces are to be seen of terrible floods, which have from time to time poured down from the mountains, and devastated tracts of land more or less large. These floods usually occur at the melting of the snow in spring, but may happen at any time of year when, either from excessive rain, or from the too rapid melting of the snow, or from a dam of ice falling and then bursting, a mountain torrent swells beyond its usual proportions, and carries down stones, earth, huge rocks, and trees, sweeping everything before it till it reaches the valley, when it spreads out, often covering acres of fertile land with rubbish, and ruining the land for ever. There is hardly a year in which some part of Switzerland does not suffer from this cause. A flood in the autumn of 1852 converted the valley of the Rhone below Martigny into a lake, and covered hundreds of acres of land with rubbish, which in 1856 remained untouched and uncultivated. The flood on the same day carried away all the bridges but one in the valley of Chamouni; whilst, above Sallenches, the river left its bed, and cut out a channel 30 or 40 ft. wide, and 6 or 8 ft. deep, through the fertile land and down to the bare rock. Great floods are described in Rte. 56A and Rte. 109. The upper part of the valley of the Rhône is now a desert in consequence of floods, and traces of great floods may be seen in the valley of the Rhine and in the vale of Sarnen, and, in fact, in nearly every valley. Those who have once seen the recent effects of a flood will soon detect them continually, though the grass and bushes in a few years conceal the traces from those who do not know where to look for them.

§ 18. GOÎTRE AND CRETINISM.

"Quis tumidum guttur miratur in Alpibus."—Juv.

It is a remarkable fact that, amidst some of the most magnificent scenery of the globe, where Nature seems to have put forth all her powers in exciting emotions of wonder and elevation in the mind, man appears, from a mysterious visitation of disease, in his most degraded and pitiable condition. Such, however, is the fact. It is in the grandest and most beautiful valleys of the Alps that the maladies of *goître* and *cretinism* prevail.

Goître is a swelling in the front of the neck (of the thyroid gland, or the parts adjoining), which increases with the growth of the individual, until, in some cases, it attains an enormous size, and becomes " a hideous wallet of flesh," to use the words of Shakspeare, hanging pendulous down to the breast. It is not, however, attended with pain, and generally seems to be more unsightly to the spectator than inconvenient or hateful to the

d

bearer; but there are instances in which its increase is so enormous that the individual, unable to support his burden, crawls along the ground under it. On the N. of the Alps women appear to be the principal sufferers from this complaint, and in the Valais scarcely a woman is free from it, and it is said that those who have no swelling are laughed at and called goose-necked. At Domo d' Ossola it seems more prevalent among the men.

Cretinism, which occurs in the same localities as goître, and evidently arises from the same cause, whatever it may be, is a more serious malady, inasmuch as it affects the mind. The cretin is an idiot—a melancholy spectacle—a creature who may almost be said to rank a step below a human being. There is a vacancy in his countenance; his head is disproportionately large; his limbs are stunted or crippled; he cannot articulate his words with distinctness; and there is scarcely any work which he is capable of executing. He spends his days basking in the sun, and from its warmth appears to derive great gratification. When a stranger appears, he becomes a clamorous and importunate beggar, assailing him with a ceaseless chattering; and the traveller is commonly glad to be rid of his hideous presence at the expense of a few sous. Cretins however are now either diminished in number or are confined, and the traveller is not pestered by them as he used to be. At times the disease has such an effect on the mind that the sufferer is unable to find his way home when within a few feet of his own door.

Various theories have been resorted to, to account for goître: some have attributed it to the use of water derived from melting snow; others, to the habit of carrying heavy weights on the head; others, again, to filthy habits; while a fourth theory derives it from the nature of the soil, or the use of spring-water impregnated with calcareous matter.

As the goître occurs in Derbyshire, Yorkshire (especially at Settle, in the limestone district of Craven), Notts, Somerset, Surrey, Hants, &c., where no permanent snow exists, and no rivers spring from glaciers—also in Sumatra, and in parts of South America, where snow is unknown—and last, but not least, as no one ever drinks snow-water, which is always dirty, it is evident that the first cause assigned is not the true one; as for the second and third, they would equally tend to produce goître in the London porters, and in the inhabitants of the purlieus of St. Giles's. If the limestone theory be true, all other rocks should be exempt from it, which is not the case, as far as our experience goes. Goître is found only in certain valleys; nor, when it does occur, does it exist throughout the valley. It appears in one spot; higher up it is unknown, and in another situation, a mile or two distant, perhaps it is again prevalent. A curious example of this is afforded by the valley leading up to the Great St. Bernard. Goître is unknown above Liddes; abounds at Verchères, 800 ft. lower down; and is almost universal at Orsières: had the disease depended upon the glacier-water, it would, of course, be more prevalent near to the glaciers, and in the upper part of the valley.

A careful attention to the circumstances accompanying its appearance will show that it is connected with the condition of the atmosphere, and is found in low, warm, and moist situations, at the bottom of valleys, where a stagnation of water occurs, and where the summer exhalations and autumnal fogs arising from it are not carried off by a free circulation of air ;—that it is, in fact, one of the many injurious effects produced by malaria. It prevails in places where the valley is confined, and shut in, as it were—where a free draught is checked by the sides being clothed with wood, or by a sudden bend occurring in its direction—where, at the same time, the bottom is subject to the overflowings of a river, or to extensive artificial irrigation. The conjecture which derives the disease from breathing an atmosphere of this kind, not liable to be purified by fresh currents of air to carry off the vapours, is, perhaps, not undeserving of consideration and further investigation on the part of the learned.

Goître usually occurs about the age of puberty. It becomes hereditary in a family, but children born and educated on spots distant from home, and in elevated situations, are often exempt from it. At Sion, in the Valais, which may be regarded as the head-quarters of goître, children and even adults are often removed to the mountains from the low ground on the first symptoms of the malady, and the symptoms disappear where this is resorted to in time. Iodine has been applied with success as a remedy in some cases; but, as it is a dangerous remedy, the administration of it must be resorted to with the greatest caution.

The late Sir Astley Cooper, who in 1834 visited Martigny for the purpose of making observations upon goîtres, considered them to be occasioned by the want of a due circulation of air; and he found the inhabitants of one side of a valley afflicted by them, while those on the other were quite free from them. (L. S. 1845.)

§ 19. HEIGHTS OF THE PRINCIPAL MOUNTAINS, LAKES, AND PASSES, ABOVE THE LEVEL OF THE SEA.

Taken principally from Leuthold's Map, and reduced to English feet.

MOUNTAINS.

	feet.		feet.
Nepaulese mountain (Himalaya)	29,002	Piz Linard	11,420
Sorato (South America)	25,250	Mittelhorn	11,300
Oertler Spitz (Tyrol)	12,885	Titlis	10,690
Maladetta (Pyrenees)	11,426	Diablerets..	10,670
Ben McDhui (Scotland)	4,390	Dent de Midi	10,531
Snowdon (Wales)	3,571	Uri Rothstock	10,376
		Sardona	10,220
Mont Blanc	15,760	Buet	10,050
Monte Rosa	15,160	Torrenthorn	9,760
Mischabel	14,924	Glärnisch	9,528
Mont Cervin	14,836	Sidel-horn..	9,500
Finster Aar Horn	14,130	Cramont	9,040
Combin	14,120	Görner Grat .. .. .. (?)	9,000
Géant	13,900	Faulhorn	8,674
Aletsch Horn	13,800	Breven	8,500
Jung Frau	13,720	Sentis	8,280
Mönch	13,510	Stockhorn	7,620
Schreckhorn	13,410	Pilatus	7,116
Dent Blanche .. .. .. (?)	13,325	Flegère	6,350
Piz Mortiratsch .. .. (?)	13,290	Montanvert	6,303
Cima de Jazi	13,240	Rigi	5,676
Eiger	13,060	Dôle	5,520
Velan	12,370	Mont Tendre	5,510
Wetterhorn	12,200	Saleve	4,560
Altels	12,180	Weissenstein	4,200
Dödi	11,880		

LAKES.

	feet.		feet.
Schwartzer See .. .. (?)	8,600	Bienne	1,410
Dauben See	7,280	Lucerne	1,406
Silser	6,000	Zug	1,400
Joux..	3,210	Constance..	1,385
Lungern .. .. (?)	2,420	Zürich	1,310
Egeri	2,360	Orta..	1,150
Brienz	1,781	Geneva	1,142
Thun	1,755	Lugano	937
Sarnen	1,715	Bourget	762
Morat	1,442	Como	692
Wallenstadt	1,420	Maggiore	680
Neuchâtel..	1,420		

PASSES.

	feet.		feet.
Weiss Thor	(?) 12,000	Col de Balme	7,550
Erin	11,760	Gemmi	7,540
St. Théodule	11,185	Grimsel	7,530
Col du Géant	11,146	Joch	7,340
Collon	10,333	Kinzig Culm	7,280
Strahleck	9,750	Ober Alp	7,140
Moro	9,640	Bernardin	7,010
St. Bernard	8,200	Splügen	6,940
Col du Bonhomme	8,195	Cenis	6,825
Furca	8,150	St. Gothard	6,808
Col de la Seigne	8,100	Surenen	6,720
Rawyl	7,960	Wengern Alp	6,690
Nüfenen	7,950	Simplon	6,580
Panixer	7,940	Scheideck, Hasli	6,480
Bernina	7,695	Lukmanier	6,340
Albula	7,680	Maloya	6,060
Julier	7,625	Dent de Jaman	4,855·
Sanetsch	7,367	Brünig	3,668
Susten	7,560	Unter Hauenstein	2,260

ABBREVIATIONS, &c., EMPLOYED IN THE HANDBOOK.

The points of the compass (not magnetic) are marked by the letters N. S. E. W.

(*rt.*) right, (*l.*) left,—applied to the banks of a river. The right bank is that which lies on the right hand of a person whose back is turned towards the source, or to the quarter from which the current descends.

Distances are, as far as possible, reduced to English miles; when miles are mentioned, they may be understood to be English, and feet to be English feet.

Where there is a railway the distances at the head of the chapters are measured from the first station or terminus. On other roads the distances are measured from each place to the next place mentioned.

The names of Inns precede the description of every place (often in a parenthesis), because the first information needed by a traveller is where to lodge, and the best Inns are placed first.

Instead of designating a town by the vague words " large " or " small," the amount of the population, according to the latest census, is almost invariably stated, as presenting a more exact scale of the importance and size of the place.

In order to avoid repetition, the Routes are preceded by a chapter of preliminary information; and to facilitate reference to it, each division or paragraph is separately numbered.

Each Route is numbered with Arabic figures, corresponding with the figures attached to the Route on the Map, which thus serves as an Index to the Book; at the same time that it presents a *tolerably* exact view of the great and minor roads of Switzerland, and of the course of public conveyances.

MAPS AND PLANS.

SECTION I.

SWITZERLAND.

ROUTE 1.

BASLE TO BERNE, BY THE VAL MOUTÍERS (MÜNSTER THAL) AND BIENNE.

BASLE or Bâle. (Germ. Basel, Ital. Basilea.)—*Inns:* Drei Könige (Three Kings), a large house, well situated on the Rhine; Sauvage (Wilder Mann), within the town ; Cigogne (Storch), near the post-office, repaired and improved; Kopf (Tête d'Or) ; Krone (Crown) ; overlooking the river. The Three Kings is superior in size and situation, but many complaints are made of it.

Basle, capital of the now subdivided canton called Basle-town, is divided by the Rhine into Great Basle on the left bank and Little Basle on the right bank, connected by a wooden bridge, 680 ft. long, partly on stone piers. The towns are now united, and with a few miles of territory form the half-canton called Basle-town. The town contains 27,500 Inhab. (21,500 Prot., 5500 Cath.); and it enjoys considerable prosperity from the residence of many rich merchants, bankers, and families of ancient descent, and from its position in an angle on the frontiers of France, Germany, and Switzerland, a few miles below the spot where the Rhine first becomes navigable. Its most important manufactures are of ribands and paper.

A large proportion of travellers entering Switzerland pass through Basle, and there are conveyances from it to nearly every part of Switzerland. Great Basle is situated on high,

sloping banks, overlooking the Rhine, which rushes past in a full broad flood of a clear, light green; and the view from it is bounded by the hills of the Black Forest on the one side, of the Jura on the other. Its appearance is still that of an old German town, with high curious roofs and large houses.

The *Cathedral*, or Münster, on the high bank on the l. of the Rhine, above the bridge, distinguished by its 2 spires (about 220 ft. high), and the deep-red colour of the sandstone of which it is built, is an interesting edifice, though not of beautiful architecture. It was begun by the Empr. Henry II. in 1010, and consecrated 1019. The oldest part of the existing edifice, however, is probably not more ancient than the 12th century; and it was mostly rebuilt in the beginning of the 15th century after an earthquake. Some figures of monsters, now in the crypt, alone may have belonged to the original. The 4 columns at the E. end, formed of groups of detached pillars, with singular and grotesque capitals ; the tomb of the Empress Anne, wife of Rudolph of Habsburg, and mother of the line of Austrian princes, whose body was removed to St. Blaize in 1770 ; and a stone font (date 1465) are worth notice in this part of the building. Very remarkable is the *Portal of St. Gallus*, leading to the N. transept, and decorated with statues of Christ and St. Peter, and of the wise and foolish virgins. It dates probably from the latter part of the

B

12th century. The wheel of fortune, above it, is of the 13th centr. In the W. front, under the towers, two equestrian statues, St. George and the Dragon, and St. Martin, stand forth with great boldness. The church is used now for the Protestant service, and the altar stands between the choir and nave, nearly underneath a rich Gothic rood-loft (*Lettner*, date 1381). On the l. of the altar, against a pillar, is the red marble tombstone of Erasmus, who died here in 1536. There is a very large new organ. A staircase, leading out of the choir, conducts into a small apartment—the Chapter House, or *Concilium's Saal*—in which some of the meetings of the Council of Basle, or rather of its committees, were held between 1436 and 1444. It is a low room, with 4 Gothic windows—distinguished not only in an historical point of view, but also as being quite unaltered since the day of the Council. It is now appropriated to the purposes of a museum, and contains many interesting antiquities. On the S. side of the Church are very extensive and picturesque *Cloisters*—a succession of quadrangles and open halls—which, with the space they enclose, still serve, as they have done for centuries, as a burial-place, and are filled with curious and interesting tombs; among which are the monuments of the 3 Reformers, Œcolampadius (Hausschein), Grynæus, and Meyer. The cloisters were constructed in the 14th century, and extend to the verge of the hill overlooking the river. It is not unlikely they may have been the favourite resort of Erasmus. Bernouilli, a native of Basle, is buried in *St. Peter's Church*, which contains many monuments of its wealthy citizens. Œcolampadius first preached the Reformation in *St. Martin's*, the oldest church in Basle.

Behind the Minster is a *Terrace*, called *Die Pfalz*, 75 ft. above the river, planted with chesnut trees, and commanding a beautiful view over the Rhine, the town, and the Black Forest hills, among them the Blauen. Close to it is the Club called *Lesegesellschaft* —including a reading-room, where 80 papers are taken in.

The Minster is situated in a square of considerable size—in one corner of which, in a recess, stands a building called " zur Mücke," in which, during the Council of Basle, the Conclave met which elected Felix V. pope.

In the narrow street leading from the Rhine Bridge to the Minster-Platz is the *New Museum*, a handsome building, containing *Paintings and Drawings by the younger Holbein*—a highly interesting collection, including the Passion of Christ, in 8 compartments, full of life, and carefully finished; also 8 sepia drawings of the same subject;—a dead Christ, formerly in the Minster; Holbein's Wife and Children, with countenances full of grief and misery (1526), a very remarkable work, from its perfect truth to nature; portraits of Erasmus, of Froben the printer, excellent—of a Mlle. von Offenburg, inscribed " Lais Corinthiaca," very good; the same lady as Venus with Cupid; two representations of a School, painted by Holbein at the age of 14, and hung up as a sign over a schoolmaster's door in the town of Basle. Among the *Drawings* are Holbein's own portrait— *a work of the very highest excellence;* heads of the family Meyer, sketched for the celebrated picture now in the Dresden Gallery, a beautiful pen and ink drawing; original sketch for the famous picture of the family of Sir Thomas More—the names of the different personages are written on their dresses; 5 sketches for the frescoes which formerly decorated the Rathhaus in Basle, with one or two fragments of the frescoes themselves; sketches in ink for glass windows, for the sheaths of daggers, for the organ in the Minster; the Costumes of Basle; 83 marginal caricatures made on a copy of Erasmus' Laus Stultitiæ, which so amused the author when shown to him, that he is said to have laughed himself out of a fit of illness, &c. &c. Here are also preserved 6 fresco fragments of the original Dance of Death, which once adorned the walls of the Dominican Church in Basle, and a set of coloured drawings of the whole series of figures. The

Dance of Death has been attributed without cause to Holbein, since it existed at the time of the Council of Basle, at least 50 years before his birth. Holbein* was born at Augsburg in 1489, and removed about 1517 to Basle : his circumstances were by no means prosperous; he was even reduced to work as a day-labourer and house-painter, and painted the outer walls of the houses of the town. It is related of him that, being employed to decorate the shop of an apothecary, who was intent on keeping the young artist close at his work, and being disposed to repair to a neighbouring wine-shop, he painted a pair of legs so exactly like his own, and so well foreshortened, on the under side of the scaffolding, that the apothecary, seated below, believed him to be constantly present and diligently employed. Erasmus, writing from Bâle a letter of introduction for the painter to one of his friends, complains that "hic frigent artes," and the want of encouragement drove Holbein to seek his fortune in England, where he met with high patronage, as is well known. Yet the city showed its esteem for his talents by granting him a salary of 50 gulden per annum, which was paid him even when in England. Here are also some curious paintings of an artist of Berne named *Manuel* (1484—1530): portraits of Luther and his wife, by *L. Cranach;* of Zwingli.

Here also are deposited some antiquities, bronzes, fragments of pottery, coins, &c., from Augst, the site of the Roman *Augusta Rauracorum,* 7 miles from Basle (see p. 9); also a silken embroidered banner, given by Pope Julius II. (1515) to the Bâlois.

The same building contains the *Public Library* of 70,000 volumes (4000 MSS.)—among them, the Acts of the Council of Bâle, 3 vols., with chains attached to the binding, many very important MSS., of which there is a good catalogue, and a few of the books of Erasmus; also, a copy of his 'Praise of Folly,' with marginal

* See Kugler's 'Handbook of Painting,' vol. ii., German School.

illustrations by the pen of *Holbein.* There are autographs of Luther, Melanchthon, Erasmus, and Zuinglius. Those who wish to see the library should apply early, as the librarian is usually absent in the afternoon.

The *University* of Basle, founded 1460, was the first great seminary for the advancement of learning established in Switzerland : it enjoyed a high reputation under Erasmus, and numbered among its professors in recent times the names of Euler and Bernouilli, the mathematicians, who were natives of Basle. Schönbein, the discoverer of gun-cotton and of ozone, is a professor.

The *Rathhaus,* in the Market-place, is a building of pleasing Gothic architecture, founded 1508. The frieze displays the emblazoned shields of the original cantons. The armorial bearing of canton Basle is said to be meant to represent the case of a cross-bow. The frescoes, designed by Holbein, were obliterated in 1817! The Great Council-Room (*Stadt-Rath-Saal*) is ornamented on the walls and roof with humorous reliefs carved in wood by *Mat. Giger* (1609). The painted glass of the windows—coats of arms of 12 of the Swiss cantons, with supporters. At the foot of the stairs is placed a statue of Munatius Plancus, the founder, according to tradition, of Bâle and of the Roman colony of Augst. Here is preserved some curious old church plate—part of the Dom-Schatz—a silver cup of open work is the oldest piece (13th century) —St. Anne with the Virgin and Child; and a relic-box with reliefs, 13th century, deserve notice.

The *Arsenal* contains a limited collection of ancient armour, of which the only curiosities are a suit of chain mail, once gilt, with plate mail beneath it, worn by Charles the Bold at the battle of Nancy; two Burgundian cannon, of iron bars bound round with hoops, and several suits of Burgundian and Armagnac armour.

English Church service in a neat chapel in the Three Kings Hotel. It is panelled with wood-work which formerly lined the chapel of the Abbot of St. Gall. Dr. Jung is a good physician.

The terraced *Garden of M. Vischer*, an eminent banker, overlooking the Rhine, is a very pretty spot.

The gateways, battlemented walls, watch-towers, and ditch, which formed the ancient defences of the town, remain in a good state of preservation. The *Spalenthor*, i. e. *St. Paulusthor* (1400), retains its advanced work or *Barbican*, similar to those which formerly existed at York, and, with its double portcullis and two flanking towers, is particularly picturesque. The machicolations are supported by strange but clever figures approaching to the grotesque. The *Gelten-zunft* and *Spiezhof* are specimens of civic architecture, with Holbeinesque ornaments.

Basle is a tolerably clean town; its streets are plentifully supplied with *Fountains*. The *Fischmarkt Brunnen* is a very elegant Gothic structure, ornamented with statues, well executed, of the Virgin, St. John, Peter, the Cardinal Virtues, &c. *Spahlen-Brunnen*, in the Spahlen suburb, is surmounted by a Bagpiper (Dudelsackpfeiffer), to whose music a sculptured group of peasants dance around the base. It is copied from a design of Holbein or Dürer.

Erasmus resided in the house *Zum Luft*, and Frobenius printed in it one of the first Bibles. The building called Kirschgarten was erected by the father of the distinguished African traveller, *Burckhardt*, who was born here.

A handsome new *Hospital* has been built on the site of the palace of the Markgraves of Baden.

Down to the end of the last century (1798), the clocks of Basle went an hour in advance of those in other places of Europe—a singular custom, the origin of which is not precisely known. According to tradition, it arose from the circumstance of a conspiracy to deliver the town to an enemy at midnight having been defeated by the clock striking 1 instead of 12.

The ancient sumptuary laws of Basle were singular and severe. On Sunday all were obliged to dress in black to go to church; even now no carriage may enter or quit the town during the hours of *morning* service. Females could not have their hair dressed by men; carriages were not permitted in the town after 10 at night, and it was forbidden to place a footman behind a carriage. The official censors, called Unzichterherrn, had the control of the number of dishes and wines to be allowed at a dinner party; and their authority was supreme on all that related to the cut and quality of clothes. At one time they waged desperate war against slashed doublets and hose.

Since the Reformation, Basle has been regarded as the stronghold of Methodism in Switzerland. The pious turn of its citizens was remarkably exhibited in the mottoes and signs placed over their doors. These have now disappeared; but two very singular ones have been recorded—

Auf Gott ich meine Hoffnung bau,
Und wohne in der *alten Sau*.

On God I build my hopes of grace,
The ancient Pig's my dwelling place.

Wacht auf, ihr Menschen, und thut Buss,
Ich heiss *zum goldenen Rinderfuss*.

Wake, and repent your sins with grief;
I'm call'd the Golden Shin of Beef.

The spirit of trade, however, went hand in hand with that of religion—and Basle has been called a city of usurers; 5 per cent. was styled a "Christian usance" (einen Christlichen Zins), and a proclamation of the magistrates (1682-84) denounced those who lent money at a discount of 4 or 3½ per cent., as "selfish, avaricious, and dangerous persons;" those who lent their capital at a lower rate were liable to have it confiscated, because, forsooth, such persons, "by their avarice, did irremediable injury to churches, hospitals, church property, &c., and are the ruin of poor widows and orphans."

Basle was for many centuries an Imperial German town, governed by its bishops, under whom it appears to have flourished. It joined the Swiss confederation in 1501; and after severe struggles its bishops were expelled. The government then fell into the hands of the aristocratic burghers, whose authority was destroyed in 1798, partially restored in 1814, and again destroyed in 1848.

The dissensions which broke out soon after the Revolution of 1830 between the inhabitants of the town of Basle and those of the country, led to a civil war between the parties, and a bloody contest near Liesthal occasioned the Swiss Diet, in 1832, to pass an act for the formal separation of the canton into two parts, called Basle Ville and Basle Campagne. Basle Ville, however, refused to submit, and attacked the Campagne with 1600 men, of whom 400 were left on the field of battle, Aug. 1833. The diet then occupied the whole canton, and a final separation was made. Basle Campagne consists of two-thirds of the territory of the whole canton, and has for its capital Liestal. Each sends a deputy to the Diet; but the two divisions enjoy only half a vote each, and when the deputies of the two divisions take opposite sides (which is generally the case) their vote does not count.

In Little Basle, beyond the bridge, are the remains of the convent of Klingenthal, whose inmates caused what is called "the Nuns' War," 1436.

Reading-room—Schweighause's, kept by Mr. Ludwig, opposite the Three Kings, where newspapers of all countries may be read, and Guide-books, maps, and views obtained.

There is very good trout and grayling *fishing* in the Birs, and also in the Wiese, about 3 m. from Bâle, on the rt. bank of the Rhine.

Railways. Baden line: to Freiburg, Heidelberg, and Frankfurt. Alsace line: to Strasburg.—See HANDBOOK FOR FRANCE. *Trains* 4 times a day. The early train in 4 hrs.; other trains 5 hrs.—Strasburg to Paris takes 15 hrs. Luggage is examined at St. Louis, the French custom-house. Baggage declared to be "en transit" is exempted from search at the frontier, and is sealed (plombé) until it quits France. Railways also to Waldshut (Rte. 7), Berne, Lucerne, Zürich, and Bienne.

Environs.—About 2 m. out of the town, just within the French frontier, is the ruined fortress of *Hüningen*, erected by Louis XV. to overawe his Swiss neighbours, and dismantled in 1815. At *St. Crischona*, about 4 m. from Basle, is an interesting missionary establishment.

The Routes to Berne by the Hauenstein (Rtes. 2 and 3) command noble views of the Alps; while that by the Val Moutiers (Rte. 1) has even greater attractions.

Basle to Berne by the Münster Thal.

Post-road, 9⅝ posts, = 81½ Eng. m.

	Posts.		Eng m.
Basle.			
Lauffen	1⅞	=	16¾
Délémont . . .	1¼	=	11¼
Münster . . .	¾	=	7¼
Malleray . . .	¾	=	6¾
Soncebos . . .	¾	=	6¾
Bienne	1⅛	=	10
Aarberg	1	=	9
Berne	1½	=	13¼

This road will still be taken, at least as far as Bienne, by those who wish to see the beautiful Val de Moutiers. With a voiturier the journey to Berne occupies 2 days, stopping the first night at one of the good inns of Malleray or Tavannes.

The *valley of the Birs*, commonly called the *Val Moutiers* (*Münster Thal*, in Germ.), through which this excellent road passes, is one of the most interesting and romantic in the whole range of the Jura. It consists of a series of narrow and rocky defiles, alternating with open basins, covered with black forests above, and verdant meadows below, enlivened by villages, mills, and forges. A road was originally carried through the Val Moutiers by the Romans, to keep up the communication between Aventicum, the Helvetian capital, and Augst, their great fortified outposts on the Rhine. As long as it runs through Basle Campagne, *i. e.* for 4 or 5 m., it passes dirty villages and mean houses.

At *St. Jacob*, about ½ m. beyond the gates of Bâle, in the angle between two roads, a small Gothic cross has been erected, to commemorate the *battle of St. Jacob*, fought in 1444, when 1600 Swiss had the boldness to attack, and the courage to withstand for 10 hrs., a French army tenfold more numerous, commanded by the Dauphin, afterwards Louis XI. Only 10 of the Swiss escaped alive, the rest were left dead on the field, along with thrice their own number of foes, whom they had slain. This almost incredible exploit spread abroad through Europe the fame of Swiss valour; and Louis, the Dauphin, wisely seeing that it was better to gain them as friends than to oppose them as enemies, courted their alliance, and first enrolled them as a permanent body-guard about his person —a practice continued by the French monarchs down to Charles X. The Swiss themselves refer to the battle of St. Jacob as the Thermopylæ of their history. The vineyards near the field produce a red wine, called Schweitzer Blut (Swiss blood).

A few miles farther, near *Reinach*, on the opposite bank of the *Birs*, is another battle-field—that of *Dornach* —where the Swiss gained a victory over a much larger Austrian force in 1499, during the Suabian war. The bone-house, in which the remains of the slain were collected, still exists near the Capuchin convent, and is filled with skulls gathered from the field. In the church of the village Maupertuis the mathematician (d. 1759) is buried. A monument, set up to his memory by his friend Bernouilli, was destroyed by the curé of the village, who was in the habit of repairing his hearthstone when broken, with slabs taken from the churchyard. It has been replaced by a fresh monument set up at the expense of canton Soleure.

Beyond *Aesch* the road enters *l'Evêché*, that part of the canton Berne which anciently belonged to the Prince Bishop of Basle; the valley contracts, increasing in picturesque beauty as you advance. The castles of *Angenstein* and *Zwingen* are passed before reaching *Lauffon*,—a curious, old, and dirty walled village. No good *Inn*.

Soyhière (Germ. *Saugern*)—a village prettily situated, with a small country

Inn (Croix Blanche), tolerably good. Here is the division of languages: part of the inhabitants speak German, part French.

The *Hôtel de Bellerive*, 3½ hrs. from Basle, good, moderate, and highly recommended as a good halting-place. Here are mineral baths.

A contracted pass, the rocks of which on the rt. are surmounted by a convent, leads into the open basin of *Délémont* (Delsberg); but it is unnecessary to pass through that little town (situated on the way to Porentruy), as our road turns to the l., and continuing by the side of the Birs, enters a defile higher, grander, and more wild than any that have preceded it. This is, properly speaking, the commencement of the Val Moutiers. Rocky precipices overhang the road, and black forests of fir cover the mountains above. In the midst of it are the iron furnaces and forges of *Courrendelin* (Germ. Rennendorf. *Inn:* Hirsch), supplied with ore in the shape of small granulated red masses, varying from the size of a pea to that of a cherry, from the neighbouring mines. The remarkable rent by which the Jura has been cleft from top to bottom, so as to allow a passage for the Birs, exhibits marks of some great convulsion of the earth, by which the strata of limestone (Jura-kalk) have been thrown into a nearly vertical position, and appear like a succession of gigantic walls on each side of the road. The gorge terminates in another open basin, in the midst of which lies Moutiers. The new road branches off to the Weissenstein and Soleure beyond the gorge, about 1 m. before reaching *Moutiers Grandval*, or *Münster* — (*Inn:* Krone, very good)—a village of 1250 Inhab., named from a very ancient *Minster* of St. Germanus on the height, founded in the 7th century, and now fast falling to ruin. [There is a good car-road from Moutiers to the *summit of the Weissenstein* (Rte. 3), a distance of about 10 m., up-hill nearly the whole way; but fit for the cars of the country, one of which, drawn by 2 horses, may be hired here to go and return for 20 fr. It passes through the villages of Grandval (Grossau) and Gänsbrunnen; the ascent occupies 2 hrs.]

At the upper end of the basin of Moutiers the road is conducted through another defile, equally grand, at the bottom of which the Birs foams and rushes, overhung by perpendicular cliffs and funereal firs. To this succeeds the little plain of Tavannes, in which are situated the villages of Court (*Inn:* Bär; whence a steep and uneven foot-path runs over the Monto to Bienne), and

Malleray (Lion d'Or, a good *Inn;* capital trout). Convenient sleeping-places on this journey either here or 3 m. further, at Dachsfelden, or

Tavannes (*Inns:* Couronne, new landlord, who speaks English ; — Croix). The valley to the E. of Court, called Chaluat (Tschaywo), is inhabited by the descendants of the Anabaptists, expelled from Berne in 1708-11. They are distinguished by their industry and simple manners : the young men wear beards — they speak French. ¾ m. above Tavannes is the source of the Birs; before reaching it our road quits the valley, mounting up a steep ascent, in the middle of which it passes under the singular and picturesque archway formed in the solid rock, called

Pierre Pertuis. It is probably a natural opening, enlarged by art. It existed in the time of the Romans, as is proved by a defaced inscription on the N. side :

NUMINI AUGUS
tor VM — ——
VIA fa CTA   PER.M —
DV rmi VM PATER num
II. VIR um. COL HELVET —

It stood on the boundary line separating the people of the Rauraci, who extended to Bâle, from the Sequani. The archway is about 40 ft. high and 10 or 12 thick. The pass was fortified by the Austrians in 1813. Here is the watershed dividing the streams of the Birs from those of the Suze.

Sonceboz—(*Inn:* Couronne, good)— a village in the Val St. Imier (Germ. Erguel), up which runs a good road to Chaux de Fonds (Rte. 48), and out

of which another branches S. to Neuchâtel from Villaret. The road to Bienne passes the forges of *Reuchenette* in the valley below, and descends the valley along the l. bank of the *Suze,* which forms several small cascades. The projecting rock of Rond Châtel was occupied in feudal times by a fort, and held by the powerful Bishops of Bâle, to whom it gave the command of this pass. The *View* from the last slope of the Jura, over Bienne and its lake, with St. Peter's Isle, and the district watered by the Aar, Emme, and Zihl, backed in clear weather by the snowy range of the Alps, from Mont Blanc to the Jungfrau, is exceedingly beautiful. On the bare limestone slope of the Jura, close to the road, are lying numbers of granite boulders. (See p. lv.)

Those who wish may go through Bienne (Rte. 3), but the voituriers prefer the road by *Büren*, turning off to the l. after descending from the Jura, and avoiding Bienne altogether.

Aarberg (*Inn:* Krone) is a town of 864 Inhab. on a rocky promontory, nearly surrounded by the Aar, which, indeed, at high water, actually converts it into an island. The road enters and quits the town by 2 covered bridges.

At *Neubrücke* the Aar is crossed by a covered bridge.

The road passes through rich and tolerably level country near

Hofwyl, long well known as the agricultural and educational institution of the late M. Fellenberg, now carried on by Dr. Edward Müller. Originally it consisted of

1. A *seminary* for young gentlemen; also a separate school of instruction for schoolmasters.

2. A *school for the poor*, who were taught according to the system of M. Fellenberg, with the double object of instructing farmers and introducing agricultural improvements.

3. An agricultural establishment, consisting of an academy for practical husbandry; a model farm; an experimental farm; an extensive collection of agricultural implements, and a manufactory for making them.

The surrounding district was little better than a bog when M. Fellenberg settled here in 1799; but he gradually brought it into cultivation; and an English agriculturist, who had been sent abroad to investigate the state of agriculture on the continent, reported that here alone he had seen really good ploughing.

A new and direct road has been opened to Berne, traversing the picturesque peninsula of Enge, nearly surrounded by the Aar, by Reichenbach, and Buchsee. A lofty bridge of 3 arches, a noble structure, has been thrown over the river. Nearly opposite the N. extremity of the lofty and picturesque promontory called Enge, lies the old *Castle of Reichenbach*, which belonged to Rudolph of Erlach, the hero of the battle of Laupen, who was murdered here, in his old age, by his son-in-law, Jost von Rudenz, with the very sword which he had wielded at that glorious victory. The assassin was pursued, as he fled from the scene of his crime, by the two bloodhounds of the aged warrior, who broke loose at their master's cries. They tracked the murderer's footsteps of their own accord, and after some hours returned with gore-stained lips, and nothing more was heard or known of Jost von Rudenz.

BERNE. (Rte. 24.)

ROUTE 2.

BASLE TO SOLEURE, BY THE OBER HAUENSTEIN.

The old road to Soleure diverged at *Liesthal* and crossed the Ober-Hauenstein 3000 ft. above the sea-level. The ascent was, until the road was improved, so steep that down to the end of the last century loaded waggons were drawn up on one side and let down the other with a rope and windlass.

Near the bottom of the descent the imposing ruins of the *Castle of Falkenstein*, surmounted by its circular Donjon, rise midway between the two roads to Basle, by the Hauenstein and by the Passwang, which unite here. This position gave to its ancient owners the powers of levying black-mail upon each of these passes. It belonged at one time to Rudolph von Wart, who was broken on the wheel for his share in the murder of the Emperor Albert, and was consoled in his agony by the presence and fortitude of his wife. (See Rte. 6, p. 16.) The castle was destroyed by the men of Basle, because a waggon laden with saffron, belonging to their merchants, had been pillaged by the lords of Falkenstein.

Ballsthal (*Inn:* Rössli, tolerable), the chief place in the valley.

The valley is suddenly closed by the advance of a rock surmounted by the still inhabited Castle of *Blauenstein*, at whose base crouches the village of Innere Klus (*Inn:* Hirsch), arranged in 2 rows of houses, at the outlet of a romantic defile or rent (*Klus*), which severs the Jura chain. It derives its name from having been closed (clausus) in ancient times by gate and wall, erected by the lords of Blauenstein. This pass is of much importance in a military point of view, as one of the main portals into Switzerland. In the iron furnaces of Klus village the pea-like iron-ore (bohnerz), so common in the Jura, is smelted. At Aussere Klus the pass terminates, and the road emerges into the valley of the Aar, affording a splendid view of the Alps.

SOLEURE.

ROUTE 3.

BASLE TO SOLEURE AND BIENNE, BY RAILWAY.—ASCENT OF THE WEISSENSTEIN.

	Eng. m.
Basle	
Liesthal	12
Laufelfingen	22
Olten	31
Herzogenbuchsee	45
Soleure	51
Bienne	65

As far as Aarburg the road is the same as in Rte. 4. Near Aarburg, which is a little beyond Olten, the road diverges and follows for some distance the rt. bank of the Aar: it then goes through a fertile but uninteresting country to

Herzogenbuchsee, Junct. Stat. (*Inn:* Sonne), a town of 4500 Inhab. Here the line to Soleure branches off from the line to Berne (Rte. 5), and turns to the W.

SOLEURE (Germ. Solothurn)—(*Inns:* Couronne, good and moderate ; Cerf; La Tour)—the capital of the canton, is prettily situated on the Aar, at the foot of the Jura range, and has 5370 Inhab. (200 Protestants). In the middle of the 17th century it was surrounded by fortifications of great extent, which took 60 years to complete, and consumed vast sums of money. In 1835 the removal of these costly and useless works was decreed by the Great Council of the canton. It is on the whole a dull town with little trade and few manufactures. The following objects are most worth notice.

At the end of the principal street, approached by a flight of steps, flanked by fountains representing Moses striking the rock, and Gideon wringing the dew from the fleece, stands the *Cathedral of St. Ursus* (a soldier of the Theban legion), a modern building, finished 1773, by an Italian, Pesoni, of Ancona; it is distinguished by its size, and on the whole handsome.

The *clock tower* (Zeitglockenthurm), in the market-place (a continuation of the same street), is stated by the guide-books to be a Roman work, while a German inscription upon it attributes its foundation to a period 500 years earlier than the birth of Christ; it may owe its origin to the Burgundian kings. It is square in form, and constructed of the most solid masonry, rough outside, originally without window or other opening, for 80 feet. If we are to believe the two Latin verses on the front of this building, Soleure is the most ancient city in N.W. Europe except Treves:

In Celtis nihil est Salodoro antiquius, unis
  Exceptis Treviris, quorum ego dicta soror.

The *Arsenal* (Zeughaus), a gable fronted house (d. 1580), not far from the Cathedral, contains the most extensive and curious collection of ancient armour in Switzerland. Here are shown numerous standards, taken by the Swiss in their victories over the Burgundians and Austrians, at Sempach, Morat, Nancy (bearing the portrait of Charles the Bold—with St. George and the Dragon), and Grandson. Some of these, in order to preserve them, have been fastened to pieces of coarse canvas; the yellow flag with the Austrian eagle was brought from Dornach. Among 800 suits of armour are many French and Burgundian. There are a few suits of chain mail, and a great many of commoner sort worn by Lanzknechts. More than 100 heads are said to have fallen under an *executioner's sword* here preserved. Several specimens of wall pieces, or long swivels, for the defence of a fortress, are curious. Some of the armour is for sale.

The *Museum*, in the Waisenhaus, close to the bridge over the Aar, contains the finest collection of Jura fossils in existence—15,000 specimens, chiefly from quarries near Soleure, which will be viewed with great interest by the geologist. There are nearly thirty specimens of fossil turtle, rarely found elsewhere, together with teeth and palates of fish, and numerous fragments of saurians, derived from a formation which is believed to correspond with the Portland stone of England. The jaws of mammalia are said to come from the same locality (?). A suite of specimens of the rocks of the Alps were collected in numerous journeys by Professor Hugi, to whom belongs the merit of forming and arranging this cabinet.

The Ambassador of France to the Swiss Confederation resided here until the French Revolution : his hotel is converted into a barrack. The Roman Catholic Bishop of Bâle lives here. The clergy are numerous and powerful, both in the town and canton. There are several convents at Soleure. The sisters of *St. Joseph's Nunnery,* outside the Berne gate, make artificial flowers, sweetmeats, and other articles, which they sell at the grating. Their pincushions are clumsy, and themselves not very interesting. Soleure was long the head-quarters for enlisting Swiss recruits in the foreign service of France, Spain, the Pope, and Naples, in which countries a body-guard of Swiss was always maintained. The town of Soleure was an ancient Imperial city, but had been long allied to Berne, and in 1481 became, with its surrounding country, a Swiss canton. Until 1793 the government of Soleure was the closest and the worst of the Swiss governments. The old government was partially restored in 1814, but completely altered and rendered democratic in 1831.

Thaddeus Kosciusko, the Pole, spent the last years of his life here; his house, in which he died, is near the Post-office, No. 5, Gurzelen-gasse. His entrails are interred in the church-yard of Zuchwyl, a mile distant on the opposite side of the Aar, under a monument inscribed "Viscera Thaddei Kosciusko."

About 2 miles N.E. of Soleure, beyond the village of St. Nicholas, lies the chapel and *Hermitage of St. Verena*, at the extremity of a pretty valley, hemmed in by rocks of gneiss and granite, embowered in trees, and traversed by a sparkling rivulet. It is rendered accessible by paths, originally formed by the French émigrés, who, at the outbreak of the French Revolution, sought an asylum here. The valley abounds in caves and grottoes, partly natural, partly artificial, and at its further extremity, within a natural shelf of over-arching cliff, stands the little *Chapel of St. Verena;* behind the altar a small cave has been cut in the rock, and now contains a representation of the holy sepulchre. This saint, a pious maiden who accompanied the Theban legion, suffered severe temptation in this solitude, according to the legend, from the devil, who, on one occasion, was on the point of carrying her off, when she saved herself by clinging fast to the rock, where the hole made by her finger-nails still

remains. On the way to the hermitage, near the church of St. Nicholas, the *Château of Waldegy* is passed; its old-fashioned gardens, laid out in terraces, are worth notice.

[*The Weissenstein.*—The most interesting excursion in the neighbourhood of Soleure is that to the summit of the Weissenstein (Whiterock, probably named from its white cliffs of limestone), the mountain immediately behind the town. The distance is about 8 miles, and the time occupied in the ascent 3 hours. The mountain is made accessible for chars-à-banc, by a road somewhat steep, passing through the villages Langendorf and Oberdorf, behind which it is carried up the face of the mountains in a series of zigzags. Pedestrians may find a short cut, and reach the top easily in 2½ hrs.; they may visit the Hermitage of St. Verena in their way to or fro.

An *Hotel and Bath-house* has been built at the expense of the town on the brow of the mountain, 3950 feet above the sea-level, and 2640 above the Aar at Soleure. It furnishes about 30 beds, and the accommodation, though homely, is good. It is rented by the landlord of the Couronne at Soleure, M. Brunner.

The dairy of the establishment is supplied by 60 cows, fed on the pasture on the summit of the mountains, so that milk and cream may be had here in perfection.

Many invalids take up their residence here during the summer months, on account of the fresh air, or for the "cure de petit lait" (goats' whey), &c., which is recommended in certain complaints. The daily charge for those who remain here more than a week "en pension," is 6 F. francs.

The greater portion of visitors, however, resort hither merely on account of the view, remaining on the summit one night to enjoy the sunset and sunrise.

The Inn of the Weissenstein, and the still more elevated summit of the mountain, called Hasematte, 1½ hour's walk from the Inn, to the W. of it, command one of the finest *distant* prospects of the Alps which can be named. The great chain of snowy peaks, &c., here seen, spread out along the horizon, extends for a distance of nearly 200 miles, from the Sentis on the E., to the Mont Blanc in the W. Immediately in front rise the Jungfrau, Schreckhorn, and other giants of the Bernese chain. In the foreground, amidst a varied expanse of wooded hill and verdant vale, are seen the lakes of Morat, Neuchâtel, and Bienne, while the silvery Aar, on which stands the town of Soleure, winds like a snake at the foot of the mountain.

. Another road, quite practicable for a char-à-banc, descends the opposite (N.) side of the Weissenstein, into the Val Moutiers (see p. 5).]

After Soleure the road crosses the Aar and runs along the S. base of the Jura. The inn on the top of the Weissenstein continues long a conspicuous object.

On the rt. of the road lie the Baths of *Grange* (*Grenchen*), a large building.

Bienne (Germ. *Biel*)—*Inns :* H. du Jura, and Couronne, both good and moderate ; Croix Blanche. Bienne is prettily situated at the mouth of the valley of the Suze, at the foot of the Jura, here mantled with vines, and about a mile from the head of the lake of Bienne (Rte. 45). It is still surrounded by its ancient walls and watch-towers, and is approached by several shady avenues. The number of inhabitants, chiefly Protestants, amounts to 4248. The town anciently belonged to the Bishop of Bâle, but the citizens, early imbued with the spirit of freedom, formed a perpetual alliance with Berne in 1352, for the defence of their liberties, in revenge for which the town was burnt by their liege lord. The Reformation further weakened the connection between the town and its ecclesiastical ruler, and at the beginning of the 17th century his authority became nominal. Bienne is an industrious town, and well situated.

On the margin of the lake, at the outlet of the Thiele, stands Nydau—(*Inn :* Bear)—and its castle, flanked by round towers and surmounted by a tall square keep. The lords of Nydau, an extinct family, to whom it once belonged, were foes of Berne ; their stronghold now bears on its front the Bernese bear, painted of colossal dimensions, and is converted into the cantonal salt-warehouse. From the slope of the hill near Belmont, a good view is obtained of the lake and of St. Peter's Isle. rt., near a fir-wood, rises an obelisk, by way of monument to the Swiss who fell here doing battle against the French 1798.

[Those who have a taste for climbing may gratify it by ascending from hence the *Chasseral* (Gestler), one of the highest mountains of the Jura, 3616 ft. above the lake, and 4936 ft. above the sea, with the certainty of being rewarded with a magnificent view if the weather be clear. The ascent can be made in a carriage in 4½ hours.]

From Bienne steamers now go to *Neuchâtel* and *Yverdun* (R. 45), where the Railway carries passengers to *Lausanne* and to Geneva. This is now one of the least fatiguing modes of reaching Geneva or Bex, and either can be accomplished from Basle in a day.

ROUTE 4.

BASLE TO LUCERNE, BY THE CENTRAL SWISS RAILWAY.

	Eng. m.
Liesthal	12
Lanfelfingen	22
Olten	31
Reiden	40
Sursee	50
Lucerne	63

This is perhaps the best and easiest way of entering Switzerland, the Rly. being now open all the way. The works on this line have been executed by the English engineer Brassey.

The Rly., on quitting Basle, crosses the valley of the Birs a little N. of the battlefield of St. Jacob (p. 5), on a lattice bridge of 3 arches. A little beyond this place the men of Basle were in 1833 drawn into an ambuscade by the men of Liesthal and defeated with considerable slaughter. A few miles further the Rly. quits the valley of the Rhine to ascend that of the *Ergolz.*

Liesthal Stat. (*Inns* not good : Falke; Schlüssel) was always opposed to its subjection to Basle, and was finally separated from Basle in 1833 (see p. 5). It is a dirty, uninteresting town of 2170 Inhab., and since the separation has become the seat of government of Basle Campagne, which includes 53 parishes, with about 36,000 Inhab. In the Council-house (Rathstube) are curious paintings and sentences on the walls, and Charles the Bold's cup taken at Nancy.

Sissach Stat. The Rly. now ascends the valley by a gradient of 1 in 20, and several side valleys are crossed on bridges, the line constantly rising until it looks down upon the village of

Bukten Stat. (*Inn :* Halb Mond), beyond which is a tunnel 900 ft. long; l. rise the picturesque ruins of the Castle of *Homburg.*

Laufelfingen Stat. Soon after this the formidable tunnel under the Unter-Hauenstein is entered. This tunnel was 3 years in progress, and at one accident in 1857 50 men were buried alive and lost. This pass has always been of great importance as an outlet for the merchandise of Switzerland, and as the most direct line of communication from W. Germany to Italy by the St. Gothard. From the summit of the pass on the old road, after crossing the boundary-line of Bâle and Soleure, a remarkable view is obtained of the great chain of the Alps, which will be entirely lost to the traveller by the Rly. Those who would not miss the view will quit the train at Laufelfingen, walk over the mountain, and rejoin the rail at Olten.

Olten (*Inns :* Krone, best ; Halbe Mond), which, though it contains but 1500 Inhab., promises to rise into a flourishing town, to the prejudice of

Soleure, of which it is becoming the rival. Its prosperity will be greatly promoted by its position near the point of junction of the railroads to Zürich, Lucerne, Berne, and Soleure, which all concentrate here to traverse the Jura. It is built on the l. bank of the Aar, and is said to be the Roman *Ultimum.* The *old parish church*, converted into a wood warehouse since the new one was built, is mentioned in records as early as 1240.

Aarburg Stat. (*Inns:* Bär; Krone), a neat town of 1500 Inhab., almost entirely rebuilt since a conflagration in 1840. It is distinguished by its extensive *Citadel* on the heights above, constructed in 1660 ; the only fortress belonging to the Swiss Confederation, but of no use as a fortification, for, although it has bomb-proof casemates hewn out of the rock, its works have been allowed to go to decay. It serves as a military storehouse for the Swiss Confederation, and forms a picturesque object in the landscape, such as is met with in the background of old German pictures. Outside the town is an extensive cotton factory, and a suspension wire bridge over the Aar. Here the Railway branches off to Berne (Rte. 5) and to Soleure (Rte. 3).

The Railroad continues along a pretty valley, distinguished by its verdant pastures, and its substantial-looking houses, many of them with gardens, whose walls are often covered with thin plates of wood overlapping each other like fishes' scales. It is bordered by a varied outline of wooded heights. In front, the snowy Alps.

Zoffingen Stat.— *Inns:* Cheval Blanc (Rössli), Ochs—a town with 3172 Inhab. Its *Library* contains curious MS. letters and drawings. A fragment of the castle of Reiden, and a solitary tree perched on a rock beside it, become conspicuous before reaching the village of

Reiden Stat. The Parsonage was originally the house of the Knights of Malta.

Dagmersellen Stat. Inn : Lion, kept by A. Bühler, good and clean.

A view is obtained of the Lake of Sempach, Mounts Rigi and Pilatus, and of a smaller lake called Mauensee, from the height above.

Wauwill Stat.

Sursee Stat.—(*Inns:* Soleil ; Hirsch ; both bad and dear)—an old walled town, whose gate-towers still bear the double-headed eagle of Austria carved in stone. " The traveller may well employ a few moments in examining the *Rathhaus*, much dilapidated, but affording a good specimen of the peculiarities of the German-Burgundian style. The general outline resembles the old Tolbooth of Edinburgh."—Sursee lies at the distance of about a mile from the N. extremity of the Lake of Sempach, which is seen over and among the orchards on the left of the road in going to Lucerne. It has no pretensions to great beauty, but is pleasing, and highly interesting historically, from the famous *Battle of Sempach* (1386)—the second of those great and surprising victories by which Swiss independence was established. It was fought on the E. shore of the lake, behind the little town of Sempach, opposite which the lake comes into full view from our road. In 1805 a portion of the water of the lake was let off, in order to gain land along its banks ; thus its extent is diminished, its surface lowered, and its form somewhat altered from what it was at the time of the battle. The Rly. runs along its W. shore.

Sempach Stat. (*Inns :* Kreutz ; Adler.) About 2 m. from this a small chapel, in the form of a portico, is erected to commemorate the victory, on the spot where Leopold of Austria (son of the Duke of the same name who had been defeated 71 years before at Morgarten) lost his life. The names of those who fell, both Austrians and Swiss, were inscribed on the walls, which also bear a rude fresco representation of the noble devotion of *Arnold of Winkelried.*

He of battle-martyrs chief !
Who, to recall his daunted peers,
For victory shaped an open space,
By gath'ring, with a wide embrace,
Into his single heart, a sheaf
Of fatal Austrian spears.—*Wordsworth.*

He was a knight of Unterwalden, who, observing all the efforts of the Swiss to break the ranks of their enemies foiled by their long lances, exclaimed, " Protect my wife and children, and I will open a path to freedom." He then rushed forward, and gathering in his arms as many lances as he could grasp, buried them in his bosom. The confederates were enabled to take advantage of the gap thus formed in the mail-clad ranks of the foe, before the Austrian lancers had time to extricate their entangled weapons from his body. In order to oppose the Swiss, who fought on foot, many of the Austrian nobles had dismounted to form a serried phalanx ; but the armour which rendered them almost invulnerable on horseback, and which, while they remained united and in close column, had formed so impenetrable a barrier to the attack of the Swiss, now that their ranks were broken, disabled them from coping with their light-armed and active foes. 600 nobles were slain, and more than 2000 common soldiers ; while the entire force of the Swiss, who achieved this victory, is said not to have exceeded 1400 men. The conquerors founded masses for the souls of those who fell, friends as well as foes, and they are celebrated even now on the anniversary of the fight, which is a popular festival. Fine view of the Righi and Pilatus from this part of the line.

At *Buttisholz,* a village about 3 m. W. of Nothwyl Stat., and on the rt. of the road, may be seen a mound, called the *English barrow,* because it contains the bones of 3000 Free Companions, or Guglers, who had formerly served on the English side in the wars between England and France. They were engaged by Enguerrand de Coucy, son-in-law of Edward III. of England, to conquer the Austrian dominion, to which De Coucy had some claim through his mother. The King of France furnished him with the requisite money, in order to liberate France from the ravages of these Free Companions, who, while pillaging in the Swiss cantons, were attacked in detail and destroyed by the Swiss peasants in 1376. The action which took place here was between the peasants of Entlibuch and a body of these Free Companions.

The approach to Lucerne is charming: on the l. rises the Rigi, in shape somewhat resembling a horse's back; on the rt. the Pilatus is distinguished by its serrated ridge. After crossing the small stream of the Emme, we reach the banks of the green Reuss, rushing out of the lake of Lucerne. Lucerne is surrounded on this side by a battlemented wall, flanked at intervals by a number of tall watch-towers, descending to the margin of the river.

At present the Railway stops at Emmenbrücke Stat., a short distance from

LUCERNE. (Route 16.)
Omnibuses await the trains.

ROUTE 5.

BASLE TO BERNE, BY THE CENTRAL SWISS RAILWAY.

	Eng. m.
Basle	
Liesthal	12
Laufelfingen	22
Olten	31
Herzogenbuchsee	45
Burgdorf	56
Berne	71

The road as far as Aarburg is described in Rte. 4. At Aarburg, a little beyond Olten, the road leaves the Lucerne line and turns to the S.W., keeping for some distance along the l. bank of the Aar; it then traverses a fertile but dull country to

Herzogenbuchsee Junct. Stat. (*Inn:* Sonne), a town of some 4500 Inhab.

Burgdorf (*Inns:* Emmenhof, Bär), a thriving town (3500 Inhab.) of large houses, pleasantly situated at the mouth of the fertile Emmenthal (Rte. 22). In the old castle here Pestalozzi (Rte. 47) first established

his school. In the ch. of *Hindelbank* are many monuments to the noble family of *Erlach*, and also the celebrated *Monument of Madame Langhans*, wife of the clergyman, who died in childbirth. It is by a sculptor named Nahl, and represents her with her child in her arms, bursting through the tomb at the sound of the last trumpet. Its merit, as a work of art, has been much exaggerated. Its chief excellence seems to be the natural manner in which the crack in the stone is represented. The epitaph was written by Haller. This tomb is formed of sandstone, and is let into the pavement of the church. The chief figure is injured by the loss of the nose, which Glütz Blotzheim asserts (it is to be hoped unfoundedly) was the wanton act of an Englishman.

The *Castle* of Reichenbach on the neighbouring height belongs to the Erlach family.

Berne (Rte. 24). The Rly. station is at present outside the town, but will, when the bridge across the Aar is completed, be brought into the town.

ROUTE 6.

BASLE TO ZÜRICH—RAILWAY.

	Eng. m.
Basle	
Liesthal	12
Laufelfingen	22
Olten	31
Aarau	
Schintznach	
Brugg	
Baden	
Zürich	

The road as far as Olten is described in Rte. 4. At the *Olten* junction the Zürich branch turns W., keeping on the rt. bank of the Aar, to

Aarau—Inns: Wilder Mann (Sauvage), comfortable; Löwe; Krone; Rössli—the chief town of the canton Argovie, which was first included in the Confederation in 1803, having previously formed a subject province of canton Berne, contains 4500 Inhab., and is situated on the rt. bank of the Aar: Simond called it, in 1817, "an odious little place;" but it has much improved and increased since then. It lies at the S. base of the Jura, here partly covered with vineyards. There are many extensive cotton-mills here.

The *Rathhaus*, in which the cantonal councils are held, has been rebuilt. In the *parish church* Protestant and Catholic services are performed alternately.

Henry Zschokke, the historian and novel-writer, resided here until his death, 1848, in a pretty villa on a hill on the l. bank of the Aar. When the armies of the French Revolution took possession of Switzerland in 1789, and destroyed its ancient form of government, Aarau was made for a short time capital of the Helvetian Republic.

There are several ruined castles visible from the Rly., the most conspicuous of which is that of *Windegg*.

Schintznach Stat. Near this are the *Baths of Schintznach*, also called Habsburger Bad, the most frequented watering-place in Switzerland. The principal buildings are the *Great Inn* (Grosser Gasthof) and the *Bath-house*, in a semicircular form. "The table-d'hôte saloon is 180 French ft. long, and 500 persons frequently sit down to dinner together in the season. There are 360 beds and 160 baths, all exactly alike, lined with Dutch tiles. Each visitor has his own bath for the time he remains, and there is an admirable contrivance for ventilating it. What pleased us most in this vast establishment was the attention which is paid to the wants of the poor. There is accommodation for 90 persons both in baths and beds, and they are provided with these, as well as with medical attendance, free of all expense. There are funds, likewise, for their maintenance, which are increased by a poor-box carried round every Sunday by a lady and gentleman at the table d'hôte. There are two resident physicians. The water is 60° Fahr.; it tastes strong of sulphur, Epsom and Glauber salts, by no means a palatable draught. The visitors are chiefly French—very few English; hence, though provisions are dear in this country, the table-d'hôte costs only 3 fr."—L. Fm. The waters are efficacious in cutaneous disorders, in rheumatism and gout, and for wounds. Schintznach owes little to nature except its waters. Some pretty walks have been made near the houses, and winding paths, under the shade of trees, lead up the hill to Habsburg.

Among the many *excursions* in the neighbourhood may be mentioned the ascent of the *Gisli-Fluh*.

Brugg, or *Bruck—Inn:* Das Rössli. Rly. to Waldshut (Rte. 7) in progress. An ancient possession of the House of Habsburg, containing 800 Inhab. The exit and entrance to it are guarded by high conical roofed towers. It is the birthplace of Zimmerman, physician of Frederick the Great, who wrote on Solitude.

The country around Brugg is interesting, both in a geographical and historical point of view. In the plain, a little below the town, three of the principal rivers of Switzerland which drain the N. slopes of the Alps, from the Grisons to the Jura, the Limmat, the Reuss, and the Aar, form a junction, and, united under the name of the Aar, throw themselves into the Rhine about 10 m. below Brugg, at a place called Coblenz.

Close upon this meeting of the waters, and on the triangular tongue of land between the Aar and Reuss, stood *Vindonissa*, the most important settlement of the Romans in Helvetia, as well as their strongest fortress on this frontier, on which they placed their chief dependence for maintaining this portion of their empire. Its works extended 12 m. from N. to S. Yet scarcely any portion of it now appears above ground; traces of an amphitheatre, a subterranean aqueduct, which conveyed water from Brauneggberg, 3 m. off, foundations of walls, broken pottery, inscriptions, and coins, have been turned up by the spade from time to time, and its name is preserved in that of the miserable little village of *Windisch.*

"Within the ancient walls of Vindonissa, the castle of Habsburg, the abbey of Königsfeld, and the town of Bruck have successively arisen. The philosophic traveller may compare the monuments of Roman conquests, of feudal or Austrian tyranny, of monkish superstition, and of industrious freedom. If he be truly a philosopher, he will applaud the merit and happiness of his own time."—*Gibbon.*

1½ m. E. of Brugg stands the *Abbey of Königsfelden* (King's field), founded, 1310, by the Empress Elizabeth, and Agnes Queen of Hungary, on the spot where, two years before, their husband and father, the Emperor Albert, was assassinated. The convent, a group of gloomy piles, was suppressed in 1528; part of it is now converted into a farm-house, an hospital, and a mad-house; the rest is rapidly falling to decay. The *Church,* though dilapidated, contains some very fine painted glass, and numerous pavement tombs, with sculptured coats of arms of a long train of nobles who fell in the battle of Sempach. The large vaults beneath were the burial-place of many members of the Austrian family, including Agnes, and Leopold, who fell at Sempach, but they were removed hence into the Austrian dominions in 1770. According to tradition the high altar stands on the spot where Albert fell. He was about to invade Switzerland with his army, had crossed the ferry of the Reuss in a small boat, leaving his suite on the opposite bank, and attended only by the four conspirators. The chief of them, John of Suabia, his nephew—who had been instigated to slay him by the wrong he endured in being kept out of his paternal inheritance by his uncle—first struck him in the throat with his lance. Balm ran him through with his sword, and Walter von Essenbach cleft his skull with a felling-stroke. Wart, the fourth, took no share in the murder. Although the deed was so openly done, in broad day, almost under the walls of the Imperial Castle of Habsburg, and in

sight of a large retinue of armed attendants, the murderers were able to escape in different directions; and the imperial retainers took to flight, leaving their dying master to breathe his last in the arms of a poor peasant who happened to pass.

A peasant-girl that royal head upon her
  bosom laid,
And, shrinking not for woman's dread, the
  face of death survey'd:
Alone she sate. From hill and wood low
  sunk the mournful sun;
Fast gushed the fount of noble blood. Trea-
  son his worst had done.
With her long hair she vainly pressed the
  wounds to staunch their tide;
Unknown, on that meek, humble breast, imperial Albert died.

Mrs. Hemans.

A direful vengeance was wreaked by the children of the murdered monarch; not, however, upon the murderers—for, with the exception of Wart, the only one who did not raise his hand against him, they all escaped —but upon their families, relations, and friends; and 1000 victims are believed to have expiated, with their lives, a crime of which they were totally innocent. Queen Agnes gratified her spirit of vengeance with the sight of these horrid executions, exclaiming, while 63 unfortunate men were butchered before her, "Now I bathe in May-dew!" She ended her days in the convent of Königsfelden, which she had founded and endowed with the confiscated property of those whom she had slaughtered. Penance, prayer, and almsgiving could avail but little to stifle the qualms of a guilty conscience for the bloody deeds which she had committed; and it is recorded that a holy hermit, to whom she had applied for absolution, replied to her, "Woman! God is not to be served with bloody hands, nor by the slaughter of innocent persons, nor by convents built with the plunder of orphans and widows, but by mercy and forgiveness of injuries." The building in which she passed 50 years of her life was destroyed; that which is shown as her cell is not so in reality. There was a grove of oaks on the spot at the time the murder was committed. The tree under which Albert fell was converted into a chest to hold Agnes' jewels, and is still preserved.

About 2 m.from Brugg, on a wooded height called Wülpelsberg, stand the remains of the *Castle of Habsburg,* or Habichtsburg (Hawk's Castle), the cradle of the House of Austria, built by Count Radbod of Altenburg, 1020, an ancestor of the family. A mere fragment of the original building now exists. The tall, square keep of rough stones has walls 8 ft. thick; and beneath it a dungeon, to be entered only by a trap-door in the floor above. The view from it is picturesque and interesting; the eye ranges along the course of the three rivers, over the site of the Roman Vindonissa and Königsfelden, the sepulchre of imperial Albert: on the S. rises the ruined castle of Braunegg, which belonged to the sons of the tyrant Gessler; and below it Birr, where Pestalozzi, the teacher, died, and is buried. It takes in at a single glance the whole Swiss patrimony of the Habsburgs—an estate far more limited than that of many a British peer—from which Rudolph was called to wield the sceptre of Charlemagne. The House of Austria were deprived of their Swiss territories by papal ban, 150 years after Rudolph's elevation: but it is believed that the ruin has again become the property of the Austrian Emperor by purchase.

On quitting Brugg, the road passes the convent of Königsfelden, traverses Oderdorf (near which are scanty remains of a Roman amphitheatre), and crosses the river Reuss. It then proceeds up the l. bank of the Limmat to

Baden (*Inn:* Waage (Balances), the best hotels are across the water at the baths, more than ½ mile from the town).—This ancient walled town, of 1800 Inhab., is squeezed within a narrow defile on the l. bank of the Limmat, here crossed by a wooden bridge. The ruins of the *Castle* overlook it from a rocky eminence, now tunnelled through by the Zürich Railway, well worth ascending for the singular view. It was anciently the stronghold of the Austrian princes, and their residence while Switzerland belonged to them. Here were planned the expeditions against the Swiss, which were frustrated at Morgarten and Sempach. At length when the Pope, in 1415, excommunicated the Archduke Frederick, the Swiss took it and burnt ît. In *the Rathhaus* of Baden the preliminaries preceding the treaty of peace which terminated the war of the Spanish Succession, were arranged by Prince Eugene on the part of Austria, and by Marshal Villars for France, in 1712.

Baden, like its namesakes in Baden and Austria, was frequented on account of its mineral waters by the Romans, who called it *Thermæ Helveticæ.* It was sacked and destroyed by Cæcina. Tacitus mentions it as " in modum municipii extructus locus, amœnus salubrium aquarum usu, frequens."—*Hist.* i. 67.

The *Baths* (*Inns:* Stadthof, best; Hinterhof; Raabe), on the borders of the Limmat, ¼ mile below or N. of the town, are resorted to between June and Sept. by numerous visitors, chiefly French and Swiss. The waters are warm and sulphureous, having a temperature of 38 Réaum., and are good for rheumatism, &c.

The *Great Baths,* on the l. bank of the river, are frequented by the upper classes; those on the opposite side by the lower orders.

The Swiss Baden, though not equal in beauty to its namesakes in other parts of Europe, has considerable attractions in the country around it. The rocky heights on each side of the river—the one surmounted by the ruined castle, the other partly covered by vineyards—form a portal through which the Limmat pours. Before this gorge was formed, Baden and the country above it must have been a vast lake.

Agreeable walks are made for invalids by the side of the Limmat, and many pleasant excursions may be made in the country around—the most interesting being that described above, to Schintznach (8 miles), by Windisch, Königsfelden, and Habsburg.

magistrates and patrician families, but everything is covered with plaster and whitewash.

The *Church of St. John* is very large.

The public walks just outside the town on the S. side command fine views of the Rhine, &c.

There are baths close to the Rhine and a swimming-bath in the river.

The celebrated wooden bridge over the Rhine, of a single arch, 365 feet in span, was burnt by the French in 1799, and is replaced by one of ordinary construction. A model of the original may be seen in the town library: the architect was a carpenter from Appenzell, named Grubenmann.

The Town Library contains the collection of books of the celebrated Swiss historian Müller, who was born here.

Railway to Winterthur and Zürich.

Diligences to Donaueschingen and Freiburg (on the road to Strasburg and Frankfurt); to Constance.

Steamers to Constance.

Omnibus to the falls (1 fr.).

THE FALLS OF THE RHINE.

The Falls are about 3 miles below Schaffhausen; the road to Zürich passes within ¼ m. of them.—(*Inns :* Weber's; Bellevue.) These quarters are convenient for those who would enjoy the aspect of the cataract at different hours, at sunrise and by moonlight.

It will take at least 2 hours to see the falls properly.

The falls may be reached from Schaffhausen by the l. bank, by the rt. bank, or by the river. The road by the l. bank is the longest, about 6 m., but reaches the castle of Laufen at once without obliging the traveller to cross the river; moreover, by approaching the fall on this side nothing is seen of it until it is at once presented in its most magnificent point of view, and the effect is, therefore, much increased. The road by the rt. bank is about 3 m. long, ugly and dusty. The charge for a carriage and pair to go and return is 8 fr., 1 fr. bonnemain, by either road. The most

pleasant mode of visiting the falls is, perhaps, to take a carriage, and drive to the place whence the boats start, then take a boat (3 fr.), and send on the carriage to bring you back. The boats are about half a mile below the town, and in one of them you may descend the river, which already forms a succession of rapids, by no means dangerous under the guidance of a boatman accustomed to the river. When the increased celerity of the current and the audible roar announce that the skiff is approaching the falls, the steersman makes for the l. bank, and lands his passengers in the garden of the castle of Laufen. This garden is situated on a high rock overlooking the fall, and is a private residence, but belongs to the canton, and is let upon condition of being exhibited. A charge of 1 fr. is made for each person admitted to the castle and the walks. Here is also a print-room; many pretty views of the Rhine, &c., may be found for sale, also maps and guide-books. There are several platforms and kiosks in the gardens, from which views of the falls are obtained, and several flights of very rude stone and wooden steps conduct to a projecting stage, or rude balcony, of stout timbers, thrown out, like the bowsprit of a ship, from the vertical cliff to within a few feet of the fall. It actually overhangs the roaring shoot, and though perfectly secure, trembles under the impulse of the water. Here, covered with the spray, the traveller may enjoy the full grandeur of this *hell of waters ;* and it is only by this close proximity, amidst the tremendous roar and the uninterrupted rush of the river, passing with the swiftness of an arrow above his head and beneath his feet, that a true notion can be formed of the stupendous nature of this cataract. The best time for seeing the fall is about 8 in the morning, when the iris floats within the spray (provided the sun shines), and by moonlight. The river is usually most full in the month of July. The Rhine, above the fall, is about 300 feet broad; the height of the fall varies from 60 feet on one side to 45 on the other; but, including the rapids above, the entire descent is not less than 100 feet. Two isolated pillars of rock, standing in the middle of the stream, divide the fall into 3 shoots. Seen from behind, these pinnacles appear eaten away by the constant friction of the water, and tottering to their fall; yet, though the rock is soft, the waste of it within the memory of man has not been perceptible.

The river, after its leap, forms a large semicircular bay, as it were to rest itself; the sides of which are perpetually chafed by the heaving billows. Here, in front of the fall, on the rt. bank, stands the *Castle of Wörth*, a square tower, containing a camera obscura, which shows the fall in another and a very singular point of view. From this tower to the foot of the rock on which the castle of Laufen stands, boats ply, to ferry visitors across, charging ⅓ fr. each! The boats are much tossed about in their passage, but make it without risk. The boatmen below the falls will land adventurous travellers on the central rock at 4 fr. each; and those who have a steady head may ascend it, and view the fall from this vantage-ground. These boatmen appear to enjoy a monopoly, and are very exorbitant and insolent.

On the rocks on the rt. bank are some iron-works, the hammers of which are worked by the fall, but the buildings materially injure the beauty of the falls. Immediately above the falls is the new and handsome stone bridge of the Schaffhausen and Zürich Railway, which passes under the Castle of Laufen and close to the falls. (Rte. 8.)

It is a curious fact that no classic or ancient author mentions the Rheinfall.

ROUTE 7A.

SCHAFFHAUSEN to CONSTANCE— LAKE OF CONSTANCE.

Post-road, 3¼ posts = 29¼ Eng. m.

	Posts.	Eng. m.
Schaffhausen.		
Diessenhofen . .	⅞	7¼
Steckborn . . .	1⅜	12⅜
Constance . . .	1	9

Diligence daily, along the S. or Swiss bank of the Rhine, in 5 hours.

A *steamer* daily, ascending the Rhine to Constance in 6 or 8 hours against the current; descending in 3 or 4 hrs. It passes under 3 bridges, lowering its chimney. Cuisine on board bad. It does *not* take carriages.

[The journey may be made by the road on the *N. side of the Rhine*, which is also provided with post-horses, but the Swiss road is shorter.

The relays (in Germ. miles) are—

1½ *Randegg*. Here is the Baden Custom-house. Beyond this is passed *Singen* — (*Inn*, poor and extortionate). Near this place you pass at the foot of *Hohentwiel*. The castle is now dismantled. The lofty rock upon which it stands gives it the appearance of an Indian hill-fort.

2¾ *Radolfszell*—(*Inn:* Poste, good) —a desolate town, with a fine church, in the true German-Gothic style.

The scenery throughout the whole of this road is exceedingly agreeable, often striking. The woods abound in most splendid butterflies. Collections of these insects may be bought at Singen, and also at Radolfszell.

The Rhine here, suddenly contracted from a lake to a river, is crossed by a wooden bridge, in order to reach

3 *Constance*. (In the next page.)]

The Swiss Road runs along the l. bank of the Rhine, past the Nunneries of Paradies and Katherinethal, the former belonging to the order of St. Clara, the latter of St. Dominic; but the revenues and the number of sisters in both are now much reduced. The Austrian army under the Archduke

Charles crossed the Rhine at Paradies 1799.

Diessenhofen—(*Inn :* Adler).

Wagenhausen—(*Inn :* Ochse, clean and fair).

[1. A little off the road lies *Stein* — (*Inns :* Schwan ; Krone) —a town of 1270 Inhab., on the rt. bank of the Rhine, belonging to Schaff-hausen, united by a wooden bridge with a suburb on the l. bank. The *Abbey of St. George* is a very ancient ecclesiastical foundation. The owners of the ruined castle of Hohenklingen, situated on the rocky height, were originally the feudal seigneurs of the town, but the citizens obtained independence from their masters by purchase.

3 miles E. of Stein, at a height of between 500 and 600 feet above the Rhine, are situated the *Quarries of Œhningen*, remarkable for the vast abundance of fossil remains of terrestrial and fresh-water animals found in them, including mammalia, birds, reptiles, fishes, shells, insects, and plants, some of them identical with species now living. The most curious discovery is that of the perfect skeleton of a fossil fox, made by Sir Roderick Murchison: a very large tortoise had previously been brought to light. The beds of rock in which the quarries are worked consist of marls, limestones, shales, and building-stone. They lie immediately above the formation called Molasse, and differ in their organic contents from all other fresh-water formations hitherto discovered.]

Above Stein the Rhine expands into a lake called *Untersee* (lower lake) connected again by the Rhine at its upper extremity with the large Lake of Constance. *Feldbach*, also a nunnery, belonging to sisters of the Cistercian order, is passed before reaching

Steckborn. "In the broad part of the Rhine, where it is still rather a lake than a river, is the *Isle of Reichenau*, anciently famed for a Monastery founded by one of the successors of Charlemagne, of which the *Church* (partly Romanesque) and Treasury remain. In the Treasury are to be seen the shrine of St. Fortunata, an ivory ciborium, a cope, a crozier, and a missal of the xth century."—F. S.

Itznang, a small village on the opposite shore of the river, within the territory of Baden, is the birthplace of Mesmer, the *inventor* of animal magnetism.

Near the village of *Berlingen* the pretty *château* of the Duchess of Dino appears; and a little further that of *Arenaberg*, once the residence of the late Duchess of St. Leu (Hortense, ex-Queen of Holland), and of her son Prince Louis (now the Emperor Louis Napoleon), before he attempted his revolution at Strasburg, since sold to a gentleman of Neuchâtel.

The Castle of *Gottlieben*, on the l. of the road, built by the Bishops of Constance 1250, on the Rhine, at the point where it enters the Untersee, is remarkable for having been the prison of John Huss and Jerome of Prague, who were confined within its dungeons by order of the Emperor Sigismund and Pope John XXIII. The latter was himself transferred a few months later to the same prison, by order of the Council of Constance. In 1454 Felix Hämmerlin (Malleolus), the most learned and enlightened man of his time in Switzerland, was also imprisoned here. The building is now private property.

Petershausen, now a barrack on the rt. bank of the Rhine opposite Constance, was a free abbey of the Empire.

CONSTANCE. *Inns:* Brochet (*Hecht*), best; looking over the lake; very attentive landlord;—Post (Golden Adler; Aigle d'Or), good ; — Hôtel Delisle (Golden Löwe), outside the territory of the Customs League, just beyond the gate, at Kreutzlingen, good.

Mr. Keppler, landlord of the *Hecht*, is an accomplished fisherman, as well as a civil and attentive host: he has excellent rods, nets, punts, and all appliances for *fishing*, which he lets out on moderate terms. He has also very extensive water privilege in and around Constance. In short *the Angler* can find no better quarters in Switzerland than in his house.

Constance, a decayed city, of 5500

Inhab., instead of 40,000, which it once possessed, is remarkable for its antiquity, since its streets and many of its buildings remain unaltered since the 15th century. Although situated on the l. or Swiss bank of the Rhine, it belongs to Baden. It is connected with the opposite shore by a long wooden covered bridge, and occupies a projecting angle of ground at the W. extremity of the Bodensee, or lake of Constance; its agreeable position and interesting historical associations make amends for the want of life perceptible within its venerable walls. It has of late, however, revived considerably; the government have formed, at a large expense, a Port on the lake, which facilitates the navigation, while it is an ornament to the town: and several manufactories of cotton and muslin have sprung up. The ancient bishopric, numbering 87 bishops, was terminated in 1802, and in 1805 Constance was ceded by Austria to Baden.

The *Minster* is a handsome Gothic structure, begun 1052, with fine open-work turrets in the W. end; the doors of the main portal between the two towers are of oak, curiously carved with a representation of the Passion of our Lord, executed in 1470 by one Simon Bainder. The nave is supported by sixteen pillars, each of a single block, and dates from the 13th century. The spot where the "Arch-heretic Huss" stood, as sentence of death by burning was pronounced on him by his unrighteous judges, is still pointed out. Robert Hallam, Bishop of Salisbury, who presided over the English deputation to the council, is buried here, in front of the high altar, under a tomb, which is very remarkable, as being of *English brass*, which is fully proved by the workmanship. It was probably sent over from England by his executors. He wears the Order of the Garter. Beneath the ch. is a very ancient *crypt*, with a passage leading from it towards the river. Two sides of the ancient *cloisters*, whose arches are filled in with beautiful tracery, are yet standing. By the side of the cathedral is a circular (?) chapel,

perhaps a baptistery, in the centre of which is a Gothic Holy Sepulchre.

There are some curious relics in the *Sacristy*, also a beautiful Gothic fireplace and piscina. In the *Vestry-room* above are a range of singular cupboards or presses of carved oak, none of a later date than the xvth century. There is a beautiful view from the tower of the cathedral, W. over the lake and mountains of Tyrol, and E. over the valley of the Rhine.

The *Dominican Convent*, now a cotton-printing establishment(Macaire's), is very interesting. The place is still shown where Huss was confined, though the stone chamber itself has been removed (at least all that remained of it) to the Kaufhaus. The church forms a picturesque ruin, in the early style of German Gothic. The chapter-house is even older. The cloisters are perfect. The little island upon which this building stands was fortified by the Romans, and a portion of the wall, towards the lake, can yet be discerned.

In the *Hall of the Kaufhaus* (built 1388, as a warehouse), close to the lake, the *Great Council of Constance* held its sittings 1414-18, in a large room supported by wooden pillars. That famous assembly, composed, not of bishops alone, like the ancient councils, but of deputies, civil and ecclesiastical, from the whole of Christendom, including princes, cardinals (30), patriarchs (4), archbishops (20), bishops (150), professors of universities and doctors of theology (200), besides a host of ambassadors, inferior prelates, abbots, priors, &c., was convened for the purpose of remedying the abuses of the church; and as those abuses began with its head, the proceedings were prefaced by a declaration that a council of the church has received, by Divine right, an authority in religious matters, even over that of the pope. It exerted its influence in curbing the Papal power, by deposing the infamous John XXIII. and Benedict XIII., and by electing in their place Martin V. It was by the act of this council that John Huss and Jerome of Prague were seized and executed, in spite of the safe-conduct granted to the former by the Emperor Sigismund, the president of the assembly.

The chairs occupied by the Emperor and Pope, a model of the dungeon, now destroyed, in which Huss was confined ; it is of the same size as the original, and in it the actual door and other fragments have been incorporated;—also the car on which he was drawn to execution; the figure of Abraham, which supported the pulpit from the Minster, and which the people mistook for Huss, and defaced accordingly, and some other relics of the council, still remain in the hall, besides a collection of Roman and German antiquities, dug up in the neighbourhood. 1 fr. is charged for admission.

The *house* in which *Huss* lodged, bearing a rude likeness of him, is pointed out in the Paul's Strasse, near the Schnetzthor. He was thrown into prison, soon after his arrival, in the *Franciscan Convent*, now a ruin, whence he was removed to a more irksome dungeon, affording scarcely room to move, in the before mentioned *Dominican Convent*.

The field, outside of the town, in the suburb of Brühl, in which he suffered martyrdom, with a fortitude which moved even his judges and executioners to admiration—nay, even the place where the stake was planted, are still pointed out; and rude images of Huss and Jerome, formed of clay taken from the spot, are offered for sale to the stranger.

Here is a capital Swimming Bath at the *Ecole de Natation* in the midst of the lake, approached by a long plank bridge, at the end of which, stuck up in large letters visible far off, may be read the temperature of the waters.

Excursions may be made hence to Reichenau (p. 22), Meinau, and Heiligenberg. The *island* of *Meinau*, about 4 m. N. of Constance, is a well-cultivated little estate, yet with no want of trees. The house was once a commandery of the Knights of the Teutonic Order. From the terrace of the garden there is a magnificent view over the lake, of the mountains of the Vorarlberg and Appenzell, among which the Sentis is pre-eminent. Nearer at hand the cultivated German shores, with the towns of Mörsberg, Friedrichshaven, &c., complete the picture. Meinau is approached by a wooden foot-bridge ¼ m. long connecting it with the shore; there is an inn on the island.

From *Hohenrain*, 1 hour's walk, is a fine view of the Alps.

Diligences : Schaffhausen, Coire, St Gall (Railway to Zürich begun).

Lake of Constance, or *Boden See*.

8 or 10 *Steamboats* navigate the lake of Constance, between Constance Schauffhausen, Ueberlingen, Meersburg, Friedrichshafen, Rorschach, Ludwigshafen, Romanshorn, Lindau and Bregenz. The time and place of starting are promulgated in a printed tariff, which will be found hung up in all the inns near the lake. It takes 5 hours to go from Constance to Lindau, and 3 to Rorschach or Friedrichshafen. The steamers take carriages. The numerous stoppages, and the shifting of passengers from one steamer to another, are annoyances for which travellers must be prepared

The lake of Constance, called by the Germans *Boden See*, and anciently known to the Romans under the name *Lacus Brigantinus* (from Brigantia, the modern Bregenz), is bordered by the territories of 5 different states—Baden, Württemberg, Bavaria, Austria and Switzerland, and a portion of its coasts belong to each of them. It is about 44 m. long, from Bregenz to Constance, and 30 from Bregenz to Friedrichshafen; about 9 m. wide in the broadest part; 964 ft. is its greatest depth ; and it abounds in fish, of which 25 species have been enumerated. It lies 1385 ft. above the sea.

Its main tributary is the Rhine which enters at its E. extremity, and flows out under the walls of Constance. The accumulated deposits of the river have formed an extensive delta at the upper end of the lake, and are annually encroaching further.

Its banks, either flat or gently undulating, present little beauty of scenery compared with other Swiss lakes; but they are eminently distinguished for their fertility, and its S. shore is studded with a picturesque line of ruined castles or hill-forts of the middle ages.

At its E. extremity it displays alpine features in distant glimpses of the snow-topped mountains of Vorarlberg, but the distant Sentis towers over the cultivated slopes which border the lake, and is a fine feature all the way from Constance.

Its waters, on an average, are lowest in the month of February, and highest in June and July, when the snows are melting: it sometimes swells a foot in 24 hours at that season.

On quitting Constance, to the rt. is the suppressed Augustine convent of Kreuzlingen, now turned into an agricultural school, with 70 or 80 pupils. The edifice dates from the end of the 30 years' war, in the course of which the preceding building was destroyed. The *Church* possesses in a side chapel some curious wood-carvings by a Tyrolese; a representation of the Passion with several hundred small figures; also a vest embroidered with pearls, the gift of Pope John XXII. in 1414. *Inn:* Goldener Löwe (H. Delisle), clean and reasonable.

The canton of Thurgovia, which occupies the S. shore of the lake from Constance to Arbon, is distinguished for its surpassing fertility. Instead of rocks and mountains, and alpine pastures, the characteristics of other parts of Switzerland, this canton presents richly-cultivated arable land, waving with corn and hemp; the place of forests is supplied by orchards; it is, indeed, the garden and granary of Helvetia. The country is at the same time thickly peopled, abounding in villages and cheerful cottages.

The nunnery of Münsterlingen, about 4 m. further, was suppressed in 1838, and converted into an hospital. The surviving sisters are allowed to occupy one wing of the building during their lifetime. The old convent near the water was the

[*Switz.*]

scene of the reconciliation between the Emperor Sigismund and Duke Frederick of Austria, 1418.

Romanshorn (Rte. 9)—(H. Bodan)—terminus of the N. E. Rly. On the N. shore of the lake is Friedrichshafen and the *Villa* of the King of Würtemberg, in which he usually passes a part of the summer; and at Friedrichshafen is the terminus of the Stuttgard Rly., which joins the Baden Rly. at Bruchsal. See HANDBOOK FOR SOUTH GERMANY.

Arbon (*Inns:* Kreutz; Traube), a walled town of 660 Inhab., close upon the lake. The Romans under Augustus built a fort here, upon the high road from Augst and Windisch to Bregenz, which they called *Arbor Felix.* It was abandoned by them to the Allemanni in the 5th century. The *Castle,* on an eminence overlooking the lake, was built 1510, but its tower is said to rest on Roman foundations. The *belfry,* detached from the church, is boarded, not walled, on the side nearest the castle, in order that no force hostile to the lords of the castle should be enabled to shelter themselves in it, or annoy the castle from thence. The monk of St. Gall is said to have died at Arbon (640), and the place was a favourite residence of Conradin of Hohenstaufen.

Rorschach (Rte. 66), on the *South-Eastern* Railway. A short distance from Rorschach is the mouth of the Rhine, beyond which is the Vorarlberg in Austria.

ROUTE 8.

SCHAFFHAUSEN TO ZÜRICH—RHEINFALL RAILWAY.

Stations.						Eng. m.
Schaffhausen.						
Andelfingen	.	.	.	.	.	9
Winterthur	.	.	.	.	.	18
Effretikon	.	.	.	.	.	
Wallisellen	.	.	.	.	.	
Zürich	.	.	.	.	.	35

The Rly. station at Schaffhausen is just outside the town on the S.W.

After leaving the town, the Rly. continues on the rt. bank of the Rhine for about 2 m., till just above the falls, when it turns and crosses the river by a very long and handsome stone bridge, and immediately afterwards enters a tunnel and passes under the Castle of Laufen, one of the most remarkable pieces of Rly. scenery in the world. On emerging from the tunnel, which is short, a rapid view of the falls may be caught on the rt. The Rly. keeps for a short distance on the cliffs close to the Rhine, but high above it, forming a road wonderfully picturesque, but frightfully expensive to the Rly. engineer, and then quits the Rhine and proceeds through a fertile country somewhat uninteresting, but with occasional fine views, towards the valley of the Thur, making a great bend in order to cross that river near

Andelfingen Stat.

The Rly. now ascends a considerable incline, in order to cross the ridge between the valley of the Thur and the valley of the Töss, and affords a fine view on the rt. before descending into the broad and fertile valley of the Töss.

Winterthur Junct. Stat. — (*Inns :* Wilder Mann, good; — Sonne) — an industrious manufacturing town of 5341 Inhab. (Protestants), consisting of two long parallel streets, crossed by eight smaller ones at right angles. The *New School* is the only conspicuous building.

The weaving of muslin and the printing of cotton are the most thriving branches of industry here.

This is the junction station of the *Rorschach* and *St. Gall* line, and of the *Romanshorn* line.

On the banks of the Töss, about 3 m. on the l. of the road, and nearly 4 m. from Winterthur, rises the *Castle of Kyburg*, memorable in history as the seat of a powerful family of counts, who, between the 9th and 13th centuries, gained possession of the N. of Switzerland, as far as the Rhine and lake of Constance, and numbered as their dependents and vassals 100 lords of minor castles,

now for the most part in ruins. The line becoming extinct in 1264, their domains fell to the share of Rudolph of Habsburg; and the Austrian family, though long since deprived of them, still retains among its titles that of Count of Kyburg.

The ancient Dominican Convent of Töss, on the road, now converted into a factory, was the chosen retreat of the Empress Agnes after the murder of her father, Albert of Austria. Here her daughter-in-law, St. Elizabeth of Hungary, took the veil, and died in the odour of sanctity : her monument, with the arms of Hungary, is visible in the existing church. The cloisters, built with the church in 1469, are ornamented with fresco paintings of Bible subjects.

After leaving Winterthur the Rly. follows the rather picturesque valley of the Töss, passing between steep green hills, leaving Kyburg on the l., and then follows another stream into the valley of the *Glatt*, up which on the l. there is a fine view of Glärnisch and other mountains.

Wallisellen Junct. Stat.

[Here the branch Rly. up the manufacturing valley of the Glatt to Rüti, and ultimately to Coire by Wallenstadt, joins.]

Shortly after leaving Wallisellen a long tunnel under the hill of Weid is traversed ; on emerging from it the Limmat is crossed, and after making some very sharp curves the Rly. reaches

ZÜRICH. — *Inns :* Hôtel Baur, a large, handsome, comfortable house, with a reading-room : and a 2nd house, a quiet family hotel, with garden, and all English comforts, close to the lake, with a fine view, called H. Baur au Lac. These are two of the best Inns in Switzerland, and M. Baur is the most polite and attentive of landlords. *Charges :* Table-d'hôte at 1 and 4, 4 frs.; beds, 2 frs.; rooms looking over the lake, 3 frs.; bougie, 1 fr.; sitting-room, 6 to 10 frs. In the reading-room the *Times, Galignani,* and 2 American papers. H. Bellevue, a new house (1858), on the lake. Also in the town, H. Bellevue. Couronne

(Krone), on the rt. bank of the Limmat, pretty good; view of the lake. Schwerdt (Epée), improved. Faucon, large new house. Storck, commercial.

Zürich, the most important manufacturing town of Switzerland, and the capital of a canton distinguished above all others for prosperous industry, has 17,000 Inhab., nearly all Protestants, and lies at the N. end of the lake of Zürich, and on the banks of the Limmat, just where it issues out of the lake in a rapid and healthful stream, clear as crystal, and another river, the Sihl, flows on the W. side of the town. A Roman station, *Turicum* (?), on this spot, probably gave rise both to the town and its name. The canton became one of the Swiss confederacy in 1351. The Reformation occasioned more bitterness here than in any other canton, and the domestic quarrels have always been very violent. The government became democratic in 1831. The flourishing condition of the town is visible in the improvements going forward in it, and in the number of the new buildings in and around it. The banks of the Lake (described in Rte. 14) and the Limmat, and all the neighbouring hills, are thickly dotted over with houses, now united with the town itself by the removal (in 1833) of the useless and inconvenient ramparts, and forming a wide circle of suburbs. This unfortunate town was the scene of a battle in Sept. 1799, when 37,000 French under Massena drove out the Russians under Korsakof, and compelled them to fall back upon the Rhine with a loss of 8000 men.

Apart from its agreeable situation, and thriving manufactures, there is not much to be seen in Zürich. There are no fine buildings here: that of the most consequence is the *Cathedral*, or *Gross Münster*, on the rt. bank of the Limmat, surmounted by 2 W. steeples. It is venerable from its age, having been built in the 10th or 11th century, and worthy of respect from having been the scene of Zwingli's bold preachings of Reformation in the church, and

amendment of morals. It is a massive Romanesque edifice; very plain within and without, but interesting in the eye of the architect and antiquary. Its nave is supported on square pillars and round arches: beneath it is a very perfect crypt. Its very fine N. doorway with detached shafts and the adjoining *cloisters* raised upon small low triple arches, with slender columns and capitals of various patterns, fantastically carved, are very curious.

The house in which the reformer *Zwingli* passed the last six years of his life is still standing : it is No. 185 in the Grosse Stadt.

The *Ch. of St. Peter* (with the large clock), on the l. bank of the Limmat, had for its minister, for 23 years, *Lavater*, the author of the renowned work on Physiognomy, who was born at Zürich. On the capture of the town by the French army, he was shot, within a few steps of his own door, by a French soldier, to whom, but two minutes before, he had given wine and offered money, and while he was in the act of assisting another soldier who had been wounded. A high reward was offered by Massena, the French commander, for the discovery of the murderer : but Lavater refused to inform against him. After lingering through three months of excruciating agony, Lavater expired, Jan. 2, 1801, at the parsonage : his grave is marked by a simple stone in the *churchyard of St. Anne*, where Ebel, author of the Swiss Guide, and Escher von der Linth (Rte. 14), are also buried.

In the council-chamber of the *Rathhaus*, a massive square building opposite the Sword Inn, where the Diet used to meet, is an extravagant painting of the Oath at Grütli, by *Henry Fuseli* (properly Fussli), who was born here.

The *Town Library*, close to the New stone bridge, in a building formerly a church (Wasserkirche), contains, in addition to 45,000 printed volumes and MSS., 100 vols. of autograph letters of early Reformers ; 3 Latin letters of *Lady Jane Grey* to Bullinger, in a beautifully clear and regular hand—a few grammatical errors have been remarked in them; Zwingli's Greek Bible, with marginal notes (chiefly Hebrew) by himself; a Roman inscription, giving the ancient name of Zürich, *Turicum*; a bust of Lavater, by *Dannecker;* a portrait of Zwingli and his daughter, by *Hans Asper;* a model in relief of a large part of Switzerland, interesting and superior to that at Lucerne; some very curious fossils from Œhningen, including one described by Scheuchzer as a human skull, though in reality a portion of a lizard—fossils of the Glarus slate, chiefly fishes, from the Plattenberg.

The *Old Arsenal* (Altes-Zeughaus), near to Baur's Hotel, contains some ancient armour; also a cross-bow, said to be (?) that with which William Tell shot the apple from his son's head; Zwingli's battle-axe; and several tattered standards, taken by the Swiss from their enemies, including one of Charles the Bold of Burgundy. This collection is inferior to those in several other Swiss cantons.

In 1832-3 a *University* was established at Zürich, and many professors, expelled from other countries for their political opinions, have repaired hither as teachers. As yet the number of students is not great. The building of the suppressed Augustine convent has been appropriated to its use, and considerable additions to it have been made. The *Library* contains many original MSS. of the early reformers; and the *Museum* of *Natural History* some good specimens of Swiss minerals and fossils, together with the Herbarium of John Gessner, and a zoological collection.

One of the most pleasing features about Zürich is its *Promenades* and points of view. One of the best of them is an elevated mound, once forming part of the ramparts, and called Cats' Bastion, now included in the *New Botanical Garden*, which is prettily laid out in walks and shrubberies, and opened to the public without restriction, a privilege not abused: it commands a delightful view of the town, lake, and distant Alps. Nothing can be more delightful than the view at sunset from this point, extending over the smiling and populous shores of

the beautiful lake to the distant peaks and glaciers of the Alps of Glarus, Uri, and Schwytz, tinged with the most delicate pink by the sinking rays. The most prominent and interesting of the Alpine peaks seen from this, beginning at the E., are the Sentis in Appenzell, barely visible; Glärnisch, Dödi, Klariden in Glarus, Achsenburg, Rossberg, and Uri Rothstock.

The *Hohe Promenade*, a raised terrace, stretching above the lake from the heights E. of the town, also commands a good view, but more confined than the former.

Environs. a. The Gasthaus *Zur Weid*, about an hour's walk on the Baden road, commands a magnificent view of the Alps, the town, and the vale of the Limmat.

b. The *Hütliberg*, about 3 m. W. of the town, one of the Albis range of hills, whose summit, 2792 ft. high, commands a complete panorama, and is easily accessible in 1 h. to the foot of the hill and another hour to the top. The Inn on the top is good and contains 10 rooms.

c. The triangular piece of ground at the junction of the Limmat and Sihl, below the town, called *Schützen-Platz*, is also a public walk; it is planted with shady avenues, but commands no view. Here is a simple monument to the memory of Solomon Gessner, author of 'The Death of Abel,' who was a native of Zürich.

Zürich is historically remarkable as the place where the Reformation first commenced in Switzerland, under the guidance and preaching of Ulric Zwingli, in 1519. It had already, at an earlier period, afforded safe and hospitable shelter to Arnold of Brescia, when driven out of Italy for inveighing against the temporal power of the Pope. It was the asylum of many eminent English Protestants banished by the persecutions of the reign of Queen Mary: they met with a friendly reception from its inhabitants during their exile. The first *entire English version* of the Bible, by Miles Coverdale, was printed here in 1535.

Zürich is the native place of Hammerlin the reformer; of Gessner the poet, and Gessner the naturalist; of Lavater; and of Pestalozzi the teacher.

The principal *Manufactures* are those of silk, the weaving of which occupies many thousands in the town and along the shores of the lake. There are one or two large cotton-factories. The cotton and silk goods made in the neighbourhood, and in other parts of the canton, are the object of an extensive commerce with Germany and Italy, and compete in price with English goods. Mr. Escher's large *manufactory of machinery* employs 700 persons, including several English overseers. Most of the iron steamers plying on the Swiss lakes are made by him, and boats, engines and all, are actually carried in pieces by carts over the St. Gothard to the Italian lakes. Many of the manufacturers of Zürich have the reputation of great wealth, without much polish; hence the expression, "Grossier comme un Zurichois." Those inhabitants, however, with whom the traveller comes in contact, are certainly more polished, and ready to oblige, than the generality of German Swiss.

A fine *Hospital* behind the new promenade, an *Orphan House* (Waisenhaus), an *Asylum* for blind and deaf (Blinden Institut), and a stone bridge over the river, have risen up within a few years.

The *Museum* Club contains a capital reading-room, where Galignani, The Times, John Bull, Examiner, Athenæum, and Literary Gazette, Quarterly and Edinburgh Reviews are taken in; besides more than 300 of the best Continental journals. Travellers can be introduced for a few days by a member. Open 8-12 a.m. and 2-6 p.m.

Those who enter Switzerland on this side will do well to provide themselves with maps, &c., here.

Leuthold (next door to H. Baur, speaks English) has a good collection of guide-books, maps, prints, stationery, &c. He is the publisher of an excellent map.

Fussli (near the stone bridge) has also a good collection of guide-books, maps, prints, &c.

Dr. Locher is a good medical man. *Keretz*, in the Wein-Platz, makes up English prescriptions.

Furrer is well recommended as a voiturier and job-master.

The *Post Office* is a handsome building, faced with Doric pillars, near the Frau-Münster Kirche, opposite H. Baur.

Railways—To Basle; terminus on the Schützenplatz; to Romanshorn (Rte. 9); to St. Gall and Rorschach; to Berne and Lucerne.

Steamboats go thrice a-day from Zürich to the other end of the lake (Rapperschwyl) and once to Schmerikon and back. Diligences convey passengers thence to Wesen, where another steamer is prepared to carry them across the lake to Wallenstadt. (Rte. 14.) The *Righi* top may be reached from Zürich in 9 hrs., and Lucerne in 7 hrs., taking the steamboats as far as Horgen across the lake of Zug (R. 15).

ROUTE 9.

ROMANSHORN TO ZÜRICH.—RAILWAY.

Eng. m.

Romanshorn.	
Weinfelden Stat. . .	14¼
Müllheim Stat. . .	19
Frauenfeld Stat. . .	25¼
Winterthur Stat. . .	35
Wallisellen Stat. . .	46
Orlikon Stat. . .	48
Zürich Stat.	51¼

Romanshorn (Hôtel Bodan), a small village on the lake of Constance. From a château on the heights above it there is a fine view over the lake (Rte. 7A).

Weinfelden, celebrated for its wines. The council of the canton Thurgau sits here.

Müllheim.—A wooden tower has been erected on the summit of *Hohen-*

rain, a hill near this, on account of the extensive view. (See p. 24.)

Frauenfeld — (*Inns:* Krone, best: Hirsch)—the chief town of the canton Thurgovie (Germ. Thurgau), has 2450 Inhab., and is situated on the river Murg, which sets in motion the wheels of several cotton, dyeing, and printing mills. It is a mean and uninteresting little place. The *Castle*, on a basement of rock fronting the Murg, was built in the 11th century, by one of the vassals of the Counts of Kyburg.

On a hill to the S. of the town stands the Capuchin Convent, founded in 1595, now occupied by only 7 or 8 brothers.

Winterthur Junct. Stat. (see Rte. 8).
ZÜRICH (Rte. 8).

ROUTE 13.

ZÜRICH TO BERNE, RAILWAY.

	Eng. m.
Zürich.	
Baden	. . . .
Aarau	. . . .
Herzogenbuchsee	. . . .
Berne	. . . . . .

The distance is about 80 m.; the fastest trains accomplish it in 4 hrs. 20 min. The road is very circuitous: as far as Olten it is the same as to Basle (Rte. 6). At Olten it joins the Basle and Berne line (Rte. 5). Most of the trains, however, run up to Olten.

ROUTE 14.

ZURICH TO RAGATZ, BY THE LAKES OF ZÜRICH AND WALLENSTADT.

Whole distance, 65 Eng. m. Road, 6 posts = 54 m. Rly. in progress.

	Posts.		Eng. m.
Zürich.			
Rapperschwyl	. .	2½	= 10
Uznach	. . .	1	= 9
Wesen	. . . .	1¼	= 11¼
Wallenstadt (by water)			= 12
Ragatz	. . . .	1½	= 13½

Diligence and boat, 13 hrs., 13 f. 90 c.

Good carriage-roads run along both sides of the lake of Zürich. The road to Wallenstadt and Coire runs along the rt. or N. bank. The steamers take carriages across the two lakes. That of Wallenstadt *must* be crossed in the steamer, there being no road.

The *Glatt-thal Railway* is now open to *Rüti*, near Rapperschwyl, and will be continued from Rapperschwyl along the precipitous S. shore of the Lake of Wallenstadt to Sargans and Coire. The expense and difficulty of the enterprise are frightful, and the Rly. does not appear very necessary, as the Rly. by St. Gall serves, though rather longer, to connect Zürich and Coire, &c.

Steamboats traverse the Lake of Zürich, to and fro, five times a day, in 2 to 2½ hours. *Steamer* also once a day to Schmerikon and back. They zigzag from one side of the lake to the other, to take in and let out passengers at the different towns. As the vessels on both lakes, and the diligences, are under the same administration, the fare may be paid at once. Even in posting, the horses, postboys, tolls, &c., may be paid for before starting, at the steam-boat office. The steamers take carriages from Zürich to Wallenstadt, Rapperschwyl, or Schmerikon; and from Wasen to Wallenstadt. For the charges for transport of a carriage see the tariff in the Post-book.

Diligences, &c., at Horgen for Zug and Arth on the way to the Rigi (R. 15); at Rapperschwyl for St. Gall

(R. 69); at Richterswyl for Einsiedeln, and Schwytz; at Lachen for Glarus.

Diligences and covered row-boats are in readiness on the arrival of the steamer at Schmerikon, to carry on the passengers to Wesen, where they embark on another steamer to Wallenstadt. There another set of coaches takes them on to Ragatz, Pfeffers, Coire, &c. Unless places are taken at Zürich, travellers may be left behind for want of room in the coaches. In one day you may see the Lakes of Zürich and Wallenstadt, and reach Pfeffers early.

The *Lake of Zürich* has no pretensions to grandeur of scenery; that must be sought for on the silent and savage shores of the lakes of Lucerne, Brienz, and Wallenstadt; but it has a charm peculiarly its own — that of life and rich cultivation. Its borders are as a beehive, teeming with population, and are embellished and enlivened at every step by the work of man. The hills around it are less than 3000 feet above the sea, and descend in gentle slopes down to the water's edge; wooded on their tops, clad with vineyards, orchards, and gardens on their slopes, and carpeted with verdant pastures, or luxuriantly waving crops of grain at their feet. But the principal feature in this landscape is the number of human habitations: the hills from one extremity to the other are dotted with white houses, villas of citizens, cottages, and farms, while along the margin of the lake, and on the high road, they gather into frequent clusters around a church, forming villages and towns almost without number. Every little stream descending from the hill is compelled to do duty by turning some mill; at the mouths of the valleys enormous factories are erected, and thus the shores of the lake, on either side, have the appearance of one vast and almost uninterrupted village.

The effect of this lively foreground is heightened by the appearance of the snowy peaks of the Sentis, Dödi, and Glärnisch, which are seen at different points peering above the nearer hills. The charms of the Lake of Zürich inspired the Idylls of Gessner: they are celebrated in an ode of Klopstock, and in the prose of Zimmerman. The lake is a long and narrow strip of water, about 26 miles in length from Zürich to Schmerikon, and not more than 3 broad at the widest part, between Stäfa and Wädensweil. The principal river falling into it is the Linth, which issues out at Zürich, under the name of Limmat.

Scarcely any of the villages or towns on the lake are remarkable, except as the seats of flourishing industry. A few only of the principal places are enumerated below, with their distance by land from Zürich. The banks are distinguished as rt. and l., in reference to the course of the Limmat.

l. The high ridge rising on the W. of Zürich, and bordering the lake for more than 12 miles, is the *Albis*.

rt. *Küssnacht*—(*Inn:* Sonne)—a village of 2114 Inhab.; not to be confounded with its namesake on the Lake of Lucerne, famous in the history of Tell.

l. *Rüschlikon:* behind this are the baths of Nydelbad, with a bath-house.

rt. *Meilen*—(*Inns:* Löwe; Sonne) —a very considerable village of 3036 Inhab., chiefly silk-weavers, with a Gothic church, built 1490-9.

l. *Thalwyl*—(*Inn:* Adler.) Lavater is said to have written a portion of his work on Physiognomy at the parsonage of the village of Ober-Rieden, about 3½ m. farther on.

l. *Horgen*—(*Inns:* Meyerhof, good; Löwe, clean). Here passengers bound for Lucerne or the Rigi, by way of Zug, disembark and cross the hills (Rte. 15).

l. *Wädenschwyl*—(*Inn:* Seehof)—a pretty village of 4357 Inhab., containing silk factories. Above it stands the castle, formerly residence of the bailiff (oberamtman), now private property.

l. *Richterswyl*—(*Inn:* Drei Könige). Here is one of the largest cotton factories on the borders of the lake.

The village is built on the boundary line of cantons Zürich and Schwytz; behind it, the road to Einsiedeln ascends the hills. The pilgrims bound to that celebrated shrine usually disembark here. (See R. 74.) *Diligences* thither in the morning, on arrival of steamers in 2½ hrs., and afternoon to Schwytz. Zimmerman resided here as physician, and in his work on 'Solitude' justly praises the extreme beauty of Richterswyl.

rt. *Stäfa*—(*Inns:* Krone; Sterne)—an industrious village, the largest on this side of the lake, with 3500 Inhab., by whom much silk and cotton is woven. Göthe resided here, 1797. The extremity of the lake beyond this lies out of the limits of the canton Zürich. It has been calculated that the number of inhabitants on each of its banks, hence to the town of Zürich, a distance of 16 miles, is not less than 12,000.

On approaching Rapperschwyl and its long bridge, the pretty little isle of *Aufnau* becomes a conspicuous feature and ornament to the landscape. It has some celebrity as the retreat and burial-place of Ulric Von Hutten, a Franconian knight, the friend of Luther and Franz of Sickingen, distinguished equally for his talents and chivalrous bravery, but withal a bit of a roué. His satirical writings contributed not a little to the spread of the Reformation, but raised up against him such a host of enemies that he was forced to fly from the court of Charles V., and take refuge from their persecution, first, with Franz of Sickingen, and, after his death, in this little island. Zwingli had procured for him an asylum here, in the house of the curate, where he died a fortnight after his arrival (1523), at the age of 36. He was buried by a faithful friend, but all record of the spot in which he lies has long since disappeared.

The *Bridge of Rapperschwyl* is one of the longest in the world: it extends from the town to a tongue of land on the opposite side, completely across the lake, a distance of 4800 ft., or more than ¾ of a mile. It is

only 12 ft. broad, is formed of loose planks laid (not nailed) upon piers, and is unprovided with railing at the sides, so that only one carriage can safely pass at a time. It was originally constructed by Leopold of Austria, 1358 : the existing bridge dates from 1819.

A small stone pier has been thrown out into the lake at Rapperschwyl, a little below the bridge, outside the gate of the town, to receive passengers and merchandize from the steamboat.

rt. *Rapperschwyl* (*Inn:* H. du Lac, very good). This is a very picturesque old town, in canton St. Gall (1600 Inhab.), still partly surrounded by walls, and surmounted by an *Old Castle* (Der Grafenburg) and a *Church*, near which, from the terrace called Lindenhof, a fine view is obtained. It is about 19 m. from Zürich, and the same distance from Wesen. Roads run from hence to St. Gall, and across the bridge to Einsiedeln (Rte. 74) and Glarus, by Lachen (Rte. 72).

At *Schmerikon* (*Inn:* Ross), at the E. extremity of the Lake of Zürich, the road quits its margin; the castle of Grynau, on the rt., stands on the *Linth*, a little above its entrance into the lake. From Schmerikon to Wesen barges or truck-boats convey passengers along the Linth canal, but the passage up the furious stream, from W. to E., is tedious. Descending the stream is quicker and more pleasant than going by the diligence. It is about 20 m. by land, and somewhat less by water. Pedestrians will find the towing-path along the Linth canal shorter than the carriage-road from Schmerikon to Wesen.

ˡ ˡ *Uznach* (*Inn:* zum Linth-hof, very fair)—a small town of 900 Inhab., on an eminence, the summit of which is occupied by a small square tower of the ancient castle and by that of the church. The road to St. Gall (R. 69) turns off here. There are mines of brown coal at Oberkirch, about a mile from Uznach, in a hill 1500 feet high. Near Uznach is an immense cotton-mill, driving 24,480 spindles, and having 100 windows on each side. It is supplied with water from a mountain-torrent descending immediately behind it.

Soon after leaving Uznach, the valley of Glarus opens out into view, with the snowy mountains near its head, a very beautiful prospect. Out of this valley issues the river *Linth*, an impetuous torrent, fed by glaciers, and carrying down with it vast quantities of débris, which had accumulated to such an extent 25 years ago, that its channel was obstructed, and its bed raised many feet above the level of the lower part of the valley. From this cause arose repeated and most dangerous inundations, which covered the fertile district on its banks with stone and rubbish, and converted the meadows into a stagnant marsh. Nearly the entire valley between the lakes of Zürich and Wallenstadt was reduced to a desert, and its inhabitants, thinned in numbers by annual fevers, arising from the pestilential exhalations, abandoned the spot. The valley of the Linth was relieved from this dire calamity by Mr. Conrad Escher, who suggested to the Diet, in 1807, the ingenious plan of digging a new bed for the waters of the Linth, and turning it into the lake of Wallenstadt, in whose depths it might deposit the sand and gravel which it brought down, without doing any damage. He at the same time proposed to improve the issues of the lake of Wallenstadt by digging a navigable canal from it to the lake of Zürich, so as to carry off the waters of the Linth, and the other streams falling into it, and cause it to drain the intervening valley, instead of inundating it. This important and useful public work was completed by Escher in 1822, and has been attended with perfect success. In consequence of it the valley is no longer sterile and unwholesome, and the high road to Wesen, which was often cut off and broken up by inroads of the river, is now carried in a straight line along its rt. bank. Immediately opposite the opening of the valley of the Linth, at whose extremity the mountains of Glarus now appear in all their gran-

deur, a simple *Monumental Tablet* of black marble has been let into the face of the rock by the roadside, to the memory of the public-spirited citizen who conferred this great benefit on the surrounding country. He earned from it, in addition to his name, the title *Von der Linth*, the only title which a republic could properly confer, and of which his descendants may be more proud than of that of count or baron. The Linth is here crossed by a bridge called Ziegelbrücke, over which runs the road to Glarus. (R. 72.) Near it are a cotton manufactory and an establishment for the education of the poor of the canton Glarus. It is called the *Linth Colony*, because it owes its origin to a colony of 40 poor persons, afterwards increased to 180, who were brought hither by charitable individuals from the over-peopled villages of the canton, and setted on this spot, which was the bed of the Linth previous to Escher's improvements, in order to reclaim it by removing the stones and rubbish, and rendering it fit for cultivation. They were lodged, fed, and allowed a small sum for wages, the expense being defrayed by subscription. After having, by these means and by the correction of the Linth, described above, restored the valley to a state fit for agriculture, and having been saved themselves from starvation, in a season of scarcity, they were dismissed to seek their fortunes with some few savings to begin the world; and, what was of more importance, with industrious habits, which they had learned while settled here. In the school which now replaces the colony, 40 children from 6 to 12 are taught, and teachers are also instructed.

Wesen (*Inn:* L'Epée, tolerable) is a village of about 500 Inhab., at the W. extremity of the lake of Wallenstadt, and in the midst of scenery of great magnificence.

The ascent of the *Speer* is made in 3½ hrs. from Wesen: it commands a noble view.

There is an interesting pass without any difficulties from Wesen to Wildhaus

(R. 71) in the Toggenburg. It crosses the ridge between the Leistkamm and the Gulmen, and may be accomplished, including the ascent of the Gulmen, in 7 or 8 hours' walking. [A carriage may be hired from Wesen to the Rigi by way of Einsiedeln (R. 74). The road turns out of that to Zürich at the *Inn*, Zum Escher Linth, crosses the canal, and proceeds through a pretty country by Galgenen and Lachen (Ox, a good inn), where it falls into the route from Rapperschwyl.]

LAKE OF WALLENSTADT.

A steamboat runs between Wesen and Wallenstadt, to and fro, 2 or 3 times a day in summer, with a tolerable restaurant and table-d'hôte on board. The voyage takes up about $1\frac{1}{2}$ hr.; fares 2 fr. 15 and 1 fr. 50. Carriages are taken at about 9 frs. (See Post Tarif), being shipped and landed free of expense, except a trinkgeld. There is no road on either side of the lake.

Diligences are provided at each end of the lake to carry on passengers, and there are plenty of vehicles for hire.

The *Railway* from Zürich to Coire will be carried along the S. shore of the Wallenstadt lake.

Previous to the construction of the Linth canal, the only outlet for the lake of Wallenstadt was a small stream called the Magg, which encountered the Linth, after a course of about 2 miles, and was arrested by the débris and stones brought down by that river, so that not only were its waters often dammed up behind, but the surface of the lake was raised several feet above its ordinary level, in consequence of which they overflowed the valley both above and below it, and laid the villages of Wallenstadt, at the one end, and Wesen, at the other, under water for many months during the spring. By Escher's correction of the course of the Linth, its waters are now carried into the lake, where they have already formed, by their deposit of mud and gravel, a delta nearly half a mile long. Another canal, deep and protected at the side

with strong dykes, now supplies the place of the Magg, and drains the lake of Wallenstadt into that of Zürich.

The lake of Wallenstadt is about 12 miles long by 3 broad; its scenery is grand, but inferior to that of the lake of Lucerne. Its N. shore consists of colossal cliffs of lime and sand-stone, regularly stratified, and so nearly precipitous that there is room for no road, and only for a very few cottages at their base, while their steep surface, almost destitute of verdure, gives to this lake a savage and arid character. The S. side consists of more gradually sloping hills covered with verdure and overtopped by the tall bare peaks of more distant mountains. Here there are several villages, and a very rough and irregular road runs along it. The lake has the reputation of being dangerous to navigate, on account of sudden tempests; but in this respect it does not differ from other mountain lakes. In Jan. 1851, however, the steamer was submerged by a squall, and every soul on board, 14 in all, perished. It was fished up from a great depth.

The precipices along the N. bank vary between 2000 and 3000 feet in height, and the stranger is usually surprised to learn that above them are situated populous villages and extensive pastures crowded with cattle. Such a one is the village of Ammon, containing 3000 Inhab., nearly 2500 feet above the lake, with a church, gardens, and orchards. It is approached by one narrow and steep path, which may be traced sloping upwards from Wesen along the face of the mountain. Several waterfalls precipitate themselves over this wall of rock, or descend, by gashes or rents in its sides, into the lake; but they dwindle into insignificance by the end of summer, and add no beauty to the scene. The principal ones are the Beyerbach, 900 feet high (above which lies Ammon), and the Seerenbach, 1200 feet high.

The hamlet of St. Quinten is the only one on this side of the lake. On the opposite (S.) side there are numerous villages at the mouths of the streams and gullies. The principal of them is Murg, near which a large cotton-factory has been built. Behind it rises the mountain Murtschenstock. Its summit, 7270 feet high, and almost inaccessible, is traversed through and through by a cavern, which, though of large size, looks from the lake like the eye of a bodkin. The hole is best seen when abreast of the village of Mühlehorn; by those not aware of the fact, it might be mistaken for a patch of snow. This peak is a favourite resort of chamois.

The N.E. extremity of the lake is bounded by the 7 picturesque peaks of the Sieben Churfirsten, or Kurfürsten. At their feet lies the village of

Wallenstadt—Inns: Aigle d'Or, near the steamer, tolerable; Hirsch (Cerf, or Poste)—a scattered township of 800 Inhab.; nearly ½ m. from the lake, of which it commands no view. The flats of the valley around and above it are marshy, and the neighbourhood was formerly very unhealthy, so long as the irregularities of the Linth obstructed the passage of the waters of the lake. Wallenstadt is a dull place, and travellers have no need to stop here.

[A steep and rugged path by the side of the Chürfursten, commanding magnificent views, leads in 1 day to Wildhaus (Rte. 71), whence Appenzell may be reached in another day (Rte. 70).]

There is considerable beauty in the scenery of the valley of the Scez, between Wallenstadt and

Sargans — (*Inns:* Kreutz (Croix Blanche); Löwe;) a picturesque old town of 723 Inhab., on an eminence surmounted by a *castle*, near the junction of the roads from St. Gall and Zürich to Coire. It stands upon the watershed dividing the streams which feed the Rhine from those which fall into the lake of Wallenstadt; and this natural embankment is so slight (about 200 paces across and less than 20 feet high) that, as the deposits brought down by the Rhine are constantly raising its bed, it is not impossible, though scarcely probable, that the river may change its course, re-

linquish its present route by the lake of Constance, and take a shorter cut by the lakes of Wallenstadt and Zürich. It was calculated by Escher von der Linth, from actual measurements, that the waters of the Rhine need rise but 19½ feet to pass into the lake of Wallenstadt; and it is, indeed, recorded that the river, swollen by long rains in 1618, was prevented taking this direction only by the construction of dams along its banks. Geologists argue, from the identity of the deposits of gravel in the valley of the Upper Rhine with those in the vale of Scez, that the river actually did pass out this way at one time. The Rly. from Zürich by Winterthur, St. Gall, and Rorschach will fall in here.

The remainder of this route up the valley of the Rhine by

Ragatz to

Coire, is described in Rte. 67.

ROUTE 15.

ZÜRICH TO LUCERNE (OR THE RIGI), BY HORGEN, ZUG, AND IMMENSEE.

	Eng. m.		hrs.	min.
Zürich.				
Horgen (steamer) . .	9	=	1	
Zug (diligence) . .	12½	=	4	
Immeneee (steamer) .	6	=	1	
Küssnach (diligence) .	2½	=		30
Lucerne (steamer) .	5	=		30
	35	=	7	0

This is a very pleasant expedition in fine weather. The times above given are those actually occupied, including stoppages, which are of course considerable. Passengers can book through from Zürich, and have no trouble with their luggage, fare 7 fr. 40. The steamers are so arranged as to meet the diligences, and, what with hills and stoppages, a tolerable pedestrian can cross from Horgen to Zug, and from Immensee to Küssnach, as fast as the diligence. [The summit of the Rigi (Rte. 17 A) may be reached from Immensee or Arth in 9 or 10 hrs. from Zürich.]

Horgen (*Inns :* Meyerhoff, pleasantly situated, said to be extortionate; Lowe). Up to this place see Rte. 14. Passengers are made to walk nearly ¼ m. from the quay to the diligence office: those who mean to hire a carriage to Zug (12 or 14 fr.) should send up for one. A brown coal or lignite is found here; not fit, however, for steam-boilers. The road immediately begins to ascend by a series of zigzags, affording fine views over the lake; and from a spot called *Bocke*, about ¼ m. off the road, a still finer view is obtained. The ascent occupies full 1½ hr., after which the descent is at once commenced, the road running for the most part along the rt. bank of the *Sihl*, crossing it at the village of

Sihlbrücke, by a covered bridge, which conducts from canton Zürich into canton Zug. From the ridge which succeeds, the Rigi and Pilatus mountains are first seen, and soon after the borders of the lake of Zug are reached.

Zug (*Inns :* Hirsch (Cerf), good ; Falken ; Couronne ; Bellevue) — capital of canton Zug, in size the smallest state of the Confederation, has 3200 Inhab., and is prettily situated at the N.E. corner of the lake. It has an antiquated look, surrounded by its old walls, and, being without trade, has a silent and deserted air. Its inhabitants, exclusively Roman Catholics, are chiefly occupied with agricultural pursuits. The rich crops, vineyards, orchards, and gardens, on the borders of the lake, proclaim a soil not ungrateful to the cultivator.

There is a *Capuchin Convent* and a *Nunnery* here. The picture by Caracci in the former, mentioned by the guide-books, is none of his, but is by an inferior artist, Fiamingo, and of no great merit.

The *Ch. of St. Michael*, a little way outside of the town, like many of the churches in the Romish cantons, has a curious *bonehouse* attached to it, containing many hundred skulls, each inscribed with the name of its owner. It is the custom for the relations of the dead to cause their skulls to be taken up, cleaned, labelled with their names and date of birth and death, and then placed in the bonehouse! The churchyard in which it stands is filled with quaint gilt crosses by way of monuments, and the graves are planted with flowers. The *Cemetery* deserves a visit; the display of armorial bearings, coats, and crests, even on the humblest tomb, is a remarkable decoration in a republican state!

It is recorded that in the year 1435 a part of the foundations of the town, weakened probably by an attempt to draw off part of the water of the lake, gave way, whereby two streets, built on the ground nearest the water, were broken off and submerged ; 26 houses were destroyed, and 45 human beings perished ; among them the chief magistrate of the town. His child, an infant, was found floating in his cradle, on the surface of the lake ; he was rescued, and afterwards became landammann of the canton.

At *Felsenegg*, on the mountain above the town, a pension has been built by the proprietor of the Bellevue in Zug.

Diligences to Lucerne and Zürich. (Rte. 16.)

[An excellent road to *Arth* (Rte. 17) winds round the base of the Rossberg, which has obtained a melancholy celebrity from the catastrophe caused by the fall of a portion of it. (See R. 17.) Near the chapel of St. Adrian a small monument has been erected on the spot where the arrow is supposed to have fallen which Henry von Hunenberg shot out of the Austrian lines into the Swiss camp, before the battle of Morgarten, bearing the warning words, "Beware of Morgarten." It was in consequence of this that the confederates occupied the position indicated, and it contributed mainly to their victory on that memorable field. Morgarten (Rte. 74) lies within this canton, about 14 m. W. of Zug, on the lake of Egeri.]

Here again the diligences stop outside the town at a considerable distance from the steam-boat pier, which is in the town, opposite the Hirsch. Ample time is allowed for dining here.

The Lake of Zug, whose surface is 1340 feet above the sea, is 8 m. long, and about ¾ broad. Its banks are low, or gently-sloping hills, except on the S. side, where the Rigi, rising abruptly from the water's edge, presents its precipices towards it, forming a feature of considerable grandeur, in conjunction with the Pilatus rising behind it. The *Rufi*, or *Ross-berg*, rising in the S.E. corner, is also lofty and steep ; the lake, at its base, is not less than 1200 ft. deep.

Immensee. A truly Swiss village, with a comfortable and cheap little *Inn.* [Horses are kept here for the ascent of the *Rigi* (Rte. 17A), which may be ascended from this place as well as from Arth (Rte. 17A), to which the steamer proceeds.]

About a mile from the village, by the roadside, stands *Tell's Chapel*. By a singular anomaly a place of worship, originally dedicated to "The Fourteen Helpers in Need" (Our Saviour, the Virgin, and Apostles), now commemorates a deed of blood, which tradition, and its supposed connection with the origin of Swiss liberty, appear to have sanctified in the eyes of the people, so that mass is periodically said in it, while it is kept in constant repair, and bears on its outer wall a fresco representing Gessler's death.

A little further on the l. it is said that a ruined wall may be seen, which goes by the name of *Gessler's Castle*, and is said to be the one to which he was repairing when shot by Tell. This event occurred in the celebrated *Hollow Way* (Chemin creux —Hohle Gasse), through which the road now passes. It is a narrow green lane, overhung with trees growing from the high banks on each side. Here Tell, after escaping from Gessler's boat on the lake of Lucerne, lay in wait for his enemy, and shot him as he passed, from behind a tree, with his unerring arrow. It is somewhat remarkable that researches into the archives of Küssnacht have clearly proved that the ruin called Gessler's Castle never belonged to him. The "Hollow Way" has been much filled up in making the new road.

Küssnacht (H. du Lac ; Hirsch ; Rössli), a small village, with nothing remarkable, situated at the bottom of one of the branches of the *Lake of Lucerne*. (Rte. 18.) The diligence here comes up to the steam-boat pier. On the l. are seen the steep sides of the Rigi, and in front are Pilatus and the vale of Sarnen. The steamer rounds a rocky point, on the islets of which are small chapels or niches placed to commemorate accidents which have happened near the place : soon afterwards are seen the spires of LUCERNE. (Rte. 17.)

ROUTE 16.

ZÜRICH TO LUCERNE, OVER THE ALBIS, OR BY RAILWAY.

The quickest method of reaching Lucerne is by Rly. to Olten (Rte. 6), thence to Lucerne (Rte. 3), which takes altogether about 5 hrs.

In fine weather, however, it is well worth while to take the carriage-road over the *Albis* for the sake of the very beautiful view of the chain of the Alps, and of a large part of Switzerland, which is seen from its summit. It skirts the shore of the lake at first, but at Adliswyl it crosses the river Sihl, and soon after in numerous zigzags begins to ascend to

Ober-Albis. Inn : Hirsch, which affords moderate accommodation and a magnificent prospect. The best point, however, for seeing the view, is the *Signal* (Hochwacht, called also Schnabel), a height off the road, about a mile above the inn : it takes in nearly the whole of the Zürichsee. At the foot of the mountain, between it and the lake, the vale of the Sihl intervenes. Its wooded slopes were the favourite retreat of the pastoral poet Gessner; they were occupied in 1799 by two hostile armies — that of the French under Massena, who encamped on the slope of the Albis, and that of the Russians, who occupied the rt. bank of the Sihl. They watched each other from hence for more than 3 months ; until Massena, by a masterly movement, crossed the Limmat, cut off part of the Russian force, and compelled the rest to a hasty retreat. On the S. are seen the little lake of Turl (Turler See), at the foot of the mountain; not far from it the church of Kappel, where Zwingli died ; farther off the lake of Zug, and behind it tower the Rigi and Pilatus mountains, disclosing between them a little bit of the lake of Lucerne. The grandest feature, however, of the view is the snowy chain of the Alps, from the Sentis to the Jungfrau, which fills up the horizon. It has been engraved by Keller.

In posting you must take an extra horse (renfort) either from Zürich or Zug up to the summit; 1 post is charged. The greatest height which the road attains is 2404 ft. above the sea, 1000 ft. above Zürich lake, after which it descends, passing on the rt. the little lake of Turl.

The road is carried along the W. slope of the Albis, from its summit to Hausen, near which village is *Albisbrunn*, a large and handsome watercure establishment, in which travellers in general are also received at the rate of 5 fr. a day, board and lodging. It is a pleasant residence from the beauties of its situation, its views of the Bernese Alps, and the salubrity of its air and water. It is under the management of Dr. Brunner.

Beyond Hausen the new road passes *Kappel* (5 m. from the Albis inn), a village of 600 Inhab., which has obtained a woful celebrity in Swiss history as the spot where the Confederates, embittered against each other

by religious discord, dyed their hands in the blood of one another, and where Zwingli the reformer fell in the midst of his flock on the 11th of October, 1531. Many of the best and bravest of the citizens of Zürich perished on that day of civil broil, overpowered by the numbers of their opponents, the men of the 4 inner cantons, Zwingli, who, in accordance with the custom of the time and country, attended his flock to the field of battle, to afford them spiritual aid and consolation, was struck down in the fight, and found by a soldier of Unterwalden, who did not know him, but who, ascertaining that he refused to call on the Virgin and saints, despatched him with his sword as a dog and a heretic. His body, when recognised by his foes, was burnt by the common hangman, and even his ashes subjected to the vilest indignities that malice could suggest. A handsome *monument*, consisting of a rough massive block of stone by the road-side, has taken the place of the tree which marked the spot where he fell. It bears, on metal plates, inscriptions in German and Latin. The *Gothic church* of Kappel, anciently attached to a convent suppressed soon after the commencement of the Reformation, was built in 1280.

Zug (Rte. 15) ; whence the traveller may proceed to Lucerne, as in Rte. 15, or by *Chaam*: or, in descending from Ober-Albis, Zug may be avoided altogether, and the shorter road by *Knonau* taken.

LUCERNE (Luzern). *Inns:* H. des Suisses (Schweizer Hof); the Englischer Hof equally good; views from the windows of both superb. H. du Rigi, comfortable, and fine views. Schwann. These 4 Inns face the lake, and are near the steamers. Balances (Waage), good; very cheap, en pension, 5 fr. a day; good Tavel wine. Æschmans' Pension, overlooking the lake, close to the Kapell Brücke, is recommended; the master obliging.

Lucerne, chief town of the canton, lies at the N.W. extremity of the lake of Lucerne, and is divided into two parts by the river Reuss, which here issues out of it. Its population is about 10,000, all Roman Catholics, except about 300 Protestants. Lucerne is the residence of the Papal Nuncio.

It is not a place of any considerable trade or manufactures, but their absence is more than compensated by the exquisitely beautiful scenery in which it is situated on the borders of the finest and most interesting of the Swiss lakes, between the giants Pilatus and Rigi, and in sight of the snowy Alps of Schwytz and Engelberg. The town is still walled in on the land side by a long wall, with numerous picturesque watch-towers, erected in 1385; but its chief peculiarity is its *bridges.* The lowest, or *Mill-bridge*, is hung with paintings, nearly washed out, of the Dance of Death: the second or *Reuss-brücke*, is the only one uncovered and passable for carriages; the upper, or *Kapellbrücke*, a cool and shady walk in a hot day, runs in a slanting direction across the mouth of the Reuss, whose clear and pellucid sea-green waters may here be surveyed to great advantage, as they rush beneath it with the swiftness of a mountain torrent. Against the timbers supporting the roof of this bridge are suspended 77 pictures; those seen in crossing from the rt. to the l. bank represent the life and acts of St. Leger and St. Maurice, Lucerne's patron saints. The subjects of those seen in the opposite direction are taken from Swiss history, and are not without some merits, but being lighted only by the glare reflected upwards from the water, are not easily distinguished. Near the middle of the Kapell-brücke, rising out of the water, stands a very picturesque watch-tower, called *Wasserthurm*, forming a link of the old fortifications of the town. It is said to have once served as a light-house (*Lucerna*) to boats, and hence some have derived the present name of Lucerne. The *Hofbrücke*, the longest of all the bridges, was entirely removed, 1852: the intervening space between it and the shore having been filled up. The Hôtel des Suisses and Swan and a fine row of houses stand on this space, which is also the landing-place of the steamboats.

In churches and other public buildings Lucerne has no very prominent objects. The *church of St. Leger*, also called Hof- or Stiftskirche, is modern, except the two towers, which date from 1506. The bells in it are fine and curious. The adjoining churchyard is filled with quaint old monuments, and the view from the cloister windows is fine.

The *Arsenal*, near the gate leading to Berne, is one of those venerable repositories common to the chief towns of all the cantons, in which are deposited the muskets, artillery, &c., for arming their contingents of troops. It contains some rusty suits of ancient armour, and several historical relics and trophies of Swiss valour, such as the yellow Austrian banner, and many pennons of knights and nobles, taken at the battle of Sempach; the coat of mail stripped from the body of Duke Leopold of Austria, who fell there : the iron cravat, lined with sharp spikes, destined for the neck of Gundoldingen, the Schultheiss and general of the men of Lucerne, who died in the hour of victory. A sword of William Tell, and a battle-axe borne by Ulric Zwingli at the battle of Kappel (R. 16) (? now at Zürich), are of very doubtful authenticity : though the malice of the enemies of Zwingli may have led to the assertion that he took active part in the fight, it is believed that he assisted his countrymen merely with exhortations and consolations of religion. Several Turkish standards deposited here were captured at the battle of Lepanto, by a knight of Malta, who was a native of Lucerne.

General Pfyffer's model (in relief) of a part of Switzerland may interest those who desire to trace on it their past or future wanderings ; but 1 fr. is demanded for admission.

The *Gothic Fountains*, which are to be observed in all parts of Switzerland, are here of singular beauty and originality.

The *English church service* is performed every Sunday at 10½ and 6 in an edifice allotted by the government for the purpose. The clergyman depends entirely on voluntary contributions of visitors, having no stipend. Müller is a good chemist. Dr. Nager has been recommended as a physician.

At Eglin Brothers, in the Kapel Strasse, books, prints, panoramas, and maps relating to Switzerland may be had.

The most interesting of the *sights* of Lucerne is, without doubt, the *Monument to the memory of the Swiss Guards,* who fell while defending the Royal Family of France in one of the bloody massacres of the first French Revolution, August 10, 1792. It is situated in the garden of General Pfyffer, a little way beyond St. Leger's ch. on the Zürich road. The design is by Thorwaldsen, executed by Ahorn, a sculptor of Constance. It represents a lion of colossal size, wounded to death, with a spear sticking in his side, yet endeavouring in his last gasp to protect from injury a shield bearing the fleur-de-lis of the Bourbons, which he holds in his paws. The figure, hewn out of the living sandstone rock, is 28 ft. long and 18 high, and whether as a tribute to fallen valour, or as a work of art, of admirable design and no mean execution, it merits the highest praise. It is the most *appropriate* monument in Europe. Beneath it are carved the names of the officers who fell in defending the Tuileries, Aug. 10 and Sept. 2 and 3, 1792. The loyalty and fidelity of this brave band, who thus sacrificed their lives for their adopted sovereign, almost make us forget that they were mercenaries, especially standing forward as they did, as the protectors of Louis and his family, at a moment when deserted or attacked by his natural defenders, his own subjects. There is a quiet solitude and shade about the spot which is particularly pleasing and refreshing. The rocks around are mantled with fern and creepers, forming a natural framework to the monument ; and a streamlet of clear water, trickling down from the top of the rock, is received into a basin-shaped hollow below it, forming a mirror in which the sculpture is reflected. One of the very few survivors of the Swiss Guard, dressed in its red uniform, acts as guardian of the monument, and cicerone to the stranger. The cloth for the altar of the little chapel adjoining was embroidered expressly for it by the late Duchess d'Angoulème.

There are many pretty *walks* and *points of view* near Lucerne; one of the most interesting is to the Lime-tree, under which is a dial pointing to the mountains on the horizon ; another is the villa called *Allenwinden,* perched on the top of the hill outside the Weggis gate, from which it may be reached in a walk of 15 minutes, by a path winding up the hill outside the town walls.

Steamers several times a-day to Fluelen and the other villages on the lake. From Fluelen diligences proceed over the St. Gotthard. Travellers book from Lucerne.

Railway to Basle, Berne, &c.

Gibraltar—a height on the opposite side of the Reuss, outside the Basle gate, also commands a fine prospect.

No one should leave Lucerne without exploring the beauties of its *Lake* (Rte. 18)—called in German Vierwaldstädter See—the grandest in Europe in point of scenery, particularly the farther end of it, called the bay of Uri; and much additional pleasure will be derived if the traveller who understands German will take Schiller's ' Wilhelm Tell' as a pocket companion, in which admirable poem so many of the scenes are localized. The lake and its scenery look much better from a row-boat than from the steamer, which is too large, and makes everything except the high mountains appear small.

Those who intend to traverse the lake, and visit the Rigi, and to return afterwards to Lucerne, should combine the two expeditions, which may be effected in two days, *thus*— go to Küssnacht or to Arth and ascend, descending next day on the opposite side, and embarking on the lake, either at Weggis or Gersau, pass up the bay of Uri, and by Tell's chapel, returning by water to Lucerne the 2nd evening.

Mount Pilate. This ascent has hitherto been somewhat long and difficult, and could only be made on foot, and occupied a long day. Now, however, an *Inn* has been built (to be opened in 1858) on a shoulder of the mountain, about half an hour from the summit; and a good mule-path has been made from *Hergiswyl*, a village on the lake, which will lead to the Inn in about 3 hrs. The traveller should beware of the innkeepers, &c., at Lucerne, who appear jealous of this mountain, and will throw difficulties in the way. After leaving the Inn on the mountain a new path zigzags up amongst some rough heaps of stones, which were formerly very difficult to climb over, and finally reaches the entrance of a cavern, called the Locher, which extends vertically about 40 ft.: it is not difficult to climb up, and the traveller emerges on the actual top of the mountain, and the whole range of the Bernese mountains suddenly burst upon him, having been previously concealed by the mountain. There is not a more striking scene in all Switzerland. There are altogether 7 summits, exceedingly rugged and precipitous.

The *Tomlishorn* is the highest, 7116 ft. above the level of the sea, and 5766 above the lake. It is however nearly 2 hrs. from the Locher, and not so well worth a visit as the *Esel*, which is a rugged eminence to the E. of the Locher, and about 20 min. distant. From this the view is even finer than from the Locher. Unfortunately Pilatus is very subject to clouds, otherwise the mountain is far more interesting than the Rigi, and the view from it finer. Large nummulites are found upon it, and there are many varieties of plants. As the present Inn was built by an inhab. of Nieddem-Wald, the canton of Ob-dem-Wald proposes to build an opposition Inn in the hollow under the Esel. If the traveller wishes to descend from the Esel by Alpnach, he will go straight down the hollow, and, keeping to the rt. at the bottom of it, he will come to a tolerably well-marked track by the side of a ravine, and finally reach the road made by some

French timber dealers, reaching Alpnach in 2½ hrs.

Hitherto the best and still a very pleasant and shady way of ascending the mountain has been to follow the Entlebuch road (Rte. 22) for about 6 miles, then leaving the road, and turning to the l., a sharp ascent of half an hour through woods leads to the beautiful hamlet of *Herrgotteswald*, where there is a tolerable country Inn, and the traveller should sleep there, in order to have ample time for the expedition. It would not be possible to find the way to the summit without a guide, and the landlord will act as guide, but charges 10 fr. The first 2 hrs. are through beautiful woods and green pastures; then comes a very steep ascent of about an hour, which brings the traveller to the Inn above mentioned.

A traveller lost his way among the rocks above Hergiswyl and was killed in 1857.

There is commonly reported to be a cave on the mountain, with a stone resembling a monk; but an English University reading party, who repeatedly ascended the mountain from Lucerne, report that they could never find either the cave or the lake mentioned in the next page.

According to a wild tradition of considerable antiquity, this mountain derives its name from Pilate, the wicked governor of Judæa, who, having been banished to Gaul by Tiberius, wandered about among the mountains, stricken by conscience, until he ended his miserable existence by throwing himself into a lake on the top of the Pilatus. The mountain, in consequence, labours under a very bad reputation. From its position as an outlier, or advanced guard of the chain of the Alps, it collects the clouds which float over the plains from the W. and N.; and it is remarked that almost all the storms which burst upon the lake of Lucerne gather and brew on its summit. This almost perpetual assembling of clouds was long attributed by the superstitious to the unquiet spirit still hovering round the sunken body, which, when disturbed by any intruder, especially by the casting of stones into the lake, revenged itself by sending storms, and darkness, and hail on the surrounding district. So prevalent was the belief in this superstition, even down to times comparatively recent, that the government of Lucerne forbade the ascent of the mountain, and the naturalist Conrad Gessner, in 1555, was obliged to provide himself with a special order, removing the interdict in his case, to enable him to carry on his researches upon the mountain.

It is remarkable that the only thing on the mountain which can be called a lake belongs to Alpnach, and is beyond the limits of canton Lucerne; so that the Town Council had no jurisdiction over that part of the mountain. It is dried up the greater part of the year, and reduced to a heap of snow, which, being melted in the height of summer, furnishes water to the herds upon the mountain, which resort to it to slake their thirst.

According to some, the name Pilatus is only a corruption of *Pileatus* (capped), arising from the cap of clouds which rarely quits its barren brow, and which are sometimes seen rising from it like steam from a cauldron. The peasants profess to be able to foretell the weather from the appearance of the clouds on the top, and have a saying,—

> "Wenn Pilatus trägt sein Hut
> Dann wird das Wetter gut.
> Aber hat er seiner Degen,
> Wird es regen."

The mountain consists, from its base to its summit, of nummulite limestone and sandstone; the strata incline to the S., and abound in fossil remains, especially near the summit, around the Bründlis Alp and the Castelen Alp.

ROUTE 17.

LUCERNE TO SCHWYTZ—THE FALL OF THE ROSSBERG.

	Leagues.	Eng. m.
Lucerne.		
Küssnacht . . .	2¼ =	7¼
Arth	1½ =	5¼
Schwytz . . .	2¼ =	8¼
	7	21

A good *post*-road to Schwytz, traversed by a diligence daily in 4 hrs.

Schwytz may also be reached rather more easily by steaming to Brunnen.

There is a steamer to Küssnacht. (Rte. 15.)

The road to Küssnacht runs nearly all the way in sight of the lake of Lucerne, and of the Alps of Engelberg and Berne beyond. On a headland at the angle of the green bay of Küssnacht, stands the ruined *castle* of New Habsburg, destroyed, 1352, by the Lucerners.

Küssnacht— Inns; H. du Lac; Hirsch; Rössli. (Rte. 15.)

Between this place and Immensee is the Hollow Way where Tell shot Gessler. (Rte. 15.)

Immensee. Comfortable little Inn. The road now skirts the lake of Zug (Rte. 15), or the tourist may take the steamer to

Arth — Inns: Schwarzer Adler (Black Eagle)—a village of 2129 Inh., occupies a charming position on the lake of Zug, between the base of the Rigi and the Rossberg. There is a Capuchin convent here. In the *Treasury* of the *Church* some interesting curiosities are preserved, including an ancient and richly-worked crucifix and chalice of silver, which belonged to Charles the Bold, and were left by him to his Swiss conquerors on the field of Grandson, besides some gaudy priests' robes.

The Rossberg, a dangerous neighbour, threatens no danger to Arth, because its strata slope away from the village. The Rigi is a source of considerable gain to Arth, from the number of guides and mules furnished by the villagers to travellers to ascend the mountain.

Goldau, about 2 m. from Arth.

FALL OF THE ROSSBERG.

> " Mountains have fallen,
> Leaving a gap in the clouds, and with the shock
> Rocking their Alpine brethren ; filling up
> The ripe green valleys with destruction's splinters,
> Damming the rivers with a sudden dash,
> Which crushed the waters into mist, and made
> Their fountains find another channel—thus,
> Thus, in its old age, did Mount Rosenberg."
> *Byron.*

On approaching Goldau (*Inn:* Cheval Blanc; good and civil people) the traveller may perceive traces of the dreadful catastrophe which buried the original and much larger village of that name, and inundated the valley for a considerable distance with a deluge of stones and rubbish. The mountain which caused this calamity still remains scarred from top to bottom : and nothing grows upon its barren surface ; but in the course of years the valley itself has in many places become green, and the fallen rocks bear trees, lichens, and vegetation, and the great similarity to mountain valleys in general shows how often in past ages such catastrophes must have happened, though no record of them has been preserved.

The Rossberg, or Rufiberg, is a mountain 4958 ft. high ; the upper part of it consists of a conglomerate or pudding-stone, formed of rounded masses of other rocks cemented together, and called by the Germans Nagelflue, or Nail-rock, from the knobs and protuberances which its surface presents, resembling nail-heads. From the nature of the structure of this kind of rock, it is very liable to become cracked, and if rain-water or springs penetrate these fissures they will not fail to dissolve or moisten the unctuous beds of clay which separate the nagelflue from the strata below it, and cause large portions of it to detach themselves from the mass. The strata of the Rossberg are tilted up from the side of the lake of Zug, and slope down towards Goldau like the roof of a house. The slanting direction of the seams which part the strata is well seen on the road from Arth. If, therefore, the clay which fills these seams be washed out by rains, or reduced to the state of a viscous or slimy mud, it is evident that such portions of the rock as have been detached from the rest by the fissures above alluded to, must slip down, like the masses of snow which fall from the roof of a house as soon as the lower side is thawed, or as a vessel when launched slides down the inclined plane purposely greased to hasten its descent. Within the period of human records destructive land-slips had repeatedly fallen from the Rossberg, and a great part of the piles of earth, rock, and stones, which deform the face of the valley, derive their origin from such catastrophes of ancient date ; but the most destructive of all appears to have been the last. The vacant space along the top of the mountain caused by the descent of a portion of it, calculated to have been a league long, 1000 ft. broad, and 100 ft. thick, and a small fragment at its farther extremity, which remained when the rest broke off, are also very apparent, and assist in telling the story. The long and wide inclined plane forming the side of the mountain, now ploughed up and scarified as it were, was previously covered with fields, woods, and houses. Some of the buildings are still standing within a few yards of the precipice which marks the line of the fracture.

The catastrophe is thus described in the narrative published at the time by Dr. Zay, of Arth, an eye-witness:—

" The summer of 1806 had been very rainy, and on the 1st and 2nd September it rained incessantly. New crevices were observed in the flank of the mountain, a sort of cracking noise was heard internally, stones started out of the ground, detached fragments of rocks rolled down the mountain; at two o'clock in the afternoon of the 2nd of September, a large rock became loose, and in falling raised a cloud of black dust. Toward the lower part of the mountain, the ground seemed pressed down from above; and when a stick or a spade was driven in, it moved of itself. A man, who had been digging in his garden, ran away from fright at these extraordinary appearances; soon a fissure, larger than all the others, was observed; insensibly it increased; springs of water ceased all at once to flow; the pine-trees of the forest absolutely reeled; birds flew away screaming. A few minutes before five o'clock the symptoms of some mighty catastrophe became still stronger; the whole surface of the mountain seemed to glide down, but so slowly as to afford time to the inhabitants to go away. An old man, who had often predicted some such disaster, was quietly smoking his pipe when told by a young man, running by, that the mountain was in the act of falling; he rose and looked out, but came into his house again, saying he had time to fill another pipe. The young man, continuing to fly, was thrown down several times, and escaped with difficulty; looking back, he saw the house carried off all at once.

"Another inhabitant, being alarmed, took two of his children and ran away with them, calling to his wife to follow with the third; but she went in for another, who still remained (Marianne, aged five): just then, Francisca Ulrich, their servant, was crossing the room, with this Marianne, whom she held by the hand, and saw her mistress; at that instant, as Francisca afterwards said, ' The house appeared to be torn from its foundation (it was of wood), and spun round and round like a tetotum; I was sometimes on my head, sometimes on my feet, in total darkness, and violently separated from the child.' When the motion stopped, she found herself jammed in on all sides, with her head downwards, much bruised, and in extreme pain. She supposed she was buried alive at a great depth; with much difficulty she disengaged her right hand, and wiped the blood from her eyes. Presently she heard the faint moans of Marianne, and called to her by her name; the child answered that she was on her back among stones and bushes, which held her fast, but that her hands were free, and that she saw the light, and even something green. She asked whether people would not soon come to take them out. Francisca answered that it was the day of judgment, and that no one was left to help them; but that they would be released by death, and be happy in heaven. They prayed together. At last Francisca's ear was struck by the sound of a bell, which she knew to be that of Steinenberg: then seven o'clock struck in another village, and she began to hope there were still living beings, and endeavoured to comfort the child. The poor little girl was at first clamorous for her supper, but her cries soon became fainter, and at last quite died away. Francisca, still with her head downwards, and surrounded with damp earth, experienced a sense of cold in her feet almost insupportable. After prodigious efforts she succeeded in disengaging her legs, and thinks this saved her life. Many hours had passed in this situation, when she again heard the voice of Marianne, who had been asleep, and now renewed her lamentations. In the mean time the unfortunate father, who, with much difficulty, had saved himself and two children, wandered about till daylight, when he came among the ruins to look for the rest of his family. He soon discovered his wife, by a foot which appeared above ground: she was dead, with a child in her arms. His cries, and the noise he made in digging, were heard by Marianne, who called out. She was extricated with a broken thigh, and, saying that Francisca was not far off, a farther search led to her release also; but in such a state that her life was despaired of: she was blind for some days, and remained subject to convulsive fits of terror. It appeared that the house, or themselves at least, had been carried down about 1500 feet from where it stood before.

" In another place, a child two years old was found unhurt, lying on its straw mattress upon the mud, without any vestige of the house from which he had been separated. Such a mass of earth and stones rushed at once into the lake of Lowertz, although 5 m. distant, that one end of it was filled up, and a prodigious wave passing completely over the island of Schwan-au, 70 feet above the usual level of the water, overwhelmed the opposite shore, and, as it returned, swept away into the lake many houses with their inhabitants. The village of Seewen, situated at the farther end, was inundated, and some houses washed away; and the flood carried live fish into the village of Steinen. The chapel of Olten, built of wood, was found half a league from the place it had previously occupied, and many large blocks of stone completely changed their position.

" The most considerable of the villages overwhelmed in the vale of Arth was Goldau, and its name is now affixed to the whole melancholy story and place. I shall relate only one more incident :—A party of eleven travellers from Berne, belonging to the most distinguished families there, arrived at Arth on the 2nd of September, and set off on foot for the Rigi a few minutes before the catastrophe. Seven of them had got about 200 yards a-head,—the other four saw them entering the village of Goldau; and one of the latter, Mr. R. Jenner, pointing out to the rest the summit of the Rossberg (full 4 m. off in a straight line), where some strange commotion seemed taking place, which they themselves (the four behind) were observing with a telescope, and had entered into conversation on the subject with some strangers just come up; when, all at once, a flight of stones, like cannon-balls, traversed the air above their heads; a cloud of dust obscured the valley; a frightful noise was heard. They fled ! As soon as the obscurity was so far dissipated as to make objects discernible, they sought their friends; but the village of Goldau had disappeared under a heap of stones and rubbish 100 feet

in height, and the whole valley presented nothing but a perfect chaos! Of the unfortunate survivors, one lost a wife to whom he was just married, one a son, a third the two pupils under his care : all researches to discover their remains were, and have ever since been fruitless. Nothing is left of Goldau but the bell which hung in its steeple, and which was found about a mile off. With the rocks torrents of mud came down, acting as rollers; but they took a different direction when in the valley, the mud following the slope of the ground towards the lake of Lowertz, while the rocks, preserving a straight course, glanced across the valley towards the Rigi. The rocks above, moving much faster than those near the ground, went farther, and ascended even a great way up the Rigi; its base is covered with large blocks carried to an incredible height, and by which trees were mowed down, as they might have been by cannon.

" A long track of ruins, like a scarf, hangs from the shoulder of the Rossberg, in hideous barrenness, over the rich dress of shaggy woods and green pastures, and grows wider and wider down to the lake of Lowertz and to the Rigi, a distance of 4 or 5 m. Its greatest breadth may be 3 m., and the triangular area of ruins is fully equal to that of Paris, taken at the external boulevards, or about double the real extent of the inhabited city. I notice, however, that the portion of the strata at the top of the Rossberg, which slid down into the valley, is certainly less than the chaotic accumulation below; and I have no doubt that a considerable part of it comes from the soil of the valley itself, ploughed up and thrown into ridges like the waves of the sea, and hurled to prodigious distances by the impulse of the descending mass, plunging upon it with a force not very inferior to that of a cannon-ball."

The effects of this terrible convulsion were the entire destruction of the villages Goldau, Bussingen, and Rothen, and a part of Lowertz; the rich pasturages in the valley and on the slope of the mountain, entirely overwhelmed by it and ruined, were estimated to be worth 150,000*l.*; 111 houses, and more than 200 stables and châlets, were buried under the débris of rocks, which of themselves form hills several hundred feet high. More than 450 human beings perished by this catastrophe, and whole herds of cattle were swept away. Five minutes sufficed to complete the work of destruction. The inhabitants of the neighbouring towns and villages were first roused by loud and grating sounds like thunder : they looked towards the spot from which it came, and beheld the valley shrouded in a cloud of dust; when it had cleared away, they found the face of nature changed. The houses of Goldau were literally crushed beneath the weight of superincumbent masses. Lowertz was overwhelmed by a torrent of mud.

The danger of further calamity from the fall of other portions of the mountain is by no means past, even now. On July 3rd, 1823, a shepherd boy climbed up to the peak of the Rossberg, called Spitzbühel, to gather herbs. In crossing over towards Zug he came to a fissure, which he leaped across ; but on his return he found it so much widened, that he could not venture to repeat his jump, and was obliged to make a circuit to reach home. By the 6th of July the rent had increased to a width of 40 or 50 feet, and to the depth of nearly twice that number of feet. Great apprehensions were entertained lest the mass thus separated should in falling take the direction of the Inn and Church of Goldau : however, on the 11th, after the crack had widened to 150 ft., with a depth of 120, and a length of 200, down came the huge fragment; it was shattered to pieces in its fall, and threw up the waters of the lake of Lowertz 5 ft., but did no damage.

Those who desire a near view of the landslip should ascend the Gnypenstock, whose summit may be reached in 3 hours from Arth.

The new church and one of the inns at Goldau stand on the site of the village overwhelmed by the Rossberg;

its inhabitants, thus destroyed in the midst of security, are said to have been remarkable for the purity of their manners and their personal beauty. The church contains two tablets of black marble inscribed with the names of some of the sufferers, and with particulars of the sad event. The high-road traverses the talus or débris, which extends from the top of the Rossberg far up the Rigi on the rt. It ascends vast hillocks of rubbish, calculated to be 30 feet deep hereabouts; but near the centre of the valley probably 200 feet, and winds among enormous blocks of stone already beginning to be moss-grown, and with herbage springing up between them. Among these mounds and masses of rock numerous pools are enclosed, arising from springs dammed up by the fallen earth.

Lowertz, or Lauerz, standing on the margin of the lake round which our road is carried on a terraced embankment, lost its church and several of its houses in the same catastrophe. The lake was diminished by one quarter in consequence of the avalanche of mud and rubbish which entered it, and its waters were thrown up in a wave 70 feet high to the opposite bank, so as to cover the picturesque island, and sweep away a small chapel which stood upon it. The ruined *Castle of Schwanau*, still existing upon it, has an historical interest from having been destroyed at the first rising of the Swiss Confederates in 1308, to avenge an outrage committed by the Seigneur, in carrying off a damsel against her will, and detaining her in confinement. " There is a wild and sombre tradition attached to this island, that 'once a year cries are heard to come from it, and suddenly the ghost of the tyrant is seen to pass, chased by the vengeful spirit of a pale girl, bearing a torch, and shrieking wildly. At first he eludes her swiftness; but at length she gains upon him, and forces him into the lake, where he sinks with doleful struggles ; and, as the waves close over the condemned, the shores ring with fearful and unearthly yellings.' "

[Near the village of Lowertz another footpath strikes up the Rigi, which is shorter than going round by Goldau for travellers approaching from Schwytz or Brunnen. About 3 m. above Lowertz it falls into the path from Goldau. (Rte. 17A.) The Rigi Culm may be reached by it in 3 hours.]

Seewen—(*Inn:* Zum Kreutz)—a village at the E. extremity of the lake, is resorted to on account of its chalybeate springs. Baths, &c., have been established here. A direct road to Brunnen here turns to the rt.; it is 1½ m. shorter than that by Schwytz, but is not good.

Schwytz—(*Inns:* Rössli, tolerable; —H. Hettinger)—is a mere village, though the chief place in the canton— "the heart's core of Helvetia"—from which comes the name Switzerland, and contains a Pop. of 5225 Roman Catholics, including the adjoining scattered houses and villages, which all belong to one parish. It lies picturesquely, about 3 m. from *Brunnen*, its port on the lake of Lucerne, at the foot of the very conspicuous double-peaked mountain, called Mythen (Mitres), the loftiest of whose horns is 5860 feet above the sea; and they flank the summit of the Hacken Pass.

Adjoining the *Parish Church*, a modern building, finished in 1774, is a small Gothic chapel, called *Kerker*, erected, according to tradition, at a time when admission to the church was denied the people by a ban of excommunication from the Pope. It was built in great haste, half of it within three days, and the mass was secretly administered within it.

In the *Cemetery* of the parish church is the grave of Aloys Reding, the patriotic leader (Landeshauptman) of the Swiss against the French Republicans, in 1798. "Cujus nomen summa laus," says his epitaph.

The *Rathhaus*, a building of no great antiquity nor beauty, in which the Council of the canton holds its sittings, is decorated with portraits of 43 Landammen, and a painting representing the events of the early Swiss history.

The *Arsenal* contains banners taken by the Schwytzers at Morgarten, and others borne by them in the battles of Laupen, Sempach, Kappel, Morat, &c.; also a consecrated standard presented by Pope Julius II. to the Schwytzers.

The *Archiv* (record-office) is a tower of rough masonry several stories high, and was probably once a castle: its walls are remarkably thick, and beneath it are dungeons.

Schwytz possesses a Capuchin convent, and a Dominican nunnery, founded in 1287. A Jesuit convent and Ch., built 1847, on the hill, has never been occupied.

Diligences to Lucerne, Zürich, Richterschwyl, Einsiedeln, St. Gall, and Glarus.

The Schwytzers first became known in Europe about the year 1200, in a dispute which the natives of this district had with the tenants of the monks of Einsiedeln. The holy Fathers, concealing from the Emperor the very existence of such a race as the men of Schwytz, had obtained from him a grant of their possessions, as waste and unoccupied lands. The Schwytzers, however, were able to maintain their own property by their own swords, until at length the Emperor Frederick II. confirmed to them their rights.

The name Swiss (Schwytzer) was first given to the inhabitants of the three Forest cantons after the battle of Morgarten, their earliest victory, in which the men of Schwytz had taken the lead, and prominently distinguished themselves above the others.

At *Ibach*, a village on the Muotta (through which the road to Brunnen passes), may be seen the place of assemblage where the Cantons-Landes-Gemeinde—consisting of all the male citizens of the canton—formerly met in the open air to choose their magistrates, from the Landammans down to the lowest officer. Here they used to deliberate and vote on the affairs of the state, decide on peace or war, form alliances, or despatch embassies —a singular example of universal suffrage and the legislation of the masses. The business was opened by prayer, and by the whole assembly kneeling, and taking an oath faithfully to discharge their legislative duties. According to the Constitution of 1833, the General Assemblies of the canton are now held at Rothenthurn, on the road to Einsiedeln. At present the meeting of the Circle only is held here.

ROUTE 17A.

THE RIGI.

The *Rigi*, or Righi (*Regina* Montium is only a fanciful derivation of the name), a mountain, or rather group of mountains, rising between the lakes of Zug and Lucerne, owes its celebrity less to its height, for it is only 5676 ft. above the sea, than to its isolated situation; separated from other mountains, in the midst of some of the most beautiful scenery of Switzerland, which allows an uninterrupted view from it on all sides, and converts it into a natural observatory, commanding a panorama hardly to be equalled in extent and grandeur among the Alps. It has also the advantage of being very accessible; no less than 4 mule-paths lead up to the summit, so that it is daily resorted to in summer by hundreds of travellers of all countries and ages, and of both sexes. The upper part of the mountain is composed, like the Rossberg, of the brecciated rock called Nagelflue. Externally, the entire summit is clothed with verdant pastures, which support more than 2000 head of cattle in summer, and the middle and lower region are girt round with forests.

Owing to the uncertainty of the atmosphere at high elevations, travellers should prepare themselves for disappointment, since the trouble of an ascent is often repaid with clouds and impenetrable mist, instead of a fine sunrise and extensive prospect. He is wise, therefore, who, in fine weather, manages *to reach the summit before the sun goes down*—he, at least, has two chances of a view. It not unfrequently happens, however, that the traveller who has commenced the ascent in sunshine and under a clear sky is overtaken by clouds and storms before he reaches the top.

Horses and Guides.

There are 4 principal bridle-paths to the top of the Rigi:—

a. from Goldau or Arth.
b. from Küssnacht or Immensee.
c. from Weggis or Fitznau.
d. from Gersau.

The summit may be reached in 10 hrs. from Zürich by Immensee or Goldau (Rte. 15), and in 4 or 5 hrs. from Lucerne by Küssnacht (Rte. 17) or Weggis. Carriages can reach Goldau or Küssnacht, and the traveller who ascends by one will do well to choose the shady side and descend by another. At all these places, and at most of the villages round the mountain, horses, guides, and porters may be procured at prices regulated by tariff.

The usual *charge for a horse* is 10 fr. to the top (including toll for road), and 6 to return next day by the same road; 7½ by a different road on the opposite side of the mountain, with a drink-money of 1 fr. or 2 fr. a-day to the boy who leads the horses. A porter, to carry baggage, 6 fr. and 3 to return. A horse may be hired for 6 fr. up to the convent of Maria zum Schnee, below which is the steepest part of the ascent. *Chaises à porteur* may be procured for ladies who do not like to ride or walk, and each bearer receives 6 fr. up or 9 fr. up and down. In the height of summer, when the concourse of visitors is immense, those who are anxious may send up a telegraphic despatch from Zürich or Lucerne (charge 1 fr.) to secure beds at the Rigi-culm inn, and for a franc extra, before starting, you may ascertain the number of the room secured for you. The pedestrian, unless he desire to be relieved of his baggage, has not much need of a guide, as the paths are most distinctly marked, and are traversed by so many persons that he can scarcely miss his way. To those who ride on horseback, the man who leads the horse will serve as guide.

a. *Ascent from Goldau, or Arth.*

	hrs.	min.
Goldau, or Arth		
Unter Dächli	1	0
Maria zum Schnee . .	0	50
Staffel	0	45
Kulm	0	40

Goldau, or *Arth,* may be reached by the road (Rte. 17) from Schwytz or Lucerne, or from Lucerne by steamer to Küssnacht ($\frac{1}{4}$ hr.), omnibus or on foot to Immensee ($\frac{1}{2}$ hr.), steamer or on foot to Arth, and thence by carriage or on foot to Goldau ($\frac{1}{2}$ hr.). The steamers are generally arranged so as to enable this to be done. The ascent is of $3\frac{1}{4}$ hrs.; descent $2\frac{1}{4}$: a good walker can ascend in $2\frac{1}{4}$, and descend in $1\frac{1}{2}$ hr. This is, indeed, the best side to ascend from, because the path runs along a deep gully in the interior of the mountain, the sides of which protect the traveller from the afternoon sun (a thing of importance), and shut out all view until the summit is reached, where it bursts at once upon the sight: the other paths wind round the exterior of the mountain.

From Goldau the path strikes at once from the inn of the Cheval Blanc up the side of the mountain; at first across fields strewn with blocks from the Rossberg, which, by the force acquired in their descent down one side of the valley, were actually carried up the opposite slope.

Near a small public-house, called *Unter Dächli,* where the guides usually stop to give breath to their animals and a glass of schnaps to themselves, the path was very steep, but has lately been improved.

This is a good point for surveying the fall of the Rossberg in the vale of Goldau below. The long train of rubbish thrown down by that convulsion can be traced stretching across to the lake of Löwertz, which it partly filled up (see Rte. 17). The steep footpath from Arth falls into our road here. Here begin "the Stations," a series of 13 little chapels, each with a painting representing an event in our Lord's Passion, which lead up to the pilgrimage church of Mary-of-the-Snow. The steepest part of the road is over at the 4th station. At the chapel of Malchus, containing the Bearing of the Cross, the path from Löwertz falls into our route, and soon afterwards there is a steep path on the rt. leading straight to the Culm, presenting no difficulty to pedestrians, and easy to find, but avoiding Maria zum Schnee and the Staffel.

Notre Dame des Neiges, or *Maria zum Schnee,* is a little church much frequented by pilgrims, especially on the 5th of August, on account of the indulgences granted by the Pope at the end of the 17th century to all who make this pious journey. Adjoining it is a small *hospice,* or convent, inhabited all the year by 3 or 4 Capuchin brothers, who do the duty of the church, being deputed by the fraternity at Arth on this service. The church is surrounded by a group of inns, the best of which (the Schwerdt and Sonne) are sometimes resorted to by invalids, who repair hither to drink goat's whey, and might even afford a homely lodging to travellers benighted or unable to find room in the two inns on the top of the mountain: the others are public-houses, chiefly occupied by pilgrims. Half an hour's walking, up gently-sloping meadows, brings the traveller to the inn called Rigi-Staffel. (See p. 51.)

The ascent from *Arth* is by a steep path which falls into the Goldau path in about an hour, as above mentioned.

b. *Ascent from Küssnacht or Immensee.*

Küssnacht is reached by steamer from Lucerne, and the ascent requires 3 hrs. to mount, $2\frac{1}{2}$ to descend. A mule-path, as long as that from Goldau, and in some places more steep. A toll is paid on this road for mules. By a détour of $\frac{1}{2}$ an hour, Tell's Chapel (see

Rte. 15) may be visited in going or returning. Leaving Küssnacht and passing on the l. the ruins of Gessler's Castle (Rte. 15), it is carried in zigzags up the steepest part of the mountain, through forests, and across the pastures called Seeboden. The lake of Lucerne is in sight almost the whole way. The path emerges on the brow of the hill in front of the Staffel inn, but a steep foot-path strikes off some distance below, and leads direct to the very top.

Ascent from Immensee.—Immensee may be reached from Zürich (R. 15). From it there is a good track, which soon falls into that from Küssnacht.

c. Ascent from Weggis.

	hrs.	min.
Weggis.		
Helligenkreutz	1	0
Kaltbad	1	0
Staffel	0	40
Kulm	0	40

Weggis. *Inns:* Eintracht; Concordia; Löwe (Lion)—a small village on a little ledge at the foot of the Rigi, on the lake of the Four Cantons, is the spot where those who approach the Rigi by water, land. It supports more than 40 horses, and guides in corresponding numbers. The steamer to and from Lucerne and Flüelen touches here 6 times daily (¾ hr.). A bad path, winding round the foot of the Rigi, connects Weggis with Küssnacht; but the chief communication is carried on by water.

The mule-path up the Rigi from Weggis is less steep than the two preceding: 3¼ hrs. up; 2¼ down. It strikes up the mountain immediately opposite the laading-place, and keeping to the rt. winds along the outside of the mountain, in constant view of the lake, passing, first, the little chapel of Heiligenkreutz (Holy Cross), and then stretching up to a singular natural arch (called Hochstein, or Felsenthor), formed by 2 vast detached blocks of nagelflue (pudding-stone), holding suspended a third, beneath which the path is carried. These broken fragments serve to illustrate the tendency which this rock has to cleave and split, and

to this cause may be attributed a singular torrent of mud, which, in the year 1795, descended from the flank of the Rigi upon the village of Weggis, destroying 30 houses and burying nearly 60 acres of good land. It advanced slowly, like a lava-current, taking a fortnight to reach the lake, so that the inhabitants had time to remove out of its way. It is supposed to have been produced by springs, or rain-water, percolating the cracks of the nagelflue, and converting the layer of clay, which separates it from the beds beneath it, into soft mud. Had there been any great fracture in the nagelflue, it is probable that a large portion of the mountain would have given way and slipped down into the lake, since the strata of the Rigi slope at a very steep angle. Had this been the case, a catastrophe, similar to that of the Rossberg, might have ensued. As it was, the softened clay was squeezed out by the weight of the superincumbent mass of the mountain, and formed this deluge of mud, traces of which are still visible on the side of the mountain.

About ½ an hour's walk above the arch lies the *Cold Bath* (kaltes Bad), where a source of very pure cold water, issuing out of the rock, supplies a small bathing establishment. (Douche is very efficacious.)

An *Inn*, of wood, has been constructed here, containing 26 bedrooms and 6 baths. It was once the custom for patients to lie down in the bath with their clothes on, and afterwards to walk about in the sun until they dried on the back; but this method is no longer regarded as essential to effect a cure. Close to the cold-bath is a little chapel, dedicated to the Virgin, to which pilgrims repair, and in which mass is daily said for the shepherds on the Rigi.

The spring is called the *Sisters' Fountain*, from a tradition that 3 fair sisters sought refuge here from the pursuit of a wicked and tyrannical Austrian bailiff, and spent the remainder of their days amidst the clefts of the rocks in the exercise of piety.

The path, after leaving the Kaltbad, passes at first over a pasture, and then turns the shoulder of the mountain, affording a fine view of the country beyond Lucerne, and reaches the *Staffel* (see below).

d. *Ascent from Gersau,* 4½ hrs. Crossing the meadows, and by a cascade of the Roehrlibach, and amongst huge blocks of fallen rock, the little inn of Unter Geschwänd is reached (1¼ hr.). After passing the chapel of St. Joseph, and taking care to keep to the l., the baths and inn of *Rigi Scheideck* are reached, commanding a fine view. The Scheideck is 3 hrs. from Gersau, and thence in 1 hr. Maria zum Schnee is reached. (Rte. 17 A a.)

There are several other paths up the Rigi more or less fit for horses; one of the most interesting is that to *Fitznau*. From the Staffelhaus this path diverges l., passing a waterfall, behind which is a cavern, the vestibule of which is 100 ft. deep, and it is said to lead to others penetrating *through* the mountain. In Fitznau on the lake of Lucerne is a neat little *Inn*. The daughters of the house are good singers. Thence by boat in 1 hr. to Buochs.

There is also a path from Löwertz.

Summit of the Rigi.

All the principal paths converge and unite in front of the *Staffelhaus,* a tolerable inn, into which travellers are sometimes inveigled by a statement that the inn on the *Culm* is full. Let them beware ere they trust such assertions. It is ¼ an hour's walk below the Culm, and it is a bad plan to stop short of it, since those who rest here must get up half an hour earlier next morning if they wish to catch the sunrise from the top.

The *Culm,* or culminating point of the Rigi, is an irregular space of ground of some extent, destitute of trees, but covered with turf. On the top stands the *Inn,* a group of large buildings, affording good accommodation, considering the height, which exceeds that of the most elevated mountain in Britain, being 5676 ft. above the sea level, and 4270 ft. above the Lake of Lucerne. An enormous building was added in 1857, containing a vast salle-a-manger, and many other rooms. Unfortunately it is so near the top, and so high, as partially to interfere with the view. *Charges:* tea or breakfast, 1½ F. fr.; supper (¾ hr. after sunset), without wine, 3 fr.; bed-room, 2 fr.; servants, 1 fr. About 20,000 persons make this ascent in a year! Tourists will do well to engage apartments beforehand, which may be done by means of the electric telegraph, at a cost of 1 fr. Travellers not on foot should bring all their cloaks with them, as the cold is often intense; and the thermometer, marking 76° in Lucerne at mid-day, was 37° on the Rigi at sunset, and 31° at sunrise. The house is warmed with stoves even in summer. The following notice is hung up in every room :—" On avertit MM. les étrangers qu'il est défendu de prendre les couvertures de lit pour sortir au sommet;" a threat which seems more likely to have suggested than prevented the commission of so comfortable an offence. In 1855 the landlord paid for a piece of ground on which the new building stands (96 ft. by 55 ft.), no less than 54,000 fr., or more than 2000l. to the canton.

During the height of summer, when travellers are most numerous, the Culm inn is crammed to overflowing every evening; numbers are turned away from the doors, and it is difficult to procure beds, food, or even attention. The house presents a scene of the utmost confusion, servant maids hurrying in one direction, couriers and guides in another, while gentlemen with poles and knapsacks block up the passages. Most of the languages of Europe, muttered usually in terms of abuse or complaint, and the all-pervading fumes of tobacco, enter largely as ingredients into this Babel of sounds and smells. In the evening the guests are collected at a table-d'hôte supper; after which most persons are glad to repair to rest. It takes some time, however, before the hubbub of voices and the trampling of feet subside; and, not unfrequently, a few roystering German students prolong their potations and noise far into the night. The beds, besides, are not very inviting to repose; and are generally very damp, or rather wet, though of the thousands who annually visit the Rigi none ever appear to suffer from it. Whether the inmate have slept or not, he, together with the whole household, is roused about an hour before sunrise by the grating sounds of a long wooden horn, which is played until every particle of sleep is dispelled from the household. Then commences a general stir and commotion, and everybody hastens out with shivering limbs and half-open eyes to gaze at the glorious prospect of a sunrise from the Rigi. Fortunate are they for whom the view is not marred by clouds and rain, a very common occurrence, as the leaves of the Album kept in the inn will testify. Indeed the following verses describe the fate of a large majority of those who make this expedition:—

Nine weary uphill miles we sped,
 The setting sun to see ;
Sulky and grim he went to bed,
 Sulky and grim went we.
Seven sleepless hours we tossed, and then,
 The rising sun to see,
Sulky and grim we rose again,
 Sulky and grim rose he.

Long before dawn an assemblage of between 200 and 300 persons is often collected on the Rigi Culm, awaiting the sunrise, to enjoy this magnificent prospect in the cold, though it may be viewed nearly as well from the windows of the salle-à-manger. A glare of light in the E., which gradually dims the flickering of the stars, is the first token of the morning; it soon becomes a streak of gold along the horizon, and is reflected in a pale pink tint upon the snows of the Bernese Alps. Summit after summit slowly catches the same golden hue; the dark space between the horizon and the Rigi is next illuminated; forests, lakes, hills, rivers, towns and villages, gradually become revealed, but look cold and indistinct

until the red orb surmounts the mountain top, and darts his beams across the landscape. The shadows are then rolled back, as it were, and in a few moments the whole scene around is glowing in sunshine. The view is best seen during the quarter of an hour preceding and following the first appearance of the sun; after that the mists begin to curl up, and usually shroud parts of it from the eye.

The most striking feature in this wonderful panorama, which is said to extend over a circumference of 300 m., is undoubtedly the lakes of Lucerne and Zug; the branching arms of the former extend in so many different directions as to bewilder one at first, and both lave the base of the mountain so closely that the spectator might fancy himself suspended in the air above them, as in a balloon, and think, by one step from the brow of the precipice, to plunge into them. The peculiar greenish blue tint which sheets of water assume when seen from a height has also something exceedingly beautiful. Eight other lakes may be seen from the Rigi, but they are so small and distant as to "look like pools ; some almost like water spilt upon the earth."

On the N. side the eye looks down into the lake of Zug, and the streets of Arth; at the end of the lake the town of Zug, and behind it the spire of the Ch. of Kappel, where Zwingli, the Reformer, fell in battle. This is backed by the chain of the Albis, and through gaps in its ridge may be discerned a few of the houses of the town of Zürich, and two little bits of its lake. Over the l. shoulder of the Rossberg a peep is obtained into the lake of Egeri, on whose shores the Swiss gained the victory of Morgarten. The N. horizon is bounded by the range of the Black Forest hills.

The prospect on the W. is more open and map-like, and therefore less interesting. Close under the Rigi lie Tell's chapel, on the spot where he shot Gessler, and the village and bay of Küssnacht. Farther off, nearly the whole canton of Lucerne expands to view;—the Reuss winding through the midst of it. Above the Reuss is the lake of Sempach, the scene of another triumph of Swiss valour. Lucerne, with its coronet of towers, is distinctly seen at the W. end of the lake, and on the l. of it rises the gloomy Pilatus, cutting the sky with its serrated ridge. The remainder of the W. horizon is occupied by the chain of the Jura.

On the S. the mass of the Rigi forms the foreground, and touching the opposite mountains of Unterwalden, only allows here and there a small portion of the lake of Lucerne to be seen. On this side the objects visible in succession, from rt. to l., are the lakes of Alpnach and Sarnen, buried in woods, by the side of which runs the road to the Brünig; the mountains called Stanzer and Buochserhorn, and behind them the magnificent white chain of the high Alps of Berne, Unterwalden, and Uri, in one unbroken ridge of peaks and glaciers, including the Jungfrau, Eiger, Finster Aarhorn, the Titlis (the highest peak in Unterwalden), the Engelberger Rothstock, and the Bristenstock, between which and the Seelisberg runs the road of St. Gothard.

On the E. the Alpine chain continues to stretch uninterruptedly along the horizon, and includes the pre-eminent peaks of the Dödi, on the borders of the Grisons, of the Glärnisch, in canton Glarus, and of the Sentis, in Appenzell. In the middle distance, above the lake of Löwertz, lies the town of Schwytz, the cradle of Swiss freedom, backed by the two singular sharp peaks called, from their shape, the Mitres (Mythen). Above them peers the craggy crest of the Glärnisch; and to the rt. of them is the opening of the Muotta Thal, famous for the bloody conflicts between Suwarrow and Massena, where armies manœuvred and fought on spots which before the shepherd and chamois hunter alone used to tread. Farther to the l. rises the mass of the Rossberg,—the nearest mountain neighbour of the Rigi. The whole scene of desolation caused by its fall (see Rte. 17); the chasm on the top, whence the ruin came; the course of the terrific avalanche of stones, di-

verging and spreading in their descent; the lake of Lowertz, partly filled up by it, and the pools and puddles caused in the valley by the stoppage of the watercourses, are at once displayed in a bird's-eye view.

The very distant bare peak seen above the top of the Rossberg is the Sentis.

The Spectre of the Rigi is an atmospheric phenomenon not unfrequently observed on the tops of high mountains. It occurs when the cloudy vapours happen to rise perpendicularly from the valley beneath the mountain, on the side opposite to the sun, without enveloping the summit of the Rigi itself. Under these circumstances the shadows of the Rigi Culm and of any person standing on the top are cast upon the wall of mist in greatly magnified proportions. The shadow is encircled by a halo, assuming the prismatic colours of the rainbow, and this sometimes doubled when the mist is thick.

Two melancholy accidents have occurred on the top of the Rigi:—in 1820 a guide who had attended an English family was struck dead by lightning as he stood watching the clouds: in 1826 a Prussian officer, who had reached the summit, accompanied by his wife and children, fell from a very dangerous seat which he had selected on the brow of a precipice (the only spot where the summit is really a precipice), and was dashed to pieces at the bottom. According to another account, the miserable man threw himself off, having previously announced his intention of committing suicide to his wife, who summoned the guide to arrest him, but, after a severe struggle, her husband got loose, and effected his purpose.

ROUTE 18.

THE LAKE OF LUCERNE.   LUCERNE TO FLÜELEN.

Steamers several times a day between Lucerne and Flüelen (26 Eng. m.) and back—to Weggis in ¾ hr.—Beckenried in 1½ hr.—Gersau in 1¾ hr.—Brunnen, 2½ hrs.—Flüelen in 3 hrs. *Fare*—1st class, 4 fr. 60, to Flüelen.

The scale of charges for conveying carriages, including embarking, is fixed by tariff in the *Indicateur*.

Boats may be hired at all the ports on the lake, and are convenient when the steamer's time is not suitable. Those who wish to see the lake to advantage, should see it from a row-boat and not from a steamer. The charges are fixed by tariff, which may be seen at the inns, but the men expect a bonne main.

Much has been said of the dangers of the lake of Lucerne, arising from storms: sudden and tempestuous winds no doubt do sometimes occur ; but the boatmen can always foresee the approach of a storm, and are very careful not to subject themselves to any risk. The clumsy flat-bottomed boats are only fit for the dead calm which generally prevails, and would be useless if there was often bad weather ; yet instances of accidents are hardly known—either the boatmen will not stir out, or put into shore, which is always near, on the slightest appearance of bad weather. Those who trust themselves on the lake in boats should implicitly follow the advice of the boatmen, and not urge them to venture when disinclined, neither they nor their boats being fit for bad weather.

The *winds* on the lake are singularly capricious and variable, blowing at the same time from opposite quarters of the compass in different parts of it, so that the boatmen say that there is a new wind behind every promontory. The most violent is the S. wind, or Föhn, which occasionally rushes so furiously down the bay of Uri as to prevent the progress of any row-boat, and renders it difficult for even a steamer to make headway. During fine weather, in summer, the north wind blows along the bay of Uri from ten to three or four, after which it dies away, and is succeeded by the S. wind. The boatmen, in coming from Lucerne, endeavour to reach Flüelen before the wind turns.

The *Lake of Lucerne*, or *of the Four Forest Cantons* (Vier-Waldstädter-See), so called from the cantons of Uri, Unterwalden, Schwytz, and Lucerne, which exclusively form its shores, is distinguished above every lake in Switzerland, and perhaps in Europe, by the beauty and sublime grandeur of its scenery. It is hardly less interesting from the historical recollections connected with it. Its shores are a classic region—the sanctuary of liberty ; on them took place those memorable events which gave freedom to Switzerland — here the first Confederacy was formed ; and, above all, its borders were the scene of the heroic deeds and signal vengeance of WILLIAM TELL, on which account they are sometimes called Tell's Country.

The lake lies at a height of 1406 ft. above the sea-level : it is of very irregular shape, assuming, near its W. extremity, the form of a cross. Its various bays, branching in different directions, are each named after the chief town or village situated on them : thus the W. branch is properly the lake of Lucerne : then come the bays of Alpnach on the S., Küssnacht on the N., Buochs, stretching E. and W. ; and lastly, the bay of Uri, running N. and S., entirely enclosed within the mountains of that canton.

Quitting Lucerne, the steamboat soon arrives abreast of a promontory on the l., called Meggenhorn, close off which lies a small island, the only one in the lake. A Frenchman, the Abbé Reynal, took upon himself to raise upon it a monument to the founder of Swiss liberty ; it consisted of a wooden obelisk, painted to look like granite, with Tell's apple and arrow on the top. This gingerbread memorial of vanity and bad taste was luckily destroyed by lightning. Thus far the shores of the lake are undulating hills, clothed with verdure, and dotted with houses and villas—a smiling scene to which the dark ridge of Pilatus adds a solitary feature of grandeur. After doubling the cape of the Meggenhorn, the bay of Küssnacht opens out on the l., that of Alpnach on the rt., and the traveller finds himself in the centre of the cross or transept (so to call it) of the lake. From this point Mount Pilate is seen to great advantage—clouds and darkness almost invariably rest upon his head, and his serrated ridge and gloomy sides have a sullen air in the midst of the sunny and cheerful landscape around. The superstitions connected with this mountain are mentioned in Rte. 16.

Looking up the bay of Küssnacht the ruined castle of Neu Habsburg is seen on the l. perched on a cliff; and, at the further extremity of the village of Küssnacht, a fort belonging to the counts of that canton. The colossal mass of the Rigi occupies the other side of the bay. Its sides are girt with forests, below which runs a fringe of fields and gardens, dotted with cottages; while, above, it is clothed to its very summit with verdant pastures, feeding a hundred flocks;—an agreeable contrast to his opposite neighbour Pilate.

After weathering the promontory of Tanzenburg, a spur or buttress descending from the Rigi, the village of *Weggis* appears in sight: it is the usual port of disembarkation for those who ascend the Rigi from the water (Rte. 17 A c), and may be reached in about an hour from Lucerne. The high precipices opposite Weggis belong to canton Unterwalden, but the narrow ledge of meadow at their base is in canton Lucerne.

Two rocky headlands projecting from the Rigi on one side, and the Burgenburg on the other — significantly called the Noses (Nasen)—now appear to close up the lake; but as the boat advances, a narrow strait, not more than 1½ m. wide, is disclosed between them. Once through these narrows, and the noses seem to have

overlapped each other, and the traveller enters, as it were, a new lake shut out by high mountains from that which he has traversed before. This oval basin is called the *Gulf of Buochs,* from the little village at the bottom of the bay on its S. shore, behind which rise two grand mountains, the Buochser and Stanzer-Horn.

Beckenried (*Inn:* Sonne) was once the place of assembly of the council of the 4 cantons. The steamers here land passengers bound for *Buochs* (3 m.) or *Stanz* (6 m.). Carriages may be hired here, and there is now an omnibus daily for Lüngern at the foot of the Brünig (Rte. 19).

There is a pleasant walk from Beckenried to Grütli, by a charming path. On the opposite shore, at the foot of the Rigi, nestles the little village *Gersau* — (*Inn:* Sonne, small, but clean)—which, with the small strip of cultivated and meadow land behind it, formed, for four centuries, an independent state, undoubtedly the smallest in civilized Europe. A path from this place leads up the Rigi (Rte. 17 A d.)

Its entire territory consists of a slope leaning against the side of the mountain, produced probably by the earth and rubbish washed down from above, by two mountain-torrents breaking out of ravines behind it. The whole extent of land cannot measure more than 3 m. by 2, which would make a very small *parish* in England; scarcely an acre of it is level ground, but it is covered with orchards, and supports a population of 1348 souls, dwelling in 174 houses, 82 of which form the village.

It is recorded that the people of Gersau bought their freedom from a state of villenage in 1390, with a sum of 690 lbs. of pfennings, scraped together after 10 years of hard toil, to satisfy the Lords of Moos, citizens of Lucerne, whose serfs they had previously been. They maintained their independence apart from any other canton, and governed by a landam-man and council, chosen from among themselves, until the French occupied Switzerland in 1798, since which they have been united with the canton Schwytz. Though Gersau possessed a criminal jurisdiction of its own, together with a gallows still left standing, no instance of a capital execution occurred during the whole of its existence as a separate state.

There is something very pleasing in the aspect of Gersau on the margin of its quiet cove, shrouded in orchards and shut out from the rest of the world by the precipices of the Rigi ; for, although there is a path hence to Brunnen, and another to the top of the mountain, they are difficult and little used. Its picturesque, broad-brimmed cottages are scattered among the fields and chesnut woods nearly to the summit of the slopes ; some perched on sloping lawns, so steep that they seem likely to slip into the lake. The steamer calls off Gersau, which is reached in 1½ hr. from Lucerne. As soon as it is left behind, the singular bare peaks of the Mythen (Mitres) start up into view,—at their foot the town of Schwytz is built, 3 m. inland, and in front of them stands the village of

Brunnen — (*Inns :* Golden Adler, Cheval Blanc)—the port of the canton Schwytz, built at the mouth of the river Muotta. Its position in reference to the surrounding scenery is one of the most fortunate on the lake, commanding a view along two of its finest reaches. Mt. Pilatus is well seen from this. The warehouse, called *Sust,* bears on its outer walls a rude painting of the three Confederates, to commemorate the first alliance which was formed on this spot between the Forest Cantons in 1315, after the battle of Morgarten. Aloys Reding here raised the standard of revolt against the French in 1798. Schwytz is 3 m. distant. (R. 17.)

Those who intend to ascend the Rigi from this, usually take a char to Goldau (charge 9 frs.) : — for pedestrians there is a shorter footpath from Löwertz (see Rtc. 17A a).

The *steamer* touches here 6 times a-day. *Diligences* for St. Gall and Zürich by Arth.

Opposite Brunnen, the lake of the Four Cantons changes at once its direction and its character. Along the bay of Uri, or of Flüelen as it is sometimes called, it stretches nearly N. and S. Its borders are perpendicular, and almost uninterrupted precipices ; the basements and buttresses of colossal mountains, higher than any of those which overlook the other branches of the lake; and their snowy summits peer down from above the clouds, or through the gullies in their sides, upon the dark gulf below. At the point of the promontory, opposite Brunnen, stands a small inn, called Treib, with a little haven in front, in which boats often take shelter. When the violence of the Föhn wind renders the navigation of the lake to Flüelen impracticable, travellers sometimes take a footpath from Treib over the mountains by Seelisberg, Bauen, Isenthal, and Seedorf. There is a similar and equally difficult path from Schwytz to Morsebach, Sisikon (or Sissigen), Tellenrüth, to Altorf, which was nevertheless traversed by the French General Lecourbe, with his army, in pursuit of Suwarrow, in the night, by torchlight, in 1799. The want of boats to transport his forces across the lake compelled him to this daring exploit. On turning the corner of the promontory of Treib, a singular rock, called *Wytenstein,* rising like an obelisk out of the water, is passed, and the bay of Uri, in all its stupendous grandeur, bursts into view.

"It is upon this that the superiority of the lake of Lucerne to all other lakes, or, as far as I know, scenes upon earth, depends. The vast mountains rising on every side and closing at the end, with their rich clothing of wood, the sweet soft spots of verdant pasture scattered at their feet, and sometimes on their breast, and the expanse of water, unbroken by islands, and almost undisturbed by any signs of living men, make an impression which it would be foolish to attempt to convey by words."—*Sir James Mackintosh.*

After passing the Wytenstein about a mile, the precipices recede a little, leaving a small ledge, formed by earth fallen from above, and sloping down to the water's edge. A few walnut and chesnut trees have here taken root, and the small space of level ground is occupied by a meadow conspicuous among the surrounding woods from the brightness of its verdure. This is *Grütli* or *Rütli*, the spot pointed out by tradition as the rendezvous of the 3 founders of Swiss freedom, — Werner Stauffacher, of Steinen, in Schwytz; Erni (Arnold) an der Halden, of Melchthal, in Unterwalden ; and Walter Fürst, of Attinghausen, in Uri. These "honest conspirators" met in secret in the dead of night, on this secluded spot, at the end of the year 1307, to form the plan for liberating their country from the oppression of their Austrian governors. They here "swore to be faithful to each other, but to do no wrong to the Count of Habsburg, and not to maltreat his governors."

"These poor mountaineers, in the 14th cent., furnish, perhaps, the only example of insurgents who, at the moment of revolt, bind themselves as sacredly to be just and merciful to their oppressors as to be faithful to each other;" and, we may add, who carried out their intentions. The scheme thus concerted was carried into execution on the following new year's day ; and such was the origin of the Swiss Confederation.

According to popular belief, which everywhere in Switzerland connects political events with notions of religion, the oath of the Grütli was followed by a miracle, and 3 springs gushed forth from the spot upon which the 3 confederates had stood. In token of this every stranger is conducted to a little hut built over the 3 sources of pure water, and is invited to drink out of them to the memory of the 3 founders of Swiss freedom. It is doubtful whether the 3 sources are not merely 1 split into 3 ; but few would search to detect "the pious fraud."

The view from Grütli is delightful. A small scar may be observed from hence on the face of the opposite precipice of the Frohnalpstock, formed by the fall of a piece of rock. The fragment which has left such a trifling

blemish was about 1200 ft. wide ; when it fell it raised such a wave on the lake as overwhelmed 5 houses of the village of Sissigen, distant 1 mile, and 11 of its inhabitants were drowned. The swell was felt at Lucerne, more than 20 miles off.

The immediate shores of the bay of Uri are utterly pathless, since, for the most part, its sides are precipices, descending vertically into the water, without an inch of foreground between. Here and there a small sloping ledge intervenes, as at Grütli, and on one or two other spots room has been found for a scanty group of houses, as at Sisikon, Bauen, Isleten, &c. The strata are singularly contorted in many places.

A little shelf, or platform, at the foot of the Achsenburg, on the E. shore of the lake, called the *Tellen-Platte*, is occupied by TELL'S CHAPEL, and may be reached in ¾ of an hour from Grütli. Here, according to the tradition, Tell sprang on shore out of the boat in which Gessler was carrying him a prisoner to the dungeon of Küssnacht (Rte. 15), when the sudden storm on the lake compelled him to remove Tell's fetters, in order to avail himself of his skill as steersman : thus affording the captive an opportunity to escape. The chapel, an open arcade lined with rude and faded paintings, representing the events of the delivery of Switzerland, was erected by canton Uri in 1388, only 31 years after Tell's death, and in the presence of 114 persons who had known him personally—a strong testimony to prove that the events of his life are not a mere romance. Once a year, on the first Friday after the Ascension, mass is said and a sermon preached in the chapel, which is attended by the inhabitants on the shores of the lake, who repair hither in boats, forming an aquatic procession.

The murder of Gessler by Tell, notwithstanding the provocation, was a stain on the Swiss revolution, marked as it was equally by the just necessity which led to it and the wise moderation which followed it, in preventing the shedding of blood, so that even the tyrannical bailiffs of the Emperor were conducted unharmed beyond the limits of the Confederacy, and there set free: an act of forbearance the more surprising considering that many of the Swiss leaders were smarting under personal wrongs inflicted by these Bailiffs or Zwing-Herrn.

Tell, acting by the impulse of his individual wrongs, had well nigh marred the designs of the confederates by precipitating events before the plan was properly matured. Yet there is something so spirit-stirring in the history of " the mountain Brutus," that there is no doubt the mere narration of it contributed as much towards the success of the insurrection and the freedom of Switzerland, by rousing the minds of a whole people, as the deep and well-concerted scheme of the 3 conspirators of Grütli. It ought to be added that there have been fierce disputes as to the existence of Tell, and that a similar story is related as having occurred in Denmark to one Toko in the 10th cent.

The view from Tell's chapel is exceedingly fine. The following are the remarks of Sir James Mackintosh on this scene : — " The combination of what is grandest in nature, with whatever is pure and sublime in human conduct, affected me in this passage (along the lake) more powerfully than any scene which I had ever seen. Perhaps neither Greece nor Rome would have had such power over me. They are dead. The present inhabitants are a new race, who regard with little or no feeling the memorials of former ages. This is, perhaps, the only place in our globe where deeds of pure virtue, ancient enough to be venerable, are consecrated by the religion of the people, and continue to command interest and reverence. No local superstition so beautiful and so moral anywhere exists. The inhabitants of Thermopylæ or Marathon know no more of these famous spots than that they are so many square feet of earth. England is too extensive a country to

make Runnymede an object of national affection. In countries of industry and wealth the stream of events sweeps away those old remembrances. The solitude of the Alps is a sanctuary destined for the monuments of ancient virtue ; Grütli and Tell's chapel are as much reverenced by the Alpine peasants as Mecca by a devout Musselman ; and the deputies of the 3 ancient cantons met, so late as the year 1715, to renew their allegiance and their oaths of eternal union."

The depth of the lake, opposite Tell's chapel, is 800 ft. After rounding the cape on which it stands, Flüelen appears in view. On the W. shore the valley of Isenthal opens out; terminated by the grand snowy peaks of the *Uri Rothstock* on one side, while in the centre the vista is closed by the grand conical peak of the *Bristenstock.*

The *Uri Rothstock*, for its height, 10,376 ft., is one of the easiest mountains in Switzerland. Those who wish to ascend it may land at Brunnen, and cross in a row-boat to Isleten, whence it is 5 m. to Isenthal, at which place there is tolerable accommodation for the night. Next morning start with one of the Imfangers as a guide (5 fr. for each person), and return at night.

Flüelen, the port of the canton Uri, may be reached by steam in 20 minutes from Tell's chapel. Here begins the carriage-road over the St. Gothard. (Rte. 34.)

ROUTE 19.

THE PASS OF THE BRÜNIG.—LUCERNE
TO MEYRINGEN OR BRIENZ.

	Eng. m.
Lucerne.	
Stanzstad (by water) . . .	4¼
Stanz (diligence)	1¼
Sarnen (diligence). . . .	8
Lungern (diligence) . . .	8¼
Meyringen (horses), or . .	9
Brientz (horses). . . .	10

There are several methods of going from Lucerne through Sarnen to Lungern, and thence across the Brünig into the Oberland. As far as Lungern the road is practicable for chars; thence a bridle-path leads over the mountain.

a. Carriage to Winkel, boat to Gestad. This route has no advantages over

b. Boat to Gestad (2 h. 20 m., 1 fr. 50 the boat, 2 fr. each man, and 1 fr. bonnemain for all), carriage to Sarnen.

c. Boat or steamer to Stanzstad; carriage to Sarnen, as in the table above. An omnibus meets the steamer daily.

d. Steamer to Beckenried; carriage to Sarnen. An omnibus meets the steamer daily.

a and *b.* Time from Lucerne to Gestad, 2 h. 20 m. Gestad to Lungern, by char, 3½ hrs. Lungern to Meyringen, on horses, 3 hrs. To Brientz, 3½ hrs. Good pedestrians will take a char only to Gyswyl, where the steep ascent of the Kaiserstuhl begins.

From Lucerne the traveller proceeds by water through a strait between the village of Stanzstad on the l. and a spur of the Pilatus, called Lopper, on the rt., into that beautiful and retired gulf of the lake of the Four Cantons, called the Lake of Alpnach. The castle of Rotzberg, on its E. shore, is remarkable as the first stronghold of the Austrians of which the Swiss confederates gained possession on New-year's day, 1308. One of the party, the accepted lover of a damsel within the castle, being, according to the practice of Swiss lovers even at the present time, admitted by a ladder of ropes to a midnight interview with his mistress, a girl living within its walls, succeeded in introducing, in the same way, 20 of his companions, who found no difficulty in surprising and overpowering the garrison. The loves of Jägeli and Anneli have, from that day forth, been celebrated in Swiss song. A series of simultaneous risings in other parts of the Forest Cantons proved equally successful, and in 24 hours the country was freed from the Austrian rule.

Gestad, or *Alpnach-am-Gestad,* at the S. end of the bay (1½ hr. from Winkel) (*Inn:* Cheval Blanc — not good), is one of the ports for travellers going to or coming from the Brünig. A 1-horse char to Lungern costs 12 fr. and drink-money 1 fr.; a 2-horse carriage 20 fr. and 2 fr. drink-money. A row-boat takes 40 min. hence to Stanzstad, where the Lucerne steamer touches once a-day going and returning, the Lake of Alpnach being too shallow to admit the steamer. Behind Gestad is seen the taper spire of

Alpnach (*Inn:* Schlüssel, Key). It is a scattered village of 1400 Inhab. at the foot of the Pilatus (Rte. 17), which extends 1½ mile from the water-side. The extensive forests which clothe the sides of that mountain belong, for the most part, to Alpnach, and would be a source of wealth to its inhabitants if they could be got at more easily. It was with a view of turning to account the fine timber growing on spots barely accessible by ordinary means, owing to their height and the ruggedness of the ground, that the celebrated *Slide of Alpnach* was constructed. This was a trough of wood formed of nearly 30,000 trees, fastened together lengthwise, 5 or 6 feet wide at the top, and 3 or 4 feet deep, extending from a height of 2500 feet down to the water's edge. It was planned and executed by a skilful engineer from Württemberg, named Rupp. The course of this vast inclined plane was in some places circuitous; it was supported partly on uprights; and thus was carried over 3 deep ravines, and, in two instances, passed underground. Its average declivity did not exceed 1 foot in 17, yet this sufficed to discharge a tree 100 ft. long and 4 ft. in diameter, in the short space of 6 minutes, from the upper end of the trough, where it was launched, into the lake below, a distance exceeding 8 Eng. m. The trees were previously prepared by being stripped of their branches, barked, and rudely dressed with the axe. The bottom of the trough was kept constantly wet by allowing a rill of water to trickle down it, and thereby diminish the friction. Professor Playfair, who has written a most interesting account of the slide, says that the trees shot downwards with a noise like the roar of thunder and the rapidity of lightning, seeming to shake the earth as they passed. Though the utmost care was taken to remove every obstacle, it sometimes happened that a tree stuck by the way, or, being arrested suddenly in its progress, leaped or bolted out of the trough with a force capable of cutting the trees growing at the side short off, and of dashing the log itself to atoms. To prevent such accidents, watchmen were stationed at regular distances along the sides during the operation of discharging the wood, and a line of signals, similar to those in use on modern railways, were established, showing, by a concerted signal, when anything went wrong. The timber, when discharged, was collected on the lake and floated down the Reuss into the Rhine, where it was formed into rafts, such as are commonly met with on that river, and sold in Holland for ship-building and other purposes. Napoleon had contracted for the greater part of the timber, to supply his dock-yards; but the peace of 1815, by diminishing the demand, rendered the speculation unprofitable, and the slide, having been long abandoned, was taken down in 1819. Similar slides, nearly as long, are common throughout the great forests of the Tyrol and Styria. (See *Handbook for South Germany.*) In 1833 some French speculators constructed a cart-road up the Pilatus into the centre of its forests, and the timber

squared or sawn into planks was brought down on the axle, drawn by 20 or 30 horses and oxen.

The *Ch. of Alpnach*, a handsome modern edifice, was built with the timber brought down by the slide.

In the canton Unterwalden, which we are about to traverse, by an ancient law every inhabitant was bound to guide the stranger who questions him on his way, without fee or charge. The road ascends the valley along the left bank of the Aa, about 7 m. to *Sarnen*. (See *c* and *d.*)

c and *d.* Lucerne to Stanzstad, ¾ hr.; char to Lungern, 4 hrs. Those coming from Lucerne will land at Stanzstad; those from Flüelen, &c., at Beckenried; at either of which places chars may be procured, and there is a diligence once a day. One-horse char to Lungern, 15 fr., 1 fr. pourboire; 2-horse, 25 fr., 2 fr. pourboire.

Stanzstad (no good Inn) is a small village on the margin of the lake, immediately opposite Winkel, under the Rotzberg. It is distinguished by its tall watch-tower, 5 centuries old. In 1315, a little before the battle of Morgarten, a vessel laden with Austrian partisans was crushed and swamped by a millstone hurled from the top of this tower. An avenue of walnut-trees leads, in 2 m., to Stanz.

[*Beckenried* is a village of 1400 Inhab., beautifully situated, where the Soleil is a good and clean *Inn*. It can furnish chars or horses.

There are pleasant walks around Beckenried; and the steamer touches there 4 times a-day. The char or diligence road runs round the bay of *Buochs*, passing through the village of Buochs, till it meets, in 6 m., the other road at]

Stanz — Inns: Krone (Crown); Engel (Angel) — capital of the lower division (Nidwalden) of canton Unterwalden, contains 1870 Roman Catholic Inhab. It was in the *Rathhaus* of Stanz that the venerable Swiss worthy Nicolas Von der Flue appeased the burning dissensions of the confederates, in 1481, by his wise and soothing counsels. In the existing building there is a picture (? daub) representing him taking leave of his family. In the market-place is a statue of Arnold of Winkelried, a native of Stanz, with the "sheaf of spears" in his arms. (See Rte. 4.) His house is also shown here, but it has been entirely modernised. The field on which it stands is called in old records "the meadow of Winkelried's children." On the outer walls of the bone-house, attached to the handsome *Parish Church*, is a tablet to the me-mory of the unfortunate people of Nidwalden (386 in number, including 102 women and 25 children) who were massacred, in defending their homes, by the French in September, 1798. In that year this division of the canton was the only part of Switzerland which refused the new constitution tyrannically imposed on it by the French republic. The ancient spirit of Swiss independence, fanned and excited by the exhortations of the priests (which in this instance must be termed fanatic, as all resistance was hopeless and useless), stirred up this ill-fated community to engage an army ten times greater than any force they could oppose to it, and consisting of veteran troops. At a time when the larger and more powerful cantons had yielded, almost without a struggle, the brave but misguided men of Unterwalden and Schwytz afforded the solitary proof that Swiss bravery and love of freedom were not extinct in the land of Tell. Their desperate resistance, however, served only to inflame the fury of their foes. After a vain attempt made by the French to starve the Unterwaldeners into submission, "on the 3rd of September, 1798, General Schauenburg, the French commander, directed a general attack to be made, by means of boats from Lucerne, as well as by the Oberland. Repulsed with great spirit by the inhabitants, only 2000 strong, the attack was renewed every day from the 3rd to the 9th of September. On this last day, towards two in the afternoon, new reinforcements having penetrated by the land side, with field-pieces, the invaders forced their way into the very heart of the country. In their despair the people rushed on them with very inferior arms. Whole families perished together; no quarter was given on either side. 18 young women were found among the dead, side by side with their fathers and brothers, near the chapel of Winkelried. 63 persons who had taken shelter in the church of Stanz were slaughtered there, with the priest at the altar. Every house in the open country, in all 600, was burnt down; Stanz itself excepted, which was saved by the humanity of a *chef de brigade*. The inhabitants who survived this day, wandering in the mountains without the means of subsistence, would have died during the ensuing winter if they had not received timely assistance from the other cantons, from Germany and England, and from the French army itself, after its first fury was abated."— *Simond.*

The attack upon Stanzstad was conducted by General Foy, afterwards so prominent a leader of the liberal party in France. That unfortunate village was totally consumed.

Kerns, a small village 7 m. beyond Stanz, with a tolerable Inn. There is a short cut to Sachselen. A mile and a half beyond Kerns is

Sarnen.—(*Inn :* Schlüssel, very fair; better than Inn at Lungern.) This village, of 3000 Inhab., is the capital of the division of the canton called Obwalden, and the seat of the Government. It is pleasingly situated at the extremity of the lake of Sarnen, at the foot of an eminence called *Landenberg*, a spot memorable in Swiss history as the residence of the cruel Austrian bailiff of that name who put out the eyes of the aged Henry an der Halden, father of one of the heroes of Grütli. This act of atrocity made a deep impression on the popular mind, contributing, with other events, to the outbreak of the Swiss insurrection. On New-year's morning, 1308, 20 peasants of Obwalden repaired to the castle with the customary presents of game, poultry, &c., for the seigneur, who had gone at that hour to mass. Admitted within the walls, they fixed to their staves the pike-heads which they had concealed beneath their dress, blew a blast as a signal to 30 confederates who lay in ambush, under the alders, outside of the gate, and, in conjunction, captured the stronghold almost without resistance. No vestige of the castle now remains: the terrace which occupies its site, and commands a most beautiful view, has since 1646 served for the annual convocations of the citizens of the canton, who meet there to exercise the privilege of electing their magistrates. Adjoining it is the public shooting-house, for the practice of rifle shooting. The upper half of the village was burnt some years ago. The lower half is very old; and there is a bridge across the river nearly 300 years old, constructed, like many of the Swiss bridges, on the modern principle of having the arch above the roadway.

The *Rathhaus*, a plain edifice, not unlike the court-house of an English county town, contains, in its " business-like council chambers," portraits of the landammen from 1381 to 1824. " The artists have been particularly successful in delineating the beards." There is one picture, however, better than the rest, of Nicholas von der Flue, one of the worthies of Switzerland, more particularly respected in this canton, where effigies of him abound. He enjoys the rare reputation of a patriot, and at the same time a peace-maker, having spent his life in allaying the bitterness and dissensions between his countrymen, which, at one time, threatened the destruction of the Helvetian Republic. In the vigour of his years he retired from the world into the remote valley of Melchthal, where he passed his time as a hermit in a humble cell, in exercises of piety. His reputation, however, for wisdom as well as virtue, was so high that the counsellors of the confederacy flocked to him in his solitude to seek advice, and his sudden appearance before the Diet at Stanz and his conciliating counsels prevented the dissolution of the confederacy. After enjoying the respect of

men during his lifetime, he was honoured after his death (1487) as a saint.

[The *Melchthal*, mentioned above, opens out to the E. of Sarnen. At its mouth, close to the chapel of *St. Niklausen*, stands an isolated tower, one of the most ancient buildings in the canton, dating from the earliest Christian times, when it was erected probably as a belfry. Melchthal was the native place of Arnold an der Halden, one of the conspirators of Grütli. (Rte. 18.) While ploughing his field near Schild, he was interrupted by a messenger sent from the bailiff Landenberg to seize his yoke of oxen. Enraged by the insolence of the servant, and the injustice of the demand, Arnold beat the man so as to break his finger; and fearing the tyrant's vengeance fled over the mountains into Uri, little anticipating that his rash act would be visited by the tyrant upon his father, by depriving him of sight.]

The valley of Sarnen, bounded by gently sloping hills, has nothing Alpine in its scenery; its character is quiet, and pastoral, and pleasing. The successful experiment of letting off the waters of the lake of Lungern has led to a similar project of reducing that of Sarnen, which will probably be carried into effect sooner or later.

The road skirting the E. shore of the lake traverses the pretty village of Sachselen (*Inns:* Kreutz, clean and good ; Engel). Within the *Parish Church*, Nicholas von der Flue, the hermit and saint, is interred. His bones lie, but do not repose, in a glass case above the high altar, the shutters of which are opened for travellers, and are also withdrawn at stated seasons in order to be exhibited to the crowds of pilgrims who repair hither to pay their vows to the saint. Within the ribs, where the heart was, there is now a jewelled cross, and from the breast hang several military orders gained by natives of Unterwalden in military service, but offered up to the use of the dead saint, who is known to the peasants by the name of Bruder Klaus. There is a wooden figure in the transept, clothed with the saint's veritable robes. The walls are lined, by devotees, with votive tablets offered to the shrine of St. Nicholas, recording miracles supposed to have been performed by him.

The village *Gyswyl*, on the rt. of the road, was half swept away in 1629 by an inundation of the torrent Lauibach, which brought so much rubbish into the valley as to dam up the waters of the Aa. A lake, thus created, lasted for 130 years, when it was finally let off by an artificial canal into the lake of Sarnen.

[The summit of the *Rothhorn*, celebrated for its view, may be reached in 6 hours from Gyswyl; the path, at least for the first 3 hours, is good; the descent into the valley above Sörenberg is not so good. (See Rte. 25 E.)]

The steep ascent of the *Kaiserstuhl* requires to be surmounted before the road reaches a higher platform in the valley occupied by the *Lake of Lungern*.

This lake was formerly a beautiful sheet of water, embowered in woods sweeping down to its margin, and partly enclosed by steep banks. The dwellers on its shores, less influenced by admiration of its picturesqueness than by the prospect of enriching themselves in the acquisition of 500 acres of good land, previously buried under water, tapped it a few years ago, lowering its surface by about 120 feet, and reducing its dimensions—and thereby its beauty—by nearly one half. The works designed to effect this object were commenced in 1788; but had been repeatedly interrupted by want of funds, and by political commotions. They owe their recent completion to a joint-stock company, consisting of the inhabitants of the district, aided by a skilful engineer, named Sulzberger. The earlier attempts had been limited to the boring of a tunnel through the ridge of the Kaiserstuhl, which, crossing the valley between the lakes of Sarnen and Lungern, forms a natural dam to the waters of the latter. The tunnel begins near Burglen, and is carried in a sloping direction gradually upwards towards the lake. Before Sulzberger took the matter in hand it had made considerable progress; but still the

most difficult part of the task remained, viz., to complete it, and break a passage into the lake without injury to the lower valley, or loss of life to those employed. Having with much labour driven the tunnel as near to the bed of the lake as the excavations could with safety be carried, it became necessary to guard against any sudden irruption. With this object in view, he at first proposed to bore a number of small holes with an auger through the intervening rock, and to close them with cocks to open and shut at pleasure. A boring-rod, 12 feet in length, driven through the rock, was followed by a discharge of mud and water, and a blow, struck with a hammer by the miner from within, reverberated on the surface of the lake so as to be perceived by persons stationed in a boat above the spot—proving that the basin of the lake had been perforated.

The engineer, however, soon discovered that the friable nature of the rock traversed by the rod, and the clay and sand above it, rendered the plan of draining the lake by a number of small perforations impracticable. He was thus compelled to have recourse to a mine, and for this purpose he enlarged the end of the tunnel by driving a shaft or chamber, about 6 feet square, upwards, so as to reach within 6 feet of the water. A cask, containing 950 lbs. of powder, was then conveyed to the end of the shaft, and finally hoisted into this vertical chamber, by propping it upon logs of wood; then, a fusee being attached to it, the end of the tunnel was rammed tight with sand many feet thick, to prevent the mine exploding backwards. Upwards of 500 men, relieving each other day and night, were employed to execute this part of the task, the difficulty of which consisted not merely in the weight to be transported along a passage nowhere more than a foot wider than the cask on any side, but in the foulness of the air inhaled by so many labourers, which soon became so bad as to extinguish all the lights; while the constant influx of water, pouring in through the crannies of the gallery, threw further impediments in the way of the miner. As it was impossible to renew the air by ventilation, it became necessary to withdraw the men for several hours at a time. In addition to all this, a great part of the operations were necessarily performed in the dark.

The length of the tunnel was 1390 feet. Strong flood-gates had been erected at its lower extremity to modify and restrain the issue of the flood. All things being thus prepared, on the morning of January 9, 1836, a cannon-shot, fired from the Kaiserstuhl, answered by another on the Landenberg, gave notice to the whole valley of what was about to happen, and a bold miner, named Spire, was despatched with two companions to fire the train. The length of the match was so regulated as to give them ample time to escape through the tunnel; and their return to daylight was announced by the firing of a pistol. A multitude of spectators had collected on the surrounding hills to witness the result of the experiment which had cost so much time and money to execute, and in which many were so deeply interested—while considerable anxiety prevailed as to its happy result. Expectation was now at the utmost stretch; ten minutes had elapsed beyond the time allotted to the match, and nothing was heard. Some began to fear;—in a minute two dull explosions were heard; but they neither shook the ground above, nor even broke the ice which at that season covered the lake. No one doubted that the mine had failed, when, on a sudden, a joyful shout from below announced its success, as a black torrent of mud and water intermixed was seen by those stationed near the lower end of the tunnel to issue from its mouth. The winter season had been expressly chosen for the consummation of the undertaking, because the waters are then lowest, and many of the tributary torrents are frozen or dried up.

The drainage of the lake of Lungern was effected gradually and safely. In six days the water fell 14 feet, and in ten days more the lake had sunk to a level with the mouth of the tunnel. The lake of Gyswyl, indeed, was filled by the water for a few days, during which it laid several houses under water, but it was soon drained off. On the shores of the lake of Lungern, appearances were at first alarming. The steep banks, deprived on a sudden of the support of the water, began to crack; large masses broke off, and a very considerable fissure appeared near the village of Lungern, which threatened injury to it, so that the church and many of the houses were dismantled and abandoned, and the bells removed from the tower. A piece of ground, several acres in extent, did indeed separate, and slide into the water, just after a house and shed which stood on it had been pulled down and removed. Fortunately this was the extent of the mischief, and church and village are still safe. The uncovered land presented, for some months, only a blank surface of mud and sand, to which the crows resorted in great numbers to feed on the worms and shell-fish left dry in the mud by the receding waters. By the latter end of the year a scanty crop of potatoes was raised on part of it. It is now divided into fields, apparently not very fertile, with a châlet in each, and looks very ugly and like the property of a freehold land society. The aqueous deposits brought down into the lake by tributary brooks, and laid bare by this drainage, will be remarked with interest by the geologist, as illustrating alluvial phenomena and the consequences of changes in the relative level of land and water. Much float-wood was found in the bed of the lake; it had assumed the appearance of brown coal.

The cost of this enterprise was 51,826 f. (5000l.) and 19,000 days' labour performed by the peasants.

Lungern (*Inn:* Löwe, moderate), about 9 m. from Sarnen, the last village in the valley, situated at the foot of the Brünig, and at the S. end of the lake, now removed by the drainage some distance from it. Here the char-road ceases, and the rest of the way must be travelled on foot, or on horses, which are kept here for hire. Return horses from Brienz or Meyringen may sometimes be found here.

From Lungern to Meyringen takes the horses about 3 hrs., to Brienz 3½. Though there is nothing very grand or striking, it is an exceedingly pretty pass, and may be achieved by those who do not wish to attempt anything fatiguing. The first part of the road is very steep, and over large blocks of stone like high steps. It is however very pretty, passing through a forest of pines growing amongst the rocks. The road is so narrow in some parts that the guide can scarcely walk by the side of the horse: a rail protects the path. [There is a short cut for pedestrians to Brienz.] The horse-path now passes through an elevated valley or passage, about 1½ m. long, which brings you to the col, ending in an abrupt descent into the vale of Hasli.

The culminating point of the pass of the Brünig is 3668 ft. above the sea-level. From a little chapel near the frontier of Canton Berne, a charming and first-rate view is obtained along the entire valley of Nidwalden, backed by the Pilatus, with the Lungern See for a foreground, forming altogether one of the most delicious scenes in Switzerland. From the brow, the valley of Hasli, with the Aar winding through the midst, opens out to the view of the traveller, backed by the gigantic and snow-white crests of the Wetterhorn, Eiger, and others of the Bernese Alps, and in front of them the Faulhorn. Close to a small tavern, formerly a toll-house, from which there is a fine view, the road divides: the branch on the rt. leads to the lake of Brienz; the other to Meyringen, seated in the midst of the rich flat which forms the bottom of the valley. From the opposite precipices two or three streaks of white may be discerned: these are the Falls of the Reichenbach, and at their foot are the Hotel and Baths. 1½ hr. will now take the traveller down to

Meyringen (Rte. 25); and 1 hr. will take him down the steep descent to the bridge on the road from Brienz to Meyringen, whence it is about 3 m. over a dull flat road to

Brienz. (Rte. 25 E.)

ROUTE 22.

LUCERNE TO BERNE [OR THUN], BY THE ENTLEBUCH AND THE EMMENTHAL.

Post road. 6⅜ posts = 57 Eng. m.

	Posts.	Eng. m.
Schachen . . .	1¼	= 10
Escholzmatt . .	2	= 18
Hochstetten . .	2	= 18
Berne	1¼	= 11

This is the best and shortest of the two *carriage*-roads to Berne, and may still be adopted by pedestrians, or by those who wish to see two of the finest pastoral valleys in Switzerland. A Rly. is projected. After a short detour the road enters a narrow valley, and follows the course of the stream past Krienz, where there are some iron-works, and then falls into the valley of the *Kleine Emme*, which it follows.

Schachen, a little beyond which the Free Corps were defeated in 1845 by the men of Lucerne.

From Schachen there is a road over the *Bramegg* pass, commanding a fine view, and falling into the main road at Entlebuch, but by the main road it takes about 4 hours from Lucerne to reach the village of

Entlebuch, at the W. foot of the Bramegg (*Inns* : H. du Port, Drei Könige), prettily situated on a slope, with the torrents Entle and Emme roaring beneath it.

From Entlebuch is a road formerly a char-road, not marked in the maps, to Alpnach (Rte. 21) by the side of the Schlierenberg.

The vale of Entlebuch is about 30 m. long, and is flanked by mountains covered with woods and pastures. The men of the valley are celebrated as the best wrestlers in Switzerland. They hold 4 or 5 great wrestling-matches, called Zwing Feste, between the months of June and Oct.; the chief on the first Sunday in Sept., when they try their skill against the athletes of the neighbouring valleys. The Bernese highlanders are formidable rivals. The Entlebuchers have been long renowned for their courage and independence. In 1405 Lucerne bought this valley from Austria, and bought up the feudal rights of the nobles over it, substituting a Lucerne bailli.

Escholzmatt (*Inns*: Krone;—Löwe —good) is a scattered village, in a very high situation. A little way beyond it the road quits the Entlebuch, and descends, by the side of the Ilfis torrent, into the canton of Berne.

Langnau (*Inns*: Cerf, quiet and good; H. zum Emmenthal, clean) is the principal place in the *Emmenthal* —an extensive, fertile, and industrious valley, famed for its cheeses (made on the high pastures near the tops of the hills, and exported all over Germany), and for its manufactures of linen. Its meadows are of the brightest verdure; the cottages neat and substantial, with pretty gardens before them. The Emme, which traverses it, and its tributaries, at times commit serious devastations, by inundating their banks and overspreading them with gravel and débris. Such an occurrence in August, 1837, occasioned by a thunderstorm, created serious injury, destroying many houses and almost all the bridges: several lives were lost.

It is not necessary to pass through Langnau, and ½ a mile is saved by leaving it on the rt. The Ilfis is crossed, and afterwards the Emme, before reaching *Signau*—(*Inn*: Ours, tolerable) — a pretty village, with a ruined castle above it.

[About 2 m. farther, the road to Thun (4½ leagues from Hochstetten) turns off on the l., and shortly falls into the high road from Berne to Thun (Rte. 25), by the Château of Niessen, 4 leagues from Berne.]

The road to Berne proceeds by *Gross Hochstetten*, and *Worb*, an industrious village, with a Gothic castle above it.

BERNE (in Rte. 24).

ROUTE 24.

LUCERNE TO BERNE, BY RAILWAY.

This is now the quickest mode of reaching Berne from Lucerne, and takes about 5 hrs.

Lucerne to Olten. (See Rte. 4.)

Olten to Berne. (See Rte. 5.)

BERNE. — *Inns:* Falke (Faucon), obliging landlord. Charges—breakfast, 1½ fr.; tea, do.; beds, 2½ fr. Couronne — clean and comfortable, the landlord has also a separate *private* lodging-house facing the river. These are both first-rate inns, and equally good—tables-d'hôte at 1, 3 fr.; at 5, 4 fr. H. des Boulangers (Pfistern), new, 1851. The *Abbayes*, or houses of the guilds, such as the Distelzwang,* or Abbaye aux Gentilshommes, and the Abbaye du Singe, afford comfortable, quiet, and moderate accommodation to travellers. A large hotel is building (1857) near the new Federal Palace.

Berne, capital of the largest of the Swiss cantons (Pop. 450,000, nearly all Protestants), and, since 1849, permanent seat of the Swiss Government and Diet, and residence of most of the foreign ministers, contains 27,475 Inhab. It was founded in 1191 by Duke Berchthold V. of Zähringen, and was so called by him because he had killed a bear on the spot, and both he and

---

* *Zwang*, a local word for guild: Distel, thistle, the emblem of the gentlemen who held their meetings or club under this sign.

the bear are still held in great respect. It joined the Swiss confederation in 1353, having been for many years an ally. Until 1798 it held Argau, Vaud, and other districts, as tributaries, and is reported to have governed them tyrannically. The government latterly fell into the hands of a small number of aristocratic families, who lost their power in 1798, partly recovered it in 1814, and lost it again in 1831. The history of Berne, which is very curious, is well related in the Hist. of Sw. published by the U. K. S. It may be mentioned that a Von Erlach led the Swiss to the battle of Laupen in 1339, and a Von Erlach led them against the French in 1798. Until 1848 the Swiss government was carried on by Berne, Zürich, and Lucerne alternately, the governing canton for the year being called the Vorort.

Berne is built on a lofty sandstone promontory, formed by the winding course of the Aar, which nearly surrounds it, flowing at the bottom of a deep gully, with steep and in places precipitous sides (stalden). The inconvenient ascent and descent by which the town could alone be reached from the E. formerly, has been remedied by a lofty *Bridge* (Pont de la Wydeck), partly of granite, derived from erratic blocks lying on the Kirchet hill, thrown over this gully. It is 900 ft. long, and the central arch over the Aar 150 ft. wide and 93 ft. high (a small toll is paid). The distant aspect of the town, planted on this elevated platform, 1700 ft. above the sea, is imposing; and there is something striking in its interior, from the houses all being built of massive stone. It has this peculiarity, that almost all the houses rest upon arcades (Lauben), which furnish covered walks on each side of the streets, and are lined with shops and stalls, like " the Rows " in the city of Chester. The lowness of the arches, however, and the solidity of the buttresses supporting them, render these colonnades gloomy and close. The chief street of shops and business runs through the town, along the top of the ridge. Overhanging the Aar, and removed from the main streets, are the more aristocratic residences of the exclusive patricians, and look really like "gentlemen's houses"—a rare thing in a continental town.

Rills of water are carried through the streets to purify them, and they are abundantly furnished with *Fountains*, each surmounted by some quaint effigy. One of these, the *Kinderfresser-Brunnen* (Ogre's-fountain), on the Corn-house-square, receives its name from a figure (probably Saturn) devouring a child, with others stuck in his girdles and pockets ready for consumption. Some bear the figures of armed warriors, such as David: another is surmounted by a female figure; but the favourite device is *the Bear*. Thus, the upper fountain in the principal street is surmounted by a bear in armour, with breast-plate, thigh-pieces, and helmet, a sword at his side, and a banner in his paw. The *Schützen Brunnen* is the figure of a Swiss cross-bowman of former days, attended by a young *bear* as squire; and two stone *bears*, larger than life, stand as sentinels on either side of the Morat gate.

Along the line of the principal street, which extends from the Bridge to the Murten-Thor, are three antique watch-towers. The *Clock-tower* (Zeitglochenthurm) stands nearly in the centre of the town, though, when originally built, in 1191, by Berchtold V., of Zähringen, it guarded the outer wall. Its droll clockwork puppets are objects of wonder to an admiring crowd of gaping idlers. A minute before the hour strikes, first a wooden cock appears, crows twice, and flaps his wings; and while a puppet strikes the hour on a bell, a procession of bears issues out, and passes in front of a figure on a throne, who marks the hour by gaping and by lowering his sceptre. Further on in the street stands the *Käficht Thurm* (cage tower), now used as a prison; and beyond it *Christopher's tower*, also called Goliath's, from the figure of a giant upon it. Projects are entertained of pulling down these curious towers, in order to widen the street.

The great charm of Berne is the view of the Bernese Alps, which the town and every eminence in its neighbourhood command in clear weather From the *Platform*, a lofty terrace, planted with shady rows of trees, overlooking the Aar, behind the Minster, six snowy peaks of the great chain are visible, and from the Enghe terrace, outside of the town, at least a dozen rise into view; they appear in the following order, beginning from the E.:—1. Wetterhorn; 2. Schreckhorn; 3. Finster-Aarhorn; 4. Eigher; 5. Mönch; 6. Jungfrau; 8. Gletscherhorn; 9. Mittaghorn; 10. Blumlis Alp; 11. In the middle distance, Niessen; 12. Stockhorn. (See Woodcut.)

There cannot be a more sublime sight than this view at sunset; especially at times when, from a peculiar state of the atmosphere, the slanting rays are reflected from the Alpine snows in hues of glowing pink. It is hardly possible to gaze on these Alps and glaciers without desiring to explore their recesses, which enclose some of the most magnificent scenery in Switzerland. The *Platform* itself, supported by a massive wall of masonry, rises 108 ft. above the Aar; yet an inscription on the parapet records that a young student, mounted on a spirited horse, which had been frightened by some children, and leaped the precipice, reached the bottom with no other hurt than a few broken ribs. The horse was killed on the spot. The rider became minister of Kerzerz, and lived to a good old age!

The *Minster*, a very beautiful Gothic building, was begun in 1421, and finished 1457, possibly from the designs of Erwin of Steinbach, who built Strasburg Minster, or one of his family; and many of the ornaments, such as the open parapet running round the roof, and varying in pattern between each buttress, are not inferior in design or execution to those of Strasburg. The chief ornament is the great W. *portal*, bearing sculptured reliefs of the Last Judgment, flanked by figures of the wise and foolish Virgins, &c. (date, 1475-85). The interior is not remarkable ; but the *Organ*

is new, and one of the lions of Berne fine, and is played on daily. In th windows, and on the roof, are the coat of arms of the aristocratic burgher of Berne. 4 tall windows of painte glass in the choir deserve notice some of them are very curious fro their grotesqueness (date, end of 15 century), *e. g.* the Pope grinding t 4 Evangelists in a mill, whence iss a number of wafers which a bish collects in a chalice. The stalls the choir are well carved with figur of the Apostles on one side, and pr phets on the other. Along the wa are tablets, bearing the names of officers and 683 soldiers, citizens Berne, who fell fighting against t French, 1798. There is also a mon ment erected by the town, in 166 and restored in 1847, to Bercht of Zähringen, founder of Berne. the vestry are rich tapestry and ve ments, part of the spoil taken fr Charles the Bold at Morat.

On the Münster Platz, opposite t W. door of the cathedral, has be erected *a bronze Monumental Statue* Rudolph v. Erlach, the conqueror Laupen, with 4 bears at the corners.

The *Museum* contains one of th best collections of the natural pr ductions of Switzerland to be fou in the country. It is open to t public 3 times a week : strangers m obtain admittance at all times by small fee.

In the zoological department ther are stuffed specimens of the bear all ages. Two young cubs, about th size of kittens, respectively 8 and 2 days old—hideous and uncouth mon sters—enable one easily to discove the origin of the vulgar error that th bear was licked into shape by it mother. The lynx of the Alps, and the steinbock, both from the Bernese chain, are interesting from their rarity; these animals have nearly disappeared from Europe. Here is deservedly preserved the skin of *Barry*, one of the dogs of St. Bernard, who is recorded to have saved the lives of 15 human beings by his sagacity. A chamois with three horns, one growing out o the nose ; a specimen of a cross breed

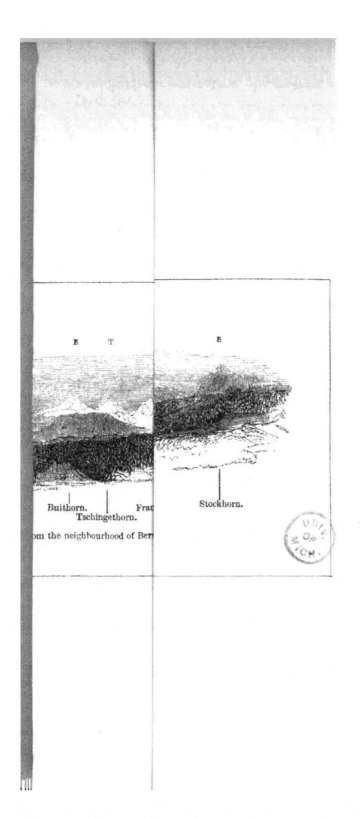

Buithorn.   Frat

        Tschingethorn.   Stockhorn.

om the neighbourhood of Ber

between the steinbock and domestic goat, which lived 7 years; a wild boar, of gigantic size and bristling mien, are also worth notice.

In the *Ornithological* department are the lämmergeyer (vulture of lambs), the feathered monarch of the Alps, and inferior in size to the condor alone among birds. It breeds only on the highest mountains.

In addition to the native birds of Switzerland, there are specimens of several foreign and tropical birds which have found their way into Switzerland by accident ; viz., a flamingo, killed near the lake of Morat, and a pelican from Constance. Possibly the flamingo came from the waters of the district around Nismes and Arles, where these birds are not uncommon.

The departments of geology and mineralogy are very rich. The geology of Switzerland may be well studied in the very complete series of fossils collected by *M. Studer* and others. There are a number of beautiful specimens of all the rarest and finest minerals from St. Gothard. The illustration of Swiss *Botany* is equally complete.

Several plans in relief of various parts of Switzerland will prove equally instructive to the student of geography and geology.

In a small collection of *Antiquities* the following objects seem to deserve mentioning:—some Roman antiquities dug up in Switzerland ; the Prie Dieu of Charles the Bold, and part of his tent hangings, captured by the Bernese at Grandson ; the pointed shoes worn by the Bernese nobles in the 16th century ; some dresses, &c. from the South Sea Islands, brought over by Weber, the artist, who accompanied the expedition, who was of Swiss origin.

The *Town Library* is a good collection of 40,000 volumes, and is well stored with Swiss history. Haller, who was born at Berne, was librarian. The butter-market is held beneath this building.

The *Arsenal* has scarcely any curiosities to show since it was robbed by the French in 1798 ; the arms for the contingent of the canton are kept in it.

The new *Bundes-Rathhaus* or *Palast*, built 1854, near the Museum and Casino Terrace, by far the largest and handsomest building in the town, includes all the departments of the Swiss Legislature, the Diet, and the various Public Offices. The Diet (*Bundesversammlung*) consists of 2 bodies, the *Stände-rath* (44 Deputies of the Cantons) and National-rath.

Berne is celebrated for the number and excellence of its Charitable Institutions: they are, perhaps, more carefully attended to than any in Europe. There is a public granary in case of scarcity, two orphan-houses, an Infirmary, and an extensive *Hospital*, bearing the inscription "Christo in pauperibus." It was for a long time the finest, indeed the only grand building in the town, a just subject of pride ; but it has of late been eclipsed by the colossal dimensions of the new Prison and Penitentiary, a circumstance characteristic of the present period perhaps in other countries besides the canton Berne. *English Church service* is performed twice a day on Sunday, in the chapel of the Burger Spital.

Since 1834 an *University* or high school has been established at Berne.

The *bear* forms the armorial badge of the town, the word "bern" signifying "bear" in old German, and he is as great a favourite here as in the house of Bradwardine. Not only is his effigy on sign-posts, fountains, and buildings, but for several hundred years living specimens of the favourite were maintained by the town, until the French revolutionary army took possession of Berne, 1798, and the bears were led away captives, and deposited in the Jardin des Plantes, where one of them, the celebrated Martin, soon became the favourite of the French metropolis. But when the ancient order of things was restored at Berne, one of the first cares of the citizens was to replace and provide for their ancient pensioners. There is a foundation for the support of the bears, who, after having been reduced to one miserable animal, have lately been renovated, and have been removed from the Aarberg Gate to near the new bridge. No traveller will quit Berne without paying them a visit, unless he wishes to have the omission of so important a sight thrown in his teeth whenever Berne is mentioned.

The fortifications of the town, no longer of use as defences, are converted into *Promenades*, and make very agreeable walks. The banks of the Aar, which they overlook, are most picturesque ; and the Alps, when visible, form a background of the utmost sublimity.

They, however, as well as the city of Berne itself, are best seen from a terrace walk called the *Enghe*, a little more than a mile outside the Aarburg Gate, the favourite resort of the citizens. N.B. Good coffee and *krimpel kuchen*. On the way to it, beyond the gate, is the *Shooting-house*, where rifle-matches take place.

Two other more distant and elevated points, which are most advantageous for commanding the panorama of the Alps, are the hill of *Altenberg*, ½ hr.'s walk on the N. of the town, reached by a footbridge across the Aar ; and the *Gurten*, a height an hour's walk to the S. of the town.

The *Casino*, a handsome building in the Ober-Graben, contains a reading-room, supplied with newspapers, a ball-room, &c. There is also a *Theatre* in the town.

Dalp, Fisher, & Co. are the principal booksellers, and keep a good supply of maps, views, and costumes, &c., of Switzerland.

Jacob König, near the Clock-tower, is an excellent watchmaker.

Passports.—The Foreign ministers to the Swiss Confederation reside at Berne, and here visas for France can be procured.

The traveller pressed for time, and wishing to avoid delay, may leave his passport with the master of the inn, to be forwarded to him by post. The English and Austrian ministers sign passports only early in the morning, from 10 to 11 or 12. The Austrian signature, *indispensable* for the travel-

ler who would enter Italy, if not obtained here, can only be got at Turin or Stuttgart, the nearest capitals where Austrian ministers reside.

Hindelbank, which is sometimes visited, on account of the tomb of Madame Langhans, is described in Rte. 5.

ROUTE 25.

THE BERNESE OBERLAND.

A. BERNE TO THUN AND INTERLAKEN.
B. INTERLAKEN TO LAUTERBRUNNEN.
C. LAUTERBRUNNEN TO GRINDELWALD —WENGERN ALP—FAULHORN.
D. GRINDELWALD TO MEYRINGEN — GREAT SCHEIDECK.
E. MEYRINGEN TO BRIENZ AND THUN— GIESBACH.

	Eng. m.
Thun, 2 posts charged . .	16¼
Interlaken (by land), 2 posts charged	15
Lauterbrunnen	7
Grindelwald, by the Wengern Alp	
Meyringen, by Scheideck .	
Brientz	8
Interlaken (by water) . .	10
Thun (by water). . .	11

This agreeable excursion may be made in 4 days, 1st to Interlaken, 2nd to Grindelwald by Lauterbrunnen, 3rd to Meyringen, 4th back to Berne ; or, if 3 days only can be given, 1st to Lauterbrunnen, 2nd to Rosenlaui, 3rd to Meyringen, and so back. Most persons, however, will feel disposed to devote longer time to it. But it is by no means necessary to return to Berne: the passes of the Gemmi (R. 38), of the Brünig (R. 19), and of the Grimsel (R. 28), connect the Oberland with the general tour of Switzerland.

It was in this magnificent highland

district that Byron " repeopled his mind from nature," and gathered many of the ideas and images which he has so exquisitely interwoven in his tragedy of Manfred, the scene of which lies among the Bernese Alps. He preferred many of the scenes among these mountains and lakes to Chamouni, and calls them " some of the noblest views in the world."

There is a regular tariff of prices for carriages, as appended to the Swiss Indicateur. One-horse carriage, 10 fr. a-day; 2 horses, 20, bonnemain not included; horse and boy, 11 fr.; more than 1 horse. 10 fr. each.

A. *Berne to Thun.*

A 3 hours' drive. Rly. in progress. Diligence 4 or 5 times a day, 2fr. 75c. Passengers can book through to Interlaken or to Brienz. A voiturier charges 18 fr. and drinkmoney (no back fare); a return voiturier 10 or 12 fr. [It is said that the voyage from Thun to Berne by the market-boats is very pleasant.]

The road is excellent, and in fine weather the snowy Alps are in sight nearly the whole way. The scenery of the valley of the Aar is very pleasing; laid out in pasture lands, with abundance of villages, and substantial farm-houses, with broad roofs, surrounded by neat gardens. The river itself runs at some distance on the rt., and is rarely visible. The principal village passed on the way is *Münsingen*, memorable in recent Swiss annals as the spot where the great public meetings of the men of the canton were held in 1831 and in 1849, which adopted new constitutions, and overthrew the rule of the oligarchy.

The *Stockhorn*, with its conical peak, and the *Niesen*, two limestone mountains, forming, as it were, the advanced guard of the high Alps, posted on the opposite side of the lake, become conspicuous objects before reaching

Thun, Fr. *Thoune* — *Inns :* H. de Bellevue, outside the town—well situated in a garden commanding a view of the Aar—belongs to MM. Knechten-

hofer, who are also proprietors of the steamboat, rather dear ;—Hôtel and Pension Baumgarten; clean and pleasant, in a nice garden; rather dear;—Freyenhof, within the town, very good, frequented by Swiss officers;—Faucon ;—Kreuz.

There is not a more picturesque town in Switzerland than Thun, 3800 Inhab. ; situated about a mile from the lake, upon the river Aar, which here rushes out of it as clear as crystal. Pre-eminent above the other buildings rise a venerable church and a picturesque feudal castle of the Counts of Kyburg (1429), almost grotesque in its antiquity. The town seems to have been of great importance formerly, and in the 14th centy. reckoned 70 noble families within its dominions. It is a very curious old town, but contains within its walls no particular object especially worthy of notice. It is also, from its position and its beautiful environs, one of the most agreeable places of residence in Switzerland, and, being the starting-place for those who visit the Bernese highlands, it is thronged with a constant succession of travellers through the whole summer.

Here is the *Military College* of the Swiss Confederation, for educating officers, and the principal cavalry barracks of the country. Reviews take place every summer in the vicinity.

The *Castle of Schadau* is a large and singular Gothic castle, built (1850) by M. Rougemont, of Paris, between the Aar and the lake.

The view from the *Churchyard terrace* " along the lake, with its girdle of Alps (the Blumlis Alp being the most conspicuous), fine glaciers, and rocks wooded to the top," is mentioned by Byron. A more extensive prospect is gained from the grounds of a pretty country house, called the *Chartreuse*, about ¼ mile above the Hôtel Bellevue. The Jungfrau, Mönch, and Eigher are visible from hence. The *Churchyard of Æschi*, about 6 m. from Thun, on the S. side of the lake, is a charming excursion, easily made and without fatigue (see Rte. 38).

M. Knechtenhofer has built a *chapel for the English service* in the grounds of his hotel.

Wald, opposite H. Bellevue, has a good stock of wood carving.

Vehicles of various kinds and guides may be hired at Thun. Travellers often send their carriages from Thun to Lucerne while they make a tour in the Oberland, beginning and ending with those places. The innkeeper will make the arrangement, and consign the carriage to the inn which the traveller may designate. Baggage may be safely left in it. The charge for a light carriage is 72 fr., everything included. Probably 1 fr. a-day will be charged for the standing of the carriage as long as it remains at the inn.

Lake of Thun—Thun to Interlaken.— Steamboats ply between Thun and Neuhaus twice a day to and fro. The voyage takes up 1¼ hr. Fare 2 fr.

The steamer does not take carriages; but a good carriage-road runs to Interlaken (2 posts), along the S. shore of the lake. The distance, about 15 Eng. m.

The lake is about 10 m. long.; 1775 ft. above the level of the sea.

The banks of the lake near Thun are occupied with neat villas and cheerful gardens ; further on, its N. shore is precipitous, and not very interesting. Among its scanty villages and hamlets, the most important is Oberhofen, distinguished by the square tower of its castle.

The S. shore is more striking. Here the two remarkable mountains, the *Stockhorn*, with a sharp peak projecting like a horn, or thorn, and the pyramidal mass of the *Niesen*, with its conical top, stand sentinels at the entrance of the Kander and Simmenthal. The river Kander, conducted into the lake by an artificial channel formed for it in 1714, has deposited around its mouth, within less than a century and a half, a delta or sand-bank of several hundred acres. The progress and extent of this recent formation, so interesting to geologists, have been ably investigated by Sir C. Lyell.

S. At the foot of the Niesen, on a projecting tongue of land, stands the picturesque castle of *Spietz*, founded according to tradition, by Attila (?) and belonging to the family of E lach. At Spietzwyler there is a nea *Inn.*

N. When about two-thirds over th lake, a projecting promontory of pre cipitous rock, called the *Nase*, passed, and a fine view is obtained the Eigher and Mönch, which fill the extremity of the lake with t white mass of their snow. To t rt. of them appear the Jungfrau a Finster Aarhorn.

In front of the Nase the lake 720 ft. deep. N. Behind the vill Merligen runs the *Justis Thal :* distance of between 2 and 2½ h. up it, in the ridge forming its boundary, is a cave called *Scha* which in the height of summer alw contains *ice.* Such ice caverns are uncommon in the Jura, and in ot parts of the world. This cave ha branches ; that in which the ice occ runs straight from the entrance about 60 ft., when it suddenly narro and dips down 12 or 15 ft.

N. Farther on, in the face of mountain overhanging the lake, is *Cave of St. Beatus*, above a small cade, which may be seen leaping the lake. St. Beatus, according to dition a native of Britain, conve the inhabitants of this part of Helv to Christianity. Being minded to up his residence on the shore the lake, he fixed his eyes up grot well suited to a hermit's ab which happened at the time to occupied by a dragon. The mon however, was easily ejected wit force, and simply by hearing a n to quit addressed to him by St. Be Among the miracles performed b anchorite, in addition to the ab must be mentioned that of his cros the lake on his cloak, which, spread out on the water, served instead of a boat. A rivulet is out of the cave, and is subject sudden rises, which fill the cave the roof, and are accompanied loud report, like that of a cannon.

may be reached in a quarter of an hour from the shore.

At *Neuhaus* a group of houses and cabarets at the end of the lake, about 10 m. from Thun, and about 2½ m. from Interlaken, the passengers are landed. A long array of carriages, porters, guides, and horses, will be found awaiting their disembarkation: also a diligence which runs to Interlaken; fare 1 fr. One-horse char, 2 frs.; two-horse, 3 frs.

Unterseen, a dilapidated Swiss village of 1000 Inhab., composed (except the *Castle* on the market-place, and *Rathhaus*) of wooden houses, many of them brown from age, being two centuries old. It suffered from an inundation Aug. 1851, which swept away its bridge and some of its houses, and the landlord of H. des Alpes was drowned at the same time. It is situated about half way between the lakes of Thun and Brienz, whence its name, and that of Interlaken, both signifying "between the lakes." There are several pensions here, where the charge is 4 to 5 fr. a day (Beausite, tolerable); but they are not so good as those of Interlaken; they are chiefly resorted to by Germans and Swiss, and the hours are more primitive, dinner being served at 1.

The manufactory of *Parquet floorings* of MM. Seiler is worth a visit.

*** Travellers having made up their minds at which house they will put up, in Interlaken, should insist on being driven to it, and not be deterred by being told that "it is full" —a common trick with persons interested in other houses.

Interlaken. Inns: H. des Alpes (Madame Hoffstetters), both hotel and pension, the largest establishment here ; H. Belvedere ; Schweizer Hof, new, 1856 ; Hotel d'Interlaken ; H. de la Jungfrau (Seiler père; charge 5 fr. a-day, with wine), recommended. There are at least a dozen pensions or boarding-houses here, where travellers are received for one day, paying as an hotel, or for a stay of 5 or even 8 days en pension, at lower charges, varying between 5 and 6 fr. a-day,

exclusive of wine, for boarding and lodging. The principal pensions are Strübe's, late Müller's;—the Casino affords as good accommodation as any in the place. At most of these houses there is a daily table-d'hôte, and during the season balls are now and then given at one or other. Pension Ober, very comfortable. Pension Ritschard, quiet and comfortable.

Interlaken has few sights or lions for the tourist or passing traveller, who need not stop here, unless he require to rest himself. Its beautiful position, however, on a little plain between the lakes, in full view of the Jungfrau, whose snowy summit is seen through a gap in the minor chain of Alps, its vicinity to numerous interesting sites, and some of the most pleasing excursions in Switzerland, together with its cheapness as a place of residence, have spread its reputation through Europe, and have converted it into an English colony, a sort of Swiss Harrowgate, two-thirds of the summer visitors being, on a moderate computation, of our nation. The village itself, a collection of whitewashed lodging-houses, with trim green blinds, has nothing Swiss in its character. Still, however, though no longer a place of retirement, Interlaken must not be disparaged; its almost endless walks and rides, its boating parties on the two lakes, its picnics and balls, would, in the society of friends, afford amusement for a season. In front of the lodging-houses runs a magnificent *Avenue of huge Walnut-trees*, most inviting from its cool shade. The wooded slopes of the *Harder*, a hill on the opposite bank of the Aar, are rendered accessible by easy paths, commanding a delightful view. Beware of the slippery and really dangerous grass along the ridge : an English lady perished here in 1850. The old *Castle of Unspunnen* is within an easy walk even for ladies ; while the Giesbach falls, Lauterbrunnen, with the Staubbach, and Grindelwald with its glaciers, are within a short morning's row or ride. The top of the Wengern Alp may be reached from this in 5 hrs., and the Faulhorn in 6 hrs. The Morgenberg, sometimes called Gumi-horn (7400 ft.), is said to be easy of ascent, and to command a fine view. Most of the surrounding mountains will repay an ascent. The streams usually terminate in small glaciers, not seen from the valley. They are described in the following tour of the Oberland. The view from the churchyard of *Aeschi*, on the S. shore of the lake of Thun, forms a deserving object of a day's excursion. You leave the carriage-road to Thun at Leissigen, and take a footpath on the l. along a narrow lane for about 5 m. The carriage may wait at Spietz. (See Rte. 38.) At *Urfer's* Subscription *Reading-room* and Library 'The Times,' 'Galignani,' "Débats,' &c., are taken in.

The *English Church Service* is performed every Sunday twice in the Old church by an English clergyman, for whom a small stipend is formed by voluntary contributions among his countrymen.

Dr. Mani, physician, speaks English, and keeps an *English dispensary.* His *goat's whey* establishment is much resorted to by invalids.

Mountain-ponies may be hired at Interlaken at 11 fr. a-day, bonnemain included. *The Guides* abound, and are paid by tariff, at the rate of 6 frs. per diem, but expect 1 fr. bonnemain. Instances of gross misconduct are very rare; but there is no remedy except an appeal to a magistrate, who usually seems to consider the tourist fair game.

B. *Interlaken to Lauterbrunnen,*

About 2 hours' walk—a drive of 1¼ h. Carriage there and back, one horse, 8 fr.; two horses, 15 fr. After passing a tract of verdant meadow-land, on which great wrestling-matches (one of which has been described by Madame de Staël) are periodically held, the road passes on the rt. the *Castle of Unspunnen:* it is in a very dilapidated state, but a square tower, with a flanking round turret, rise picturesquely above the brushwood surrounding them. It is the reputed residence of Manfred,

and its position in front of the high Alps renders it not unlikely that Byron may have had it in his eye. The real owners of the castle were the barons of Unspunnen, a noble and ancient race, who were lords of the whole Oberland, from the Grimsel to the Gemmi. Burkard, the last male descendant of this family, had a beautiful and only daughter, Ida, who was beloved by a young knight attached to the Court of Berchtold of Zähringen, between whom and Burkard a deadly feud had long subsisted. Under such circumstances the youthful Rudolph of Wadenswyl, despairing of obtaining the father's consent to their union, scaled the castle-walls by night, carried Ida off, and made her his bride. Many years of bloody strife between the two parties followed this event. At length Rudolph, taking his infant son by Ida along with him, presented himself, unarmed and without attendants, to Burkard, in the midst of his stronghold. Such an appeal to the old man's affections and generosity was irresistible; he melted into tears, forgot his wrongs, and, receiving his children into his bosom, made Rudolph's son the heir of his vast possessions. At the time of the reconciliation, the old baron had said, "Let this day be for ever celebrated among us;" and rural games were in consequence, for many years, held on the spot. These were revived in 1805 and 1808, and consisted of gymnastic exercises, wrestling, pitching the stone, &c., in which the natives of the different cantons contended with one another, while spectators from far and near collected on a natural amphitheatre. A huge fragment of rock, weighing 184 lbs., which was hurled 10 ft. by an athlete from Appenzell, may still be seen half buried in the ground.

Leaving behind the villages of Wylderswyl and Mühlinen, whose inhabitants are sadly afflicted with goître (§ 18), the road plunges into the narrow and savage gorge of the torrent *Lütschine*. Not far up, the road passes a spot of evil repute as the scene of a fratricide—"just the place for such a deed." It was marked by an inscription in the face of a projecting rock, called, from the murder, the Evil Stone (Böse Stein), or Brother's Stone. The encroachments of the river upon the road rendered it necessary to blast a portion of the rock in order to widen the carriageway, in doing which the inscription has been displaced. The murderer, according to the story, was lord of the Castle of Rothenflue, which stood on the opposite side of the valley. Stung with remorse, he fled away from the sight of man, wandered an outcast among the wilds like Cain, and perished miserably.

At the hamlet of Zweilütschinen, about two miles from the entrance of the valley, it divides into two branches: that on the l., from which flows the Black Lütschine, is the valley of Grindelwald, terminated by the gigantic mass and everlasting snows of the Wetterhorn (Rte. 25 D); that of the rt., traversed by the White Lütschine, is the valley of the Lauterbrunnen, and it ought to be visited first.

The valley of Lauterbrunnen is remarkable for its depth, its contracted width, and for the precipices of limestone, nearly vertical, which enclose it like walls. Its name, literally translated, means "nothing but fountains;" and is derived, no doubt, from the number of streamlets which cast themselves headlong from the brows of the cliffs into the valley below, looking at a distance like so many pendulous white threads.

The road to Grindelwald crosses the Lütschine: that to Lauterbrunnen passes under the base of a colossal precipice, called Hunnenflue, whose face displays singular contortions in the limestone strata. If the clouds permit, the summit of the Jungfrau now bursts into sight; and soon after, surmounting a steep slope, we reach

Lauterbrunnen. Inn: Capricorn (Steinbock) ; 20 horses are kept here. This village contains about 1350 Inhab., dwelling in rustic houses, scattered widely apart, along both banks of the torrent. It lies 2450 ft.

above the sea, so sunk between precipices that, in summer, the sun does not appear till 7 o'clock, and in winter not before 12. Only the hardier species of grain grow here, and the climate is almost too rough for pears and apples. About 30 shoots of water dangle from the edge of the ramparts which form the sides of the valley; and, when their tops are enveloped in clouds, appear to burst at once from the sky: many of them are dried up in summer. These minor falls, however, are all eclipsed by that of the *Staubbach,* distant about ½ a mile from the inn. It is one of the loftiest falls in Europe, measuring between 800 and 900 feet in height; and from this cause, and from the comparatively small body of water forming it, it is shivered by the wind into spray like dust long before it reaches the bottom (whence its name—literally, *Dust*-stream).

Strangers, who expect in the Staubbach the rushing and roaring rapidity of a cataract, will here be disappointed; but, in the opinion of many, this want is atoned for by other beauties peculiar to this fall. The friction of the rock, and the resistance of the air, retard the descent of the water, giving it, when seen in front, the appearance of a beautiful lace veil suspended from the precipice, and imitating, in its centre, the folds of the drapery. When very full, it shoots out from the rock, and is bent by the wind into flickering undulations. Byron has described it admirably, both in prose and verse:—

"The torrent is in shape, curving over the rock, like the *tail* of a white horse streaming in the wind—such as it might be conceived would be that of the 'pale horse' on which Death is mounted in the Apocalypse. It is neither mist nor water, but a something between both : its immense height gives it a wave or curve—a spreading here or condension there —wonderful and indescribable."— *Journal.*

"It is not noon—the sunbow's rays still arch
The torrent with the many hues of heaven,
And roll the sheeted silver's waving column
O'er the crags headlong perpendicular,

E 2

And fling its lines of foaming light along,
And to and fro, like the pale courser's tail,
The giant steed to be bestrode by Death,
As told in the Apocalypse."   *Manfred.*

The Staubbach is seen to perfection before noon, when the iris formed by the sun falling full upon it, "like a rainbow come down to pay a visit—moving as you move," and the shadow of the water on the face of the rock, give an additional interest. At other times it is as well seen from the inn as from the nearest point which can be reached without becoming drenched with spray. Wordsworth has called it " a sky-born waterfall;" and when the clouds are low and rest on the sides of the valley, it literally appears to leap from the sky. In winter, when the torrent is nearly arrested by the frost, a vast pyramid of ice is formed by the dripping of the water from above, increasing gradually upwards in the manner of a stalagmite, until the colossal icicle reaches nearly half way up the precipice. There is a smaller upper-fall above the one seen from Lauterbrunnen. A footpath leads up to it in ¾ of an hour, but few think it worth the trouble of the ascent.

By ascending at the side of the Staubbach, turning off about 200 yds. beyond Lauterbrunnen,

Mürren, a small village, is reached, where refreshments may be obtained. This village is on the route to the Furce. (Rte. 26.) The view of the Bernese chain from this point is very fine, and is still finer from one of the peaks of the *Schilthorn*, half an hour above the village. The descent may be varied by passing through *Grünenwald* and the *Seefinen-Thal* (Rte. 26) to the upper valley of Lauterbrunnen.

Ulrich Lauener, of Lauterbrunnen, is a celebrated guide. His brother Johann lost his life in pursuit of chamois on the precipices of the Jungfrau.

Upper Valley of Lauterbrunn.

Of the multitudes who visit Lauterbrunn, a very small proportion trouble themselves to explore the upper part of the valley. The fall of the *Schmadribach* is quite a sufficient object for a day's excursion; being, in truth, inferior to few in Switzerland. It is a large body of water, which, issuing from the glacier, throws itself immediately over a precipice of great height, and again makes two more leaps, of inferior height, but great beauty, before reaching the bottom of the valley. Horses can go for about two hours from Lauterbrunn to the hamlet of Trachsel Lauinen, opposite which will be seen the remains of an avalanche, called by the same name, which falls annually from the Jungfrau, and spreads its ruins over a surface of many hundred acres. An hour farther, in which there is a steep ascent to be surmounted, stands a single châlet, near the foot of the lower fall; from which there is ½ an hour's sharp ascent to the foot of the upper fall. Deciduous trees cease below Trachsel Lauinen; thence to the fall, the way lies generally through pine forests, and the pasturage is abundant to a much greater height. High above tower the summits of the chain, which, branching from the Jungfrau, is continued in an unbroken line of ice to the Gemmi.

On returning, the curious little cascade of the Trümmelbach, issuing from a deep ravine under the Jungfrau, may be visited.

c. *Lauterbrunnen to Grindelwald,*—a. *By the char-road.* b. *By the Wengern Alp.*

Both Lauterbrunnen and Grindelwald may be visited in one rather long day from Interlaken, returning in the evening. If the Wengern Alp route is chosen, a char may be taken at Interlaken, and the saddle-horses may be used to draw the char, saddles being taken with it. The char may then be left at Lauterbrunnen, and will be run down by boys to the junction of the Grindelwald road, where it will be found by the tourists, who will in the mean time have crossed the Wengern Alp, and come down from Grindelwald on the char-horses. One horse, 20 fr.; two horses, 40 fr. for this expedition.

a. By the high-road the time occupied in going from Lauterbrunnen to Grindelwald is about 2 hrs.—the distance about 9 m.; but this route should be taken only by those who can neither ride nor walk, or who prefer the jolting of a char to avalanches, Alps, and fatigue—or in case of bad or cloudy weather. It is necessary to return down the valley as far as the Zwei-Lutschinen, then, crossing the White, to ascend, by the side of the Black Lutschine—a toilsome steep, through a gloomy valley, closed up by the precipices of the Wetterhorn and the peaks of the Eigher. Nearer to Grindelwald the two glaciers appear in sight.

The traveller in the Oberland is sadly subjected to the persecution of beggars—some under the pretext of offering him strawberries, or flowers, or crystals,—others with no other excuse but their poverty, not unfrequently united to goître and cretinism, as an additional recommendation to the compassion of strangers—many of them without even the pretence of poverty, but apparently children of peasants in tolerable circumstances, with no excuse whatever. Every cottage sends forth its ragged crowds of dishevelled and unshod children; behind every rock is an ambuscade of native minstrels, who, drawn up in line, assail the passers-by with the discordant strains of their shrill voices.

b. In fine weather there is not a more interesting or exciting journey among the Alps than that over the *Wengern Alp*, or *Lesser Scheideck*. Independently of the view of the Jungfrau, and other giants of the Bernese chain (unrivalled, owing to its proximity to these sublime objects), it is from the Wengern Alp that avalanches are seen and heard in greatest perfection, and no one should abandon the expedition without an effort. The path is practicable for mules, and is about 5 hrs. walking; but on horseback, from its steepness, its great elevation, and the time spent in enjoying the view from the top, it occupies

about 7 hrs., including a halt at the summit. It is constantly traversed by ladies on horseback, or even in a chaise à porteur (§ 9). The traveller is likely to lose his way on the ascent, but no guide is required on account of any dangers. Those who are at all able to walk should take a horse to the summit only, for which one day is charged; for the whole journey, $1\frac{1}{2}$ day.

The bridle-path turns off at the chapel nearly opposite the Staubbach, and after crossing the river ascends steep zigzags, which lead out of the valley of Lauterbrunnen, in order to surmount the ridge separating it from that of Grindelwald. After nearly an hour of toilsome ascent, passing the houses of a scattered hamlet, it reaches a more gradual slope of meadow land. The valley of Lauterbrunn, beneath whose precipices the traveller has previously crept with some little awe, presents from this height the aspect of a mere trench; the Staubbach is reduced to a thin thread, and its upper fall, and previous winding, before it makes its final leap, are exposed to view and looked down upon. The path winds to the rt. round the shoulder of the hill, and then, becoming steep and slippery, crosses the meadows advancing towards the Jungfrau, which now rises in front of the spectator, with its vast expanse of snow and glacier, in all its magnificence. Not only its summit, but all the mass of the mountain above the level of the spectator, is white with perpetual snow of virgin purity, which breaks off abruptly at the edge of a black precipice, forming one side of a ravine separating the Jungfrau from the Wengern Alp. It appears to be within gun-shot of the spectator—so colossal are its proportions, that the effect of distance is lost.

About half an hour's walk below the col, at a place called Manlich, a rustic but very tolerable *Inn*, *H. de la Jungfrau*, containing 20 beds to accommodate strangers who choose to await the sunrise at this elevation, has been built on the brow of the ravine, 5350 ft. above the sea-level, directly facing the Jungfrau. From this point the mountain is best seen, as well as the avalanches descending from it. The precipice before alluded to, which forms the base of the mountain, is channelled with furrows or grooves, down which the avalanches descend. They are most numerous a little after noon, when the sun and wind exercise the greatest influence on the glacier in loosening masses of it, and causing them to break off.

The attention is first arrested by a distant roar, not unlike thunder, and in half a minute, a gush of white powder, resembling a small cataract, is perceived issuing out of one of the upper grooves or gullies; it then sinks into a low fissure, and is lost only to reappear at a lower stage some hundred feet below; soon after another roar, and a fresh gush from a lower gully, till the mass of ice, reaching the lowest step, is precipitated into the gulf below. By watching attentively the sloping white side of the Jungfrau, the separation of the fragment of ice from the mass of the glacier which produces this thunder, may be seen at the moment when disengaged and before the sound reaches the ear. Sometimes it merely slides down over the surface, at others it turns over in a cake; but in an instant after it disappears, is shattered to atoms, and, in passing through the different gullies, is ground to powder so fine, that, as it issues from the lowest, it looks like a handful of meal; and particles reduced by friction to the consistence of dust, rise in a cloud of vapour. Independent of the sound, which is an awful interruption of the silence usually prevailing on the high Alps, there is nothing grand or striking in these falling masses: and, indeed, it is difficult, at first, to believe that these echoing thunders arise from so slight a cause in appearance. The spectator must bear in mind that at each discharge whole tons of ice are hurled down the mountain, and that the apparently insignificant white dust is made up of blocks capable of sweeping away whole forests, did any occur in its course, and of overwhelming

houses and villages. During the early part of the summer three or four such discharges may be seen in an hour; in cold weather they are less numerous; in the autumn scarcely any occur. The avalanches finally descend into the valley of Trümeleten, the deep and uninhabited ravine dividing the Jungfrau from the Wengern Alp; and, on melting, send forth a stream which falls into the Lutschine, a little above Lauterbrunnen. A part of Lord Byron's 'Manfred' was either written or mentally composed on the Wengern Alp, in full view of the Jungfrau, and (he says in his Journal) within hearing of its avalanches.

"Ascended the Wengern mountain; left the horses, took off my coat, and went to the summit. On one side our view comprised the Jungfrau, with all her glaciers; then the Dent d'Argent, shining like truth; then the Little Giant, and the Great Giant; and last, not least, the Wetterhorn. The height of the Jungfrau is 11,000 feet above the valley. Heard the avalanches falling every five minutes nearly.

"The clouds rose from the opposite valley, curling up perpendicular precipices, like the foam of the ocean of hell during a spring tide—it was white and sulphury, and immeasurably deep in appearance. The side we ascended was not of so precipitous a nature; but, on arriving at the summit, we looked down upon the other side upon a boiling sea of cloud, dashing against the crags on which we stood—these crags on one side quite perpendicular. In passing the masses of snow, I made a snowball, and pelted Hobhouse with it."—*Swiss Journal.*

> " Ye toppling crags of ice—
> Ye *avalanches,* whom a breath draws down
> In mountainous o'erwhelming, come and crush
>   me!
> *I hear ye momently above, beneath,*
> *Crash with a frequent conflict;* but ye pass,
> And only fall on things that still would live ;
> On the young flourishing forest, or the hut
> And hamlet of the harmless villager.
> The mists boil up around the glaciers ; *clouds*
> *Rise curling* far beneath me, white and sulphury,
> *Like foam from the roused ocean of deep hell!"*
>   *Manfred.*

Beyond the inn it is tolerably level, and in about 2 miles the col or summit of the pass is attained, 6690 ft. above the sea-level, where there is a tolerable *Inn*, said to be better than that at Manlich. The view is very fine, including, besides the Jungfrau, the Mönch, the two Eighers, and the Wetterhorn, and from the Lesser *Lauberhorn* (1½ hr.) at the back of the inn a magnificent view is obtained. The *Jungfrau*, or Virgin, received its name either from the unsullied purity of the snow, or because (till lately) its crest had never been reached or trodden by human foot. She has now lost her claim to the title on the latter score, the highest peak having been attained in 1828 by 6 peasants from Grindelwald ; and, in August, 1841, by M. Agassiz, of Neuchâtel, accompanied by Professor Forbes, of Edinburgh, and a Swiss and French gentleman. The course they pursued was by the Ober-Aar glacier to that of Viesch, and then by following up the Aletsch glacier from the lake Moril. It has since been ascended by M. Studer and others. The Jungfrau rises to an elevation of 13,720 ft. above the sea-level. The Silber-hörner are, properly speaking, inferior peaks of the Jungfrau. Farther on appear the Mönch, or Klein Eigher, 13,510 ft., and the Great Eigher (Giant), 13,060 ft. On approaching Grindenwald, the Schreckhorn (Peak of Terror), 13,410 ft., comes into sight. The sharp, needle-formed point of the Finster-Aarhorn, the highest of the group, 14,130 ft. above the sea-level, is only visible at intervals peering above his brethren. This mountain was ascended in 1857 from the inn on the Æggishorn by Mr. Matthews and others, sleeping out two nights. The glaciers, which cling around these peaks, and fill up the depressions between them, extend without interruption from the Jungfrau to the Grimsel, and from Grindelwald in canton Berne, nearly to Brieg in the Valais. The extent of this glacier has been calculated at 115 square miles, or about one-sixth of all the glaciers among the Alps, and it is the largest glacier in Switzerland or Savoy, perhaps in Europe.

The descent to Grindelwald takes up about 2½ hrs. The path is steep and difficult, strewn with fallen rocks, · and for 20 min. lies over marshy ground. It passes within sight of a forest * said to have been mown down by the fall of avalanches, but more probably decaying, as is not unusual on the higher grounds at present. The trunks, broken short off close to the ground, still stand like stubble left by the scythe. Byron describes " whole woods of withered pines— all withered; trunks stripped and barkless; branches lifeless; done by a single winter—their appearance reminded me of me and my family."

In descending into the valley, the *Wetterhorn* (ascended by Mr. Wills in 1855) is seen in front, and on the l. the Faulhorn, surmounted by its inn. On the rt., low down, appears the white lower glacier of Grindelwald, issuing out of a gorge, on a level with the habitations of the valley.

Grindelwald.—*Inns :* Bär (Bear) at the W. of the village; Adler (Eagle) at the E. end; both tolerable. They are more than a mile distant from the lower glacier : in summer they are often very full.

The village of Grindelwald, consisting of picturesque wooden cottages, widely scattered over the valley, stands at a height of 3250 ft. above the sea, from which cause, and from its vicinity to the glaciers, the climate of the valley is cold, and unstable even in summer. Its inhabitants are chiefly employed in rearing cattle, of which 6000 head are fed on the neighbouring pastures. Some of the peasants act as guides. The Grindelwald guides, Christian Bleuver, Hildbrand Burgner, are highly recommended for difficult mountain excursions. Christian Bohren has been well spoken of as a general guide. The younger females pick up a few halfpence by singing Ranz de Vaches at the inns, and most of the children are beggars — occupations arising from the influx of strangers

* Of which Mr. Barnard has given an admirable representation in his *Swiss* Views.

into the valley, which has exercised an injurious influence upon its morals and ancient simplicity of manners. The valley has not been inhabited above 400 years, and the peasants assert that the climate becomes gradually worse, and give instances which seem to bear out their statement. It is certain that there were in former days several paths into the Valais which are now impassable; and it is said that the peasants of Grindelwald used to cross to the Valais to be married.

Grindelwald owes its celebrity, as a place of resort for travellers, to the grandeur of the mountains which surround it, and to its two *Glaciers* (§ 16), which, as they descend into the very bottom of the valley below the level of the village, and almost within a stone's-throw of human habitations, are more easily accessible here than in other parts of Switzerland. Three gigantic mountains form the S. side of the valley—the Eigher, or Giant; the Mettenberg (Middle Mountain), which is, in fact, the base or pedestal of the magnificent peak called Schreckhorn; and the Wetterhorn (Peak of Tempests), at the upper end. Between these three mountains the two glaciers of Grindelwald issue out. They are branches of that vast field or ocean of ice mentioned above as occupying the table-land and high valleys amidst the Bernese Alps, and, being pushed downwards by the constantly-increasing masses above, descend far below the line of perpetual snow (§ 16). Their chief beauty arises from their being bordered by forests of fir, which form, as it were, a graceful fringe to the white ice, while the green pastures, with which they are almost in contact near the base, contrast agreeably with their frozen peaks. Though inferior in extent to those of Chamouni, of the Aar and of Aletsch, the traveller who has seen even them will do well to explore the Glaciers of Grindelwald.

The Lower Glacier, also called the smaller, although four times as large as the upper one, forces its way out between the Eigher and Mettenberg,

and its solid icebergs descend to a point only 3200 feet above the level of the sea. A path ascends along its left margin, beneath the precipices of the Mettenberg, commanding a most interesting view of the bristling minarets of ice, rising in the most various and fantastic shapes, and affords means of paying a visit to the Lower Glacier, which is one of the pleasantest excursions on the Alps; with a local guide occupying 5 or 6 hrs. in the whole, including, if it is desired, 1 or 2 on the ice, and not fatiguing. It is not good for timid persons, as the path skirts some formidable precipices; but it is taken by ladies, who may ride on horseback for the first three quarters of an hour, and be conveyed the rest of the way in a chaise à porteur. It offers to those who cannot mount heights one of the grandest and wildest glacier views imaginable, the cultivated valley being completely hidden, and nothing visible but the enormous peaks of the Eigher, Schreckhorn, Viescherhörner, &c., which form a superb amphitheatre, very little inferior to the scene from the Jardin. The path, after passing through meadows towards the rt. side of the glacier (l. side of the traveller ascending), begins to ascend through a steep forest, and in about an hour comes out on the cliff bordering the glacier, and continues along a narrow ledge in the face of the cliff for some distance. The glacier, which is narrow at the bottom, now gradually widens, and spreads out into what is called the Sea of Ice (Eismeer), where its surface, though traversed by crevices, is less shattered than below. In 1821 M. Mouron, a clergyman of Vevay, was lost in one of the crevices. Suspicions were entertained that the guide who accompanied him had murdered him, and search was immediately commenced for the body. After 12 days of fruitless attempts, it was at length drawn out of an abyss in the ice, said to have been 700 ft. deep (?), by a guide named Burgener, who was let down from above at the peril of his life, by a rope, with a lantern tied to his neck. He was twice drawn up without having been able to find it, nearly exhausted for want of air; the third time he returned with it in his arms. It was much bruised, and several limbs were broken, so as to lead to the belief that life, or at least sensation, had departed before he reached the bottom; but the watch and the purse of the unfortunate man were found upon him, so that the suspicions regarding the guide were proved to be groundless. He was buried in the church of Grindelwald.

Following the path along the cliff we arrive at a singular depression in the rocks, called *Martinsdruck*, pointed out to the traveller, and opposite to it, in the crest of the Eigher, a small hole, called *Martinsloch*, through which the sun's rays shine twice a-year. Once on a time, according to the tradition, the basin now occupied by the Eismeer was filled with a lake, but the space between the Mettenberg and the Eigher being much narrower than at present, the outlet from it was constantly blocked up, and inundations produced, which ruined the fields of the peasants in the valley below. At length St. Martin, a holy giant, came to their rescue; he seated himself on the Mettenberg, resting his staff on the Eigher, and then, with one lusty heave of his brawny back, not only burst open the present wide passage between the two mountains, but left the marks of his seat on the one, and drove his walking-stick right through the other.

A very fine avalanche is occasionally seen from this path to fall from the precipices on the other side of the glacier. In about 2 hrs'. walk from Grindelwald the path reaches a place where it becomes necessary to take to the ice, and some planks are usually placed here to facilitate the passage. At this point nothing is to be seen in any direction but rocks, ice, and snow, with here and there a patch of pasture. The path thus far is the beginning of the Strahleck pass (Rte. 28 A). The tourist may now either return, or take a promenade on the ice, or to the châlets of Stiereck.

The *Upper Glacier* may be visited in going over the Scheideck. Blocks of clear ice cut from this glacier are exported to Berne to serve the purposes of Wenham Lake ice.

Ascent of the Faulhorn.

The Faulhorn is a mountain 8674 ft. above the sea-level, situated between the valley of Grindelwald and the lake of Brienz, and commanding, from its summit, an excellent *near* view over the neighbouring chain of Bernese Alps. On this account it is ascended in the summer-time, like the Rigi, by travellers.

It is accessible by horses. Ladies who do not ride may be carried in "chaises à porteurs," with 4 bearers to each chair, at 6 fr. each; or if the party sleep on the Faulhorn, 9 fr. A *guide* to the top is well paid with 6 frs., or 9 if they remain all night: a horse 15 frs. up and down. The inn on the summit, which is only tenanted for 4 months of the year, and is abandoned in October, affords tolerable apartments and bed-rooms, in all 24 beds, of course none of the softest. The ascent is free from danger, and not very difficult. It may be made in less than 5 hrs., and the descent in 3. The larder of mine host is pretty well furnished, and the charges are not high; 25 cents. for the stove in the principal room. In the height of summer you must secure beds beforehand, or be early on the top. The path from Grindelwald leads over the Bach Alp, by the side of a small lake, 1000 ft. below the summit, 3½ hrs. from Grindelwald. The view of the Bernese Alps from the top forms the chief feature of the panorama, which in this respect, and from the proximity of the Faulhorn to those snowy giants, far surpasses the prospect from the Rigi. On the other hand, though the lakes of Thun and Brienz are both visible, only a small strip of each appears, which is but a poor equivalent for the wide expanse of blue water which bathes the foot of the Rigi.

E 3

There is a footpath from the top of the Faulhorn, passing the waterfall of the Giesbach above the lake of Brienz: the distance is about 14 miles, but it is difficult and even dangerous, slightly marked, and not to be attempted without a guide. Travellers about to cross the Scheideck need not return to Grindelwald, but, turning to the l. at the Bach Alp, may follow a path, in places indistinct and boggy, which will bring them down upon the summit of the Scheideck, close to the *Inn*, in 2 hours' walk, on the way to Rosenlaui.

Those who cannot reach the summit of the Faulhorn will be well repaid for mounting its slope for an hour or two on the road, in order to get the fine view of the S. side of the Grindelwald valley, which cannot be seen from Grindelwald itself or from the bottom of the valley.

D. *Grindelwald to Reichenbach or Meyringen, by the Great Scheideck.*

	Hours.
Grindelwald. }	
Scheideck	3
Rosenlaui	2
Reichenbach	2½
	—
	7½

About 20 Eng. m. ; 6 hrs. good walking. On horseback, for ladies, it is a ride of at least 9 hours, including halts. No guide is required.

[An hour's walk up the valley from Grindelwald, and a slight détour to the rt. of the direct path to Meyringen, leads to the *Upper Glacier.* It does not materially differ from the one below, nor is it finer; but it sometimes has a larger vault of ice at its lower extremity. These two glaciers are the chief feeders of the Black Lutschine.]

The first hour from Grindelwald is through the meadows in the valley; afterwards the ascent is easy, and during the whole of it the *Wetterhorn* (Peak of Tempests) overhangs the path, an object of stupendous sublimity. It rises in one vast precipice of alpine limestone, apparently close above the traveller's head, though its base is more than a mile off. Avalanches descend from it in the spring and summer through four different channels ; some of them reach to the path, and travellers have been exposed to danger from them. The top of the Wetterhorn consists of a cornice of ice, which it is necessary to *cut through* with axes. Several persons have reached the cornice, but it seems that Ulrich Lauener and others, in company with Mr. A. Wills in 1855, were the first who ever reached the narrow ridge forming the top. Mr. Wills published an account of that and of other difficult excursions in the Higher Alps. Upon the slope in front of the Wetterhorn is usually stationed one who blows the *alpine horn*, a rude tube of wood, 6 or 8 ft. long. A few seconds after the horn has ceased, the few and simple notes of the instrument are caught up and repeated by the echoes of the vast cliff of the Wetterhorn, and return to the ear refined and softened, yet perfectly distinct, as it were an aërial concert warbling among the crags.

[Travellers may make the ascent of the Faulhorn from the summit of the Scheideck in about 3½ hrs.]

The view down the valley of Grindelwald, from the Scheideck, is very striking : its green pastures contrast agreeably with the bare wall of the Wetterhorn. Beyond it, on the l., rises the sharp crest of the Eigher, resembling the up-turned edge of a hatchet. On the Scheideck (6480 ft. above the sea-level) stands an *Inn*, Steinbock, with rough sleeping and other accommodation.

The prospect in the opposite direction, into the vale of the Reichenbach or of Rosenlaui, is not remarkable. High up on the rt. appears the glacier of Schwarzwald, between the Wetterhorn and Wellhorn ; further on, between Wellhorn and Engel-hörner (angels' peaks), the *Glacier of Rosenlaui* lies embedded. An hour and a half's walking from the Steinbock inn, partly through a wood of firs, brings the traveller to the

Baths of Rosenlaui, a homely but clean *Inn*, Bär, 2 hrs. from the summit, very prettily situated, near a source of mineral water, resembling closely that of Harrogate, which supplies 5 or 6 rude tubs of wood, serving as baths. The number of guests who resort hither for the use of them is very limited. Wood carving is very well executed here. A few yards behind it the Reichenbach torrent issues out of a cleft in the rock. About 20 min. from the baths is the *Glacier of Rosenlaui*, which is smaller than those of Grindelwald, but is celebrated above all others in Switzerland for the untarnished purity of its white surface, and the clear transparent azure of its icebergs. This peculiarity arises doubtless from its having no medial moraine (see § 16). The advance and retreat of the glacier may be very well observed here, as its bed is a flat rock, and this glacier is well worth a visit. A steep path on the l. of the glacier leads in about ½ an hour to the summit of a cliff which projects midway into the icy sea, and bends its course considerably. It forms a good point of view. The torrent issuing from this glacier has worn a deep chasm in the mountain side, in which, from the frail bridge thrown across it, the waters may be seen boiling some 200 ft. below.

The path to Meyringen runs by the side of this stream, first crossing a charming little green plain, carpeted with soft turf, like that of an English lawn, and dotted with châlets. The view up the valley from this point deserves particular notice : it is a favourite subject for the pencil of the artist. The Wetterhorn, the Wellhorn, and the craggy peaks called Engel-hörner, form a mountain group unrivalled for picturesqueness.

Below this the valley contracts; numerous waterfalls are seen dangling from its sides : one of them, from its height and tenuity, is called the Ropefall (Seilbach) ; and now a bird's-eye view opens out into the vale of *Hasli*, or Meyringen, which, in comparison with the narrow glens of Grindelwald and Lauterbrunnen, deserves the name

of a plain, though bounded by mountains high and steep.

The latter part of the descent leading into it is steep and rugged, and is paved with smooth and slippery blocks of stone. On this account travellers are usually invited to dismount, and descend on foot. The stream of the Reichenbach performs this descent of nearly 2000 ft. in a succession of leaps, the longest of which are the celebrated *Falls of the Reichenbach*. The upper fall is situated at a short distance to the l. of the road near the village called Zwirghi. A small fee is exacted for the liberty to cross the meadow between it and the road, and a hut called Belvedere is built beside it. But it is best seen from a rocky headland shooting out in front of the bare amphitheatre of cliffs over which the cataract dashes, and just above the struggling torrent, hurrying downwards after its fall. A little lower is another but inferior fall ; and by a third, still lower, the stream gains the level of the valley, and hastens to join its waters to the Aar. The lowest fall is very near to the

Reichenbach Hotel, 2½ hrs. from Rosenlaui, is a comfortable house, making up 40 beds, at the foot of the mountain near the hamlet of Willigegn, and is provided with hot and cold baths. Table-d'hôte 3 frs., bed 2 frs., breakfast 2 frs. H. des Alpes, also very comfortable. In fact, since the Reichenbach Hotel has been built and furnishes horses and chars, there is no necessity for going to Meyringen either on this route or on the Grimsel route. Latterly, however, complaints have been made of the charges at these hotels, which are distant about ½ m., by a footpath and ferry over the Aar, from the village of

Meyringen — (*Inns :* Sauvage, best and moderate ; — Couronne, comfortable, good horses; ask for the fish called "Lotte")—on the rt. bank of the Aar, the chief place in the vale of Hasli, is an excellent specimen of a Swiss village (2359 Prot. Inhab.). The picturesqueness of its situation is much praised. Brockedon says,

" The vale of Meyringen concentrates as much of what is Alpine in its beauties as any valley in Switzerland." Its precipitous and wooded sides, streaked with white cascades almost without number, and here and there overtopped by some snow-white peak, are indeed beautiful features ; yet the flat plain, 3 m. broad, half marsh and half dry gravel, from inundations of the river, is unpleasing from many points ; and as a dwelling-place it has serious drawbacks from the danger to which it is exposed of being swept away or inundated, if not buried, by the neighbouring torrents. It was to guard against such accidents that the stone dyke, 1000 ft. long and 8 wide, was constructed ; but its protection has not been altogether effectual. The chief cause and instrument of all the mischief is the *Alpbach*, a mountain torrent pouring down from the height behind the village, out of a narrow gorge. The district in which it rises, and through which it takes its course, is composed of the rock known to geologists as the lias marl. Being very soft, it is easily disintegrated and washed away, so that the torrent, when swollen by rain or snow, collects, and bears along with it heaps of black sand and rubbish, intermixed with uprooted fir-trees, and is converted almost into a stream of mud, on which masses of rock float like corks. A torrent of such consistence is easily interrupted in its course through the narrow crevices which it seems to have sawn for itself by the force of its current : it then gathers into a lake behind the obstacles which impede it, until it is increased to such an extent as to bear everything before it, and to spread desolation over the valley through which its course lies. A catastrophe of this sort, in 1762, buried a large part of the village of Meyringen, in one hour, 20 ft. deep in rubbish, from which it has hardly yet emerged. The church was filled with mud and gravel to the height of 18 ft., as is denoted by the black line painted along its walls, and by the débris which still covers many of

the fields and gardens around. In 1733 an inundation of the same stream carried away many houses.

There are 2 churches here, and the Swiss Government has lately given up one of them for the English service. The Rev. E. J. May, head master of the Brewer's Company School, London, has made himself responsible for the expense of fitting up the ch., and solicits subscriptions.

Travellers should visit the Fall of the *Alpbach* about 9 in the morning, on account of the *triple bow*, or iris, formed in its spray when the sun shines on it. The inner iris forms nearly a complete circle, and the outer ones are more or less circular as the water in the falls is abundant or not. The spot whence it is visible is within the spray from the cataract, so that those who would enjoy it must prepare for a wetting.

On a rock above the village rise the ruins of the *Castle of Resti:* it belonged to an ancient and noble family, to whom the praise is given of never tyrannizing over their humble dependents. The men of *Hasli* are celebrated for their athletic forms and strength. They hold Schwingfeste, or wrestling matches, every year, in July, August, and September, with their neighbours of Unterwalden and Grindelwald. The women, again, enjoy the reputation of being prettier, or rather less plain, than those of most other Swiss valleys. Their holiday costume is peculiar and not ungraceful, consisting of a bodice of black velvet reaching up to the throat, starched sleeves, a yellow petticoat, and a round black hat, not unlike a soup-plate, and about the same size, stuck on one side of the head, and allowing the hair to fall in long tresses down the back.

Six roads concentrate at Reichenbach or Meyringen: 1. to Brienz (a char road); 2. to Lucerne, by the Brünig (Rte. 19); 3. over the Susten to Wasen on the St. Gothard road (Rte. 32); 4. to the Grimsel (Rte. 28); 5. to Grindelwald, by the Scheideck; 6. to Engelberg, by the Joch Pass, Gadmenthal, and Genthil Thal. The magnificent *Fall of the Aar* at Handeck, on the way to the Grimsel (Rte. 28), is about 14 m. distant. Travellers, not intending to cross the whole pass, may make an interesting excursion thither from Meyringen; as they may also to the summit of the *Brünig*, about 6 m. distant, whence there is a beautiful view of the vale of Hasli. (Rte. 19.)

E. *Meyringen to Interlaken, by Brienz and the Giessbach Falls.—Rothhorn.*

1½ hr. drive or 7 Eng. m. to Brienz, and thence to Interlaken by water. 10 m.   Char 6 fr.

There is an excellent char road down the valley, passing numerous cascades leaping down the wall of rock. After proceeding for about 4 m. along the l. bank of the Aar, it crosses the river by a wooden bridge, just at the point where the branch of the Brünig road leading to Brienz (Rte. 19) descends into the valley. The Aar pursues its course through monotonous marsh and flat meadow land; but near its influx into the Lake of Brienz, the form of the mountains on its l. bank, above which towers the Faulhorn, is grand. In skirting the margin of the lake, the road crosses vast heaps of débris, covering acres of land once fertile. A torrent of mud, in 1797, destroyed a considerable part of two villages near Kienholz; and a land-slip from the Brienzergrat, the mountain immediately behind Brienz, over-whelmed, in November, 1824, 40 acres of land, and swept 6 persons into the lake.

Brienz — Inns :   L'Ours, good ; Weisses Kreutz (Croix Blanche), clean, at Tracht. There is also an hotel at Kienholz, the Bellevue, about a mile from Brienz, towards Meyringen. Horses may be hired at Brienz, over the Brunig Pass to Lungern : also carriages to Meyringen or Reichenbach. The landlord of L'Ours (an intelligent man who speaks German, French, English, and Italian) furnishes, for the use of ladies and invalids passing over the Brünig, *chaises à porteur.* Brienz is a small village at the E. end of the lake, on a narrow ledge at the foot of the

mountains, remarkable only for its beautiful situation, and its vicinity to the Giessbach Fall. Ask for the *Lotte,* a fish of the lake (gadus mustela). This is a good place for buying carved wood-ware. From Brienz the traveller may ascend the *Rothhorn,* the highest point of the chain running behind (N. of) Brienz, which commands a view nearly as fine as the Faulhorn. Its top may be reached in about 4 hours by a stout walker, in 5 by a horse, and in 6 by a chaise à porteurs. The upward path lies at first through a region of fine forest-trees, chiefly beech, but including many oaks : to these succeed larch, and above them one-third of steep ascent over a bare and barren track. On the ascent, fine views are obtained through vistas in the forest of the Lake of Brienz. On the top a *châlet* was built, but it has been destroyed by fire and is not rebuilt (1851). The summit is higher than the Rigi, and not so high as the Faulhorn. It takes 2 or 3 hrs. to descend. The chief features of the view are—S. the whole range of Bernese Alps, seen to great advantage in all their majesty, with a foreground of the lake of Brienz close under the mountain, and a peep of the lake of Thun in the gap above Interlaken. Besides this, the vale of Meyringen, from the lake of Brienz up nearly to the Grimsel, the lake of Sarnen, with a small lake that may be seen in the foreground, a considerable part of the lake of Lucerne, the Rigi rising from it, and a bit of the lake of Zug, are visible. Pilate makes a prominent figure. The lake of Constance also appears, and a long strip of the lake of Neuchâtel. The view of the high Alps from the Rothhorn is not so fine as that from the Faulhorn, but that of the lower country is finer.

Lake of Brienz.—Giessbach Falls.

A small *Steamer* runs daily, in 1 hr., between Brienz and Interlaken, touching at the Giessbach every trip. If the traveller misses the steamer or prefers a row-boat, it takes about 3 hrs., including a digression to Giessbach. Boat, 10 fr., 2 fr. bonnemain.

There is a very rough road, which has been partly made good and widened for vehicles (it may be finished in 1857), along the N. shore of the lake: the guides with the horses may be sent round by it, and desired to meet the travellers close to the bridge at Interlaken. There is also a very pretty foot-road along the S. side of the lake by the Giessbach. It takes 25 minutes to row from Brienz to the landing-place, close to the outlet of *the Giessbach*, where travellers begin to ascend the steep height leading to the *Falls*. They are a succession of cascades, leaping step by step from the top of the mountain; and, though inferior in height to the Reichenbach, surpass it in beauty, and in the adjuncts of a rich forest of fir, through the midst of which they break their way. The Giessbach is one of the prettiest of waterfalls; there is nothing wild about it, and the immediate contact of green turfy knolls and dark woods has the effect of a park scene. It is possible to pass behind the third fall by means of a gallery constructed beneath the shelving rock, from which it casts itself down; and the effect of the landscape seen athwart this curtain of water is singular. A very comfortable *Inn* has been built at the foot of the falls. The cottage opposite the Falls is inhabited by the schoolmaster of Brienz, whose family and himself are celebrated as the best choristers of native airs in Switzerland. He is now a patriarch of 80, and most of his children are married; but he is training his grandchildren to the same profession of songsters. The concert, accompanied by the Alpine horn, with which travellers are saluted on their departure, is very sweet. Good specimens of the Swiss manufacture of carved wood may be purchased at the Giessbach. There is a path from the Giessbach to the top of the Faulhorn, a walk of nearly 5 hrs., but difficult. The lake of Brienz is about 8 m. long; its surface is 1781 ft. above the sea level; near the mouth of the Giessbach, 500 ft. deep, but in the deepest part 2100 ft. ? Its surface is about 30 ft. higher than the lake of Thun.

ROUTE 26.

LAUTERBRUNNEN TO KANDERSTEG, BY THE PASSES OF THE SEEFINEN, FURCE, AND DÜNDENGRAT.

This path is not practicable for mules, but there is probably no route among the Alps so free from danger, which leads through such a succession of magnificent scenery. The *two* passes, however, make it very laborious. The descent into the valley of Oeschinen is awkward after dark, and the traveller, however good a walker he may be, will do well to allow himself 14 hrs. of daylight.

On leaving Lauterbrunnen there is a choice of routes: one by the valley, following the char road to Stechelberg, and then turning to the right of the course of the stream which drains the Seefinen Thal; the other, which is in many respects preferable, mounts at once from Lauterbrunnen to

Mürren (Rte. 25 B); after which an ascent is commenced in order to turn the flank of a ridge which descends here from the Schilthorn on the rt. This brings the tourist again to a position right opposite the Jungfrau, at about the height of the Wengern Alp, but with a view still more magnificent. The great chain of Alps from the Wetterhorn to the Breithorn is in front, its continuation through the Tschingel Horn to the westward, as also the Frau, being from this point of view shut out by the nearer precipices of the Gspaltenhorn. Still farther to the west is visible the

Furce; and descending from it, the torrent and the valley of the Seefinen. The ground slopes rapidly away from the foot down to the depths of the Ammerten Thal. The Jungfrau is from this point of view, and from this alone, measured in one glance from the snow on her summit to the level road at her feet: in a word, of her 13,718 ft. of altitude, more than 10,000 rise at once in precipices before the eye. The track now winds away along the slope of the mountain, and falls in with the valley path just at the foot of the pass. This Furce is a very remarkable depression between the Schilthorn and Gspaltenhorn; and an enormous buttress of the latter here turns the direction of the route from W. to S.W. The ascent is rather steep, but the ground is favourable, and clear of snow; which lies, however, in long slopes to the left. The view from the summit is very fine, including the Faulhorn, and below it the Wengern Alp and its hotel, which is easily discernible. The upper part of the Kien Thal is filled up with a great glacier, over which it is said to be possible to gain the level of the Tschingel. The descent into the Kien Thal requires from this point rather an awkward circuit, which leads to a long slope of slate débris, forming a very unstable and somewhat dangerous footing—a fall sometimes occasions a serious cut. Next succeeds a long slope of snow, and then the green sward. The route taken by the guides leads to a bridge near the hamlet of Tschingel, so low down the valley as to increase considerably the toil of the next ascent; and if the tourist is fatigued, or the sun much past the meridian, he will do well to take the opportunity which here presents itself of descending to the char road at Reichenbach. The ascent of the Dündengrat is steep, but over good ground, and a view is soon obtained of the pyramidal Niesen, and the lake of Thun beyond it. Near the top it becomes rather rough, and the stones are succeeded by a bed of snow, which adds a good deal to the fatigue of the last half-hour of ascent:

from the snow to the top of the ridge is but one step, and the next is downhill. Here a new scene of magnificence opens. The glittering Frau, which is here quite close, with a triple glacier streaming down from her side into the gulfs beneath, and farther off the Doldenhorn, and the beautiful lake of Oeschinen encompassed by it, form a scene unparalleled in the Alps; though resembling in some of its features the lake and glacier scenery near the summit of the Malöya. The descent from the high pastures to the level of the lake is practicable only by one route, where a path has been cut in steps here and there along the faces of the rocks. The path leads along the W. shore of the lake through a pine wood beyond it, in about 2 hrs. to the village and inn of Kandersteg. —See Rte. 38.

ROUTE 27.

LAUTERBRUNNEN TO KANDERSTEG, BY THE TSCHINGEL GLACIER AND GASTEREN THAL.

"From Lauterbrunnen to the Châlet on the Steinberg is not more than 3 hrs. walking—I only took 2½. The view of the Jungfrau and Breithorn during all the latter part of this walk is magnificent.

"Having slept in the châlet, I started at 5½ A.M.; reached the foot of the glacier in half an hour—after half an hour's walk over the ice, came to the bottom of a steep cliff, up which we had to climb. Here there is some danger;* for the glacier hangs over the further end of the rock, and pieces are constantly falling down, and down just the easiest way up the rock, just *the* place one would choose to ascend

* There was formerly a ladder by which another route could be taken.

by without a guide. After having got to the top of the rock, take care to keep on the snow. We went up a long fall of loose earth and stones, and narrowly escaped being knocked on the head by some large stones that came bowling down. But on the snow there is no danger. Reached the top of the Pass in 2½ hours after climbing the rock, having made a détour to the Gamschilücke, a favourite lurking-place of the chamois-hunters, whence you look straight down the Kienthal to Thun and the Niesen. It is a gap in the range of the Gspalten-hörner and Blumlis Alp. Descended the glacier to Seldon, which I reached about 12: thence down the Gasteren-thal (a scene of the most savage and gloomy grandeur) to Kandersteg by 2½; having thus spent 9 hrs. in the day's walk, allowing time for a full hour's halt; of this about 4 or 4½ hrs. was upon the glacier. The only danger—or rather the only difficulty —is in climbing the steep rock mentioned above: though if the snow be soft, of course the fatigue must be very great. If not, the walk is easy enough.

"On the top of the Pass, it is possible to strike to the left under the Tschingel-horn into the Lötsch-thal. But this is seldom tried."—H. L.

ROUTE 28.

PASS OF THE GRIMSEL AND FURCA— MEYRINGEN OR REICHENBACH TO HOS-PENTHAL.

	Hours.
Meyringen or Reichenbach .	
Guttanen	3¼
Handek	1¼
Grimsel	2
Mayenwand Inn	1¼
Furca	2¼
Realp	2
Hospenthal	1¼

To the Grimsel Hospice 7 hrs. = 18 Eng. m., 6 hrs. walk. From the Hos-pice across the Furca to Hospital, 7½ hrs., 6¼ hrs. walk. Guide to the Grimsel not necessary.

A good char-road has been carried past Reichenbach Baths over the Kir-chet to Imhof, beyond which is a much-frequented, but rather difficult, bridle-path.

It is one of the grandest and most interesting passes across the Alps.

To those coming from Brientz or down the Scheideck (p. 82), Reichenbach is the best starting point, and it is unnecessary to go to Meyringen. But those coming across the Brünig or from Meyringen cross the Aar by a wooden bridge, and in about 20 min. fall into the Reichenbach road. The vale of Hasli now contracts, and in about 2 m. is crossed by a mound or hill of considerable height, called the *Kirchet*, which appears at one time to have dammed up the waters of the Aar. At present they force their way through a singularly narrow rent, which cleaves the eminence from top to bottom. At this point is a remarkable arched cavern, called the *Finster Aar Schlucht*, which extends by a precipitous but quite practicable descent, from the summit of the Kirchet to the Aar. It is a fissure in the limestone rock through which water has formerly flowed; and from the great size of the opening, it would seem that a stream as large as the Aar must at one time have passed through it. It lies to the left of the path leading from Meyringen to Im-Grund, about 8 m. from the former place, and may be seen without occasioning the traveller more than an hour's delay. The beautiful scenery at the upper mouth of the cavern, and the savage grandeur of the perpendicular rocks, as the path emerges upon the margin of the Aar, will amply compensate the labour of the descent. On the Kirchet are erratic blocks of granite on the limestone, which M. Agassiz is of opinion must have been brought down these existing valleys by the ancient glaciers. The path, leaving for a short time the river on the l. and the char-road on the rt., mounts the steep eminence of the Kirchet in zigzags, and then descends into the retired green valley of Upper Hasli, which is in the form of a basin, surrounded by hills, and was once probably a lake. [Two valleys open out into it; on the S. that of Urbach, on the E. that of Gadmen, up which runs the path leading by the pass of the Susten (Rte. 32) to Wasen. By taking the path to the rt. on descending from the Kirchet, a detour may be made into the Urbach Thal, the scenery of which is wild and striking. An ill-traced path along the W. slope of the valley of the Aar leads from the opening of the Urbach Thal to Guttanen.] On the l. lies the village Im-Grund, and, crossing the Aar, another village, called *Im-Hof*, situated between it and the Gadmen river, is passed;—all in the little plain. The char road here ceases. From Im-Hof (*Inn*, good wine) a path branches off to Engelberg over the Joch pass (Rte. 33). Another ravine is succeeded by a second enlargement of the valley called Im-Boden. Higher up is " the small and lonely village" of *Guttanen—Inn*, tolerable, but extortionate. The best place for a mid-day halt to rest the mules is the châlet of *The Handek*, about 1½ hour's walk beyond Guttanen. It can furnish a bed upon an emergency, and tolerable provisions, coffee, milk, &c. It stands at the distance of a few yards from the *Falls of the Aar*, perhaps the finest cataract in Switzerland, from its height (more than 200 ft.), the quantity and rush of water, the gloom of the gorge into which it precipitates itself, and the wild character of the rocky solitude around it. It is also remarkably easy of access, so that the traveller may form a full estimate of its grandeur; surveying it, first, from below, through the vista of black rocks into which it plunges, and afterwards from above, stretching his neck over the brow of the precipice from which the river takes its leap, and watching it (if his nerves be steady) till it is lost in the spray of the dark abyss below.

The view from this point, not more than 5 or 6 ft. above the fall, which few will hesitate to call the best, is exceedingly impressive and stimulating. So plentiful is the rush of water that it reaches more than half way down in one unbroken glassy sheet before it is tossed into white foam; and, what adds to its beauty, is, that another stream (the Erlenbach or Handek), pouring in from the right at this very spot, takes precisely the same leap, mingling its tributary waters midway with the more powerful column of the Aar. Between 10 o'clock and 1 the iris may be seen hovering over the fall.

The dark forest of fir through which the route has wound for a considerable distance, now dwindles away into a few dwarf bushes, and disappears entirely a little above Handek. To them succeed the scanty vegetation of rank grass, rhododendron, and lichen; and even this partial covering disappears prematurely, in some places being abraded and peeled off. There is a spot about 2 m. above Handek, called *Böse Seite*, or *Höllenplatte*, where the path crosses the bed of an ancient glacier which, in former times extending thus far down the valley, has ground smooth and polished, by its weight and friction, the surface of the sloping and convex granite rock, leaving, here and there upon the surface, horizontal grooves or furrows, which may be compared to the scratches made by a diamond upon glass. This polished rock (roche montonnée) extends for a space of nearly ¼ m. Professor Agassiz has here left his autograph in the granite. It used to be customary and prudent to dismount here, and cross this bad bit of road on foot, since the surface of the rock, though chiselled into grooves, to secure a footing for the horses, was very slippery; but a secure path, and a stout post and rail on the side of the abyss, is now carried over the slippery rock. The valley of the Aar, up which the narrow path is carried, looks stern and forbidding from its sterility, and the threatening cliffs of granite which overhang it. The Aar is crossed several times by dizzy bridges of a single arch, formed of granite slabs without a parapet. There is but one human habitation between Handek and the Hospice, the miserable châlet of the Räterichsboden, where the ravine expands once more into a basin-shaped hollow, probably once a lake bed, with a marshy bottom, affording scanty herbage for a few goats, with a dismal valley leading to the mountain Nägelis Grättli on the left. A little above this the path quits the Aar, which rises in the Aar-glacier, about 2 miles higher up on the rt., and ascending a glen, strewed with shattered rocks, reaches

The *Hospice of the Grimsel*, a homely *Inn*, was originally a conventual establishment, and after the Reformation was supported by the neighbouring communes, in order to shelter those who travel from necessity, and to afford a gratuitous aid to the poor. It is now daily occupied during the summer months by travellers for pleasure, sometimes to the number of 200 at once, who sit down at a table-d'hôte usually about 7 o'clock in the evening : the fare is good, the bedrooms very small, but the charges are not high. It is often so full in summer that those who arrive late are liable to fare ill, and it is often impossible to secure *single-bedded* rooms. It is a massy building of rough masonry, designed to resist a weight of snow, and with few windows to admit the cold. It contains about 40 beds, and affords good fare, better far than might be expected in a spot more than 6000 ft. above the sea, and removed by many miles from any other human dwelling. The establishment includes a man cook, a washerwoman, and a cobbler, and they have clothes to lend to drenched travellers while their own are drying. It is occupied by the innkeeper who rents it from March to November. One servant passes the winter in the house, with a sufficient provision to last out the time of his banishment, and two dogs, to detect the approach of wanderers, for even in the depth of winter the hospice is resorted to by traders from Hasli and the Valais, who exchange the cheese of the one valley for the

wine and spirits of the other. Its situation is as dreary as can be conceived, in a rocky hollow, about 700 ft. below the summit of the pass, surrounded by soaring peaks and steep precipices. The rocks around are bare and broken, scarcely varied by patches of snow, which never melt even in summer, and by strips of grass and green moss, which shoot up between the crevices, and are eagerly browsed by a flock of 150 goats. A considerable supply of peat is dug from a bog within a few yards of the door. In the bottom of this naked basin, close to the house, is a black tarn, or lake, in which no fish live. Although entirely covered with deep snow in winter, it is said never to be frozen, as it is supplied from a warm spring. Beyond it lies a small pasturage, capable of supporting for a month or two the cows belonging to the Hospice, and the servants cross the lake twice a-day, in a boat, to milk them. It is a landscape worthy of Spitzbergen or Nuova Zembla. This wilderness is the haunt of the marmot, whose shrill whistle frequently breaks the solitude ; and the chamois, become rare of late, still frequents the neighbouring glaciers ; both animals contribute at times to replenish the larder of the Hospice.

On the 22nd March, 1838, the Hospice was overwhelmed and crushed by an avalanche, which broke through the roof and floor, and filled all the rooms but that occupied by the servant, who succeeded with difficulty in working his own way through the snow, along with his dog, and reached Meyringen in safety. The evening before, the man had heard a mysterious sound, known to the peasants of the Alps and believed by them to be the warning of some disaster : it appeared so like a human voice that the man supposed it might be some one in distress, and went out with his dog to search, but was stopped by the snow. The next morning the sound was again heard, and then came the crash of the falling avalanche. The Hospice has been rebuilt and enlarged since a fire caused, 1852, by an incendiary (the landlord, an old man 62 years of age, in order to obtain a renewal of his lease, which ran out 1853). His crime was discovered, owing to a change of wind, before the building was destroyed, and the criminal tried, and sentenced to 20 years' imprisonment.

"In August, 1799, the Grimsel became the scene of one of the most remarkable skirmishes in the campaign. The Austrians were encamped upon the Grimsel with the view of preventing the French from penetrating into the Valley of the Rhone by means of that pass. They had possession of the whole declivity from the summit of the pass to the Hospice, and also of the platform on which the Hospice stands. Their force consisted of rather less than 1500 men. The French troops under General Gudin, consisting of about 3600 men, were posted in the Oberhasli valley in the neighbourhood of Guttanen. The Austrian commander, Colonel Strauch, naturally relied upon the strength of his position, which had not only the advantage of a great declivity, but of the numerous narrow fissures in the rocks, which might be defended by a few men, protected by the upright masses of granite, against a large army. The French General also considered the position to be impregnable to an attack in front, and was therefore placed in a situation of great anxiety by receiving positive orders from Massena, who had then the chief command of the French army in Switzerland, to force the pass of the Grimsel on the 14th of August. Fahner, the landlord of the Inn at Guttanen, then undertook for a reward to guide the French over a mountain called Nägeli's Grätli to the summit of the Grimsel at a higher level than the Austrian position.

"The next morning early Gudin confided about 400 men to the guidance of Fahner ; and at the same time he sent a small detachment over and round the Sidelhorn, who were also to descend from the higher parts of that mountain upon the Grimsel, and

there meet the party guided by Fahner over the mountain on the opposite side. Gudin himself advanced with the main body of his troops up the Oberhasli valley to the platform on which the Hospice now stands, and attacked the Austrian position in front —with the characteristic impetuosity of French soldiers. The Austrian commander was convinced that the attack could not succeed in this direction, but drew down the greater part of his force from the summit of the Grimsel in order to repel it with effect, and some sharp fighting ensued. Suddenly the Austrians were alarmed by firing on the heights to their rear : and its continuance, together with the appearance of French soldiers in that direction, convinced them that an important attack was commenced in a quarter from which they least expected it. The appearance of the enemy in their rear, with numbers as unknown as the means by which they came there, induced the Austrians to waver ; and the impetuous advance of Gudin produced a panic which ended in a disorderly flight up the Grimsel in the direction of Obergestelm, in the valley of the Rhone. On the summit of the Grimsel, however, they again met with the enemy ; for by this time the troops despatched by Gudin over the Sidelhorn had nearly reached their destination, and had almost effected their junction with the party led by Fahner ; so that the two ends of the formidable serpent were nearly brought together just as the flying Austrians had reached the top of the pass. The soldiers, finding themselves surrounded, are said to have beaten their sabres and muskets to pieces upon the granite rocks ; and this tradition is countenanced by the fact that fragments of arms, evidently broken by violence, are still occasionally found at this very spot. The number of the killed is supposed not to have exceeded 150, of which the French composed not more than a fifth part. The wounded Austrians were necessarily left to their fate, the nature of the ground rendering it impossible for such of their companions as escaped to remove them, and the French troops passing directly over into the valley of the Rhone. The landlord at the Hospice found a decayed musket lying by a skeleton under a rock about 12 months ago, at some distance from the scene of the skirmish."

The source of the Aar lies in two enormous glaciers, the *Ober* and *Unter-Aar-Gletscher*, to the W. of the Hospice. The Unter-Aar glacier is the best worth visiting, and the lower extremity of the ice may be reached in 1½ hr. from the Hospice. It is remarkable for the evenness of the surface of ice and the rareness of cavities on its surface. It is about 18 m. long, and from 2 to 4 broad. Out of the midst of it rises the Finster-Aarhorn; the Schreckhorn is also conspicuous. These Aar glaciers are among the most interesting in Switzerland for those who would study the natural history of those singular natural phenomena, their progression, moraines, &c. (§ 16.) They are accessible by a bad path, but without danger (§ 13), and with little difficulty, and the scenery around is sublime in the extreme. The line of junction of the two glaciers of the Upper and Lower Aar is marked by a high and broad ridge of ice, covered with fragments of rocks, the combined moraine from the two glaciers. It rises in some places to a height of 80 ft., and resembles an artificial causeway or pier. The progressive annual march of the glacier is marked by the present situation of a huge block of white granite, which afforded shelter to a rude hut now in ruins, built by M. Hugi in 1827, at the foot of the rock *Im Abschwung*, the last projecting promontory separating the two glaciers, which, in 1840, had advanced 4600 ft. from that spot. It takes about 4½ hours, of which three are on the ice, to reach this, and 3 to return. On this glacier *M. Agassiz* of Neuchâtel erected a cabin of dry stones, under an enormous block of mica schist, known as Hôtel des Neuchâtelois, and here he carried on a series of interesting investigations and experiments respecting the glaciers for several seasons in succession. This also is no longer tenable; the huge rock which covered it has split in two; but a more permanent hut has been erected on the l. bank of the glacier, by *M. Dollfus* of Mühlhausen, 7885 ft. above the sea-level, by means of which observations were made in the way introduced by Prof. Forbes, 1842.

A *Panorama* of the Grimsel and the neighbouring peaks and glaciers may be seen from the top of the *Sidelhorn*, a mountain on the rt. of the path leading to Brieg and the Furca; its summit may be reached in 3 hours from the Hospice: it is 9500 ft. above the sea-level. The ascent is not very difficult, and the view magnificent. It is possible to descend from the summit of the Sidelhorn to the Ober-Aar glacier, and thence by very rough ground to the lower end of the Unter-Aar glacier.

Grimsel to Hospenthal by the Furca.

About 7½ hrs. = say 19 Eng. m. It is 5¼ or 6 hrs. walk, except when snow lies thick, when it may take 8. The bridle-path is by no means dangerous, and not very difficult, excepting the part between the summit of the Grimsel and the glacier of the Rhone called *Mayenwand*, which it is better to cross on foot than on horseback. Guide not necessary except to show the path in one or two places.

The summit of the pass of the Grimsel (7530 ft. above the sea, 700 ft. above the Hospice) is 2 m. from the Hospice, 1 hr. — a steep path, marked by tall poles stuck into the rock to guide the wayfarer, leads up to it. On the crest lies another small lake, called *Todten See*, or Lake of the Dead, either from the dead sterility around, or because the bodies of those who perished on the pass were thrown into it by way of burial. There is a little-known pass from this point to the Gadmenthal (Rte. 28 A b). Along the crest of the mountain runs the boundary between Berne and the Valais, and here the path divides, that on the rt. going to Ober-Gesteln (Rte. 28 B).

The pedestrian without a guide should be careful which path he takes. If he is bound for the Furca he will soon see the glacier of the Rhone below him as a guide.

The path leaves on the rt. hand the gloomy little Lake of the Dead, and skirting along the brink of a precipitous slope, descends very rapidly. This portion of the way is the worst of the whole, being very steep, slippery, and muddy. However, it soon brings the traveller in sight of the Glacier, though at a considerable depth below him. On attaining the bottom of the Mayenwald, he will find a rustic *Inn*, affording accommodation both for eating and sleeping, but where he will be subject to extortion : let him be on his guard. [By keeping to the l. on the descent the pedestrian may avoid part of the Mayenwand and the Inn, and cross the glacier, which presents no difficulties ; having crossed it he will fall into the path to Furca.]

[About ½ m. above the Inn the Rhone issues out to day at the foot of the *Rhone Glacier*, one of the grandest in Switzerland, fit cradle for so mighty a stream. It fills the head of the valley from side to side, and appears piled up against the shoulder of the Gallenstock, whose tall peak overhangs it. The source of the Rhone, in a cavern of ice, is about 5400 ft. above the sea. If you pursue a track up the W. side, or rt. bank of the glacier, you come suddenly upon a very fine waterfall, rushing forth from the summit of the glacier, and dashing without a break into an icy cavern about 150 ft. below, sending forth clouds of freezing spray. This large body of water, after forming a passage for itself under the glacier, issues forth from the cavern at its foot.]

The path leading to the Furca ascends along the E. side of the vast basin, having the glacier on the l. for a considerable distance. From this point the best view is obtained of this magnificent sea of ice, and a correct idea may be formed of its extent and thickness as the traveller passes within stone's throw of its yawning crevices. The path then leaves the glacier to mount upwards through a valley of green pastures to the summit of the pass, or *Fork*, between two mountain peaks, from which it receives its name. There are numerous tracks, but they all lead to the Furca. From this point, 8150 ft. above the sea, near the Cross which marks the boundary of the cantons of the Valais and of Uri, there is a beautiful view of the Bernese Chain, the Finster-Aar-Horn being pre-eminent among its peaks. The top of the Furca is never altogether free from snow : there is no plain or level surface on it. On the Furca is a good *Inn*, comfortably furnished, with 25 beds. It serves as convenient quarters for those who would enjoy the view from the *Furca Horn* (1 hr. above the inn) at sunset or sunrise. The descent commences as soon as the crest is crossed, over the Sidli Alp, which is covered with pastures, but monotonous and uninteresting in its scenery, and destitute of trees. The traveller must pick his way, as he best may, among a multitude of deep holes cut by the feet of mules and cattle to

Realp. Here the Capuchin monks have a small chapel and convent of ease, and receive travellers. There is also a tolerable Inn here. From Realp the ascent of the Galenstock, 10,370 ft., and also of the Gollenstock, which is said to be very accessible, may be made. It is about 4 m. of level walking hence to

Hospenthal, on the St. Gothard (Rte. 34) (*Inn :* Golden Lion, civil landlord) ; or 2½ m. farther to Andermatt (Rte. 34).

The traveller must not trust the representations of the innkeepers on this road as to the goodness or badness of the Inns at the other stations.

ROUTE 28A.

PASSES LEADING FROM THE GRIMSEL.

Besides the mule-paths leading over the Grimsel there are several passes in different directions, suited only to those who are accustomed to ice.

a.—STRAHLECK—GRINDELWALD TO GRIMSEL.

A very difficult pass indeed, suited only to skilful mountaineers. In fine weather it is free from danger. It is one of the most striking in the Alps, and is now not uncommonly performed. It may be accomplished in 14 or 15 hrs. This hard day's work may be broken by sleeping in the highest châlets at the foot of the Viescherhörner, 3 easy hrs. from Grindelwald.

The path, on leaving Grindelwald, ascends rapidly on the l. hand of the lower glacier, and is practicable for horses for about ½ an hour; it then becomes very narrow, being a mere groove in the rock overhanging the glacier. After crossing two or three planks laid across some crevasses in the glacier at the angle of a rock, we reach the châlet of Stiereck, a short 2 hrs. from Grindelwald, and so far it is the excursion described Rte. 25 c. A few minutes beyond the pastures of the Stiereck, the mountains again close in upon the ice, and the path mounts rapidly for some distance, when the mountains again recede, and one continues for a time on tolerably level ground. At the extremity of this it is necessary to get on the glacier; after a few minutes it is again necessary to return to *terra firma*, to turn a projecting rock, a matter of considerable difficulty and danger late in the season when the glacier has subsided. This accomplished, the path ascends rapidly for nearly an hour, when some overhanging rocks are reached, which seem to be the established resting-place. Soon afterwards the glacier is again reached, and all path terminates. From this point the view of the Schreckhorn, which rises immediately over you on the left, is truly magni-

ficent. This is by far the finest part of the excursion. Continuing along the glacier (which is here without crevasses, but difficult to walk on, on account of its steep slope from the left), and passing immediately below two lateral glaciers, which almost overhang you, a nearly precipitous wall of snow is reached, forming the end of the valley. At this point you turn to the left, and, ascending the glacier a few hundred feet, reach a shady ridge of rocks rising very steeply, and at right angles to the former route. This is ascended for about 1½ hr., when a platform of snow is reached, across which, after another short but steep ascent, the summit is gained in ½ an hour. " The descent, which occupied us 2½ hours, need not occupy one-fifth of that time, when there is an abundance of new snow; but it was at the time in a very dangerous state, on account of the thin coating of snow on the ice, which is inclined at a very steep angle. In consequence, though the descent is not more than 600 or 800 feet at the utmost, it occupied us 2½ hrs."

The summit of the Strahleck is, indeed, the perfection of wild scenery. Vegetation there is none, save a few of the smallest gentianellas. From the foot of the passage, the Abschwung, where Professor Agassiz's hut was situated, may be reached in 1½ hour: thence to the hospice of the Grimsel will take a good walker 3 hours, two of them on the ice

The demands of the guides at Grindelwald for this pass should not be submitted to. On one occasion they asked 180 fr. and took 30 fr. The pass is about 9750 ft. high, and it is perhaps more easy to descend from the Grimsel than to ascend from Grindelwald. The day may then be shortened by sleeping a night at the hut of M. Dollfus at the Aar glacier.

This pass was crossed by an English lady in 1841, by the aid of 12 guides and porters.

b.—GADMENTHAL TO GRIMSEL.

Though this is a very beautiful pass, it has been but seldom traversed, and has not as yet received a name.

" Having engaged Arnold Kehrli of Muhlethal as my guide, I set out from a little inn near Obermatt, at the foot of the Susten pass, at ½ past 5 o'clock on the morning of the 22nd Aug. 1854. The ascent for some way is along the l. of the ravine, down which flows the stream from the Triften glacier. In 2½ hrs. we got upon the lower part of this glacier; at first it was a good deal crevassed, but soon became more even: we continued our way along it for 1 h. and 20 min., when it became steeper, and was no longer practicable. We then ascended a rock on our l. hand, as steep as that of the Strahleck, but of a firmer kind of stone, which affords good hold for hand and foot, and in 1 h. were again on the upper part of the glacier, which is covered with snow, and not much crevassed. In 2 hrs. more of gradual ascent we arrived at the summit, which I believe is above 10,000 ft. high, and is a rounded ridge covered with snow, at right angles to the chain of mountains whose highest peak is the Galenstock, and to that called the Naglis Grat, a precipitous ridge whose sides are too steep for much snow to rest upon. The view from hence is very fine, the Galenstock being a prominent object in the foreground. From the summit, the descent of the Rhone glacier to the place where it begins to tumble into the valley occupied nearly 2 hrs. There are many small crevasses in part of this glacier which, when I crossed, were concealed with fresh snow, and we found the rope by which we were tied together very useful. The moraine on the right of the glacier and the mountain side were then followed till we came to the range of hill over which the Grimsel pass runs. We struck into it, and, after a refreshing bathe in the Tödten See, arrived at the hospice of the Grimsel at 5 o'clock. Including stoppages this pass took 11½ hrs., of which about 5¼ were upon the ice."—R. F.

c.—OBERAARJOCH—GRIMSEL TO VIESCH.

This is one of the most magnificent passes in Switzerland. It is a hard

day's work, and the descent of the Viescher glacier is very difficult, but the grandeur of its scenery, in the heart of the Bernese Oberland, will well repay any traveller who may explore it in fine weather.

" On the morning of the 27th Aug. 1854, I set out from the Grimsel at 10 min. before 3 o'clock, with Melchior Anderegg of the Grimsel, and Arnold Kehrli as my guides, both of whom I strongly recommend. As far as the foot of the Unteraar glacier the route is the same as that of the Strahleck pass: here it turns along the edge of the Oberaar glacier on its right side, as far as some châlets, where we had to wait for 40 min., till the rising sun dispersed the mists which lay upon the glacier. At 6 o'clock we took to the ice ; it is but little crevassed, and resembles much the Unteraar glacier, but it rises with a more rapid slope. Towards the summit of the pass the ice is covered with snow; we tied ourselves together with a rope, and some care was necessary to avoid the concealed crevasses. We reached the summit of the pass at 9 o'clock, and soon commenced the descent, which, at first, is down snow slopes, then upon the glacier, over and among the enormous crevasses for nearly 2 hrs. Having passed at the foot of the glacier which descends between the Rothhorn and the Viescherhörner, we left the ice for a while, and descended by the foot of the latter mountain; afterwards we sometimes followed the glacier (which always is much crevassed), sometimes its moraine or the mountain on its right, till at last, by a very steep descent, Viesch was reached at 50 min. past 3 P.M. Including stoppages of 1½ h., this pass took me 13 hrs., of which 6 were on the ice."—R. F.

The inn on the Æggishorn would now be better than Viesch.

d.—TO MEYRINGEN, OVER THE LAUTERAAR AND GAULI GLACIERS.

" We set out from the hospice of the Grimsel a little after 5 A.M. For some distance the route is the same as that of the Strahleck, but, instead of turning to the l. up the Finsteraar glacier, it inclines to the rt. along the Lauteraar to near its head, where the ridge of the Lauteraarsattel runs across from the Schreckhorn to the mountain marked in Keller's map Berglistock, but called by Anderegg, Schneehorn. Here we turned to our rt. and commenced the ascent of the steep ridge of rock which, running from the last-named mountain, forms the boundary between the Lauteraar and Gauli glaciers. After having reached about half its height, we turned again to our rt. for some distance, parallel to the Lauteraar glacier, till we came to where the passage of the ridge is to be made. The ascent is up rock and loose shingle to the summit, which is very narrow. On the northern side the descent is down an extremely steep slope of hard frozen snow, which occupied nearly 1 h. before we reached the Gauli glacier, down which we slid, and before 2 o'clock were off the ice. The route then is down the Urbach Thal, and in parts is very steep. At Hof we struck in upon the road to Meyringen, and reached that town a little after 6 o'clock, having been 13 hrs., including stoppages, in coming by this pass from the Grimsel; 5½ hrs. were upon the ice."—R. F.

c.—GRIMSEL TO ROSENLAUI.

This is the same as the route to Meyringen for a considerable distance, but after crossing the Reufen and Gauli glaciers the head of the Rosenlaui glacier is found, and by descending this the inn at Rosenlaui (Rte. 25 D) is reached. The path is described as difficult, and requiring a long day from Rosenlaui to Prof. Agassiz's Pavillon des Alpes. The view from the top of the Rosenlaui glacier is very fine.

ROUTE 28 B.

GRIMSEL TO BRIEG, BY OBERGESTELN— ÆGGISHORN.

On reaching the summit of the Grimsel Pass (Rte. 28) the path leads to the rt., whilst the Furca path goes to the l. It is a walk of 2¼ hrs. from the Grimsel to Ober-Gesteln.

[It would be worth the while of the traveller bound to Ober-Gesteln to make a détour of about 6 m. by the l. hand path to visit the glacier and source of the Rhone (Rte. 28). Below the glacier, the Rhone plunges through a magnificent gorge before reaching Oberwald. The path is rough and stony : it is 1¾ hrs. walk from the Rhone glacier to Ober-Gesteln.]

Ober-Gesteln (Fr., Haut Châtillon) (*Inn*, Cheval Blanc ; clean and civil), the highest village but one (Oberwald being the highest) in the Upper Valais, 4360 ft. above the sea-level. It is situated on the rt. bank of the Rhone, about 8 m. below its source in the glacier. It is the depôt for the cheese transported out of canton Berne into Italy, and is a place of some traffic, as it lies at the junction of the 4 bridle-roads over the Grimsel, Furca, Nüfenen, and Gries (Rte. 29).

In 1720, 84 men were killed here by an avalanche, and lie buried in one grave in the churchyard.

The descent of the Upper Valais from Ober-Gesteln to Brieg, a distance of 8 hrs., is tame and uninteresting above Niederwald, below which, especially about Viesch, its scenery is singularly beautiful. The road runs along the rt. bank of the Rhone. From Oberwald a path diverges over the col of the Gerenhorn to the Nüfenen. Between Oberwald and Viesch in descending, the peak of the Weisshorn is a noble object, and, though 40 m. off, seems to block up the valley. Looking up, the Gallenstock appears in view with like grandeur. Opposite the village of Ulrichen, the valley of Eginen opens out — up it runs the path leading over the Gries

d the Nüfenen (Rte. 35). The
pper Valais (Ober-Wallis) is very
opulous, and numerous unimportant
llages are passed in rapid succession.
ne of the largest is

Münster, containing about 400 In-
ab., and a good *Inn,* La Croix d'Or,
full view of the peak of the Weiss-
orn, a neighbour of Monte Rosa.
he landlord, J. B. Guntren, is a trust-
orthy guide. Horses for hire. The
atives of the Upper Valais are a
istinct and apparently superior race
those of the Lower. The language
German. The Romans never pe-
etrated into the higher part of the
hone valley.

Viesch (a capital country *Inn,* H.
a Glacier) lies at the entrance of a
de valley, blocked up at its upper
ttremity by a glacier, above which
se the peaks called Viescher-Hörner.
here exists a tradition that a path
nce led up this valley to Grindel·
ald: it is now entirely stopped by
e glacier, and this circumstance is
pposed to prove a great increase of
e mass of ice. Good char-road to
rieg.

Laax (Croix Blanche, good). [Hence
Kippel over the Aletsch and Lotsch
laciers, is a fine pass, but difficult.
Rte. 60).]

[From Viesch the *Æggishorn* or
tishorn (9000 ft. above the sea, 6000
bove Viesch) can be conveniently
scended. A mule-path leads to the
ry good *Inn,* which has now been
uilt upon the mountain, 2 hrs. from
iesch, 1 h. 30 m. from the summit.
his inn forms an admirable starting-
lace for numerous excursions to ob-
cts and views hardly surpassed
mongst the Alps :—1. to the summit;
. to the *Aletsch* glacier, 2 hrs. (Rte.
5 c); 3. to the Col de Jungfrau,
hrs.; 4. over the Viesch glacier to
he Grimsel (Rte. 28 A, c); 5. by the
Ioerel to Brieg; 6. ascent of the Fin-
teraarhorn (Rte. 25 c, b); 7. ascent
f the Jungfrau.

The summit of the Æggishorn is a
harp pile of stones forming an insu-
ated point, commanding a superb view
f the S. side of the Bernese Alps, and
f the mountains of the Valais, from

[*Switz.*]

the Furca to the Matterhorn, and
perhaps to Mont Blanc. Immediately
below, at the bottom of one branch of
the great glacier of Aletsch, is a small
lake, of deep cerulean blue, studded
with floating icebergs—a most picturesque and singular feature in the
scene. Travellers sometimes descend
on a cheese-sledge, fitted up for the
occasion with a cushion, &c., with
great ease, rapidity, and satisfaction.

Whether for the purpose of enjoying the panorama from the Æggisch-
horn, or for exploring the upper portion, the great Aletsch glacier, and
ascending the peaks which surround
it, the new *Inn* offers very great convenience. The landlord is extremely
attentive and obliging, and the charges
are moderate.]

[Opposite to Viesch, a pass, by the
Binnen Thal, apparently of no particular beauty, leads into the Val Formazza. (See Rte. 29.)]

Mörill (*Inn:* Venals).

The stream of the Massa, descending from the N., is supplied by the
great glacier of Aletsch, a branch of
that vast expanse of ice which extends
to Grindelwald in Canton Berne.

Naters, a village of 600 Inhab.,
lies in a beautiful situation and in a
milder climate, where the chestnut
begins to flourish. Above it rises the
ruined castle of Auf der Flüh, or
Supersax.

A wooden bridge leads across the
Rhone to the great high road at

Brieg (*Inn,* Post), at the foot of
the Simplon (Rte. 59 B).

F

ROUTE 29.

PASS OF THE GRIES, OBER-GESTELN
TO DOMO D'OSSOLA, BY THE VAL
FORMAZZA (POMMAT), AND THE
FALLS OF THE TOSA.

About 14 hrs. It is a walk of 8
hrs. over the Gries to Formazza. A
carriage-road ascends the valley from
Domo d'Ossola to Premia and San
Rocco. A guide is necessary over the
Col as far as Frutval, or he may be
dismissed safely when you have descended from the Col ¾ hr. 'Thus he
may get home the same day, and back-
hire be saved. Münster, having a
good *Inn* (Rte. 28 B), is a better
starting-point than Ober-Gesteln.

It is a mule-path, not dangerous,
though it crosses a glacier, except
when there is much snow on the col,
but difficult and very fatiguing. The
traveller who follows it will be rewarded by the scenes of wildness and
grandeur of the Val Antigorio and
Formazza, which are nowhere exceeded among the Alps. It is not a
pass for ladies.

On the Italian side of the Pass the
Baths of Crodo are *good* quarters, and
at Premia is an Inn. From either of
these places it is easy to go in one day
across the pass of the Val Tosa into
canton Tessin. The passage of the
Gries requires a long summer's day,
as, notwithstanding the apparently
short distance on the map, the walk
up the valley from Crodo to Formazza
requires full 6 hrs., and thence to
Ober-Gesteln 8 hrs.

In crossing the Nüfenen or Gries
from Brieg it is useless to go to Ober-
Gesteln. The traveller ascending the
Valais can pass the Rhone by a bridge
a little above Münster (*Inn* good), and
reach the Eginenthal in an hour.

Below *Ober-Gesteln* (Rte. 28 B) a
bridge leads across the Rhone, and
the path follows the l. bank as far as
the village Im Loch, where it turns
to the l., and begins to ascend the
Eginenthal, a barren and uninteresting valley, crossing the stream of the
Eginen above a pretty cascade 80 ft.

high. A hard climb of about 2 hrs.,
first through larch-wood, then across
a sterile, stony tract, and finally over
a little plain of green meadow, dotted
with the châlets of Egina, brings the
traveller to the foot of the final and
most difficult ascent. Near this point
a path, striking off on the l., leads
over the pass of the Nüfenen (Rte.
35) to Airolo. Here vegetation ceases,
snow appears first in patches, and at
last the glacier blocks up the termination of the valley, and the path
makes a short cut over an elbow of it.
It takes about 20 min. to cross. The
direction of the path over it is marked
by 2 or 3 poles stuck upright in the
ice. Along the crest of the mountain
runs the frontier line separating Switzerland from Sardinia. The summit of
the pass is 7900 ft. above the sea.

"Bare and scathed rocks rose on
either side in terrible grandeur out
of the glaciers to an immense height.
The silence of the place added greatly
to its sublimity; and I saw, in this
most appropriate spot, one of the large
eagles of the Alps, the lämmergeyer,
which was whirling its flight round
a mountain-peak, and increased the
deep emotion excited by the solitude
of the scene."—*Brockedon.*

In clear weather a magnificent view
presents itself from this point of the
chain of Bernese Alps. The descent
on the Sardinian side of the pass (as
usual among the Alps) is steeper than
on the N.; it is also more difficult.
The upper part of the Piedmontese
valley of Formazza, or Frutval, presents four distinct stages or platforms,
separated by steep steps, or dips, from
each other. The first is called Bettel-
matt; the second Morast (morass), on
which the miserable group of châlets
called Kehrbächi (the highest winter
habitations) are situated. The third
is Auf der Frutt, with another hamlet
of châlets, and a small chapel. Before
reaching it, the traveller falls in with
the river Toccio, or Tosa, which rises
in the upper extremity of the valley,
and terminates in the Lago Maggiore.
Beyond the hamlet the path crosses
to the l. bank of the stream, and
descending the fourth steep decli-

vity, arrives at the *Falls of the Tosa*, the approach to which has for some time previously been proclaimed by the increasing roar of the water. It is one of the most remarkable cataracts among the Alps, less on account of its form than for its vast volume of water, in which it is surpassed only by that of the Schaffhausen. It does not descend in one leap, but in a succession of steps, forming an uninterrupted mass of white foam for a length of perhaps 1000 ft., while the entire perpendicular descent is not much less than 500. Seen from below, it has a triangular appearance; above, not more than 80 ft. wide, and expanding gradually towards the bottom. It is the only Swiss fall combining great height with a large body of water. At the back of the falls a mule-path leads in 4 hrs. to Hospice All' Acqua in the Val Bedretto (Rte. 35).

2 m. below the Falls is the village of Frutval, situated on the 4th plateau. 2 m. farther are the villages of *Pommat* and *Wald*, where is a tolerable *Inn*, 3 rooms and 6 beds. The inhabitants of the upper part of the valley, as far as Foppiano, are of German descent, speaking that language, and, according to tradition, descendants of a colony from the Entlebuch. Owing to this intermixture of languages, almost all the villages have a German as well as Italian name.

Formazza (An der Matt), about 33 m. from Domo. A tolerable *Inn*. Here is the principal church of the valley.

The lower part of the vale of the Tosa abounds in exquisite scenery. The Gorge of Foppiano (Germ. Unter-Stalden), 5 m. below Formazza, is particularly grand. Lower down it expands, and displays all the softer beauties of high cultivation, luxuriant vegetation, and thick population. Below the village called Premia, where there is a dear *Inn* (All' Aquelle), a stream descending from the W. joins the Tosa, and the valley changes its name into Val Antigorio.

"The savage grandeur of the Val Formazza, down which the river takes its passage, and the delicious region through which it rolls in the Val Antigorio, cannot be painted in too glowing colours. In these high valleys, fully exposed to the power of the summer sun, there is truly a 'blending of all beauties.' The vine, the fig, and the broad-leafed chestnut, and other proofs of the luxuriance of the soil of Italy, present themselves everywhere to the eye, intermixed with the grey blocks resting on the flanks and at the feet of the high granite ridge, out of whose recesses you have not as yet escaped. Instead of the weather-stained and simple habitation of the hardy Vallaisan, sheltered by the black belt of forest, upon which alone I had glanced yesterday, I now saw, on the southern declivity of the same range, the substantial Italian structure, with its regular outline, and simple yet beautiful proportion, and the villa, the handsome church, or the stone cottage, surrounded by its girdle of vines—the vine not in its stiff and unpicturesque Swiss or Rhenish dress, but the true vine of Italy and of poetry, flinging its pliant and luxuriant branches over the rustic veranda, or twining its long garland from tree to tree.'—*Latrobe.*

This charming valley is the chosen retreat of numerous retired citizens, such as bankers, jewellers, &c., who have built themselves villas in it. The mica-slate rocks occurring near Premia and San Michele are stuck as full of red garnets as a pudding is with plums. There are several timber-slides for bringing down trees from the high forests. The trees are floated down the Tosa, and thus conveyed to Milan. An excellent carriage-road has been carried up to *Premia* from Domo d'Ossola, 4½ hrs. walking.

[A short distance below Premia is a pass by the *Binnen-Thal* to the Upper Valais. " Three hours, mostly of very steep ascent, past the village of Croveo, and through chesnut and walnut woods, brought me to the Osteria di Devorio, a mountain-inn, where a pedestrian might pass the night, charmingly situated. Two hours more, through short mountain-basons, separated by steep ascents, over rich pastures and through noble larch woods, to the last châlets, near the upper end of a mountain-lake. Here I changed the barber of *Baicno* for another guide, and commenced the last ascent, which is like one of the grandest Scotch passes on an enlarged scale. There is no permanent snow I believe, but plenty on the 19th of June. From Baieno to the summit about 6 hrs. leisurely walking. Downwards, a long tract of snow, then bare pastures, then a long and grand ravine, with magnificent larch and spruce: here there is a good horse-path, but skirting deep precipices, with some very queer corners. The descent to the village of Aernen took 4 hrs. : there is a good Swiss inn, and capital wine. Another hour to Lax. I believe that, by varying the route, a traveller might reach Brieg without lengthening his day's work more than 2 hrs. There are two other practicable passes from the Osteria di Devorio, higher, shorter, and considerably harder. From Formazza also there is a pass, 2 hrs. E. from the châlets, with 2 hrs. glacier—*ma tutto piano.* A continuous glacier from this valley eastward to the Gries. Vincenzo Proletti of Croveo, usually at the châlets in summer, seems to know his country well, and is well content with 5 francs."]

At *Crodo* (Germ. Crot) there is an *Inn.* At Ponte Maglio is the Sardinian Custom-house. 2 m. below Crodo, 2¼ hrs.' walk below Premia, are the *Baths of Crodo,* a large and well-furnished house, opened 1848 : charge en pension 5 frs. a-day, baths extra. The waters contain iron. A spring rises in the gardens. Near this are gold-mines. Carriages and horses may be hired here.

Below Crodo the carriage-road crosses the river twice before it reaches San Marco, and then enters the *Simplon road*, at the lofty and beautiful bridge of Crevola, near the new cemetery, at the junction of the Vedro with the Tosa. (Rte. 59 B.)

3 m. farther on lies *Domo d'Ossola.* (Rte. 59 B.)

ROUTE 31.

STANZ TO ENGELBERG.   ENGELBERG TO ALTORF, BY THE SURENEN PASS.   THE TITLIS.

A walk of 10½ to 15 hrs. The best plan is to sleep at Engelberg and cross the pass next day.

There is a good char-road from Stanz (Rte. 19) to Engelberg (4½ hours' walk; car, 1 horse, 12 fr.; ditto 2, 20 fr.); thence to Altorf, across the pass, a horse-path.

The road from *Stanz* to Engelberg follows the course of the Aa upwards, gradually ascending, and passing Wolfenschiess with its ruined castle, and Gràfenort, where there is a small inn. Beyond this the valley contracts. The road is carried up a steep ascent nearly 6 m. long, traversing thick woods, amidst scenery of the highest sublimity. In the midst of it, in the depth of the valley, lie the village and *Abbey of Engelberg*—(*Inns:* Engel, good and clean ; Rössli) —3220 ft. above the sea. It is hemmed in on all sides by lofty mountains topped with snow, and based by precipices from which, in winter time and in spring, numerous avalanches are precipitated. At their base, upon a verdant slope, contrasting agreeably with rock and snow, the Benedictine Abbey rises conspicuous among the ordinary habitations of the village. It was founded in 1120, and received from Pope Calixtus II. the name of *Mons Angelorum,* from a tradition that the site of the building was fixed by angels—

" Whose authentic lay,
Sung from that heavenly ground, in middle air,
Made known the spot where Piety should raise
A holy structure to th'Almighty's praise."
Wordsworth.

Having been three times destroyed by fire, the existing edifice is not older than the middle of the last century. " The architecture is plain and unimpressive, but the situation is worthy of the honours which the imagination of the mountaineers has conferred upon it." The convent is independent of any bishop or sovereign but the Pope himself, or his legate : its revenues, once more considerable, were seriously diminished by the French, but it still possesses valuable alpine pastures, and the cheeses produced on them are stored in an adjacent warehouse and cellars. It contains, at present, only 19 brothers: it has a large Church and a Library of some value, rich in Swiss early printed books and illuminated MSS. ; the roof of the apartment in which it is placed has been cracked by an earthquake. Travellers are received and entertained in the convent—those of the poorer classes gratuitously.

The *Titlis*, the chief of the mountains which overhang this romantic solitude, rises on the S. of the convent to a height of 7000 ft. above the valley, and 10,690 ft. above the sea-level. Its principal peak, the Nollen, composed of limestone, is said to be visible (?) from Strasburg : it is frequently ascended, and more easily from the inn in the Engstler-Thal (Rte. 33) than from Engelberg. The first hour from Engelberg can be accomplished on horses, after which there is a sharp ascent for an hour through woods ; the path then continues over pastures which gradually become rocks mixed with patches of snow, and the last hour is over a snowy ridge. The ascent occupies 6 or 7 hours. It is covered with a cap of snow or névé, from which numerous avalanches fall, in spring, with a roar like thunder.

The *Pass of the Joch* (see Rte. 33) leads from Engelberg to Meyringen in 10 hrs.

[Two passes lead from Engelberg into the head of the Melchthal, the *Jöchli*, somewhat difficult, and the *Storegg*, shorter, less high, and more frequented. The path, however, is indifferent and ill-defined in places. It leaves the small lake, called Luter See, on the rt., and ascends the l. hand mountain ; 6 hrs. are required from Engelberg to Sachselen.]

From Engelberg to Altorf, by the Pass of the *Surenen*, is a walk of 8 hrs. When there is fresh snow on the pass 9 or 10 hrs. should be allowed. The footpath reaches, after about 3m., the dairy belonging to the convent, called Herrenreuti, where good cheese is made : 50 cows are attached to it ; the pastures are refreshed by more than 20 springs rising upon them. From the steep sides of the Hahnenberg, on the N.E., a beautiful waterfall bursts forth, called Dätschbach. The path now winds round the base of a projecting mountain, beyond which the valley makes a bend in a N.E. direction, and, following the course of the Aa torrent for about 6 m., crosses it, and then turns nearly due E. The Stierenbach, the principal feeder of that stream, is now seen descending in a pretty cascade into the deep abyss. Half an hour's walk below the summit stand a few châlets, and beyond them the traveller has generally to traverse patches of snow, to the summit of the pass, or Surenen Eck, a narrow ridge 6720 ft. above the sea, not more than 5 ft. wide, between the Blakenstock on the l. and the Schlossberg on the rt. During the greater part of the ascent the Titlis shines forth an object of the greatest magnificence, and a long line of peaks and glaciers extends from it uninterruptedly to the Surenen. Another view now opens out on the opposite side into the valleys of Maderan and Schächen, and is bounded in the extreme distance by the snowy top of the Glärnisch in canton Glarus. On the side of the Surenen, lying within the limits of canton Uri, the surface of snow to be crossed often is greater, and the descent is steeper. Traversing the snow, and a desolate tract covered with broken rocks beyond, the châlets of Waldnacht are passed; and then, by the frightful gorge of Boghy, the path is conducted into the valley of the Reuss, forking off on the rt. to Erstfeld, for those who wish to ascend the St. Gothard—and on the l. to Attinghausen, for those who are bound to Altorf.

In 1799, a division of the French army, under Lecourbe, crossed this pass with cannon to attack the Austrians in the valley of the Reuss, but were soon driven back the same way by the impetuous descent of Suwarrow from the St. Gothard.

Altorf (Rte. 34).

ROUTE 32.

PASS OF THE SUSTEN, FROM MEYRINGEN
OR REICHENBACH TO WASEN.

11½ hrs. 10 hrs.' walk.

In 1811, when the Valais was added by Napoleon to the French empire, a char-road was constructed from Meyringen to Stein, and on the side of canton Uri from Wasen to Ferningen, to enable the inhabitants of canton Berne to convey their produce into Italy through the Swiss territory. It has fallen out of repair in many places, and can only be regarded as a bridle-path. It is a fine pass ; the Gadmenthal being very grand, in parts somewhat like the Trosachs, on a grander scale. It is a much frequented path : no guide required in clear weather. It enables a stout pedestrian to proceed in one long day from Meyringen to Wasen, on the St. Gothard, but the distance is almost too much, and it is usual to stop for the night at Stein. The word Sust means toll or custom-house, whence the name.

The route of the Grimsel is followed from Meyringen as far as Im Hof (Rte. 28), where, quitting the side of the Aar, the path follows the course of the Gadmen, ascending the valley called, at its lower extremity, Muhli-thal, and higher up Nessel-thal. Here the narrow Trift-thal opens from the S., with fine glimpses of the Triften-stock and gletscher. Beyond this the valley is named Gadmenthal.

The road passes through a fine grove of venerable sycamores, above which the Titlis rises superbly, before you reach in 4½ hrs.

Gadmen. (*Inn :* Bear, shaded by sycamores, clean and tolerable.) There is a little-known pass hence to the Grimsel (Rte. 28 A b). This village of 550 Inhab. is 3750 ft. above the sea-level, and is composed of 3 distinct groups of houses, Eck, Ambuhl, and Obermatt, ¾ mile higher up. The char-road was not carried further than the châlets of Steinen, and a portion of it was destroyed a few years ago by the sudden advance of the glacier of Steinen, which 30 years ago was more than a mile distant from it, descending from a valley on the S. The appearance of the glacier is remarkable, as it assumes a fan shape at its termination. At the foot of the Steinen glacier is a clean little *Inn*, the only good halting-place. It is 6 hours' walk from Stein to Meyringen. A steep ascent of 2 hours brings the traveller to

The top of the Susten Pass, 6980 ft. above the level of the Mediterranean. The view is very fine ; the serrated ridges, and the many pointed peaks of the mountains bounding the May-enthal, through which the descent lies, especially arrest the attention. There is always some snow on the E. declivity of the Pass, fringed by heaths, juniper, and Alp roses. The first châlets are met with on the Hunds-alp. The stream of the Mayen-Reuss, issuing out of the Susten glacier (rt.), under the Susten Horn, is crossed several times, until at the Hauser-brücke, a considerable distance below Fernigen, the unfinished char-road again commences. Near Fernigen the deeply engulfed and foaming Gurez-mittlerbach is crossed. Lower down is the village of Mayen, or Meyen, where there is an *Inn*, not so good as those at Gadmen or Stein. Most of the houses in this valley are protected from the descending avalanches by a stone-dyke, or well-propped palisade of wood raised on the hill-side behind them, to turn away the falling snow from their roofs. Near the junction of the valleys of the Mayen and the Reuss are shattered remains of an hexagonal redoubt (schanze), which was fortified by the Austrians in 1799, and stormed and taken from them by the French under Loison, who forced the enemy back up the vale of the Reuss, and, after five assaults, made himself master of Wasen, an important point. A very steep and rough road leads down from this into the village.

Wasen, on the St. Gothard (Rte. 34). Hours' walking *from* Wasen 4½ to the Pass ; ¾ to Stein; 1¾ to Gadmen; 3 to Im Hof; 1½ to Meyringen = total, 10¾ hours.

ROUTE 33.

THE JOCH PASS, FROM MEYRINGEN TO ENGELBERG.

Distance about 10 hrs. This Pass, though practicable for horses, and a good deal used, is a very high one, and steep. It is a fine Pass, with considerable variety of scenery, commanding beautiful views of the Titlis. As far as Im Hof it is the same as Rte. 28.

The village of *Wyler,* on the summit of the rise above Im Hof, is reached in 1¼ hr. from Meyringen. The Gadmen torrent is there crossed, and the path ascends rapidly for another hour, when the pastures at the lower extremity of the Gentel Thal are reached, in which is a pure spring, very grateful after the hot ascent from Wyler. From this point the path continues on a very gradual rise for 1½ hour up the pastures of the *Engstlen Alp,* celebrated for the *Schwing-Feste,* or gymnastic games held here by the youths of Hasli and Unterwalden at the end of July; it then enters the forests, and after another hour reaches the best châlets, near the *Engstlen See,* a considerable lake, which is, however, not visible from them. The best accommodation on the Pass is to be found in these châlets. Near them is a remarkable intermittent *Spring,* called *Wunderbrunnen.* It flows from spring to autumn, always running from 8 A.M. to about 4 P.M., when it ceases.

" Before entering the forest the path crosses the Engstlerbach, just below a very pretty fall of the Gentbach, and recrosses the stream some way higher up. After leaving the châlets, the path descends a very little towards the lake, and, keeping for a few minutes along the brink, rises in about ½ hour to the summit of the Pass, about 7380 Eng. ft. above the sea-level. Near the summit a very comfortable little *Inn* has been built, from which many excursions may be made, and the ascent of *Titlis* (Rte. 31) may be very well accomplished. The landlord will find good and cheap guides. The Wenden Stock and glaciers, and the Titlis, are fine objects from here. There are two paths down to Engelberg,—the horse-path, scarcely marked, leading to the l. of the Trüb See; the other and shorter one, only practicable on foot, continuing along a ridge in the direction of Engelberg for a short distance, and then descending abruptly on the rt. to a plain, on which, at ½ mile on the left, is situated the Trüb See, fed by glaciers descending from the Ochsenberg on the rt. It is necessary to bear away to the rt.-hand extremity of this plain, where there is a gap, from which a very rough and precipitous path, called the Pfaffenwand, descends for 20 minutes over grass, and afterwards débris, to the pastures, crossing which it enters the forest for ¼ hour, and shortly reaches "

Engelberg (Rte. 31).

ROUTE 34.

THE PASS OF ST. GOTHARD, FROM FLÜ-
ELEN, ON THE LAKE OF LUCERNE, TO
BELLINZONA.

16 posts = 81¾ miles.

Distances from Flüelen to Bellinzona :—

	French Posts.
Flüelen to Andermatt	5
Andermatt to Airolo	4¼
Airolo to Faido	2
Faido to Bodio	2
Bodio to Bellinzona	2¼
Posts	16

Steamers start twice a day from
Lucerne, reaching Flüelen, and thence
diligences (places in which must be
secured on board the steamer) go to
Bellinzona in 15 hrs., Milan in 25
hrs. Travellers should book from
Lucerne. By the diligence some of
the finest portions of the route are
passed in the dark.

The price of a carriage and 2 post-
horses to Hospenthal is 30 fr., to
Airolo 60, to Faido 75, to Bellinzona
100, to Magadino 115, to Lugano 125,
and to Como 150 fr., not including
the pour-boire of 2 fr. to the postilion
at each stage, or the extra horses for
crossing the mountain. Vetturini
carriages may be obtained at Lucerne,
for the whole journey to Como, for
about 250 fr., including all charges.
They perform the journey in 3 days,
reaching Como on the 3rd, in time for
the last Rlwy. train for Milan. These
carriages are more comfortable than
those furnished by the postmasters,
and will accommodate 6 persons.

Pedestrians should drive as far as
Amsteg, where the ascent properly
begins.

On this pass minerals are found,
and may be purchased better than in
any other part of Switzerland.

This was anciently perhaps the
most frequented passage over the
Alps, as it offered the most direct and
practicable line of communication between Basle and Zürich, from Northern Switzerland and W. Germany, to
Lombardy, and the important cities of
Milan and Genoa. Not less than
16,000 travellers and 9000 horses
crossed it annually on an average,
down to the commencement of the
present century; but being only a
bridle-path, it was almost entirely
abandoned after the construction of
the carriage-roads over the Simplon
and Bernardin. Deprived of the traffic
across it, the inhabitants of the villages traversed by the road, chiefly
innkeepers and muleteers, were reduced to ruin, and the revenues of the
canton, which before drew 20,000
florins annually from the tolls upon it,
were seriously diminished. The cantons of Uri and Tessin, through which
this road runs, at length became sufficiently alive to their own interests to
perceive the necessity of converting it
into a carriage-road, and thus rendering it fit to compete with the rival
routes as a channel of communication
and of transport for merchandise.
In consequence, in 1820 the work
was begun, and in 1832 finally completed and opened. The expenses
were defrayed by a joint-stock company, formed in Uri and the neighbouring cantons. The construction
of the road was intrusted to an engineer of Altorf, named Müller.

The poverty-stricken canton of Uri
had scraped together, with great difficulty, funds sufficient to execute her
portion of the undertaking, but a
storm, such as had not been known in
the memory of man, bursting on the
summit of the pass, in August, 1834,
in the course of a few hours swept
away nearly one-third of the road,
together with bridges and terraces
without number, which had been
constructed with so much labour,
cost, and difficulty. A similar tempest in 1839 effected nearly equal de-

struction. Considering the previous drain upon the resources of the canton, it is surprising how soon the mischief was repaired.

At present the road is excellent, not inferior in its construction to any other of the great Alpine highways, and certainly not surpassed by any in the interest and grandeur of its scenery.

The passage is usually free from snow for 4 or 5 months of the year; and in the depth of winter carriages are safely transported across on open sledges, except immediately after a snow-storm, when the road is sometimes blocked up for a week. It is still one of the best routes for Italy.

The canton of Uri and the valley of the Reuss possess an historical celebrity, as the theatre of the memorable campaign of 1799, when the armies of the three nations of France, Austria, and Russia, dispossessing each other in turns, marched, fought, and manœuvred, on heights whence the snow never disappears, and previously deemed accessible only to goatherds and hunters. In the month of June, in the above-named year, the Austrians, aided by the natives of Uri, had expelled the French from the valley. Satisfied with the possession of it, they passed nearly 2 months in entire inactivity, when, by a combined movement, planned by Massena, they were attacked at all points by French corps, poured in upon them from the lake of Lucerne, which was crossed by a flotilla of boats, and from every western passage leading over the Alps and into the valley of the Reuss. Lecourbe crossed the Surenen, Loison the Susten, and Gudin, with a large force, fought his way over the Grimsel and Furca, threatening the Austrians in front, in flank, and in the rear. In an engagement which took place on the 14th of August, and which lasted 5 hours, they were driven step by step up the valley, as far as Andermatt. On the two following days the French pursued them out of the valley of the Reuss into the Grisons by the Oberalp, where a bloody encounter took place. A little more than a month after this, intelligence was brought to Lecourbe, the French commander, that another large army had appeared at the S. foot of the St. Gothard. While still at a loss to imagine to what European power it might belong, fresh tidings announced that it was the veteran Suwarrow, who, at the head of a Russian army of 18,000 foot and 5000 Cossack horse, had broken up from his encampment in the plains of Lombardy, and now began to force the passage of the St. Gothard. The French retired slowly but steadily before him as far as the lake of Lucerne, where Lecourbe, after removing all the boats from Flüelen, entrenched himself in a strong position at Seedorf, on the l. bank of the Reuss. Suwarrow, whose object was to unite himself with the Russian army before Zürich, of the defeat of which by Massena he had not yet heard, here found himself without the means of transporting his army, threatened on all sides by enemies. He took little time to consider, but immediately planned and executed his wonderful and almost incredible retreat over the Kinzig Culm and into the valley of Muotta; and though constantly annoyed by the French in his rear, finally conducted his army into the valley of the Rhine, with a loss of 3000 men, of whom far more perished from cold, fatigue, and hunger, than from the enemies' bullets. (See Rtes. 72, 75, 76.)

Flüelen—(Italian *Fiora*—*Inn:* Croix Blanche, Adler)—the port of Canton Uri, at the S. extremity of the lake of the Four Cantons, is a small village in a not very healthy situation. The malaria from the marshy ground produced by the deposits of the Reuss at its entrance into the lake has been abated by means of works undertaken on a large scale to deepen the mouth of the Reuss, and thus drain the upper country. *Conveyances* and *Post-horses* may always be had here.

The *Steamer* touches here twice a day from Lucerne, and returns after a short stay; it takes carriages. (See

Rte. 18.) A pier, alongside of which the steamers are moored, offers a convenient landing-place. About 2 m. off lies

Altorf—Inns: Bär (Post); Löwe (Lion); Clef d'Or, civil people; Aigle, good. This is the capital of the canton Uri, the poorest and least populous in the Confederation, numbering altogether only 13,500 souls: it is a dull, lifeless village of 1664 Inhab., without trade or manufactures, and still exhibiting signs of the conflagration of 1799, which reduced the larger part of it to ashes. It was the early home of the great Guelph family, and, if credit is to be given to tradition, it was on the open square in the centre of Altorf that William Tell shot the apple from off his son's head. The place where he stood to take aim is marked by a stone *Fountain,* surmounted with statues of the dauntless cross-bowman and his child. The lime-tree, upon which Gessler's cap was stuck, for all men to do obeisance to it as they passed, and to which the child was bound, to serve as a mark for his father's bolt, existed a withered trunk, down to 1567, when it was cut down and replaced by another fountain, about 200 ft. distant from the first.

The tall *Tower,* ornamented with rude frescoes, representing Tell and Gessler, has been stated erroneously by some writers to occupy the site of the lime-tree; but it is proved by records still in existence to have been built before the time of Tell.

On quitting Altorf the road crosses the mouth of the vale of Schächen, traversing, by a bridge, the stream in which, according to tradition, William Tell lost his life (1350) in endeavouring to rescue a child from the waterfall of Bürglen. He plunged in, and neither he nor the child was seen after. Tell was a native of the Schächenthal, having been born in the village of Bürglen, a little to the l. of our road. The small *Chapel,* backed by an ivy-clad tower, rudely painted with the events of his life, was built in 1522 on the spot where his house stood, near the churchyard. The inhabitants of this valley are considered the finest

race of men in Switzerland. A path runs up it, and across the Klausen Pass (Rte. 72) to the baths of Stachelberg, in canton Glarus, and another over the Kinzig Culm (Rte. 79), into the Muotta Thal.

On the l. bank of the Reuss, opposite its junction with the Schächen, stands Attinghausen, the birthplace of *Walter Fürst,* one of the three liberators of Switzerland: his house is still pointed out. Above it rise the ruins of a castle, whose baronial owners became extinct in 1357, when the last of the race was buried in his helmet and hauberk. At *Bötzlingen,* 3 m. above Altorf, the parliament (Landesgemeinde) of the canton Uri is held every year, on the first Sunday in May, to settle the affairs of the state. Every male citizen above the age of 20, except a priest, has a vote. The authorities of the canton, on horseback, with the Landammann at their head, preceded by a detachment of militia, with military music, and the standard of the canton attended by the beadles in their costume of yellow and black, and by two men in the ancient Swiss garb of the same colour, bearing aloft the two celebrated buffalo horns of Uri, march to the spot in procession. From a semicircular hustings, erected for the purpose, the business of the day is proclaimed to the assembled crowd, and the different speakers deliver their harangues, after which the question is put to the vote by show of hands. When all affairs of state are despatched, the Landammann and other public officers resign, and are either re-elected or others are chosen in their place. It is possible that alterations have been made in these things, under the great political changes which have recently taken place in Switzerland.

After leaving Altorf the road passes through pretty meadows shaded with fine walnut-trees as far as Amsteg. l. rises the rocky wall of the Windgelle, a continuation of the Klareden-Grat, and Scheerhorn. A flat surface on the precipice returns a very distinct echo. A little way from Klus, a vil-

lage half-way to Amsteg, the wild
defile of the Surenen opens rt. (Rte.
31). At Klus the road approaches
the margin of the Reuss, and beyond,
at the hamlet of Silinen, it is partly
cut through the rock, passes under the
ruins of a tower, by some supposed to
be the castle of *Zwing Uri* (Restraint
of Uri), the construction of which by
the tyrant Gessler, to overawe the
peasants, roused the suspicion and indignation of the Swiss; so that it was
demolished by them in 1308, on the first
outbreak of the revolt against Austria.

Amsteg (*Inns:* Hirsch, not over
clean ; Croix Blanche ; Stern), delightfully situated, and although not a
post station, it is a convenient place for
those to stop at who cross the lake by
the 2 P.M. steamer from Lucerne. It
stands at the mouth of the *Maderaner*
or *Kerstelen Thal,* which stretches E.
as far as the base of the Clariden
Grat, a valley little visited, but well
worth exploring; abounding in waterfalls and glaciers, and fir woods without their equal. (See Rte. 80.)

At the new bridge of Amsteg the
road first crosses the Reuss and now
begins to ascend, having on the l.
hand the gigantic mass of the Windgelle and snow-peak of the *Bristenstock*
(a very rugged and difficult mountain),
and the river below, dashing from rock
to rock in an almost uninterrupted
cataract.

Intschi. A second bridge carries it
back to the rt. bank ; and, after traversing a wood, a third, called Pfaffen-
sprung (priest's leap), from a fable of
a monk having leaped across it with
a maiden in his arms, brings the traveller to the wild torrent Mayenbach,
descending from the Susten Pass (Rte.
32), which joins the Reuss immediately below.

Wasen (*Inn:* Ochs, fair), a village
of 550 Inhab., on the l. bank of the
Reuss, at the mouth of the Mayenthal. Winding from side to side, the
road slowly toils upward to Gösche-
nen, where the valley assumes a
more savage character, contracting
into the narrow ravine of Schellinen,
bounded for nearly 3 m. by impending
cliffs of granite. One vast fragment,

skirted by the road, was dropped
here, according to the popular legend,
by the devil, and is thence called
Teufelstein. This defile is a scene of
desolation and awful grandeur; the
walls of rock seem almost to exclude
the light of day, scarce a blade of
grass is to be seen, and nothing
heard but the wild dashing of the
Reuss at the foot of the precipice
below the road, from which hoarse
sounds this part of the valley gets the
name of Krachenthal. The road
hereabouts is much exposed in spring
to danger from avalanches. Here and
there niches are cut in the rock to
shelter passers, and a part of the road
is roofed by a stone *gallery.* The remains of the former road are seen on
the opposite side of the valley. The
difficulties of the ascent are next overcome by the skill of the engineer, who
has constructed a series of complicated
zigzag terraces, first on one side of the
Reuss and then on the other, by means
of which, and of numerous bridges,
the traveller at length reaches

The *Devil's Bridge,* situated in the
midst of the most stern but magnificent scenery of the whole pass. The
Reuss leaps down into the head of this
savage gorge in a lofty cataract, and
in the very midst of its din and spray.
Very precipitous rocks of granite,
remarkable for the stern nakedness of
their surface, hem in the bed of the
river on both sides; those on the left
bank leaving not an inch of space for
the sole of a foot at their base, except
what has been hewn out of it by
human art. For ages this must have
been a complete cul-de-sac, until, by
human ingenuity, the torrent was
bridged and the rock bored through.
The old bridge, a thin segment of a
circle, spanning a terrific abyss, had
originally an air at once of boldness
and fragility, much of which it has
lost by the contrast with the towering
and more solid structure that has now
entirely superseded it, and seems, as it
were, to domineer over it. The single
arch of slight masonry, suspended in
the air at a height of 70 ft. above
the Reuss, with scarce a parapet at
the side, and with barely breadth to

allow two persons to pass, almost seemed to tremble with the rushing of the torrent under the feet of the traveller. Modern improvements have deprived the bridge and its vicinity of much of its terror and sublimity. A commodious and gradually sloping terrace, hewn out of the solid rock at the foot of the precipice, leads to the broad and massive new bridge, which, though nearer to the fall than the old, may be passed without the slightest emotion of the nerves, thanks to its solidity and high parapets. It is of granite; the arch 25 ft. span: it was finished 1830. The construction of this part of the road presented great difficulties to the engineer from the hardness and smoothness of the precipitous rocks and the want of easy access to them: indeed, the mines necessary for blasting the granite could only be formed by workmen suspended by ropes from above, and dangling in the air like spiders at the end of their threads. The ancient bridge was first founded by Abbot Gerald, of Einsiedeln, in 1118, so that, in the naming of it, the devil has received more than his due: it has been allowed to remain beneath the new bridge, though no longer of any use. During the extraordinary campaign of 1799, the Devil's Bridge and the defile of the Schellinen were twice obstinately contested within the space of little more than a month. On the 14th of August the united French column, under Lecourbe and Loison, having surprised the Austrians, drove them up the valley of the Reuss, as far as this bridge, which, having been converted into an entrenched position, was defended by them for some time. The ancient Devil's Bridge was approached from the lower part of the valley by a terrace abutting against the precipice, interrupted in one place by a chasm. The road was continued over this upon an arch of masonry which supported a sort of causeway. At last even this was carried by the French, who, in their impetuous pursuit, followed their enemies across this arch. In a moment, while a crowd of combatants were upon it, it was blown into the air, and

hundreds were precipitated into the abyss below. During the night the Austrians, alarmed by the appearance of another French force in their rear, evacuated altogether the valley of the Reuss. On the 24th of the following September the tide of war took an opposite turn. Suwarrow, pouring down from the summit of the St. Gothard, at the head of 5000 horse and 18,000 foot, compelled the French, in their turn, to retire before him. The progress of the Russians was arrested here for a short time, as they found the road broken up, the Urnerloch filled with rocks, and the passage down the valley interrupted by the gap in the causeway beyond the bridge, caused by the blowing up of the arch. A murderous fire from the French swept away all who approached the edge of the chasm; but the Russian columns, eager for advance, by their pressure, pushed the foremost ranks into the foaming Reuss. The impediments in the road were soon removed; an extemporaneous arch was constructed by binding together beams of wood with officers' scarfs; and over this the Russian army passed, pursuing the enemy as far as Altdorf. This is the picturesque version of these actions in some modern histories; the truth, however, seems to be that the bridge (as its venerable appearance testifies) was not blown up, but that one of the arches leading to it was destroyed; and the Austrians took up so strong a position, that the French were unable to force the pass, and waited a day or two till they had sent troops over the mountains, threatening the flanks and rear of the Austrians, who then retreated. Nearly the same thing took place when the Russians advanced; in fact, these passes were never forced if tolerably defended, but the attacking party were always obliged to avail themselves of their superior numbers and turn the passes, coming down upon the flanks and rear of the enemy (see Rte. 28). For correct accounts of the extraordinary actions among these mountains, only Jomini, the military historian, can be relied on.

Immediately above, after passing the Devil's Bridge, the road is carried through a tunnel, bored for 180 feet through the solid rock, called *Urner-loch*, or *Hole of Uri*. It is 180 ft. long, 15 ft. high, and 16 ft. broad. Previous to its construction, in 1707, the only mode of passing the buttress of rock which here projects into the river, so as to deny all passage, was by a bridge, or shelf of boards, suspended on the outside by chains from above. By means of this the traveller doubled, as it were, the shoulder of the mountain, enveloped in the spray of the torrent, within a few feet of which the frail structure was hung. The Gallery of Uri was originally constructed by a Swiss engineer named Moretini; but was only passable for mules, until, in reconstructing the St. Gothard road, it was enlarged to admit carriages.

Out of this gallery the traveller emerges into the wide basin-shaped pastoral valley of Urseren, which, in contrast with the savage gorge of Schellinen, and from the suddenness of the transition, has obtained from most travellers the praise of beauty and fertility. Taken by itself, however, it has little but its verdure to recommend it: owing to its great height, 4356 ft. above the sea, scarcely any trees grow in it, and the inhabitants supply themselves with corn for bread from more fortunate lands. The lower part of it was probably once a lake, until a passage was opened for the Reuss through the rocks of Schellinen. It was originally colonised, it is supposed, by the Rhætians. The usual entrance to it was by the pass of the Oberalp. Its inhabitants spoke the language of the Grisons, and the valley was a dependence of the abbot of Disentis. Down to the 14th century it remained closed up at its lower extremity, and had no direct communication with the lower valley of the Reuss. About that time, however, a path seems to have been opened; and the men of Urseren, allying themselves with those of Uri, threw off the yoke of their former feudal lords. A mile from the gallery of Uri lies

Andermatt, or *Urseren* (Ital. *Orsera*) —(*Inns:* Poste, fair; Drei Könige; Hôtel du St. Gothard, good). It is a village of 600 Inhab., and the chief place of the valley, 4450 ft. above the sea-level. The honey and cheese made on the surrounding pastures are excellent; and the red trout of the Oberalp See enjoy the reputation, with hungry travellers, of being the finest in the world. They are at least an excellent dish, either at breakfast or dinner. The *Church of St. Columbanus* is said to have been built by the Lombards. On the slope of the mountain of St. Anne, which is surmounted by a glacier, above the village, are the scanty remains of a forest, the last relic of that which perhaps at one time clothed the sides of the valley entirely. "It is of a triangular form, with one of its angles pointed upwards; and is so placed as not only to break the fall of heavy bodies of snow, but to divide the masses, throwing them off on its two sides. It is now a slight and seemingly a perishable defence." The improvidence of the inhabitants, at an early period, had reduced it to a small grove, which those of later times had learned to value for the protection it afforded to their dwellings from falling avalanches. They therefore guarded it with the utmost care, abstaining from cutting down a stem of it; but, in 1799, foreign invaders, reckless of the consequences, felled a great part of it, and consumed it for firewood, or to repair the Devil's Bridge.

This was but one of the evils which that calamitous year brought upon this remote and peaceful valley, when the armies of three nations chose it for the arena of their combats, letting loose the furies—fire, famine, and slaughter—upon its unfortunate inhabitants. Suwarrow's hordes arrived at Andermatt in that year, famished with hunger. Like ravenous wolves, they seized and consumed everything they could lay hands on. They greedily devoured a store of soap which they found in the larder of the inn; and, cutting into pieces some skins which had been hung out to dry previously to being tanned, boiled and ate them also.

A bridle-path stretches up the steep lateral valley behind Ander-matt, across the Oberalp and past its lake, to Dissentis, in the Grisons. (Rte. 77.)

The vale of Urseren is about 9 m. long, and nearly 1 broad. It contains 4 villages, and 1360 Inhabs., who gain a subsistence by rearing cattle and keeping dairies, and by forwarding the transit of goods across the St. Gothard, for which purpose 300 horses are kept in it. At Andermatt, Hos-pital, and Airolo, are many mineral-dealers, from whom specimens may be purchased of the numerous rare and valuable minerals with which the range of the St. Gothard abounds. The variety of species is surprising, and the cabinet of the mineralogist derives some of the rarest substances from these Alps.

On the l. of the road, in going to Hôpital, two rude stone pillars may be, or lately might have been, seen; they are the *potence* or gallows be-longing to Andermatt, dating from the time when the valley of Urseren was an independent state, and An-dermatt, the chief place in it, enjoyed the right of criminal jurisdiction, now removed to Altdorf. It is cu-rious to observe to what an extent the possession of a gallows, and the right of hanging criminals there-on, was an object of pride in an-cient times. Such relics were once found throughout Switzerland: they seem everywhere to have been preserved almost with veneration, and were kept in constant repair, though destined never more to be used.

2 m. above Andermatt is

Hospenthal, or *Hôpital—Inn:* Gol-dener Löwe (Golden Lion), good. Excellent honey and trout, and stout horses and good carriages.

Hospenthal receives its name from an hospice which no longer exists. Above the village rises a venerable tower, said to be, like the church of Andermatt, a work of the Lombards. There is a fine collection of minerals for sale, formed by two monks: the prices seem high.

[The mule-path over the Furca (Rte. 28) leads hence to the glacier of the Rhone, and the hospice of the Grimsel.]

The high road now quits the valley of Urseren, and following the course of the Reuss, begins to ascend by nu-merous zigzags to the summit of the St. Gothard, which may be reached in about 2¼ hours from Hospenthal.

Under the name of St. Gothard are comprised, not merely the depression, or col, over which the road passes, but a group or clump of mountains, all exceeding in elevation the snow line, situated between the cantons of Uri, Valais, Ticino, and Grisons; and con-taining the sources of the Rhine, the Rhone, the Reuss, and the Ticino, all of which, with innumerable tributaries, rise within a circle of 10 miles, de-scribed from the summit of the Pass.

The river Reuss may be said to fall, rather than flow, into the lake of the Four Cantons. Between Urseren and Flüelen it descends 2500 feet, and be-tween Urseren and the top of the Pass 2000 feet, forming a succession of cata-racts. Near the summit of the Pass, the road crosses it for the last time by the bridge of Rodunt, which marks the boundary of the cantons Uri and Ticino. The source of the Reuss is in the small lake of Lucendro, a short distance on the right of the road. The summit of the Pass (6808 feet above the sea) is a valley, or saddle-shaped depression, in the great granite ridge of the central chain, overlooked by snow-clad peaks varying between 8000 and 10,000 feet in height. It is a scene of the most complete sterility and desolation: the road winds among several other small lakes or ponds, some of which flow N., but the greater part are feeders of the Ticino, on the S. side of the Pass. They may, in-deed, be regarded as the head-waters of that river, which gives its name to the canton Tessin, or Ticino.

The *Hospice*, a massive and roomy building, constructed at the expense of the canton Ticino, which has also caused several houses of refuge to be built, is designed for the accommodation of travellers, being fitted up roughly as an inn, containing 15 beds, under the management of a priest. Attached to it are warehouses for goods. A very humble hospice and a chapel have existed on this spot ever since the 13th century, owing their origin to the Abbot of Disentis, who stationed a monk here to minister to the spiritual as well as physical wants of distressed travellers. In the 17th century St. Carlo Borromeo suggested the construction of a hospice on a larger scale, which, after his death, was executed by his brother. This building was swept away in 1775 by an avalanche : another, which succeeded it, was gutted by the French, while encamped on this spot in 1799-1800, and every particle of wood burnt as fuel. This older hospice, however, is still kept up. It was until lately the only house for the reception of travellers on the summit. There is an *Inn*, of a humble kind, close to the road.

The passage in winter and spring is by no means free from danger: the snow is sometimes heaped up in drifts 40 feet high on the summit, and the descent towards Airolo is much exposed at times to tourmentes and avalanches (§ 17). A year seldom passes without the loss of 3 or 4 lives, and at times melancholy catastrophes have occurred. The spot called Buco dei Calanchetti is so named from a party of glaziers from the Val Calanka, who, persisting in pushing on from the hospice, in spite of the warnings of the inmates, were buried here beneath the snow. In 1478 an avalanche swept away a troop of 60 Swiss soldiers ; in 1624, another, which fell from the Cassadra, buried 300 persons ; and one in 1814 overwhelmed 40 horses laden with goods. The new line of road is carried as much as possible out of the course of these dangers, and, though it is unprotected by any covered galleries, accidents of this kind are more rare.

The descent towards Italy displays much skilful engineering ; and the difficulties of a slope, much steeper on this side than on the other, have been overcome by a series of 28 zigzag terraces not exceeded in numbers and tortuous direction on any other Alpine pass. They begin a little beyond the hospice, and continue nearly all the way to Airolo. The turnings are less sharp than on many other passes ; and a carriage drawn by horses accustomed to the work may trot down at a quick pace. Near the uppermost zigzag the words *Suwarrow Victor*, in large letters on the face of the rock, record the success of the Russians in gaining the Pass from the French in 1799. It was on this ascent that the Russian grenadiers were for some time arrested by the fire of the French riflemen posted behind rocks and trees. The aged Suwarrow, indignant at being foiled for the first time in his life, caused a grave to be dug, and, lying down in it, declared his resolution to be buried on the spot where " his children " had been repulsed. This appeal was responded to by his soldiers with warmth, and, when he once more put himself at their head, they drove the republicans from their position. The gully down which the road passes is called Val Tremola (Germ. Trümmeln Thal), Trembling Valley, from its supposed effect on the nerves of those who passed it. Since the new road has been made, its terrors, whatever they were previously, have been much softened. It is, however, exposed to some danger from avalanches in spring. A very pretty mineral, named from this locality, where it was first found, Tremolite, abounds in the rock of the valley, and specimens of it occur even in the walls and loose stones at the road-side. The old road lay along the l. bank of the Ticino ; the new keeps on the rt. side of it, and before reaching Airolo makes many wide sweeps along the flank of the mountain, up into the Val Bedretto, traversing the forest of Piotella, where the slate rocks are full of crystals of garnet. The view up and down the vale of the Ticino and over the snowy mountains on the opposite side of it is extremely grand.

Airolo (Germ. *Eriels*)—*Inns:* Post,

best; Tre Re, good. Airolo lies on the l. bank of the Tessin, near the junction of the branch flowing out of the Val Bedretto with that rising on the St. Gothard. It is 3794 feet above the sea-level, and its inhabitants, both in habit and language, are Italian. The situation at the foot of St. Gothard, and the consequent transit of travellers and goods, are its chief sources of prosperity. It possesses a relic of antiquity: the stump of a tower called *Il Castello*, and Casa dei Pagani, built, it is said, by Desiderius King of the Lombards, A.D. 774. The Lombard kings constructed a line of similar forts from this all the way to Como, many of which will be passed by the traveller in descending the valley.

The summit of the Pass may be reached from Airolo by a *light* carriage in 2½ or 3 hrs.; a leader must be taken up to the Hospice = 1½ poste is charged; by means of the old road and short cuts a pedestrian may ascend, and perhaps descend, in less time than a carriage.

[Several mule-paths concentrate at Airolo. Up the Val Bedretto to the Nüfenen Pass (Rte. 35), and to the Gries (Rte. 29): 2. Over the Lukmanier into the Grisons (Rte. 78); 3. Into the Val Formazza by the Nüfenen and Gries ; this can be effected by the Korner pass without descending to Nüfenen. The landlord at Bedretto will guide (1857). 4. A summer path, and difficult, ascending by the N.W. side of the Val Canaria, past the beautiful waterfall of Calcaccia (?), and over the Sella-Grat to Andermatt, in 5 hours.

The head of the Val Canaria is occupied by a small lake, the scenery is wild and rugged; and there does not appear to be any practicable track from the upper end of the valley either towards Andermatt or into the Grisons ; but a good mountaineer might probably effect a passage in either direction.]

At the mouth of the picturesque glen of Stalvedro is a Lombard tower of King Desiderius, near Quinto. This pass was defended Sept. 1799, by a body of 600 French against 3000 grenadiers of Suwarrow's army for 12 hrs., after which they effected their retreat over the Nüfanen into the Valais. The part of the valley of the Ticino traversed by the road from this to Biasca is called *Val Levantina* —*Livinen Thal* in Germ. A few miles lower down the river threads another defile, named after a toll-house within it

Dazio Grande,—a rent in the Monte Piottino (Platifer), nearly a mile long, and one of the most picturesque scenes on the whole route. The old carriage-road threaded the depths of the gorge, supported for a great part of the way on arches and terraces, and crossing the river thrice on bridges. During the storms of 1834 and of 1839, the swollen Ticino swept away nearly the whole of these costly constructions. A new line is now constructed at a higher level above the river, out of the reach of inundations, to replace that which has been destroyed ;—a proof of the immense difficulty of maintaining a road over the Alps. The descent is less rapid than the old line; it passes 3 short tunnels. On emerging from the last of these a waterfall is seen on the rt. resembling that (now defunct) of the Pelerins near Chamouni,—a shoot of water projected forwards and upwards.

Chestnut-trees first appear soon after quitting the defile of Dazio, and vines are cultivated at

Faido — (*Inns:* Angelo, good ;— Sole)—the principal place in the valley, a small town of 615 Inhab.

There is a pretty *waterfall of the Piumegna* opposite Faido, worth visiting, especially the upper fall, a short walk from the inn.

A revolt of the people of the Val Levantina, in 1755, against their tyrannical lords and masters the cowherds of Uri, to whom they had been subject since the 15th century, was terminated on this spot by the execution of the ringleaders, whose heads were fastened to the trunks of the vast chestnut-trees, in the presence of 3000 men of the valley. The troops of the Confederation had previously surrounded and disarmed this ill-starred band of rebels, and afterwards compelled them, on bended knees, to sue for mercy. The revolt was, perhaps, not to be justified ; but one thing at least is certain, that the freedom which had been the boast of the Swiss republicans was, down to the end of the last century, denied by them to the states dependent on them, who groaned under a bondage more intolerable than that of any monarchical despotism !

A footpath runs from Faido over the Lukmanier (Rte. 78) to Disentis.

Through a highly cultivated tract the road reaches another fine defile full of chestnut-trees.

Giornico (Germ. *Irnis* : *Inn*, La Corona, dirty), a village of 700 Inhab. A high tower: the *Ch. of Santa Maria di Castello*, whose substructure is said to exhibit traces of a fort, attributed to the Gauls (?), and the Ch. of San *Nicholas da Mira*, regarded by the vulgar as originally a heathen temple. Both these churches are certainly examples of the earliest form of Christian buildings, and highly deserve the attention of the architect and antiquary. " Service is not performed in St. Nicholas, though it is kept in repair. The architecture is of the rudest Romanesque style, and the E. end offers, perhaps, the most unaltered specimen of the choir raised upon substructions that can hardly be called a crypt, found in the ancient Lombard churches of Italy, distinguished by staircases, whereas it here subsists in its primitive form. The whole neighbourhood is exceedingly picturesque, and deserving at least of quite as much attention as many places which enjoy much more extended reputation."—P. The number and height of the church-towers on the side of the Alps, even on spots where wealth and population appear most scanty, are among the most striking features of this country. Instead of being surmounted by spires, as in the Roman Catholic valleys of the neighbouring Grisons, they are here piled story upon story in the Italian fashion, sometimes reaching even to an eighth tier, and ending in a ridge roof.

Half way to

Bodio, a heap of large rocks (Sassi Grossi) serves as a monument of the victory gained here in 1478 over the Milanese by the Swiss, who had made a foray across the St. Gothard as far as Bellinzona, under pretext of redressing the injury done by the Milanese, in having felled some trees belonging to canton Uri. The winter had set in with severity, and the main body of the Swiss had returned across the pass with their plunder, leaving behind only about 600 men under Captains Stranga of Giornico, and Troger of Uri. The Milanese, 15,000 strong, pressed forward to expel the highland invaders, who, resorting to stratagem to counteract the preponderance of numbers, laid the flat land in this part of the valley under water, and, placing themselves behind it, awaited their enemies at the foot of some rocks. In the course of the night the water froze hard, and next morning, while the advance of the Italians across the ice was naturally slow and faltering, the Swiss, accustomed to cross their native glaciers, rushed down upon them in a furious charge, and at once put them to the rout. Their confusion was increased by vast masses of rock hurled from the cliffs above by parties stationed for the purpose, and the slaughter was enormous. According to some accounts 1400, according to others 4000, of the Milanese fell on this occasion.

The Val Levantina terminates a little beyond Pollegio, at the junction of the Blegno. After crossing that river the traveller reaches

Biasca (*Inn*: Union, poor and slovenly), which also contains a very ancient *church*, situated on the slope of the hill. A chain of chapels, or Via Crucis, leads from it up to the Chapel of St. Petronilla, whence there is a pleasing view.

In 1512 an earthquake shook down from the mountain of Val Crenone, near the entrance of the *Val Blegno*, so vast a mass of earth and rock that it arrested the course of the river, and extended high up on the opposite side of the valley. For nearly two years, so great was the strength of this dam that the waters accumulated behind it into a lake many miles in extent, inundating numerous villages, and driving out the inhabitants by the rising flood. At length, in 1514, it began to flow over the barrier, which, being thus loosened and weakened, suddenly gave way about Easter. The deluge thus occasioned swept off everything before it—towns, villages, houses, and trees, as far as Bellinzona (a part of which was destroyed), and the Lago Maggiore. The accumulated débris of rocks and mud which it carried down with it covered the cultivated land with desolation, and marks of the ruin thus caused may be still traced along the valley. Various causes, conformable with the superstitious notions of the times, were assigned for this catastrophe. Some attributed it to the vengeance of God against the sins of the inhabitants of Biasca, called forth by the power of a Papal Brief; others traced it to the influence of "certain magicians from Armenia." It is satisfactorily accounted for by the supposition of an earthquake, since at the same time a similar fall took place from the opposite side of the mountain, which buried the village of Campo Bagnino, in the Val Calanca.

Osogno. About 8 m. below Biasca the Moesa is crossed and our road falls into that from the pass of the Bernardin (Rte. 90), near the battle-field of Arbedo, which was as fatal to the Swiss as that of Giornico was to their opponents. An account of it, as well as a full description of *Bellinzona*, is given in Rte. 90.

ROUTE 35.

PASS OF THE NÜFENEN (NOVENA), FROM OBERGESTELN TO AIROLO.

9 hours = 29 Eng. m. This is neither a difficult nor a very fine pass. The way is tolerably clear, and by travellers accustomed to mountains might be found without a guide. It is a horsepath, ascending the vale of Eginen, as in Rte. 29, but, before reaching the Gries Glacier, turns to the l., and crossing the ridge of the

Nüfenen, 7975 ft. above the sealevel. Unlike the summit of the Gries, which is covered with a glacier, this pass has grass on its very top, which commands a fine view of the S. side of the Bernese Oberland mountains. The summit is a ridge, requiring 20 min. to cross, the highest part being on the Valaisan side. The path across is marked by poles. There is at times a good deal of snow on the other side. The path descends into the Val Bedretto, in places faintly marked, and scarcely distinguishable from tracks of cattle. On the S. slope of the pass one of the branches of the river Ticino takes its rise. The path descends along its l. bank to the

Hospice al' Acqua, a house of refuge to accommodate travellers, 5000 ft. above the sea, dirty and full of fleas, 3 hrs. walk from Airolo. The Hospitalier is a good guide. A path ascending rapidly through the rough pine forest, crosses the valley from this S. into the Val Formazza to the Falls of the Tosa, 3½ hrs.' walk (see Rte. 29). The Val Bedretto, from its elevation, has but an inhospitable climate; long winters, and frosts not uncommonly in the height of summer, morning and evening. It is clothed with forests and pastures, from which its 612 inhabitants derive support in summer; while in winter the males migrate to Italy, to seek employment as servants. It is flanked on either side with glaciers, and is dreadfully exposed to avalanches (§ 18). The masses of fallen snow often remain unmelted on the margin of the Ticino till the end of September. At

Bedretto (small *Inn*), the principal hamlet, the church-tower, which has been once swept away. along with the parsonage, is now protected by an angular buttress, directed toward the side from which the avalanches fall, so as to break and turn them away. The valley leading to Airolo is very pleasing. In the lower part of the valley a scanty crop of rye is grown.

Airolo, in Rte. 34.

Route reversed.—From Airolo the path, which is good and partly paved, descends to the river, crosses it, and ascends to

The Villa recrosses the river, and chiefly through fields reaches,

Bedretto. The river is crossed and recrossed to 1 hr. 20 min. Hospice al' Aqua. Thence to the highest châlets 1 hr., and to the commencement of the summit 1 hr. 20 min. ; 2 hrs. 40 min. summit. A descent of 30 min leads into the Gries path ; 3 hrs. Münster (Rte. 28 B). Total, 8 hrs. 50 min.

From Bedretto there is a path into the Val Formazza (Rte. 34).

ROUTE 38.

PASS OF THE GEMMI, THUN TO THE BATHS OF LEUK (LÖÈCHE), AND LEUK IN THE VALAIS.

Thun to Frutigen	16 Eng. m.
Frutigen to Kandersteg . .	8¼ „
Kandersteg to Schwarenbach	3¼ hours.
Schwarenbach to Leukerbad	3¼ „
Leukerbad to Leuk . . .	8¼ miles.

Carriage from Thun to Frutigen, 20 fr., 2 fr. bonnemain. Dil. 4 hrs., 2 fr. 20. A pleasanter route is to take a boat to Spietz (4 fr.), a very pretty place, whence a walk through

fields of 10 miles leads to Frutigen. Char from Frutigen to Kandersteg, with bonnemain, 8 fr. 50. Horse to Leukerbad, 20 fr. To Dauben See, 10 fr.

There is also an excellent road from Interlaken to Frütigen ; distance about the same as from Thun.

The Gemmi (pronounced Ghemmi) is one of the most remarkable passes across the Alps. Its scenery is, perhaps, extraordinary rather than grand, and to be seen to advantage it ought to be approached from the Valais. There is a good char-road for a mile and a half beyond Kandersteg, to the N. foot of the pass : the pass itself, and the space between it and the Baths, can only be surmounted on foot or on horseback.

The first part of the route lies along the beautiful shores of the lake of Thun. Near the tall tower of Strättlingen it crosses the Kander by a lofty bridge. That river originally avoided the lake altogether, and, flowing for some distance parallel to it, behind the hill of Strättlingen, joined the Aar below Thun. Owing to the quantity of mud and gravel which it brought with it, and the slight inclination of its channel in this part of its course, it converted the surrounding district into an unhealthy marsh, and gave rise to a project, which was executed in 1714 at the expense of the canton, of turning the river into the lake of Thun. This was effected by cutting a canal, 3000 ft. long, and 272 ft. broad, into which the river was turned; and which, seen from the bridge in crossing, has much the appearance of a natural ravine. By this change of course the land on the banks of the Aar has been drained and made profitable, while the deposit of sand and stones brought down by the river into the lake has so accumulated as to form a delta around its mouth, extending already nearly a mile from the shore, and annually increasing.

The road passes the mouth of the Simmenthal (Rte. 41), guarded on one side by the Stockhorn, and on the rt. by the Niesen, two noble mountains, between which the valley opens out a scene of exceeding beauty, with the *castle of Wimmis* standing as it were in its jaws. On the margin of the lake rises another picturesque castle, that of Spietz. Skirting the base of the pyramidal Niesen, we enter the valley of Frutigen, which is remarkable for its verdure and fertility, and may be said to exhibit Swiss pastoral scenery in perfection.

At *Wyler* (5 m. from Thun) a road turns l. up to the village of *Aeschi*. The ascent of ½ hr. will be well repaid by the *view* from the *churchyard*. At your feet the Lake of Thun, with a peep into the singular Justis Thal on its N. side; beyond Thun the range of the Jura. On the l., close at hand, the rival mountains Niesen and Stockhorn tower above the Simmenthal. To the rt. stretches the Lake of Brienz; the Rothhorn and Pass of the Brünig rising from its shores, topped by the Titlis. To the S. the snowy giants of the Oberland rear their massive forms. There is a carriage road from Aeschi direct to Mühlinen. At

Mühlinen (about ¾ way from Thun to Frutigen) is a nice little *Inn*, The Bear. At *Reichenbach* the *Kienthal* opens out to the S.E. (Rte. 26.) Ascending by the side of the Kander we reach

Frütigen (*Inns*: Helvetia and Post, both tolerable ; guides and mules for the Gemmi may be hired here), a village of 900 Inhab.: its houses are for the most part not older than 1826-7, at which time nearly all were destroyed in two consecutive conflagrations. Johann Wandfluh is a good guide. Behind it the valley divides into two branches; that on the W. leads to the Adelboden; that on the E. (down which flows the Kander) to the Gemmi.

The road passes under the castle of Tellenburg, the former residence of the amtman, or bailiff of the district, and, crossing the Kander, proceeds up its rt. bank to

Kandersteg. (*Inn*: Victoria, formerly Ritter; new and civil master.) N.B. *Return* chars to Thun may be got here for 8 to 10 frs.; with 2 horses,

12 to 20 frs. Horses to cross the Gemmi to the baths of Leuk, cost 15 fr. before 10 A.M., 20 fr. after; 10 fr. to the Dauben See. Horses are usually hired here, but those who wish to avoid fatigue can go on in the char 1½ m. further. From Kandersteg to Leukerbad is about 7 hrs. ; the path is easy to find, and except in thick weather there is no occasion for a guide. Kandersteg is the last village in the valley: its scattered habitations contain about 700 individuals. It is beautifully situated 3280 ft. above the sea, at the N. base of the Gemmi. Wood cut in the mountain forests around is here set afloat in the Kander, and thus conveyed into the lake of Thun, where the logs are collected and separated by the various proprietors.

[*Excursions.*—*a.* Those who have time to spare should on no account omit to walk hence about 3 m. through a sublime gorge (see Rte. 27) into the side *Valley of Œschinen*, running directly E. from Kandersteg, where, hemmed in by precipices and glaciers, they will find a beautiful clear lake, which mirrors on its smooth surface the snowy peaks of the Blumlis Alp, at whose base it lies.—*b.* From the Œschinen lake there is a path over the Dündengrat into the Kienthal, descending which you may reach the road to Thun between Reichenbach and Mühlinen.—*c.* Another path leads over the *Furce* into the Seefinenthal, and thence to Lauterbrunnen (Rte. 27), but it is difficult, especially from the side of the Kienthal. The valleys of *Œschinen* and *Gasteren* include scenery as grand and impressive as any to be met with in the central chain of the Alps.—*d.* The excursion from Kandersteg into the Lötsch Thal and to Tourtemagne is described Rte. 60.—*e.* A path of no great difficulty leads W. in 5 hours, over the Bonder-Grat, to *Adelboden* (*Inn* tolerable.) It turns out of the char-road just above Kandersteg, crosses the grassy slopes to the foot of some rocks, which it surmounts by a ladder. From the summit (2 hrs. 50 min. walk) the view is fine, comprising the Monch, Jungfrau, and the whole of the

Œschinen-thal and lake. From Adelboden to Frütigen, a walk of 2 or 3 hours, through a deep but rather monotonous valley. Above Adelboden is a fall of some magnitude. From Adelboden there is an easy path over the *Hahnenmoos* pass, in 3¼ hrs., to Lenk (Rte. 39).]

At 1½ m. above Kandersteg the char road ceases; and the ascent of the Pass of the Gemmi commences in earnest. (An *Inn* has been built here. New landlord 1858.) The path lies for the first 1½ hr. through forests in a steep ascent; it then passes the boundary line of the cantons Berne and Wallis, and then emerges upon a tract of open pasture land, rendered desolate by the fall of an avalanche from the Rinder Horn in 1782. The path winds, for a considerable distance, among the fragments of rock brought down by it. Farther on stands the

Solitary *Inn* of *Schwarenbach*: it affords good refreshments and sleeping accommodations, which are often most acceptable in such a situation. The German poet Werner has laid in this gloomy spot the scene of a still more gloomy tragedy, 'The 24th of February.' The extravagant and improbable plot has no foundation in any real event which happened here.

About 2 m. above this the path reaches and winds along the E. margin of a small lake called *Dauben See*, supplied by snow, not by springs, which often swell it so as to cover the path: for 8 months of the year it is frozen. Nothing can exceed the dreary aspect of the seared and naked limestone rocks which form the summit of the pass: they seem too barren for even the hardiest lichens. The culminating point traversed by the road is 7540 ft. above the sea level, and about 1 hr. from Schwarenbach. From a rocky eminence on the l. of the path, a superb view is obtained of the chain of Alps beyond the Rhone, separating the Valais from Piedmont. Monte Rosa cannot be seen from the Gemmi, being completely hidden by the Weisshorn, a mountain of graceful form and magnificent dimensions from

whatever side it is seen. The highest summits in the view, reckoning from the W., are these:—1. The Pigno d'Arolla, N.W. of the Collon; 2. the Collon itself, easily recognised by the deep cleft in its side; 3. the Dent Blanche. Then come three or four minor peaks of the range at the head of that valley, among which is the mountain there called the Dent Blanche. Above this range are seen—4. the Dent d'Erin; and, 5. the Cervin: both peaks of bare rock, the former being from here the most remarkable. The series is terminated by—6. the Weisshorn, the loftiest and nearest mountain visible; and, 7. the Mont Fée, which is almost in itself a complete group of snowy peaks. It is one of the most striking views in Switzerland.

Near the verge of the descent stands a small shed, capable of affording partial shelter in a storm. A little lower down the traveller finds himself on the brink of a precipice, from which a plumb-line might be thrown into the valley below, nearly 1600 ft., almost without touching the rock, so vertical are its sides. It is principally upon the faces of a buttress of this vast wall that one of the most extraordinary of all the alpine roads, constructed in 1736-41, by a party of Tyrolese, has been carried. Its zigzags have been very ingeniously contrived, for in many places the rocks overhang the path, and an upper terrace projects farther out than the one immediately below it. It varies in width from 3 ft. to 5 ft., is bordered at the side by a dry wall, or railing, and is practicable for mules. *There is no danger in it;* and the terrors have vanished of late before improvements in the path and balustrades at the side. It is not pleasant to ride down, but on most of the passes there are places quite as alarming to weak nerves.

The wonders of this pass are greatly increased to those who approach it from the side of Leuk.

" The upper end of the valley, as you look towards the Gemmi, has all the appearance of a cul-de-sac shut in by a mountain wall. Up to the very last moment, and until you reach the foot of the precipice, it is impossible to discover the way out, or to tell whither the road goes, or how it can be carried up a vertical surface of rock. It is a mere shelf—in some parts a mere groove cut in the face of the huge cliff, just wide enough for a mule to pass ; and at the turns of the zigzags you constantly overhang a depth of nearly 500 ft. Down this difficult road invalids are carried to the baths : it is the only way of approaching them from the N., unless you were to make a *slight* détour of 200 m. by Berne, Friburg, Vevay, and Martigny." On the face of a rock, near the foot, is a small building said to have been formerly used as a guard-house to give notice of any invasion from the Bernese side.

The following clause, relative to the transport of invalids, is copied from the printed regulations issued by the director of the baths:—" Pour une personne au-dessus de 10 ans il faudra 4 porteurs ; si elle est d'un poids au-dessus du commun, 6 porteurs: si cependant elle est d'un poids extraordinaire, et que le commissaire le juge nécessaire, il pourra ajouter 2 porteurs, et jamais plus." This provision for excessive corpulence is somewhat amusing. The ascent from the Baths to the summit takes 2 hrs. ; a mule costs 4½ fr. up and down.

Baths of Leuk (Leukerbad, — Fr. Lôèche). Inns: Maison Blanche, very good; H. de Bellevue, good ; H. de France ; Hôtel des Alpes, a stone house. The accommodation at Leuk is good, considering that most of the houses are of wood, not very well built, shut up and abandoned from October to May. The fare is tolerable, everything but milk and cheese being brought from the valley below. A *bath* costs 2 fr.

The baths consist of 5 or 6 lodging-houses, attached to a hamlet of about 300 Inhabs., situated more than 4500 feet above the level of the sea, *i.e.* higher than the highest mountain in Great Britain, and at the end of a valley terminated on all sides by

tremendous precipices, which will remind the traveller of a *cirque* in the Pyrenees. The hot springs annually attract a number of visitors, chiefly Swiss and French, during the season, viz. in the months of July and August, though the inns are open from May to October. From the dreariness of the situation, the coldness of the climate, and the defects of the lodging, few English would desire to prolong their stay here, after satisfying their curiosity by a sight of the place. The baths and adjacent buildings have been three times swept away by avalanches since their establishment in the 16th century ; and, to guard against a recurrence of the calamity, a very strong dyke is now built behind the village to ward off the snow. Such danger, however, is past before the bathing season begins. One of the first patrons of the baths was the celebrated Cardinal and Archbishop of Sion, Matthew Schinner.

The springs, to the number of 10 or 12, rise in and around the village, and nine-tenths of them run off into the Dala torrent without being used. *The chief spring of St. Laurence* bursts forth out of the ground between the inn and the bath-house—a rivulet in volume at its source, with a temperature of 124° Fahr. It is used for the baths after being slightly cooled. The other springs vary somewhat in temperature, but little in contents. They contain only a small portion of saline matter, and seem to owe their beneficial effects less to their mineral qualities than to their temperature and the mode of using them. The patient begins with a bath of an hour's duration, but goes on increasing it daily, until at length he remains in the water 8 hours a day—4 before breakfast, and 4 after dinner. The usual *cure time* (kur) is about 3 weeks. The want of the accommodation of private baths, and the necessity of preventing the ennui of such an amphibious existence, if passed in solitude, has led to the practice of bathing in common. The principal bath-house is a large shed divided into 4 compartments or baths, each about 20 ft. square, and capable of holding 15 or 20 persons. To each of these baths there are two entrances, communicating with dressing-rooms, one for the ladies, the other for the gentlemen. Along the partitions dividing the baths runs a slight gallery, into which any one is admitted, either to look on or converse with the bathers below. The stranger will be amazed, on entering, to perceive a group of some 12 or 15 heads emerging from the water, on the surface of which float wooden tables holding coffee-cups, newspapers, snuff-boxes, books, and other aids, to enable the bathers to pass away their allotted hours with as small a trial to their patience as possible. The patients, a motley company, of all ages, both sexes, and various ranks, delicate young ladies, burly friars, invalid officers, and ancient dames, are ranged around the sides on benches, below the water, all clad in long woollen mantles, with a tippet over their shoulders. It is not a little amusing to a bystander to see people sipping their breakfasts, or reading the newspapers, up to their chins in water—in one corner a party at chess, in another an apparently interesting *tête-à-tête* is going on; while a solitary sitter may be seen reviving in the hot water a nosegay of withered flowers. The temperature of the bath is preserved by a supply of fresh water constantly flowing into it, from which the patients drink at times. Against the walls are hung a set of regulations and sumptuary laws for the preservation of order and decorum in the baths, signed by the burgomaster, who enforces his authority by the threat of a fine of 20 fr. for the highest offence against his code.

"Art. 7. Personne ne peut entrer dans ces bains sans être revêtue d'une chemise longue et ample, d'une étoffe grossière, sous peine de 2 fr. d'amende.

"Art. 9. La même peine sera encourue par ceux qui n'y entreraient pas, ou n'en sortiraient pas, d'une manière décente."

Four hours of subaqueous penance are, by the doctor's decree, succeeded by one hour in bed; and many a fair nymph in extreme *négligé*, with stockingless feet and uncoifed hair, may be encountered crossing the open space between the bath and the hotels. From their condition, one might suppose they had been driven out of doors by an alarm of fire, or some such threatening calamity. The higher patients go away in September, and late in the autumn, when only the poorer patients remain, the sight of the bath is rather disgusting.

a. The principal curiosity of the neighbourhood is the *Ladders* (Leiter). A path through the woods, on the l. or E. side of the Dala, 1½ m., half an hour from the baths, leads to the foot of the precipice, which, as before observed, hems in the valley of Leuk on all sides, as with a colossal wall. Upon the sloping pasturages about a mile above the summit of this precipice, however, stands a village called *Albinen;* and the only mode by which its inhabitants can communicate directly with the baths is by a series of 8 or 10 ladders placed nearly perpendicularly against the face of the cliff. It can hardly be called difficult to climb to the top, but it would not do for any of weak nerves and a dizzy head, as the ladders, which are pinned to the crevices of the rock by hooked sticks, are often awry, and rather unsteady: yet they are traversed at all seasons, day and night, by the inhabitants of the village above—by children, as well as men and women, often with heavy burdens. The use of the ladders, which the nature of the sides of the valley renders indispensable, has given rise to a singular modification of the dress of the female peasants, which here includes those nether habiliments confined in other parts of the world to men and shrews. Nor are they ashamed of this portion of their attire, as, in climbing the mountains, the petticoat is tucked up, and the wearers do not differ in appearance from boys.

N.B.—There is an easy sloping path from Albinen to Inden.

b. A day may be well devoted to the *ascent of the Torrent-horn,* a mountain rising E. of Leuk baths, if the weather be clear. The summit (9760 ft. above the sea), which may be reached in 4 hours on a mule, except the last hour (8 fr. and bonne-main), commands a wonderfully fine panorama of the Alps—an unbroken series of peaks from Mont Blanc to the Simplon; both the compeers of Monte Rosa (Weisshorn, &c., on the S. side of the Rhone, and the Altels, Gspalthorn, and Blumlis Alp on the N.). The Gemmi road lies deep below, and its summit is seen through a gap in the chain. The ridge ends in a frightful precipice surrounded by isolated rocks, whose sides are equally vertical. Pedestrians will require a guide to find the path up. The first 1200 ft. and the last 700 are a steep climb. Descent in 3 hours.

The rocky pass, called Felsen Gallerie, on the opposite side of the Dala, on the way to Siders, is a very striking scene. (See below.)

Mules are kept at the baths, under the direction of a commissaire, to transport travellers: the prices are fixed by a printed tariff. (§ 10.)

There are two ways from the baths to the valley of the Rhone.

a. The new carriage-road from the Baths to the Simplon road follows the course of the *Dala* torrent through one of the finest gorges in Switzerland; and the new road is, for its length, one of the finest roads, descending by numerous zigzags, and crossing the river by a solid and lofty bridge, 420 ft. above the torrent, opposite Albinen (omnibus daily in summer), and conducts, in about 8½ m. (2½ hrs. walk), to Leuk. Toll 3½ fr. for a small carriage.

Leuk (*Inns:* Kreutz; Stern, not good), a village of 620 Inhab., traversed by a narrow dirty street, on the rt. bank of the Rhone, near its junction with the Dala. A covered bridge over the Rhone connects it with the Simplon road (Rte. 59 A). Above it are ruins of two castles, destroyed by the Valaisans in 1414.

b. The other way, a mule-path carried along the W. side of the valley of the Dala, but high above that river, conducts at once to the town of Sierre (Siders), 12 m. distant, and is a short cut for those who wish to *descend* the valley of the Rhone towards Martigny and Geneva. It traverses the high pasturages, and beyond them a forest of larch; and passes the village of Inden, near which a most extensive view is gained over the valley of the Rhone, its towns, villages, farms, and old castles. The unsightly débris brought down by the furious torrents issuing from the opposite valley, and the wide expanse of bare gravel overflowed by the Rhone in spring, and converted into a river-channel—but in summer left bare and arid—give a desolate character to the scene.

Between Inden (where is a toll of 1 fr. per mule) and a village called Varen the road makes an abrupt turn, and the traveller finds himself beneath the shadow of a tremendous overhanging precipice, forming the corner of the Löéche valley. The effect of approaching it from the side of Sierre is grand in the extreme, and totally unexpected, after turning a corner of the rock. The path is carried along a narrow ledge in front of the cliff; beneath it is a gaping abyss, extending nearly down to the bed of the Dala, and above, the rocks lean so far forward that stones falling from their tops would descend upon the road, and it is therefore partly protected by a roof. This spot is called the *Gallerie*, and was the scene of a bloody combat in 1799, when the Valaisans defended this spot for several weeks against the French, effectually checking all attempts to pass, by rolling down stones and logs from above.

A rough and steep descent leads from this, in about 1½ hour, to

Sierre, upon the Simplon road (Rte. 59 A).

ROUTE 39.

PASS OF THE RAWYL.—THUN, OR IN-
TERLAKEN, TO SION OR SIERRE.—
THE GRIMMI.

The pass of the Rawyl begins at
An der Lenk, at the N. foot of the
pass, a good halting-place, about 40
m. from Thun ; thence to Sion, over
the mountain, forms a day's journey
of fully 10 hrs. It is difficult, but
scarcely deserves to be called dangerous ; it is traversed sometimes on
horseback, but is better calculated for
the pedestrian. Indeed, there must
be considerable hazard in attempting
to ride up on the N. side from An der
Lenk. From Sion to the top of the
pass there is a good mule-path, recently much improved. Nothing but
a little milk is to be had between An
der Lenk and Sion, therefore provisions ought to be taken. The scenery
on both sides of the pass resembles
that on the S. side of the Gemmi.

The village of An der Lenk may be
reached from the lake of Thun, either
by following the Simmenthal, along
which there is a good char-road, or
by the Diemtigen Thal and the pass
of the Grimmi, a route accessible only
to pedestrians. The scenery by the
Diemtigen Thal is inferior ; and in
going from Thun there is little saving
of time, but in going from Interlaken
the way by the Diemtigen Thal is
decidedly shorter.

The road up the *Simmenthal* is described (Rte. 41) as far as Zweisimmen (33 m. from Thun), whence the
char-road is continued, bearing to the
rt. up the Ueber Simmen Thal, about
10 m. to An der Lenk.

The route by the *Diemtigen Thal*
follows the Simmenthal (Rte. 41) as
far as Lattenbach 10 m. A path
there strikes off up the Diemtigen
Thal, crosses the stream of the Chivel,
and follows its l. bank through Diemtigen and Narrenbach, then recrosses
it to

Thiermatten, where there is an inn.
About a mile beyond this it again
passes the stream, and, leaving it on

[*Switz.*]

the l., gradually ascends to the pass
of the *Grimmi* (5580 ft.). Descending
through the *Fermel Thal* (a fertile
valley, only 6 m. long), it reaches

Matten, in the Upper Simmenthal,
on the char-road leading from Zweisimmen to An der Lenk, 4 m.

"*From Interlaken to Lenk* I followed a path but little known, passing
through Wimmis, and behind the
rocky point that overhangs the Simmen, continuing on the rt. bank of
that river till I reached the Diemtigen Thal, up which I proceeded by a
well-defined but rather rough path
until I joined the char-road to Thiermatten at Narrenbach. By this route
the walk from Interlaken to Thiermatten (where there is an *Inn*) will
occupy a good walker 8 hrs.; from
Thiermatten to the summit of the
Grimmi 3 hrs. more; to Andermatten
on the Simmen 1½ hr.; and another
hour to An der Lenk.

"The *Diemtigen Thal* does not possess any great degree of beauty, nor
is the view commanded from the summit of the Grimmi, although extensive
and fine, of that remarkable character
that would make the pass worth visiting on its own account. I should say
that the cattle of the Diemtigen Thal
are the finest I have seen in the Oberland. The timber is also very fine.
The Fermel Thal, by which one descends to the valley of the Simmen, is
very pretty. By this route I reached
An der Lenk from Interlaken in one
day."—*J. D.*

An der Lenk (*Inns:* Etoile ; Bär),
beautifully situated, surrounded by
high peaks and glaciers. "The *Wild-
strubel* (10,800 ft.), with the waste of
snowy glaciers beneath, forms the
most striking and prominent feature,
rising into the air above an unusually
long line of grey precipices, down
which ten or twelve cascades are seen
rolling into the country at the base."
—*Latrobe.*

A guide should be taken from An
der Lenk, as the path is in many
places difficult to find.

The Simmen rises about 6 m. above
An der Lenk, at the foot of the
glacier of Räzliberg, from a source

G

called the Seven Fountains. In the source itself there is little to compensate for the trouble of the ascent to it, but the scenery around it is of great grandeur. Between it and An der Lenk, the Simmen forms several cascades.

It is a walk of 10 hrs. without stopping, from An der Lenk to Sion. The path, instead of proceeding towards the source of the Simmen, ascends the l. bank of its tributary, the Iffigenbach; and the gorge of that torrent, flanked by vast precipices, is in places very grand.

The solitary traveller should beware of losing time by crossing a tempting bridge about half-way to Iffigen, a little below a very picturesque waterfall.

Iffigen, a group of farm-houses at the N. base of the Rawyl, near which the Iffigenbach makes a very fine fall, is a good 2 hrs. walk from Lenk. Another 2½ hrs. will bring you to the cross on the summit by proceeding leisurely.

A series of zigzags lead from Iffigen up the mountain, over some patches of snow. The path in several parts of this distance is very narrow, and runs along the edge of the precipice: some people might call it dangerous; there is, however, no real danger to a pedestrian of ordinary firmness. In this part of the pass, two small falls or jets dash down the face of the rock across the path, threatening the traveller with a shower-bath when they are increased by heavy rains. At the second fall the path is narrow, but as it is constantly washed by the water no loose stones rest on it, and as it slopes inwards away from the abyss it is not dangerous. A somewhat difficult and fatiguing zigzag surmounts the steep part of the ascent. From the brow of the precipice, looking N., a fine view expands over the valley of An der Lenk, and the mountains of the Simmenthal covered with fine pastures and farmhouses. By crossing a bed of snow lying on the W. side of a small lake, the Rawyl See, the path leads up to

The *summit of the pass of the*

Rawyl, marked by a cross (7960 ft.). The summit is probably 2 m. broad: the path across it is tedious from the number of gullies, and the alternately crumbling and slippery nature of the soil, consisting of clay-slate, which gradually changes into clay. Another small lake is reached before the traveller gains the brow of the S. declivity of the mountain, consisting of precipices similar to those on the side of Berne. The view hence of the mountains on the S. side of the vale of the Rhone, especially of the Matterhorn and its glaciers, is very sublime. A zigzag path conducts down the cliffs to the châlets of Rawin in 1 hr. 15 min. The descent is good, the path having been recently reconstructed. Close to these châlets two large bodies of water burst, one on either hand from the cliffs, forming fine falls. That on the rt. has an uncommonly fine and singular appearance, bursting out of a black cleft in the face of a broad and precipitous rock, in 5 or 6 distinct columns, and afterwards forming a fine wild tumble of foaming water. Though apparently clear when issuing from the rock, it has no sooner touched the ground than it becomes a river of liquid mud, a large portion of which is a short way below separated from the torrent, and conducted very ingeniously along the face of the mountain, and at one part against a perpendicular cliff, till, after a course of several miles, it fertilises the meadows near Ayent.

Two paths branch off at the châlets of *Rawin;* the one leading through the village of Lens, and in 5½ hrs. to Sierre; the other through Ayent to Sion in 4½ hrs. The walk from the châlets of Rawin to Sierre is very fatiguing, owing to the frequent ascents and descents. For nearly half an hour from Rawin, the rt.-hand path runs nearly on a level: it next rises for some distance to turn a rocky barrier, and then descends on *Ayent.* Foot passengers can avoid this ascent by following the bank of the water-course before mentioned, which saves nearly an hour. The most dangerous part takes 10 min. or ¼ hr. to traverse. The only way of passing is along trees supported on cross bars over the water. The scene here is very grand. The rock hangs over on the rt. side, and on the l. recedes beneath to a depth of 1000 ft. The trees are placed singly above the bed of the water-course, and are not more than a few inches wide, and not very firmly secured, which increases the danger.

The other and longer road is practicable for mules from Sion up to the top of the pass. For some distance it lies amidst forests of fir. It unites with the footpath before reaching

Ayent (no Inn), about 3 hrs. walk, passing the hamlet of Grimseln.

Sion (Rte. 59 A.), in 1¼ hr.

At Sion, experienced guides and mules may be obtained for the ascent of the Rawyl.

ROUTE 39 A.

LENK TO LAUENEN BY THE TRÜTTLIS-BERG.—LAUENEN TO GSTEIG BY THE CHRINEN.

This is a mule-road of 7 hrs., and does not require a guide in fine weather. Beyond the church of An der Lenk, the path, after traversing meadows, begins to ascend on the N. side of the valley to the Ober Staffel, a plain which is reached in 2¼ hrs. An hour more brings the traveller to the Col of *Trüttlisberg* (about 5900 ft.), between the Dauben and the Stublen. A steep descent leads in 1¼ hr. to

Lauenen (*Inn:* Bär), whence in 2 hrs. over the Chrinen (5000 ft.).

Gsteig. (Rte. 40.)

ROUTE 40.

PASS OF THE SANETSCH.—SAANEN TO SION.

About 12 hrs.

This is a long, steep, and tedious horse-pass, but not dangerous except in very bad weather. The village of Saanen (or Gessonay) and the road between it and Thun are described in Rte. 41. Char-road to Gsteig, about 11 m.

At *Staad* the path turns S. by the valley of the *Saane*, the upper end of which is called Gsteig-Thal, to

Gsteig — (*Inns:* Bär ; Rabe, tolerable)—the highest village in it, situated close under the lofty and precipitous Mittaghorn, and near the foot of the Sanetsch, the most westerly of the passes over the Bernese chain.

[From Gsteig there is an easy pass by the *Col de Pillon* (5150 ft.), to Bex and to Aigle in the lower Valais.]

It is advisable to sleep at Gsteig (Châlet in French), from which Sion is distant full 10 easy hrs., or 8 hrs. hard walking. The pass rises from this place in a very precipitous manner, and often resembles the pass of the Gemmi. ¾ hr. above Gsteig the Saane makes a beautiful *fall*, clearing the face of the rock by at least 100 ft. In the evening it is crowned by an iris. The path continues by the side of the Saane up to its source. Lovely view looking back on Gsteig. After a climb of

2 hrs. a grassy plain is entered, which is surrounded with abrupt rocky mountains, and which leads by a gentle ascent of an hr. to

The *summit*, 7560 ft. above the sea-level, a wild, rocky, solitary plain 3 or 4 m. long, called Kreutzboden, barely relieved by a few patches of vegetation.

It is not a very grand pass, but the mountains of the great chain of the Alps are finely seen, from Mt. Velan and Mt. Combin to the Dent d'Erin and the Dents Blanches, in the neighbourhood of the Matterhorn. But neither that remarkable peak nor any part of the Weisshorn, Rothhorn, or Monte Rosa, are visible. The whole of the straight, steep Val d'Erin from the Valais, and the glacier of Ferpêcle, are seen directly in front. On the other side the descent is steep but grassy all the way down to the pine forests, through which the road to Sion is tedious, but still interesting.

2 m. from the summit the *Morge* river is crossed, and after 4 m. of bad winding road, passing a chålet, is again crossed by the Pont Neuf, a substantial stone foot-bridge 200 ft. above the black stream. "There is a very pleasing yet grand view from this point. The black slate rocks rise on the E. to a height of about 2500 ft. Portions of rock have been detached and stand upright from the valley, each the height of a small mountain. The hill on the W. is covered with fir-trees. A white horizontal line will be observed on the face of the slate mountain (rt.); this is the wall of a watercourse constructed at the sole expense of a farmer's wife to supply her native village with water for irrigation, of which she had felt the want in her lifetime, and for which she left the whole of her fortune at her death." The descent continues for about 5 m. through the ravine of the Morge. Near its mouth is a ruined castle, and fine view over the valley of the Rhone, the Matterhorn, &c. The only village,

Champignol is the first place from Gsteig where refreshments can be procured. Here and at Saviese are many narrow lanes, through which the way is intricate to find. Fine view, as you descend, of the 3 castles of

Sion (Rte. 59 A.). (*Time from Sion:* walking to Champignol, 1 hr.; to summit of pass, 4 hrs.; to Gsteig, 3½ hrs.)

ROUTE 41.

THUN TO VEVAY, BY THE SIMMENTHAL; SAANEN, CHÂTEAU D'OEX, AND GRUYÈRES:—PASS OF THE DENT DE JAMAN.

27 leagues = 80 Eng. m.

Thun	Leagues.	Eng. m.
Zweisimmen . .	11 =	32½
Saanen (Gessonay)	2½ =	8½
Château d'Oex . .	2½ =	7½
Montbovon . . .	3 =	9
Bulle	3½ =	10½
Vevay	4½ =	12½

An excellent carriage-road has been made through the Simmenthal, but it has lately fallen into disuse. The inns and the means of travelling are not good. It is a little longer than the highway by Berne and Freyburg (Rte. 42). The valley abounds in rich cultivation, fields, orchards, and gardens, meadows reaching to the tops of the hills, with houses and villages lying along the banks of the river, varied with fir forests, rocky gorges and open basins, entirely of a pastoral character.

The entrance to the Simmenthal lies between the Stockhorn on the rt. and the Niesen on the l., and is approached from Thun by the road along the margin of the lake (see Rte. 38), and the banks of the Kander, as far as its junction with the Simmen, a little below the picturesque castle of Wimmis, which our road passes on the l.

About 2 m. farther is *Erlenbach.* From this parsonage Latrobe started on those Alpine expeditions which he has described in so admirable and interesting a manner in his *Alpenstock* (an excellent English guide with a foreign name). The Stockhorn rises almost immediately behind the village of Erlenbach.—(*Inns* Löwe and Bär.)

Weissenburg [has a poor *Inn*, where mules may be hired, and chairs with bearers, to convey persons who do not choose to walk, to the *Baths of Weissenburg*, distant between 2 and 3 m. from this. There is an ascent immediately on leaving the village, but after that the path winds through the most beautiful and picturesque defile, narrowing at every step into a profound chasm, till suddenly the Bath-house, singularly situated in its recesses, bursts upon the view. This large building is placed in a little nook between the boiling torrent Büntschi and the rocks, leaving barely space sufficient for the house and baths. In this retired spot the traveller is surprised to find himself surrounded by a *crowd* of peasants. In July there were 75 of that class, and 30 of a higher class of visitors : later in the year the latter preponderate. It is difficult to imagine how they pass their time in this solitude. Three weeks is the " cure " or period allotted to the trial of the remedy of the waters, which are sulphureous, and are supposed to be most efficacious in removing all internal obstructions. Great must be their power to induce patients to remain in so melancholy a place ; yet the scenery around is highly picturesque, but inaccessible to all but stout climbers, except along the road to Weissenburg. The source is situated about ½ m. higher up in the gorge, and the water, which has a temperature of above 22° Réaum., is conveyed to the baths in wooden pipes carried along the face of the precipice. The bath-house is entirely of wood. The food is said to be coarse, but good ; table-d'hôte at 12 ; salle à manger large, but low ; bed-rooms small. The whole expense, baths included, 9 fr. a-day for the superior class, and about half for the peasants. Some way up the ravine the peasants have formed a pathway out of it to the upper pastures, by cutting notches or rude steps in the face of the rock, and partly by attaching ladders to it. By this means they scale a dizzy precipice between 200 and 300 ft. high. The pedestrian bound for the upper

Simmenthal need not retrace his steps to Weissenburg, as there is a short cut direct from the baths to Oberwyl, on the high road.]

Boltingen (*Inn:* Bär ; trout-fishing here), a village situated 2600 ft. above the sea, a little to the S. of the old castle of Simmeneck. The ruined castle of Laubeck overlooks the road, which is now carried round the eminence, avoiding a steep ascent. The gorge of *Laubeck* is a scene of grandeur. Near Reidenbach there are coal-mines. The river is crossed 3 times before reaching

Zweisimmen, a village of 1200 Inhab., composed of old brown and red wooden houses (no good *Inn;* Lion best), situated at the junction of the great and lesser Simmen. The *Castle of Blankenburg* crowns the height about a mile above it. Until the democratic revolutions in canton Berne, it was the residence of the landvogt, who now occupies his own humble farm-house beside it. It is still the seat of the government, and the prison. A char-road runs hence past St. Stephan (*Inn:* Alter Schweitzer), in 1½ hr., to Matten (see Rte. 39).

The road to Bulle and Vevay now quits the Simmenthal by a very steep ascent, through scenery blackened with grand forests of pine, and, turning to the S.W., crosses an elevated tract of pasture-land called the Saanen-Moser, till it descends upon

Saanen (Fr. *Gessonay*)—*Inns :* H. de Kranich, best, and highly recommended ; l'Ours). The principal place in the pastoral valley of the upper Saane (Sarine), whose inhabitants are almost exclusively cattle-owners, or occupied in their dairies, and in manufacturing excellent cheese, exported to all parts of the world as Gruyères cheese. A kind peculiar to the valley, too delicate to bear exportation, is called Fötschari-käse. The ascent of the Sanetsch Pass (Rte. 40) is made from this.

The road beyond this is hilly. A mile below Saanen we pass out of Berne into canton Vaud. German, the language of the upper extremity of the valley, is soon exchanged for a French patois, in the lower portion, which is called Pays d'en haut Romand. The first Vaudois village is Rougemont (Germ. Rothberg—*Inn:* Kreutz). Its château was formerly a convent.

Château d'Oex (Oesch) — (*Inns:* L'Ours ; Maison de Ville)—a village of 612 Inhab., 3030 ft. above the sea, rebuilt after a conflagration which almost entirely consumed it. The château, after which it is named, is replaced by a *church* on the height where once it stood. The road next crosses the Saane to *Moulins*, whence a path strikes off leading into the Val des Ormonds (Rte. 41A) by the Monette, and also into that over the Dent de Jaman. At *Rossinière*, on the rt. bank of the Saane, the Pension kept by Mr. Herschoz is highly praised ; charge for bed and board, 4 fr. 50 c. a day. The pass of the Tine between very grand rocks and pines leads to

Montbovon — (Bubenberg. *Inn:* Kreutz)—which Byron calls " a pretty scraggy village, with a wild river and a wooden bridge:" it is situated in canton Freiburg. A few horses are kept here for hire. It is better to order them from Vevay the day before.

[A horse-path over the highly interesting *Pass of Dent de Jaman* (Jommen-Pass), 4890 ft. above the sea-level, descending upon the Lake of Geneva above Montreux, will bring the traveller to Vevay in 6 hours, a walk of 5 hrs. Byron, who crossed it, describes the whole route as " beautiful as a dream." " The view from the highest points (we had both sides of the Jura before us in one point of view, with alps in plenty) comprises, on one side, the greatest part of Lake Leman ; on the other, the valleys and mountain of the canton of Freiburg, and an immense plain, with the lakes of Neuchâtel and Morat and all which the borders of the Lake of Geneva inherit. The music of the cow's bells (for their wealth, like the patriarch's, is cattle) in the pastures, which reach to a height far above any mountains in Britain, and the shepherds shouting to us from crag to crag, and playing on their reeds, where the steeps appeared almost inaccessible, with the surrounding scenery, realized all that I have ever heard or imagined of a pastoral existence—much more so than Greece or Asia Minor, for there we have a little too much of the sabre and musket order, and if there is a crook in one hand, you are sure to see a gun in the other ; but this was pure and unmixed—solitary, savage, and patriarchal. As we went they played the ' Ranz de Vaches ' and other airs by way of farewell. I have lately repeopled my mind with nature."—*Byron's Journal.*

The view from the Col commands great part of the lake, but to see the Oberland range you must climb the *Dent* itself, 2 hrs. from the Col. From Vevay to the Col is 4 hrs. climb.

At the Châlets of Avents you may have a chamber and tolerable fare.]

The carriage-road from Montbovon to Vevay makes a very long détour : descending the valley of the Saane, and passing around the base of the *Moleson* (6181 ft.), the highest mountain in canton Freiburg, it passes under the hills crowned by the castle and town of

Gruyères (German, Greyerz)—*Inns:* said not to be good. This dirty little mouldering town of 375 Inhab. is extremely picturesque from its position on the face of a hill, the top of which is crowned by the *Castle*, very commanding from its situation, and well preserved. Its owners, the Counts of Gruyères, were sovereigns of the surrounding district down to 1554, when the family became bankrupt, and the creditors seized and sold the lordship to Berne, so that the last descendant died in a strange land. It is now falling into decay, only one portion being occupied by the Préfet. The gloomy antiquity of the interior corresponds with the character of its watch-towers, battlements, and loop-holes, as seen from without. The walls are 14 ft. thick, the halls vaulted and dimly lighted by small windows : in one is a fireplace at which oxen were roasted whole. The *torture* chamber at the top of the stairs contained the rack which had been used within the present century to inflict punishment. The old *Ch. of St. Theodule*, containing a monument with marble effigies of a Count of Gruyères, in singular costume—is remarkable for its antiquity. The inhabitants of the town are a lazy set, many of them pensioners of a very rich *Hospital* here.

The language spoken by the people of the district, a dialect of the Romansch (called, in German, Gruverin-Welsch), is thought to prove their descent from the Burgundians. It is a subject worthy the attention of travellers. The district is also famous for its *cheeses*, and supplies from its rich pastures a great part of the 40,000 centners (cwt.) of cheese which canton Freiburg manufactures yearly, and which is chiefly exported under the name of Gruyère.

The watch-tower of La Tour de Treme was an outpost of the Counts of Gruyères.

Bulle (Boll)—(*Inns:* Cheval Blanc ; Maison de Ville)—one of the most industrious towns in the canton. It contains 2000 Inhab., and is the chief depôt for the Gruyère cheese made in the valleys of the Saarine and of Charmey, and in the elevated plateau of which it is the centre. It is 2300 ft. above the level of the sea; and if the ages inscribed on the tombstones form any test, it must be one of the healthiest places in the world. There is a curious old chateau, but the town is modern, having been burnt in 1805. The bize or N.E. wind blows keenly over the plateau. It is distant about 18 m. from Freiburg, and the same from Vevay. A diligence daily between those two towns runs by Bulle. It is a *post road.*

[From Bulle may be made the ascent of the *Moléson* (6181 ft.), commanding a magnificent view.]

Our course now turns S. along the high road between these two places, skirting the W. base of the Moléson to

Chatel St. Denis (Kastels) — (*Inn:* Maison de Ville)—a picturesque vil-lage with an elevated castle on the l. bank of the Veveyse. ¼ m. S. of it the road enters canton Vaud.

An excellent road, admirably engineered, carried by an easy descent in zigzags down the steep hill towards the beautiful lake Leman, conducts the traveller to

Vevay (Rte. 56). The view from this road is nearly as fine as from the Jaman, so that you have no reason to regret the enormous bends which it makes, though they lengthen the journey by several miles.

ROUTE 41A.

CHÂTEAU D'OEX TO AIGLE, BY THE VALLEY DES ORMONDS.

6½ hours' walk.

A road, at present practicable only for mules and foot passengers (carriage road projected, 1857) diverges to the l. from the grand route from Thun, at Moulins, near Château d'Oex (Rte. 41), and leads the tourist by the Val d'Etivar and the valley of the Mausse, at an elevation of 3500 ft. above the level of the sea, a distance of 3 leagues to Comballaz, a small village which is never free from snow before the month of June. On one side of this mountain route rise in all their grandeur the Moléson, the Dent de Jaman, and all their train of frowning and fantastic satellites; and on the other the glaciers of the Diablerets, with the Dent du Midi and Vallaisan alps in the distance. Above les Isles the valley terminates in a wonderful horseshoe precipice of gigantic height (not unlike the Cirque of Gavarnie in the Pyrenees), over which dash 5 or 6 waterfalls, called *Plain des Isles*, while behind rise the snow and peaks of the Diablerets. This scene is well worth a visit. By the *Col de la Croix* the traveller may descend to Bex and the Rhone valley.

At Comballaz there is a comfortable *Inn* and boarding-house 5000 ft. above the sea (charge 5 frs. a-day), much frequented in summer, for the benefit of the mountain air and a sulphureous mineral spring of some celebrity which takes its source here. From hence by a rapid descent, and amidst pine forests, rushing cascades, valleys, and mountains, the traveller arrives through the picturesque valley of Les Ormonds at

Sepey, a distance of 1 league.— (*Inns:* l'Etoile (fair) is one of 3 pensions of a homely kind—moderate in their charges, as well as in accommodation, which is quite inferior to the hotels at Vevay or H. Byron, though suited to the Swiss who resort to them from June to the end of August.) Nothing can be more primitive and original than this little mountain town. The houses, or rather châlets of a superior description, entirely composed of wood, and most of them carved, and in general covered with verses and texts from the Bible. The inhabitants of les Ormonds are a powerful and hardy race, celebrated as the best rifle-shots in Switzerland. In fact, their unerring aim at immense distances is truly astonishing. The pasturages in this valley are much celebrated, and the cheese, cream, and butter of les Ormonds equal any in the canton.

At Sepey 2 paths fall in—*a.* that from Comballaz (N.), and *b.* that leading from the Upper Ormonds, up which runs a path (E.) by l'Eglise (2 hrs. from Sepey) and Les Isles, over the Col de Pillon, to Gsteig (Rte. 40) and Saanen. The latter pass is not difficult.

"From Sepey to Aigle (3 short leagues) the descent is made in any description of carriage in about an hour, the ascent in 2½ hrs., by a road which, perhaps, for beauty of construction is not surpassed in Europe. It was commenced by the Vaudois Government in 1836, with the intention of connecting the Simplon with Thun, In-

terlaken, and the German cantons at Château d'Oex, but owing to the enormous expense which has attended its formation, and the continual repairs that are necessary in winter, from the snow and other causes, it has not been continued farther than Sepey. The road is wide, and its gradual and easy ascent around the sides of a seemingly impracticable mountain, to a height of nearly 3000 ft., reflects the highest credit upon the engineer who superintended the work, M. Pichard, a Vaudois. It is remarkable for the boldness of its construction upon the sides of and through enormous rocks. At the bottom of the valley, beneath the feet of the traveller, rushes the Grande Eau in a continual series of torrents and cascades. Frightful precipices frown above him ; and the Contour Bleu, an immense work, composed of 3 long and high walls upon which the road passes on the edge of a precipice, adds to the grandeur of the scene. In the distance, near Aigle, the snowy tops of the Dent du Midi glisten in contrast to the dark forests of the Ormonds, and the Dent de Chammosaire rears its grey peak above the pasturages and châlets that are everywhere scat-on the mountain sides."—*J. D.*

Aigle, the first stage from Villeneuve, on the Simplon road, is the best starting-point for exploring the valley des Ormonds.

The expedition from Montreux, or Villeneuve, to Sepey and back, is both easy and interesting, and there are numerous paths amongst these mountains by which the route may be varied.

ROUTE 42.

BERNE TO VEVAY, BY FREYBURG.

6¼ posts = 56 Eng. m.

	Posts.		Eng. m.
Berne.			
Neueneck (Singine?)	1	=	9 ·
Freyburg . . .	1¼	=	11¼
Bulle	1⅞	=	17
Vevay	2½	=	19

Diligences 11 and 13 hrs.

Quitting Berne by the gate of Morat, flanked by its two bears, we traverse a fertile but not very interesting country. At Neueneck, where there is a good *Inn* (the Hirsch), the stream of the Sense, which separates canton Berne from Freyburg, is crossed. About 4 m. lower down this stream is *Laupen,* famous for the battle in which the Swiss confederates, under Rudolph of Erlach, defeated the mailed chivalry of Burgundy and Suabia, 1339.

The farm-houses and buildings along the road are remarkable for their size. At Neueneck (Singine ?) the canton of Freyburg is entered.

The gauze wings and dark dress of the female peasantry of Berne are exchanged for broad-brimmed, flapping straw hats and red petticoats; while the numerous crosses at the roadside announce a Roman Catholic canton.

Quitting Neueneck the admirably constructed road turns, immediately after crossing the bridge, along the bank of the river, and amidst beautiful scenery gradually reaches high ground which commands a fine view of the Alps in clear weather.

The appearance of Freyburg from the Berne road is singularly striking and picturesque, as the road, winding round the shoulder of the steep hill overlooking the valley of the Saarine, brings the traveller suddenly in view of the antique battlements and numerous towers, crowning the summit of a precipitous rock on the opposite side of the gorge. Near the top of the hill is seen a staring modern building, like a manufactory, with 5 stories and many windows, once a Jesuits' Pensionnat; not far from it the former Jesuits' college and convent ; next, the Gothic tower and church of St. Nicholas ; beyond appears the suspension-bridge, hung by 4 ropes of iron across the river, and linking together the two sides of the valley. Previous to its construction the only way of reaching the town from Berne was by descending the steep hill on the one side, and following numerous circuitous zigzags which led to the water side. The road then crossed the river 3 times by 3 different low bridges, after which it immediately ascended another slope equally steep. A diligence, or heavy carriage, performing this meandering and difficult route, required not much less than an hour to pass through the town ; at present the traveller rolls luxuriously over this beautiful bridge, and, without either ascending or descending, is transported in 2 minutes through a breach formed in the old houses, on the edge of the precipice, into the centre of the town. A moderate toll for every person, horse, and carriage, is paid on crossing.

FREYBURG.—(*Inns:* Zähringer Hof, close to the bridge, very good ; beds, 2 fr. ; table d'hôte at 12½, 3 fr. ; at 5, 4 fr.; tea 1½ fr. Beer excellent. The view of the two bridges from the platform behind is very fine. H. des Merciers or Marchands, near the church, good and cheaper.)

This town (9000 Inhab., chiefly Rom. Cath.), the capital of canton Freyburg, is situated on a promontory formed by the windings of the Saarine (Saane). Many of the houses stand on the very edge of the precipice overhanging the river, and their quaint architecture, the long line of embattled walls stretching up hill and down dale, varied by the chain of feudal watch-towers, and gateways of the ancient fortifications which still exist in a perfect state, together with the singular and romantic features of the gorge of the Saarine, make the distant view of the town at once imposing and highly picturesque. The narrow dirty streets and mean buildings of the interior do not altogether correspond with these outward pro.mises of interest.

Freyburg was founded in 1175, by Duke Berchthold of Zähringen, father of him who founded Berne, and was long a free town. In 1343 it entered into alliance with Berne, but afterwards became subject to the Dukes of Savoy; but having again become free, was in 1481 admitted into the Swiss confederation.

The Suspension Bridge, the longest of a single curve in the world, was completed and thrown open in 1834. The engineer who constructed it is M. Chaley, of Lyons. Its dimensions, compared with those of the Menai bridge, are as follows:—.

	Length.	Elevation.	Breadth.
Freyburg	905 ft.	180 ft.	22 ft. 11 in.
Menai	580	130	25

Another account makes it 840 feet between the piers.

It is supported on 4 cables of iron wire, each containing 1056 wires, the united strength of which is capable of supporting 3 times the weight which the bridge will ever be likely to bear, or 3 times the weight of 2 rows of waggons, extending entirely across it. The cables enter the ground on each side obliquely for a considerable distance, and are then carried down vertical shafts cut in the rock, and filled with masonry, through which they pass, being attached at the extremity to enormous blocks of stone. The materials of which it is composed are almost exclusively Swiss; the iron came from Berne, the limestone masonry from the quarries of the Jura, the wood-work from the forests of Freyburg: the workmen were, with the exception of one man, natives who had never seen such a bridge before. It was completed between 1830 and 1838, at an expense of about 600,000 fr. (24,000*l.* sterling), and in 1834 was subjected to various severe trials to prove its strength. First, 15 pieces of artillery, drawn by 50 horses, and accompanied by 300 people, passed over it at one time, and were collected in as close a body as possible, first on the centre, and then at the two extremities,

to try the effect of their concentrated weight. A depression of a metre (39¼ inches) was thus produced in the part most weighed upon, but no sensible oscillation was occasioned. A few days after the bridge was opened by the bishop and authorities of the town, accompanied by about 2000 persons, who passed over it twice, in procession, preceded by a military band, and keeping step. The passage of 2 or 3 heavy carriages or carts across it causes only the slightest perceptible oscillation; and nothing is more extraordinary in this beautiful structure than the combination of stability with such apparent fragility. The bridge has now stood for upwards of 20 years, and certainly does not contain one-tenth of the iron used in suspension bridges of English construction. It is well seen from the platform of the Zähringer Hof, from the old road below it, and from the singular gorge of Gotteron.

Another Wire Bridge, 640 feet long and 317 high, has been suspended across the gorge of Gotteron, on the opposite side of the river Saarine. It was finished in 1840. Though not of such large dimensions as that built in 1834, it is very curious, as the wire cables are attached immediately to the solid rock on each side, and the point of suspension is higher on one side than on the other, which gives it the appearance of half a bridge. The object of this mode of construction is economy, the expense of building piers of solid masonry from the bottom of the valley being saved.

The principal *Ch. of St. Nicholas* is rather a handsome Gothic building (date 1285–1500). The portal under the tower (date 1452) is surmounted by a curious bas-relief, representing the Last Judgment. In the centre stands St. Nicholas, and above him is seated the Saviour; on the l. hand an angel is weighing mankind in a huge pair of scales, not singly but by lots, and a pair of imps are maliciously endeavouring to pull down one scale, and make the other kick the beam; below is St. Peter, ushering the good into Paradise. On the rt. hand is the reverse of this picture—a devil, with a pig's head, is dragging after him, by a chain, a crowd of wicked, and carries a basket on his back, also filled with figures, apparently about to precipitate them into a vast cauldron suspended over a fire, which several other imps are stirring. In the corner is Hell, represented by the jaws of a monster, filled up to the teeth with evil-doers, and above it is Satan, seated on his throne.

The *Organ*, built by the late Aloys Moser, a native of the town, is one of the finest instruments in Europe. The organist is allowed to play on it for the gratification of travellers only at hours when the mass is not going on—at ½ past 1 and ½ past 5 in the afternoon, and on fête days not at all. An arrangement is made with the organist by which strangers may have an opportunity of hearing the instrument at certain hours at 1 fr. each. Tickets are obtained at the hotels. His fee is 11 fr. for a party at any other time. The performance terminates with the imitation of a storm, introducing the howling of the wind, and the roaring of the thunder, interspersed with a few flashes of lightning from 'Der Freischutz.' The instrument has 64 stops and 7800 pipes, some of them 32 ft. long.

Down to 1847 Canton Freyburg presented a remarkable instance of a state with a constitution purely democratic, in which the chief influence was exercised by the hierarchy. The town of Freyburg was a stronghold of the Romish priesthood: it is the see of a bishop, who still styles himself Bishop of Lausanne, although, since the Reformation, the canton Vaud is cut off from his diocese. It contained no less than 9 convents (5 for monks and 4 for nuns), 12 churches, and 10 chapels. The *Jesuits*, while interdicted from most other states of Europe, were here openly tolerated, having been recalled, in 1818, by a decree of the Grand Council of the canton. The *Jesuits' Convent*, or college, was founded in 1584 by Father Canisius, who died in the odour of sanctity at the age of 77,

and is interred in the Jesuits' church, awaiting the honours of canonisation, which have been, it is said, long promised to his remains. Henry IV. of France subscribed towards the building of the church, and presented the high altar, little aware of his coming fate from the dagger of a Jesuit. The college was suppressed by a decree of the Diet, 1847. The building of the convent is of very humble kind, rather mean than otherwise, and contains nothing remarkable. Its walls are lined with bad portraits of the generals of the order of Jesus, and of the rectors of the establishment.

The Pensionnat, or Jesuits' School, the most conspicuous building in the town, situated on a spot overlooking the other edifices, was destined for the reception of about 400 pupils, many of them children of the Roman Catholic noblesse of France and Germany, who were sent hither for their education. The School and Convent have been turned into a Cantonal school since 1848; but the loss of the Jesuits' School is felt severely by the tradesmen of the town, who were also the owners of the building.

Among the curiosities of Freyburg is the ancient trunk of a *Lime-tree*, planted, according to tradition, on the day of the battle of Morat, in 1476. The story relates that a young Freyburgois, who had fought in the battle, anxious to bring home the good news, ran the whole way, and arrived on this spot, bleeding, out of breath, and so exhausted by fatigue, that he fell down, and had barely time to cry "Victory!" when he expired. The branch of lime which he carried in his hand was immediately planted, and grew into the tree, of which this decayed trunk, 20 ft. in circumference, is the remains. Its branches are supported by stone pillars.

Near to it is the ancient *Rathhaus*, a building of no consequence, but standing on the site of the Duke of Zähringen's castle.

A long flight of steps leads from this down to the lower town and river side: it is called the *Rue Court Chemin*, and the roofs of some of its houses serve as pavement for the street above it, called *Rue Grande Fontaine.*

The canton Freyburg is singularly divided between the German and French languages; and the line of separation, extending from the S.E. corner to the N.W., passes through the town of Freyburg, so that in the upper town French is spoken, and in the lower German. This distinction, however, is wearing out.

The walls and gates of the town are perfect specimens of ancient fortification, and contribute, along with the general air of antiquity, to carry back the spectator to a remote state of society. One tower, near the Préfecture (thrown across the street, and now converted into a prison), has acquired the name of *La Mauvaise Tour,* because it contained the rack. Though the torture had been disused in the canton for many years, it was not legally abolished until 1830 !

The romantic character of the winding gorge of the Saarine, on whose margin Freyburg is planted, has been before alluded to. Close to the old bridge of Berne, another gorge, deep sunk between rocks of sandstone, called *Gorge de Gotteron,* opens into the Saarine. It is a wild spot, with strange old tumble-down mills on the stream, and the wire bridge, spanning the ravine high over head with its web-like filaments, increases its picturesque character. The larger suspension-bridge is also well seen from it.

About 3 m. lower down the valley of the Saarine is the *Grotto of St. Magdalene,* a hermitage and chapel cut out of the sandstone rock, by a native of Gruyères named Dupré, between 1670 and 1680. Its wonders have been exaggerated by the guide-books, and it is scarce worth a visit.

Morat is about 10 m. from Freyburg (Rte. 43). Coaches run thither. [There are three diligence roads from Freyburg to Lausanne; 1, by Romont, hilly and bad; 2, by Payerne, see Rte. 43 ; 3, by Yverdun, and thence by Rly (Rte. 45).]

Diligences to Vevay, 7 fr. 85 c.

Leaving Freyburg by the Romont gate, the *Glane* is passed by a fine bridge, and the road leaving the celebrated Cistercian convent of Hauterive on the l. follows the valley of the Saarine to

Bulle, the road from which to Vevay is described in Rte. 41.

Vevay. (Rte. 56.)

ROUTE 43.

BERNE TO LAUSANNE, BY MORAT AND AVENCHES (AVENTICUM).

Post road.   6¼ posts = 56¼ Eng. m.

	Posts.		Eng. m.
Berne.			
Güminen . . .	1¼	=	11¼
Morat	¼	=	6¼
Payerne . . .	1¼	=	11¼
Lausanne . . .	3	=	27

2 diligences daily, in 11 hrs.

Soon after leaving Berne a distant view of the Alps is obtained on the l. The Saarine is crossed by a covered Bridge at

Güminen, and a little farther on the road enters Canton Freyburg.

Morat — Germ. Murten — (*Inns:* Couronne ; Croix Blanche)—a thriving town of 1853 Inhab., situated on the E. shore of the lake of Morat, on the high road from Berne, Basle, and Soleure, to Lausanne. Its narrow and somewhat dismal streets are overlooked by an old *Castle ;* and it is still partly surrounded by feudal fortifications—the same which, for 10 days, withstood the artillery of Charles the Bold.

" There is a spot should not be pass'd in vain—
Morat! the proud, the patriot field! Where man
May gaze on ghastly trophies of the slain,
Nor blush for those who conquer'd on that plain.
Here Burgundy bequeathed his tombless host,
A bony heap through ages to remain ;
Themselves their monument." *Byron.*

The battle of 1476, which has rendered the name of this otherwise insignificant town famous all over the world, was fought under its walls. The Swiss were drawn up along the heights a little to the S.W., and nothing could resist their impetuous charge. The loss of the Burgundians was immense : 15,000 dead bodies were left on the field, and thousands perished in the lake. The bodies of the slain were collected by the Swiss in an Ossuary, which, after standing 300 years, was destroyed in 1798 by the soldiers of the Burgundian Legion in the Revolutionary French army, anxious to efface this record of their ancestors' disgrace and defeat. The ringleaders were the band of the 75th half-brigade.

It should, however, be recollected that the Swiss were not here defending their own country, but were invading the territories of the Duke of Savoy, of which the present Pays de Vaud then formed part, because the nobles there had taken the part of the Duke of Burgundy, and that the war with Charles of Burgundy had been partly occasioned by the intrigues and bribery of Louis XI.

Byron, who visited the spot in 1816, says—" A few bones still remain, notwithstanding the pains taken by the Burgundians for ages (all who passed that way removing a bone to their own country), and the less justifiable larcenies of the Swiss postilions, who carried them off to sell for knife-handles—a purpose for which the whiteness, imbibed by the bleaching of years, had rendered them in great request. Of those relics I ventured to bring away as much as may have made a quarter of a hero, for which the sole excuse is, that, if I had not, the next passer-by might have perverted them to worse uses than the careful preservation which I intended for them."—*Byron.*

Since Byron visited the spot, the scattered remains have been collected and buried, and an obelisk has been set up over them (in 1822), by the canton, at the road-side, about ¼ m. S. of Morat, on the site of the bone-house. The inscription belonging to it, and one or two cannon, made of

iron hoops, used in the battle, are still preserved in the *Town-house* of Morat.

The best view of the battle-field and lake is from the hill of *Münch‧wyler,* near an enormous lime-tree, 36 ft. in circumference, and 90 ft. high, still in full vigour and luxuriant foliage : it is probably at least 600 years old, since, according to tradition, the Swiss held a council of war before the battle under its shade. According to Ebel, the tree is 36 ft. *in diameter;* and the American, Cooper, in consequence, took a long walk up the hill, under a hot sun, to see it. " There we went, dragging our weary limbs after us, to discover that for ' diamètre ' we ought to have read ' circonférence.' I wish the erratum had been in his book instead of mine."

The lake of Morat is about 5 m. long and 3 broad : it is separated by a narrow flat tract of land from the lake of Neuchâtel, but empties itself into it through the river Broye.

About 5 m. beyond Morat is *Avenches* — Germ. Witlisburg — (*Inns:* Couronne; Hôtel de Ville), an ancient walled town of 1650 Inhab., situated in the S.W. angle of the area once occupied by *Aventicum,* the Roman capital of Helvetia. It appears to have existed before the time of Cæsar. it attained the height of its prosperity, and a population of 60,000 souls, in the reign of Vespasian and Titus; and it was destroyed, first by the Alemanni, and afterwards by Attila. The ancient walls may be traced for nearly 4 m., in some places 14 ft. thick and 15 ft. high; they extended down to the lake, where they formed a small mole and harbour. The modern town fills but one-tenth of the space they enclosed—the rest is meadow-land or corn-field. About a mile before reaching Avenches the road from Morat is carried through a breach in these ancient fortifications. On the l. is seen a tower, which, though ruined, is the most perfect of the Roman edifices here. They owe their total destruction to their massy masonry having been for ages regarded as a quarry out of which the neighbouring houses and villages have been built. Close to the modern town, on the l. of the road, a solitary Corinthian column, 37 ft. high, is still standing, and has, for a long time, served the storks as a pedestal to build their nests on, whence it is called the Cigognier.

"By a lone wall, a lonelier column rears
A grey and grief-worn aspect of old days:
'Tis the last remnant of the wreck of years,
And looks as with the wild bewildered gaze
Of one to stone converted by amaze,
Yet still with consciousness ; and there it
   stands,
Making a marvel that it not decays,
When the coeval pride of human hands,
Levell'd Aventicum, hath strew'd her subject
   lands."

Other traces of fallen splendour, such as the line of city walls, broken cornices, inscriptions, distinct remains of an *amphitheatre*, and fragments of an aqueduct, exist, and are interesting evidence of the extent of the largest Roman colony in Helvetia.

Tacitus has recorded the history of Julius Alpinus, the chief man of the city, who was condemned to death for aiding and abetting an insurrection against the Roman Emp. Vitellius, in ignorance of the murder of his rival Galba (A.D. 69).

1500 years after this event an Inscription was reported to have been found here, bearing these words:— "Julia Alpinula: Hic Jaceo. Infelicis patris infelix proles. Deæ Aventiæ Sacerdos. Exorare patris necem non potui: Male mori in fatis illi erat. Vixi annos xxiii. (I, Julia Alpinula, lie here—unfortunate child of an unfortunate parent, priestess of the Goddess Aventia. I failed in averting, by my prayers, the death of my father: the Fates had decreed that he should die ignominiously. I lived to the age of 23.)" Byron says—" I know of no human composition so affecting as this, nor a history of deeper interest. These are the names and actions which ought not to perish, and to which we turn with a true and healthy tenderness, from the wretched and glittering detail of a confused mass of conquests and battles, with which the mind is roused for a time to a false and feverish sympathy, from whence it recurs at length with all the nausea consequent on such intoxication."

" ...oh! sweet and sacred be the name !—
Julia—the daughter, the devoted—gave
Her youth to Heaven ; her heart, beneath a
   claim
Nearest to Heaven's, broke o'er a father's
   grave.
Justice is sworn 'gainst tears, and hers would
   crave,
The life she lived in ; but the judge was just,
And then she died on him she could not
   save.
Their tomb was simple, and without a bust,
And held within one urn one mind, one
   heart, one dust."

The critical acuteness of an English nobleman (Lord Mahon) has destroyed the romance of this story by proving incontestably that the above pathetic epitaph, the cause of such poetic sympathy, is an *impudent modern forgery* of the 17th century,* and that no such person as Julia Alpinula ever existed.

The *feudal Castle* was built by a Count Wivilo, in the 7th century, whence Wiflisburg, the German name of Avenches. The country here is interesting by the richness of the cultivation, the beauty of the fruit-trees, and the comfort apparently enjoyed by the population.

At *Domdidier*, 2 m. from Avenches, a road strikes off on the rt. to Freyburg (Rte. 42).

Payerne — German *Peterlingen* — (*Inns:* Bär, is newer, but not better than the Hôtel de Ville). There are two churches in this walled town— the one, now turned into a *Halle au Blé*, is in the Romanesque style, and very ancient. Bertha Queen of Burgundy, the founder of it and of the adjoining convent (suppressed since the Reformation, and now a school), was buried in it. The curiosity of the place is Queen Bertha's Saddle, a cumbrous machine kept in the *parish* church, from which it appears that, in her days, it was the fashion for ladies to ride *en cavalier;* but Bertha spun as she rode, having a distaff planted on the pummel. In the same church is Bertha's tomb, an antique

* See, 'Quarterly Review,' June, 1846.

sarcophagus discovered 1818, now covered with a slab of black marble.

A carriage-road runs from Payerne by Estavayer to Yverdun, partly near the lake of Neuchâtel. That to Lausanne ascends the valley of the Broye, past Lucens (Lobsingen) and its castle to—

Henniez, and

Moudon—Germ. *Milden—(Inn :* H. Victoria, not good.) This town (1500 Inhab.) was the Roman *Minidunum,* hence its modern name.

[At the village of *Carouge,* a road turns off on the l. to Vevay.]

The stage to Lausanne, about 13 m., consists of nearly 7 of long and incessant ascent, and 5 of descent. Extra horses (Renfort) are required for the first. From the summit and S. slope of the *Jorat,* for that is the name of the hill, a beautiful view expands over the Leman Lake; and in clear weather the snows of Mont Blanc and the high Alps border the horizon.

It is a drive of 3 hrs. from Moudon to

LAUSANNE (Rte. 56).

ROUTE 44.

BERNE TO NEUCHÂTEL AND LAUSANNE.

3¼ posts = 29 Eng. m.

	Posts.	Eng. m.
Berne.		
Aarberg	1¼ =	10
Anet	1 =	9
Neuchâtel	1¼ =	10

Post-road. 2 diligences daily in 5¼ hrs. to Neuchâtel. Steamer to Yverdun. Rly. to Lausanne. Or by Rly. to Bienne (Rte. 305), steamer to Neuchâtel and Yverdun (Rte. 45), and Rly. to Lausanne.

The road passes by *Seedorf,* a village named from the pretty little lake, to *Aarberg* (Rte. 1). Travellers desirous of visiting Rousseau's Island, on the lake of Bienne (Rte. 45), may

proceed from this by Walperswyl and Teuffelen to Gerolfingen, on the margin of the lake, about 4 m. from Aarberg. The road to Neuchâtel is carried through Siselen and

Anet, or *Ins (Inn:* Bär), a village on an eminence, from which the Alps are well seen in clear weather, with the lake of Morat and Neuchâtel near at hand. The lake of Bienne lies about 3 m. to the N. of this place. You overlook from this the Aarberger moor, a tract of morass, 9 m. long by 6 m. wide, which has never been drained, owing to the great cost of embanking. An excellent road has been made from Anet to Morat, opening a ready communication between Neuchâtel and Freyburg. Skirting the hill of Jolimont we cross the river *Thiel,* or *Zihl,* through which the waters of the lake of Neuchâtel are discharged into that of Bienne. It forms the boundary line of cantons Berne and Neuchâtel. The Castle, close to the bridge, is now a prison. A road runs from this to *Erlach* (Cerlier), a town of 1000 Inhab., on a spur of the *Jolimont,* which projects into the lake like a wall or causeway, nearly as far as Rousseau's Island. The castle of Erlach was the cradle of the noble family of that name: among its members was Rudolph, the hero of Laupen in 1339.

Near St. Blaize the road, macadamized and improved, reaches the margin of the lake of Neuchâtel, and continues along it at the foot of the Chaumont, as far as

NEUCHÂTEL (Germ. Neuenburg)— (*Inns:* Faucon;—H. des Alpes, at the waterside, best; capital trout;—H. de Commerce, or Ancre; H. du Lac, new and clean).

The chief town of the canton (8000 Inhab. Prot.) is built upon the steep slope of the Jura mountains, and along a narrow shelf of level ground between the hills and the lake, formed for the most part of alluvial deposits brought down by the river Seyon, partly gained by embankments from the water. Several new streets have been built on the land thus acquired. Except as the threshold of Switzerland, it has little to interest the passing traveller: it has but little trade, and not much activity, except on market-days. Its objects of curiosity are few and unimportant; and the scenery of the lake, though agreeable, is tame, compared with that of other Swiss lakes. On the other hand, to one newly arrived in the country, the first, and, under all circumstances, glorious view of the Alps from the heights of the Jura above the town, and occasionally from the upper windows of the hôtel, must appear magnificent; and should the sky be clear, and the traveller's temper even, the objects around will assume a different aspect, and Neuchâtel, with its picturesque old castle, its numerous white country-houses, its vine-clad hills, and its blue expanse of lake, will be pronounced beautiful.

The French princes of the house of Châlons (Longueville) were, at least nominally, the sovereigns of this little state : though the subjects maintained jealously their privileges and liberties, allowing their princes but very limited authority. When the house of Châlons became extinct in 1707, the King of Prussia was chosen, as the nearest descendant by the female line, to be sovereign or stadtholder. The sovereignty of the house of Brandenburg was interrupted by Napoleon, who made Marshal Berthier Prince of Neuchâtel, but was resumed in 1815, and continued until lately. Though long an ally of the Swiss cantons, Neuchâtel was not formally incorporated as a member of the Confederation until 1814. There was a great struggle in 1848 between the aristocratic and the democratic parties, the latter assisted occasionally by French sympathisers from across the frontier. The constitution, as settled in 1848, is upon the regular French republican model.

In Sept. 1856 the watchmakers of Locle, headed by several of the aristocracy, rose in arms with the intention of putting down the new constitution and increasing the power of the King of Prussia. The diet, however, marched bodies of men into the canton and put down the insurgents, not without bloodshed. This affair had for some time a very threatening appearance, but was finally settled under the mediation of the great powers, the prisoners taken by the Diet being liberated, and the King of Prussia renouncing his rights and title.

The *Old Castle* on the height, now converted into government offices, was originally the residence of the French princes.

The *Church*, adjoining the castle, is a Gothic building of the 12th century: but the E. end, in the round style, is older. Within it are curious monuments of several Counts and Countesses of Freyburg in Breisgau, decorated with their effigies. Farel, the reformer, was buried on the terrace in front of the building, but the situation of his grave is unknown. There is a pleasing view from this terrace.

The *Hôtel de Ville*, in the lower town, is a large modern edifice, faced with a Grecian portico. In it the meetings of the Grand Council of the canton are held.

The *Gymnasium*, a handsome new building near the lake, erected by the town, as a public school, contains a very interesting *Museum of Natural History*, including good collections in zoology, conchology, and geology. The specimens of rocks and fossils illustrating the structure of the Jura mountains are very complete and instructive. This institution owes much to the zeal and talents of Professor Agassiz, a native of Orbe in Vaud, whose interesting discoveries in the history of fossil fishes have thrown as much light on that branch of study as Cuvier's labours had done for other departments of comparative anatomy. The Professor is also a hardy mountaineer, and has paid great attention to and thrown much light upon the nature of glaciers. The town has also built a *Ladies' School* (1853), where a good cheap education is given to girls.

The charitable institutions of this town, for which it is indebted to its own citizens, are on a very splendid scale. In 1786 one David Pury left his whole fortune of 4,000,000 of livres (166,000*l.*) to endow an hospital and poorhouse, and for other purposes connected with the improvement of his native town. He had quitted it a poor lad, without money or friends, had gradually, by industry and talent for business, increased his means, becoming, in turn, jeweller, owner of mines, banker, and, finally, millionnaire, at Lisbon, where he died.

The *Hospital Pourtales* is a similar monument of the benevolence and public spirit of a townsman. It is open to people of all religions and countries alike.

Several of the richest bankers, merchants, &c., in France, are Neuchâtelois by origin.

Those who would enjoy one of the finest distant views of the Alps, with the lakes of Neuchâtel, Morat, and Bienne in the foreground, and the long range of the Jura on the N., should ascend to the *summit of the Chaumont*, the hill immediately above Neuchâtel. It is but 1½ hour's walk, and a good carriage road leads thither in 1½ hour. It is 3580 feet above the sea-level. The view comprehends the whole array of Alps, from the Titlis to Mont Blanc, and is said to be finer even than that from the Weissenstein. It must, however, be borne in mind, that the atmosphere is seldom perfectly clear. There is a tolerable *Inn* on the top.

On the slope of the hill, about 2 m. above the town, lies the largest boulder-stone known on the Jura; it is called *Pierre à Bot* (toad-stone), and is situated in a wood, near a farmhouse; it is 62 feet long by 48 broad, and is calculated to contain 14,000 cubic feet. It is of granite, similar to that of the Great St. Bernard, from which part of the Alps it probably came, as there is no similar rock nearer at hand; yet it exhibits no symptoms of attrition, all its angles being perfectly sharp. The entire S. slope of the Jura, a limestone formation, is strewed with these granite blocks, which, from the nature of the stone, must have all been derived from the high Alps. Their presence in this spot was long a mystery, but is now pretty generally attributed to the operation of enormous glaciers covering a large portion of Switzerland and carrying these blocks on their surface, or else to the operation of floating icebergs operating as rafts on a great lake or inland sea.

The *Gorge of the Seyon* (the stream passing through the town), immediately behind Neuchâtel, is a singular scene, and those who find little to amuse them in the town will not repent a walk to explore it, though its recesses are only to be reached by scrambling and climbing. It is a deep narrow fissure, cleaving the centre of the chain of the Jura, and allowing the river Seyon to escape from the Val de Ruz into the lake of Neuchâtel. The section it presents of the strata of the Jura limestone will prove particularly instructive to the geologist. In one spot they may be observed curved and fractured, probably by the upheaving force from below, which first broke this crevice in the mountain. Outside the town, near a singularly-placed water-mill, the rent, or gorge, makes a sudden bend at right angles to its former direction, and the rocks nearly close over the stream, which there sweeps round the eminence on which the castle stands, and flows into the lake after passing through the centre of the town. Though in winter a furious torrent sweeping everything before it, it is reduced in summer to a noisome driblet of water, exhaling unwholesome effluvia. A tunnel *de la Troué du Seyon* has, in consequence, been made through the rock at the bend before alluded to, for the purpose of carrying its waters entirely clear of the town into the lake, at a considerable distance S. of its former outlet. This public work was executed out of the Pury fund without levying any imposts on the townsfolk.

The road to Vallengin has been carried up this gorge, following nearly the line of the conduit which supplies Neuchâtel with water. It is cut through the limestone rock for nearly 2 miles, and avoids altogether the painful ascent and descent which the old road made.

The principal produce of the canton is wine ; the best sorts resemble Burgundy, but are much inferior. The red wines of Cortaillod and Derrière Moulins, and the white grown between Auverquier and St. Blaise, are most in repute ; they are agreeable as sparkling wines. The chief manufacture is that of watches and clocks, of which 130,000 are exported annually : the central seat of it may be said to be the valley of Chaux de Fonds and Locle (Rte. 48) ; but much is done in the town of Neuchâtel. Most of the watches sold at Geneva are made in the canton of Neuchâtel ; the dealers at Geneva contracting for all the good ones, and leaving the bad. But the manufacturers of Neuchâtel are now beginning to cultivate for themselves this branch of industry.

There are *steamers* daily in 2½ hrs., and *diligences* in 3½ hrs. to Yverdun (Rte. 45), whence Rly. to Lausanne. (Rte. 45.)

There are *steamers* and *diligences* also to Bienne and thence to Basle (Rte. 1).

Railway to Locle and Chaux de Fonds, and thence into France, in progress. Also Rlys. to Bienne and to Yverdun in progress.

ROUTE 45.

BIENNE TO YVERDUN AND LAUSANNE, BY THE LAKES OF BIENNE AND NEUCHÂTEL.—RAILWAY.

Bienne to Neuchâtel, 18 m. Steamer, 2h., or omnibus, 3 hrs.

Neuchâtel to Yverdun, 23 m. Steamer 2½ hrs., omnibus 3½ hrs. Rly. in progress.

Yverdun to Lausanne or Morges, 26½ m. Rly. 1¼ hr.

Bienne is described in Rte. 3.

A *steamer* proceeds (omnibus down to the lake) along the lake of Bienne through the shallow waters of the *Thiele* into the lake of Neuchâtel. At Neuchâtel there is a larger steamer which takes passengers on to Yverdun.

The *Lake of Bienne* (German *Bieler See*) is about 10 m. long, and nearly 3 broad. It is 8 feet lower than the lake of Neuchâtel, whose waters it receives at its S. extremity by the Thiel, discharging them again at the N.E. corner, through a continuation of the same river. Its banks are neither bold nor striking, but it possesses much quiet beauty of scenery, although it owes its celebrity chiefly to Rousseau's residence on it, and to his somewhat extravagant praises. The *Isle St. Pierre*, on which he took refuge for 2 months, in 1765, after his proscription at Paris, and his pretended stoning at Motiers (Rte. 49), is situated about 6 m. from Bienne. Boats may be hired at almost all the villages on the lake to row to it. Carriages may be sent on from Bienne to Gleresse, a village opposite the island, to wait. The island, a pretty object, is a ridge of sandstone, rising 12 ft. above the lake, and prolonged southwards, under water, to the hill called Jolimont. It is crowned by a grove of magnificent old oaks, the shade of which in summer is most refreshing.

Rousseau's room is preserved nearly in the state in which he left it, except that its walls, doors, shutters, and windows are scribbled over with names of visitors of all nations. To escape the importunities of curious visitors he used to climb up by a stove, through a trap-door (still shown) into the garret, and frequently, when informed by his host that a party had come expressly to see him, refused to appear—"Je ne suis pas ici dans une ménagerie."

Neuceville (Germ. *Neuenstadt*), a little town of 1200 Inhab., on the edge of the lake, at the foot of the Chasseral, whose summit may be reached hence in 3½ hrs., and a little to the S.W. of the two islands.

On the opposite side of the lake, near its S. extremity, stands *Erlach* (Cerlier), at the foot of the *Jolimont*, a hill of sandstone, which sends out the spur prolonged into the Isle St. Pierre, producing shallows covered with reeds stretching into the lake.

The borders of the lake of Neuchâtel are reached at St. Blaise, and an improved road, skirting the edge of the vineyards, conducts thence to NEUCHÂTEL (Rte. 44).

A little more than a mile from the gates of Neuchâtel the road crosses the glen of Serrières by a handsome stone bridge, built by Marshal Berthier. The bottom of it is occupied by a little hamlet, composed of a group of water-mills, turned by a remarkable stream, rising in the head of the dell and falling into the lake, after a course of not more than ½ a mile. Though it remains, as it were, but a few minutes above ground, it rises in sufficient force and volume to turn a wheel within 200 yards of its source, and subsequently sets in motion several others, both above and below the bridge. It is fed from secret reservoirs within the mountain, and is probably to be identified with some of those singular streams which bury themselves in various places among the cavernous range of the Jura.

About 3 m. farther is Columbier, once the seat of the Scotch Marshal Keith, the friend and general of Frederick the Great; he was governor of Neuchâtel. Cortaillod, by the water-side, produces one of the best wines in the canton. The village Boudry, on the Reuse, was the birthplace (1764) of the demagogue and Jacobin of the French Revolution, Marat.

St. Aubin — (*Inn*: Couronne;) — a village half-way to Yverdun. Near it are the castles of Gorgier and Vaumarcus. An excursion may be made from this over the hills to the Creux de Vent (Rte. 49), 4 m.

Grandson — (*Inns*: Lion d'Or; Croix Rouge, not good)—a town of 890 Inhab., with a venerable *Castle*, now converted into a snuff-manufactory, on an eminence above the lake. It is historically remarkable because before the battle of Grandson it resisted for 10 days the assaults and artillery of the Burgundian army. When at length the garrison, reduced by famine and invited by the offer of free pardon, by a spy or deserter who had entered the castle by stealth, surrendered it, Charles, with a ferocity peculiar to his character, caused them to be stripped and hung by hundreds on the surrounding trees, and as many more to be drowned in the lake. But two days after, on the 3rd of March, 1476, he expiated this atrocious crime, and experienced the vengeance of the Swiss in the memorable defeat of his host, 50,000 strong, by the army of the confederates, amounting to not much more than ⅓ of that number; and was himself compelled to fly for his life across the mountains, with only 5 followers. The spoil of his camp, which fell into the hands of the victors, included 120 pieces of cannon, 600 standards, all his jewels and regalia, costly hangings, and military chest; on that day gold and diamonds were dealt out to the Swiss by handfuls. In this battle, however, as in these of Morat and Nancy, the Swiss were invading the then territories of the Dukes of Savoy or of Burgundy. The scene of the battle lies between Concise—(*Inn*: l'Ecu de France, comfortable)—and Coreilles, near which 3 rough obelisks of granite 8 or 10 ft. high were set up by the Swiss to mark their victory. (? May they not be Druid stones?)

The *Church* of Grandson is very ancient, 10th or 11th cent., and curious. The prior's stall of wood is worth notice. Farel preached the reformed doctrines from its pulpit. There is a path over the hills from Grandson to Motiers Travers.

Yverdun (German *Ifferten*)—(*Inns*: H. de Londres; Maison Rouge)— a town of 3461 Inhab., at the S. extremity of the lake of Neuchâtel. It is built upon the site of the Roman

Ebrodunum, whose name, with a little change, it still inherits.

The *Castle*, built in the 12th century by Conrad of Zähringen, became the school-house and residence of Pestalozzi, from 1805 to 1825. Although the founder of a system of education, and of many schools both in Europe and America, he was a very bad practical schoolmaster himself; and this establishment, the headquarters as it were of his system, turned out a signal failure.

A very delightful excursion may be made from this up the *Val Orbe* to the *Lac de Joux* (Rte. 50). The road hence to Geneva passes through Val Orbe.

Steamers to Neuchâtel and Bienne.

Railway 26½ m. long to Lausanne and Morges. The country through which it runs is fertile, but does not present anything very remarkable. The Rly. at first follows the valley of the Thiele; it then takes nearly the course of the unfinished canal (Rte. 50), till it reaches the valley of the *Venoge*, which it follows to *Bussigny* Junct. within a few miles of the lake of Geneva, when it separates into two branches, one to *Geneva* (Rte. 53), the other to

LAUSANNE (Rte. 56).

ROUTE 48.

NEUCHÂTEL TO CHAUX DE FONDS
AND LOCLE.

About 20 m. Rly. from Chaux de Fonds to Locle. Rly. from Neuchâtel in progress.

The road to Vallengin conducts directly through the profound chasm of the Seyon (Rte. 44).

Vallengin — (*Inn*: Couronne) — is the principal place in the fertile Val de Ruz—430 Inhab. Its *Castle* (now a prison) is in part as old as the 12th century: its base is washed by the Seyon. The *Church*, a perfectly regular Gothic structure, was built by a Count of Vallengin, on his return from the crusades, in consequence of a vow made to the Virgin in a storm at sea that he would build a church upon the water; accordingly the stream of the valley is conducted under the building.

A steep and long ascent up the Tête de Rang leads by

Hautes Geneveyes (Hôtel Reybaud) to the Col des Loges, whence is a fine view over the Vosges, Jura, and Alps (H. la Vue des Alpes, good *Inn*), to

Chaux de Fonds—(*Inns*: Fleur de Lys, Balances, Lion d'Or)—a scattered village of 15,000 Inhab., in a bleak, upland, and desolate valley, bare of wood, and from its great elevation of 3070 ft. above the sea, capable of producing only a scanty crop of oats. The village covers an area not less than that of the city of Oxford, each cottage being an isolated cube, surrounded by a croft or garden half an acre or an acre in extent; it was, however, burnt in 1794. Its inhabitants are reputed to be very rich. After Locle, it is the chief seat of the manufacture of clocks and watches. This is not carried on in large factories, but in the separate dwellings of the workmen. Each man usually makes only one particular piece of machinery, leaving even the finishing of it to others. The number of persons here and at Locle, and in the neighbouring district, engaged in different branches of watchmaking is about 12,000; the wages vary from 2½ fr. to 10 fr. a day. The number of gold and silver watches made in 1851 was 156,122, and in Locle 83,684; in 1774 the total number of watches made was 300. There are two *subterranean mills* here, turned by the stream of the valley previous to its sinking underground; the rocks have been blasted to afford space for the mills; but those at Locle are even more curious. *Diligences* to Porentrui; — to Basle; —to Sonceboz, by the St. Immerthal; —to Besançon.

A pleasant day's excursion from Chaux de Fonds may be made by driving along the fine road to Maison Monsieur (Inn), situated on the Doubs. Thence on foot, and partly by water, down the stream, to the Saut du Doubs. Thence to Morteau, and through the Roche Fendue to Locle.

The *Doubs*, which separates Switzerland from France, traverses one of those singular fissures common in the Jura limestone, and descends in a fall (le Saut du Doubs) 80 ft. high. Above the fall the river, dammed up by rocks, spreads out into a sort of lake; below, for the space of nearly 6 m., it runs between rocks 800 or 1000 ft. high, presenting to the pedestrian both here and lower down, as far as Goumois and St. Ursitz, many scenes of beauty and interest.

The Saut du Doubs is 4 m. from Locle.

The Rly. is now open to

Locle—(Inns: Fleur de Lys ; Trois Rois)—another scattered village, occupied by an industrious population of 8514 souls; the men chiefly watchmakers, the women lacemakers; rebuilt since a fire which consumed it in 1833.

The little stream of the *Bied*, which traverses the valley, loses itself, at a short distance from Locle, in a chasm in the rock. This outlet, however, proved insufficient to drain the valley; and the district around the town was, in consequence, inundated at the season of the melting of the snows— and not much better than a morass at any time. To remedy this evil, a tunnel, 950 ft. long, was pierced through the screen of solid limestonerock which encompasses the valley in 1802-6, and this now effectually carries off into the Doubs the previously stagnant waters. At Cul des Roches, a short distance from this artificial drain or emissary, and about a mile from Locle, the river disappears in a natural opening, sinking into the heart of the mountain, through a vertical abyss, more than 100 ft. deep. This water-power, or privilege, as an American would call it, is not lost; but, in order to render it available, 3 or 4

mills have been constructed, one below the other, in the cavernous cleft—each receiving, in turn, the stream, which puts its wheels in motion. "You go down flights of broken and slippery stairs, cut in the rock, to these mills, placed one under another, in very frightful situations undoubtedly, but rendered more so to the imagination of the beholder from the circumstances of darkness and ignorance of the means by which the works are secured, by the noise, the unfathomable depth below, &c."—*Simond.*

3 m. from Locle is *La Roche Fendue*, an aperture bored in the rock, dividing Switzerland from France, commenced 1779, and only lately finished, by which the road to Besançon is shortened by 6 m. : it opens a singular view over the Val de Doubs.

There is another road from Locle to Neuchâtel, by Chaux de Milieu, Les Ponts, the heights of La Tourne, and Corcelles.

ROUTE 49.

PONTARLIER (IN FRANCE) TO NEUCHÂTEL, BY MOTIERS TRAVERS.

3¼ posts = 29 Eng. m.

	Posts.	Eng. m.
Pontarlier.		
Motiers	1¼ =	14¼
Neuchâtel . . .	1¼ =	14¼

A diligence daily. Rly. in progress, and also Rly. from Pontarlier to Salins and Dôle.

Pontarlier—(Inns: La Poste, good — Lion d'Or) — the last town in France.

The road first ascends by the side of the river Doubs, and through the pass of La Cluse, which may be called a mountain gateway between France and Switzerland, to St. Pierre de Joux. The defile is commanded by the *Château de Jour*, situated on the summit of a precipice, at the foot of which the roads from Pontarlier and Salins, and those from Neuchâtel and Geneva, by Jougne, unite. This frontier-fort was the prison of the unfortunate Toussaint l'Ouverture, when treacherously carried off from St. Domingo by command of Napoleon. He ended his days here, some say by violent means; but the sudden transition from the climate of the tropics to a dank dungeon on the heights of the Jura sufficiently explains the cause of his death, without the need of violence. Here also was confined, previously, another remarkable prisoner, *Mirabeau*, who was sent hither by virtue of a lettre de cachet obtained by his father, " l'Ami des Hommes," as he called himself, and the tyrant of his own family, as he proved himself. Mirabeau, having by his insinuating manners obtained leave from the governor to visit the town of Pontarlier on parole, made love to Madame de Monnier, the young wife of an old magistrate there, and eloped with her to Holland. She was the Sophie to whom he addressed some of his obscene writings.

Between the villages of Verrières de Joux and Verrières de Suisse, the French frontier is crossed. The Custom-house regulations on this part of the French frontier are more than usually rigorous. In some places there is a treble line of douaniers, which makes it advisable to have the luggage plombé at the first station. In some places the douaniers attend only during certain hours of the day, and persons arriving in their absence must await their return. Travellers should ascertain by previous inquiry what these hours are (?).

The country now becomes exceedingly romantic—the hills clothed with forests, the valleys carpeted with the richest verdure, and sprinkled with neat cottages in the picturesque style of architecture peculiar to the chain of the Jura and Alps. Cheese, nearly as good as that of Gruyères, and sold under that name, is made on the upland pastures of the Jura.

The descent from the summit so the ridge into the Val Travers if through another narrow gorge, called La Chaîne, because the passage was at one time stopped by a massy chain drawn across the road, and fastened to staples in the rock. This primitive fortification is said to have been a relic of the Burgundian wars, intended to arrest the artillery of Charles the Bold.

At the village of St. Sulpice the river Reuse, which waters the Val Travers, rises out of the rock. This abundant source is said to be the outlet of the Lac d'Etalières, situated about 10 miles off, among the hills.

From Motiers to Verrières extra horses must be taken at the ascent.

Motiers Travers—(*Inn:* Maison de Commune)—is a village inhabited by watch and lace makers, on the rt. bank of the Reuse, which has obtained some notoriety as the place of residence of Jean Jacques Rousseau after his banishment from Geneva. In the house occupied by him his desk is shown, at which he wrote his celebrated ' Lettres de la Montagne ;' and up stairs, in a wooden gallery, two peeping-holes, through which he could observe people out of doors without being seen himself. He quitted the place under the pretence of having been persecuted, and because the boys threw stones at his windows.

The Val Travers is highly picturesque. A few miles lower down it is bounded on the rt. by a remarkable mountain called *Creux de Vent*, 4800 ft. above the sea. " Its summit is hollowed out into a vast and profound cavity, 500 ft. deep, surrounded by an amphitheatre of limestone rock from the top to the bottom." It is more than 2 m. in diameter. " At times, when a change of weather is impending, the crater of the mountain is seen to become suddenly filled with a cloud of white vapour, working and rising and falling with an easy but perceptible motion, until the whole hollow presents the appearance of an immense cauldron of boiling vapour, which seldom rises above the edge. If any escape, it is by the opening towards the defile; and I have seen it repeatedly issue in a thin white line, and float gradually down the centre of the valley till imperceptibly diminished and dissipated."—*Latrobe.*

The echo produced by firing a gun within the Creux de Vent is like a scattered fire of musketry, or a succession of discharges from a battery; and the hollow may be called the very cradle of the winds, which appear to be perpetually blowing from it.

La Clusette, near Brod, is a very picturesque defile—the road hanging over the precipice. A steep ascent carries the road out of the Val Travers; and at the top of the ridge, near the site of what once was the robber castle of

Rochefort, a beautiful view opens through the gap of the defile, over the lake of Neuchâtel, and the Alps along the horizon.

From this place the Rly. to Chaux de Fonds will branch off, the main line leading to

NEUCHÂTEL (Rte. 44).

ROUTE 50.

YVERDUN TO THE LAC DE JOUX.

18 m. Diligence daily to Le Brassus. After leaving Yverdun the road reaches in 6 m.

Orbe—(*Inn:* La Maison de Ville) —a picturesque and ancient town of 1927 Inhab., built on a hill nearly insulated by the Orbe, which is crossed by 2 bridges—a lower one of great antiquity, and an upper and

modern one of a single arch, 124 ft. span, in use at present. It was the Roman station *Urbigenum*, and a place of importance in the middle ages, under the Burgundian Kings, who had a *Royal Castle* here. The fair but cruel Brunehilde, Queen of the Franks, took refuge here, with her granddaughter, but was soon put to death. The three sons of Lothaire I. met here, in 855, to divide his kingdom. In 1475 the Swiss took Orbe by assault; but the *Castle*, whose venerable ruins, reduced to two solitary towers of antique structure, are now included in a terrace which serves as a public walk, made a lengthened resistance. The garrison, yielding step by step, disputed the possession of each chamber, stair, and passage. The last remnant were pursued into a tower, which the Swiss set fire to, and the few who fell into their hands alive were thrown over the battlements.

An attempt was made in 1689 to connect the lakes of Geneva and Neuchâtel by a canal between the rivers Orbe and Venoge; it was cut as far as Entre Roche, about 12 m., but was never carried further. It lies about 1½ m. E. of the road.

There is a post road into France from Orbe, along the l. bank of the Orbe, by Jougne (1¾ p.) and Pontarlier.

About 2 m. above Orbe, near Mont Charand, is a cavern, with stalactites. called Grotte aux Fées . not far from it is a cascade of the Orbe.

The carriage road now turns away from the river, and proceeds through Romainmotier, under the singular mountain called *Dent de Vaulion*, to *Le Pont*, on the Lac de Joux. The vale of the Orbe is one of the most beautiful in the Jura, and the pedestrian may find a footpath along its banks, up to its source, in the cliff below

Pont, a little village, named from a bridge across the channel, which connects the *Lac de Joux* with the small *Lac des Brenets*, is the best head-quarters, as it has a tolerable inn. It is prettily situated at the S.

base of the *Dent de Vaulion*, whence that mountain may be ascended in ½ hr.; *fine view*. One side of it is a sheer precipice of bare limestone 2000 ft. high—the other a steep slope, or inclined plane, covered with verdant turf. It requires a steady head to look from the top over the verge of the precipice.

About 3 m. N. of Pont, and the same distance above Vallorbe, is the source of the Orbe, which rises at once a copious stream, supplied, it is supposed, by subterranean conduits from the Lac de Joux.

The valley in which the *Lac de Joux* is situated contains two other lakes, Le Ter and Brenet, and is entirely shut in by high hills; so that, although these sheets of water are fed by all the streams of the valley, they have no visible outlet above ground. There are, however, large cavities and orifices in the beds of these lakes, called *entonnoirs*, through which the waters escape. These fissures are sometimes rendered incapable of carrying off the waters from internal obstructions, and thus inundations are caused in the valley. A tunnel, of no very great extent, might drain the lake entirely. The *Lac de Joux* is 3210 ft. above the level of the sea. The source of the Orbe is about 700 ft. lower than the surface of the lake. The scenery of the Valley de Joux is very romantic, and will alone compensate for a visit. Along the S.E. side of the lake rises the imposing mass of the *Mont Tendre*, 5510 ft. high: its lower slopes are well wooded. The view from its summit, extending to Mont Blanc on the one side, and to Soleure on the other, will repay the trouble of the ascent. There is a path down the opposite side of the mountain, leading, in 2 hrs., to the village of Mont Richer. An unfortunate English gentleman, named Herbert, who was drowned in a well near the châlets of the Mont Tendre in 1837, is buried at Mont Richer. Henri Chenu, fruitier, is said to be a good guide for the Mont Tendre. There is a cross-road along the N.W. shore of the Lac de Joux, from Pont to Les Rousses, on the old post-road from Dijon to Geneva. Another cross-road, winding round the shoulder of the Mont Tendre, runs direct from Pont to Aubonne, on the way to Geneva, rendering it unnecessary to return to Orbe.

ROUTE 53.

MACON TO GENEVA (RAILWAY).

In former days the main road from Paris to Geneva passed through *Dôle*, *Les Rousses*, and *Gex*, commanding in fine weather a magnificent view of the Alps.

The Rly. from Paris now branches at *Macon*, passing through *Bourg, Amberieu, Culoz*, and *Bellegarde*. Near Bellegarde is the celebrated Perte du Rhône (Rte. 53 e). At *Challex* the Swiss territory is entered about 7 m. from

GENEVA. (*Germ.* Genf; *Ital.* Ginevra.) *Inns :* H. du Métropole, an immense establishment opposite the Jardin Anglais; L'Ecu de Genève; Hôtel des Bergues; Couronne—three excellent inns, facing the lake. It is not easy to say which is best. H. d'Angleterre, also on the quay, good; H. des Chemins de Fer, on the Grand Quai; H. du Rhone, clean and reasonable; La Balance, most comfortable as a 2nd class inn. Niederhausen's *Pension. Restaurant*, Richter (Lion d'Or), Rue du Rhône, No. 62, good. *Cafés*, Du Nord, facing the lake, one of the best in Switzerland; La Poste.

Passports are generally required at Geneva.

Geneva, though the capital of the smallest of the Swiss cantons, except Zug, is the most populous town in the Confederation, since it contains

32,000 Inhab. (9322 Rom. Catholics), or, including its suburbs, 37,724. It is well situated, at the W. extremity of the lake of Geneva, at the point where "the blue waters of the arrowy Rhone" issue out of it. The river divides the town into two parts; the smaller on the rt. bank being called Quartier St. Gervais. The intensely blue colour of the waters of the Rhone, alluded to by Byron, is certainly very remarkable, and resembles nothing so much as the discharge of indigo from a dyer's vat. The cause of it has not been satisfactorily explained. Sir Humphry Davy attributed it to the presence of iodine. The extreme purity lasts but for a short space, since a mile below the town it is polluted by the admixture of the waters of the turbid Arve, and retains the same dingy hue all the way to the sea.

Geneva, when seen from the lake, presents a very imposing appearance, in consequence of improvements, made since 1830, for which it is indebted, in no slight degree, to the circulation of the gold of English travellers among its inhabitants. Several new quarters have started up on the banks of the Rhone and the margin of the lake, displaying handsome fronts of tall houses, lined with broad quays towards the lake. The Quai de Mont Blanc is a continuation of Quai des Bergues, and forms a row of magnificent houses. On the S. bank of the Rhone the unsightly houses which lined the margin of the lake have been refaced and beautified, while a broad belt of land has been gained from the water, and converted into a line of Quais. This is connected with the Quai des Bergues by two handsome bridges, thrown across the lake, and united with a small island, formerly a part of the fortifications, now occupied by a very inferior statue of Rousseau. Since 1848 the fortifications have been razed, those near the Porte de Rive partly thrown into the lake, so as to form another new Quai, occupied by new streets and houses. Geneva is divided into the upper and lower town; and this distinction, arising from the uneven nature of the ground, is perpetuated in the rank and condition of the inhabitants of the two divisions. The upper town consists almost entirely of the large and handsome mansions of the burgher aristocracy, heretofore the senators and magistrates of the republic, between whom and the inhabitants of the lower town, consisting of shopkeepers, a strong social line is drawn. The Quartier de St. Gervais is the abode of the workmen, the seat of democracy after the French pattern—the Faubourg St. Antoine of Geneva:—its streets are narrow, its houses lofty, and it has something of the air of the old town of Edinburgh. The feuds arising between the high and low town were not few, nor void of interest; indeed, they would fill a long and amusing historical chapter: they often led to bloodshed; but the democrats below generally brought their exalted neighbours to reason by the simple expedient of cutting off the water-pipes, taking especial care to guard the hydraulic machine which furnished the supply to the upper town, and which is situated in their quarter. The disputes are now between the upper town and St. Gervais, the lower town siding sometimes with one, sometimes with the other.

History. Geneva is of Roman origin, and in the middle ages up to 1530 was governed by its bishop, with whom the citizens had many struggles. In 1401, the Counts of Savoy became powerful enough always to obtain the bishopric for one of their own family. One portion of the citizens, leagued together under the name of Eidgenossen (from which "Huguenot" is probably derived), after many struggles with the Counts or Dukes, in 1518 concluded an alliance with Freyburg and soon afterwards with Berne, and in 1530 compelled the Duke of Savoy to sign a treaty by which they regained their independence. The struggles between the different classes of citizens in the following 250 years are exceedingly curious. After a sort of reign of terror Geneva was annexed to France in 1798. In 1814 it became

[*Switz.*]   H

a member of the Swiss confederation, and the aristocratic government was re-established, but after many changes a democratic government was established in 1846, every citizen having a a vote. The aristocratic party however still are sometimes in a majority.

If looked at in an historical point of view, Geneva may be said to possess an interest, for the intelligent traveller, far greater than that to be derived from the individual objects of curiosity contained within its walls. The influence which she has exercised, not only over Europe but over the world, by means of her children, or those whom she has adopted as her citizens, is quite out of proportion to the limited extent of a territory which one may traverse from end to end in a morning's ride. Voltaire ridiculed its diminutiveness by saying, "Quand je secoue ma perruque je poudre toute la république ;" and the Emperor Paul called the disputes of its citizens a tempest in a tumbler of water : yet from Geneva emanated those religious doctrines from which Scotland, Holland, and a large part of France, Germany, and Switzerland, derive their form of faith, and which were transported by the Pilgrim Fathers to the opposite shores of the Atlantic. Here also were sown those political opinions which bore fruit in the English revolution under Charles I., in the American and the French revolutions.

Some few memorials still exist in the town serving to recall the events which have occurred in it, and the great names connected with it.

Although Geneva is deservedly a great focus for travellers of all nations, it possesses within it few objects of interest to the passing stranger. As a town, it is not very prepossessing; it has no fine public buildings; in short, scarcely any *sights*. It is owing to its beautiful environs, to its vicinity to Chamouni, to the charming scenery of its lake, and to its position on the high road from Paris to Italy, that it has become a place of so much resort.

The *Cathedral*, or *Ch. of St. Pierre*, is of an extreme simplicity of archi-

tecture. Its fine Corinthian portico added on the outside is a blemish where it is placed, but its interior possesses interest as a very early and uncorrupted specimen of the Gothic of the 11th century. It contains the monuments of Agrippa d'Aubigny, the friend of Henry IV., and grandfather of Mad. de Maintenon, and that of the Comte Henri de Rohan, a leader of the French Protestants in the reign of Louis XIII., slain near Rheinfelder, 1638. A statue of plaster now replaces one of marble, ruthlessly destroyed at the French Revolution. The canopy of the pulpit is the same under which Calvin preached.

The *Palais Electoral*, outside the Porte Neuve, is a new and handsome building for the government.

The *Musée Rath*, so named after its founder, General Rath, who left the reversion of his fortune to it, is a building in the Greek style, close to the Porte Neuve; it contains a collection of pictures and other works of art, of no very great merit, the greater part by native artists. Among the Genevese painters, Calame, Diday, Hornung, and Töpfer deserve to be mentioned.

The *Musée d'Histoire Naturelle*, No. 209, Grande Rue, is chiefly interesting to the student as containing the geological collections of Saussure, the fossil plants of MM. Brongniart and Decandolle, and the collections of M. Necker. It is principally filled with the native productions of Switzerland, and contains specimens of the chamois, of the Bouquetin, the dog of St. Bernard, of all the fishes of the rivers and lakes of this country ; among them the *ferra*, the lotte, and a trout weighing 43 lbs. from the lake of Geneva. There is the skin of an elephant, which lived a long time in a menagerie in the town, but at length becoming unruly was shot.

There is also a cabinet of *antiquities;* some of them found in the neighbourhood, such as a silver buckler, with fine bas-reliefs, discovered in the bed of the Arve, inscribed "Largitas Valentiniani Augusti;" some instruments of sacrifice found near the rocks of Neptune in the lake, &c. &c. Also the lantern dropped in the town ditch by one of the Savoyard soldiers engaged in the unsuccessful attempts to scale the walls in 1602 (see p. 148).

The *Post Office* is a handsome edifice on the Place Bel Air, Rue de la Corraterie. The *Electric Telegraph Office* is in the rear.

The best and most respectable Club in Geneva is that called the *Cercle* de la Rive.

The *Public Library*, Rue Verdaine, attached to the *College*, a scholastic looking building, of no architectural pretensions, behind St. Pierre, founded by Calvin, contains 40,000 volumes. The following curiosities are shown to all who desire to see them:—394 MS. letters of Calvin, almost illegible, but with fair transcripts (there is one addressed to Lady Jane Grey while a prisoner in the Tower); 44 vols. of his MS. sermons between 1549 and 1560; 12 vols. of letters addressed to him, and many important documents relating to the Council of Basle; several volumes of letters of Theodore Beza; the manuscript of the ' Noble Leçon,' a work of the ancient Waldenses; part of the account-book of the household of Philip le Bel, for 1308, written with a style upon waxed tablets, but now almost effaced; a translation of Quintus Curtius, taken along with the baggage of Charles the Bold at Morat. The Discourses of St. Augustine, a MS. on papyrus of the 7th century. Letters of St. Vincent de Paul, J. J. Rousseau, &c. The library is opened every day but Saturday and Sunday, from 11 to 4, and on Tuesday, to *consult* books, from 1 to 3.

- On the island, in the middle of the Rhone, not far from the Hydraulic Machine, traces may, it is said, be discovered of a Roman structure, supposed to be the foundations of one of the *towers* erected by Julius Cæsar, to prevent the Helvetians crossing the river. The earliest mention of Geneva occurs in his Commentaries, where it is described as "the last fortress of the Allobroges, and nearest to the Helvetian frontier."

A *Prison*, remarkable for its arrangement on the cellular system, now occupies the site of the Evêché, near St. Peter's church, originally the palace of the bishops.

John Calvin, the reformer, is supposed to have lived in the house, No. 116, in the rue des Chanoines, and he probably died there. It was in the year 1536 that he passed through the town a fugitive, on his way from Italy to Basle. Two years had not elapsed since the Genevese had abolished Roman Catholicism, expelled their bishop, and adopted the Reformation. Farel, who was the means of introducing it, was then preaching at Geneva, and, aware of Calvin's talents and powerful eloquence, entreated him to remain. Calvin obeyed the call, and, in a short space, the itinerant preacher and foreigner was raised to be the dictator of the republic, ruling its turbulent democracy with a sway not more mild than that of the dukes of Savoy and bishops of Geneva, under which the citizens had groaned for ages, and from which the Reformation had at length released them. From the pulpit of St. Peter's Church, which became at once the tribune and judgment-seat of the reformer, he denounced the prevailing immorality of the town with such eloquence and force that profligacy was obliged to hide its head. His hearers, running into an opposite extreme, adopted a rigorous and puritanical austerity of manners, and every transgression of Calvin's code of morals was visited with punishment of the utmost severity.

But Calvin's influence was not confined to the pulpit; he was elected president of the Consistory, of which one third of the permanent members were ministers, and the remainder laymen holding office for a year only. This council assumed an authority far more despotic than that of the bishops: it exercised the power of an inquisition, to examine into men's private lives, and into the affairs of families of whatever rank.

The sumptuary laws enacted by

Calvin were severe, but were rigidly enforced by the Consistory. They contained such enactments as the following: a dinner for ten persons was limited to five dishes; plush breeches were laid under interdict; violations of the sabbath were followed by a public admonition from the pulpit; adultery was punished with death; and the gamester was exposed in the pillory, with a pack of cards tied round his neck.

Calvin was equally rigorous in the maintenance of orthodoxy. Servetus, condemned by him for holding antitrinitarian doctrines, which, however, he did not attempt to disseminate in Geneva, was burnt at the stake in the *Champ de Bourreau*, the ancient place of execution outside the walls. The hole in which it was planted is now filled up, and the destination of the spot is changed.

Geneva, thus become the metropolis of Calvinism, and "the Rome of Protestantism," was resorted to by many foreigners, who sought refuge here from religious persecutions in their own country. Among a number of English and Scotch exiled by the cruelties of the reign of Queen Mary, was John Knox. He was made a citizen of Geneva in 1558, and did not finally quit it till 1560. Calvin died in 1564, at the age of 55, after 23 years of uninterrupted power: he was buried in the *cemetery of the Plain Palais*, but he forbade the Genevese to mark the spot where his remains were laid with a monument— the site of his grave is pointed out, and distinguished by the letters J. C. A Genevese law limits the property in a grave to 15 years, after which it may be opened for a fresh occupant, but the right to retain it longer may be bought at the rate of 300 frs. for 15 years, or 1000 frs. in perpetuity.

The Duke of Savoy, after his authority within the town had been destroyed (p. 145) was unwilling, notwithstanding, to abandon his claim to the possession of it. For many years after that event, he was engaged in repeated open contests with the citizens; nor did he omit to maintain, within the walls, spies and secret partisans, in the hopes of gaining possession of it by surprise. The street called *Corraterie*, at the period in question, A.D. 1602, the town ditch, was the scene of the most memorable of these attempts, known in Swiss history as *the Escalade*. The inhabitants, lulled to security by a display of pacific intentions on the part of the reigning Duke Charles Emanuel, had neglected all precautions to guard against an attack, even though warnings had been given them of approaching danger. On the night of Dec. 20th the townsfolk were aroused from sleep by the firing of musketry, and by an alarm that the enemy was already in possession. It appeared that a sentinel, in going his rounds with a lantern, had fallen among a party of armed men, who had quickly despatched him, but not before his cries and the report of his matchlock had aroused the rest of the guard. It was quickly discovered that a party of Savoyards, 200 strong, detached from a still larger force of 2000 men, who had approached the city in the darkness, and were posted on the Plain Palais, a little distance beyond the walls, had descended into the fosse of Corraterie, and by the aid of scaling-ladders, painted black, in order that they might not be seen, had surmounted the ramparts, were proceeding in small parties to burst open the Porte Neuve, and thus admit their associates on the outside. The Savoyards had already despatched a messenger announcing to their commander the capture of the town; but the citizens, though completely taken by surprise, were by no means seized with the panic which such an occurrence was likely to produce. Every man, armed as he might be, issued out into the streets; the small body of Savoyards who had gained the ramparts were quickly overpowered; the first gun fired from the walls, by a chance shot, swept away three of the scaling-ladders; and the enemy on the outside, on approaching the Porte Neuve, found that, instead of being blown up, it was strongly guarded, with the portcullis down. Many anecdotes are told of the prowess of the townspeople on that night; and an iron saucepan, with which an old woman knocked down a soldier, is still preserved in the arsenal, along with a piece of the scaling-ladders. The storming party, thus unexpectedly attacked, and at the same time cut off from their friends, were quickly killed or made prisoners. Those who fell alive into the hands of the Genevese were hung next day as housebreakers : 67 heads were planted along the ramparts, but many more than these fell in the ditch and outside the town. In the *cemetery of St. Gervais*, on the rt. bank of the Rhone, a monumental epitaph was set up to commemorate the names of 17 Genevese who were killed on the occasion ; and the venerable Theodore Beza, at that time 80 years old, gave out from the pulpit next day the 124th Psalm, which has been sung ever since on the anniversary of the Escalade.

Jean Jacques Rousseau, son of a watchmaker of Geneva, first saw the light in a street of the Quartier St. Gervais, since named after him (Rue de Rousseau), and in the house No. 69. It is no longer in its original condition, having been altered, and partly rebuilt. The accident of his being shut out of the town one evening, on his return from a walk, induced him to fly from his native town, as he feared to face his master next morning. His book, the *Emile*, was burnt, in conformity with an order of the Council of Geneva, by the common hangman, in front of the Hôtel de Ville, in 1762. The instigators of this act were Voltaire and the Council of the Sorbonne, who, by a singular coincidence, in this instance acted in unison. The Council at the same time issued a warrant for the arrest of the author.

The *Botanic Garden* behind the theatre, and near the Porte Neuve, deserves mention, as having been laid out under the direction of the eminent botanist Decandolle ; but the funds are so limited that the collection of plants is of no great importance. The ground it occupies has also painful historical associations. On this spot, in 1794, took place fusillades and butcheries too horrible to be detailed, in which the blood of the most respectable citizens of the town was shed, condemned to execution by a band of wretches, most of whom were their fellow-citizens, though directed by a deputy from the Comité du Salut Public at Paris.

Besides the names of Calvin and Rousseau, which are connected with Geneva—the one by adoption, the other by birth—it is the birthplace of many illustrious men, whose reputation may be styled European. The list includes the names of Isaac Casaubon; of Lefort, the friend and councillor of Peter the Great; of Necker, the weak and ill-starred minister of Louis XVI., and father of Madame de Staël; of the naturalists Saussure (who first ascended Mont Blanc), Bonnet, De Luc; and Huber, the biographer of the bee and ant; Decandolle, the botanist; of Dumont, the friend and adviser of Mirabeau and Jeremy Bentham ; and Sismondi, the historian. Among the living there are Neckar, the geologist ; De la Rive, the chemist ; Maunoir, the oculist ; and Merle d'Aubigné, author of the *History of the Reformation*, and a preacher at the Oratoire.

Geneva may be regarded as the intellectual metropolis of Switzerland; and strangers who choose it as their residence, if provided with good introductions, will find, among the upper classes, a very agreeable society, including many individuals distinguished for their literary and scientific acquirements.

The staple manufacture of Geneva, from which it derives its chief commercial prosperity, is that of *watches, musical boxes,* and *jewellery*. The first watch was brought to Geneva in 1587, and at the end of the last century 4000 persons were employed within the town, and 2000 without the walls, on this manufacture. At present the number is diminished to less than 3000, though, from improvements in the mechanical processes and increased skill of the workmen, the number of watches made is much greater than before, 100,000 being now manufactured annually. Upwards of 50 watchmakers' and 70 jewellers' workshops are kept in constant employment in the town ; and it has been calculated that in good years, 75,000 ounces of gold, 5000 marks of silver, and precious stones to the value of a million of francs, are used in them. A committee of master workmen with a syndic at their head, called *commission de surveillance*, are appointed by the government to inspect every workshop and the articles made in it, to guard against fraud in the substitution of metals not of legal alloy, and thus to prevent any deterioration in a branch of industry productive of so great an advantage to Geneva. Among the best establishments for jewellery and watches is that of Rossel et Fils, Rue du Rhône: also Mr. Geo. Roch, 183, Rue du Rhône. A good watch costs from 300 to 500 francs.

At the French custom-house, musical snuff-boxes, of Genevese manufacture, and watches pay a duty of only 5 fr. each. Smuggling, once carried on to an enormous extent between the Swiss and French frontiers, has greatly diminished, owing to the modifications of the French tariff.

Theatrical performances, for centuries interdicted in Geneva by one of the austere laws of Calvin, are now tolerated, and a *Salle de Spectacle* has been built close to the Porte Neuve. Voltaire greatly shocked the prejudices of the citizens by acting plays, as it were under their very nose, at Les Délices and Ferney. Rousseau writes to him, " Je ne vous aime pas ; vous avez corrompu ma république en lui donnant des spectacles." A *Conservatoire* de Musique has also been erected.

A very well executed *model of Mont Blanc*, the work of an artist named Sene, who employed 10 years upon it, is placed in a building erected for the purpose, in the Jardin Anglais. It is interesting to study either before or after a visit to Chamouni.

On the grand Quai, close to the port where the steamers land, a *Limnimètre* (lake measure) has been erected to mark the rise and fall of the waters of the lake, which amounts to 50 inches or more, and makes a very great difference in the appearance of the town.

At the *Boucheries*, near the Post-office, the town maintains, at the public expense, a brace of Eagles. These birds are the armorial bearings of Geneva, as the bear is of Berne.

A British Vice-Consul was appointed at Geneva, 1846. The gentleman who fills the office is most obliging and anxious to be useful.

American (U.S.) Consul, Mr. Bolton, 15, Quai des Bergues.

The *English Church*, near the Bergues Hotel, built by subscription, on the site of the former fortifications (granted by the Swiss Government), was consecrated and opened in 1853 by the Bishop of Winchester. Mr. George Haldimand gave 1000*l.* towards it. Service is performed every Sunday at 11.

Railways: to Lyons or Paris by Fort l'Ecluse; to Lausanne.

Diligences to Chambéry and Turin, by way of Annecy (Rly.); over the Simplon to Milan, in 67 hours.

Steamboats daily to Lausanne and Villeneuve in 8¼ hours. (Rte. 56 and 57.) Rly. in progress.

To *Chamouni.*—Diligences daily to St. Martin: chars onward—making the whole journey in 9 or 10 hours.

Voituriers charge for a carriage with one horse 10 to 12 fr., with two horses 22 fr. per diem (Kölliker lets carriages).

Post-horses—120, Rue du Cendrier. ¼ a post extra is charged on quitting Geneva.

Geneva is lighted with gas (1845). The coal is brought from St. Etienne. The English traveller, especially if he be proceeding to the French or Austrian dominions, will do well to provide himself here with those little English comforts which he will not find beyond the next custom-house.

At the shop of Archinard and Bordier, in the Rue Basse, all kinds of English cutlery and household goods may be had genuine. The Demoiselles Lacour, in the Grande Rue, are celebrated for gloves and ladies' shoes; Clerc Bonnet, Quai des Bergues, has the best supply of cigars, tobacco, and snuff. Brachard, Grande Rue, and Wesel, opposite, are good stationers. Briquet has published good maps. Viguet, 49, Rue des Allemands, a good chemist.

Monroe, bookseller, 1, Place des Bergues, has a *reading-room*, and keeps a store of maps, guides, English books, &c.; also lists of the campagnes and apartments to be let, in or about Geneva ; a visitors' and strangers' book; and receives subscriptions for the English Church. Good tea may be had of Monroe.

Dr. Coindet is an eminent and friendly *physician*. Dr. Lombard also is well informed, kind, and experienced: both studied at Edinburgh.

The *Ramparts*, formerly so conspicuous, are entirely swept away, and their site built over as though they had never existed. The extremity of the Quai du Mont Blanc, or the Isle Jean Jacques Rousseau, formerly the *Isle des Bergues*, is a good point of view to see the lake and Mont Blanc.

In the *Cemetery* of *Plain Palais*, a little way beyond the Porte Neuve, Sir Humphry Davy, who died here in 1829, and near to him Decandolle, the botanist, Dumont and Pictet, are buried. The site of Calvin's grave is shown here.

In the bed of the lake lie many granitic boulders, transported from the high Alps. Two of these, a short distance beyond the port of Geneva, and a little to the S.E. of the town, are so large as to project above the water. They are called *Pierres de Niton*, from a tradition that sacrifices were offered upon them to the god *Neptune* by the Romans. Indeed, instruments of sacrifice have been found near them.

Environs of Geneva.

Omnibuses run to Carouge, Laney, and Ferney every hour, from the Places de Bel Air, de Rive, de la Porte Neuve, and Porte de Cornavin.

It has been already observed that Geneva is chiefly distinguished for its beautiful situation on the margin of an enchanting lake, whose gently-sloping banks are scattered over with villas, surrounded by gardens, and looking more like English country-houses than any to be found in other parts of the Continent.

The rides, walks, and views in the vicinity are delightful, and almost endless; but the great charm of every prospect is the *Mont Blanc*, and the range of Alps of Savoy, when they deign to show themselves, which they do not, in perfect distinctness, more than 60 times a year on an average. There cannot be a more lovely sight than that of Mont Blanc, and the surrounding Aiguilles, tinged with the pink hue which the departing sun sheds upon them in certain states of the atmosphere.

a. The *junction of the Arve with the Rhone* is well worth visiting, and is best seen either from the tongue of land between the two rivers, which is reached on foot over the wire bridge to the rt. of the Porte Neuve, along the l. bank of the Rhone by the gasworks, or from the grounds of a country-house called Châtellaine, or Campagne Matthieu, on the rt. bank of the Rhone, about 1½ m. beyond the Porte de Cornavin. On the way to it, Les Délices, a country-house of Voltaire, is passed.

The Arve, a furious torrent fed by the snows and glaciers of Mont Blanc, looks like a river of mud. The pellucid blue waters of the Rhone, driven on one side by the furious entrance of its new ally, for a long time refuse to mix with it, and the line of separation between the blue and white water is distinctly marked. At length the Arve gains the mastery; and the Rhone, once polluted, does not recover its purity before reaching the sea.

b. On the S.E. side of Geneva rises the *Mont Salève,* a long line of limestone precipices, seeming to impend over the town, though it is, in reality, 5 m. off, and within the Sardinian territory. Those who are acquainted with Edinburgh may be reminded of Salisbury Crags in looking at it. The S. side of this mountain is a gentle slope, covered with verdant pasture and sprinkled with houses. The whole of this vast inclined plane, facing the Alps, is strewn over with fragments of rock, identical with that of which Mont Blanc is composed (p. lv.). The largest of these masses is 7 ft. long.

The summit of the Salève (4560 ft.), more than 3100 ft. above the lake, is frequently scaled by the inhabitants of Geneva, who make picnic parties to enjoy the view from its summit. The shortest road to it is by Carouge and Veyrier (taking the junction of the Arve on the way: there is a shorter road back, 3 m.); whence a very steep path, practicable only on foot, partly formed by steps cut in the rock, and called *Pas de l'Echelle,* leads up through a remarkable gap in the mountain to the village of Monetier (pronounced Monté) 2½ m. Those who cannot walk may reach Monetier by a carriage-road, which makes a détour of 8 m. from Geneva, through the beautiful village of Mornex, at the back of the mountain. The pleasantest way is to be driven to Monetier, thence to ascend the Petit or the Grand Salève on foot, and to descend the Pas de l'Echelle on foot to Veyrier, whither the carriage may be sent round to wait for the party.

From *Monetier* to the top is about an hour. Near the top are the Chalets des Treize Arbres (3850 ft.), so called from the presence of a few trees. The view extends S. up the valley of the Arve over the Mole to Mont Blanc; E. over a vast expanse of the lake; N. to the town of Geneva, the Rhone, and the Jura behind; W. the eye follows the valley of the Rhone as far as the gap in the Jura mountain, through which the river forces its way into France. The path is easily missed, owing to the tracks made by the winter

snow and rain being mistaken for paths; but the chief danger arises from attempting to descend through the cleft or gorge in the centre, where a very steep slope ends in an abrupt precipice. For any one accustomed to mountains there is no danger whatever; but in 1853 one English gentleman was killed, and his companion broke his thigh, in wandering about on the mountain, after losing their way.

c. On the S. shore of the lake, about 2 m. from Geneva, and a little to the l. of the high road to Thonon, is the *Campagne Diodati,* Lord Byron's residence in 1816, where he wrote 'Manfred,' and the third canto of ' Childe Harold.' Deodate, professor of theology, it will be remembered, was a friend and correspondent of Milton, who visited him here.

d. Ferney, the residence of Voltaire, an object of great attraction to travellers, is situated within the French territory, about 5 m. N. of Geneva, on the road to Paris by Gex. On the way thither, near Grand Saconnex, an eminence presents one of the best points of view of Mont Blanc.

Voltaire resided for nearly 20 years at Ferney, from 1759 to 1777. He may be said to be the founder of the village, which, before his time, consisted of but 6 or 8 hovels. He collected industrious colonists, introduced useful manufactures among them, and improved his estate, of about 900 acres, by draining, &c., besides building on it the *Château,* which still exists, but has been so much altered by its present proprietor, M. Griolet, a weaver of broadcloth. On the l. hand, as you enter the gates, stands the *Church,* originally inscribed with the words "Deo erexit Voltaire," now used as a hayloft. The *Theatre* stood opposite, in which his own tragedies were acted by amateurs, but it has been pulled down. The Château is rather handsome, and before the recent alterations two rooms were preserved nearly in the state in which Voltaire left them. The furniture was faded by time, and decayed, principally through the depredations of mischievous relic-hunting visitors.

The curtains of his bed were reduced to one-third of their original length by such thefts; and if the practice had been continued would soon have disappeared altogether. On the walls of his bed-room hang some bad prints, selected and placed there by himself; and worse paintings of his friends, Frederick the Great (a present from that king), Le Kain the actor, Catherine II. of Russia (executed in needle-work by her own hand), and Madame de Châtelet. The Russian Empress, it will be remembered, sent an embassy from St. Petersburg to Ferney to compliment the Nestor of poets. On one side of the room is a *monument* of earthenware—almost the only relic still remaining here—intended to hold his heart, which was removed to Paris by the French. It is inscribed, "Mes mânes sont consolés puisque mon cœur est au milieu dè vous." It was set up by his adopted daughter, the Marquise de Villette, and bears a strong resemblance to a German stove. By the side of it hang portraits of his seamstress, of the Savoyard boy his servant, and of Pope Ganganelli. In the ante-room is a singular picture, painted by some artist of signpost capacity, but designed by Voltaire himself. On the l. hand he appears in the act of being introduced to Apollo by Henry IV., who holds in his hand a copy of the 'Henriade.' On the opposite side the same Voltaire is seen conducted in triumph by the Muses to the temple of Memory, while his enemies and detractors, prostrated before him, writhe in torments beneath his feet.

The situation of Ferney is charming, in full view of the Alps and of Mont Blanc; but the windows of the house, excepting those of the Library, were turned directly away from the landscape. In the garden is a long berceau walk, closely arched over with clipped horn-beam—a verdant cloister, with gaps cut in it here and there, admitting a glimpse of the prospect. Here Voltaire used to walk up and down, and dictate to his secretary. Among the trees of the grove round the house is an elm planted by his own

hand in 1763: it was struck by lightning in 1824. The old gardener of Voltaire, who was living till 1845, related some curious particulars of his master. He was always addressed by the people of the village as "Monseigneur." He drove out every day in a gilt coach, drawn by 4 horses; and he was a terror to all the little boys he met in his walks.

e. Perte du Rhône.—The excursion to the Perte du Rhône at Bellegarde, on the French frontier, may be recommended. The distance is about 16 m., and, now that the rly. is opened, may easily be accomplished in a day. The carriage-road from Collonges to Bellegarde is very fine. You enter

——" where the swift Rhone cleaves his way
between
Heights which appear as lovers who have parted."

The lofty Vuache on the side of Savoy, and the huge mass of the highest part of the Jura chain, slope precipitously down to the torrent of the Rhone. The road hangs midway in this prodigious passage; and the *Fort de l'Ecluse*, the fortress which gives its name to the pass, commands this entrance of France. Infinite labour and expense have been used by the French government to strengthen this position since its destruction by the Austrians, 1814. Additional batteries have been hewn in the rock above the lower fortress, and these communicate with the guard-rooms below by a broad staircase, more than 100 feet in height, hewn inside the solid mountain. Leave may sometimes be obtained from the governor to view the fortress; but at any rate the road passes through it, and enables the traveller to see something of its remarkable defences.

From Collonges to Bellegarde (*Hôtel de la Poste*) the road sweeps along the wild gorge through which the Rhone pours. At Bellegarde it crosses the narrow and rocky bed of the Valserine. The traveller will walk from the inn to the Perte du Rhône (¼ of a mile); he will find plenty of squalid guides to show him the spot where the river, which he has accompanied from the clear cistern of its waters through the rough mountain pass, plunges at once beneath an accumulation of broken rocks which have fallen from above and covered its bed from side to side. When the waters are tolerably low, as in the spring or winter, the whole river is absorbed for a distance of 120 yards; but the Sardinian government, to facilitate the floatage of timber, &c., has blown up a considerable portion of the covering rocks and laid bare the channel. The bed of the Valserine is more picturesque, and scarcely less curious than the Perte. It is also deeply cut in the rock, but not so deep as the bed of the Rhone, consequently has to make a leap to join it. At the junction are some very picturesque mills (*Moulin de Mussel*), one of which was nearly annihilated by a falling rock, 1844. It is worth while to descend from the garden of the inn into the worn channel of this little river, which is almost dry in summer time, except where a runlet of its water burrows into the clefts and fantastic bends of the calcareous rock.

f. Another pleasant excursion may be made to *D'Ivoune*, where the river Versoix takes its rise in a pretty grotto at the foot of the Jura; and people go to eat the small delicate trout which are taken in it. The view from the terrace of the Château d'Ivoune is very fine. The best road to go is by Coppet and Celigny (where the waterfalls should also be visited), and to return by Ferney. The distance from Geneva to D'Ivoune is 12 m.

Chamouni and the shores of Lake Leman may be explored in 4 days from Geneva —thus, 1st, by early steamer to Lausanne or Vevay—by 2nd steamer on to Villeneuve—in the evening by the Milan Rly. and diligence to Martigny; 2nd, by the Tête Noire or Col de Balm to Chamouni (Rte. 115); 3rd, at Chamouni; 4th, back to Geneva.

ROUTE 56.

GENEVA TO VILLENEUVE, BY LAUSANNE, VEVAY, AND CHILLON. LAKE OF GENEVA.

6½ posts = 58 Eng. m.

	Posts.	Eng. m.
Geneva.		
Coppet		= 10
Rolle		= 22
Morges		= 31
Bussigny Junct. .		= 35
Lausanne . . .		= 39
Vevay	1¼	= 11¼
Villeneuve . . .	¾	= 7¾

The Rly. is now open to Bussigny and Lausanne. As far as Coppet it belongs to the Lyons and Geneva Co. From Coppet it belongs to the Western Rly. of Switzerland. But for those who are not in a violent hurry a far more pleasant route is by

Steamboats.—*Steamers* leave Geneva and Villeneuve, at the two extremities of the lake, twice a-day. They make the voyage from one end to the other in about 5 hours. The *steamers do not take carriages*. They stop to land and receive passengers at Coppet, Nyon, Rolle, Morges, Ouchy (the port of Lausanne), 3 hrs., Vevay 4 hrs., and Villeneuve — all situated on the N. shore of the lake, and described below. Another steamer plies between Geneva and the towns on the S. (Savoy) side of the lake. (Rte. 57.)

Lake Leman, in a Calm.

" Clear, placid Leman! thy contrasted lake,
  With the wild world I dwelt in, is a thing
  Which warns me, with its stillness, to forsake
  Earth's troubled waters for a purer spring.
  This quiet sail is as a noiseless wing
  To waft me from distraction ; once I loved
  Torn ocean's roar, but thy soft murmuring
  Sounds sweet as if a Sister's voice reproved,
That I with stern delights should e'er have
  been so moved.

It is the hush of night, and all between
Thy margin and the mountains, dusk, yet
    clear,
Mellowed and mingling, yet distinctly seen,
Save darken'd Jura, whose capt heights
    appear
Precipitously steep; and drawing near,
There breathes a living fragrance from the
    shore,
Of flowers yet fresh with childhood; on the
    ear
Drops the light drip of the suspended oar,
Or chirps the grasshopper one good-night carol
    more.

*   *   *   *   *   *

At intervals, some bird from out the brakes
Starts into voice a moment, then is still.
There seems a floating whisper on the hill,
But that is fancy,—for the starlight dews
All silently their tears of love instil,
Weeping themselves away."

Lake Leman, in a Storm.

" The sky is changed!— and such a change!
    Oh night,
And storm, and darkness, ye are wondrous
    strong,
Yet lovely in your strength, as is the light
Of a dark eye in woman! Far along,
From peak to peak, the rattling crags among
Leaps the live thunder! Not from one lone
    cloud,
But every mountain now hath found a
    tongue,
And Jura answers, through her misty shroud,
Back to the joyous Alps, who call to her aloud!

Now, where the swift Rhone cleaves his way
    between
Heights which appear as lovers who have
    parted
In hate, whose mining depths so intervene
That they can meet no more, though broken-
    hearted!
Though in their souls, which thus each other
    thwarted,
Love was the very root of the fond rage
Which blighted their life's bloom, and then
    departed :
Itself expired, but leaving them an age
Of years all winters,—war within themselves to
    wage.

Now, where the quick Rhone thus hath cleft
    his way,   [stand:
The mightiest of the storms hath ta'en his
For here, not one, but many, make their
    play,   [hand,
And fling their thunder-bolts from hand to
Flashing and cast around : of all the band,
The brightest through these parted hills hath
    fork'd
His lightnings,—as if he did understand,
That in such gaps as desolation work'd,
There the hot shaft should blast whatever
    therein lurk'd.

And this is in the night :—Most glorious
    night!
Thou wert not sent for slumber! let me be
A sharer in thy fierce and far delight,—

A portion of the tempest and of thee!
How the lit lake shines, a phosphoric sea,
And the big rain comes dancing to the earth!
And now again 't is black,—and now, the glee
Of the loud hills shakes with its mountain-
    mirth,
As if they did rejoice o'er a young earthquake's
    birth.

Sky, mountains, river, winds, lake, light-
    nings! ye!
With night, and clouds, and thunder, and a
    soul
To make these felt and feelings, well may be
Things that have made me watchful ; the far
    roll
Of your departing voices is the knoll
Of what in me is sleepless,—if I rest.
But where of ye, oh tempests! is the goal?
Are ye like those within the human breast?
Or do ye find, at length, like eagles, some high
    nest ?"   *Byron.*

The Lake of Geneva, called by the
Romans Lacus Lemanus, has nearly
the shape of a half-moon, its horns
being turned towards the S. It is the
largest lake in Switzerland, being 55
m. long, measured close to its N. shore,
and about 40 m. along its S. bank; it
is 6 m. wide at the broadest part (between Rolle and Thonon), and its
greatest depth (between Evian and
Ouchy) is 900 ft. Its surface is about
1142 ft. above the level of the sea, but
the height often varies in the year
more than 50 inches, being usually
lowest in the winter, between Jan. and
April, and highest in Aug. and part of
July and Sept., owing to the supplies
then derived from the melting snows
and glaciers. Besides these periodical
variations, the Lake is subject to other
more arbitrary changes of level, called
seiches. This phenomenon consists of
a sudden rise and fall of the water in
particular parts of the lake, independently of the agency of the wind or of
any other apparent cause. It is most
common in the vicinity of Geneva.
During these oscillations the waters
sometimes rise 5 ft., though the usual
increase is not more than 2; it never
lasts longer than 25 minutes, but it is
generally less. The cause of these
seiches has not been explained with
certainty, but they are observed to
occur most commonly when the clouds
are heavy and low. The lake never
freezes over entirely, owing to its
great depth; but in severe winters

the lower extremity is covered with ice. The sand and mud brought down by the Rhone and deposited around its mouth have caused considerable encroachments upon its upper extremity: even within the records of history Porte Valais stood on its margin, and its basin is reported to have originally extended upwards as far as Bex.

"Mon lac est le premier," are the words in which Voltaire has vaunted the beauties of the Lake of Geneva; and it must be confessed that, though it wants the gloomy sublimity of the Bay of Uri and the sunny softness of the Italian lakes, with their olive and citron groves, it has high claims to admiration. It also possesses great variety of scenery. The vine-covered slopes of Vaud contrast well with the abrupt, rocky precipices of Savoy. Near Geneva the hills subside, admitting an exquisite view of Mont Blanc, whose snowy summit, though 60 m. distant, is often reflected in its waters.

" Lake Leman woos me with its crystal face,
  The mirror where the stars and mountains view
  The stillness of their aspect in each trace
  Its clear depth yields of their far height and hue."

At its E. or upper extremity it extends to the very base of the high Alps, which by their close vicinity give its scenery a character of increased magnificence.

The boats on the lake are very picturesque, having lateen sails like the craft of the Mediterranean. It is generally calm, but not the dead calm of the mountain lakes ; occasionally the bize, a cold E. wind, is very strong, and causes considerable motion in the steamers from Geneva until they get beyond Lausanne. The S.W. wind is described as still stronger. These are the only winds which materially affect the lake.

Among the fish of the lake trouts are rare; the Lotte, on which Rousseau's Julie makes her last repast, is described as "une espèce de barbeau, assez fade, peu cher, et commun."

The first part of the road out of Geneva lies among villas and pleasure grounds not unlike English country-seats. Few spots in Europe present so many admirable sites for a dwelling as the shores of Lake Leman in full view of Mont Blanc. After a mile or two Mont Blanc is hid behind the intervening mountains of Voirons, and does not reappear until near Nyon.

The parish of *Versoix*, through which the road passes, formerly belonged to France. The Duke de Choiseul, minister of Louis XV., irritated with some proceedings of the inhabitants of Geneva, proposed to raise a rival city at Versoix which should deprive Geneva of its trade. A pier was projected into the lake to form a port, a grand Place was laid down, streets running at right angles were marked out; but beyond this the plan was never carried into execution. Hence the verses of Voltaire :—

" À Versoix nous avons des rues,
  Mais nous n'avons pas de maisons."

A little beyond Versoix (now an inconsiderable village) we pass out of the canton of Geneva into that of Vaud.

Coppet—(*Inn:* Ange)—a small village of 600 Inhab., only remarkable for the *Château*, immediately behind it, but so placed as to command no view of the lake. It is now the property of Madame de Staël Vernet. It is a plain edifice, forming three sides of a square, the front towards the lake being flanked with a tower at each end. It was the residence of Madame de Staël the author, as well as of her father, the French minister Necker. There are portraits of her by *David*, of her parents M. and Madame Necker, and a marble bust of M. Rocca, Madame de Staël's second husband. One room is pointed out as the study in which the authoress of Corinne composed many of her works. Her inkstand and desk are still preserved. The grounds are traversed by shady walks; and a clump of trees surrounded by a wall, in a field a little to the W. of the house, shrouds from view a sort of chapel in which Necker and his daughter are buried.

Nyon (*Inn:* Couronne ; not good), a town of 2682 Inhab., stands on a height ; but its suburbs, through which the high road runs, extend down to the lake. It was the Roman Novidunum. From the Terrasse des Marroniers near the fine old château once the seat of the Bailli de Nyon, there is a very fine view.

[An excellent carriage-road ascends the Jura from this in zigzags to St. Cergues, from which the *Dôle*, the highest summit of this part of the chain of the Jura, can be most easily ascended. Mules and guides can be procured at the small *Inn* of St. Cergues, which affords tolerable accommodation for a night. The ascent of the Dôle from St. Cergues requires about 3 hours' march ; but it is neither fatiguing nor dangerous. Perhaps there is no mountain in Switzerland which better repays the traveller for his fatigue, and no view more wonderfully extensive, and admirably diversified than that which it commands."]

Rolle. (*Inns:* Couronne; Tête Noire.) The hills around this village are covered with vineyards, producing a tolerable wine. One of the best Vaudois wines is grown on the slope between Rolle and Aubonne, called La Côte.

On the opposite shore of the lake is discerned the Gulf of Thonon, and the snowy head of Mont Blanc peering over the mountains of the Chablais, is visible all the way from Morges to Geneva. A little further on the rocks of Meillerie and the entrance of the Valais appear.

[A few miles above Rolle is *Aubonne*—*Inns:* Couronne ; Lion d'Or)—an ancient town of 1667 Inhab., with an Eastern-looking *castle*. Byron says of it—"The entrance and bridge something like that of Durham : it commands by far the fairest view of the lake of Geneva (and of Mont Blanc behind it) ; a grove on the height of very noble trees. Here Tavernier, the Eastern traveller, bought (or built) the château, because the site resembled and equalled that of Erivan, a frontier city of Persia. Here he finished his voyages." The *Church* contains the monument of the brave French Admiral Duquesne, the conqueror of De Ruyter—the chastiser of the Turkish and Algerine corsairs, whose services Louis XIV. refused to recompense, and whose body that monarch for a long time denied to his son,—exiled to Aubonne by the revocation of the Edict of Nantes, because Duquesne was a Protestant, and refused to adopt the king's religion. Aubonne is less than 3 m. distant from the lake. On the hills sloping down towards the lake called *La Côte*, between Aubonne and Nyon, grows the best Swiss wine, called *le Moulart*.

The *Signal de Bougy*—above Aubonne, 2730 ft. above the sea-level, is a celebrated point of view.]

Morges. (*Inn:* La Couronne.) Close to the small port of this little town of 2800 Inhab. rises the old *Castle of Wufflens*, distinguished by its tall white square donjon and group of minor turrets, built of brick, with deep machicolations. It is said to have been built by Queen Bertha in the 10th cent. It is well preserved and highly picturesque.

Bussigny Junct. Here the Rlwy. from Yverdun (Rte. 45) joins.

The distant view of Lausanne, seated on sloping hills and surmounted by its cathedral and castle, is pleasing. Between it and the lake, at the distance of ¾ m., stands the suburb or village of *Ouchy*, which may be termed the port of Lausanne. (*Inn :* Ancre, at the water-side, very good and cheap; Hotel and Pension Bachoffner also good ; both houses are kept by English landladies. Families may live here *en pension* at the rate of 30 or 40 fr. a-week each person.) Lord Byron wrote the Prisoner of Chillon in the Ancre inn, in the short space of *two days*, during which he was detained here by bad weather, June, 1816 : " thus adding one more death-less association to the already immortalized localities of the lake." There is a branch of the Rlwy. to Ouchy, but omnibuses also run between Ouchy and Lausanne—fare ½ fr. or 1 fr. with luggage.

Traversing the shady *Promenade* of *Montbenon*, renowned for its fine prospect, the old road entered

LAUSANNE. (*Inns:* Hôtel Gibbon, large and excellent ;—Faucon, good and quiet ;—Bellevue, quiet, reasonable, well kept and finely situated, with an open country view.) Lausanne, capital of the canton Vaud, contains 17,108 Inhab. (970 Roman Catholics). The Pays de Vaud (Germ. Waadtland) was originally subject to the Dukes of Savoy, but, having been conquered by the Bernese, remained tributary to that republic for 2½ centuries, until 1798, when it acquired its independence, which, however, it retained in 1814 only by the payment of a large sum of money, and then became a member of the Swiss Confederation. The constitution was rendered more democratic by changes in 1830 and 1845 ; and it is now one of the cantons the most imbued with the revolutionary opinions common on the continént. The language spoken is French. 200,000 Inhab. ; 192,000 Prot. The town stands on the lower slope of the *Mont Jorat*, which sinks gradually down to the lake, but is intersected by several ravines, giving it the form of distinct eminences. From this cause the old streets ranging over broken ground are a series of ups and downs: many are very steep. A causeway and viaduct, called from its builder *Pont Pichard*, have been made to span the valley from the front of the Hôtel Gibbon, and a winding road, carried on a level along its E. bank, renders the centre of the town and cathedral much more accessible than formerly. The older streets are mostly narrow and not very clean, and few of the houses stand on the same level. A very good point of view is

The Cathedral (at the foot of the flight of steps leading to it from the market-place ask for the keys of the door, kept at the sexton's house, No. 6), a very extensive building, and internally the finest Gothic church in Switzerland, " was founded A.D. 1000, and some traces of the original edifice may be noticed in the groined arches behind the altar. With this exception the building dates from 1275. The interior is singular in its construction, and very beautiful, though modern

arrangements have closed the choir—removed the stalls—in a manner incongruous with all precedent. Upon entering the W. door, two piers are seen on the rt. and l., each consisting of a thick central column, surrounded by six distinct and detached columns of the same height but smaller diameter. Each of these piers is surmounted by another, which would altogether resemble its subordinate, if a wall projecting from the side did not take the place of one of the smaller columns ; —these groups of columns stand at the angles of a porch of four arches, the singularity and beauty of which are greatly increased by two apses which are attached to it on the N. and S. sides. Beyond this is another porch, in which the vaulting, ribs, and arch mouldings are most beautifully supported by a series of detached slender columns. On entering the nave, 2 wide arches are seen on the right and on the left ; and these are succeeded, on each side, by 6 narrower arches, the arrangement of which is so peculiar, that they suggest the idea of their having been experiments in architectural construction during the transition period. They are thus described by Mr. Willis :—' Each alternate pier consists of 12 parts, or shafts—namely, 3 on each face for the vaulting of the nave and side aisles respectively, and 3 for the pier arches. But of the interposed ones, the first has coupled columns for the pier arch, and a lateral sub-shaft for its sub-arch ; the next has a single round shaft for the pier arch, and a stout detached shaft in front of it, which, running up to the roof, carries 3 vaulting ribs in a group upon a round abacus ; the next, with a similar arrangement for the pier arch, has a slender shaft in front, supporting the simple rib of a six-partite vault, of which this is the only compartment, the rest of the nave having quadri-partite vaults.'— The circular apse, at the eastern end, is singular and complete, both as a continuation of the nave and of the aisles. The Triforium Gallery is carried continuously along the nave, the transept, and the apse ; above it is a second gallery, equally complete, but it is arranged in compartments of triple arches, for the purpose of enabling it to conform to the openings of the windows. Within the central tower, but at a higher level, are 2 similar galleries, equally complete. At the eastern sides of the transept are 2 compartments, which form, as it were, 2 aisles to that part of the building;— the walls of these, as well as of the side aisles and the apsidal aisles, are lined throughout with a succession of low columns supporting trefoil or quatrefoil arches."—*F. L.*

Among the monuments within the church are a mailed effigy of Otho of Granson, whose ancestor, Otto de Grandeson, held several important offices in England, under Henry III. and Edward I. ; and the tomb of Victor Amedeus VIII. (Voltaire's " Bizarre Amédée "), who was Duke of Savoy, Bishop of Geneva, and Pope under the title of Felix V., but resigned in succession all these dignities, preferring to end his days as a monk in the convent of Ripaille, on the opposite shore of the lake. It is much mutilated. The monument of Mrs. Stratford Canning, a vase with a bas-relief, by *Bartolini* (not by Canova, as most guide books have it), is poor and not in good taste. Here also is interred the venerated Bernard de Menthon, founder of the Hospice of the Great St. Bernard.

On another platform, a little way behind the Terrace of the Cathedral, stands *the Castle*, a picturesque, massive square tower with 4 turrets at the angles. It was originally the residence of the Bishops of Lausanne, but is now the council-house of the canton. The Bishop's apartments, well restored, are worth seeing.

Lausanne possesses a *College*, founded 1587, and a *Cantonal Museum*, in which are some objects of interest, —such as a collection of minerals from Bex and a model of the salt-mines there. It is not deficient in the other branches of natural history. A specimen of the silurus glanis, one of the largest fresh-water fishes, came from the lake of Morat. Many *anti-quities* discovered within the canton, at Aventicum, and on the borders of the Lake Leman, also some relics of Napoleon, his Waterloo saddle, fowling-piece, &c., are preserved here.

The *Blind Asylum*, founded by Mr. Haldemand, an Englishman of Swiss descent, is admirably managed by Mr. Hirzel.

The house of Gibbon, in which he completed the History of Rome, was in the lower part of the town, behind the church of St. Francis, and on the right of the road leading down to Ouchy. Both it and the *garden* have been entirely changed. The wall of the Hôtel Gibbon occupies the site of his summer-house, and the *berceau* walk has been destroyed to make room for the garden of the hotel, but the terrace overlooking the lake, a lime and a few acacias, remain.

" It was on the day, or rather the night, of the 27th of June, 1787, between the hours of 11 and 12, that I wrote the last line of the last page in a summer-house in my garden. After laying down my pen I took several turns in a berceau, or covered walk of acacias, which commands a prospect of the country, the lake, and the mountains. The air was temperate, the sky was serene, the silver orb of the moon was reflected from the waves, and all nature was silent." *Gibbon's Life.*

The *English church service* is performed every Sunday in the Chapelle du Culte, but an English chapel has been built. The Lutheran service is also performed in the same building in the course of the day.

The *Post* and *Diligence office* is in the Place St. François, near the church. Hignou and Co., 7, Rue de Bourg, have an excellent *Reading-room* well supplied with English papers, and a circulating library.

Diligences daily to Vevay and Bex, and to Berne. The office for *post-horses* is in the Rue Martheray, No. 57.

Railways to Yverdun (Rte. 45), Geneva and Basle.

Steamboats touch at Ouchy, the port of Lausanne, at the water-side, twice a-day, on their way to either extremity of the lake. Omnibuses convey travellers to and fro. Rlwy.

The neighbourhood of Lausanne is unrivalled for the number and beauty of the walks which it presents. Partial and pleasing glimpses of the lake are obtained from the *terraces* within the town, and from that of Montbenon, just outside the walls, on the way to Geneva ; but far more extensive and beautiful prospects are presented from the heights above it. The best spot for an extensive survey is the elevated platform called the *Signal*, accessible by a carriage road. Near it is the extensive forest of Sauvabellin (Silva Belini), in which it is said the Druids once worshipped the god Bel, and thence its name. There are a great number of country-seats in the vicinity ; that of *Vernant* is highly praised ; its grounds have the character of an English park, with the Alps and the lake in addition. Cooper, the American novelist, thus describes the view from the heights above Lausanne :—" The form of the lake prevents an entire view of it from any single spot. One is as well placed at Lausanne as at any other spot perhaps for such a purpose ; but even there the W. end of the sheet is quite concealed by the curvature. If the foot of the lake is hid from the eye, its head, on the contrary, lies open before the spectator, and it offers one of the grandest landscapes of this the noblest of all earthly regions. In that direction the mountains of Savoy rise like ramparts, and the valley of the Rhone retires in the distance until it is lost in the sublimity of mystery (?). Whichever way the eye wanders over the wide range of hill-sides, villages, vineyards, mountains, and blue water, it never fails to return to this one spot, which on the whole offers one of the nicest combinations of the great and the enchanting in scenery of any place within my knowledge." Mont Blanc is not visible from the Signal, but may be seen from the top of the Jorat, on the road to Berne.

About 2 m. out of Lausanne, beyond the Calvaire, on the Berne road, is the *Cemetery of Pierre de Plain.* John *Philip Kemble*, the tragedian, is buried within it. His tomb is a plain flat slab, one of 9 or 10 in a row, all English graves. The house where he died is called Beau Site ; the plantations were all laid out by himself.

———

The road to Vevay runs along the slope of the Jorat, here covered with vineyards (Lavaux), industriously terraced high up the hills extending to Vevay. The road continues in view of the lake, and is improved by levelling and widening, though at times narrow, and partly enclosed between the walls of vineyards, rendering it very hot in summer, being unsheltered by trees. Near Vevay, the gorge of the Rhone appears in sight, overlooked by the snowy peaks of the Dent de Midi.

At Pully an inferior sort of coal, abounding in sulphur, is dug from a mine in the hill-side.

Vevay. Inns: Trois Couronnes, kept by Monnet ; close to the lake: one of the best Inns in Switzerland, comfortable and clean: a very large house and a civil landlord; *reading-room* well supplied with papers: charges not out of proportion with the comfort, but the traveller will frequently find it full, and the other hotels are far inferior. From Oct. 15 to May 1 you may live here moderately *en pension.* H. du Lac Leman, new 1853, small, clean, and comfortable : view over lake. Charges, lodging 1 fr. 50 c. ; dinner 3 frs. ; breakfast 1 to 2 frs. ; servants 50 c. The Château de Vevay is a respectable boarding-house. Trois Rois.

Vevay (Germ. Vivis, the Roman Vibiscum) is the second town in canton Vaud, and has 5200 Inhab. It is principally distinguished for the exceeding beauty of its situation, at the mouth of the gorge of the Veveyse, on the margin of the Lake Leman, at a point where the scenery of its banks is perhaps most beautiful. The writings of Rousseau have contributed not a little to its celebrity in this respect.

From the little terrace at the end of the market-place, or from the roof of the Trois Couronnes, or, better still, from the villa called Hauteville, about 2 m. above Vevay, the eye surveys on the E. the village of Clarens, Montreux, Chillon; beyond it Villeneuve and the gorge of the Rhone, backed by the gigantic Alps of the Valais, the Dent de Midi, and Pain de Sucre (neighbours of the Great St. Bernard); while on the opposite shore of the lake rise the rocks of Meillerie, surmounted by the peaks of the Dent d'Oche, and the village of St. Gingough, at the foot of the mountains. The walks in the immediate neighbourhood are somewhat dull, as the whole country consists of vineyards, surrounded by stone walls.

In the *Ch. of St. Martin,* a little above the town, situated amidst trees and vineyards, and used only in summer (date 1438), Ludlow the regicide is buried, as well as Broughton, who read the sentence of death to Charles I., Love, and Cawley, all four republicans. They died here in exile, a price having been set upon their heads; and repeated applications were made to the canton of Berne to deliver them up, which the government very properly refused to accede to. *Ludlow's house* still exists on the road to La Tour de Peil; he placed over his doorway this inscription—" Omne solum forti patria." The tablet is removed to England. The castle was removed to make way for Monnet's hotel.

The *English Ch. Service* is performed on Sundays in St. Clair at 11 and 3.30.

Many excursions may be made from Vevay by land or water. Boats at 1 fr. the hour. *Chillon* is a morning drive (the route may be varied by taking the upper road).

The *Frères Weibel,* 53, Rue d'Italie, are recommended as voituriers.

The *wines* of the neighbourhood of Vevay, especially of the sunny district extending hence to Lausanne, and called Lavaux, enjoy a considerable reputation for Swiss wines. The Romans are believed to have first planted the vine on these hills; and the discovery of a stone inscribed " Libero Patri Colliensi" proves that they had erected a temple to Father Bacchus at Collium, a little village now called Cully, on the margin of the lake, between Vevay and Lausanne.

A society or guild of high antiquity, called *l'Abbaye des Vignerons,* exists at Vevay to promote the cultivation of the vine; and for this purpose it despatches every spring and autumn " experts," qualified persons, to survey all the vineyards of the district, and upon their report and testimony it rewards the most skilful and industrious vinedressers with medals and pruning-hooks (serpes d'honneur) as prizes.

In accordance with a custom handed down from very ancient times, which is possibly a relic of pagan superstition, this society celebrates once in 15 or 20 years a festival called *la Fête des Vignerons.* As many as 700 persons took part in the last festival, and one of the ballet-masters of the French opera was employed to drill and instruct the rustics in dancing. The last anniversaries were in 1819, 1833, and 1851, and multitudes of spectators flocked from all parts to witness them.

The road from Vevay to Freyburg by Bulle is described Rte. 42.

The beautiful Pass from Vevay over the Dent de Jaman, and the road thence to Thun, in Rte. 41.

A pleasant shady road on the slope of the hills, above the dusty highway, leads in 6½ m. to Montreux and Chillon.

About 2 miles off, on a swelling eminence overlooking the lake, stands the ancient *Castle of Blonay,* which has belonged to the same family for 700 years. Further on, above Clarens, is *Chatelard,* another castle.

About a mile out of Vevay the hamlet of La Tour de Peil, with a castle built at the water-side in the 13th century, is passed. 3 m. further lies *Clarens,* so sentimentally described by Rousseau in the Nouvelle Héloïse. It commands certainly one of the finest views over the lake—the mountains of the Rhone valley and of the opposite shore, but in itself is a poor village, far less attractive than many of its neighbours, and it probably owes its celebrity to a well-sounding name, which fitted it for the pages of a romance. Rousseau's admirers have puzzled themselves with endeavouring to identify the localities, though he has himself stated that they are "gros-sièrement altérés." The spot on which the beautiful "bosquet de Julie" is sought for is now a potato-field. Byron says that the trees were cut down by the monks of St. Bernard, and lavishes some unworthy and un-deserved abuse upon those hospitable ecclesiastics; but he has forgotten to ask whether the bosquet really ever had any existence except in Rous-seau's imagination. Byron, indeed, viewed the spot with a poet's eye, and the exquisite beauty of the sur-rounding scenery, which has been accurately described by Rousseau, called up all the poet's enthusiasm and inspiration.

" Clarens! sweet Clarens, birthplace of deep
      Love!
  Thine air is the young breath of passionate
      thought:
  Thy trees take root in Love; the snows above
  The very glaciers have his colours caught,
  And sunset into rose-hues sees them wrought
  By rays which sleep there lovingly: the rocks,
  The permanent crags, tell here of Love, who
      sought
  In them a refuge from the worldly shocks
Which stir and sting the soul with hope that
      woos, then mocks.

" Clarens! by heavenly feet thy paths are
      trod—
  Undying Love's, who here ascends a throne
  To which the steps are mountains; where the
      god
  Is a pervading life and light,—so shown
  Not on those summits solely, nor alone
  In the still cave and forest; o'er the flower
  His eye is sparkling, and his breath hath
      blown,
  His soft and summer-breath, whose tender
      power
Passes the strength of storms in their most
      desolate hour.

" All things are here of him; from the black
      pines,
  Which are his shade on high, and the loud
      roar
  Of torrents, where he listeneth, to the vines
  Which slope his green path downward to the
      shore,

  Where the bow'd waters meet him, and adore,
  Kissing his feet with murmurs; and the wood,
  The covert of old trees, with trunks all hoar,
  But light leaves, young as joy, stands where it
      stood,
Offering to him and his a populous solitude—

" A populous solitude of bees and birds,
  And fairy-form'd and many-colour'd things,
  Who worship him with notes more sweet than
      words,
  And innocently open their glad wings,
  Fearless and full of life: the gush of springs,
  And fall of lofty fountains, and the bend
  Of stirring branches, and the bud which
      brings
  The swiftest thought of beauty, here extend,
Mingling, and made by Love, unto one mighty
      end.

" 'T was not for fiction chose Rousseau this spot,
  Peopling it with affections; but he found
  It was the scene which passion must allot
  To the mind's purified beings; 't was the
      ground
  Where early Love his Psyche's zone unbound,
  And hallow'd it with loveliness: 't is lone,
  And wonderful, and deep, and hath a sound,
  And sense, and sight of sweetness; here the
      Rhone
Hath spread himself a couch, the Alps have
      rear'd a throne."

The swelling hills and vine-clad slopes, which form the banks of the lake nearly all the way from Geneva, here give place to beetling crags and woody precipices rising abruptly from the water's edge. The road sweeps in curves round the retired bays at their feet.

Montreux (*Inn:* Cygne, at Vernex— the only tolerable one in the neigh-bourhood.

This village, seated on an eminence (l.) above the road, with its church spire a little apart from its houses, is much prettier in itself and in its situa-tion than Clarens. It abounds in *Pen-sions* long established, and much fre-quented by foreigners.

" It is celebrated as the most shel-tered spot on the banks of the lake of Geneva, and the remarkable salu-brity of its climate renders it desirable winter-quarters for invalids who can-not cross the Alps. The statistical researches of Sir F. d'Ivernois have shown that Montreux is the place in the world where there is the smallest proportion of deaths and of imprudent marriages."—*R.*

At *Glyon,* at a considerable height,

directly above Montreux, in a bracing situation for invalids, several hotels and pensions have been established. Heimberger's strongly recommended. H. du Rigi.

About 1¾ m. from Montreux stands the picturesque and renowned *Castle of Chillon*, on an isolated rock nearly surrounded by deep water, but within a stone's throw of the shore and of the road, with which it communicates by a wooden bridge. It was built in 1238 by Amedeus IV. of Savoy, and was long used as a state prison, where, among other victims, many of the early reformers were immured. When Byron, in the Prisoner of Chillon, described the sufferings of an imaginary captive, he was not acquainted with the history of the *real* prisoner, Bonnivard, prior of St. Victor, who, having rendered himself obnoxious to the Duke of Savoy by his exertions to free the Genevese from the Savoyard yoke, was seized by the Duke's emissaries, and secretly carried off to this castle. For 6 long years he was buried in its deepest dungeon, on a level with the surface of the lake. The ring by which he was attached to one of the pillars still remains, and the stone floor at its base is worn by his constant pacing to and fro. Byron afterwards wrote the sonnet on Bonnivard, from which the following lines are taken:—

' Chillon ! thy prison is a holy place,
  And thy sad floor an altar ; for 't was trod
Until his very steps have left a trace
  Worn, as if the cold pavement were a sod,
By Bonnivard ! May none those marks efface !
  For they appeal from tyranny to God."

At length, in 1536, the Swiss wrested the Pays de Vaud from the hands of Charles V. of Savoy. Chillon was the last place which held out for him; but an army of 7000 Bernese besieging it by land, while the galleys of the Genevese assaulted it by water, soon compelled it to surrender, and Bonnivard, with other captives, was set free. The changes which had occurred during the years of his imprisonment almost realised the legend of the Seven Sleepers. He had left Geneva a Roman Catholic state, and

dependent on the Duke of Savoy; he found her free, and a republic, openly professing the reformed faith.

The castle is now converted into a magazine for military stores. The curious old *Chapel* is well worth seeing. Strangers are readily conducted over other parts of it, and (independently of the associations connected with the building) may find something to interest them in its "potence et cachots." The former is a beam, black with age, extended across one of the vaults, to which the condemned were formerly hung. The cachot is an *oubliette*, whose only entrance was by a trap-door in the floor above. There is a small spiral staircase of three steps; the prisoner found no fourth step, and was precipitated to a depth of 80 feet. The dungeon of Bonnivard is airy and spacious, consisting of two aisles, almost like the crypt of a church; its floor and one side are formed by the living rock, and it is lighted by several windows, through which the sun's light passes by reflection from the surface of the lake up to the roof, transmitting partly also the blue colour of the waters. Formerly it was subdivided into small cells by partition walls between the pillars. Byron inscribed his name on one of the pillars, and his example has been followed by many others, as Dickens, &c., but it is far more lastingly associated with the spot.

" Lake Leman lies by Chillon's walls ;
  A thousand feet in depth below
  Its massy waters meet and flow ;
Thus much the fathom-line was sent
From Chillon's snow-white battlement (? ?)
Which round about the wave enthrals ;
A double dungeon wall and wave
Have made—and like a living grave.
Below the surface of the lake
The dark vault lies wherein we lay ;
We heard it ripple night and day.
In Chillon's dungeons deep and old
There are seven columns massy and grey,
Dim with a dull, imprison'd ray,
A sunbeam which hath lost its way,
And through the crevice and the cleft
Of the thick wall is fallen and left,
Creeping o'er the floor so damp,
Like a marsh's meteor lamp."

It is by this castle that Rousseau has fixed the catastrophe of his Héloïse, in the rescue of one of her children by Julie from the water; the shock of which, and the illness produced by the immersion, is the cause of her death.

Between Chillon and Villeneuve, 10 minutes' walk from either, stands the *Hôtel Byron*, a comfortable *Pension*, on the lake, table-d'hôte liberal, and great cleanliness and civility; rooms lofty and airy : charge 7 fr. a day.

Villeneuve (*Inns:* Aigle Noir ; Croix Blanche; H. du Port, clean and low charges) is a small and ancient walled town of 1480 Inhab. (*Pennilucus* of the Romans), situated at the E. extremity of the lake, where the road quits its borders to enter the valley of the Rhone.

About a mile from Villeneuve lies a small island, one of three in the lake: it is thus mentioned by Byron in the 'Prisoner of Chillon:'—

" And then there was a little isle,
Which in my very face did smile,
    The only one in view ;
A small green isle, it seem'd no more,
Scarce broader than my dungeon-floor ;
But in it there were three tall trees,
And o'er it blew the mountain-breeze,
And by it there were waters flowing,
And on it there were young flowers growing,
    Of gentle breath and hue."

The commencement of the valley of the Rhone is dreary and uninteresting. The low ground is a flat alluvial deposit, formed by mud brought down by the river, and still remaining in the state of a barren and unwholesome morass. The encroachments of the land upon the lake, even within the period of historical record, have been very great. Port Valais, Portus Valesiæ of the Romans, in their time stood on the margin of the lake, but is now more than a mile and a half inland; the intervening tract has been gained since. The Rhone itself creeps slowly along, impeded by its own windings, and as it were burdened with mud, very unlike the torrent of azure and crystal which bursts out of the lake at Geneva. Upon this plain, at the mouth of the valley of the Rhone, Divico, the first Helvetian chief mentioned in history, defeated, B.C. 107 (the 646th year of Rome), the Roman forces under Lucius Cassius,

slaying their general and compelling his army to pass under the yoke.

The top of the mountain above *Yvorne* was thrown down by an earthquake, 1584. A wine of some reputation in Switzerland now grows on the slope.

It is worth while to go out at night and see the process of catching trout in the torrents, affluents of the Rhone, by means of a lanthorn and knife. The fisherman enters the water up to his middle, furnished with an oval lantern, water-tight, and having a long tube projecting from its top, which serves both as a handle and to convey air to the flame. This he plunges into the water ; and when the fish, attracted by the light, approach, he slowly raises it towards the surface, until the trout, who follow, come within reach, when he deals them a deadly blow with the knife, which sends them dead to the bottom, to reappear in a few minutes and be thrown into a basket which the man carries behind him. In this way a considerable number of fish are caught.

ROUTE 56A.

VILLENEUVE TO MARTIGNY.

	Post.	Miles.
Villeneuve.		
Bex		15
Martigny . . .	1 =	9
		24

The Rlwy. is now open to Bex (50 min.), and will be open to Martigny in Sept. 1858, whence it is to be continued up the Valais.

Villeneuve in Rte. 56.

Aigle—(*Inns:* H. du Midi ; H. de Ville) — a village of 1650 Inhab. (*Aquileia.*) Black marble is quarried near this. The Val des Ormonds opens behind Aigle. (See Rte. 41A.)

Bex (pronounced *Bey*) — *Inn:* l'Union, good: it comprises a boarding-house and an establishment of baths, supplied from a sulphureous spring rising in the vicinity, which causes Bex to be resorted to as a watering-place in summer. Board, 4½ frs. a day, for not less than a week. Guides, horses, and chars-à-banc for excursions among the mountains may be hired here.

Bex, a village of 3000 Inhab., situated on the high road to the Simplon, is chiefly remarkable for its *Salt Mines* and *Salt Works*. Salt has been obtained from brine-springs here since the middle of the 16th century. For a long time they belonged to a merchant family of Augsburg named Zobel, but they are now the property of the government of the canton. Down to 1823 the brine-springs alone furnished the salt, and they were gradually failing, when M. Charpentier suggested the plan of driving shafts and galleries into the mountain in search of rock-salt. The result was the discovery of a large and rich vein of the mineral, which has been traced for a distance of 4000 ft. and for a height of 600 ft., varying in thickness from 2 ft. to 50 ft.; and the annual produce of salt is now augmented to 20,000 or 30,000 quintals. Strangers arriving at Bex commonly pay a visit to the mines, which are situated about 2 m. off in the valley of La Gryonne. A carriage road leads through most beautiful scenery to the entrance of the mines. The salt is obtained either from the brine-springs, six or seven of which, of various degrees of strength, burst forth in different parts of the interior of the mountain, or from the rock-salt, which, after being extracted by the help of gunpowder, is broken into pieces, thrown into large reservoirs, called dessaloirs, cut in the anhydrite rock (sulphate of lime without water) in the interior of the mountain, and there dissolved in water. Each reservoir is usually filled with water 3 times. The 2 first solutions (lessivages) furnish a liquor with 25 or 26 per cent. of salt; the 3rd is much weaker, having only 5 or 6 per cent. The brine, either from the sources or from these reservoirs, containing above 20 per cent. of salt, is conveyed in pipes made of fir-wood at once to the boiling-house (maison de cuite); that which is less strong must be subjected to the process of graduation in the long buildings or sheds, open at the sides, which are passed at Bexvieux and Devins, between Bex and the mines. These evaporating-houses, or *maisons de graduation*, are filled up to the roof with stacks of fagots of thorn-wood, over which the salt water, after being raised to the roof by pumps, is allowed to trickle drop by drop. The separation of the water in passing through colanders, and its exposure to the atmosphere as it falls, produce rapid and considerable evaporation of the watery particles, while the gypsum dissolved in it adheres, in passing, to the twigs, and crystallizes around them. The water is thus made to ascend and descend several times; it becomes stronger each time, and at length is brought to the condition of saturated brine, fit for boiling in the salt-pans. It will easily be perceived how much fuel is thus spared by not subjecting the weak solution to the fire at first.

The principal mines are those called *Du Fondement* and *Du Bouillet;* the latter contains a gallery driven horizontally into the mountain for 6636 ft., 7½ ft. high and 5 ft. wide. At 400 ft. from its entrance is the round *reservoir*, 80 ft. in diameter and 10 ft. deep, excavated in the rock, without any support to its roof. In it the weak water is collected, which requires to undergo the process of graduation. A little farther on is another irregular reservoir, 7933 ft. in extent, supported by pillars, and destined to hold the stronger brine fit for the salt-pans without undergoing any intermediate process.

Many beautiful minerals are obtained from the salt-mines of Bex—such as very clear crystals of selenite, muriacite, anhydrite, &c.

It occupies ½ a day to visit the salt mines.

[There is a short but difficult path

(Rte. 58) from Bex to Sion by the Bergfall of Les Diablerets; a guide would be required for this journey, and a practised mountaineer would find an interesting excursion by ascending to the small glacier de *Martinet*, below the perpendicular crags of the *Dent de Morcles* (9513 ft.) In favourable weather a magnificent view of the Alps would be obtained.]

"Journeying upward by the Rhone,
That there came down a torrent from the Alps,
I enter'd where a key unlocks a kingdom:
The mountains closing, and the road, the river
Filling the narrow space."   *Rogers.*

Such is the scene presented to the traveller at the old *Bridge of St. Maurice*, which spans the rapid river with one bold arch 70 ft. wide, leaning for support on the rt. side upon the Dent de Morcles, and on the l. upon the Dent du Midi, whose bases are pushed so far forward as barely to leave room for the river.

The bridge, erroneously attributed to the Romans, is not older than the 15th century, but may possibly rest on Roman foundations. It unites the canton Vaud with the canton Valais; and a gate at one end, now removed, formerly served to close the passage up and down: a circumstance alluded to in the lines of Rogers. A small fort was erected by the Swiss in 1832, above the road, to defend the pass. Here the road is joined by the road from Geneva along the S. shore of the lake through St. Gingough. (Rte. 57.)

No one can cross the bridge of St. Maurice without being struck with the change in the condition of the inhabitants of the two cantons. The neatness and industry of the Vaudois are exchanged, within the space of a few hundred yards, for filth and beggary, equally apparent in the persons and habitations of the Valaisans. Their physical condition is lamentable; no part of Switzerland is afflicted to a greater extent with the maladies of goître and crétinism (§ 18), and the victims of them shock the traveller's sight at every step.

Immediately beyond the bridge, squeezed in between the mountain and the l. bank of the Rhone, stands

St. Maurice — (*Inn:* L'Union) — a town of 1050 Inhab., occupying the site of the Roman Agaunum. It owes its present name to the tradition that the Theban Legion, under the command of St. Maurice, suffered martyrdom here by order of Maximian, A.D. 302, because they refused to abjure Christianity.

The *Abbey*, the oldest Christian foundation among the Alps, established in the 4th century, founded in honour of *St. Maurice*, and endowed by Sigismond, King of Burgundy, was for many centuries one of the most celebrated of abbeys, and the town itself was the capital of one of the Burgundian kingdoms. In the *Treasury* are preserved an agate cameo cup of antique Greek art, and a bottle or ampaule of Saracenic workmanship, presented by Charlemagne; a crozier of gold, in the shape of a spire, the niches of it filled with figures an inch high, most elaborately worked; a chalice, given by Bertha Queen of Burgundy, and several besides, of a very early date. The *Church* was much damaged by fire in the 17th century, but the tower is unaltered, and several Roman inscriptions are built into its walls.

On quitting the town we perceive on the right bank of the Rhone the Bath-house of *Lavey*, erected 1831 over a warm sulphureous spring discovered in the river bed, at the expense of canton Vaud. The water is employed in supplying medicinal baths, the healing properties of which are attributed to the quantity of azote gas contained in the water. Upon a projecting platform of rock considerably above the road, rises the Hermitage of Notre Dame du Sax. Lower down on the road is the chapel of Veriolez, raised on the precise spot of the Theban massacre (!), and covered with rude frescoes.

In the autumn of 1835 a torrent of mud descended from the summit of the Dent de Midi into the Valais near Evionaz. It cut a passage for itself through the forest, which clothes the side of the mountain, snapping the stoutest trees short off like twigs. It covered the high road for a length of 900 ft., interrupting for some time the communication, and overwhelmed many fields and orchards, and some few houses; but no lives were lost, as the slow progress of the current allowed every one time to remove out of its way. On the 25th of August a violent storm of rain had burst upon the Dent de Midi, accompanied by thunder; and it is said that the lightning struck the peak several times. It is supposed that a mass of the mountain was loosened by the rain, and in falling broke through and carried down with it a considerable part of a glacier. The rain and melting ice mixing with the fragments and with the débris of moraines converted the whole mass into a thick mud, which swept slowly downwards like a lava current. Blocks of limestone of many tons weight, and some of them 12 ft. high, were carried along with it. It is a remarkable fact that the stream of mud contained scarcely one-tenth part of water; the fluidity of the mass was no doubt promoted by the character of the rocks and soil which covered the mountain, and which consisted of a black splintery limestone, shale, and loam. The wretched hamlet Evionaz occupies the site of an old town, Epaunum, destroyed by a similar mud-torrent in 563.

This part of the valley has a dreary and barren aspect, from the quantity of bare gravel and broken rock strewed over it, and the traces of the terrible flood of 1852 are still very visible. A steady but not very heavy rain began at 2 A.M. 16 Sept. 1852, and continued without intermission for 36 hrs. It seems to have been warm rain, which thawed the snow, for by 18 Sept. the rivers had swollen terribly; the bridge at Trient was carried away and deposited in a field below, and the valley from Martigny to Bex was laid under water, many of the fields being covered with débris, and ruined for years to come.

About 6½ m. from St. Maurice,

2 from Martigny, is the famous *Waterfall of the Sallenche,* which here descends into the valley of the Rhone out of a narrow ravine, apparently excavated by its waters. The perpendicular descent of the stream is about 280 feet, but the final leap of the cascade not more than 120 feet. It is a fine object, both from its volume and height, visible from a considerable distance up and down. It is best seen in a sunny morning before 12 o'clock, when the iris, formed in the cloud of spray, hovers over it. In the floods of 1852 it was a magnificent sight, the spray reaching nearly to the road, which was all under water. The neighbouring village of Mieville sends forth an importunate crowd of beggars and self-appointed guides to conduct travellers from the road to the fall, a distance of a few hundred yards.

Near Vernuyaz we cross another stream, the *Trient,* descending from the Pass of the Tête Noire (Rte. 116), and issuing out of a singular rent in the side of the valley. It is worth while to climb up the l. side of the ravine, and creeping to the edge, to look down into the chasm worn smooth and hollowed out by the force of the water.

On the banks of this river a desperate action was fought in 1841 between the ultra-Catholics of the Upper Valais aided by Lucerne, and the men of the Lower Valais, in which the latter were defeated with considerable slaughter, and their partisans were subsequently banished till 1848.

On the outskirts of Martigny, upon a commanding rock, rises the *castle of La Bâtie* (irreverently likened by Mr. A. Smith to " an insolent lighthouse ") formerly a stronghold of the archbishops of Sion; it was taken and burnt by George Supersax in 1518. The deep dungeon beneath its tall tower is only accessible by a trapdoor in the floor of the chamber above. The river Dranse passes out into the Rhone, between La Bâtie and *Martigny* (Rte. 59 A).

ROUTE 57.

GENEVA TO MARTIGNY, BY THONON AND
MEILLERIE, ALONG THE SOUTH SHORE
OF THE LAKE OF GENEVA.

Post-road 21 leagues = 62½ Eng. m.

	Leagues.	Eng. m.
Geneva.		
Douvaine . . .	3¾ =	11
Thonon	3 =	9
Evian	2 =	6
St. Gingough . .	4 =	12
Vionnas	2½ =	7½
St. Maurice . .	2½ =	8
Martigny . . .	3 =	9

A steamer plies along the S. shore
of Chablais from Geneva, touching at
Evian, Thonon, Meillerie, St. Gingough, and Boveret. The road itself
is the original Simplon road, but is
now almost deserted, though from
Evian to Boveret the scenery is very
grand, finer than that of the N. shore.
After quitting Geneva by the
Quartier de Rive, a fine view opens
out rt.; beyond the Salève rises
the Môle, and the valley of the
Arve is terminated by the Buet, by
Mont Blanc and its glaciers. The
shore of the lake is dotted over with
villas of the Genevese. One of these,
near the village of Cologny, the *Campagna Diodati*, is interesting as having
been the residence of Lord Byron in
1816. He wrote here the 3rd canto
of Childe Harold and the tragedy of
Manfred.

Beyond the village of Corsier the
Genevan territory is left, and we enter
the kingdom of Sardinia and the ancient province of Chablais, which extends along the lake as far as St. Gingough. A monotonous plain is traversed in order to reach

Douvaine, the first Sardinian post-

station, where passports and baggage
are examined.

Thonon — (*Inns :* H. de l'Europe,
fair, adjoining the Terrace; Les Balances)—an ancient town of 3740 Inhab., originally capital of the Chablais.

On quitting Thonon we pass on the
left, between the road and the lake,
Ripaille, anciently an Augustine convent, founded by Amedeus VIII. of
Savoy, in which he passed the latter
portion of his life, having assumed the
cowl of an Augustine monk. He ab-
dicated, in turn, the dukedom of Savoy, the Papacy (into which he had
been installed with the title of Felix
V.), and the bishop's see of Geneva.
He resided here after his second abdication, passing his time not in the
austere penance of an anchorite, but,
according to the popular belief, in ease,
feasting, and dissipation. Hence the
French proverb — "Faire Ripaille."
Recent historical investigations, however, make it probable that, even to
the last, he had not abandoned the
path of ambition, and that far from
being inactive and exclusively devoted
to luxury, he was still weaving political intrigues. The castle, with 7
towers, built by Amedeus for himself
and the six knights whom he chose as
companions, has nearly disappeared.
The relic of the convent is converted
into a farm-house.

A long bridge of 24 arches carries
the road over the Dranse, a torrent
descending from the mountains of the
Chablais, and augmented to a large
volume by the melting snows during a
small part of the year.

[There is a char-road for a short
distance up the valley of the Dranse
to some gypsum-works, after which
the road passes through numerous
villages to La Vernaz and by the
ruins of the Abbey of *Aulph*, and
then branches on the l. to the Val
d'Illier, on the rt. over the Col de
Jourplan (6270 ft., no view) through
the Val Valentine to Samoens (Rte.
115 A), about 12 hrs.' walk.]

Through groves of magnificent
chestnut-trees we pass *Amphion*, a
gay watering-place frequented by the
Genevese, where are baths supplied

by a chalybeate (? sulphur) spring, and reach

Evian (*Inn:* H. du Nord; Poste), a town of 1670-Inhab., at the water-side; also provided with a bathing establishment.

The *Rocks of Meillerie*, celebrated by Rousseau and Byron, were, under the orders of Napoleon, and with the help of gunpowder, blasted to form a passage for the magnificent road of the Simplon, which is here carried partly through them, partly on a ter-race 30 or 40 feet above the lake. Previous to its construction, the little village of Meillerie was barely ac-cessible, except by boats. About a mile off the shore, at Meillerie, the lake attains its greatest depth, 920 Fr. ft. Here Byron was nearly lost in a storm. Rousseau, in the N. Héloïse, has conducted St. Preux and Mad. Wolmar also to this port for shel-ter from a tempest. On the opposite shore is seen Clarens, and the white wall of the castle of Chillon (Rte. 56).

St. Gingough—(*Inn:* Poste, an enor-mous building, once a convent, good. Mosquitoes very troublesome all along the S. shore of the Lake. A deep ravine here divides Savoy from the Swiss territory of the Valais; tra-vellers entering from the Valais are subjected to custom-house regulations here.

Boveret—(*Inn:* La Tour)—the next village, lies within the valley of the Rhone, here a broad, flat, dreary swamp (p. 164). Port Valais, in the days of the Romans, stood on the waterside; all the ground between it and the lake has been pro-duced since the records of history, by the deposits of the river. At Porte du Siex the rocks on the rt. encroach so far upon the Rhone as barely to leave a passage for the road at their base. Advantage was taken of this pass in ancient times to construct a fort with loopholes for arrows, and embrasures for cannon, which effectu-ally closed the entrance to the Valais, the only passage being over its draw-bridge and through its gate. At Porte du Siex is a bridge over the Rhone. A road leads from it to Vil-

leneuve on the opposite side of the lake by Chessel and Noville across the plain, strewed with hillocks and débris of limestone, the remains of a landslip from the Grammont, 7000 ft. high, on the l. bank of the Rhone, A.D. 563. A huge fragment from the summit of the mountain fell down the ravine of Evouettes, all across the valley as far as Roche and Rennaz, burying a Roman station, so as to dam up the Rhone and form a tem-porary lake, reaching up to the rocks of St. Tryphons, which at last burst its barrier near Porte du Siex.

The canal of Stockalper, running nearly parallel with the road, was cut about a century ago, to drain this portion of the valley. At Vouvry is a good country *Inn.*

Vionnaz. Above this village are some most remarkable boulders.

Monthey. [Behind this village is the Val d'Illier extending towards the Dent du Midi, and accessible to mules. The scenery of this valley is highly praised by those who have visited it, and an hotel has lately been built at *Champery* in the upper part.]

Evionaz. Owing to an abrupt bend in the valley, and a projecting rock which hides the upper portion from view, the road comes suddenly upon the town of

St. Maurice (Rte. 56).

Martigny (Rte. 59A).

ROUTE 58.

BEX TO SION, BY LES DIABLERETS AND COL DE CHÉVILLE.

11 hrs., a walk of 9½ to 10 hrs, ex-cluding stoppages.

Bex is described in Rte. 56A. This is a highly interesting pass, both from the geological phenomenon of its Berg-

I

fall, or mountain slip, and for the extreme picturesqueness of its scenery; but for some unknown reason the whole region of the Diablerets, though yielding to few in ruggedness and in commanding views over the Alps, has been unvisited and neglected : The part which runs high above the Liserne would not be very secure to ride, but is perfectly safe for foot passengers.   At *Grion* there is a tolerable and very cheap inn, and in the season one or two boarding-houses.   As the pass is long, it is advisable to sleep at Grion, 2½ hrs. from Bex.   (There is, however, a much shorter path to Anzeinde, passing through Frenières.)   After Grion there is no inn (worthy the name) by the way.   The path ascends the valley of the Avençon, running in a direction nearly due E. from Bex, passing Bexvieux to the châlets of Charnemey (2 hrs.), and the châlets of La Lex (2 hrs.), through some of the most pleasing pastoral scenery in Switzerland.   Here the path begins rapidly to ascend in a tortuous course to the châlets of *Anzeinde* (1 hr.), and thence (3¼ hrs.) to the summit of the *Col de Chéville*.   [An exceedingly steep and rugged path leads from this place over the Col de Chéville to the Sanetsch and Gsteig.]   The path then leads to the rt., and winds down a steep rock near a small waterfall to the bottom of the valley, where the stream is crossed.   The valley into which it descends on the E. side of the pass is nearly filled by the wreck of the fall of the *Mont Diablerets*, a name given to the spot by the peasantry, it is said, because they regard it as the vestibule of hell.   This mountain is composed of limestone strata, much deranged and steeply inclined.   The lower beds, being soft and shaly, are disintegrated by the infiltration of water from the vast glaciers on the N.E. ; and, after the supports and foundation are thus removed, large masses are detached from the mountain into the valley below, forming éboulemens of the most tremendous kind.   During the last century two catastrophes of this kind

occurred, in 1714 and 1749.   By the former, 15 human beings, 100 head of cattle, and 55 châlets were buried alive.   Subterranean noises, produced by the commotion in the mountain, gave warning for several days beforehand, so that most of the peasants and their cattle removed out of the way.   Among those who did not profit by this was a man belonging to the village of Avers in the Valais.   His friends gave him up for lost, his wife was looked upon as a widow, and his children as orphans.   Three months afterwards, on Christmas-eve, he suddenly made his appearance in the village, pale, haggard, with scarcely a rag to cover him, having all the appearance of a spectre.   The door of his own house was shut in his face, and the people in the village repaired in the greatest terror to the minister, begging him to lay the ghost.   It was with great difficulty that he at length convinced them that it was himself.   He had been overwhelmed in a châlet on the mountains, but escaped being crushed to death by two masses of rock forming an angle over it.   He had managed to support life upon a store of cheese laid up for the winter, and with water from a brook which found its way through the fallen rocks.   After many weeks passed in the dark, and many vain efforts to extricate himself, he at length, by creeping and scratching among the rocks, formed a passage through which a gleam of daylight appeared, and through it succeeded at length in working his way out.   At the moment of the fall, the surrounding district shook as with an earthquake, a thick cloud of dust rose high into the air from the friction of it, masses of rock were hurled a distance of 6 miles, and the current of air produced by it threw down trees which were not touched by the avalanche itself.   The inhabitants of one of the neighbouring villages derive this singular advantage from the fall of the peak of the mountain, that they enjoy summer at a certain season of the year several minutes earlier than they did before the event occurred. The fall of 1749 arrested the course of the Liserne, forming two small lakes, called Derborenze, which still exist.

After crossing the stream the path gently rises to a wooden cross, and soon after reaches a small lake and some châlets. The path then crosses on the W. side of the lake, for the space of two leagues, heaps of rubbish and fallen rocks. The scene is one of the utmost desolation; overhead towers the ridge of the Diablerets, 10,670 ft. above the sea-level. Three of its five peaks have already fallen, and the two which remain threaten, sooner or later, to follow. The mountain is again rent with fissures, and scarcely an hour passes in which a slight noise is not heard or a fragment of stone does not fall. The accumulated débris of the mountain is said to cover a space of 8 miles. At one point, on reaching the borders of the Liserne, a narrow and dangerous path has been formed across the talus, at the edge of a precipice overhanging the stream: it is called *Le Saut du Chien.* The beech woods in the valley of the Liserne through which the path runs for some distance are unusually fine, and the whole valley most picturesque, and peculiar in character, owing in part to the enormous depth at which the stream runs below, and the extreme steepness of the mountains on either side. No road, as far as I can recollect, except the Gemmi, skirts such precipices.

Thenceforth the path follows the l. bank of the Liserne as far as the chapel of St. Bernard, where it bears away to the E., descending upon St. Severin and Haut Couthey, and thence enters the valley of the Rhone and the high road of the Simplon, within 2½ miles of

Sion (Rte. 59 A).

Time, walking leisurely from Sion
to the châlet of Chéville ... 6h. 0m.
Châlet to top of the pass ... 0 48
Top—to Bex 4 30
———
Total 11 18

ROUTE 59A.

PASSAGE OF THE SIMPLON. MARTIGNY
TO BRIEG.

Post-road: to Brieg 5⅔ posts = 52 m., 10 hrs; to Domo d'Ossola 10¾ posts = 96 miles.

	Posts.		Eng. m.
Martigny.			
Riddes	1	=	9
Sion	1	=	9
Sierre	1½	=	10
Turtman . . .	1	=	9
Visp	1	=	9
Brieg	⅔	=	5¼

The grand and celebrated Simplon road was almost destroyed by two successive storms in 1834 and 1839, but the damage has been repaired for the most part. With post-horses the journey may barely be accomplished in 3, or easily in 3½ days, resting 1st night at Brieg, 2nd at Domo, 3rd at Milan.

Diligences daily to Milan from Lausanne, making numerous halts, and performing the distance in 50 hours. It should be recollected that when the days begin to grow short, the diligence passes through the best part of the Simplon after dark.

Railway from Martigny in progress.

Martigny (German Martinach).— *Inns:* Cygne ; La Tour—both tolerable. Grande Maison et Poste (Morands), comfortable and reasonable. Hotel Clerc, the newest.

Martigny (Octodurus of the Romans) consists of two parts—the one situated on the Simplon road, the other, Bourg de Martigny, more than a mile distant up the valley of the Dranse. Its position on the high road of the Simplon, at the termination of the char-road from the St. Bernard, and the mule-path from Chamouni, renders it the constant resort of travellers. The scenery around is grand : a flat, open valley bordered by mountains of great boldness. The ruins of the *Castle of La Bâtie* (see p. 167) are a pleasing feature in all the views. It is a small town of no prepossessing appearance, 1520 ft. above the sea, placed near the spot where the Rhone receives the Dranse, a torrent by which Martigny itself and the village of Bourg de Martigny have been twice nearly destroyed, in 1545 and in 1818. Marks of the last inundation (Rte. 109) are still visible on the walls of many of the houses ; and the massive construction of the lower walls of the post-house is designed to protect it from the effects of similar catastrophes. The bridge is one of the finest specimens of the Swiss covered wooden bridges, with the arch above the roadway. The monks of St. Bernard have their head-quarters in a *convent* within the town, from which the members stationed on the Great St. Bernard are relieved at intervals. The monastery of the Great St. Bernard is a journey of 10 hours from hence. (Rte. 108.)

The valley of Chamouni may be reached in 7 or 8 hours by the Tête Noire (Rte. 116), or Col de Balme (Rte. 117). The Forclaz and the beautiful view from it is an easy walk. From Martigny to Visp (Zermatt) is 9 hrs.' posting.

The *waterfall of the Sallenche* is 4 miles from Martigny, lower down the valley. (See p. 167.)

At Martigny the Rhone makes an abrupt bend, forming nearly a right angle. For many miles above the town, the bottom of the valley through which it flows is a flat swamp, rendered desolate and unwholesome by the overflowings of the Rhone and its tributaries, which, not being carried off by a sufficient declivity in their beds, stagnate, and exhale an injurious malaria under the rays of a burning sun, and generate gnats not much inferior to mosquitoes. Tra-

vellers do not suffer from the malaria, but the inhabitants of the valley are dreadfully afflicted with goître (§ 18), crétinism, and ague; and the appearance of decrepitude, deformity, and misery arrests the traveller's attention at every step. A tolerable wine, called Coquempin, is grown upon the hills; the low flats produce little except rushes, rank grass, and alders. The mountains which here bound the valley have a bare and desolate aspect.

Riddes. After crossing the Rhone the road passes the footpath leading to the Diablerets (Rte. 58), and soon after the twin castles of Sion appear in sight.

Sion (Germ. *Sitten*).—*Inns :* Lion d'Or; Poste, very good, 1855. There is a comfortable *pension* 2 minutes' walk from Sion, kept by Madame Muston, late landlady of the Lion d'Or. Sion has no less than three extensive castles, which give the town a picturesque and feudal aspect from a distance. *Tourbillon*, the castle seen on the l. in advancing from Martigny, built 1492, and long the bishop's residence, is now a complete ruin. The hill immediately above the town is crowned by the *Old Cathedral*, which includes a votive chapel to St. Catherine and some old frescoes. The present cathedral is in the town below, and close to it is the modern Bishop's Palace. The castle on the l. or S. peak, called *Valeria*, contains a very ancient church, and serves now as a Catholic seminary. Beneath there is a third castle, called *Majoria*, from the majors, or ancient governors of the Valais, its first occupants; it was burnt in 1788 by a conflagration which destroyed the greater part of the town. In the *Jesuits' convent* is a collection of the natural history of the Valais.

The *Hospital*, under the care of the Sœurs de la Charité, contains many victims of goître and crétinism, the prevailing maladies of the district.

Sion contains 2590 Inhab. and is the capital of the Valais (Germ. *Wallis*)—one of the most miserable and melancholy districts in northern Europe. It was formerly a flourishing country, as the ruins of the numerous castles and the remains of former splendour at Sion and Visp attest; and in the commencement of the 16th century the celebrated Matthew Schinner, Bishop of Sion, was a powerful prince, whose alliance was courted by all the sovereigns of Europe—principally, it is true, for the sake of procuring the services of the Swiss mercenaries. At present, with the exception of the hotels, nothing appears prosperous in the Valais itself or in the numerous lateral valleys, and the race of man seems to have deteriorated. This has been attributed sometimes to the long-continued residence in the deep valley, sometimes to poverty caused by the influence of the powerful Roman Catholic priesthood: the cause is doubtful, the fact indisputable. It is said that Sion has been besieged and taken more than 30 times, and, like many Swiss towns, it has been burnt nearly down. There has been fighting very lately in the canton, and at present the democratic party prevail.

Omnibus daily to Leuk Baths (Rte. 38).

There is a mule-path from this over the mountains to Bex, passing the Diablerets (Rte. 58).

S. of Sion the Val d'Erin stretches far into the main-chain of the Alps (Rtes. 106 B, 106 D).

Sierre (Germ. Siders).—*Inn:* Soleil (Post): good.

A steep but romantic path leads to the Gemmi by the Baths of Loèche, turning out of the post-road a little way beyond the town, before reaching the bridge. (Rte. 38)

Opposite Sierre another valley stretches S. into the main-chain of Alps, the Val d'Anniviers or Einfisch Thal. Its entrance from the Valais is so small that its very existence is said to have remained unknown until the 12th century, when the Bishop of Sion discovered it, and converted its inhabitants from heathenism! (Rte. 106 D.)

The post-road, after crossing the Rhone, and winding for some distance among irregular hillocks, passes, on the rt. bank of the river, at the mouth of the gorge of the Dala, the picturesque village of Leuk (Rte. 38).

Pfynn (ad fines) is on the boundary between the German language, which prevails above this, as far as the source of the Rhone, and the French, which is spoken below 'this. The l'finger Wald, behind Sierre, is a strong military position, stoutly defended against the French in 1798.

Süsten, where there is a small but comfortable inn.

Tourtemagne (Germ. Turtman.)— *Inns:* Soleil, fair ; Poste, better. The Turris Magna, from which the place is named, is now used as a chapel. 15 minutes' walk behind the inn is a *Cascade* of some repute. The volume of water is considerable, and its height by actual measurement is 150 ft. Though on the whole inferior to the fall of the Sallenche near Martigny, it is still worthy of a visit by those who are amateurs of waterfalls: the scene is interesting on account of its entire seclusion. The neighbourhood is overspread with marshes and stagnant pools. A wild gorge behind the town leads up to the Turtman Thal (Rte. 106 D).

Visp or *Vispach* (*Viége*)—(*Inns:* Soleil and Weisses Pferd, both tolerable) —once the seat of numerous noble families, some of whose houses still remain. They had a church of their own which was presented to the inhabitants by the family of Blindra, the last of the noble families—is a miserable village, but finely situated at the junction of the Visp with the Rhone. Its misery was increased by the repeated shocks of an earthquake, which began on July 25, 1855, with a very severe shock and lasted with diminished force for several months, leaving only 7 houses in Visp habitable, and forcing the inhabitants to encamp. The roof of one of the 2 huge churches was thrown down, and one half of the Soleil Inn was destroyed. Visp was the centre of the earthquake, which was felt over an area of 300 miles N. and S., 250 E. and W. The Visp-Thal leads to Saas and Zermatt (Rte. 106).

The Gamsen and other torrents

which fall into the upper end of the Valais are very dangerous neighbours to the villages and cottages on their banks. The bed of the river Visp is nearly 13 ft. above a part of the village, and the Saltine is nearly 11 ft. higher than Brieg. The miserable and poverty-stricken inhabitants are in consequence obliged to construct very considerable dykes to restrain them, but even these defences are liable to destruction every 2 or 3 years.

The desolation which the torrents spread over the fields, by their débris, will attract the remark of every traveller; and the evil is constantly increasing, as the beds of the torrents rise as fast as the dykes are raised to restrain them, till they flow along the top of a colossal aqueduct or wall of loose rocks, which the road ascends and descends like a hill.

The ascent of the Simplon originally began at Glys, a village distinguished by its large church and *charnel - house* filled with skulls!—10,000 at a rough computation. Now, however, a détour of about 1 m. is made to pass through

Brieg — Inns : Poste ; clean and comfortable ; civil landlord; good cuisine;—H. d'Angleterre. Brieg is the usual halting-place of travellers before or after crossing the Simplon. It is a small town of 751 Inhab., situated on a sunny slope by the side of the Saltine, and overlooking the course of the Rhone, which here makes a sharp bend. The most conspicuous buildings are, the château of the family Stockalper, whose 4 turrets are crowned with tin cupolas, and the *Jesuits' College.* There is also an *Ursuline Convent.*

[The upper valley of the Rhone above Brieg, and the route to the Grimsel and Gries, are described in Rtes. 28 and 29. An interesting excursion up it may be made as far as Viesch, where the scenery is very beautiful.]

ROUTE 59B.

BRIEG TO DOMO D'OSSOLA — SIMPLON PASS.

	Posts.	Eng. m.
Brieg.		
Beresal	1	9
Simplon . . .	1¾	15½
Isella	1	9
Domo d'Ossola. .	1¼	11¼

Brieg to Domo 4½ posts=45 miles, 12 hrs. posting or diligence. Voiturier 60 or 70 fr.

On foot the distance may be shortened, but it will require full 12 hrs.' steady walking. N.B. In September the diligence does not reach the finest part of the pass till dark.

The construction of a route over the Simplon was decided upon by Napoleon immediately after the battle of Marengo, while the recollection of his own difficult passage of the Alps by the Great St. Bernard (at that time one of the easiest Alpine passes) was fresh in his memory. The plans and surveys by which the direction of the road was determined were made by M. Céard, and a large portion of the works was executed under the superintendence of that able engineer. It was commenced on the Italian side in 1800, and on the Swiss in 1801. It took 6 years to complete, though it was barely passable in 1805, and more than 30,000 men were employed on it at one time. To give a notion of the colossal nature of the undertaking, it may be mentioned that the number of bridges, great and small, constructed for the passage of the road between Brieg and Sesto, amounts to 611, in addition to the far more vast and costly constructions, such as terraces of massive masonry miles in length; of 10 galleries, either cut out of the living rock or built of solid stone; and of 20 houses of refuge to shelter travellers, and lodge the labourers constantly employed in taking care of the road. Its breadth is throughout at least 25 ft., in some places 30 ft., and the slope nowhere exceeds 1 in 13.

To use the eloquent words of Sir James Mackintosh, "the Simplon may be safely said to be the most wonderful of useful works, because our canals and docks surpass it in utility, science, and magnitude, but they have no grandeur to the eye. Its peculiar character is, to be the greatest of all those monuments that at once dazzle the imagination by their splendour, and are subservient to general convenience." It may be observed in addition that (except the Cenis) the Simplon was the first of the great carriage-roads opened across the W. Alps; and though others, since constructed, surpass it in some respects, especially in the elevation attained (*e. g.* the Stelvio), yet this has the merit of originality, and the others are in some respects mere copies.

The cost of this road averaged about 5000*l.* a mile. In England the average cost of turnpike-roads is 1000*l.* per mile. The object of Napoleon in its formation is well marked by the question which, on two different occasions, he first asked of the engineer sent to him to report progress—"Le canon quand pourra-t-il passer au Simplon?"

The ascent of the Simplon begins at once from *Brieg.* About ½ a mile above the town the road leaves, on the rt., the lofty covered bridge over the Saltine, now little used, since most vehicles make the détour by Brieg instead of going direct to or from Glys, whither this bridge conducts. The road then makes a wide sweep, turning away from the Glyzhorn, the mountain which bounds the valley on the rt., towards the Breithorn, on the opposite side, approaching a little hill dotted with white chapels and crowned by a calvary. It then again approaches the gorge of the Saltine, skirting the verge of a precipice, at the bottom of which the torrent is seen at a vast depth, forcing its way among black and bristling slate rocks, which seem still shattered by the convulsion which first gave a passage to its waters. At the upper end of the ravine, high above his head, the traveller may discern the glaciers under which the road is carried, but which he will require at least 3 good hours to reach, on account of the sinuosities of the route. Looking back, he will perceive the valley of the Rhone, as far as Turtman, spread out as a map at his feet; Brieg and Naters remain long in sight. It is a constant pull against the collar from Brieg to the second refuge. Here the road, carried for some distance nearly on a level, is compelled to bend round the valley of the *Ganther* until it can cross the torrent which traverses it by another lofty bridge, called *Pont du Ganther.* The upper end of this wild ravine is subject to avalanches almost every winter, the snow of which nearly fills it up, and reaches sometimes to the crown of the arch. This bridge is left uncovered, from the fear justly entertained by the engineers that the terrific gusts or currents of air which accompany the fall of an avalanche might blow the arch entirely away, were much resistance of flat timber-work presented to it. The road originally traversed a gallery cut in the rock near this, but it has been removed. After crossing the bridge the road turns down the opposite side, and then ascends by a zigzag to the third refuge, called

Béresal, or *Persal,* an Inn, consisting of 2 buildings connected by a roof across the road, where 16 post-horses are kept, affording tolerable fare and beds. It may be reached in 2½ hours from Brieg.

The first gallery which the road traverses is that of Schalbet, 95 ft. long—3920 ft. above Glys. Near this and hence to the summit, should the sky be clear, the traveller's attention will be riveted by the glorious view of *the Bernese Alps,* which bound the Valais and form the rt.-hand wall of the valley of the Rhone. The glittering white peaks of the Breithorn, Aletsch-hörner, and Viescher-hörner, are magnificent objects in this scene, while below them two strips are visible of the glaciers of Aletsch, one of the most extensive in the Alps.

Fifth Refuge, called *Schalbet.*—

the Valais, consists of a few miserable huts, grouped round a singular, tall building, 7 stories high, erected, like the tower at Simplon, by the old Brieg family Stockalper, in ancient days, for the refuge of travellers.

An hour's walk by the side of the torrent, which falls in a cascade down the rt.-hand wall of the valley, leads to the gold-mine of Zürichbergen, which, though it barely produces a few particles of the precious metal, is still worked in the hope of gain. In the winter of 1842-3 the snow was drifted to such a depth in the gorge below Gondo, that the sledges on which carriages were placed passed about 100 ft. above the road. The traveller enters Italy a short while before reaching the Sardinian village of

Isella (*Inn* good and clean, though small, better than at Simplon), where the custom-house and passport office are situated.

The tempests of 1834 and 1839 fell with tremendous violence upon this part of the road, which they destroyed for a space of nearly 8 m. Every bridge of stone was swept away ; in some instances, even the materials of which the bridge was built disappeared, and the very place where it stood was not to be recognised, and it was many years before the road was repaired. The Gallery of Isella, a narrow arch of rock a little below the village, was flooded by the torrent pouring through it, so high were the waters swollen. At the mouth of the Val Dovedro, a handsome new bridge, which supplied the place of the one demolished by the torrent over which it passes, was itself carried off, together with a temporary wooden one, in 1850.

Hereabouts a change comes over the valley, from nakedness to the rich green foliage of the chestnut, which shades the road, and to that of the dark fir which clothes the summits of the hitherto bare mountains above. The last gallery is traversed a little before reaching Crevola, where the Doveria is crossed for the last time by a fine lofty bridge of 2 arches, nearly 90 ft. high, previous to its

flowing into the river Toccia, or Tosa, which here issues out of the Val Formazza, and the Val Vedro terminates in the Val d'Ossola. The mule-path from the Gries and Grimsel, passing the falls of the Tosa (Rte. 29), falls into the Simplon route at Crevola.

It is now that the traveller really finds himself in a different region and in an altered climate : the softer hues of earth and sky, the balmy air, the trellised vines, the rich juicy stalks of the maize, the almost deafening chirp of the grasshoppers or tree-crickets, and, at night, the equally loud croakings of the frogs—the white villages, with their tall, square bell-towers, also white, not only scattered thickly along the valley, but perched on every little jutting platform on the hill-sides—all these proclaim the entrance to *Italy.* Eustace has remarked that "the valley which now opens out to view is one of the most delightful that Alpine solitudes enclose, or the foot of the wanderer ever traversed ;" a remark which, though true, will bear much modification in the opinion of those who quit Italy by this route instead of entering it. It is only by those who approach it from the north that its charms can be fully appreciated.

Domo d'Ossola (*Inns:* H. Albasini, new and highly recommended ; H. d'Espagne; H. de Ville or Ancienne Poste), a small and unimportant town, with few points of interest, save that it is Italian—in every stone. Houses with colonnades, streets with awnings, shops teeming with sausages, macaroni, and garlic, lazy-looking, loitering lazzaroni in red nightcaps, and bare, mahogany-coloured legs, intermixed with mules, burly priests, and females veiled with the mantilla, fill up the picture of an Italian town.

There is a very curious *Calvary* above the town well worth a visit by those who do not intend to see Varallo.

Omnibus daily to Pallanza.

The ascent from this to the head of the Simplon occupies 7 hrs.

Several very interesting *Excursions* may be made from this : *a.* up the lovely *Val Anzasca* (Rte. 105), by Pié di Mulera, to Ponte Grande, in the centre of it, is a drive of 5 hrs. from Domo.

b. The *Val Vigezzo*, scarcely known to travellers, abounds in beauties; Sta. Maria Maggiore, the chief place in the valley, is 3 hrs.' drive. (*Inn:* Lion d'Or.) Many elegant villas belong to retired jewellers, natives of the valley, who have made fortunes in the capitals of Europe. The ch. of Craveggia may vie in splendour with those of Genoa. The sides of the mountains are beautifully wooded.

c. The *Falls of the Tosa,* in the Val Formazza, are accessible partly by a char-road as far as Premia, 3⅓ leagues, and the rest of the way by a mule-path. The best quarters are at the Baths of Crodo. (Rte. 29.)

ROUTE 59c.

DOMO D'OSSOLA TO MILAN.   LAGO MAGGIORE.

	Miles.
Domo.	
Vogogna	10
Pallanza or Baveno . . .	15 or 14
Milan	40

From Domo to Baveno takes up 5 hrs. posting, exclusive of stoppages. Travellers can join the steamers, which go up and down the lake 4 times a-day, either at Pallanza or Baveno. Hitherto travellers have generally taken the steamer at Baveno, but now that the new road is completed Pallanza seems much more convenient. The *Inn* is no worse, and every steamer touches there, whilst passengers are obliged to go off from Baveno in boats, and the Borromean islands are not much further off.

The road descends the valley of the Tosa, the bridges over which, below Domo d'Ossola, and again 6 m. below Vogogna (at Magiandone), were carried off by the storms of 1834 and 1849. Till lately rude ferry-boats still supplied their places. In 1856, however, one of the bridges was rebuilt, and the other is now in progress, and the whole of the road is now in very good order on the Sardinian side. After leaving Domo the valley widens and loses its beauty.

Vogogna.—(*Inn:* Alb. della Corona.) The Tosa, in spite of its rapidity, is navigable a short distance above this place; the barges are towed up by double teams of 6 or 8 horses on each bank.

Near Ornavasca are the white marble quarries which have supplied the stone for Milan Cathedral.

At *Gravellona* a large bridge crosses the Strona, a stream which drains the Lago d'Orta, and a carriage-road, running up its l. bank, leads, in 2 hrs., to the lake of Orta. (See Rtes. 101, 102.)

Here another road leads to *Pallanza* (R. 92), whilst the main road continues to

Fariolo (*Inn,* Lion d'Or, attentive landlord. Steamers come here once a day only). Here the Lago Maggiore bursts into view, with the Isola Madre, the northernmost of the Borromean Islands, in the distance. A little further are quarries of a beautiful rose granite, which derives its colour from the prevalence of felspar in it. That mineral is obtained here in beautiful flesh-coloured detached crystals. Steamers call off here and Baveno at 9½ A.M. descending, and at 1¼ P.M. on ascending the lake.

Baveno.—*Inn:* La Posta, lovely situation, but dear and uncivil. A large new inn was opened in 1858. There is a tolerable inn at Stresa, Albergo Reale.

The principal object in going to Baveno is to visit the *Borromean Islands* (which, however, may be as well visited from Pallanza).

By starting tolerably early the islands may be visited from Baveno, or Pallanza, and Milan reached on the same day. The steamers touch at the Isola

Bella. It takes 25 minutes to row from Baveno to the Isola Bella (boat there and back 5 fr., or 2 fr. an hr.), passing, on the way, the Isola dei Pescatori, so called because its inhabitants are chiefly fishermen, whose rude semi-plastered houses contrast with the stately structures on the neighbouring island. The *Isola Bella (Inn :* Delfino, tolerable ; fully as good as the old inn at Baveno, and much more convenient for persons arriving by the steamers ; passengers are conveyed free of charge to and from the steamers) belongs to the Count Borromeo, who resides a part of the year in the vast palace. An ancestor of the family, in 1671, converted this mass of bare and barren slate-rock, which lifted itself a few feet above the surface of the lake, into a beautiful garden, teeming with the vegetation of the tropics. It consists of 10 terraces, the lowest founded on piers thrown into the lake, rising in a pyramidal form one above another, and lined with statues, vases, obelisks, and black cypresses. Upon these, as upon the hanging gardens of Babylon, flourish in the open air, not merely the orange, citron, myrtle, and pomegranate, but aloes, cactuses, the camphor-tree (of which there is a specimen 40 ft. high)—all inhabitants of tropical countries—and this within a day's journey of the Lapland climate of the Simplon, and within view of Alpine snows.

The proverbial disagreement of doctors is nothing in comparison with the discord of travellers on the merits of this island. To *Simond* the sight of the island at a distance suggests the idea of " a huge Perigord pie, stuck round with the heads of woodcocks and partridges;" *Matthews* extols it as " the magic creation of labour and taste . . . a fairy-land, which might serve as a model for the gardens of Calypso;" *Saussure* calls it " un magnifique caprice, une pensée grandiose, une espèce de création;" while *Brockedon* sternly pronounces it as " worthy only of a rich man's misplaced extravagance, and of the taste of a confectioner." To taste it may have

little pretension; but, for a traveller fresh from the rigid climate of the north, this singular creation of art, with its aromatic groves, its aloes and cactuses starting out of the rocks— and, above all, its glorious situation, bathed by the dark blue waters of the lake, reflecting the sparkling white villages on its banks, and the distant snows of the Alps — cannot fail to afford pleasure, and a visit to the Isola Bella will certainly not be repented of.

Every handful of mould on the island was originally brought from a distance, and requires to be constantly renewed. It is probable that its foundation of slate-rock favours the growth of tender plants by long retaining the heat of a noon-day sun; but few persons are aware that, in addition to this, the terraces are boarded over during winter, and the plants protected from the frost by stoves heated beneath: thus converting the terraces into a sort of hothouse. The orange and lemon blossoms perfume the air to some distance.

A laurel (bay) of gigantic size is pointed out, as well for its remarkable growth as for a scar on its bark, where Napoleon, it is said, cut with a knife the word " battaglia," a short while before the battle of Marengo. Rousseau once thought of making the Isola Bella the residence of his Julie, but changed his mind on reflecting that so artificial an abode would not be consistent with the simplicity of her character.

The *Palace*, which, with the gardens, is liberally shown to strangers at all times by permission of its owners, contains pictures by the *Procaccini*, the Charity of *And. Sacchi*, and 50 by *Tempesta*. In the *Chapel* are 3 fine sepulchral monuments of the Borromeo family, removed from churches in Milan at the time of the Cisalpine republic : one, of the 15th century, was erected to hold the relics of St. Giustina, an ancestress of the family; another, on the rt. of the altar, is by Ant. Busti, and is praised by Vasari. The large unfinished building which separates the two wings was intended for a great central hall and staircase, but has never been covered in. The whole establishment is in a melancholy state of dilapidation, and appears to have never been touched since its construction.

The *Isola Madre* is well worth a visit by a horticulturist; from its greater distance from the mountains, which screen the sun earlier from the others, it enjoys a milder climate in winter. The plants of New Holland grow luxuriantly out of doors; the two species of tea are generally in flower in October. The Chilian Araucaria here attains a great size; tropical plants grow luxuriantly on the rocks around; on the island are many pheasants, a rare sight in Italy, these birds being as it were imprisoned, from their inability by flight to gain the opposite shores. The small Island of St. Giovanni, forming the 4th of the Borromean group, is situated near Pallanza; it offers nothing remarkable.

The *Monte Monterone*, rising behind the village, commands a fine panoramic view of the Alps, and has at its feet the Lago d'Orta on one side, and Lago Maggiore on the other. Asses are kept for the ascent, 4 fr. It takes 3½ hrs. from Baveno to reach the top, 4350 ft. above the sea-level. You may descend the opposite side to Orta in 2½ hrs., and return in car or boat to Omegna, 2 hrs. walk from Baveno. (See Rte. 102).

One of the most pleasant routes which can be taken is from Baveno to Luino by steamer, Luino to Lugano by carriage, Lugano to Porlezza by steamer, Porlezza to Menaggio by carriage, Menaggio to Bellaggio (Rte. 93).

There are now two lines of excellent steamers on the Lago Maggiore, the Austrian and Sardinian. The boats of the latter, built by the eminent Swiss engineers, Escher of Zürich, are of iron, and extremely well appointed. The Austrian steamers usually run to Sesto Calende; the Sardinian to Arona. As the lake is in the Swiss, Austrian, and Sardinian territories, luggage is examined wherever the traveller lands, on the ground

that it *may* have come from another territory.

The *steamers* call at Pallanza. For fuller description of *Lago Maggiore* see Rte. 91.

———

The Simplon road, where it skirts the lake, is an almost uninterrupted terrace of masonry, studded with granite posts at intervals of a few feet. Travellers coming from Milan may embark on the lake to visit the Borromean islands at

Stresa (Albergo Reale, fairly good), where boats are kept.

Belgirate, and *Lesa*, the summer residence of the celebrated Manzoni, pretty villages, remarkable for the number of villas with terraces and gardens in front. The colossal statue of *St. Carlo Borromeo* appears on the hill above the road on the rt., before reaching

Arona (*Inns:* Albergo d' Italia, extortionate; Posta, near the station, good; A. Reale) — an ancient and rapidly improving town of 4000 Inhab. It is built on the very margin of the lake; the principal street is so narrow that only one carriage can pass. The Simplon road runs through the upper part of the town. The steamers touch here frequently, and carriages can be embarked here. The *railroad* from *Arona* to *Novara*, by which travellers can reach *Genoa* in 6, and *Turin* in 7 hrs., was opened 1855. The station is close to the steamboat pier. In consequence of this railway, and the improvements of the harbour in progress, Arona has become the great entrepôt between Genoa and Switzerland, and a very thriving place.

The principal *Ch.* (*Santa Maria*) contains a very beautiful picture attributed to Gaudenzio Ferrari, who has signed Vinci after his name—a Holy Family, with shutters, bearing figures of saints, and the portrait of a Countess Borromeo, by whom it was presented to the church; it is retouched. San Carlo Borromeo was born in the old castle above Arona, 1538; destroyed by the French 1797.

On a hill, about half an hour's walk from the town, stands the *Colossal Statue* of *St. Charles Borromeo*, 66 ft. high, and placed on a pedestal 40 ft. high. The head, hands, and feet, alone, are cast in bronze; the rest of the figure is formed of sheets of beaten copper, arranged round a pillar of rough masonry which forms the support of it. The saint is represented extending his hand towards the lake, and over his birthplace Arona, bestowing on them his benediction. There is grace in the attitude, in spite of the gigantic proportions of the figure, and benevolence beams from the countenance; altogether the effect of it is good, and very impressive. It was erected, 1697, by subscriptions, principally contributed by the Borromean family. It is possible to enter the statue and to mount up into the head, but the ascent is difficult and fatiguing, and not to be attempted by the nervous. It is effected by means of two ladders, tied together (provided by a man who lives hard by), resting on the pedestal, and reaching up to the skirt of the saint's robe. Between the folds of the upper and lower drapery the adventurous climber squeezes himself through—a task of some difficulty, if he be of corpulent dimensions; and he then clambers up the stone pillar which supports the head, by placing his feet upon the iron bars or cramps by which the copper drapery is attached to it. To effect this, he must assume a straddling attitude, and proceed in the dark till he reaches the head, which he will find capable of holding 3 persons at once. Here he may rest himself by sitting down in the recess of the nose, which forms no bad substitute for an arm-chair. In the neighbouring church several relics of San Carlo are preserved.

From the top of *la Rocca*, or hill above Arona, there is a fine view. The geologist will find near the quarries of limestone (Dolomite) an interesting contact of the magnesian limestone and red porphyry.

Opposite Arona, on the other side of the lake, stands *the Castle of Angera*, a fief of the Borromeos, on a similar limestone peak, at the foot of which is the neat modern village of the same name.

Diligences daily to Martigny and Geneva over the Simplon.

Omnibus to the *Lago d' Orta*.

A good carriage-road leads from Arona, by Borgomanero, to Orta (Rte. 101), 13 kil. = 9½ m.

————

The view of the peaked snowy ridge of the Monte Rosa, from the lower part of the Lago Maggiore, is magnificent. A ferry-boat conveys the traveller across the Ticino, which forms the outlet of the lake, into the territory of Austrian Lombardy, and the small town of

Sesto Calende (*Inns:* none good; Post, best), 5 m. from Arona, charged as 1 Piedmontese post or 1½ Austrian post. Sesto is said to have been a Roman station, and to have received its name from a market held here on the 26th or 27th of the month—*Sexto Calendas*. It stands on the left bank of the Ticino, just below the spot where it quits the Lago Maggiore. The *Ch. of St. Donato* is a structure of the middle ages.

There is a road from this place to Como by Varese, passing through a rich and beautiful district.

Steamers for the head of the lake, stopping at Arona, and calling off the Borromean Islands. There will soon be railway communication to Milan. At present the coach-road to Milan lies over the beginning of the great plain of Lombardy, between avenues of cabbage-headed mulberry-trees, hedges of Robinias, and rows of vines trained between trees, not so as to intercept the splendid views of the Alps which in places bound three-fourths of the horizon.

The country is excessively fertile, but the road usually disagreeable from the dust. The posting is not on a good footing, and the rate of driving is very slow—even the prospect of double buonamano has little effect in accelerating the postilions. The name of every village is written on the wall at the entrance. The first which we pass is Somma, containing an ancient castle of the Viscontis, fringed with swallow-tailed battlements, and a remarkable cypress-tree of great age, one of the largest known. It is stated to have been a tree in the days of Julius Cæsar (?); it is 121 ft. high and 23 ft. in girth. Napoleon respected it at the time of the construction of the route of the Simplon, causing the road to diverge from a straight line on account of it.

Near this was fought the first great battle between Scipio and Hannibal, commonly called the battle of the Ticinus, in which Scipio was worsted.

Gallarate, a large town surrounded by a fertile country.—Beyond this is *Cascina del Buon Jesu*. At Busto, 2 miles to the W. of this, is a church designed by Bramante, and containing frescoes by *Gaudenzio Ferrari*. The Olona is crossed soon after at Castellanza, where there are several manufactories—the road following the bank of the river to

Rho.—Outside the town is a very large and handsome church designed by Pellegrini; the façade, recently finished, is by Pollack. Near this are extensive rice-grounds, the vicinity of which is very unhealthy.

The road terminates at, and enters Milan by the arch of the Simplon (*Arco della Pace*), commenced by Napoleon, and finished by the Austrian government 1838.

MILAN.—(*Inns:* Bairr's Hotel, La Villa, on the Corso Francesco, the Regent-street of Milan, excellent, and not dear; Albergo Reale, very good; Gran Bretagna; Bella Venezia.) For a description of Milan see HANDBOOK FOR NORTH ITALY.

ROUTE 60.

TURTMAN TO THE BERNESE OBERLAND, BY KIPPEL. PASSES FROM KIPPEL.

There is no difficulty in going from Turtman to Kippel, from which the following passes may be taken :

a. to Kandersteg by the Lötschen.
b. to Lauterbrunnen by the Upper *Lötschthal*.
c. to .Viesch by the Lötschsattel.

From *Tourtmagne or Turtman* (Rte. 59 A) to Kippel.

"A mile or so above Tourtemagne a bridge over the Rhone leads to the village of Gampel, at the mouth of the Lötschthal, a very narrow and steep valley rising, not in terraces, but with a rapid and continuous ascent. After crossing the Lonza at Gampel a steep ascent succeeds (now mastered by a good road), commanding fine views over the Rhone. The path next enters a gorge. About an hour from Gampel there is a fall, not visible from the road, of no great height, but a large volume of water. Beyond the chapel of Koppigstein, which is constantly swept away by avalanches, you recross the Lonza to its rt. bank. For the first 1½ hr. not a green field or patch of corn is passed; at the end of that time a group of cottages occurs in a lovely scene of meadow, wood, and rock, overhung by superb peaks, after which the character of the valley is more cheerful as far as

Ferden, where it turns sharply to the east. At the angle, the view along both branches of the valley is superb; the upper portion is wider and longer than that which has been passed, extending to the great Lötschgletscher, a branch of the sea of ice around the Jungfrau, overhung by the Lauterbrunn Breithorn on one side, and the Aletsch-hörner, or some of their offsets, on the other; while on the south the Nesthorn and other very lofty mountains rise almost perpendicularly in icy peaks. The curé's house at

"*Kippel*, 15 min. from Ferden, affords the best, if not the only, accommodation. Good guides may be had. Joseph Appener is celebrated. The curé is a capital mountaineer, but few or none can speak anything but their own German patois."

a. Kippel to Kandersteg.

The passage of the Loetschberg presents some difficulty; guides with ropes should be provided. The first hour is through magnificent larch woods, after which there is about 3 hrs. over pastures, bare stony slopes, and beds of snow to the Col, 6960 ft. above the sea-level, overhung by the grand precipices of the Balm-horn, which forms the eastern end of the Altels group. By giving about 3 hrs. more to the excursion, a high peak to the E., called the Hoch-horn, may be ascended. A less time might probably suffice if the shortest route from Kippel were taken; our guide did not suggest it till we had nearly reached the Col, from which it is 1½ hr., chiefly over ice. Some fearfully steep slopes are to be crossed, from which the eye plunges down right into the Gasterenthal, 5000 to 6000 ft. beneath. A singular and most striking scene occurs in passing round an insulated steeple of rock, rising out of the ice, with a pool of clear blue water at its foot. Between it and the peak lies a narrow isthmus of ice, sloping steeply down on either side; after passing this, the icy shoulder of the mountain is to be wound round, with empty space on two sides; and then the last ascent, up a sharp pile of stones, which we estimated at 5 min., and found to take 15. The view is superb. To the S. and S.W. Monte Rosa, the Matter-horn, and Mont Blanc towering far above nearer mountains, are the leading objects. To the E. the Tschingel-horn and other points of the chain on which we stood, extending to the Jungfrau and the Aletsch-hörner. To the W. a sea of lower mountains towards the Simmenthal, and an extensive view over the Bernese lowlands. Retracing our course for a good way, we then de-

scended over bare rocks and beds snow to the lower part of the Balm gletscher, and reached in a short 2 h from the Hoch-horn the point whe the direct route across the Lötschberg quits the glacier, after lying across probably for 1½ to 2 m. Thence there is about 1¼ hr. of very steep descent into the Gasterenthal. The river is to be crossed by a bridge, which must not be missed: thence to Kandersteg, about 2 hrs. (Rte. 27.)

"This, though over the ice, was formerly a mule path of some traffic, but fell into disuse when the road over the Gemmi was made; it is now impassable for mules. The glacier is much crevassed, but not dangerous. 8 hrs. is abundantly sufficient to go from Ferden or Kippel to Kandersteg, so that the whole distance from Tourtemagne to Kandersteg might be accomplished in one long day, and the bad quarters of the Lötschthal avoided. From Ferden two or three parallel passes lead to the baths of Leuk in 5 or 6 hrs."

b. Kippel to Lauterbrunn.

"A little above the village of Zneisten, and about 2 hours' walk from Kippel, is a narrow valley, leading up into the main chain of the Bernese Alps; the name, as well as I could catch it from the pronunciation, is Mindere-Thal; there is no indication of it in Keller's map, which is not very minutely accurate in its topography of these mountains; but it runs nearly N. and S., and must originate near the S. side of the mountain called by him Tschingel-horn, but which is in fact the Gspalt-horn. This valley or gorge is followed till the glacier is approached which fills up its head, and which is here inaccessible en face; a détour has therefore to be made to the l., over very steep ground, and the glacier is again approached at a point where its inclination is smaller, and at a height where it is already covered with perpetual snow. Here the rope came into requisition, and the day's work began in earnest. Slope after

slope of snow was passed, the few crevasses which the snow had not completely hidden being approached by
Appener just in the right place;
until after nearly 3 hours of walking
up to the calf of the leg in snow, we
reached a long range of weather-beaten
rocks which shut out all view in front,
and were announced to form the summit of the range. The scenery hitherto had been more remarkable for the
novelty of the different mountain-peaks
within sight, than for the magnificence
of any one in particular: the southern
faces of the Bernese Alps, and the
northern pinnacles of the Aletsch-
hörner (mountains not usual to be
looked at from this point of view, and
not a little difficult to identify), with
the sloping fields of snow across which
our track was visible for a foreground.
The ridge we had attained was in no
sense of the word a Col or pass, but a
tolerably level and uniform elevation,
with a wall of rocks of no great height,
forming a continuous crest or battlement; but the grand *coup d'œil* was to
come. Stepping through an interval
between the rocks, the scene changed
at once. In place of the gradual slope
by which we had ascended, immediately beneath our feet the ground
fell away in front and on either hand,
to the level of the Great Tschingel
Glacier, several hundred feet below
us, with just enough snow heaped up
against the ridge on which we were
standing to make the descent practicable. We were at a point immediately above the centre of the glacier,
of which we could see the two extremities sinking, one into the Gasterenthal,
and the other into the valley of the
Ammerten; directly in front, on the
opposite side of the glacier, was the
Kien-thal, with the Niesen at the far
end of it; but the mist was hanging
over the Lake of Thun. Appener's
knowledge of the pass was here criti-
cally tried: at the base of the snowy
precipice on which we were standing,
just where the bank of snow touched
the glacier, was evident to the rt. and l.,
as far as we could see, an enormous
crevasse, or *bergschrund*, gaping to receive the avalanche of snow which

would be inevitably occasioned by our
attempting to descend that way; while
immediately beneath us, the convexity
of the descent intercepted our view of
the bottom of the ridge. My Kandersteg guide and I turned to Appener in
despair; he, however, laughed, and
said that we should soon see that below
where we were standing there was no
schrund at all; and so it proved, or
rather, as is most probable, the convex
configuration of the descent at that
point had thrown the snow more forward, and filled it up. Once upon the
level of the glacier we felt all our
anxieties over, and ran quickly over
the hard snow, and, after one or two
faults among the crevasses below the
Mutelihorn, reached the track usually
taken between Gasteren and the Steinberg."

" *Time,* Kippel to the snow, 3 hours;
over snow to the summit, nearly 3
hours; descent to Lauterbrunnen (very
quick), 5 hours; total, 11. At the
Capricorn I found the route was unknown to any of the guides; Joseph
Appener is the only safe man to take.
He told me he had tried it with Professor Studer of Berne some years before, but the bad weather turned them
back."—E. W.

c. Kippel to Viesch by the Lötschsattel.

"This is a hard day's work, but,
with the exception of a small part of
the Lötschen glacier, presents no great
difficulties. By this route the traveller
is brought into the centre of the great
mountains of the Oberland, and traverses the great Aletsch glacier, the
largest in the world; yet it seems to
be but little known. I was indebted
to Professor Stüder, of Berne, for the
information which led me to explore
it. On the morning of the 19th Sept.
1854, at a little after 3 o'clock, I left
the house of the curé of Kippel, where
I had been hospitably received, accompanied by Ignatz Lehner and François
Hassler, a student at Sion, as my guides;
they had been upon the glaciers, but
neither of them had gone over the
pass. There was no moon, and fe

some time we walked by the light of a lantern carried by Lehner. After near 4 hrs. walking, up the valley and along the mountain side on the rt. of the Lötschen glacier, we got upon the ice. At first the glacier was easy, but, as it rose more rapidly, it became much crevassed, and we found the snow-slopes impracticable; and, after about ½ an h. of difficulties, came to a more even part, covered with hard snow, gradually rising to the Sattel, which we reached at 10 min. after 9 o'clock. The descent of the great Aletsch glacier is easy, and at 1 o'clock we left it near where the lake of Mar-jelen had been: it had burst its banks, and there was only a little stream run-ning in the centre where the lake once was. After a tedious descent we came into the same route as I had followed in coming down from the Oberaarjoch (Rte. 28A, c.), and at ½ past 4 o'clock reached Viesch. We were, including stoppages, nearly 13½ hrs., of which a little more than 6 hrs. were on the ice. We should have crossed in shorter time had any of us before been over the pass, for our ignorance of the route caused us some détours, particularly on the Lötschen glacier. I believe some guides for it may be found at Viesch."—R. F.

This pass might be more easily taken to or from the inn on the Æggishorn. (Rte. 28B.)

ROUTE 66.

ZÜRICH TO RORSCHACH—SOUTH-EAST-ERN RAILWAY.—ST. GALL.

	Eng. m.
Zürich to Winterthur	16¼
Winterthur to Wyl	17¼
,, to Flawyl	27
,, to St. Gall	36
,, to Rorschach	45

The total distance being about 62 m. ?^{st} (!) trains in 4 hrs., ordinary

trains in 6 hrs. This Rly. is now carried on to Coire (Rte. 66). The possible continuation of this line over the Lukmanier pass seems the most feasible of all projects for crossing the Alps by Rly.

Zürich to *Winterthur Stat.*, in Rte. 8.

The Rly. now leaves the Romanshorn line and follows the valley of the Töss as far as Elgg 7 m.; 6 m. further it crosses the Murg and reaches

Wyl Stat., a small town of 2000 Inhab. with several convents; it then crosses the valley of the Glatt by a lattice bridge of 3 arches 380 ft. long and 120 ft. high.

About 8 m. from St. Gall the valley of the Sitter is crossed by a wrought iron lattice bridge, of clever device, 560 ft. long, in 4 arches or spans. It is raised upon cast-iron piers 200 ft. above the river, resting on stone foun-dations. These lattice bridges are very common in America, but do not seem to have found favour in England.

A long Tunnel is then passed through close to

St. Gall (St. Gallen). — *Inns:* Lion, very good, and thoroughly com-fortable; Hecht (Brochet), good; Rössli (Cheval).

St. Gall, capital of the canton, is situated in an elevated valley on the banks of a small stream called the Steinach. Pop. 13,000 (3100 Roman Catholics). It is one of the principal seats of manufacturing industry in Switzerland. The manufacture of *Swiss muslins* is the most flourishing, but the spinning of cotton is also ra-pidly increasing. There are extensive bleacheries in the town, and the neighbouring slopes are white with webs. The embroidered curtains and ladies' collars are very pretty and cheap here.

The antique walls, however, which still surround the town, and the ditch, now converted into gardens, tell of a totally different period and state of society, and recall to mind the ancient history of St. Gall. If we may believe the legend, it was in the early part of the 7th century that St. Gallus, a Scotch monk (? Irish), left his convent in the Island of Iona, one of the Hebrides, and, after travelling over a large part of Europe converting the heathens, finally settled on the banks of the Steinach, then a wilderness buried in primæval woods, of which bears and wolves seemed the rightful tenants rather than men. He taught the wild people around the arts of agriculture, as well as the doctrines of true religion. The humble cell which the Scotch missionary had founded became the nucleus of civilization : and fifty years after his death, when the fame of his sanctity, and the miracles reported to have been wrought at his tomb, drew thousands of pilgrims to the spot, it was replaced by a more magnificent edifice, founded under the auspices of Pepin l'Heristal. This abbey was one of the oldest ecclesiastical establishments in Germany. It became the asylum of learning during the dark ages, and was the most celebrated school in Europe between the 8th and 10th centuries. Here the works of the authors of Rome and Greece were not only read but copied; and we owe to the labour of these obscure monks many of the most valuable classical authors, which have been preserved to modern times in MSS., treasured up in the Abbey of St. Gall ; among them Quintilian, Silius Italicus, Ammian Marcellinus, and part of Cicero, may be mentioned. About the beginning of the 13th century St. Gall lost its reputation for learning, as its abbots exchanged a love of piety and knowledge for worldly ambition, and the thirst for political influence and territorial rule. The desire of security, in those insecure times, first induced the abbot to surround his convent and the adjoining building with a wall and ditch, with 13 towers at intervals. This took place at the end of the 10th century, and from that time may be dated the foundation of the town. He and his 100 monks of the Benedictine order thought it no disgrace to sally forth, sword in hand and helmet on head, backed by their 200 serfs, in the hour of danger, when the convent was threatened by ungodly laymen. The

donations of pious pilgrims from all parts of Europe soon augmented enormously the revenues of the abbots. They became the most considerable territorial sovereigns in N. Switzerland ; their influence was increased by their elevation to the rank of princes of the empire ; they were engaged in constant wars with their neighbours, and were latterly entangled in perpetual feuds with their subjects at home. These bold burghers, who, in the first instance, owed their existence and prosperity to the convent, became, in the end, restive under its rule. In the beginning of the 15th century the land of Appenzell threw off the yoke of the abbot; at the Reformation St. Gall itself became independent of him ; and in 1712 the ecclesiastical prince was obliged to place the convent under the protection of those very citizens whose ancestors had been his serfs.

The French Revolution caused the secularization of the abbey, and the sequestration of its revenues followed in 1805. The last abbot, Pancratius Forster, died in 1829, a pensioner on the bounty of others, in the convent of Muri.

The *Abbey Church*, now cathedral, was so completely modernized in the last century that it possesses little to interest the stranger.

The vast buildings of the deserted *Monastery* date from the 17th and 18th centuries ; and the part of it which formed the abbot's *Palace* (*Die Pfalz*) now serves for the public offices of the Government of the canton. In it is preserved the *Convent Library* (Stifts Bibliothek), which still contains many curiosities, such as numerous Latin classics, MSS. of the 10th and 11th centuries, Greek New Testament of the 10th century, Psalms of the 9th century, various ancient MSS. either from Ireland or transcribed by Irish monks ; also a MS. of the Niebelungen Lied, and many letters relating to the Reformation.

The finest edifice is the *Orphan House*, outside the town, to the N.W.

At the *Casino Club* will be found an excellent *reading-room.*

The *Freudenberg*, the neighbouring mountain on the S.E. of the town, commands from its summit, about 2 m. off, a fine panorama, including the lake of Constance and the mountains of St. Gall and Appenzell, with the Sentis at their head. A carriage-road leads up to the inn on the top.

Excursion.—From St. Gall to Trogen, Gais, Appenzell, Weissbad, and back to St. Gall—a delightful day's drive (Rte. 68).

Rorschach — Inns : Hirsch, good and moderate. Post (Krone). This little lake-port and town of 1650 Inhab. is the principal corn-market in Switzerland, held on Thursday. The grain required to supply the greater part of the Alpine districts of N. Switzerland is imported from Suabia, in boats, across the lake, and is deposited temporarily in large warehouses here. Much muslin is made at Rorschach.

The deposits of the Rhine are, it is said, forming themselves into shallows between Rorschach and Lindau, which may soon impede the direct navigation of the lake between these two places. On the slope, a little above the town, is the large dilapidated building, called *Statthaltery*, or Marienberg, a palace once of the proud abbots of St. Gall, now a government *School*. Its Gothic cloister, and vaulted refectory with bas-reliefs, deserve notice (date 1513). It commands a fine view from its terrace. Near it, perched on a projecting sandstone rock, is the desolate *Castle of St. Anne*, with its square keep. From the top of the hill, behind Rorschach (1 hour's walk), you may obtain a view over the whole lake of the influx of the Rhine, and of the town of Bregenz.

ROUTE 67.

RORSCHACH TO COIRE, BY RAGATZ AND THE BATHS OF PFEFFERS.

62 Eng. m. Rly. open.

		Eng. m.
Rorschach.		
Altstetten	. . . .	16
Sennwald	. . . .	26
Sewelen	. . . .	37
Ragatz	. . . .	48
Coire	. . . .	62

Rorschach may be reached from Zürich or Schaffhausen by the South-Eastern Railway (Rte. 66), which is now continued to Coire.

Steamboats go daily between it and Friedrichshafen in Würtemberg ; and the steamers from Constance, Romanshorn (Rte. 7A), and Lindau also touch here regularly, corresponding with the diligences to Milan.

After leaving Rorschach the road skirts the foot of low hills clad with vineyards, beneath which the yellow-bellied pumpkins may be seen basking in the sun, but soon quits the margin of the lake to cross the flat delta of the Rhine. The district around the mouth of the river abounds in marsh, and is by no means healthy.

Rheineck (Inns : Brochet, Post ;— Krone)—a village of 1370 Inhab., on the l. bank of the Rhine, about 4 m. above its embouchure, situated under vine-clad hills. There are several other castles on the neighbouring heights.

St. Margarethen, a pretty village completely embowered in a grove of walnut and fruit trees, is situated near the *Austrian ferry, over the Rhine*, which must be crossed in going to Bregenz, or Lindau (see *Handbook for South Germany*) ; but it is not passable after dark. Our road leaves it on the l., and turns soon afterwards due S. up the valley of the Rhine, through a highly cultivated country rich in grain, especially maize, and abounding in orchards. The Rhine here is a wide, shallow, muddy, and unsteady stream, constantly changing its channel and overflowing its banks: it is not navigated except by wood-rafts, which float down it.

Altstetten — (*Inns:* Post ; Rabe)— a town of 6429 Inhab., in a fruitful neighbourhood, and in a lovely spot commanding views of the Alps of Vorarlberg. There is a road from this over the hill of *Stoss* to Appenzell, by Gais, ½ p. (Rte. 68), and St. Gall, 3 leagues: very steep, but quite practicable for light carriages. It takes 2 hrs. to reach the top with leaders. The view from it over the Alps of the Vorarlberg is fine, and the route interesting. Another road, over the Ruppen, leads in 3 hrs. to St. Gall, by Trogen (Rte. 68). The female inhabitants of the lower Rheinthal are all diligently occupied in tambouring muslin; much of which goes to England. [Altstetten to Feldkirch in Austria beyond the Rhine is 1¼ p. by Oberied—*Inn:* H. du Cheval.]

Sennwald — a village at the foot of the *Kamor* (5320 ft. high, 3 hours' walk, commanding a fine view over the Alps of Appenzell, Vorarlberg, and Grisons: its summit is called Hohekasten).

Down to the 17th century, the district which we now traverse belonged to the powerful barons of Hohen Sax, many of whose castles, reduced to ruins by the Appenzellers, may still be discerned upon the heights on the W. of the Rhine valley. One of this family, a brave and noble soldier, and a Protestant, escaped with difficulty from the massacre of St. Bartholomew at Paris, and on his return home was murdered by his nephew. After this foul deed, it is the popular belief that the blessing of God was withdrawn from the race: it is certain they never prospered. In 1616 their vast domains were sold to Zürich, and the family became extinct soon after. The body of the murdered man is still preserved in a perfect condition, in a coffin with a glass lid, dried like a mummy, under the church-tower of Sennwald. This circumstance, and the story connected with it, have given to the remains a reputation for sanctity; so that, though a Protestant, the Catholics have stolen

some of the limbs as relics, and once actually carried off the body across the Rhine; it was, however, speedily reclaimed.

Werdenberg — (*Inn:* Kaufhaus).— was the seat of a noble family of that name, who played an important part in early Swiss history. The *Stammschloss*, the cradle of the race, still stands, a conspicuous white building, in good preservation, above the town. A cross road runs hence through the vale of Toggenburg to Wyl (Rte. 71).

Sevelen (*Inn:* Traube). Rt. on the height the ruined castle Wartau ; l. beyond the Rhine, lies Vaduz, capital of the principality of Lichtenstein; and at the entrance of the Luziensteig pass (see p. 192) Schloss Gutburg. In the background rises the grey head of the Falkniss with its chaplet of snow: the whole landscape is splendid, grand, and full of variety.

At *Sargans*, which we pass a little on the rt., the road from Wallenstadt (Rte. 14) falls in, and the Rly. from Wallenstadt will also join here.

Ragatz—*Inns:* Hof Ragatz, originally the summer residence of the abbots, and now a bathing establishment, and supplied with water from the hot springs of Pfeffers, conveyed hither in wooden pipes, 12,500 feet long; a large house with a fine view. The charges to persons staying in the house to take the baths are very low, but for *passing* travellers the charges are the same as at other inns in Switzerland.—Hôtel de la Tamina. Ragatz is a village of 600 Inhab., situated at the mouth of the gorge (töbel), through which the torrent Tamina issues out to join the Rhine. It thrives from its central position at the junction of the great roads from Zürich, St. Gall, Feldkirch, Coire, and Milan, to all which places *Diligences* run daily, and from its vicinity to the mineral springs of Pfeffers, which cause it to be much resorted to as a watering-place, especially since the gloomy and uncomfortable old baths have been supplanted by the cheerful new establishment. There is an English chapel here.

[No one should omit to visit the

OLD BATHS OF PFEFFERS (properly Pfäffers), situated a little way up the vale of the Tamīna, *one of the most extraordinary spots in Switzerland*, and now made accessible by a car-road cut in the rocks of the gorge. The distance, not being more than 2½ m.. is performed in ¾ of an hour, and it takes only 20 minutes to return in a char. The charge for a char at the hotel is 5 frs. Those who are able should walk; it is not possible to miss the way; you may reach the baths within an hour on foot, and so miss none of the beauties. It is a delightful walk, the scenery very romantic; the torrent forming waterfalls at every step, and floating down the logs of wood. Much of the interest and original singularity of the spot, however, is destroyed by the improvement of the access to it.

The Old Baths are situated in two large piles of building connected together by a chapel. They are built on a narrow ledge of rock, a few feet above the roaring Tamīna, and so deeply sunken between the rocks that they may be said to be half buried, so that in the height of summer, the sun appears above them only from 10 to 4.

The hot springs of Pfeffers were not known to the Romans. There is a story that they were discovered by a hunter, who, having entered into the abyss of the Tamina, in the pursuit of game, remarked the column of vapour arising from them. For many years nothing was done to facilitate access to them, and patients desirous of profiting by their healing virtues were let down to the source from the cliffs above, by ropes, and, in order to reap as much benefit as possible, were accustomed to pass a week together, both day and night, in them, not only eating and drinking, but sleeping, under hot water, instead of under blankets. The cause of the virtue of the water is not very evident, as a pint contains scarcely 3 grains of saline particles; it has a temperature of about 98° Fahrenheit. The patients are almost exclusively of the lower orders, and if they survive a residence of some weeks in this place they certainly ought to be capable of surviving any illness.

The situation of the old baths is both gloomy and monotonous, hemmed in between dripping walls of rock, and shaded by dank foliage, with only a narrow strip of sky overhead, and with small space or facilities for locomotion and exercise, unless the patient will take the road to Ragatz or scale the sides of the valley above him. To one fresh arrived from the upper world, its meadows and sunshine, a visit to Pfeffers has all the effect of being at the bottom of a well or a mine, except for a few hours at midday. The atmosphere is kept at one regular temperature of chilliness by the perpetual draught brought down by the torrent; and the solitary and imprisoned ray of sunshine which about noon, and for an hour or two afterwards, finds its way into these recesses, is insufficient to impart permanent warmth or cheerfulness. It is to be presumed that few English travellers would be disposed to make any stay here. A passing visit of a few hours will satisfy the curiosity of most persons. No one, however, should depart without visiting the

Source of the hot spring.

A few yards above the old baths. the sides of the ravine of the Tamīna contract in an extraordinary manner, so as to approach within a few feet of each other; a little farther they even close over and cover up the river, which is seen issuing out of a cavernous chasm. The springs are reached through the bath-house, whence a bridge of planks across the Tamīna leads to the entrance, which is closed by a door. The bridge is prolonged into the gorge. in the shape of a scaffolding or shelf, suspended by iron stanchions to the rocks, and partly laid in a niche cut out of the side. It is carried all along the chasm as far as the hot spring. and affords the only means of approach to it, as the sides of the rent are vertical, and there is not an inch of room between them and the torrent, for the sole of a foot to rest. Formerly the passage was along two, sometimes one plank, unprotected by railings ; at present a platform, 4 feet wide, furnished with a hand-rail, renders the approach to the spring easy for the most timid, and perfectly free from risk. Each person pays 1 fr. for admittance. A few yards from the entrance, the passage is darkened by the overhanging rock. The sudden chill of an atmosphere never visited by the sun's rays, the rushing and roaring of the torrent, 30 or 40 feet below, the threatening position of the rocks above, have a grand and striking effect ; but this has been diminished by modern improvements, which have deprived the visit to the gorge of even the semblance of danger. In parts, it is almost dark, where the sides of the ravine overlap one another, and actually meet over-head, so as to form a natural arch. The rocks in many places show evident marks of having been ground away, and scooped out by the rushing river, and by the stones brought down with it. For several hundred yards the river pursues an almost subterranean course, the roof of the chasm being the floor, as it were, of the valley. In some places the roots of the trees are seen dangling through the crevice above your head, and at one particular spot you find yourself under the arch of the natural bridge leading to the staircase mentioned farther on. Had Virgil or Dante been aware of this spot, they would certainly have conducted their heroes through it to the jaws of the infernal regions.

The shelf of planks extends more than ¼ m. from the baths. At its extremity, at the bottom of a cavern in the rocks, rise the springs, the temperature being about 100° Fahrenheit; the water is received into a reservoir nearly 15 feet deep, from which it is conducted in pipes to the baths. The first baths were miserable hovels, built over the spring, and suspended, like swallows' nests, to the face of the rock : the only entrance to them was by the roof, and the sick were let down into them by ropes and pulleys. Marks of these hovels are still to be seen on the rocks. The springs generally cease to flow in winter, but burst forth again in spring ; they are most copious when the snow has fallen in abundance, and continue till autumn, after which their fountains are again sealed. The water has little taste or smell ; it bears some resemblance, in its mineral contents, to that of Ems, and is used both for bathing and drinking.

After emerging from the gorge, at the bath-house, the traveller may ascend the valley above it by a well-marked track ; ascending the steep l. bank, and then keeping to the l., and descending a little, he will in about half a mile cross by a natural bridge of rock, beneath which the Tamīna, out of sight and hearing from above, forces its way into the gorge of the hot springs. A steep path or staircase (Steige) formed of trunks or roots of trees, on the rt. bank, is then met with, ascending which, you reach an upper stage of the valley, formed of gentle slopes, and covered with verdant pasture on one side, and with thick woods on the other. The two sides are separated by the deep gash and narrow gorge, along the bottom of which the Tamīna forces its way. This is, perhaps, the best point for obtaining a general view of the baths and this singular spot in which they are sunken. On looking over the verge of the precipice, you perceive, at the bottom of the ravine, at the depth of 300 feet below, the roofs of the two large buildings, like cotton factories in size and structure. The upper valley, also, with its carpet of bright green, its woods, and the bare limestone cliffs which border it on either hand, and above all, the huge peak of the Falkniss, rising on the opposite side of the Rhine, form a magnificent landscape.

A char-road runs from the top of the Steige along the rt. bank of the Tamīna, through a wood and meadows, to

The *Convent of Pfeffers,* a vast edifice, but not otherwise remarkable : it was built 1665, in place of one destroyed by fire. It encloses a church in the centre, like all the convents of the Benedictine order. It is finely placed on an elevated mountain-platform, commanding, on one side, the valley of the Rhine, backed by the majestic Falkniss ; on the other, opening out towards the lake of Wallenstadt and the peaks of the Sieben Kurfürsten. This Benedictine monastery, founded 713, was suppressed, after an existence of 10 centuries, in 1838, by a decree of the government of the canton of St. Gall, in consequence of the finances of the convent having become involved, and at the request of a majority of the brethren. The Government pensioned the abbot and the monks; agents of the canton took possession of the convent and all that belonged to it, and have converted it into a lunatic asylum.

The convent once possessed a very extensive territory; its abbots were princes; but the French, as usual, appropriated their revenues; and at the termination of the French rule, but a small part of their property was restored to them, including the baths. This is now appropriated to pious works, the education of the people, &c. The revenues of the convent were valued at 216,365 Swiss florins. .

Near the convent stands the ruined *castle of Wartenstein.*

A pretty, but bad, char-road zigzagging down through woods leads from the convent back to Hof Ragatz.

The pedestrian going to Coire need not return to Ragatz after ascending the Steige, but may pass the convent and proceed to the Untere-Zoll-Brücke; or he may proceed to Reichenau by *Kunkels* (see below, *d*).

The *Kalanda,* or Galandaberg (the mountain on the rt. bank of the Tamina, above the old baths, which separates the valley from that of the Rhine), is sometimes ascended on account of the view from its top—a 5-hours' walk. Many other interesting *Excursions* may be conveniently made from Hof Ragatz, but there appear to be no saddle-horses.

a. To *Luziensteig,* a remarkable for-

tified pass, beyond the Rhine, league from Ragatz, between Fläschberg and the Falkniss. T ascent of the *Fläschberg* from Luzie steig is now made by a carriage-ro reaching in succession the vario forts, and the view from its top, a down the tremendous precipice whi scarps one side of it, is very striking

b. To the *Prättigau* and *Fide* (Rte. 81), returning by the Schalfik

c. To the top of the *Graue Hörne* an ascent requiring 5 hrs.—8760 ft. whence you may see the Lake Constance over the peaks of tl Kurfürsten.

d. By the *Kunkels* pass to Reichen: on the Splügen. This pass is n very striking, but is a change fro the high road. There is a tolerab char-road to Vättis, and in fact a ch: might be taken to the foot of the co The char-road goes past the conven but the pedestrian can go by th old baths, and ascend the Steige, th path from which falls into the cha road. The char-road proceeds alon the rt. bank of the Tamina, pa: many small slate-works, to the hamle of Vadura. The valley is here tole rably wide and fertile; soon afterward however it contracts and become walled in with tremendous precipice on each side, pines growing on then wherever there is room. In 1 h 15 m. from the top of Steige th valley turns to the rt. and opens out then *Vättis* is reached, a small villag at the entrance of the Kalfeuser Thal where bread and wine, and perhaps bed, might be procured. The patl now keeps to the l. over green mea dows, the bare precipices of the Ca landa overhanging on the l. The numerous châlets of *Kunkels* are next reached, and then the foot of the col where the l. path must be taken; and a steep ascent of 20 min. leads to the head of the pass. There is not much view from the col itself. Keeping again l., the path plunges into the ravine of *Foppa,* and by a very steep descent, affording occasionally fine views of the valley of the Rhine, Tamins is reached and then Reiche nau (Rte. 87). Time, fair walking—

Ragatz.	hrs.	min.
Steige	1	0
Vättis	2	0
Kunkels	1	25
Col	0	50
Reichenau.	1	20
Total . . .	6½	0

A French detachment crossed this pass in 1799, drove out the Austrians, and plundered Tamins.

e. The excursion up the Kalfeuser-Thal towards the glaciers of the Sar-ona is seldom made, but the scenery is very grand. As far as Vättis the path is the same as that over the Kunkels. There is a tolerable path to Glarus by the Weissthanen-Thal (Rte. 76 A), and a very difficult path to Flims (Rte. 77).

f. Those who do not intend to cross into Italy may visit the *Via Mala* and return in a long day.

The Rly. now crosses the Rhine and passes out of canton St. Gall into the Grisons. The valley of the Rhine has a grand appearance from this point. The peak of the Falk-niss is a conspicuous and striking object in the view to the N.E. The Rhine alone is unpicturesque, from the width of its bed and the large space of unsightly sand and gravel left bare in summer. Its bed is constantly rising, so as to threaten more fearful inundations; and a plan has been proposed, by M. la Nicca, of cutting a new channel for its unruly stream, from this point as far as the Lake of Constance. The road is carried over the *Landquart*, an impetuous torrent, descending from the valley of Prettigau (Rte. 81), which here enters the Rhine.

Beyond this, the Convent of Pfeffers is visible from the road; the snowy heights of the *Calanda* rise into sight on the opposite bank of the Rhine; and the ruins of feudal castles, perched upon rocky knolls, overlooking the valley, give a highly picturesque character to the scene. One of the most conspicuous is Haldenstein, nearly opposite Coire.

The manner in which mountains may be worn down and converted into hills in the course of ages is very well illustrated along this valley. From the valleys on each side between the mountains proceed torrents, which have borne down the debris of the mountains, and have thereby formed long hills, reaching to the Rhine. The highest parts of these hills, next the mountains, must be several hundred feet high, whence they gradually slope away. The road regularly ascends the hills, crosses the bed of the torrent at the top, and then descends.

Coire (Germ. *Chur;* Romansch, *Cuera.*)—*Inns:* Weisses Kreutz (White Cross), and Freyeck, very good. Capricorn, or Steinbock, outside the town, civil people, the best here, 1855. *Times* is taken in. The wine of the Valteline is generally consumed in the Grisons, but *Completer*, which grows on the Rhine, near Malans, is very good, and should by all means be tried here.

Coire, capital of the Grisons, the *Curia Rætorum* of the Romans, is an ancient walled town of 5483 Inhab. (900 Rom. Catholics), about a mile from the Rhine. Its prosperity arises almost entirely from the high roads upon which it stands, which form the channel of communication from Italy into Switzerland and Western Germany. Coire is the staple place of the goods transported over the two great Alpine carriage-roads of the Splügen and Bernardin. It is the place of meeting of the Council of the Grisons; a member of which claims the title of "Your Wisdom" ("Euer Weisheit").

The town has narrow streets, and stands on uneven ground, at the entrance of the magnificent Glen of the *Schalfik-thal;* some curious domestic architecture will be found in it. The *Bishop's Palace* and the quarter around it, inhabited by the Roman Catholics, occupy the summit of an eminence and are separated from the rest by walls and battlements, closed by double gates, one to keep the Roman Catholics in, the other to keep the Protestants out. Here is situated the *Ch. of St. Lucius,* or the *Dom,* a curious example of early pointed Gothic, including fragments of earlier buildings. It is entered from the W. by a round-arched portal supported on monsters.

The choir is raised on steps, leaving open to the nave the crypt beneath, which rests on a single pier, whose base is a monster. The statues of the Four Evangelists, Janus-like, in pairs, standing upon lions, are very ancient. There are singular old carvings and paintings, and numerous monuments of the noble Grison families. There is a sacramental shrine with metal door, and two other fine shrines, and some candlesticks of metal. In the sacristy are preserved the bones of St. Lucius, a British king, and the founder of St. Peter's Ch., Cornhill, and some specimens of church plate, a bishop's crozier, a monstrance of the 14th centy., shrines, &c.

The *Episcopal Palace* (Hof), near the church, is an antique building; the staircase and halls are singularly decorated with stucco work. The bishop's private chapel is in the heart of an old Roman tower called *Marsöl*, attached to the N.E. side of the palace. St. Lucius was put to death in this tower. In another wing is a rude Dance of Death, much mutilated. There is a second Roman tower, *Spinöl*, in an angle of the walls.

Behind the Palace is a kind of ravine, lined with vineyards, across which a path leads to the *Roman Catholic Seminary*, from which is a picturesque view of the town. There is a considerable collection of Romansch literature in the *Library* of the *Cantonal Schools*.

Besides the roads from Coire to Italy, by the Splügen (Rte. 87 and 88) and Bernardin (Rte. 90), several new lines lead in different directions through the Grisons. A carriage road between Coire and the Engadine, over the Julier Pass, is now finished. (See Rte. 82.)

Diligences every day to Milan, by the Splügen, in 29 hrs.; to Bellinzona, by the Bernardin, in 17 hrs.; to Samaden (daily) in 12 hrs.

Rly. from Rorschach.

The Romansch or Rumonsch Language.

The *Romansch* (properly the *Ræto-Romansch*) language is one of those which, in the course of the middle ages, took their rise from the common or Rustic Latin (Lingua Romana rustica), spoken in different parts of the Roman empire in Europe. The Provençal of the S. of France is another, and the Wallachian (Romouni) is a third of these tongues still existing. The Ræto-Romansch was at one time spoken all through the Roman province of *Rætia*, which included the modern countries of the Grisons, the Tyrol, and the adjacent districts of Switzerland and S. Germany, where many Romansch proper names of places still remain, though the inhabitants speak German. Besides a considerable mixture of pure German, the Ræto-Romansch contains several hundred words, relating to Alpine life and occupations, derived from the aboriginal Alpine tribes, whom Livy asserts to have been related to the Etruscans.

The population of the Grisons, in 1850, amounted to 88,935, of whom about 50,000 speak Romansch, 30,000 German, and 8000 Italian (in the S. districts of Misocco, Bergell, and Peschiavo). As regards grammatical differences, the Romansch of the Grisons is divided into three principal dialects, which prevail in—1. The Upper Engadine; 2. Lower Engadine; 3. The Oberland, or country "above and below the forest."

The literature of the Ræto-Romansch language dates back to the latter half of the fifteenth century, beginning with popular songs relating to warlike exploits, succeeded in 1525 by an epic poem by Johannes Travers, a chief actor in the events he describes. The first printed book was the translation of the New Testament into the dialect of the Upper Engadine by Tachem Bifrun, a lawyer of Samaden. It was published 1560, and had great influence in the extensive spread of the Reformation through the whole Rætian Valley of the Inn. It was followed by other translations of the whole Bible, by books of prayer, catechisms, &c., throughout the Romansch Grisons; and the example set by the Protestants was quickly followed by the Roman Catholics.

Most of the inhabitants of the Grisons are bilinguals, who, if they speak Romansch, speak Italian or German likewise. The laws are written and the edicts of Government are published in Romansch, and there are two Romansch newspapers — 'Amity del Pievel' (the Friend of the People), ultramontane, published at Coire in the dialect of the Oberland, and the liberal 'Gazetta d'Inngiadina,' in that of the Lower Engadine.

The traveller in the. Grisons may be reminded that, the Romansch names of places, of two syllables, generally have the accent on the last syllable, as Ardéz, Cernéz, Lavín, Mascín, Ragátz, Sargáns, and that the Romansch names of many places differ materially from the German: *e.g.*, Disentis, *Rom.* Muster; Brigels, *Rom.* Breil; Waltersburg, *Rom.* Uors; Ems, *Rom.* Dommat.

History and Government of the Graubunden or Grisons.—It must not be supposed that the conspiracy on the Grütli, in 1307, and the exploits of Tell,' gave freedom to the whole country now called Switzerland, or even influenced more than a very small part of it—the Forest cantons—except in as far as such a spirit-stirring example is capable of influencing the minds of a neighbouring people. For more than a century after the first Swiss union, that part of the country of Rætia now called Grisons groaned under the tyranny of almost numberless petty lords, who, though they possessed but a few acres of land, or even no more than the number of square feet on which their castle stood, yet assumed the rights of independent sovereignty, waging perpetual petty war with their neighbours—oppressing their own subjects, and pillaging all travellers — the ancient form of levying duties and customs. The best notion of the state of society which existed during this period of the Faustrecht (club law), may be formed from the quantity of feudal ruins which stud not only the main valleys of the Rhine, but even the lateral valleys and gorges of the Rætian Alps. At last a day of retribution came. The peasants rose in revolt and threw off the yoke of the nobles—with less violence than might be expected, chiefly because the great ecclesiastical potentates, the Bishop of Coire, the Abbots of St. Gall and Disentis, and some of the more influential barons, sided with the peasants, directing, instead of opposing, the popular feeling.

The result of this was the Grison Confederacy (1471), quite distinct from the Swiss Confederacy, composed of *Three Leagues* (Bünden)—the Upper, or Grey League (Ober, or Graue Bund), 1424 (named from the simple grey home-spun coats of those by whom it was formed) ; the League of God's House (Ca Dè in Romansch, in Germ. Gotteshaus Bund), so called from the church of Coire, the head and capital of this league, 1396 ; and the League of the Ten Jurisdictions (Zehn-Gerichte), of which Mayenfeld is chief town (1428).

The government produced by this revolution presented a remarkable example of the sovereignty of the people and of universal suffrage. Not only every valley, but in some cases every parish, or even hamlet, in a valley, became an independent commonwealth, with a government of its own, with peculiar local administrative rights and privileges. Sometimes one of these free states, sometimes several together, formed a commune or schnitze, literally slice (gemeinde or gericht) ; each commune had its own general assembly, in which every citizen of the age of 18, sometimes younger, had a vote, and by which the magistrates and authorities, down to the parson and schoolmaster, were elected. With such a complication of machinery, it is difficult to understand how any government could have been carried on ; and we accordingly find the history of the Grisons little better than a long series of bickerings, feuds, revolts, conspiracies, massacres, intrigues, and peculations. The wisest decisions of the diet of the canton were annulled or frustrated by the votes of the general assemblies, accordingly as the interest or caprice of the most influential popular leader might sway these meetings at the moment. Two great families, those of

K 2

Planta and De Salis, in the end, long monopolised the chief influence, as well as the patronage and offices of the federal government. Such, then, was the *practical* result of this democracy of the purest form *in theory.*

Towards the end of the 15th centy. the Grisons concluded a permanent alliance with the Swiss, and in 1525 conquered Chiavenna and the Valteline, which remained subject to them till 1798. In 1814 the Grisons became a Swiss canton.

A new local and administrative organization of the canton of the Grisons was introduced in June, 1851. According to this new law the old historic names and divisions are abolished, and the canton is portioned out into 14 districts, 39 circles, and 205 communes or parishes.

ROUTE 68.

ST. GALL TO ALTSTETTEN, BY GAIS AND THE STOSS; GAIS TO APPENZELL; WITH EXCURSIONS TO THE WEISSBAD, THE WILDKIRCHLEIN, AND THE HOCH SENTIS.

There are 2 roads from St. Gall to Altstetten—by Trogen or by Gais, and either of them is perfectly practicable for a light carriage. It is about 15 m. by either road, but that by Trogen is less steep, and takes nearly an hour less time. The excursion to Appenzell may be made from Gais. The road from St. Gall to Altstetten (an excellent and less hilly one), by *Trogen,* a neat little town (*Inn:* Krone, clean), whose environs are charming, is carried over the Ruppen. A diligence to Feldkirch follows it: time 3¼ hrs. with 6 horses.

The other road from *St. Gall,* by Gais, quits the canton of St. Gall and enters that of Appenzell (Ausser-Rhoden) a little before reaching, by an excellent but hilly road,

Teuffen—(Inns: Hecht, good; Bär). The inhabitants of this flourishing village of neat cottages are chiefly engaged in the manufacture and embroidery of muslin. Grubenmann, the carpenter, who built the celebrated bridge of one arch at Schaffhausen, was born here, and built the Ch.

Gais—Inns: Ochs, largest and best; Krone; Lamm, small, but clean and cheap; goats' whey is brought from the high Alps every morning. The bread is very good here. This little village of neat timber cottages, mostly converted into lodging-houses by the peasants their owners, irregularly scattered over lawn-like meadows, is situated in an open country, with nothing but green pastures around, at an elevation of 2900 ft. above the sea-level. Yet the reputation of its pure and bracing air, and of its cure of goats' whey (molkenkur ; cure de petit lait), annually attract hither many hundred invalids from all parts of continental Europe ; and during the season, in July and August, the principal inns are generally full.

The peasants' houses are particularly clean, trimly painted outside, as though they had just issued from a bandbox.

Gais lies in view of the Sentis and its chain; a noble object; and at the S. side of the *Gäbris.* The view from the top of that mountain is delightful, and may be attained with little trouble, in 1 hr., on horseback. Guide 2 fr.

The native songs of the cow-herds and dairy-maids of Appenzell are highly melodious.

There is a char-road from Gais to Herisau (see Rte. 69), about 5 hrs. walk.

2 m. to the E. of Gais, on the road to Altstetten, is the *Chapel of Stoss,* erected on the summit of the steep pass leading down to the Rhine Thal. to commemorate the almost incredible victory gained by 400 men of Appenzell over 3000 Austrians in 1405. The Archduke of Austria and the Abbot

of St. Gall had hoped to take the Swiss by surprise with this preponderating force. But a handful of the mountaineers, under the conduct of Count Rudolph of Werdenberg, assembled in haste, gave them battle, and defeated the invaders, with a loss of 900 men, losing only 20 of their own party. The blood of the slain is said to have discoloured the mountain-torrent which flowed past the battle-field as far as its influx into the Rhine. The view from the Stoss over the valley of the Rhine, 2000 ft. below, and of the snowy mountains of Tyrol and Vorarlberg beyond, is of the highest beauty.

A very steep descent leads from the Stoss to Altstetten. You hire a spare skid at the top of the hill, and go down with both wheels locked. From Stoss to Altstetten, in the valley of the Rhine, is 1 hour's drive, about 5 m. (Rte. 67). It takes 2 hrs. to ascend.

———

It is a distance of 3½ m. S.W. (there is a footpath shorter) from Gais to

Appenzell — Inns: Hecht (Pike), a clean, homely farm-house. Though the chief place of the district of Inner Rhoden, this is but a large village of 1400 Inhab., consisting of old houses, with two convents, and a modern *church* attached to a Gothic choir, painted with representations of banners and flags taken by the Appenzellers in the 15th cent., and contains nothing remarkable in it. It derives its name from the country-seat of the Abbot of St. Gall (Abten-zelle, Abbatis Cella), having been anciently built here, when the country around was an uninhabited solitude.

The *Landesgemeinde*, or Assembly of the canton, meets on a square, near a lime-tree, every year. In the Record Office, *Archiv*, are preserved a number of banners, conquered by the Appenzellers of old, and the only surviving trophies of their valour. Here are the flags of Constance, Winterthur, Feldkirch ; the Tyrolese banner and free ensign, inscribed " Hundert Tausend Teufel," conquered at Landek, 1407 ; the Genoese banner of St.

George, and two captured from the Venetians, 1516, in the battle of Agnadel.

The *canton Appenzell* lies somewhat out of the beat of travellers, completely surrounded (enclavé) by the territory of canton St. Gall, and shut in, at its S. extremity, by the Alps ; on which side no great high roads pass through it. Appenzell itself lies in a cul-de-sac of the mountains, except for such as will take the difficult paths over the high Alps and glaciers. On this account, it is but little visited by English travellers. It originally belonged to the league of Imperial Towns under a bailli, but in 1513 it joined the Swiss cantons as the 13th and last canton of Switzerland before 1708. The canton is divided into 2 parts or districts, called *Rhoden*, quite independent of each other, but enjoying only one vote at the diet. Outer Rhoden is a very thickly peopled district, having 8781 Inhab. to the Germ. sq. mile, who are Protestants. These are almost exclusively engaged in manufactures, chiefly of cotton, muslin, tambouring, &c. Inner Rhoden, on the contrary, is a land of herdsmen, and is Roman Catholic; its high and bleak mountains produce nothing but rich pasturage and sweet grass, upon which vast herds of cattle are fed. The government, in both states, is a pure democracy : the General Asembly, or Landesgemeinde, is composed of every male born in the canton. In travelling through this somewhat primitive district, two unusual objects may attract the traveller's attention,— the pillory, by the road-side, furnished with a collar (carcan), a hole for the neck, a padlock, and a chain ; and the bone-house, or *ossuaire*, in the churchyards, destined to receive the skulls and bones, which, after lying a certain number of years below ground, are dug up to make room for others; and, having been ticketed and labelled with the names of their owner, are laid out for show on shelves in the bone-house.

There is an appearance of prosperity, of cleanliness and neatness in

Ausser Rhoden, which is very pleasing. The green hill-sides to their very top are studded with cheerful looking houses, the dwellings of the peasants. The villages of Trogen, Teuffen, and Speicher are highly interesting, for, though the houses are of wood, they are tastily and comfortably built, and most of them with a well-tended garden before them. In fact many persons of ample fortune reside in these little towns, much of the Swiss muslin being made or embroidered here for St. Gall houses. Every cottage is filled with females assiduously busied in embroidery. But a remarkable change greets the traveller, on entering Roman Catholic Inner Rhoden, from Protestant Outer Rhoden. He exchanges cleanliness and industry for filth and beggary. What may be the cause of this is not a subject suitable for discussion here. The Appenzellers are passionately fond of gymnastic exercises; and a part of every holiday is devoted to wrestling and boxing matches. Hurling the stone is another frequent exercise. A mass of rock, varying in weight from half to a whole cwt., is poised on the shoulder, and then cast forward a distance of several feet. In 1805 a man of Urnäsch hurled a stone, weighing 184 lbs., 10 ft. The Appenzellers are also capital shots: rifle-matches are held in summer on almost every Sunday, and the cracking reports resound on all sides. The laws of the canton (especially of Outer Rhoden) restrict dancing to 3 or 4 days of the year; but, as the people are much addicted to this amusement, the law is frequently infringed, and the peasants will often cross the frontier of the canton in order to enjoy unmolested their favourite amusement.

There is a road from Appenzell to Herisau (Rte. 69) by Gonten.

About 2½ m. S.E. of Appenzell is *Weissbad*, a homely boarding-house and bathing establishment, situated in a beautiful and retired spot, at the foot of the Sentis, surrounded by grounds, from which walks lead up the mountains. The house is capable of accommodating 120 visitors, but the visitors and accommodation are inferior to those at Gais.

In addition to the cure of goats' whey, there are mineral springs as Weissbad, and the bath-houses contain 80 baths.

Excursions.— a. To the *Alpensee*, 1 hour's walk: very pretty scene, suited for ladies.

Three small torrents, the Bären (or Sentis)-bach E., the Schwändebach S., and the Weissbach W., issuing out of 3 Alpine valleys deeply furrowed in the sides of the Sentis, in whose glaciers they take their rise, unite at Weissbad, and form the river Sitter.

b. About 5 m. up the middle valley, 1½ hour's walk, is the singular hermitage and chapel of the *Wildkirchlein*. It is reached by crossing the Alpine pasture of the Bodmenalp, which, in spite of its elevation, is in summer a perfect garden, unfolding a treasure to the botanist, and affording the sweetest herbage to the cows.

In a recess scooped out of the face of a precipice, 170 ft. above these pastures, a little *chapel* has been perched. It was built 1756 by a pious inhabitant of Appenzell, and dedicated to St. Michael, and on that saint's day mass is celebrated here annually. A bearded Franciscan occupies the hermitage adjoining, and will conduct strangers through the long caverns hung with stalactites, which perforate the mountain behind his dwelling. The pilgrimage will be repaid by the charming prospect from the door which he opens.

Through this rocky vault is the sole outlet upon another fine pasturage, the Ebenalp, 5090 ft. above the sea-level, commanding a far more extensive and a different view, extending over the lake of Constance and the Suabian hills, 20 minutes' walk from Wildkirchlein.

c. The *Sentis*, the highest mountain in Appenzell, 8280 ft. above the sea-level, may be ascended from Weissbad in 6 hours. The view from the top is much extolled, and a panorama of it has been engraved. Various paths lead up to it; the best and easiest, which is also perfectly safe in the company of a guide, leads by way of the Meglisalp—*Inn*—(3 stunden); Wagenlücke (2 stunden); to the summit, where is an *Inn* (1 stunde), a walk of nearly 20 m.

d. From Weissbad to the top of the Kamor, called *Hohkasten*, is a walk of about 2¼ hours. From the top (a small *Inn*) is a fine view over the Rhine valley, part of the Lake of Constance, the Alps of Vorarlberg. There is a path from Weissbad by Brüllisau, and thence by the Kamor or by the Hohkasten, to Sennewald in the Rheinthal, in 5 hours.

The paths are not easy to find without a guide. The summit of the *Kamor* commands a remarkable panorama. Even from the paths to Sennewald, the traveller has a delightful prospect over the Sentis and Canton Appenzell on one side, and over the lake of Constance, Tyrol, and the Rhine, on the other. A 3rd path leads over to Sax in the Rheinthal from the lower end of the Fakler See at the head of the Säntisthal.

A steep and rather difficult but not dangerous path, commanding some fine views, leads S. over the ridge of the Sentis by the Krayalp from Weissbad to Wildhaus, the birthplace of Zwingli, in Toggenburg (Rte. 71), in 7 hrs.; whence in another day Wesen, or Wallenstadt, may be reached. The paths are difficult to find without a guide.

ROUTE 69.

ST. GALL TO RAPPERSCHWYL, BY HEINRICHSBAD AND HERISAU.

4¾ posts = 39 Eng. m.

	Posts.	Eng. m.
St. Gall.		
Herisau	1½	= 11
Wattwyl . . .	1¼	= 10
Uznach	1	= 9
Rapperschwyl . .	1	= 9

Diligences daily. Time shorter by Wyl.

About 2 m. from St. Gall, a little beyond the village of Bruggen, the road crosses the gorge of the Sitter by the magnificent *Krätzeren Brücke*, a bridge 590 ft. long, and 85 ft. above the stream, built 1810. A little after we enter canton Appenzell.

[About a mile to the E. of Herisau is the watering-place called *Heinrichsbad*. The *Badhaus* is the most elegant establishment of the sort in Switzerland, after Schintznach, surrounded by agreeable pleasure-grounds, the creation of one Heinrich Steiger, a rich manufacturer. Two springs rising out of gravel, and variously impregnated with iron, carbonic acid, &c., are used for drinking, and to supply the baths. Goats' whey and asses' milk are also furnished to those invalids for whom they are prescribed. Accommodation in a cowhouse is provided for invalids suffering from diseases of the chest. The neighbourhood is exceedingly picturesque.]

Herisau—Inns: Löwe (Lion), the best; Hecht (Brochet)—the industrious chief village of Ausser-Rhoden, contains 8387 Inhab., stands 2334 ft. above the sea, and is advantageously situated at the junction of two streams, the Glatt and Brühlbach, which turns the wheels of its numerous manufactories. It is a very singular place from its extraordinary irregularity of construction. There are beautiful walks on the surrounding heights; two of them are topped by ruinous castles, the Rosenberg and Rosenburg, which, according to the story, were once connected together by a leathern bridge. The lower part of the *Church Tower*, in which the Archives are deposited, is the oldest building in the canton, dating probably from the 7th century.

The articles chiefly manufactured here are muslins, cottons, and silk, the last a recent introduction: 10,200 persons are employed in Ausser-Rhoden in weaving muslins, and a very large number in embroidering them.

The *Hundswyler Tobel*, a very singular gorge or chasm, deep and wild, about 3½ m. from Herisau, deserves to be visited.

There is a direct road from Herisau to Appenzell (Rte. 68), by Waldstadt (1¾ hours); Urnäsch (1½), and Gonten (1): in all 5 stunden = 16¼ m.

Schönengrund. •

Through an undulating country, we reach the frontier of Appenzell, and re-enter that of its grasping neighbour, St. Gall, before arriving at

Peterzell: 3 m. beyond the ruined Castle of Neu-Toggenburg lies

Lichtensteig, (*Inn:* Krone,) a town. of 744 Inhab. on the rt. bank of the Thur, the ancient county of Toggenburg. A picturesque and handsome old *Place*, composed of lofty buildings with porticoes, forms the principal street.

Wattwyl (*Inns:* Lion d'Or; Rössli), a pretty manufacturing village, about 1½ m. farther, stand the convent of Santa Maria and the Castle of Iberg.

The road soon after surmounts the steep ascent of the ridge of Himmelwald. From its top a beautiful prospect expands to view; in front the lake of Zürich, with the castle, town, and bridge of Rapperschwyl, in full relief on its margin; behind it the pine-clad and snow-topped Alps of Schwytz and Glarus; on the E. the remarkable peaks of the Sieben Kühfirsten, and behind the fertile vale of Toggenburg (Rte. 71). The road divides on the opposite side of the hill.

Utznach.

Rapperschwyl (Rte. 14).

ROUTE 71.

WYL TO COIRE.   THE TOGGENBURG.

7⅜ posts = 62 Eng. m.

	Posts.	Eng. m.
Wyl.		
Wattwyl . . .	1⅜	= 12¼
Neu St. Johann .	⅞	= 7⅜
Wildhaus . . .	1⅛	= 10
Sewelen. . . .	1¼	= 11¼
Coire	2¾	= 24⅜

Diligence 2 or 3 times a-week. *Post road.*

Wyl on the Railway (Rte. 10).

The road, after leaving Wyl, continues on the l. bank of the Thur, to Dietfurth, where it crosses the river to *Lichtensteig* and *Wattwyl* (Rte. 69).

Ebnat (Inn: Pfau).—*Toggenburg,* as the long and fertile valley of the Thur is called, extends for nearly 40 m., from Wyl up to the source of that river, and a splendid specimen of a Swiss valley it is, embracing within its range almost all the various features of Alpine scenery, save that there is scarcely a tract of level alluvial bottom to be found in its whole extent; its sides being everywhere steep or undulating. It is bounded by high mountains; on the N. by the Sentis, and on the S. by the peaks of the Kurfürsten. It was anciently governed by counts of its own. When their line became extinct, 1436, the district was claimed by canton Zürich, and a memorable war on the subject ensued, in which the Swiss cantons for the first time fought with one another. It finally, in 1460, fell to the abbot of St. Gall, whose successors had continual disputes with the inhabitants, especially after the Reformation. In 1712 the abbots, after much fighting, were expelled, but restored in 1718. Since 1803, the Toggenburg has formed part of canton St. Gall. It is thickly peopled; its inhabitants, an industrious race, are chiefly occupied with the manufacture of muslin and cotton.

Neslau.—Inn : Krone.

Neu St. Johann. An extra horse up the ascent.

Upon the high ground dividing the valley of the Thur from that of the Rhine, stands the remote village

Wildhaus — (*Inn :* Sonne, Hirsch), 3450 ft. above the level of the sea, and at the S. base of the Sentis. It is remarkable as the birthplace of the Swiss reformer, Ulrich Zwingli. The house in which he first saw the light (Jan. 1, 1484) still exists; it is an humble cottage of wood; its walls formed of the stems of trees, its roof weighed down by stones to protect it from the wind. It has resisted the inroads of time for more than 350 years; and the beams and trunks which compose it are black with age. Zwingli's family were humble peasants; he quitted home when 10 years old, to go to school at Bâle.

[There is a pass, difficult but not dangerous, over the Kray Alp from Wildhaus to Appenzell.]

The road descends into the valley of the Rhine near Grabs, and soon after reaches

Werdenberg, which, with the following stations, is described in Rte. 67.

Coire (Rte. 67).

ROUTE 72.

LACHEN OR WESEN TO GLARUS, THE
BATHS OF STACHELBERG. — PASS OF
THE KLAUSEN TO ALTORF.

	Posts.	Miles.
Wesen		
Glarus	1	= 9
Linth-thal . . .	1¼	= 13¼

Diligences leave Lachen and Wesen (Rte. 14) for Glarus on the arrival of the diligence from Zürich (2 fr. 40.) It is a drive of 1½ hour from Wesen to Glarus; 2 hours more to Lint-thal.

Lachen (*Inn :* Ours) is a village of 1200 Inhab., on the margin of the Lake of Zürich, where coaches to Zürich, Schwytz, and St. Gall cross and take on passengers.

The canton of Glarus, or Glaris, consists of one great Alpine valley, and of several secondary or tributary valleys, branching off from it, and penetrating deep into the high Alps. There is but one carriage-road into it, which terminates, after a distance of 6½ leagues = 19½ Eng. m., at the baths of Stachelberg ; and for carriages there is no egress save the portal which has admitted the traveller. It is a truly Alpine district, abounding in very wild scenery.

The road from Wesen crosses the Linth canal (Rte. 14) by the Ziegelbrücke, and enters the jaws of the valley of Glarus, flanked by precipices almost perpendicular, and backed by the vast mass and snowy head of the Glärnisch Mountain.

[The road from Zürich and Rapperschwyl to Glarus passes through Lachen on the S. side of the Lake of Zürich, and along the l. bank of the Linth canal to Nieder-Urnen, where that from Wesen joins it.]

Näfels—(Inns: Hirsch ;—Schwerdt) —in the gorge of the valley, a village of 1800 Inhab., and the chief place in the Roman Catholic division of the canton, is a Swiss *battle-field* of some celebrity. 11 simple stones, set up on the meadow of Reuti, hard by, mark the spot where, in 1388, 1300 men of Glarus met a force of 6000 Austrians, who, having taken Wesen by treachery, had burst into the canton, ravaging and plundering the country as they advanced. When tidings of this reached the ears of Matthias am Buhl, the lands-captain, he hastily collected a handful of shepherds, and not only checked the career of the foragers, in spite of the disproportion of numbers, but after 11 distinct charges, aided by volleys of stones and rocks discharged from precipices above, which threw the Austrian cavalry into confusion, finally repulsed the invaders, with a loss of 2500 of their number left dead on the field.

The anniversary of the fight of

Näfels is still celebrated through the canton by an annual festival. An engagement took place at Näfels, in 1799, between the Austrians and French.

From *Möllis*, the village opposite Näfels, the river Linth is conducted into the lake of Wallenstadt by the artificial canal constructed by Escher (see p. 33). In the churchyard of Mollis the heroes of Näfels are buried.

The valley of the Linth is subject to much danger and injury from its sudden rises, and the swelling of its tributary torrents. The broad fringe of unsightly sand and gravel visible on both sides of the Linth, the common drain of the district, will show what mischief that river occasions after storms of rain, and during the melting of the snows. The whole of the lower part of the valley is at times converted into a lake; and the little patches of ground, which have cost the peasant much hard labour and care to cultivate, are at once overwhelmed and ruined. The limestone mountains of this district abound in caverns, which serve as reservoirs for the melting glaciers. In the spring and early summer, the rocks appear to stream from every pore, while every gorge and hollow sends forth a raging torrent.

Glarus was formerly subject to the Abbey of Sächingen, to which rights Austria succeeded. Glarus joined the Swiss cantons in 1352, and after the battle of Näfels gained partially its independence; and towards the end of the 11th centy. the canton honestly purchased their feudal rights of Austria, and finally made peace with Austria. The Reformation divided the canton and occasioned severe struggles and fighting. In 1798 the canton lost several dependencies. It contains 30,000 Inhab.; 26,000 Prot., 4000 Roman Catholics, all speaking German.

Glarus (Glaris, Fr.)—(*Inns:* Aigle d'Or, fair; Rabe). This little village, the capital of the canton, is chiefly remarkable for its secluded situation at the base of the Glärnisch and Schilt, encompassed and shut in by the Alps, whose bare and bleak precipices and tops contrast remarkably with the milder verdure about their base. The inhabitants, 4320 in number, are distinguished by their industry and enterprise, which has converted Glarus into a place of manufactures, especially of cotton, printing of muslins, &c. They are reported to retain that simplicity of manners which their seclusion from the rest of the world would lead one to expect.

They possess a *Club* (Casino), a modern house of fine masonry, and a *Free School* for 700 children, erected by private subscriptions, and reflecting much credit on the public spirit of the citizens. The houses, chiefly of stone, and many of them ancient, are frequently ornamented outside with fresco paintings, and contrast strikingly with the huge modern factories in the neighbourhood. In the old *Rathhaus* is some fine painted glass, and enormous horns of steinbock decorate the antechamber. The Gothic *church* is open to Protestant and Romanist alike. Zwingli was the pastor here, 1506 to 1546. The Linth is crossed by two bridges.

The name *Glarus* is said to be a corruption of *Hilarius*, a saint to whom a shrine was built among these mountains at a very early period.

The *green cheese* called *Schabzieger* is peculiar to the canton Glarus. It owes its peculiar appearance, smell, and flavour, to an herb (Melilotus cærulea; blue melilot; Germ. Honigklee), which is partly cultivated for this purpose in gardens within the canton, and partly imported from others. To fit it for use, it is dried, ground to powder, and, in that state, mixed with the curds, in the proportion of 3 lbs. of the herb to 100 lbs. of curds. The cheese is said to be made of cows' milk, like any common cheese, and not of goats'. The curds are brought down from the high pastures into the valley in sacks, and, after having a due proportion of herb incorporated with them, are ground in a mill resembling that used for making cider. After being thoroughly kneaded by this process for an hour or two, it is fit for pressing. The cheese is ripe for use after a twelvemonth's keeping. A large quantity of it is exported to America; and the manufacture of it is considered a lucrative trade. The natives attribute its peculiar character to some virtue in the pastures on which the cows are fed.

It is a pleasant 2½ hrs. drive from Glarus to *Obstalden* or Narexen, where is a fine view over the whole lake of Wallenstadt and part of that of Zürich. A broad road leads thither from Mollis. N.B. The charge for horses, guides, and porters in the valley of Glarus is very high, and the beasts are very bad.

Many mountain paths ramify in various directions from Glarus.

a. The Pragel pass (Rte. 75) by the Klönthal; a beautiful pastoral valley: the finest part of it is not more than 8 m. from Glarus, and may be reached in a char.

b. The pass of the *Klausen* to Altorf. —(Described below.)

c. 4 passes into the Valley of the Vorder Rhine:—

(1) To Disentis over the *Sand Alp.* About 12 hrs. walk. The path crosses the snow, but is said to be neither difficult and dangerous. The head of the pass is 9000 feet (?) above the sea. From the châlets of the Kaurein, about half way between the Sand Alp and Disentis, a little-known pass leads over glaciers into the Maderaner Thal.

(2) To Brigels, by the *Limmernthal* and *Kistengrat* (Rte. 73).

(3) To Panix, by the *Panixer pass* (Rte. 76).

(4) To Flims, by the *Segnes pass* (Rte. 76).

d. The most interesting excursion is that to Lint-thal and Stachelberg, up the valley of the Linth, where first the Glärnisch, and, higher up, the Dödi, with its snowy satellites, are objects of extreme grandeur and beauty.

A good road leads up the valley of the Linth, 13 m. to the village of *Lint-thal* (*Inn :* Löwe. Resorted to only by the peasantry of the neighbourhood.) The Diligence crosses the river below Lint-thal, and will leave or call for strangers proceeding to the handsome *Hotel* and

Baths of *Stachelberg,* an excellent and most comfortable house, built on an eminence on the opposite side of the Linth, surrounded by torrents, rocks, and glaciers. It has greatly risen in repute as a watering-place, and on account of the exquisite beauty of its situation, and the virtues of its concentrated alkaline sulphureous *spring,* which distils, drop by drop, from a fissure in the Braunberg, is much resorted to. The period of the "cure" is fixed at between 20 and 24 days. The hotel is surrounded by walks and pleasure-grounds. It is resorted to by a mob of holiday-makers on Sundays, when the house is very noisy. An interesting expedition may be made hence to the little-visited glacier of Bisserten.

About 1 m. from Lint-thal is the Fall of the *Fätschbach.* About 1 hr. above Lint-thal is the fine *fall* of the *Schreyenbach,* of the Staubbach kind, which when seen from below appears to issue from the sky. At the bottom it spreads over 30 yards of rock, coming down in a shower of water-rockets.

Above the baths the vale of the Linth becomes grander and more savage, and at length contracts into a chasm, low in the depths of which the river worms its way, while a narrow and steep path alone leads along the edge of the precipice. 5 miles up (2 hours' walk), at a spot where the gorge is deepest, was a singularly bold bridge of a single arch of stone, 20 ft. span, and 140 ft. above the torrent, and 400 years old. This was the *Pantenbrücke,* an object of considerable romantic beauty. It was swept away by an avalanche, 1852, and is replaced by a wooden bridge. The gorge above the bridge becomes even more romantic and wild; it is surpassed by few in the Alps. 2 hrs. walk above the bridge brings you to the foot of the *Dödi Glacier.* The path runs near the stream all the way. About ½ hr.'s climb in zigzag up the base of the Dödi brings you to the "Sand Alp," whence is a striking view of the valley you have traversed; a verdant basin encircled with peaks. No guide is needed.

The Gorge, ¼ hour's walk above the Pantenbrücke, is one of the grandest in the Alps.

The valley of the Linth terminates in a group of magnificent mountains, whose tops are occupied by vast fields of never-trodden glaciers. The Dödi or Todiberg (11,880 ft.) is the giant of this portion of the chain of Alps, and its summit has been rarely ascended. Six persons only have reached the top. No Englishman. The guides ask 100 fr. A difficult and dangerous path, practicable only in the height of summer, leads across these glaciers to Disentis, over the Clariden-Grat.

Klausen Pass—Stachelberg to Altorf.

Stachelberg.	h.	m.
Summit	4	15
Unterschächen . .	2	0
Spiringen	1	0
Altorf	1	15
	9	30

Charge for a horse from Stachelberg to the summit, 12 fr.; to Altorf, 24 fr. and a trinkgeld. The path is so well marked that guides may be dispensed with; it is practicable for horses. It turns out of the valley of the Linth to the W. at Aue, about a mile above the baths, and ascends the valley of the Fätsch, or Urner Boden, keeping along its l. bank; a very stiff pull of 1¾ hours. Within a mile above the junction of the Fätsch and Linth, the valley belongs to canton Uri. It abounds in fine mountain pastures, and many of the inhabitants of the Schächen-thal pass their summer here among the cows. Urner Boden is a scattered hamlet of 80 houses, with a church, extending the whole length of the valley. The culminating point, or Klausen pass, is a ridge of 6150 ft. high, connecting the snowy chain of the Clariden Alps on the S. with the shattered Zingel, Glatten, and Camli. On the top stands a little chapel. A little further on the path divides, leading l. by a rapid descent, or straight on along the higher level until it falls in with that from the Kinzig Culm, and descends upon Spi-

ringen. This, though the longest, is said to be less fatiguing: it is probably also the less beautiful track.

The other and more frequented path descends by long and steep zigzags, by the rocks of the Balmwand, into the *Schächen-thal;* on the l. hand is seen the very pretty cascade of the *Stäubi.* Opposite the chapel of St. Anne a bergfall occurred in 1833, which arrested for some time the course of the Schächen, and produced a small lake. At the village of

Unter Schächen, the first on the Uri side (a small *Inn*), another branch of the valley opens S., and sends forth the main stream of the Schächen, which some consider to rise from the Stäubi. The Spitze, the mountain on the l. bank of the torrent, discharges dangerous avalanches in spring. At *Spiringen,* and a little lower down, near the chapel of St. Anthony, there are inns, tolerably good for this country. It was over the steep and barely accessible ridge of the *Kinzig Culm* (Rte. 79), which walls in this portion of the valley to Muotta, that Suwarrow's memorable retreat was conducted, 1799.

Bürglen, the birthplace of Tell, stands at the mouth of the Schächenthal. (Rte. 34.)

Altorf (Rte. 34).

ROUTE 73.

STACHELBERG TO BRIGELS, OVER THE KISTENGRAT.

" After crossing the Pantenbrücke (Rte. 72), which is nearly 2 hrs.' good walking from the baths of Stachelberg, the path over the Kistengrat turns rather sharply to the l., and ascends through pleasant woods and green pasturages for a time. 2½ hrs. from the Pantenbrücke, always rising, brings you to the summit of the little secluded nook in which the châlet of the Limern Alp, the highest belonging to the Lint-thal, is built. It consists of 3 miserable hovels of loose stones, one a piece for the cows, the goats, and the men. This is separated from the black precipitous face of the Selbsauft Mountain by a deep chasm, the bottom of which can scarcely be seen from the edge. Here a man and 2 boys, with 3 or 4 cows and some goats, pass 3 months of the year in seclusion, taking with them their supply of flour and bread. After quitting the Limern Alp, there was no semblance of a path, and the snow, which in the middle of the day before had been declared by the guide and peasantry to be quite impassable from its softness, had become early in the morning so hard and icy as to be nearly impassable in the steeper parts from its slipperiness; so great is the difference made by a few hours. It took us quite 5½ hrs. to go from the châlet on the Limern Alp to the village of Brigels, and of these 3½ were on the snow. We passed close by the Mütten See, leaving it on our left. It was then a mass of snow and ice, no water being visible. In a different state of the snow a path is sometimes taken across a lower part of the mountain, leaving the Mütten See on the right, but it was too steep and slippery for us to attempt. We crossed a higher part of the mountain by aid of the solitary foot-tracks of some shepherd, (made when the snow was softer, as the guide said, in search of some lost sheep,) and which we luckily discovered just at the steepest part, where a slip would have carried one down over a precipice of unknown depth. The views of the distant Alps from the summit are very fine, and the descent into the valley of the Vorder Rhine, near Brigels, affords one continuous view of that valley from above Disentis, almost to its junction with the valley of the Hinter Rhine, and is also very fine; but the expedition was hardly worth the trouble and danger, although it enabled me to see the upper part of

the Lint-Thal and the Pantenbrücke, and the greater part of the valley of the Vorder Rhine, without returning on my footsteps. Much depends on the season, the weather, and the state of the snow; but it is at least 9 hrs. from the baths of Stachelberg to Brigels, and one should start at ½ past 4, or at latest 5, o'clock in the morning. The Auberge at Brigels is poor. The village itself was nearly destroyed by fire a few years since, and many of the houses are new. The châlet on the Limern Alp is a little out of the way, and it would save time to carry refreshment and avoid it."

ROUTE 74.

WESEN OR RICHTERSCHWYL TO SCHWYTZ — EINSIEDELN — MORGARTEN.

	Miles.
Wesen to Lachen	15
Lachen to Schindelezi . . .	8
Richterschwyl to Schindelezi	3
Schindelezi to Rothenthurm .	7
Rothenthurm to Schwytz .	8

Total, Wesen to Schwytz, 38 m.; Richterschwyl to Schwytz, 18 m.

Diligence from Richterschwyl to Schwytz, and from Wesen to Lachen.

The road from Wesen after crossing the Linth keeps by the side of the hills to Lachen ; then passes through Pfäffikon near the long bridge of Rapperschyl, and soon afterwards begins to ascend the steep slope of the *Etzel* or Teusisberg, and crosses the Sihl at Schindeleri, ascending again. Many delightful views are obtained in ascending, over the lake of Zürich, and the summit commands a good view of the Mythen (Mitres), Rigi, and other mountains in that direction. The holy hermit Meinrad, the founder of Einsiedeln, originally fixed himself on the top of the Etzel, but the concourse of people attracted to the spot by his reputation for holiness drove him in search of solitude deep into the wilderness. A little *chapel* stands on the spot supposed to have been occupied by his cell. Near it is an inn. From this chapel the first view of Einsiedeln is obtained; the descent thither occupies 1½ hour.

[The road from Richterschwyl immediately begins to ascend and joins the other at Schindelezi.]

A mile and a half from Schindelezi is

Biberbrücke. Here the road to Einsiedeln turns off.

[The road is studded at intervals with chapels called *stations*, each containing a representation of some event in the Passion of our Lord, according to the Romish tradition, at which the pilgrims may stop and tell their beads.

EINSIEDELN (French, Notre Dame des Erémites; Lat., Monasterium Eremitarum). *Inns:* there are 55 inns and 20 alehouses here, mostly designed for the reception of poor pilgrims, and distinguished by a singular variety of signs. The best is the Hirsch (Cerf), clean and good; the charges are raised during the pilgrimage.—Pfau (Paon); good.—Adam and Eve.

The Abbey of Einsiedeln, which forms the nucleus of a village of a few hundred inhabitants, is situated on a naked undulating plain 3000 ft. above the sea, producing little but pasture. It is partly sheltered by a range of wooded hills on the S.E.

The *Monastery* itself, an extensive building in the modern Italian style, is imposing, less from its architecture than its size and its situation in so remote and naked a solitude. The existing edifice dates from the 18th century (1719), and is the 6th or 7th raised on this spot since the first foundation of the abbey, the others having been destroyed by fire. It occupies a stately site upon the hill side, separated from the humbler buildings of the village by a wide square.

The origin of the abbey is thus ac-counted for in the histories published under the authority of the monks :—In the days of Charlemagne a holy anchorite named Meinrad, of the noble house of Hohenzollern, repaired to this remote wilderness (then called the Finsterwald) to end his days in solitude and prayer, devoting himself to tend a little black image of the Virgin which had been given to him by St. Hildegarde, abbess of Zürich. This holy man was murdered by two robbers in 861; but their foul deed, which they had hoped would escape detection on a spot so remote from the haunts of men, was brought to light by two pet ravens reared by Meinrad, which pursued the murderers with croaking cries, and flapping wings, over hill and dale, as far as Zürich, where their guilt was detected, and they suffered for it on the place now occupied by the Raven inn. The reputation of sanctity, however, surrounding the spot where the saint had lived, increased so much after his death, that his cell was rebuilt, and a church founded by a community of Benedictine hermits (Einsiedlern). The first abbot was Eberard, and it is affirmed by the monkish legend, and perpetuated in the bull of Pope Pius VIII., that when the Bishop of Constance was about to consecrate the church on the 14th of September, 948, he was aroused at midnight by the sounds of angelic minstrelsy, and was informed next day, by a voice from heaven, that there was no need for him to proceed with the sacred rite, as the church had been already consecrated by the powers of heaven, and by the presence of the Saviour! The Pope pronounced this a true miracle, and, in consideration of it, granted plenary indulgence to all pilgrims who should repair to the shrine of Our Lady of the Hermits, in the words inscribed upon the church, "Hic est plena remissio peccatorum à culpâ et à pœnâ." The consequence of this has been that during 9 centuries there has been an almost uninterrupted influx of pilgrims from the surrounding countries to this shrine, and of wealth to the monastery. In process of time these pious bene-factions increased its revenues and domains to an enormous extent ; it ranked second to St. Gall alone of all the monasteries in Switzerland. Its abbot became a prince of the holy Roman empire, with a seat in the diet. He had his hereditary officers, his chamberlain, marshal, and cup-bearer ; and these posts were filled by personages of noble or princely rank. He also enjoyed the right of criminal jurisdiction and the power of life and death in several parishes and circles. Down to the 16th century the abbots themselves were of noble families.

The French revolutionary invaders of 1798 stripped Einsiedeln of its re-sources and treasures, and carried off the figure of the Virgin to Paris ; but the monks, on abandoning the con-vent, transported with them into Ty-rol a duplicate figure, which they assert to be the authentic original. Notwithstanding these untoward cir-cumstances, the abbey remains at the present day the richest in Switzer-land, and the Black Virgin, whether an original or a copy, has lost none of her reputation. The average annual number of pilgrims who receive the sacrament in the church is 150,000. In the course of the year 1700 there were 202,000 ; in 1834, 36,000 pil-grims repaired to the shrine within a fortnight. Every parish of canton Schwytz, and most of the other Roman Catholic cantons, send an annual deputation hither, headed by the landamman and the authorities. The Roman Catholics of Switzerland, in-deed, for the most part, make 2 or 3 journeys hither in the course of their lives. Many of the pilgrims are de-puties paid by others, wealthier sin-ners, to do penance for their princi-pals, who remain at home, and a pilgrimage thus performed by proxy is rendered equally efficacious with one made in person.

In 1835 the convent contained 77 monks of the Benedictine order, in-cluding lay-brothers, novices, &c.

In the square in front of the convent stands a fountain with 14 jets of water, from all of which the pilgrims drink, as it is traditionally reported that our Saviour drank from one, but from which of them is not known. In the centre of the pile of conventual buildings stands, as is usual in Be-nedictine monasteries, the *Church*, which has been compared with that of St. John Lateran at Rome. The interior is somewhat gaudily orna-mented with inferior paintings, marble and gilding. A few feet from the entrance stands the *Shrine* or *Chapel of the Virgin*, of black marble, with a grating in front, through which, by the glare of an ever-burning lamp, the spectator perceives the palladium of the temple, a little black figure of the Virgin and Child, attired in gold bro-cade, glittering with jewels, and bear-ing crowns of gold on their heads. The space in front of the shrine is rarely free of worshippers, and com-monly hundreds, nay, at times, thou-sands of devotees may be seen pros-trate before it. The walls of this part of the church are covered with votive tablets, rude paintings in oil, on which no kind of accident or misfortune is omitted, though they are chiefly de-voted to representations of escapes from fire and water, all effected by the supposed miraculous interference of the image. Its influence, however, is not limited to incidents of private life; many of the great events of history, such as the victory of the Roman Ca-tholic cantons at Kappel, are classed among the triumphant interpositions of our Lady of the Hermits. 250 new votive tablets were hung up in 1835, older ones being removed to make way for them.

In the *Chapel of the Magdalene*, a church of itself in size, on the l. of the choir, are 28 confessionals, over each of which is written the language in which confessions will be received in it, either German, Italian, French, or Romansch.

The *Treasury*, once so rich in church plate, was plundered by the French in 1798, and one splendid monstrance alone remains, but it is not readily shown. The monastery includes, be-sides the lodgings for the Abbot and the brethren, a handsome refectory, a kitchen, an hospital, a *library* containing 26,000 vols., a museum containing some fossils and minerals, a free school and boarding-school, the pupils of which are taught by the monks, and a large cellar running under the greater part of the edifice. During meals, passages of some approved author, such as Lingard's History of England, Cobbett's History of the Reformation, &c., are read aloud to the assembled brotherhood, and even at times portions of newspapers.

Zwingli, the reformer, was curate of Einsiedeln from 1516 to 1519. Theophrastus Paracelsus von Hohenheim was born here, or in the neighbourhood, in 1498.

There is a rough foot path under the Mythenberg (Mitres hill), called the *Hacken*, by Alpthal, from Einsiedeln to Schwytz, shorter than the carriage-road. It takes 4½ hrs. to walk : a guide is needed. Near the top is an inn, from which the peak, called *Hochstückli* (4470 ft.), is ¼ hr's. walk.

The carriage - road to Schwytz makes, at first, a considerable détour : the footpath is shorter, crossing the Katzenstrick, a large tract of upland meadow or common, direct to Altmatt.]

Rothenthurm (*Inn* dirty and extortionate ; it is better to stop at Lachen), a village of nearly 800 Inhab., is the place of meeting of the general assembly of the canton Schwytz, convened here every two years, in the open air, on the first fine Sunday in May. The Landamman is president, and every citizen above the age of 18 has a vote. These meetings afford no favourable specimen of the working of universal suffrage, as they frequently terminate in rioting and violence. For example, in May, 1838, 9000 voters collected here ; the show of hands was declared to be in favour of the government ; but the Liberal party being dissatisfied with the result, a battle ensued, in which the hustings were broken and many persons much injured. The democrats, enraged at their defeat, published a manifesto, calling on the "Liberals to meet in

their districts, and expel the rich from their assemblies as their ancestors expelled Gessler, since the government of the rich has become a government of murderers."

Rothenthurm receives its name from a Red Tower still standing and forming part of the defences of a long wall or rampart (letze), erected by the Schwytzers along their W. frontier, to ward off the inroads of their lordly and lawless neighbours. It extended hence as far as Arth.

About 2 m. W. of Rothenthurm, on the confines of the canton of Zug, and on the margin of the small lake of Egeri, is MORGARTEN, memorable in Swiss annals as the scene of their first struggle for independence; as the spot where the chivalry of Austria were worsted, and their leader, Duke Leopold, compelled to fly with disgrace, on the 15th of November, 1315, 8 years after the expulsion of the Austrian bailiffs. Fired with the hope of revenge and with feelings of hereditary hatred, the duke led on his mail-clad cavalry along the narrow strand between the lake and the hills. Just where the ascent into the upland country of Schwytz commences, running up a narrow defile, the Austrians were met by the confederates, a mere handful of men in comparison with their host, but of hardy frame and resolute spirit, posted on the ridge of the Sattel, near Haselmatt. The first bold charge of the Swiss, rushing on with swords and clubs, was aided by a discharge of rocks from the heights above, which quickly threw into confusion the ranks of heavy-armed knights. They attempted to fall back, but their evolutions were prevented by the infantry pressing on in their rear. Without room to manœuvre, or even to turn (for the naturally confined margin of the lake was at that time diminished by an unusual increase of its waters), the proud knights were totally at the mercy of their light-armed foes. Many, in order to escape the sword, perished by plunging into the lake ; the rush of the cavalry overwhelmed the infantry behind, and in a short time the whole army was thrown into panic and disorder. The Austrians lost the flower of their nobility, and Leopold with difficulty escaped. This astounding victory, the Marathon of Swiss history, was gained in 1¼ hr., over a force of 20,000 well-armed men, by 1300 mountaineers, who now for the first time met an army in the field.

The appropriate memorial of their success erected by the Swiss was, according to custom, a *Chapel*, dedicated to St. James; and service is performed in it annually, on the anniversary of the fight. It is still standing on an eminence above the lake, at the foot of the hill of Morgarten, close to the village of Schorno, by the road-side as you descend from Rothenthurm.

The little village of *Biberegg*, on the opposite (E.) side of Rothenthurm, was the cradle of the family of Reding, one of the oldest and noblest in the canton, and whose name appears oftener with credit than any other. There is scarcely a battle in which they are not mentioned, and they have 45 times filled the office of landamman, the highest in the state. In 1798 Aloys Reding, a hero worthy of such an ancestry, led on the brave inhabitants of these mountains to oppose, in defence of their liberties and constitution, a far outnumbering force of French under General Schauenberg. The Swiss met the invaders in the valley of Rothenthurm, and drove them back as far as the lake of Egeri and the field of their ancient victory of Morgarten. This proved but a temporary gleam of success. Their victory had cost them so large a number of men, that they were unable to renew the contest; and an overwhelming force of French marching into the canton rendered all further resistance hopeless.

A long descent, commanding a fine view of Schwytz, of the singular and picturesque Mythen (Mitre) mountains behind it, and of the lake of Lowertz, with part of the fall of the Rossberg (Rte. 17), leads through Sattel, past the chapel of Ecce Homo, to *Steinen*, a small village, having two *Inns* (Rössli, Krone), memorable as the

birthplace of Werner Stauffacher, one of the three conspirators of the Grütli, nearly 4 hours' drive from Einsiedeln. A small *chapel*, adorned with rude frescoes of scenes from his life, and the battle of Morgarten, is dedicated to his memory. It was built in 1400. The *Bonehouse* is as old as 1111.

Schwytz. (Rte. 17.)

Travellers bound from Einsiedeln to the Rigi or Lucerne need not enter Schwytz. Soon after leaving Steinen, a path branching off to the rt. leads, in about 1¼ hour, to Goldau (Rte. 17).

ROUTE 75.

SCHWYTZ TO GLARUS, BY MUOTTA, THE PRAGEL PASS, AND THE KLÖNTHAL.

Schwytz.	hrs. m.
Muotta	3 0
Highest cross	2 30
Col Pragel	0 30
Vorauen	2 0
Glarus	2 15
	10 15

(These times are for good walking from Muotta. Horses would take longer.)

A very rough char-road ascends the valley as far as Muotta, and the char is slower and more fatiguing than the walk would be. There is also a footpath from Schwytz by which Muotta may be reached in 2¼ hrs. The road crosses the plain to Ibach, a village of scattered houses at the mouth of the Muotta Thal, which here assumes the character of a contracted gorge; higher up it opens out, and exhibits considerable capabilities for cultivation. The road ascends the l. bank of the stream, traversing Ober Schönenbach, down to which point the Russians, under Suwarrow, drove the French commanded by Massena, Mortier, and Soult, in his desperate attempt to force his way through them to join the Russian army at Zürich, in 1799. The stone bridge (long since swept away by the torrent and replaced by a covered wooden bridge at a higher elevation) near this, which carried the road over to the rt. bank, was taken and retaken many times ; the mingled blood of the two nations crimsoned the stream which swept down their floating bodies.

Beyond *Ried* there is another bridge, near which is a pretty waterfall, and a third brings the traveller to

Muotta, or *Mütten* (a neat and cheap little *Inn*, Zum Hirsch—between the church and the bridge), the principal village of the valley, on the rt. bank of the stream. The parish contains 1480 Inhab. In the neighbourhood is the *Nunnery of St. Joseph*, a very ancient and primitive convent, founded 1280. The sisters are poor, and their mode of living homely; they make their own clothes and their own hay; the superior is called Frau Mutter. They receive visits from strangers without the intervention of a grating, and will even give a lodging to a respectable traveller. Whoever avails himself of this must remember that the convent is too poor to afford gratuitous hospitality. They speak no French.

From Muotta a path leads by the Kinzig Culm to Altorf. It was by this path that Suwarrow brought his troops (Rte. 79).

On the night of Sept. 27th and 28th, 1799, the inhabitants of the remote and peaceful valley of Muotta were surprised by the arrival of an army of an unknown nation and tongue, whose very name many of them had never heard, which came pouring down upon their cottages and green fields from the heights of the Kinzig Culm, by paths and precipices usually resorted to only by a solitary shepherd. These were the 24,000 Russians under Suwarrow, whose previous march out of Italy has already been detailed in Rtes. 34 and 72. Here the general first heard the news of the defeat of Korsakow and the main Russian army at Zürich. He at first gave no credence to the report, and would have hung the peasant who communicated it as a spy and traitor, but for the intercession of the lady mother of St. Joseph's nunnery. He was now beset on all sides; part of Lecourbe's division followed his rear, Molitor occupied the summit of the Muotta Thal, and Mortier and Massena blocked up its mouth. The bold attempt to cut his way out, through the forces of the latter general, was defeated, as already mentioned, chiefly by the unexpected arrival of a fresh reinforcement under Lecourbe in person, though with vast loss to the French. The veteran conqueror was compelled, for the first time in his career, to order a retreat, and to adopt the only alternative of crossing the Pragel into Glarus. The detachments of Molitor's advanced guard were quickly driven in before him, and the greater portion made prisoners. Suwarrow's rear-guard, however, encumbered with sick and wounded, was greatly harassed by Massena; but the republicans were again repulsed with loss, and driven back nearly to Schwytz. Suwarrow expected to be able to reach Zürich from Glarus, there to join and rally the broken forces of Korsakow; but Molitor, in person, warned of his approach, took possession of the position of Näfels, blocking up the outlet of the Linth Thal, as Massena had intercepted his passage down the Muotta Thal, and the Russian once more found his plans foiled and baffled. Fearing to be hemmed in on all sides by the French, he gave his troops a few days of rest at Glarus, rendered absolutely indispensable by the fatigues they had undergone, after which he once more took to the mountains, ascending the Sernft Thal (Rte. 76) and crossing the Panixer Pass to the Grisons.

A little beyond the nunnery, at the end of the village, the view into the Bisithal is very beautiful.

The Pragel pass is exceedingly steep and stony on the Muotta side, and sometimes marshy, and is scarcely fit for horses, which moreover are not easily to be found at Muotta. There are no difficulties on the Glarus side. There is not the least occasion for a guide, except perhaps to point out the best track over the boggy patches. The pass seems much used by the natives.

From the inn at Muotta the path continues for about 25 min. among the fields and houses, then crosses the stream which descends from Pragel, and immediately ascends rapidly the l. bank of the stream, very rocky and rugged for the first 2 hrs., after which and at the top there are large marshy or boggy patches with planks and stones laid across them. There is nothing striking in the scenery on this side.

The col (5200 ft.) is called Pragel, and is flat, and there is a châlet where bread, wine, &c., can be procured, but it is abandoned in the first week of Sept., and snow is said to melt late and fall soon on the pass.

The first part of the descent is gentle ; but in about 20 min. the Klön-thal opens and the path turns to the rt. and descends more rapidly among pines till it reaches the pretty hamlet of Richisau. Below this the valley is blocked up by a huge barrier, which appears to be an ancient moraine; and the path makes a détour and ascent to surmount it ; · from this there is a short and sharp descent to the little *Inn* of Vorauen, situated in the plain of the Klönthal.

The Klönthal, into which the tra-veller now descends, is exceedingly beautiful. On the rt. hand it is walled in by the Glärnisch rising in an ab-rupt and sheer precipice, terminated by a sharp edge of ice, and on the l. by the Wiggis, scarcely less abrupt. Deep in the recesses of this charming valley lies the *Klönsee*, a lake about 2 m. long, embedded deeply at the foot of the Glärnisch, whose vast grey precipices descend at this point almost perpendicularly into the water. It is surrounded by meadows of the most verdant green, covered until the end of autumn with flowers. The precipitous tracks along the side of the valley, along which some

adventurous French pushed forward in pursuit of the Russians, are pointed out. Ebel calls the Klönthal "une des vallées les plus gracieuses qu'il y ait dans les Alpes." Two Swiss have inscribed on a rock at the foot of the Glärnisch, by the side of a waterfall, an epitaph in memory of Solomon Gessner, the pastoral poet, author of the 'Death of Abel,' who used to re-pair hither from Zürich, and spend the summer in a châlet.

The Vorauen appears to be a fa-vourite excursion from Glarus, and is a good starting point for the ascent of Glärnisch ; and there is an excellent char-road from it. The char-road fol-lows the l. bank of the lake for about 3 m., and then begins to descend into the valley of Glarus. Keeping to the rt. where two roads meet, the manu-facturing village of *Riedern* is reached, from which the road or a footpath on the rt. over the hill leads to

Glarus (Rte. 72).

ROUTE 75A.

FROM MUOTTA TO THE BATHS OF STA-CHELBERG, BY THE BISI-THAL.

A laborious walk of 10 hours. The pass is not a very interesting one.

From Muotta a good horse-path leads up the Bisi Thal to the hamlet of Eigen ; the scenery is very wild ; it is much narrower than the Muotta Thal, with overhanging precipices, and well wooded. In 2½ hours

Eigen, a scattered hamlet. A bad path, practicable only for the pedes-trian, leads across the mountains to the baths of Stachelberg · and the Linth-Thal. No one should attempt this without a guide. After leaving the Bisi Thal the scenery is the most savage conceivable. The summit of the mountain between the valleys, across which the path runs, is a rugged sunken plain of bare rock, many miles in extent, without vegetation of any kind except on a central green oasis (a little verdant plain), where the soil has collected, the whole surrounded by snowy peaks. The path is only traceable in many parts by the little piles of stones put up by the shepherds to guide themselves; and the streams, instead of finding their way into the valley as usual, tumble in cascades into the bowels of the mountain. This arises from the strata of the rock being perpendicular, or nearly so, which has also caused the soil to be washed down by the rain, leaving the upturned strata of the rock naked and bleached by the weather, something like a crevassed glacier turned to rock, and rugged in the extreme. On the side of the Linth - Thal this savage plain is bounded by awful precipices which overhang the baths of Stachelberg, and it is flanked by two bold peaks right and left. The descent to the Baths is very steep and fatiguing: there is no auberge by the way.

ROUTE 76.

GLARUS TO ILANZ, UP THE SERNFT-THAL, BY THE PANIXER.

A good char-road as far as Elm; beyond that a footpath, difficult and fatiguing.

About 3 m. above Glarus the valley of the Linth divides into two branches. Out of the l. or E. branch issues the Sernft: it is sometimes called Kleinthal, to distinguish it from the larger W. branch, or Linththal.

About ½ way to Enghi (Inn), rt. there is rather a fine waterfall; ¼ h. beyond this an isolated view of the Glärnisch, very noble. This mountain, owing to its position, is one of the

most striking in Switzerland, seen from whatever side.

Matt, another village, stands on the rt. bank of the Sernft, and at the mouth of the minor vale of the Krauchthal, up which runs a path to Sargans, over the Riseten pass, 7 stunden.

The quarries in the Plattenberg, a mountain of the grauwacke and clayslate, on the l. side of the valley, opposite Matt, furnish excellent slates for roofing or for writing. Most of the schools in Switzerland are supplied from hence; and the slate was formerly exported down the Rhine to Holland and the Indies. This slate is well known to geologists for the beautiful and perfect casts of fossil fish, in which it abounds. The lower portion of the valley is unhealthy, as may be learned from the occurrence of goître and cretinism (those afflicted with the latter are here called Tölpel —dolt, blockhead—§ 18); but the inhabitants of the upper extremity are a fine and hardy race.

Elm, the highest village, is situated amidst first-rate scenery, and has a capital little *Inn* opposite the Ch. (Widow Freulers).

[*Passes from Elm.—a.* To the Baths of Pfeffers, a fatiguing walk of 12 hrs.; dangerous without a guide. The path ascends the Unterthal, and crosses the ridge of the *Ramin*, whence the panoramic view is singularly grand, into the Weisstannen Thal. There is a tolerable path as far as a châlet on the E. slope of the pass; beyond this there is scarcely any trace of one, and the passage is not practicable for mules. From this châlet you turn to the S. of E., and cross 2 ravines into the *Kalfeuser Thal*, a mile or two below the source of the Tamina, which rises at the head of that valley, in the glacier of Sardona, leaving the peak of the Sardona, the giant of this chain (10,218 ft.), on the rt. The scenery of the Gorge of the Tamina is magnificently grand. The Kalfeuser Thal terminates at Vättis (Rte. 67 d), under the Kalanda-berg, where the river suddenly alters its course, and bends to the N. There is no village where refreshment or accommodation can be obtained between Elm and Vättis, where there is a poor *Inn.*

b. From Matt to Sargans by the Weisstannen-Thal in about 8 hrs. The path crosses the Riseten Grat to Weisstannen about 5 hrs., and thence descends to Niels, near Sargans.

c. Elm to Flims in the Rhein-Thal, by the *Segnes Pass,* 7 hrs. fair walking. This is the direct road to Coire, but a guide is indispensable. The path ascends steeply in zigzags, and crossing deep slopes, generally covered with snow, reaches in 4 hrs. the summit under the Martinsloch, a hole or gap in the precipice through which the sun shines March 4 and 5, and Sept. 14 and 15, upon the village of Elm. The summit (7500 ft. above the sea level) is generally a continuous field of snow. You turn suddenly rt., and descend rapidly for 20 minutes through a deep basin of snow (glacier?) immediately under the S.E. side of the Martinsloch. A glorious view of the Alps. By striking off to the l. it is possible to reach the Kalfeuser-Thal.

20 minutes through a flat boggy basin, apparently a drained lake. A stream flows through and out of it, in a cascade. A rough bridge leads over it. Keep to the L of the stream; descend rapidly to some châlets, the first since leaving Elm (5½ hrs. walk). Splendid view over the valley of Flims, with snowy peaks for a background. *Flims.* (Rte. 77.)]

⁎ Any additional information respecting the Segnes pass derived from personal knowledge would be very acceptable to the Editor.

Elm to *Ilanz* in the *Rheinthal* by the *Panixer* pass, 7 hrs.

An hour and a quarter's walk from Elm brings the traveller almost to the head of the Sernft Thal, and in front of the opening to the S., which leads to the Panixer Pass. The ascent of the pass occupies 2½ hours, and for the last two hours the track is marked by poles. The scenery is hardly to be surpassed for wild and desolate grandeur; the ground rises in stages, or, as it were, in gigantic steps, forming open flats borne up by great pre-

cipices. The first of these flats, gained in ¾ of an hour from the Sernft Thal, is the wild Jäzer Alp. Here are found the last châlets.

The summit of the pass (7942 ft.) commands a very comprehensive view over the southern mountains of the Grisons, but is not remarkable, except for extent.

The commencement of the descent into the Grisons is marked by poles, and turns towards the W. in the direction of a large glacier fed by the snow-fields of the Hausstock. The traveller is then left at the edge of a steep declivity to find his own way down. Here it is necessary to turn to the S., and descend the declivity, loose, wet, and it may be said trackless, in order to gain the path which may be perceived on an Alp or mountain-pasturage beneath. Before reaching this Alp, the stream, just sprung in a considerable volume from its glacier, must be waded through. The way then lies for a time over the half-barren surface of the Alp, which is raised on immense precipices above the lower valley of Panix. The path then recrosses the stream (which runs in a deep chasm, hardly a yard in width, intersecting the alp), and then ascends for some distance along the face of the precipices on the E., passing in one place along a shelf cut out of the rock. There is no danger whatever here in summer; but after a fall of snow the passage might not be unattended with peril.

The path now opens upon a wide green pasturage, partially sloping down towards the S., and turning by degrees, first E. and then N.E., so as to double round the head of the ravine. The rest of the way to the village of *Panix* presents no great difficulty, though some little embarrassment may be experienced in the woods. Panix is a long 2 hours distant from the pass to which it gives name. From here it is well worth while to look back upon the pass. All approach seems so barred by precipices that its accessibility would be considered almost impossible.

Below Panix there is a good path,

running at a great elevation above the stream along the mountain-side, and eventually emerging upon the heights overlooking the valley of the Fore Rhine, which sweeps along far below. The views of this valley, seen on the descent, are of extraordinary beauty. The path leads for a long time through pleasant fields and woodland scenes, but at length descends more rapidly upon Ruvis, immediately below which village it falls into the high road which conducts to Ilanz. From Panix to Ilanz (Rte. 77) is a walk of 2 hours.

Suwarrow, after the almost incredible march detailed in the preceding route, remained like a stag at bay for three or four days at Glarus for the purpose of resting his wearied troops, though not a day was passed without skirmishes more or less severe with the enemy. At length, finding it hopeless to attack a French force now so greatly superior in numbers to his own, he adopted the only remaining alternative, of again leading his exhausted and diminished followers over the high crest of the Alps, in order to rescue them from annihilation, and enable him to unite himself with the scattered fragments of the Russian army in the Grisons. He broke up from his quarters on the 5th of October. The lateness of the season, the difficulties of the passage, and the vastly superior force pressing on the heels of his dispirited soldiers, rendered this a far more hazardous enterprise than that which he had previously accomplished. The miserable path up the valley would barely admit two men abreast: along this the army painfully wound its way in single file. The difficulty of the ascent was greatly increased by a fall of snow 2 feet deep; but, as though the hardships of the way were not enough, the indefatigable French, ascending the opposite bank of the Sernft, allowed the Russians no respite from their harassing assaults. Numbers lay down, exhausted from fatigue, to perish on the snow; many, slipping down the insecure fragments of slate, and along the rocks, polished by the frost, were hurled over the precipices, and crushed in the abyss below, while the enemy's bullets were not slow in further thinning their ranks. After five days of toil, and four nights of little repose, since they were spent on the bare surface of the snow and the glaciers, where many men were frozen to death, Suwarrow crossed the ridge of Panix, between 7000 and 8000 ft. above the sea, and on the 10th of October gained the valley of the Rhine at Ilanz. Even on reaching the descent into the Grisons, many perished in attempting to cross the fearful chasm of the Araschka Alp. For months the foul birds and beasts of prey were gorged with their bodies, and the bones of many a warrior are still blanching in the crevices and ravines of the Jätzer. Thus terminated a march of 18 days' duration, perhaps the most extraordinary ever performed by an army. incessantly engaged, fighting a battle almost every day, and obliged to traverse a country unknown, and completely destitute of resources. This remarkable retreat was accomplished with the loss of all his artillery, the greater part of the beasts of burden, and one-third of his men.

ROUTE 77.

COIRE, UP THE VALLEY OF THE VORDER RHEIN, TO DISENTIS, AND ACROSS THE OBERALP TO ANDERMATT.

Coire to Disentis 47½ m.

	Eng. m.
Reichenau	6
Flims	9
Ilanz	12½
Truns	13
Disentis	7½

Disentis to Andermatt 8 hrs. The char-road has been carried as far as Somvix beyond Truns, and is now probably open to Disentis, where horses can be obtained.

It is scarcely possible to walk from Reichenau to Andermatt in less than 2 days. As far as Disentis the scenery is, in parts, very fine, not unlike Deeside in Scotland. Thence to Andermatt is chiefly over open Alpine pasturages. The number of small castles on heights above the Rhine is remarkable; it is as much the castellated Rhine here as below Mayence.

The Great post-road from Coire (Rte. 67), up the valley of the Rhine, is followed as far as

Reichenau—Inn : Adler (Rte. 87) —where the waters of the Vorder and Hinter Rhein unite. The new carriage-road, planned by the engineer, M. La Nicca, is well constructed, though narrow. The want of roads and of inns (except at Ilánz), the pothouses which supply their place being of a very inferior kind, has hitherto prevented this beautiful district being visited by travellers as much as it deserves.

Quitting the highway, the new road strikes up the side of the hills on the l. bank of the Rhine, to the village of Tamins, directly over Reichenau.

For some distance, along the road on the N. bank, the traveller enjoys a beautiful view up both valleys of the Rhine. The entrance of that of Hinter-Rhein, up which runs the road to the Splügen, is guarded by the castle of Ræzúns, backed by villages and church-towers without number. Beyond *Trins* our road turns aside from the Rhine, and bends round a little monticule rising by a considerable and steep ascent into a small sequestered upland basin, in the midst of which lies

Flims (Rom. Flem.)—*Poste,* rough— a village 3360 ft. above the sea, named from the number of sources around it, *ad flumina.* Here the path to Glarus, by the Segnes pass (Rte. 76 c), strikes off. After continuing some time out of sight of the Rhine, we join it again after a steep descent, about 3 miles beyond Lax.

[From Flims is a long and difficult pass over the Sardona glacier into the Kalfeuser Thal (Rte. 76). Ascending the Segnes pass (Rte. 76), and then keeping to the rt. and crossing the dangerous Sardona glacier, the summit is passed by the side of the Scheibe mountain, and descending the glacier some châlets, called Milch Moos, in the Kalfeuser Thal, are reached. It would be a very long day from Flims to Vättis in the Kalfeuser Thal.]

Ilanz (in Romansch, Glion, or Ilon).—(*Inns :* Croix Blanche, clean, good beds; an obliging and honest landlord; charmingly situated, close to the bridge over the Rhine, opposite Ilánz;—Zum Lukmanier.) Ilánz is the only place in the valley deserving the name of town, and is the capital of the Graue Bund, or Grey League, p. 216. Its 568 Inhab. speak Romansch, and this dialect prevails in a large portion of the valley. This place, situated on the rt. bank of the river, exhibits marks of poverty, though the country around is fertile; its walls are in a state of dilapidation. It was once the abode of many noble families.

[The Pass of the Valserberg to Splügen is described Rte. 80 B. Road narrow but level to Trûns. The Panixer pass to Glarus is described Rte. 76 c.

From Ilanz to Tusis is a day's walk of 10 or 11 hrs. by the rt. bank of the Vorder Rhein, the Savien Thal (Rte. 80 c), and the pass of the Stäge (Rte. 80 c). Scarcely any route could repay the traveller better than this; but the path is not always good. There is also a pass to Olivone, in the Val Blegno (Rte. 77 A).]

Obersaxen (Rom., Sursaissa), a village on the same side of the Rhine as Ilánz, and about 4 m. higher up, is German, while all the villages around it are Romansch. In its vicinity stand 4 ancient castles, now picturesque ruins, about 1½ mile apart from one another. Their names are Mooreck, Schwartzenstein, Riedburg, and Axenstein. Before reaching Obersaxen, the road crosses the river, but again crosses to the l. bank before arriving at

Trûns (Rom., Tron)—(*Inns,* "not well reputed"—*J. F.*)—a village in a singularly beautiful situation, at a little distance from the Rhine. Its 800 Inhab. are Rom. Catholics, and speak Romansch. There are iron-works in the vicinity. Trûns is chiefly remarkable, however, as the cradle of liberty among the Rhœtian Alps, the Grütli of Grison history. Beneath the shade of the neighbouring forest the peasants met at the beginning of the 15th century, to concert plans for liberating themselves and their children from the oppression and slavery of their feudal lords, three or four of whose castles, now in ruins, may still be seen frowning down from the neighbouring crags.

Near the entrance of the village, on the side of Ilánz, stands the decayed but venerated trunk of a *Sycamore* (Acer Pseudoplatanus; German, Ahorn), now probably 6 or 7 centuries old, a mere trunk, cloven and hollow, beneath whose once-spreading branches the deputies of the peasants met the nobles who were favourable to their cause, in March, 1424, and took the oath of fidelity to one another, and to their free constitution then established. Such is the origin of the GREY LEAGUE, *Graue Bund* (Rte. 67), so called from the grey beards or the grey homespun garb of the venerable assembly. A vigorous young shoot has sprouted forth from the hollow trunk, and is protected by a railing. Close to the sycamore tree stands the little *Chapel of St. Anne*, whose portico is adorned with Bible texts, "In libertatem vocati estis;" "Ubi Spiritus Domini, ibi Libertas;" "In te speraverunt Patres;" &c., and with two fresco paintings. One represents the first formation of the League, the principal figures being the Abbot of Disentis, in the robes of his order; the Count of Sax, with a white flowing beard; and the lord of Rhœtzuns. The other picture shows the renewal of the oath in 1778: the deputies here appear with starched frills, and hair powdered and frizzled; in silk stockings and walking-sticks. It is recorded that the deputies on the former occasion brought their dinners in sacks on their backs, which they hung up by nails to the rocks, while

they quenched their thirst in the brook which traverses the meadow of Tavanasa. The more courtier-like deputies of the second meeting were more sumptuously feasted in the mansion of the Abbot. In the so-called *Ritter-saal*, a building belonging to the Abbey of Disentis, the arms of all the magistrates since 1424 are painted on the walls.

The inhabitants of the upper part of the valley, about Disentis, are Roman Catholics, as will become apparent from the increased number · churches and crosses. The mountain which bound it change from lime stone to primitive rocks, and give · different character to its scenery.

Opposite *Somvix* (Rom., Sumvig; Lat., Summus-vicus), abounding in cherry-trees, the valley of that name opens out; through it is a path to Olivone by the Greina pass. Beyond it the eye is arrested by the view of the Abbey and village of

Dísentis — (*Inns :* Croix Blanche, tolerable; Krone).—Living is cheap : 5½ frs. board and lodging a-day. Game plentiful. The *Benedictine Abbey* of Disentis (Rom., Mustär ; Lat., Monasterium) is one of the oldest ecclesiastical establishments in Switzerland, founded, it is said, by the Scotch monk Siegbert, a companion of St. Gall, and as the nucleus of early civilization in this wild and remote country. It stands on an elevated terrace, 3700 ft. above the sea-level, with a small village clustered round its base, and near the head of a rather long ascent. It is protected by a forest above it from falling avalanches, on the l. bank of the Vorder-Rhine, at the junction of the two Alpine torrents which unite in forming that branch of the river. The Abbey has twice been burned down in modern times, first in 1799, when the French invaders burnt it, and along with it the library formed in the 7th and 8th centuries. It must be allowed that provocation was given for this act of vengeance, by the cruel murder of a party of French soldiers, who had been disarmed and taken prisoners by the Swiss Landsturm, and who were here set upon by the infuriated inhabitants of this part of the valley, and literally cut or torn to pieces. The abbey, again burnt in 1846, but rebuilt, and now used as a school for the Canton, has an imposing appearance, from its size and position, towering above the humble hovels of the village below, as its rich and powerful abbots, in the middle ages, lorded it over their vassals. They were, at one time, firm allies of the House of Habsburg, and the abbot and his banner occupied the van at the battle of Morgarten. At a later period, however, 1424, Abbot Peter of Pontaningen was one of the founders of Grison liberty, who met under the sycamore at Trüns.

There is a path hence up the Medelser Thal to Santa Maria, and thence over the Lukmanier to Bellinzona (Rte. 78), or over the Uomo Pass and down the Val Piora to Airolo, of 10½ hrs. (Rte. 80A); a third, difficult and dangerous, runs N. over the Dödi-Grat, by the Sandalp, to the Baths of Stachelberg (Rté. 72); a fourth by the Kreutzli Pass and Maderaner Thal (Rte. 80) to Amsteg, 10 hours' good walking.

A *Railway* through the ridge of the Lukmanier (Rte. 78) has been surveyed. (See Introduction, § 8.)

Disentis is a convenient station for travellers bent on exploring these and other passes. The charge is rather high for very poor cattle, viz. 11 frs. a-day for each horse, with a bonnemain of 1 fr. a-day to each of the guides. But in summer time the horses are sent up to the High Alps to carry hay, &c., and require to be fetched a long distance.

The path from Disentis up to the Oberalp leaves the Medélser Thal on the l., and ascends the vale of Tavétsch by the l. bank of the Vorder-Rhine, now reduced in breadth and volume to a mountain-torrent. The path passes the villages Mompetavétsch, Sedrûn, or Tavétsch, the chief place in the valley, and Ruaras.

Ruaras (Rom., St. Giacomo). Lodging may be had in the priest's house, who also has some minerals. On a hill nearly surrounded by the Rhine

[*Switz.*]

stand the ruins of the *Castle of Pultmenga* or *Pontaningen*. 10 min. walk above Ruaras the path to the Oberalp splits; and the rt.-hand branch, commonly followed in summer, is shorter and better, and commands finer views, owing to its keeping more to the heights, which it at once ascends, and rapidly. It joins the other path at the N. end of the Oberalp See.

Above Ruaras a narrow gorge now leads out of the lower into an upper valley. This part of it is dreadfully exposed to avalanches. In 1808 one fell from the Ruenatsch upon the village of Selva, and killed 42 human beings and 237 head of cattle. Here begins the last and most difficult part of the ascent; all regular track disappears, and the numerous furrows worn by the feet of the cattle perplex the traveller, who will hardly be able to find his way without a guide.

Ciamot is the last village in the Tavetsch deserving that name, and provided with a church; it is 5000 ft. above the sea. The valley of Ta-vetsch is the cradle of the Vorder-Rhine: it is supplied from 3 branches, having their source in the vast mountains and glaciers which wall in its upper extremity; the *Crispalt*, on the S. side, the Sexmadan (Cima de Badus), and the Cornäre. At Ciamot the l.-hand branch is crossed, and the middle branch followed for about a mile, after which, adieu to the Rhine; a constant ascent leads the traveller to the summit of the pass, 7172 ft. above the sea.

On reaching the opposite declivity, a small lake, famed for its trout, lies at the foot of the traveller. This is the *Oberalp See*, one of the head-waters of the Reuss: it is beset with bogs, across which the traveller must pick his way cautiously. This spot was the scene of a hard struggle between the French and Austrians, in 1799. The path winds along the N. or rt. side of the lake. The vale of Urseren, with Hospital in the distance, now opens out to view, and a long and wearisome descent, first through a naked valley of pastures, and then down an

L

arduous and broken declivity, brings the traveller to

Andermatt, on the St. Gothard (Rte. 34.) To walk hence to Disentis will require 7¼ hrs.

ROUTE 77 A.

ILANZ TO OLIVONE IN THE VAL BLEGNO, BY THE PASSES OF THE DISRUT AND GREINA.

This route (14 hrs.) leads S. from Ilanz up the valley of the *Glenner* as far as *Kumbels* (1½ hr. from Ilanz), where the paths to the *Disrut* and the Valserberg diverge. The road to the Disrut, after leaving Kumbels, passes for a very long time over an elevated and extensive tract of open fields, dotted with several villages and hamlets, and commanding a view up the main valley of the Glenner as far as the pass of the Valserberg. At length the narrow upper valley of *Vrin* is entered, and, after crossing a deep ravine, the village of Vrin, which gives its name to the valley, is reached (5 hrs. from Ilanz). Here is the last, if not the only *Inn* to be found on the way.

On leaving Vrin the path descends to and crosses the river, which it recrosses almost directly afterwards. The last hamlet is *Buzasch* (1½ hr. from Vrin). From Buzasch to the summit of the Disrut is an ascent of nearly 2 hrs. For the first hour there is a path marked; the rest of the way may be called pathless. By a gap, in which snow lies, is at last attained, not the crest of the Disrut, but the narrow edge of the sharply serrated ridge which divides the hollow leading down to Buzasch from another leading down to Camps. The edge of this ridge is gained close to the point where it diverges from the chain which separates the valleys of Somvix and Vrin. The ascent from here to the Disrut is difficult but short (about ½ of an hour). Immediately on the left is seen a shallow gully partly filled with snow, the sides of which are composed of small loose fragments of rock. The head of this gully is the pass of the Disrut. As the surface of the snow is too hard and steep to be practicable, it is necessary to make one's way as well as possible up the loose rocks and stones, which slip away beneath the feet. The summit of the Disrut (7280 ft.) is thus gained, 8½ hrs. after leaving Ilanz. The view of rugged mountains from the point is exceedingly fine.

From this point there is a very bad descent into a plain below (the ascent must be extremely difficult). After a short ½-hr. of what cannot be called walking, but rather scrambling and slipping, down a crumbling declivity and a bed of snow lying in the depths of a rift, the highest part of the great plain is reached. Right above the head, but just at a safe distance, a glacier is seen pushing itself forward to the edge of a precipice, and strewing the ground at its foot, almost close to the passer by, with heaps of fragments of ice.

The ascent to the *Greina* (6520 ft.) is all but nominal. The Greina is in fact merely the western edge of this long plain. The descent on the other side into the *Val Kamadra*, the highest part of the *Val Blegno*, is rather difficult. After crossing a wet stony flat, it is requisite to ascend the right hand of the two spurs into which the broken ridge is split, and then to make a very steep descent among stones and blocks of rock into the head of the valley, which is gained in about half an hour after leaving the summit of the Greina. The head of the Val Kamadra is partially occupied by a great bed of snow, and is overhung on the W. by the vast Kamadra glacier, a portion of the same field of ice to which the Medelser glacier belongs. Once in the head of the Val Kamadra all the difficulties of the passage are surmounted. The rest of the way to *Olivone* is sufficiently easy, but will occupy full 3 hrs. more. It is advisable to manage to reach Olivone by daylight, as there is a ravine between Ghirone and Olivone, where the path skirts the edge of unguarded precipices, which makes the way rather awkward after nightfall.

The Greina may also be passed either from Somvix or Trons in the Grisons by following up the valley of Somvix. From Olivone downwards there is a carriage-road through the Val Blegno (Rte. 78).

ROUTE 78.   *

PASS OF THE LUKMANIER — DISENTIS TO OLIVONE IN THE VAL BLEGNO.

11 hrs.

A path, much frequented in summer, and practicable throughout on horseback, though very steep towards its two extremities. It is a long and not very interesting pass, but has acquired importance from the comparative facilities it offers for the construction of a Railway with tunnels through the Alps—so as to connect Switzerland, W. France, and South Germany, with Sardinia, Lombardy, and the cities of Milan, Turin, and Genoa. A succession of long and comparatively level valleys on either side of the Pass have caused it to be surveyed for the construction of a *Railway*, and Mr. Hemans, an English engineer of great experience, has ascertained that it is practicable (see p. xxiv) by means of a tunnel 15 m. long, which is to enter the mountain at Perdatsch and to emerge at Camps in Val Blegno.

The valley of *Medels*, up which this route lies as far as Sta. Maria, runs in a direction nearly due S. from Disentis, and is traversed through its whole length by the Middle Rhine.

The entrance to it is by a rocky and wooded gorge, about 2 m. from Disentis, called Conflons, because the Vorder and Mittel-Rhein unite in it. In the midst of it the Rhine forms two cascades, and beyond it the valley opens out into a wide basin, lined with pastures and forests, in the remoter parts of which the bear is still found, while the chamois abounds on the granite peaks forming the highest summits of the surrounding Alps. The path scales the steep and craggy ridge to the rt. of the gorge, of which it affords but a very imperfect view, and then descends into the Thal, opposite Curaglia, the highest village on the rt. bank of the M. Rhine, placed just above the influx of the torrent which descends from the Medelser Gletscher. A little further up the Rhine is crossed to

Platta, the principal place in the Medélser Thal. In 1 hr. more, passing through the hamlet St. Rocco, a spot is reached, whence, looking back, the view of the Dödi is superb. ¼ hr. higher is Perdätsch—situated at the opening of the Val Cristallina, which runs in a S.E. direction, and sends forth one branch of the Middle Rhine. It is celebrated for its rock-crystals, out of which the shrine of St. Carlo Borromeo, in the Duomo of Milan, was formed. The ascent here becomes more rapid, and the scenery wilder and finer. Huge rocks are jumbled about, and the Mittel-Rhein plunges, in a fall 100 ft. high, into a deep gulf. The little *hospices* of St. John and St. Gall, each with its warning bell, are passed, and in about 5 hrs. from Disentis, Sta. Maria is reached. Here a stream descends from the W. out of the Lake Dim, at the end of the Val Cadelina; and a third, between these two, issues from the foot of the Monte Scuro.

Sta. Maria is a hospice kept up for the benefit of travellers, and, though very wretched in appearance, the traveller may procure forage for horse, and a meal of coarse bread and drinkable wine for himself.

½ hr's. walk above Sta. Maria brings you to the culminating point of the

Pass of the *Lukmanier* (in Latin, Mons Lucumonius ; in Romansch, Lukmajn, or Culm Sta. Maria), 6340 ft. above the sea.

It is said that the army of Pepin passed this way, A.D. 754, on his invasion of Italy. Poles, stuck into the rocks, mark the direction of the path across the Col. A horse-path over the Uomo Pass (Rte. 80A) branches off from the hospice to Airolo, through the Val Termini, or Val Forno, the Val Piora, by Altanca, Brugnasco, and Madrano.

A cross on the summit of the Lukmanier marks the boundary of the Grisons and Canton Tessin. Hence the path to Olivone and the Val Blegno descends the Alpine Val Casaccia, in 1 hr. to

The Hospice of *Casaccia;* and, a few miles lower, to that of

Camperio, both founded, it is said, by St. Carlo Borromeo, for the reception of travellers.

The first glimpse of the spires and plain of

Olivone, from the wooded steeps of the Lukmanier, is very striking, the descent to it beautiful, and the village itself is one of the most charming spots in the Alps. The small *Inn* of Stefano Bolo is comfortable, though of no inviting exterior, and rather high-priced.

Olivone is the highest village in the Val Blegno, and stands at the point where the lateral valley of Casaccia joins it; it has about 740 Inhab.

The Val Blegno (Germ. Polenzerthal) is traversed by the stream of the Brenno, which enters it from a narrow cleft in the mountain; and a tolerable char-road, in part carriage-road, has recently been formed along the L bank of the stream, from Olivone to Biasca, on the route of the St. Gothard (Rte. 34), a distance of 14 m. All the valley on the W. is very beautiful.

Many of the chocolate-sellers and chestnut-roasters, who swarm in the streets of the cities of Italy, come from the Val Blegno.

ROUTE 79.

MUOTTA TO ALTORF, BY THE PASS OF THE KINZIG KULM.

" The path is the same as that to the Pass of the Pragel (Rte. 75) for a short distance above Muotta, but diverges from it to cross the first bridge over the river. From the bridge it strikes straight S. up the mountains; and, having ascended in that direction for a little while, turns off towards the W., away from the entrance to the Bisi Thal. The ascent is continued obliquely up a steep broken slope, till the path arrives eventually upon the wooded edge of a chasm, in which the invisible stream, which issues from the high valley leading up to the Pass, is heard descending in cataracts into the Muotta Thal. A track up the mountain side, on the right bank of this stream, is now pursued: and, after an hour's walking from Muotta, the abrupt ascent ceases, and the valley above is entered. Having passed through a wood, the path crosses the river for the first time by some châlets (1½ hour from Muotta). The river is recrossed after another quarter of an hour: a second forest is traversed, and a third bridge crossed (2½ hours from Muotta). The part of the valley below this bridge is narrow and picturesque, shut in on both sides by high white precipices. Over the E. range the sun did not appear, on the last day of July, till 8 o'clock. The rich green slopes N. of Muotta, speckled with châlets, and surmounted by vast cliffs, may be seen from favourable positions, whenever the eye is thrown back, through the opening of the valley. After the third bridge is crossed, a wild open basin is found, out of which the track is seen ascending from the S.W. corner. At this corner the river is again crossed. 1¼ hr. more are requisite before the summit of the pass is attained. As far as some châlets, about half-way up, the path may be traced without much difficulty, as it takes for its guide the falling stream, now reduced to a mere rill. Towards the summit, however, it is faintly marked, and liable to be confounded with other tracks. The stream is left behind, the direction of ascent being towards the south, among little hillocks and hollows filled with snow; over open ground, where many directions might be taken, and the proper route lost. A short pole marks the crest of the Pass (7280 feet), which is gained in about 4 hrs. from Muotta.

"Great interest is attached to the Kinzig Kulm, in an historical point of view, as being the scene of Suwarrow's disastrous march from Altorf in 1799. Having pounced down, as it were, upon the French from the heights of the St. Gothard, and driven them before him to Altorf, he there found his progress barred by the lake of Lucerne, without a boat to cross it, his troops exhausted by fatigue and famine, and the country so completely drained by war as to be quite incapable of supporting them. The only alternative that remained to him, was to attempt to join the forces of the allies, through the horrible defile of the Schächen; and to cross the rarely-trodden summit of the high Alps. The only passage up this valley was by a mere path; so that his army was obliged to advance in a single file, abandoning much of their artillery and baggage. Their march lasted 14 hours; and before the rear-guard had left Altorf, the van had reached Muotta. Many of the Russians sank from fatigue by the wayside, and perished; others fell into the hands of the French, who hovered in their rear; the valley was strewn with dead bodies of men and horses, with arms and equipments. The remainder of this memorable march is described in Rte. 75. Its picturesque attractions are also of the highest order, as the view which it commands is of great extent, and of a most magnificent and comprehensive character. This view is rather improved by being seen from an eminence to the E., reached in 10 m. from the Col.

"The descent into the *Schächen* Thal is long and steep, but the path is well traced, and the pole on the *Kinzig Kulm*, being seen for a long time, would help to guide the ascending pedestrian on this side, though it is useless for that purpose on the other. The path lies throughout down the pastures on the right bank of the stream, but generally at a considerable distance from it. The Schächen Thal is reached at a point a little below Spiringen, after a descent of 2½ hrs. From thence to Bürglen it is a walk of ¾ of an hour, and another ½ hour brings the traveller to *Altorf*."—R. E.

ROUTE 80.

AMSTEG TO DISENTIS, BY THE PASS OF THE KREUZLI.

This Pass requires from 10 to 11 hrs., and should not be tried without a guide. Anton Tresch, of Amsteg, is a good guide.

"The path runs at starting up the *Maderaner Thal*, on the l. bank of the Kerstlenbach, which joins the Reuss at Amsteg. For a few minutes it is by its side: the ascent to gain the level of the fields above the closing gorge then commences, and continues for about ¼ hr. through the forest. The valley behind the gorge is thus entered and followed up; the chapel of St. Antony and little hamlet of Bristen are passed, and a little further on the river is crossed (40 min. from Amsteg), and recrossed 10 min. afterwards. An hr. after leaving Amsteg the stream from the Ezli Thal is crossed. This valley leads to the

Kreuzli, and the Maderan Thal is now left. A considerable ascent is necessary to get into the Ezli Thal, as the path has to mount above the head of a high fall. The first bridge over its stream, above the fall, is not crossed, but the three following are. Soon after crossing the third of these bridges (about 2 hrs. from Amsteg), the last trees are passed, and the path mounts continually for nearly another couple of hours along the W. flank of a naked desolate ravine. It skirts on its way, in the bed of the stream, the remains of an immense avalanche which fell 1849—a mass of snow, dirt, and fallen rocks, probably ½ a mile long. Beside it stands a cross with the date 1834. A small marshy basin succeeds the ravine, the valley here changing its direction from S. to W. At this basin the way to the Kreuzli quits the valley, passing the river and ascending the eastern mountains. There is, however, no bridge; and the track is not perceptible in the neighbourhood of the river, though it soon reappears during the subsequent ascent.

" It is well worth while to follow up the valley for half a mile or a mile above the basin just mentioned, instead of immediately leaving it for the pass. The river is pursued towards the W., till it is lost in a short defile beneath the snow, with which the bed of the narrow passage is choked up. A multitude of gigantic blocks, heaped one above another, form one side of this cleft in the mountains. The snow affords good walking, and the defile soon gives admittance into a large hollow of the highest savage character. It is utterly sterile and uninhabited ; a mere receptacle for fallen rocks and snow. The glaciers of the Crispalt sweep down upon it ; craggy mountains of the boldest elevation girdle it in; their splintered summits rise on all sides high into the sky. To visit this spot in the journey over the Kreuzli would not increase the duration of the day's walk by much more than half an hour.

" The track which leads to the Kreuzli pass, after the marshy basin is left and the river crossed, continues to ascend towards the E. up an uneven slope, until it reaches the opening of a kind of high, short valley, by pursuing which the summit is to be gained. From this point there is an unexpected view of the bay of Uri, and of the plain at the entrance of the Reuss into the lake. The last ascent to the Kreuzli is gentle but rough, the ground being covered with loose blocks, alternating with patches of snow. The track only appears at intervals, generally upon the snow ; but the course of the little valley is in itself a sufficient guide. The crest of the pass, marked by a pole, is reached in 5 hrs. direct from Amsteg, or 6½ allowing halts to enjoy the view, and has an elevation of about 7500 feet above the sea.

" The views from the Kreuzli are on both sides of an extremely savage nature, amongst the neighbouring mountains and glaciers. There is also an extensive view, looking down the valley, of the snowy mountains between the Grisons and the canton Ticino.

" It is a bad descent into the valley of Strim down a steep declivity, broken by numbers of jutting crags. Occasional goat-tracks supply the place of a regular path. Neither is the track down the valley—when its bed is attained, and the ice-cold river, just sprung from its glaciers, waded through —anything like a good path. It requires two long and rather fatiguing hours from the summit of the pass to reach the village of Sedrun or Tavetsch in the valley of the Fore Rhine. The valley of Strim is uninhabited, and its nakedness is not relieved by a single tree, not even a stunted fir. From Sedrun to Disentis down the valley of the Fore Rhine is an easy walk of 2 hrs. (See Rte. 77.)

ROUTE 80A.

DISENTIS TO AIROLO, BY THE UOMO PASS. (11 hrs.).

"As far as the hospice of Santa Maria, 5 leagues from Disentis, the way to this pass is the same as that to the Lukmanier. (Rte. 78.) A little tributary valley of the Medelser Thal opens from the S.W. into the plain of Santa Maria, and leads to the Uomo pass. The path ascends from the plain on the rt. bank of the stream which waters this valley. There is no difficulty on the ascent, which is rapid and continuous. The valley is narrow and barren, and presents nothing remarkable. The summit of the pass is reached easily in an hour and a half from Santa Maria. Its height is 7160 ft.; the ground is flat and boggy, and not adapted for a path: it is accordingly traced along a gentle slope on the S. edge of the marsh, where there are one or two rude châlets.

"The descent is scarcely begun before a commanding view of the knot of the St. Gothard Alps opens out in front above the lesser mountains. The pastures, or 'Alp' of Piora, down which the path lies, produce a cheese of considerable repute in the canton. The descent is at first rapid, but then reaches a little plain and lake, and then the lake of *Rotom.* The descent from the lake is abrupt and long, the river forming in quick succession three very fine falls.

"After passing the third fall, the path is fairly out of the Val Piora, and on the flanks of the Val Levantina, having been throughout, during the descent from the pass, on the rt. bank of the stream, which it now abandons. The rest of the way to Airolo is very interesting. The Val Levantina and the St. Gothard road are left far beneath, and the path continues high on the slopes of the mountains, passing through the village of Madrano, and over the thin transverse ridge, pierced by the Ticino, which separates the Val Bedretto from the Val Levantina. Here the opening of the Val Canaria breaks the side of the chain: the path descends, crosses the stream issuing from it, and falls into the St. Gothard road a little below Airolo."—R. E.

ROUTE 80B.

SPLÜGEN TO ILANZ, BY THE PASS OF THE VALSERBERG (10 or 11 hrs.).

"The great road of the Bernardin is followed as far as Nüfenen, rather more than an hour above Splügen. Some 3 or 4 minutes after passing through Nüfenen, the footpath to the Valserberg branches off to the rt. by the side of a little stream, reaches in a few minutes more the base of the chain rising from the valley on the N., and continues to ascend along its side at the foot of a line of cliffs. These cliffs extend to the top of the pass, and are an excellent guide to it, the way up being always at a short distance from their base. A wooded spur separates the hollow looking towards Nüfenen from that leading down to Hinterrhein. After an ascent of less than an hour, this spur is crossed nearly at its point of divergence from the northern chain, and just above the wood which clothes its lower part. The high pastures overlooking Hinterrhein are now reached, and the path from that village falls in. There is a very good view from this point.

"The last ascent to the Valserberg is rather steep, but is marked by poles, and the highest point of the pass is attained in something less than 3 hrs. from Splügen. The Col is a narrow gap in the crest of the chain, covered with snow, and elevated nearly 7500 feet above the sea-level.

"The view to the north is very wild. Several bare mountain ranges are seen, and above them the whole line of the

Alps of Glarus, from the Dödi to the Scheibe, an unbroken bank of snow from end to end.

"For nearly an hour after the summit of the Valserberg the way is marked by poles: the highest châlets are then reached, and a stream from the right crossed. An hour and a half more are necessary to gain St. Peter's Plaz (a small *Inn*), where the main valley of the Glenner is entered. This is divided into three districts; the lower valley of Lugnetz, the side valley of Vrin, and the upper valley of Vals, called also St. Peter's Thal. In this last district the language is German, as well as in the valley of the Rheinwald and the neighbouring Savien Thal. In the districts of Lugnetz and Vrin Romansch is spoken.

"A very high and narrow gorge above Plaz cuts short in that direction the little plain in which the village is situated. Another defile terminates it to the N. about half a mile below Plaz. This ravine, through which the path, having crossed the river, is now conducted, is one of the grandest gorges by which the Alps are riven. The river is again crossed to its right bank, where a landing from the bridge has only been effected by hewing a shelf out of the rock. The way is afterwards cut with some difficulty along a broken declivity, till the valley opens out at the châlets of Feistenberg and Montasg, finely placed on the green slopes. A second gorge succeeds, and the path is forced to ascend, scarcely finding ground for its course, until a little oratory by its side marks the close of the ascent and of the long defile (6 m.), and the fertile valley of Lugnetz opens out to the N.

"Into its fields the path now descends. The river is crossed some distance lower down, by a bridge just above the baths of Pleiden. A rather long ascent then leads to Kumbels, where perhaps the most perfect of all the views of this singularly picturesque valley is commanded.

"The village of Kumbels may be reached in less than an hour and a half from Ilanz, and might therefore easily be visited, and is well worth a visit.

"The path from Kumbels continues long on the heights. It is only at a little distance from Ilanz that it leaves them, and descends into the valley of the Rhine. This river is crossed to its N. bank—the Croix Blanche, the best *Inn* at Ilanz (Rte. 77), lying on that side, close to the bridge. From St. Peter's Plaz to Ilanz is a walk of full 5 hrs."—*R. E.*

ROUTE 80c.

REICHENAU TO SPLÜGEN, BY THE SAVIEN-THAL AND PASS OF THE LÖCHLIBERG.

11½ hrs. A bridle-path the greater part of the way. Our road runs up the rt. bank of the Vorder-Rhein, as far as the German Protestant village *Versam*, where the fearful gulf of the Versamer Tobel is crossed by a very remarkable wooden bridge, with a span of 200 ft. (probably the widest wooden bridge on this principle existing), and 232 ft. above the torrent Savien. The builder is the engineer La Nicca. Here a path turns S. up the wild valley of the Savien or Rabbiusa, a very remarkable ravine, "wilder than the Via Mala," of which the W. side only is cultivated and inhabited by a German Protestant population of about 1000 souls, who were settled here in the days of the Hohenstaufen Emperors. The almost uninhabited E. side is in places formed by precipices, the rocky escarpment of Mount Heinzenberg. The path is carried up the l. or W. bank of the Rabbiusa, by the hamlets of Tenna, Areza, Neukirch, *Platz*, where the Rathhaus *Inn* is ill provided.

1. A deep path strikes off hence over the col called *Stäge* across a shoulder

of the Piz Beveren to Tusis, 4 hours. The beginning of the ascent is very steep, but afterwards lies over the grass. The summit of the pass is about 6000 ft., and is reached in 1½ hr. from Platz. It commands a fine view over the Grison Alps. The descent to Tusis traverses the remarkable plateau of the Heinzenberg, an open plain rising by degrees above the valley of Domlesch. The original path continues over the meadows of the Camana Alp to Thalkirche, the oldest and highest church in the district. Now begins the ascent of the *Löchliberg*, 8442 ft. above the sea-level.

A steep descent leads down to the village *Splügen*, in Route 87.

ROUTE 81.

THE PRÄTTIGÄU—RAGATZ TO SÜSS IN THE ENGADINE, OR PLATZ.

	Eng. m.
Schiers	10
Klosters	13

To Klosters 23 m.; Klosters to Suss 10 or 11 hrs. This is the most difficult of 4 or 5 practicable passes which connect the valley of the Rhine with the Engadine.

Opposite to Ragatz is

Mayenfeld (*Inn*, Alte Post), an ancient walled town of 1200 Inhab., on the rt. bank of the Rhine, but at a little distance from the river. It stands on the high road from Bregenz to Coire, about 12 m. N. of the latter place, opposite to Ragatz, with which it is connected by a ferry. It is the chief town of the League of the 10 Jurisdictions (Zehngerichten-Bund).

The pass is usually considered to begin from Mayenfeld; but from that place or Ragatz it is about 3½ m. to

Maláns, a village of 1054 Inhab., overlooked by several ruined castles,

and situated near the mouth of the *Prättigäu* (Rom. Val Parténz). The entrance of that valley is through the narrow gorge or defile of *Klus*, giving passage to the waters of the *Landquart*, a furious torrent which traverses the valley. This pass was once commanded by the castle Fragstein, whose ruins are still visible ; a wall, extending down to the Landquart, once closed the passage into the valley. The valley, 20 m. long, abounds in fine scenery, is shut in by high mountains and glaciers, is nowhere of any expanse, but rich in pasture-land, and famed for its large breed of cattle. It contains a population of about 10,000, who all speak German, though Romansch was the language down the 16th cent., and the names of places are still all Romansch. The rt. or N. side of the valley is occupied by the Alpine chain of the *Rhætikon*, which separates it from the Vorarlberg and from the vale of Montafun. Its most remarkable summits are the Falkniss, overlooking the Rhine, the *Scesa Plana*, 9207 ft. the highest on the N. side of the valley. The *Piz Linard* (11,420 ft.) and other mountains unite this chain with that to the N. of the Inn, which forms the division or watershed between the North Sea and the Euxine, as the Bernina chain on the S. separates the waters flowing to the Euxine from those flowing to the Adriatic. The Fermûnt (*Ferreus Mons*) is on the borders of the Engadine. It is crossed by several passes—one is called Druser-Thor.

The *Prättigau* may be approached by the traveller coming from Coire by a cut branching off from the main road a little below *Zizers*, without going round by Mayenfeld or Maláns. A tolerable carriage-road has been made up the valley as far as Kloster.

The road ascends on the rt. bank of the Landquart; on the l. bank is

Jenatz (Heims' *Inn*). ¼ hr. further is Niggli's *Inn*. The village of Fideris stands on a height 2 m. off the road, and is not visible from it (Donau's *Inn*).

A very bad road leads to the *Baths*

L 3

of Fideris, 2 m. S. of the village, in a wild and romantic gorge, not unlike that of Pfäffers. The baths, considered efficacious in chest complaints and intermittent fevers, are supplied by several alkaline acidulous springs, the strongest of their class in Switzerland, and strongly resembling Seltzer water. The visitors, almost exclusively Swiss, are received in two *Bath-houses*, capable of lodging more than 200 persons.

The accommodation at the Baths is quite second-rate, although the baths are often crowded to excess, and the landlord has made a fortune by them ; however, the table-d'hôte is well supplied.

On the rt. bank of the Landquart, opposite Fideris, rises the ruined castle of Castels, which was stormed and taken, in 1622, by the peasants, armed with sticks alone, from the soldiers of the Emperor Ferdinand, who at that period wanted to make himself master of the passes of the Grisons, to extinguish the Protestant religion in this country, and to seize and banish its ministers. A path leads S. in 3½ hrs., over the mountains, into the Schalfik thal.

Passing through *Küblis* and *Saas*, we reach

Klosters (*Inn*: near the bridge, not good), a scattered village chiefly of new houses, named after a suppressed Convent, on the rt. bank of the Landquart, 3700 ft. above the sea, in view of the glacier of Fermunt.

There are one or two difficult passes direct to Süss, but it is easier to go by the Davos-thal. A road practicable for chars ascends by the Schwarze See to (2 hrs.) Davos See.

St. Wolfgang, the highest point of the Stütz Pass, 4936 ft. above the sea. Passing on the descent a small lake, we come to

Davós (Rom. Tavoise, behind), the name of a valley in which the chief place is called *Platz* or *Am Platz*, 3 hrs. from Klosters. The *Rathhaus*, now an *Inn*, and in its primitive style these mountains perhaps do not afford a better, was formerly decorated with more than 30 wolves' heads slain in the neighbourhood—proof of the pre-

valence of these animals. A wolf-net (wolf-garne) is still hung up here, but the animals have nearly disappeared.

The Davos-thal, below Plaz, retains its pastoral character as far as Glaris. Farther down it is much contracted, and at Schmelzboden were formerly zinc, lead, and silver works.

"At Alveneu you find yourself again in a more peopled and cultivated region: on the l. appears Filisur (Rte. 83), at the debouchure of the Albula, and the Davos Thal ends at the junction of the streams."—*J. F.*

Süss by the Fluela pass (Rte. 81 B).

ROUTE 81A.

COIRE TO PLAZ, BY THE PASS OF THE STRELA (9 hrs.).

" The Schalfik Thal (before the mouth of which Coire is built, on the banks of the Plessûr, which issues from it) leads up to this pass. The path runs along the heights on the rt. of the river ; and after a continuous ascent of nearly an hour from Coire, reaches *Maladérs*, the first village of the valley. The Col of the *Strela* is visible from this point, but 7 hrs. more will be required to surmount it. The Schalfik Thal is a very extraordinary valley. There are no villages in its bed: all are on the mountains, at a vast elevation above the Plessûr, and having apparently no communication with one another. From Maladers to Langwiesen, a distance of nearly 5 leagues, the path can scarcely ever be less than 1000 feet above the river. It passes, on its way, through several villages, occupying tracts of ground on the tops of spurs or promontories projecting from the northern mountains, and divided from one another by lateral ravines, which have to be dipped into and doubled round. To the S. of the river, and also on the

W., where the Julier road runs, the character of the country is of a similar kind. One of the finest views of the Schalfik Thal is from Calfreisen, a village with an ancient tower crowned with trees. The snowy mountains of the Kalfeuser Thal are seen through the opening of the valley.

" The houses in the Schalfik Thal are well built. At St. Peter's and Langwiesen, the parsonages are marked by inscriptions, and the school-house at Peist has, besides, a few verses on its front.

" *Langwiesen* is reached in 5¼ hours from Coire ; in 2¼ more the col is gained, the last half-hour being stiff work in zigzags. The height of the pass is nearly 7700 ft. From it the whole course of the Schalfik Thal, the Galanda, the Alps of the Kalfeuser Thal, may be seen. The view in the other direction is best seen after a short descent, and comprises all the summits of the chain towards the Engadin, from the valley of the Albula to the Tyrolese frontier, including Piz Linard (11,420 ft.), over the central line of peaks from the side of the Engadin.

"A steep descent of an hour from the Strela brings one to *Plaz.*" (Rte. 81).

ROUTE 81B.

PLAZ TO SÜSS, BY THE FLUELA PASS (6 or 7 hrs.); BATHS OF TARASP.

" The valley leading up to this pass opens into the Davos Thal at Dörfli about a mile above Plaz. The path runs on the rt. bank of its stream nearly the whole way, crossing to the other side only for a very short time, when about half the length of the valley has been traversed. The ascent is easy throughout, and the path distinctly marked. There is little remarkable in the scenery, which is of a wild and dreary nature. The summit of the Flüela (7900 ft.) is a small plain occupied by two pools, and within 4 hours' walk from Davos.

" After a gradual descent for a time towards the S., a wild barren valley is overlooked, running down from W. to E. The path, turning to the l., is conducted along the mountain side above this valley, into which it descends by degrees. It then follows the l. bank of the stream for a long while, only crossing to the rt. a little distance above Süs, where it joins the road of the Engadin. *Süs* is a good 2½ hours' walk from the top of the Flüela.

" It is a walk of 5 hours down the Engadin from Süs to the baths of *Tarasp*. The path branches off from the main road on the heights near Ardetz, passes through that village, descends into the gorge of the Inn to a hidden bridge, crosses it, and ascends to the heights on the S. of the river. The position of Tarasp is marked by its old castle, perched on a conical hill in the elevated plain where the village stands. From here there is a splendid view of the Engadin and its mountains, both up and down the valley. Some very grand rocky peaks rise directly at the back of the plateau of Tarasp ; the high village of Fettan is conspicuous on the other side of the Inn ; and the Schwarzhorn closes the view to the W. The inns attached to the baths are not at Tarasp, but a mile or two farther on, at the village called by Keller Vulpera. Here, at the Albergo Conzetti, very good accommodation is to be had (Rte. 84). The mineral spring is ½ an hour's walk above the hotels, at the foot of a cliff by the side of the river Inn."— *R. E.*

ROUTE 82.

PASS OF THE JULIER, FROM COIRE TO SAMADEN.

5⅞ posts = 53 miles.

	Posts.		Eng. m.
Coire.			
Churwalden . .	¾	=	6¾
Tiefenkasten . .	1¼	=	11¼
Molins	1¼	=	11¼
Silva Plana . .	1¾	=	15¾
Samaden . . .	⅞	=	8

A carriage-road finished 1839. Engineer, M. la Nicca. It is traversed daily in summer except Sunday, by a *diligence* as far as Samaden, in 15 hrs.

On quitting Coire, the traveller leaves on the l. the entrance to the Schalfik-thal, and passes through the villages of *Malix* (near which rises the picturesque castle *Strasberg*) ;

Churwalden (*Inn:* Poste); and Parpan; then, over a barren heath, to

Lenz — (*Inn:* Krone ; a tolerable dining-place.) Beyond Lenz, the Romansch tongue (Rte. 67) is almost exclusively spoken ; even German is rarely understood, except in the inns.

The river *Albula*, which enters the Rhine through the remarkable Schyn Pass near Tusis, is crossed in order to reach

Tiefenkasten (Rom. Casté), (*Inn* execrable), a village, situated, as its name implies, in a deep hollow, at the entrance of the Oberhalbstein, or valley, running up to the foot of the Julier and Septimer, a distance of about 20 m. It is scattered over with ruins of castles ; no less than 10 of which may still be counted, "and concentrates in itself the most extraordinary combination of grand features in the whole pass."—J. F.

The path leading to the *Albula* Pass (Rte. 83) turns to the l. at the entrance of the *Oberhalbstein*. There is a short cut from the village of Lenz.

Immediately above Tiefenkasten, the road is carried through a remarkable gorge called the *Stein*, which has been compared, in the grandeur of its scenery, with the Via Mala.

The valley near Tinzen is very bleak and bare. A constant and steep ascent through more picturesque scenery brings you to the village of

Molins, *Mühlen* (*Inn*, tolerable), in a little amphitheatre, amidst the finest scenery of the Oberhalbstein. To reach Mühlen, the road crosses the stream of the Falleer, and recrossing it to the next village, Marmels, brings you at length to

Bivio or *Stalla* (Bivium)—*Inn:* Löwe —at the foot of the Pitz d'Emet. This very poor and inhospitable-looking village lies at the branching of two passes, the Julier and Septimer. The Septimer leads into the Val Bregaglia (Rte. 89); it takes 2 hrs. from Bivio to reach the summit. Bivio is placed in a secluded basin, shut in by high mountains, in a climate so severe that all vegetation is stunted. Not a tree can grow in the neighbourhood, and the people are reduced to burn sheep-dung for fuel. Potatoes rarely ripen at this height—5630 ft. above the sea.

It takes about 2 hrs. to ascend from Stalla to the summit of the *Julier Pass*, 7625 ft. above the sea level. The ascent is not difficult, and the pass is remarkably safe from avalanches. Its scenery is not particularly grand, the outline of the mountains being round. On the top, the road passes between two rudely hewn pillars of granite (derived from the neighbouring mountains), called *Julius's Columns*. They are about 4 ft. high, and destitute of inscription. Down to the 16th cent. it is known from records that only one column existed, which in 1538 fell down and broke. It may have been a mile-stone. Augustus caused a highway to be carried from Chiavenna over the passes of the Malöja and Julier. A carriage-road was formed across this pass to St. Moritz, in 1823 ; but as no attempt was made, till very lately, to improve the approach to it through the Oberhalbstein, little advantage was gained by it. Flocks of Bergamesque sheep are often found on the highest pastures, near the summit of the pass, in summer. A still more easy descent leads into the Engadine, to the village of

Silva Plana (*Inn:* Croix Blanche), situated between two small lakes, which are feeders and reservoirs of the river Inn, at the junction of the roads from the two passes of the Julier and Malöja, 5560 ft. above the sea.

On the l. bank of the Inn stands

St. Moritz.—Inns: Obere Gasthof, called Pension Fahler, kept by M. Bahrutt, the only one affording tolerable accommodation: Untere Gasthof. A new *Inn* is projected (1854). Very crowded during the bathing season. This little village is rising into repute in Switzerland as a watering-place, upon the strength of its very powerful chalybeate waters, first described, 1539, by Paracelsus. The spring rises at the foot of Mount Rosegg, on the rt. bank of the Inn, in a marshy meadow, 20 min. walk from the village. A *Kurhaus* has been built over it. The water is heated to supply the baths.

The village contains but 160 Inhab. Its situation on the W. and S. slopes of a hill 5581 ft. above the sea is really delightful, overlooking the Inn, and several beautiful green lakes which that river forms in this part of its course. The climate is too cold to allow even barley to flourish; the surrounding land is chiefly laid out in pastures, and there are some forests of larch on the neighbouring mountains. The little lake close to the village, which is generally frozen over from St. Andrew's-day (the end of November) to the beginning of May, furnishes capital trout.

A traveller repairing to church on a Sunday, at St. Moritz, found the parish fire-engine drawn up by the side of the pulpit—the church, in this and other villages, being somewhat profanely used as an engine-house. He found the office of watchman filled, and its duties discharged, by a woman, and a female also occupied the situation of baker, the bakehouse being the property of the parish.

The principal *Excursions* to be made from St. Moritz are up the valley to the Lugni See, the source of the Inn (Rte. 89); to the great Bernina glacier (Rte. 85); and down the valley to the pass of Finstermünz (Rte. 84).

Samåden, in Rte. 84.

ROUTE 83.

COIRE TO PONTE IN THE ENGADINE, BY WEISSENSTEIN AND THE ALBULA PASS.

46½ miles.

Char road as far as Filisur; this is a much more interesting route than that by the Julier pass. It is 12 hrs.' moderate walking from Lenz to Samaden. This road was formerly much more used than it is now. As far as

Lenz, it is identical with the preceding route, but at Lenz it turns round the shoulder of the mountain to the E., leaving Tiefenkasten on the rt., and passing the village of (1 hr.) Brienz, ascends the vale of Albula. On the l. towers the castle of Belfort, on an almost inaccessible rock.

Alveneu. The baths of Alveneu, on the rt. bank of the Albula, are between 1 and 2 m. from the village. Here is a sulphur spring and fair accommodation. Crossing the mouth of the Davos Thal and the stream running out of it, we follow the Albula, ascending, in a S.E. direction, to

Filisur, a large white and picturesque village on its rt. bank, having a marked resemblance in its peculiarities to the villages of the Engadine. Near it stand the ruins of Schloss Greifenstein. The inhabitants of this and the adjoining valley emigrate from home to various parts of Europe, where they exercise the craft of pastrycooks, frequently returning hither to end their days in opulence earned by industry. Two miles above Filisur are the abandoned iron-works of Bellaluna, and 4 miles from hence the path enters the narrow ravine called *Berguner-Stein,* which, like that near Tiefenkasten, has been compared with the Via Mala; "and certainly in some respects bears a strong resemblance, though of far inferior extent and sublimity. Its outlet, however, is singularly fine."—J. F. For a distance of more than 1000 ft. the path is hewn, or blasted, out of the face of the rock, and the Albula roars at a depth of 500 or 600 ft. below.

Bergün (Rom. Bergogn), a village of about 600 Inhab., chiefly Protestants, speaking Romansch, and muleteers or carters by profession, who established themselves here when this route was more frequented. It is beautifully situated among the mountains.

A steep ascent leads to the inn or châlet of

Weissenstein, 4900 ft. above the sea, in the vicinity of a small lake, the fountain-head of the Albula, which furnishes a supply of delicious red trout. It is said to be possible for an active mountaineer to cross the ridge S. of the Weissenstein and descend by the Val Bivers to the high road near Samaden, but guides are not easily to be found here. The ascent from this point is very rapid; the path lies along the N. side of the lake; traces of the Roman road may be discovered near this. A savage ravine, filled with broken rocks, hurled from the heights above, along with the avalanches, which render this part of the pass dangerous in spring, brings the traveller to

The summit of the *Pass of the Albula*. The culminating point, marked by a cross, is 7680 ft. above the sea-level; near it is another small lake. It is a scene of complete desolation. On the N. of the path rise the two peaks of the Albula—Crap Alv, or White Rock; and on the S.E. that of Piz Err.

The descent into the Ober Engadine is also at times exposed to avalanches.

Ponte or *Punt* (*Inn:* Couronne, not very bad). The village lies just at the foot of the pass, and in one of the most striking and populous quarters of this singular valley. It is not more than 5 miles by a char-road to Samaden, where there are good quarters.—See Rte. 84.

ROUTE 84.

THE ENGADINE; SILVA PLANA TO NAUDERS, AND THE PASS OF FINSTERMÜNZ.

28 stunden = 65 miles.

	Eng. m.
Silva Plana.	
Samáden	8½
Scanfs	10¼
Zernetz	10
Schuols	20
Muders	17¼

A char-road traverses the Engadine as far as Lavîn, tolerably well constructed.

The Engadine (Engiadina), or Valley of the Upper Inn, is nearly 60 miles long, and is one of the highest inhabited valleys among the Alps, varying between an elevation of 5600 ft. above the sea, at Sils, the highest village, and 3234 ft. at Martinsbruck, the lowest. There is no other valley among the Alps where so many and such large and populous villages are to be found at so high an elevation. It has at least 20 tributary valleys. Owing to this high elevation, and the icy barrier of enormous glaciers which separates it from Italy on the S., it possesses a most ungenial, nay, severe climate. In the language of its inhabitants it has 9 months of winter and 3 of cold weather. In May 1799 the French artillery crossed the lakes on the ice. The only grain grown in it is rye and barley, a stunted crop; and, in the upper portion, potatoes rarely come to maturity; yet it is one of the most opulent valleys among the Alps; but the source of its wealth must be sought for in another theatre than the valley itself. Its inhabitants, aware of the inclemency of their climate and of the barrenness of its soil, are but little addicted to agriculture. The surface, where not actually bare rock, is either covered with forests or converted to pasture, with the exception of small patches on the lower grounds, set apart for the plough or spade. Owing to the want of hands the natives let their pastures to Bergamesque shepherds, and intrust the gathering of the hay-harvest to Tyrolese and Swiss haymakers, who repair hither at the season when their labour is required. The sons of the valley, for the most part, emigrate at an early age, scatter themselves over all parts of the Continent, and may be found in most of the great capitals exercising the professions of pastrycooks, confectioners, distillers of liqueurs, clerks in warehouses, keepers of cafés, and sellers of chocolate. Many of them, in the exercise of their calling, acquire considerable wealth, and become millionnaires in florins, with which they retire to end their days by the side of the stream of their native valley. They display their wealth especially in the architecture of their houses, which are distinguished by their large dimensions, by their decorations of whitewash and fresh paint. They are occasionally decked out even with fresco friezes, and pillars ; reminding one of the pretension to taste of a cockney citizen's box near London, combined with the studied neatness of a Dutchman's country-house, both equally unexpected and out of place amidst the savage landscape of a Grison valley. "But the unvarying features are their magnitude and solidity, the brilliancy of their whitewash, and their little windows, frequently only a single pane, imbedded 1½ foot in the massive stone wall, and better adapted to exclude the cold than to admit the light."—(J. F.) Poverty is rare, beggary almost unknown ; and the people, who are, except at the village of Tarasp, Protestants, are creditably distinguished for their morality. Their pastors are held in great respect, but their pay is miserable. The sabbath is strictly ob-

served ; strangers only are allowed on that day to ride or drive, and that not until after church time.

The accommodation of travellers is not much studied in the Engadine. The *Inns* (except at St. Moritz, Samåden, and Tarasp) are very inferior, and the traveller who resorts to them must be prepared often to content himself with hard rye-bread, baked only once a quarter, eggs, cheese, and perhaps coffee. The universal language is the *Romansch* (see Rte. 67) ; but among the returned emigrants, in almost every village, may be found individuals speaking French, Italian, or even English, so that it is seldom that the stranger will not find an interpreter. The wine of the Valteline may be had good and cheap. The valley contains 10,600 Inhab.

Some of the higher Alpine pastures of the Engadine are let out every summer to Bergamesque shepherds, from the valleys Seriana and Brembana, on the Italian side of the Alps— a wild, dark, and scowling class of men, but hardy and honest, clad in homespun brown and white blankets, and feeding frugally on water pollenta of maize-meal, and a little cheese. They arrive about the beginning of July, with their flocks lean and meagre, after their long march, performed generally in the cool of the night. After a solitary sojourn of nearly 3 months, spending often the night as well as day in the open air among their flocks, they return home with fattened kine and long fleeces, which are sold to the wool manufacturers of Bergamo. Silva Plana, at the junction of the Julier and Maloyer roads, is the highest post-station.

Just below St. Moritz (Rte. 82), the Inn, on quitting the small lake, forms a pretty fall. The first villages passed are Cresta, Celerina (*Rom.* Schlarigna), and

Samåden (*Rom.* Samedan), the principal and wealthiest village in the Upper Engadine, with 500 Inhab. *Inns:* à la Vue de Bernina, new and good, 1854 ; intelligent host ; Krone. Here are mansions of the ancient families Salis and Planta. *Eilwägen* to Coire daily. Opposite to Samåden, the valley of Pontresina opens out, up which runs the road to the Bernina (Rte. 85).

At *Ponte*, beyond Bèvers, the path from the Albula (Rte. 83) descends into the valley. Further on is

Mudulein, and over the latter village towers the ruined Castle of *Gardoval*, connected with which the following story is told:—In the days of the Faustrecht, before Switzerland was free, this castle was held by a tyrannical and licentious seigneur or bailiff, who greatly oppressed the peasantry around, retaining in his pay a body of lawless soldiers for the purpose of overawing his neighbours. This libertine lord, in an evil hour, cast his eyes on the fair daughter of Adam, a farmer of the opposite village of Camogask. The maiden was still of a tender age, but of surpassing beauty, like an opening rosebud. One morning her father, who doted fondly on her, was surprised by a summons brought by two of the bailiff's servants, to convey his daughter to the castle. The father stifled his indignation, promised obedience, and next morning set out, conducting his daughter, attired as a bride, and accompanied by a number of his friends in festive garments as to a wedding, but with mournful mien. The lord of the castle watched the approach of his victim with impatience, and rushing down to meet her was about to clasp her, when, ere his polluting lips could touch her fair cheek, her father's dagger was buried deep in his breast, and his companions, throwing off their peaceful garb, and brandishing their concealed weapons, fell upon the guards, and made themselves masters of the tyrant's stronghold.. This took place in the beginning of the 15th centy., and led to the revolt of the entire Engadine, which then joined and has since remained part of the Caddè in the Grison league.

Zutz, or *Suoz* (*Inn:* Kreutz), is a village of 550 Inhab. An old tower still remains of the Stammhaus, or original castle of the family of Planta, who, as far back as 1139, held the Engadine in feof. The climate here first becomes a little milder, Zutz being sheltered from the cold blasts descending from the Maloya.

[From Zutz a path leads in about 15 hrs. over fine passes to Bormio.]

Scanfs is one of the finest and most populous villages in the valley. Here the smooth road of the Upper Engadine terminates, and the characteristic features of the habitations begin gradually to disappear. The villages below this scarcely differ in aspect from those of Tyrol. There is a path from Scanfs to Davos, over the *Scaletta* pass, 7820 ft., a distance of about 20 m.

At the Ponte Alto, under the Casannaberg, is the division between Upper and Lower Engadine. The country is poor, and not very interesting, while the road is much rougher and more hilly.

Cernétz, or *Zernets* (*Inns:* Poste; Lion d'Or, wretched), is a considerable village, with a handsome church and two feudal towers, one of which anciently belonged to a branch of the Planta family, and is called Wildenberg. [Up the opposite valley of Forno runs a path into the Münster Thal, by the *Buffalora Pass*— " 6 hours' hard walking. It is a tolerable char-road, but may be mistaken without a guide. After a gradual ascent from Zernetz, it descends into a desolate valley, where is a wretched inn (2 hrs.), the only house between the two places. The top of the pass is reached in 2½ hrs. from this, and a fine view is obtained of the Münster Thal, which is reached at Tschierf (1½ hr.) : 2 hrs. more bring you to Santa Maria." By keeping to the S. or rt. hand branch of the stream in ascending from Zernatz, the Val Livigno is entered. From Livigno a pass of no great difficulty leads in 5 hrs. to Bormio at the foot of the Stelvio pass. By keeping up the Val Livigno you can re-enter Switzerland, either by a pass to the S. which takes you into the Bernina, or E. into the Val di Fieno near Pontresina.]

The names Lavin, Zutz, and Ardetz, 3 villages in this part of the Engadine, are said to be a Romansch corruption of the Latin Lavinium, Tutium, and Ardea.

The road winds much up and down to reach the villages, which are often perched on the top of steep heights, as in the case of Guarda. Between Ardetz and Fettan, it also makes a wide sweep away from the river Inn.

Tarasp, about 1½ m. from the road, on the rt. bank of the Inn, opposite Fettan, is the only Roman Catholic and German village in the Engadine. Its inhabitants differ from their neighbours in another respect, that they do not emigrate. Though less enlightened, perhaps, they devote themselves to tilling their own land. "Tarasp has been brought into notice recently by the discovery of a *mineral spring* close to the margin of the Inn, below the castle, which has proved very attractive. Various hotels and lodging-houses have sprung up along the face of the steep. In 1845 the number of visitors was estimated at nearly 400. The spot is charming; and very tolerable accommodation, with great civility, and a plentiful table d'hôte, will be found at the Albergo Conzetti, the principal *Inn*. It is by far the best resting-place for travellers going up or down the Engadine."—*J. F.*

Schuols or *Schulz* (no good accommodation), the most populous place in the valley, contains 1143 Inhab., and is prettily situated. There is much corn-land near this. Avalanches sometimes fall from the hill of Balluns behind.

Perhaps the most picturesque scene in the Engadine is near Remus, where a wooden bridge, 60 ft. span, is thrown over the deep gorge called Wraunka Tobel, through which a torrent issues out of the vale of Ramosch. Above the bridge, which is called Ponte Piedra, rises the ruined castle Chiamuff, burnt by the Austrians in 1475.

The scenery of the valley of the Inn is very grand on approaching.

Martinsbrück (Pomartino). Here the traveller, after crossing the river, leaves the Inn to find its way directly through the pass of Finstermünz; the path takes a more circuitous route, and ascends a considerable wooded eminence, forming the boundary between Switzerland and Tyrol, and enters the Austrian dominions a short while before reaching

Nauders, where the Post is a tolerable *Inn*, about a mile distant from the remarkable defile of Finstermünz. (See HANDBOOK FOR SOUTH GERMANY.)

ROUTE 85.

PASS OF THE BERNINA, FROM SAMADEN IN THE ENGADINE TO TIRANO IN THE VALTELINE.

37½ miles.

	Eng. m.
Samáden.	
Pontresina	4
Bernina Inns	5¼
Piscadella	11¼
Puschiavo	5¼
Brusio	6
Tirano	3¼

A carriage-road, in part very well constructed, has been (1855) completed, except over some of the upper part of the pass, where it is very rough and only fit for chars. On foot the distance may be shortened some 5 miles. This pass offers several magnificent views.

Between Samaden and Madonna di Tirano tolerable accommodation is to be found at Pontresina, where also resides one of the few good *guides* for the Engadine, Colani, a miller and a good shot.

The *Bernina* is a very lofty chain of mountains, separating the valleys of the Engadine and of Bregaglia on the N., from the Valteline on the S. They vary in height between 8000 and 13,000 ft.; the highest summits, reduced into English feet are as follows, but it does not appear that any very accurate measurements have been made:—Piz Mortiratsch, 13,290; Scersen, 12,940; Palu, 12,830; Monte delle Disgrazie, 12,070; Caspoggio, 11,980; Piz Scalino, 10,930. These form, after the great chain of the Alps and the Bernese Alps, the largest range of mountains in the Alps. Their glaciers have been very imperfectly explored. Several arduous paths cross the chain, but the most frequented is that called *par excellence* the *Bernina Pass*.

From *Samaden* (Rte. 84) the road turns S., ascending the Val Pontresina, by the rt. bank of the torrent Flatz. There is a footpath from St. Moritz to Pontresina, which crosses the Inn between the lake and the waterfall, and leads by a pool and through a wood over the shoulder of the low spur between the Inn and the Flatz. There are fir forests in this valley 7000 feet above the sea-level.

Pontresina (*Inn:* Aigle, clean and well served, the best in these mountains), a considerable village; a good specimen of the style of the Engadine. *Chars* and *guides* may be procured here for the ascent of the pass. The great glacier of Mortiratsch is passed almost close to the road, about an hour above Pontresina. It fills to its mouth the lateral valley in which it lies; seeming to be kept in by a fir-clad ridge of rock, which, with the exception of a slight cleft in the middle, completely closes the entrance of the valley. Being squeezed, as it were, upwards, in consequence of the opposition to its longitudinal expansion offered by this obstruction, it rises to a good height above its fringe of trees. This glacier is of the largest size, and has an immense central moraine. Its head is encircled by a number of snowy peaks, among them the Piz Mortiratsch and the Palu.

The glacier may most easily be reached from its eastern side, whence, after a certain distance, there is no difficulty in descending on to the ice and crossing to the opposite side.

Bernina Inns—three cabarets in a desolate place, 1½ hr. below the summit, the halting-place for the mules.

The culminating point, 7695 ft. above the sea-level, lies between 2 small lakes, the *Black* (Leg Nair), which discharges into the Inn, and the *White*, which runs into the Adda. Near the Lago Bianco the new road turns off to the l., and crossing the neighbouring ridge of the Camin, passes down by La Rosa (a wretched mountain inn), and Piscadella, into the beautiful valley of *Puschiavo*.

The old path is continued along the rt. (W.) margin of the lakes, passing close to them for about 3 m., with the very fine glacier descending close upon it from the Bernina. The stream which issues from the lakes falls too precipitously into the valley to be followed by a char, and accordingly the path takes a sweep to the rt., turning a shoulder of the mountain, and thus accomplishing the 1st stage of the descent at a small village called Cavaglia, with a miserable auberge. Bears are not at all uncommon here. At this part of the road you obtain a magnificent view over the glacier of *Valpalu*, one of the most beautiful configurations of glaciers which can be seen in Switzerland. These glaciers give an interest to this path far superior to that by La Rosa. Hence the stream makes another rapid descent to the level of Puschiavo, of which, and of the beautiful lake beyond, a fine prospect is opened during the 2nd descent. The track lies over ledges of rock, and down narrow watercourses. The main road, which is excellent, is entered a short distance above Puschiavo.

This route, however, is so full of obstructions and difficulties, that horsemen generally prefer the circuit by Piscadella, though it adds 5 or 6 m. to the journey.

Puschiavo (*Inn:* Croix Federale, or Croce Bianco), a town of 1015 Inhab., in the Italian fashion, the principal place in the valley, is mainly supported by the considerable traffic of goods through it. Above it, on a height, stand the ruins of the castle of Oligati.

Nearly one-third (1500) of the inhabitants of this populous valley are

Protestants ; but owing to the jealousy of the Roman Catholics, their church is almost a fortress, and capable of defence against attacks. The language spoken by them is a corrupt Italian.

About 3 m. lower down, the road, which is here excellent, skirts the W. margin of the charming little lake of Puschiavo, famed for its trout.

Brusio is the last Swiss village. On quitting the lake, the torrent Puschiavo passes through a very narrow defile, barely allowing room for the road and the stream. It is a raging torrent, and, as it approaches the Adda, requires to be restrained within stone dykes of solid masonry, which have nevertheless proved insufficient to protect its banks from inundation. Beyond this, the Valteline, or Vale of the Adda, opens out at

Madonna di Tirano (*Inn*, zur Madonna, good). See HANDBOOK FOR SOUTH GERMANY.

It is a walk of 11 hrs. hence to St. Moritz, by Cavaglia ; 3 hrs. to Puschiavo ; 4 hrs. to summit of pass ; 4 hrs. to St. Moritz.

Pedestrians going to the Stelvio should leave the high road near Piscadella, whence Bormio may be reached in 4 or 5 hrs. by the Val Viola Pass. The path is badly marked, and appears only known to a few shepherds. In ascending from the Bernina side, it seems best to keep on the N. of the valley. Two or three small lakes are passed, the peak of Dosdè (10,640 ft.) towering above. The last châlet is by a torrent which enters the valley N. ; ascend directly thence, keeping the line of the main valley over débris and rocks. Descending towards Bormio the path is well traced on the N. side, at a considerable height above the stream ; it descends at Semogo and meets the char-road to Bormio at Isolaccia. The path seems correctly marked in Leuthold's map.

ROUTE 87.

COIRE TO SPLÜGEN, BY THE VIA MALA.

4¼ posts = 38 miles.

	Posts.		Eng. m.
Coire.			
Tusis	2	=	18
Andeer	1	=	9
Splügen	1¼	=	11

The posting arrangements on this road are or were lately very imperfect. Diligences daily by the Splügen to Como and Milan, and over the Bernardin ; but by the diligence one side or the other will be passed in the night. The road is excellent all the way. It is a drive of about 8 hrs., posting, from Coire to Splügen, and about 4½ hrs. from Splügen to Coire.

From *Coire* (Rte. 67) to Reichenau there is not much deserving notice in the scenery of the valley of the Rhine ; but the mountain Kalanda, on its l. bank, is a conspicuous object ; and on the same side of the Rhine, the village of Felsberg, partly buried by a slip from threatening rocks above it. The road runs along a nearly level bottom as far as

Reichenau—Inn, zum Adler (Aigle), good and moderate—a group of houses situated at the junction of the two Rhines. Its chief building is the handsome whitewashed *Château*, with garden, a seat of the Planta family. At the end of the last century it was converted into a school by the burgomaster Tscharner. In 1793 a young man calling himself Chabot arrived here on foot, with a stick in his hand and a bundle on his back. He presented a letter of introduction to M. Jost, the head master, in consequence of which he was appointed usher ; and for 8 months gave lessons in French, mathematics, and history. This forlorn stranger was no other than Louis Philippe, late King of the French, then Duke de Chartres, who had been forced, by the march of the French army, to quit Bremgarten, and seek concealment here in the performance of the humble duties of a schoolmaster, and in that capacity made himself equally beloved by masters and pupils. His secret was known only to M. Jost. His cheerful room is still pointed out, and 2 paintings—scenes from his own life—presented while he was King. During his residence here he must have heard the news of his father's death on the scaffold, and his mother's transportation to Madagascar. [Those who are descending, and have already traversed the main road, may take the *Kunkbels* Pass to Ragatz (Route 67 d).]

At Reichenau the road is carried first over the united Rhine and then over the Vorder Rhein by covered wooden bridges, each of one fine arch. The lower bridge is 237 ft. long and 80 ft. above the river. The more abundant waters of the Hinter Rhein coming from the Bernardin and the foot of Mount Adula are of dirty blue; while those of the Vorder Rhein, rising in the glaciers of the Crispalt and Lukmanier, are observed to be of a whitish grey tint. The road up the Vorder Rhein to its source, and to Andermatt, on the St. Gothard, is described in Rte. 77.

The road to the Splügen follows the course of the Hinter-Rhein. On the top of a commanding rock on the l. bank of the Rhine, and approached by a long bridge, rises the Castle of Rhœtzuns (Rhœtia ima): it is still inhabited.

This part of the Rheinthal, called the valley of *Domleschg* (Vallis Tomiliasca), is particularly remarkable for the vast number of *castles* (21) which crown almost every rock or knoll on either side of the river, mostly in ruins, sometimes standing out boldly from a dark background of forest, at others so identified by decay, by the weather tints, and by the lichen growth, with the apparently inaccessible rocks on which they stand, as barely to be distinguished. Their picturesque donjons and battlements contribute not a little to enhance the charms of the landscape; they serve at the same time as historical monuments to commemorate the revolution by which the power of a tyrannical feudal aristocracy, the lords of these fastnesses, was broken, and their strongholds burnt by the peasants of this valley, whom they had long oppressed.

Another peculiarity of this district is the intricate intermixture of language and religion. There are scarcely two adjoining parishes, or even hamlets, speaking the same tongue and professing the same faith. Thus at Coire German is the prevailing language, and Protestant the religion of the majority; at Ems, the first village on the road, Romansch (Rte. 67) is spoken. Tamins and Reichenau are Catholic and German; Bonaduz, divided from them by the Rhine, is Catholic, and speaks Romansch. Rhœtzuns and Kätzis are two Roman Catholic villages; but in the first the language is German, in the second Romansch. The inhabitants of Heinzenberg and Tusis, are Protestant and German; of Zillis and throughout the valley of Schams, Protestant and Romansch. Splügen and Hinter Rhein form the boundary at once of the Romansch language and Protestant religion.

The castle of *Ortenstein*, on the rt. bank of the Rhine, is one of the finest and best preserved in the valley: it is still inhabited by the Travers family.

Near the village of *Kätzis* a beautiful view opens out, on the opposite side of the Rhine, up the valley of Oberhalbstein, with the snows of Mount Albula (Rte. 83) at the termination of the vista. The river Albula enters the Rhine between Kätzis and Tusis.

The Rhine valley hereabouts exhibits dismal traces of the ravages produced by the torrent *Nolla*, which, rising at the base of the Piz Beveren, on the W. of our route, joins the Rhine nearly at right angles to the direction of the course of that river. It at all times pollutes the waters of the Rhine with its mud, and is subject to very sudden swells after rain, when it rushes down, tearing up the rocks and carrying along with it heaps of stone, mud, and gravel, which not only overspread its own banks, but frequently block up the bed of the Rhine and cause desolating inundations. Thus a district, previously fertile and beautiful, has been transformed since 1807 into a desert, and its fields either buried under stony rubbish or converted into marsh. The evil has been annually increasing for several years past, but hopes are entertained of arresting it and recovering the land. With this view, extensive dykes are being constructed along the banks of the Rhine.

Tusis (*Inns:* H. de la Via Mala, very good;—Aigle d'Or, Poste, good)—a village of 670 Inhab., finely situated on a terrace at the mouth of the Via Mala gorge. Tusis, according to some, is only the word *Tuscia*, the country of the Tuscans, who first colonized these valleys, changed in the Romansch dialect. Tusis was almost entirely destroyed by fire in 1845, and is now a street of new houses.

Immediately on the outside of Tusis the Nolla is crossed by a handsome bridge. On the rt., at the end of the valley, appears the peak of the Piz Beveren.

[Opposite Tusis the Albula enters the Rhine from the S.E., through the *Schyn Pass*, one of the most remarkable defiles in the Grisons. The path at the upper end of the gorge is cut out of the sides of precipices at a height of 1500 to 2000 ft. above the Albula. From the head of the Schyn Pass, Coire may be reached by Obervaz and the Lenzerhuss. Another path leads down into the valley of the Albula to Tiefenkasten (4 hrs. from Tusis), and towards the Oberhalbstein, Rte. 83.]

Above Tusis the valley of the Rhine seems closed up by the mountains; it is only on a nearer approach that the eye discovers the opening of that singular chasm which has cleft them through, affording a passage for the river, and in modern times, by artificial means, for the road. The l. or E. side of this colossal portal is guarded by the castle of *Realt* (Rhætia Alta), standing in the fork between the Albula and the Rhine, and from its lofty platform, 400 ft. high, looking down upon both valleys. It is accessible only from the E., and by crossing the Rhine; on all other sides the rock is a precipice. These mouldering ruins are traditionally reported to owe their origin to Rhætus, chief of the Etruscans, who, driven out of Italy by an invasion of the Gauls, established his stronghold on this spot B.C. 287, and transplanted into the Alps the people and language of Etruria. The ruined chapel of St. John, on a neighbouring height, is stated to have been the earliest, and for a long time the only Christian temple in the valley, where heathenism prevailed to a comparatively late period.

It is not above ½ m. from Tusis to the Via Mala, and, as the ascent begins immediately, the traveller should at once set off and traverse the Via Mala on foot; the carriage will be some time in overtaking him.

The VIA MALA, which commences about ½ m. above Tusis, and extends for a distance of more than 3 miles, is, perhaps, the most sublime and tremendous defile in Switzerland. It is difficult to give with any precision the dimensions of this gorge, which has cleft the mountains through the chine. The precipices, which often rise perpendicularly on both sides of it, sometimes even overhanging their base, are certainly in some places 1600 ft. high, and in many places not more than 10 yards apart. The Rhine, compressed within this narrow stony bed, to the width of a pigmy rivulet, is barely audible as it rushes through the depths below the road.

The rocks of slate and limestone, composing the walls of the ravine, are so hard that they appear to have suffered no disintegration from the weather; the fracture is so fresh and sharp that, were the convulsive force from below, which divided them, again called forth to unite them, it seems as though the gulf would close, and leave no aperture behind.

When the traveller enters the mouth of the defile, the sudden transition from the glare of sunshine to the gloom of a chasm, so narrow that it leaves in some places but a strip of sky visible overhead, is exceedingly striking. The walls of rock, at intervals on both sides, afford naturally not an inch of space along which a goat's foot could clamber; and, in ancient times, this part of the pass was deemed quite inaccessible. The peasants gave it the name of the Lost Gulf (Trou perdu, Verlohrenes Loch); and, when they wanted to go from Tusis to the higher valley of Schams, they ascended the vale of the Nolla for some distance, clambering over the tops of high mountains, round the shoulder of the Piz Beveren, and descended on the opposite side at Suvers. A second road, formed in 1470, crossed the mountains as before, but dipped down, from the village of Rongella, into the depths of the Via Mala, near the first bridge; still avoiding altogether the Trou perdu. This inconvenient path, after being used for more than 300 years, was superseded by the present magnificent highway constructed by the engineer Pocobelli. Avoiding the useless détour, and the fatiguing ascent and descent, he at once plunged into the defile, and pierced the projecting buttress of rock, which had previously denied all access to it, by the gallery or tunnel of the Verlohrenes Loch, 216 ft. long, through which the road now passes. The view, looking back from this, through the dark vista of black rock, and the fringe of firs, upon the ruined tower of Realt and the sun-lit valley of Domleschg, is very pleasing. The grooves of the boring-rod, by which the very hard slate rock is everywhere streaked, indicate how arduous was the labour of constructing this part of the road. It was literally forcing a passage through the bowels of the earth; and the whole width of the carriage-way has been gained by blasting a notch, as it were, in the side of the mountain. For more than 1000 ft. it is carried along beneath a stone canopy, thus artificially hollowed out. The road is protected by a parapet wall, below which, at a depth of many hundred

feet, the contracted Rhine frets the foot of the precipice. The road is in places steep, and fit for only one carriage to pass. A little higher up, the gorge bulges out into a sort of basin, in the midst of which stands a solitary house; but it soon contracts again, and the scenery of the pass may be said to attain the height of grandeur beyond the first of the 3 bridges, by means of which the road is conveyed from side to side of the Rhine.

This portion of the pass at least should be traversed on foot; the traveller hurrying through in his carriage is quite incapable of appreciating its awful magnificence.

The *Middle Bridge*, a most striking object, from its graceful proportions, and the boldness with which its light arch spans the dark and deep gulf below, is approached by a second small gallery, protected by a wooden roof to ward off falling stones. Hereabouts, the lofty precipices on the one side actually overhang those on the other, the direction of the chasm being oblique, and the smooth wall of rock on either side being nearly parallel, and scarcely wider apart above than below. Looking over the parapet of this bridge, the Rhine, reduced to a thread of water, is barely visible, boiling and foaming in the depths below. Indeed, in one place it is entirely lost to view—jammed in, as it were, between the rocks, here so slightly separated, that small blocks and trunks of fir-trees, falling from above, have been caught in the chink, and remain suspended above the water. The ordinary height of the bridge above the river is 400 ft.; and the water, as mentioned above, is in one place invisible at ordinary times, yet, at the commencement of the fearful inundation of 1834 (already alluded to in several routes), the postmaster of : Tusis, who drove up the Via Mala during the storm, found that the water had risen to within a few feet of the bridge; the roar was terrific; and, as he drew up a little further on, in consequence of the road being destroyed, two mangled human bodies were swept past him by the flood.

The road, again, is no more than a shelf hewn out of the face of the precipice overhung by the rock, so as to be almost a subterranean passage, and the width of the defile is, in places, not more than 24 ft. Near the 3rd, or upper bridge, however, a fine structure—built to replace the one swept off in 1834—it widens out, and the road emerges into the open valley of Schams (Sexamniensis, from 6 brooks, which fall into the Rhine from its sides), whose green meadows and neat white cottages have a pleasing effect when contrasted with the gloomy scene behind. It has, however, suffered much from the inundation of 1834, which converted the valley into a lake, destroyed a great part of the road, and rendered a new line necessary. The first village is *Zillis*; between it and Andeer, a stone, bearing the following inscription, was set up, by the road-side, on a bridge, after the completion of the great highways over the Splügen and Bernardine :—" *Jam via patet hostibus et amicis. Cavete, Rhæti ! Simplicitas morum et Unio servabunt avitam libertatem.*"

[In descending the pass travellers by voiturier should leave the carriage at the first bridge and walk through the Via Mala to Tusis. It is not above 3 m., and the voiturier will stay 2 hrs. at Tusis.]

Andeer—Inns : H. des Bains ; or Poste: the *mineral baths* are not much used. This is the chief village in Schams, and has 400 Inhab., who, like their neighbours, are Protestants, and speak Romansch. Over the doors of many of the cottages, quaint verses and mottoes in that language are inscribed.

Above Andeer a very large landslip or bergfall occurred in 1835, by the giving way of a mountain, which buried the road, and, for 16 days, cut off all communication up and down the valley. Luckily it happened in the night, so that no one was hurt.

The ruined castles visible in the valley of Schams have an historical interest, from being monuments of the dawn of Grison liberty. In the last half of the fourteenth century they served as the residences of bailiffs, zwingherrn, or landvoghts, dependents of the Counts of Vatz or of the Bishop of Coire, petty tyrants and oppressors of the poor—akin in character to Gessler, the victim of Tell's vengeance. At length a peasant of the Schamser Thal, named Jean Chaldar, exasperated at the sight of two horses which the chatelain of Fardun had turned out to graze in his field of green corn, gave vent to his anger by killing the animals. He suffered punishment for this act by being long detained prisoner in a dark dungeon. One day after his release, the chatelain of Fardun, in passing his cottage, entered as the family were at dinner, and, when invited to partake of their humble meal, evinced his contempt by spitting in the dish. Chaldar, roused by this filthy insult, seized the oppressor by the throat, and thrusting his head into the smoking dish, compelled him to partake of it, saying, "Malgia sez la pult cha ti has condüt"—"Eat the soup thou hast thus seasoned." This bold deed served as a signal for a general rising ; the peasants flew to arms, and the castles were stormed and burnt. One of the first that fell was Bärenburg, which is passed on the l. of the road after quitting Andeer.

[The Val Aversa, or Ferrara, on l. of road, is a wild Alpine glen. It is worth the traveller's while to stop his carriage at the mouth of the Val, and ascend it as far as the falls of the Aversa, 10 minutes' walk. The second and finest Fall is 35 min. walk from the entrance of the vale. The lower part of the valley is well wooded and picturesque. In about 4 hrs. the large village of Cresta is reached, and the valley opens out into wide sloping pastures, which, though elevated, support large herds of cattle. Though there are no difficulties, the want of a regular path renders a guide advisable over the *Forcella* Pass, from the summit of which the path descends over snowy slopes to the mule-track of the Septimer Pass, and thence to Casaccia. Though not very interesting, this is a convenient route from Andeer into the Engadine in 10 hrs. walk.]

As soon as the road has crossed the mouth of the Val Aversa it begins to mount in zigzags into the gorge of the *Rofla*, which closes up the S. end of the oval vale of Schams, as the Via Mala does the N. Its scenery, though fine, is inferior to the lower pass. The Rhine here descends in a cataract, called the fall of the Rofla. It does not rank as a first-rate waterfall, but the scenery around is very picturesque—the sides of the valley being thickly wooded, and the river studded by saw-mills, where the timber of the neighbouring forests is sawn into planks. A timber-slide, similar to that of Alpnach (Rte. 19), was constructed to convey the trees to the borders of the Rhine.

The old mule-path which traversed this valley to Coire crossed the river by a wooden bridge, still standing, to Suvers, where it began painfully to ascend the mountains, and proceeded along the high ground to descend again at Tusis.

The new road leaves the bridge on one side, traverses a small gallery cut in the rock, then crosses to the l. bank of the Rhine, and soon reaches

Splügen (Ital. Spluga)—*Inn :* Post, tolerable. This little village is situated on the Rhine, at the point of departure of the two Alpine passes of the Splügen and Bernardin, at a height of 4711 ft. above the sea. It suffered severely from the flood of 1834, which swept away more than a dozen houses, in some of which the owners had been seated at their evening meal not an hour before. Five human beings perished by this catastrophe, the effects of which are still painfully visible. The covered bridge over the Rhine escaped almost by a miracle; that over the Serända was soon annihilated.

Splügen is the chief place in the desolate pastoral vale of the Rhein-

wald, and anciently belonged to th lords of Sax, in the vale of Misocc on the S. slope of the Bernardin, b it afterwards joined the Grey Leagu

The climate is very chilly here, an barley scarcely ripens.

The village prospers by the con stant passage of goods and travelle to and from Italy. In autumn it thronged with drovers; large herd of cattle and many horses then cro the Alps for the Milan market.

An excursion, which lies within th compass of a day, returning to slee may be made from Splügen to th *Source of the Hinter-Rhein.* It wi occupy 5 hrs. going; 2 along the pos road, 2 on horseback, and 1 on foo it is described in Rte. 90.

Travellers going N. from Splüge who have seen the Via Mala, ma pursue with interest the wild path ove the *Löchliberg* and down the *Savie Thal* to Coire. (Rte. 80c.)

ROUTE 88.

PASS OF THE SPLÜGEN,—FROM SPLÜGE TO CHIAVENNA AND THE LAKE C COMO.

5 posts = 45 Eng. m.

	Posts.	Eng. m.
Splügen.		
Campo Dolcino. .	1¼ =	17
Chiavenna . . .	1¼ =	10
Riva	1 =	9
Colico	1 =	9

This pass may be said to begin Rorschach or Ragatz. Rly. to Coir diligence from Coire to Chiavenna, 13 hrs. (18 fr. 20). Splügen to Chi venna in 6 hrs. (8 fr. 40). Voituri in 2 days from Ragatz to Chiaven 130 fr. The inns at Ragatz and Tusis on this road are excelle Coire and Reichenau, fair ; And and Splügen, tolerable.

The route of the Splügen was completed by the Austrian Government in 1823, to counteract the new Swiss road over the Bernardin, which, had the Splügen been allowed to remain in its original condition, would have withdrawn from it all the traffic into Italy. The engineer employed in this undertaking was the Chevalier Donegani.

N.B. Without an Austrian minister's signature on the passport, the frontier cannot be passed; and the traveller unprovided with it will inevitably be turned back on the summit of the mountain.

The Splügen road, turning to the l. from the village of that name, crosses the narrow wooden bridge over the Rhine, and, quitting the river, begins at once to ascend. Fine views of snow-peaks are obtained on the ascent. It is carried up the valley of the Oberhausen-bach, a small torrent which joins the Rhine at Splügen, by an entirely new line, the old one having been demolished by the disastrous tempest of 1834. This little valley presented one scene of desolation: road and bridges having been entirely carried away, and enormous piles of broken rocks spread over its sides and bottom. The new line, however, on this side of the mountain, constructed by a Swiss engineer, employed by the canton of the Grisons, is, in every respect, a great improvement upon the old one. A little way above Splügen it is carried through a short tunnel, supported by a Gothic arch.

After surmounting the district of fir forests by an uninterrupted slope, the road reaches the Summit of the Pass, 6940 ft. above the sea, by means of 16 skilfully conducted zigzags, by which the face of the mountain is scaled. Along this narrow ridge, which is 4¾ m. from Splügen, and more than 1800 ft. above it, runs the boundary line of Switzerland and of Lombardy. Almost immediately after surmounting it the road begins to descend. Upon this slope lies the first cantonièra, or house of refuge; and, lower down, a series of tourniquets conduct to the

Austrian Custom-house and Passport-office—a melancholy group of buildings, including several very common taverns for the entertainment of waggoners. Here passports are examined and luggage searched, and the traveller must often reckon upon no inconsiderable delay, especially if he arrives between 12 and 2, the douanier's dinner-hour. The custom-house stands at one end of a sort of oval basin, surrounded by lofty mountain peaks, among which, on the rt. of the road, rises that of the Splügen, and the glaciers which feed the rivers running towards Italy. It is a scene of extreme dreariness and desolation; not a shrub of any kind grows here; no vegetation is seen but lichen, mosses, and a little coarse grass. The snow often reaches up to the windows of the first story of the houses.

The old road, a mere bridle-path, proceeded from this elevated valley, or basin, direct to the village of Isola, through the defile of the *Cardinel*, a very perilous spot, from its dire and constant exposure to falling avalanches.

The French army of Marshal Macdonald, who crossed the Splügen between the 27th November and 4th December, 1800, long before the new road was begun, in the face of snow and storm, and other almost insurmountable obstacles, lost nearly 100 men, and as many horses, chiefly in the passage of the Cardinel. His columns were literally cut through by the falling avalanches, and man and beast swept over to certain annihilation in the abyss below. The carriage-road very properly avoids the gorge of the Cardinel altogether, but the way to it turns off from the second wooden bridge crossed on quitting the custom-house.

Near the scattered hamlet Teggiate the descent recommences, and soon after the road is carried through the first great Gallery, more than 700 ft. long, 15 ft. high and wide, followed by a second, 642 ft. long, and, after a short interval, by a third, 1530 ft. long. These galleries, the longest on any Alpine high road, are constructed of the most solid masonry, arched, with roofs sloping outwards, to turn aside the snow, supported on pillars, and lighted by low windows like the embrasures of a battery. They were rendered necessary to protect this portion of the road from falling avalanches which habitually descend the face of the mountains, and which, if not warded off, would have swept away the road the first year after it was made.

From the entrance of the second gallery there is a most striking view down upon the roofs of the houses of Isola, and the long line of zigzags, abandoned since 1838, by which the traveller originally descended to Chiavenna. At the village of *Pianazzo* (a cluster of. pitch-coloured hovels), the new line, after descending 2 angular terraces, turns off to the l. This alteration, by which nearly 3 m. of distance are saved, was rendered necessary on account of the injury done to the whole line by the storm of 1834, and also by the great dangers to which that part of the route, between Isola and the Cascade of the Medessimo, was exposed from avalanches, which fall regularly into the savage glen of the Lira, below Pianazzo, producing an almost annual loss of life. In 1835 5 peasants and 8 horses were overwhelmed by the snow in this glen as they were returning from conducting the diligence on a sledge over the mountain. The postilion, being nearest the rock, which fortunately somewhat overhung the road, drew the horse he rode under the cliff as. soon as he heard the crash ; to this circumstance he and the animal owed their preservation. Although buried like the rest, who perished, they were rescued· and dug out after an imprisonment of some hours.

Pianazzo stands at the same height above the sea as the bridge over the Rhine at Splügen. The road, after passing through it, crosses the little stream of the *Medessimo*, within a few yards of the verge of the precipice, over which it throws itself in a beautiful fall, 800 ft. high. The view, looking down the fall from a terrace near the bridge, is very fine ; it is also well seen from the different winding terraces down which the road is carried. After crossing the bridge, the road traverses some galleries, and gradually descends by numerous zigzags down the face of something nearly approaching to a precipice. This is a most extraordinary piece of engineering, and well deserves examination. It is of course best seen on the ascent.

Campo Dolcino, which, in spite of its sweet-sounding Italian name, is but a poor village, with a tolerable *Inn* (Post), civil people, on a small grassy plain, on the borders of the *Lira*.

A further improvement has been made in the continuation of the road, which, on quitting the plain, threads the gorge of *St. Giacomo ;* an inscription, by the road-side, commemorates its completion by Carlo Donegani, in the reign of the Emperor Francis II. It has been effected at considerable labour and expense, by cutting through the rock. The vale of the Lira presents a singular aspect of desolation, from the quantity and size of the masses of fallen rock which entirely filled the lower part of it. They are fragments of the neighbouring mountains, which are composed of a species of white gneiss, exceedingly brittle, and which, after exposure to the weather, assumes a red colour. It must have been a difficult task to carry a road through such a wilderness, between such a labyrinth of detached blocks ; and it is accordingly in many places narrow, the turnings very sharp, and the terraces too short. The aspect of desolation in this fractured valley would be greater were it not for the rich dark foliage of the chesnut-trees, of very large size, which now begin to sprout out from among the rocks so as to mask their barrenness. The tall white Italian campanile of the church of Madonna di Gallivaggio, amid such a group of foliage, contrasting with the tall precipices around, forms an agreeable picture. Near it, at the village St. Giacomo, whence the valley is named, the Lira is spanned by a new and bold bridge.

A mile or two farther on, the valley opens out, and Chiavenna expands to view, a picturesque town, beautifully situated, under an Italian sun, surrounded by hills clothed with the richest vegetation, with vines and fig-trees.

Chiavenna (Germ. Clefen, Clavenna of the ancients)—*Inns* · Conradi's, fair for an Italian inn ; Chiave d'Oro— a town of 3040 Inhab., is charmingly situated in the midst of vineyards, close under the mountains, which appear to impend over it, at the junction of the valley of St. Giacomo with that of the Meira, called Val Bregaglia. Beyond this beauty of situation there is very little here to interest the passing traveller. The town presents a decayed appearance, but derives much benefit from its position on the Splügen road, and maintains several spinning-mills for silk and cotton. An ingenious manufacturer named Vanossi at one time wove here a fire-proof cloth of asbestos, a mineral which abounds in the mountains of the neighbourhood. Opposite Conradi's inn, at the foot of a rock, is a large ruined *Palazzo* which once belonged to the Salis family : strangers are admitted to enjoy the fine *view* from the summit of the rock. The principal *Ch. of St. Lawrence* has a tall campanile standing within a square enclosure, surrounded by a cloister. On one side are two bone-houses, filled with skulls, arranged in patterns, and, adjoining them, in the octagonal *Baptistery*, is a curious ancient stone font, sculptured with rude bas-reliefs, which will interest the antiquary. The citizens keep their Valteline wine in natural grottoes at the foot of the mountains, which form excellent cool cellars and are called Ventorali.

Near Pleurs, about 3 m. up the Val Bregaglia, memorable for the fate of its inhabitants, who were buried by the fall of a mountain (Rte. 89), is a peculiar manufacture of a coarse ware for culinary purposes, made out of potstone (lapis ollaris). This stone is easily cut, or turned in a lathe, and is able to endure heat. Pliny calls it lapis Comensis, from its being exported from the lake of Como : the manufacture has greatly dwindled down at present.

The description of the road up the beautiful Val Bregaglia and over the pass of the Maloya, by way of Pleurs, is given in Rte. 89.

Chiavenna belonged to the Dukes of Milan down to the 16th century, when the Swiss became possessed of it, and it formed, with the Valteline and Bormio, a state subject to the canton of the Grisons. Napoleon added it to the kingdom of Italy, as lying on the S. side of the Alps ; and the Congress of Vienna, by the same rule, transferred it to the Emperor of Austria.

At Chiavenna, as in the Valaisan towns, are to be seen large houses, the former residences of noble families, now half ruinous or inhabited by poor people. It is difficult to understand how Chiavenna could have flourished in a place hardly accessible to mules, and why it should afterwards have decayed. At present it affords signs of reviving prosperity.

The *Fall of the Gardona*, about 4 m. from Chiavenna, is worth notice. At the distance of ½ hr. from the town on the Riva road, the river on the rt. must be crossed. A walk of ½ hr. leads thence to the Fall.

The diligence through Chiavenna to Coire in 13½ hrs. passes at a very early or late hour. A voiturier to Ragatz in 1854 charged 125 fr., sleeping the first night at Andeer, and arriving in the afternoon of the second day at Ragatz. A bargain should be made that he should change horses at Campo Dolcino, and so go at a better pace and avoid waiting 2 hrs. at that dull spot.

———

Omnibus every morning from Chiavenna to Colico, to meet the steamer from Como, returning in the afternoon.

The lower valley of the *Maira*, from Chiavenna to the lake of Riva, is by no means pleasing in its scenery, and the low ground is occupied by marsh rather than meadow.

Riva stands near the N. extremity

of the Lago Mezzola, called also
Lago di Riva. It is a most picturesque small lake, so walled in• by
mountains that, until a few years,
there was no road by the side of it,
and travellers were carried across it
in flat barges by a tedious navigation,
rendered difficult and intricate by the
annually increasing deposits of mud,
which form shoals between this lake
and that of Como, and prevent the
steamboat ascending to Riva. The
naked and savage mountains around
have a very peculiar outline. Their
sides are furrowed with ravines, down
which furious torrents precipitate
themselves at some seasons, strewing
the margin of the lake with wreck.
The engineers who constructed the
capital new road, finished in 1835,
experienced the greatest obstacles in
crossing the débris at the mouth of
these ravines. The Codera, one of
the most furious torrents, spreads
out its waste of rocks and gravel in
the shape of a fan, for a breadth of
at least half a mile. This river at
ordinary times trickles through the
stones in 3 or 4 paltry driblets, crossed
by wooden bridges, under which the
water is turned by the construction
of artificial canals, flanked by wedge-
shaped dams and dykes. After traversing this desolate space, the road
is carried through two galleries excavated in the rock, and soon after
emerges upon the delta of the river
Adda, flowing from the E. out of the
Valteline into the lake of Como.
There can be little doubt that the
lake originally bathed the feet of the
mountain on this side; but, in the
course of ages, the deposits brought
down by the Adda and Maira have
so far encroached on it as to form an
extensive plain of swamp and morass,
through which the river Adda now
winds. The new causeway stretches
in a straight line across this morass,
passing the Adda upon a long wooden
bridge, too narrow for more than one
carriage at a time. Near the centre
of the plain the great road to the
Stelvio branches off on the l. (See
HANDBOOK FOR SOUTH GERMANY.)
The Spanish Fort Fuentes, built 1603,

as the key of the Valteline, on a rock
once, perhaps, an island near the
mouth of the Adda, is left on the rt.,
and the margin of the lake of Como is
reached at

Colico, a village situated under
the Monte Legnone, immediately S.
of the embouchure of the Adda. It
is less unwholesome than formerly,
owing to the drainage of a large portion of the marsh-land. It is not,
however, a good halting-place; the in•
different Inns, All' Isola Bella and Angelo, are poor and filthy.

Steamboats from Como arrive of
Colico every day, about noon, and return in half an hour. On some days
in the week there is also a steamer
early in the morning. They will embark or disembark a carriage; fare,
first class, 3 frs. Boats may at all times
be hired here to cross or descend the
lake, but they are dear, and are scarcely
safe for carriages. The magnificent
carriage-road of the Stelvio is carried
along the E. shore of the lake, traversing several remarkably long tunnels excavated in the solid rock; it is
well worth exploring, at least as far
as Varenna (11 m. from Colico), where
the Inns are good. (Rte. 93.)

Diligences daily—to Bormio Baths
at the foot of the Stelvio; to Milan;
to Sondrio, across the Splügen.

Lecco
Como   Rail. Como to Milan.
Milan   HANDBOOK NORTH ITALY.

ROUTE 89.

CHIAVENNA TO SILVA PLANA AND THE
SOURCE OF THE INN, BY THE VAL
BREGAGLIA AND THE PASS OF THE
MALOYA.

9 leagues = 27 Eng. m.

	Leagues.	Eng. m.
Chiavenna.		
Vico Soprano	4	12
Silva Plana	5	15

The carriage-road up the Val Bregaglia and over the Maloya has been finished within the Swiss territory, beginning at Castasegna; thence to Silva Plana it is a first-class carriage-road. The first few miles within the Austrian territory are unfinished, in some places steep, and paved with stones, so that, though quite passable by chars, it might be dangerous for a heavily laden carriage. Within the Grison territory it is excellent as far as Vico Soprano. The inns in the Val Bregaglia are bad; the best is that at Vico Soprano. There is no *good* inn between Chiavenna and Silva Plana.

The road ascends by the rt. bank of the Maira, in face of a pretty cascade formed by the Acqua Fraggia descending from the N. About 3 m. above Chiavenna it passes, on the opposite side of the river, the grave of the village of *Pleurs* or *Piuro*, buried, with its 2430 inhabitants, by the fall of Monte Conto, on the night of the 4th of Sept. 1618. It was a beautiful and thriving place, peopled by industrious inhabitants, and contained numerous villas, the summer resort of the citizens of Chiavenna. It now lies beneath a heap of rocks and rubbish, 60 ft. deep, which fills up the valley. Every soul within it perished, and the long-continued excavations of all the labourers that could be collected from far and near failed in rescuing anything alive or dead, except a bell and two lamps, from the ruins. All traces of the catastrophe are now nearly obliterated, and the spot is grown over with a wood of chestnuts. The inhabitants received many previous warnings, which were unfortunately despised. For ten years previous large crevices had existed on that side of the mountain; and heavy rains preceded the catastrophe. Masses of rock fell the day before, rents were formed in the mountain, and the shepherds had observed their cattle fly from the spot with marks of extreme terror. For two hours after, the course of the Maira was dammed up by the fallen débris, but luckily the river soon worked its way through, without producing a débâcle.

The *Val Bregaglia* (Germ. Bergell) is fertile and very picturesque: it is shut in by high mountains. Many of its inhabitants emigrate, and adopt the profession of chimney-sweepers, which they exercise in some of the large towns of the Continent. After passing through Santa Croce, and Villa (Pontella), the road quits the Austrian territory and reaches the Swiss frontier at

Castasegna. Above this the white mulberry no longer flourishes, and this is therefore the limit of the culture of the silkworm. A little way within the frontier (rt.) is the *Castle of Bondo*, belonging to that branch of the Salis family (Soglio) which is settled in England. The ruined Castle of Castelmur on the l. bank of the Maira is conspicuous by reason of its tall donjon, 100 ft. high, from which two walls, 15 ft. high and 10 thick, descend into the gorge to the river side. The valley was formerly closed here by a gate, and the castle formed the key of the valley.

Vico Soprano (Vespran) (*Inn*: Krone), a German and Protestant village of 504 Inhab., on the l. bank of the Maira, 3380 ft. above the sea.

[The *Zocca* pass leads from Vico Soprano to the Baths of San Martino and to Morbegno in the Valteline in about 11 hrs. This route is not often traversed, but is very fine. It leaves the high road about half way to Casaccia, and follows the course of the Albigna, where there is a fine waterfall; it then traverses a glacier for a short distance, and then across patches of snow with very little track to the head of the pass near the Zocca. A solitary châlet is after some time reached, and then the village and baths of S. Martino in the Val Masino, a wild and striking valley, down which there is a good road to Morbegno. A guide is indispensable.]

Casaccia (*Inn* fair for the locality; obliging host, Bartho. Zoani), a village situated on the l. bank of the torrent, which after passing Chiavenna flows into the Lago Mezzola, at the S. side of the Septimer, and on the W. of the Maloya, over both of which mountains the Romans conducted highways in the age of Augustus.

[Several passes lead from Casaccia.

a. To Andeer by the Forcella (Rte. 87).

b. The *Septimer*, now an indifferent horse-path, but well traced and not difficult, leads from Casaccia to Bivio (Rte. 82), 4 or 4½ hours' walk. The S. side is much more steep and stony than the descent on Stalla. The summit is 7840 ft. above the sea-level. There is no inn on the summit, though one is marked in Keller: only ruins of a hut. The view from this is fine; the Piz Muretto and Monte del Oro being conspicuous features in it. Though now impracticable for any kind of vehicles, this was once the ordinary highway between Italy and Switzerland until the formation of the carriage-road over the Splügen, which, being a lower pass, and 10 m. shorter, is of course preferred to it. On the Monte Lunghino, between the passes of Septimer, Julier, and Maloya, are situated the sources of the Maira flowing into the Adriatic, and of the Oberhalbstein Rhein flowing into the North Sea; and the river Inn rises out of a small lake and flows into the Black Sea. Thus, one single mountain distributes its rills between the three great seas which bathe the continent of Europe, and in this respect it is unique.

c. The *Muretto* to Sondrio in the Valteline, 10 hrs.—a pass very seldom traversed.]

Above Casaccia *the Maloya road* is zigzagged for 1 hour of ascent, up to the summit of the pass (6060 ft.); but on the N. side the descent is so gradual as not to require the skill of an engineer. The scenery it presents is not so grand as that on most of the passes in the main range of the Alps; but the combination of the lofty and snow-clad summits of the Bernina, and the glaciers descending from them, with the lakes, close to the shore of which the road is carried, gives this pass an air of singular picturesqueness, to which I remember no parallel among the Alps. If the road were made good from Chiavenna

to Vico Soprano, it would be the natural highway between Milan and Innsbrück, being lower than the neighbouring passes. A little way down the N.E. side of the ridge the road falls in with the infant *Inn* (in Romansch Oen or Ent), here a mere torrent, which hastens to pour itself into the *lake of Sils*, a picturesque mountain basin, 5 m. long, extending as far as Sils. This lake (in Romansch Leg de Selgio) is fed by the much smaller lake of Lugni, 2 m. higher up in the flank of Mont Longhino, the true source of the Inn.

Sils, the highest village of the Engadine. The most conspicuous building here is the villa of a chocolate manufacturer, named Josti, a native of Davos, who, having quitted Switzerland a beggar, made a large fortune in one of the capitals of N. Germany, a part of which he expended on this huge and unprofitable structure.

The lake of Sils is succeeded by two other small lakes of Silva Plana, and of Campfeer, through both of which the Inn passes. At *Silva Plana* the Julier road (Rte. 82) enters the Engadine.

ROUTE 90.

PASS OF THE BERNARDIN—SPLÜGEN TO BELLINZONA.

Post road, 45 miles.

	Eng. m.
Splügen.	
Hinterrhein	9
St. Bernardino	12
Misocco	9
Bellinzona	15

Distances doubtful.

The road over the Bernardin is the same as that over the Splügen up to Splügen. Coire to Bellinzona, 17 hrs. Splügen to Bellinzona, 10 hrs. Voiurier from Ragatz in 2½ days, 160 fr. The *Inns* on this road are better than on any other pass. Ragatz, Tusis, and Bernardino are excellent. It is he custom to stop at Bellinzona, but t is better to go on to Locarno, a much prettier place, and the hotel no worse than at Bellinzona. The supply of post-horses on this road is very small, and difficulties are therefore experienced in getting on.

The road over the Bernardin was constructed in 1822, under the direction of the engineer Pocobelli, at the joint expense of the Sardinian and Grison governments. About 6-7ths of the sum required were advanced by the King of Sardinia, who duly appreciated the advantages to his dominions to be derived from a highway which should connect, by a direct line, the port of Genoa and the capital Turin with Switzerland and W. Germany.

The road, leaving the bridge of Splügen (Rte. 88) on the l., advances up the valley of Hinter-Rhein, whose stern and barren features have less of beauty than of wildness, along the l. bank of the Rhine through Nüfanen, distant about 7 m. to

Hinterrhein (*Inn:* Post), the highest village in the valley; no grain but barley grows.

[Hence to the source of the Rhine will take up 6 or 7 hours going and returning, exclusive of stoppages. The excursion should not be made except late in summer or in autumn, when there is little danger from avalanches. A multitude of streamlets trickle down from the crevices in the surrounding mountains, where deep snow rests almost all the year round, to feed the infant Rhine. But the *Source of the Rhine* lies about 10 miles higher up the valley, ½ of which distance, or ⅔ late in the summer, can be performed on horseback, the rest on foot; the latter part of the walk especially is difficult and fatiguing, over débris of fallen and melting avalanches, and the assistance of a guide is necessary to find the way. The scenery of the upper part of the valley is savagely grand, and well deserves the notice of

travellers. The river takes its rise at the very extremity of this frost-bound valley, from beneath the Rheinwald glacier, filling a depression between the Piz Val-Rhein (or Vogelberg, 10,300 ft.) and Zapotta. At the end of about 4 miles the path begins to ascend, and is soon lost in crossing steep slopes covered with débris of rock, so that a previous knowledge of the direction will alone enable the traveller to reach the source by himself. A small rocky and swampy green spot, on which a few sheep may be seen feeding immediately beneath the glacier of the Moschel Horn, surrounded on all sides by snow and glaciers, is called ironically " Paradies." Immediately opposite, and on the other side of the Rhine, here struggling through the stones, is a savage gorge or rent in the rock called " Hölle." The narrow path skirts its edge. To this succeeds a rapid rise. In ¼ an hour more you come to the head of the valley, a small verdant flat plain, whence you look down on the fountain-head in the glacier, which is sometimes hollowed out into a magnificent dome or cavern.]

There is a fine *Pass, the Valserberg,* from Hinter-Rhein to Ilanz (Rte. 80 B).

The road over the Bernardin bids adieu to the Rhine at Hinter-Rhein, crossing it by a stone bridge, after which you immediately begin to ascend, breasting the steep slope of the mountain by sixteen zigzags; many of the turnings are very abrupt.

A striking view opens out on the rt., over the head of the Rhine valley and the glaciers, whence it bursts forth. On the rt. of the road rises the gigantic mass of the Moschel-Horn, and on the l. the black peak of the Mittag-Horn overhangs the pass.

This passage over the Alps is said to have been known to the Romans: it was called the Vogelberg down to the beginning of the fifteenth century, when a pious missionary, St. Bernardin of Sienna, preached the Gospel through these remote Alpine valleys, and a chapel dedicated to him, on the S. side of the mountain, gave rise to the name which it still retains. It was traversed, in March, 1799, by the French army of Lecourbe, at a season when winter still reigns on these elevations, and before the mountain possessed any other road than a miserable mule-path.

The summit of the pass, about 7010 ft. above the sea, and 2400 ft. above the village of Splügen, is partly occupied by a lake called *Lago Moesola*, the source of the Moesa, along whose margin the road runs. At this point a very substantial but homely inn, or house of refuge, has been erected. The head of this pass is grander and less dreary than the heads of the other great passes.

A little way down the S. slope of the mountain, the Moesa is crossed by a handsome bridge of a single arch, 110 ft. above the river, named after Victor Emanuel, King of Sardinia, who contributed so largely to the construction of this road. The carriage-way is here covered over for some distance with a substantial roof, supported on solid buttresses, to protect it from avalanches and whirlwinds of snow, to which this gully is much exposed at times. A few straggling and stunted pines here make their appearance; a little lower down, trees 40 or 50 ft. high may be seen clinging to the rock, with barely 2 ft. depth of soil beneath them; their roots scarcely strike downwards at all, but spread far and wide in a horizontal direction, so that when a tree is thrown down by the wind, roots and soil are peeled off at once, and nothing but bare rock remains below. The S. face of the mountain is also far more abrupt and precipitous than the N.; but the road is so skilfully carried down it, and so gradually, that a postilion, accustomed to it, trots quickly down the whole way, turning sharp round the corners of the zigzags. The traveller beholds the road almost beneath his feet, extending like an uncoiled rope below him, and as he moves backwards and forwards, following its turns, he appears to hover over the valley below, and might fancy himself fastened to

the end of a pendulum, and balanced in mid-air. The passage of the mountain from Hinter-Rhein to St. Bernardino is effected in about 3½ hrs.; and on a comparatively level spot is

St. Bernardino (*Inns:* H. Brocco, large and good; H. Ravizzo; H. Motto), a village and watering-place, the first and loftiest in the valley of Misocco, consisting of a few houses planted half way down the descent on a small plain or ledge, in a romantic situation. There is a mineral spring with *Baths* here, having a temperature of about 40° Fahr., and a strong taste of ink. It is one of the highest mineral sources among the Alps, and annually draws a considerable number of patients to the spot, for whom large hotels and pensions have been built.

After leaving St. Bernardino the road ascends for about 2 m., and then plunges by a series of curious and complicated zigzags into the lower valley of *Misocco* (in Germ. Masox or Misox Thal; Ital. Val Mesolcina), which is celebrated for its beauty. Near the road are two very fine falls of the Moesa.

Near *St. Giacomo* there are quarries of gypsum: here there is also a fall of the Moesa. It is a continued descent as far as Misocco and the Ponte di Soazza, which is only a few hundred feet higher than Coire, in the valley of the Rhine. This will give some idea of the abruptness of the southern descent from the Alps contrasted with the northern.

Misocco (*Inn:* Post, dirty, wretched), a village of about 900 Inhab., called also Cremao. The views from its churchyard and old castle are fine.

In the neighbourhood of Misocco the luxuriant growth of the chestnut and walnut, the abundant crops of maize, the presence of the vine and the mulberry, which succeed each other within the space of a few miles, remind the traveller that he is indeed in Italy; and he soon becomes otherwise aware of this change by the altered language, the laziness and filth of the inhabitants, and their miserable habitations. The situation of

Misocco is charming. A little way below it, in the middle of the valley, rises up the ruined *Castle of Misocco*, a feudal seat of the powerful lords of Masox, sold by them, 1482, to the celebrated Milanese general Trivulzio, taken and destroyed by the Graübündtners, 1526. The valley is here bounded by precipices, over and among whose rocky sides a number of waterfalls dash, assuming the shape of that which in Scotland is called the Mare's Tail. The knoll on which the castle stands seems formed to command the passage up and down.

From *Soazza* a very steep and difficult path, not practicable for horses, ascends the E. side of the valley, and leads to Chavenna in 8 hrs. by the *Forcola* pass.

The valley of Misocco has lost much of its beauty and cheerfulness since the fearful thunderstorm and inundation of August, 1834, which overwhelmed the land in many places with torrents of rocks, and has left behind beds of gravel and alluvium in places 90 ft. high, thus condemning it to eternal sterility. 50 houses, 200 châlets, and many bridges were swept away. An inscription has been attached to a huge mass, stating that it and others descended from the Forcola.

Below *Soazza* the new road runs along the rt. bank of the Moesa. On the rt., the graceful cascade of Buffalora precipitates itself from the top of a rock.

Lostallo. A tolerable *Inn* here. The general legislative assemblies of the men of the valley are held here.

Reggio.

At Grono the Val Calanca opens out from the W.

Roveredo—(*Inns :* Croce Bianca, tolerable; Canone d'Oro)—a village containing nearly 1000 Inhab., with the ruined castle of Trivulzio in its vicinity. The Prior of Roveredo and 11 old women were burnt for practising witchcraft by Carlo Borromeo, in 1583, at his first visitation of the diocese. The rivers hereabouts are used to float down the timber cut in the forests of the higher transverse valleys.

St. Vittore is the last village in the canton of the Grisons : below it we enter the canton Tessin and the Val Levantina, and our road joins that descending from the St. Gothard (Rte. 34). Below the junction of the rivers Moesa and Ticino stands *Arbedo*, memorable in history for the severe defeat which the Swiss sustained here from the Milanese, commanded by the celebrated generals Della Pergola and Carmagnola, in 1422. Near the Church of St. Paul, called Chiesa Rossa, from its red colour, 2000 Swiss lie buried under 3 large mounds, still distinguishable. Defeat was at that period so unusual to the Swiss, even from a greatly superior force, that they retired across the Alps abashed and discouraged.

The distant aspect of Bellinzona, surrounded by battlemented walls, which once stretched quite across the valley, and overhung by no less than 3 feudal castles, is exceedingly imposing and picturesque. It looks as though it still commanded, as it once did, the passage of the valley. The luxuriance of vegetation, and the magnificent forms of the mountains around, complete the grandeur of the picture.

Bellinzona (Germ. *Bellenz*).—*Inns :* Angelo, best; Aquila—Aigle d'Or— (Post), outside S. gate, dirty, but reasonable; Grand Cerf. All the inns here are indifferent, and the traveller must not expect, here or at Locarno, the comforts of a Swiss hotel.

Bellinzona, situated on the l. bank of the Ticino, here restrained by a long stone dam (Tondo Ripario), and containing 1926 Inhab., guarded by not less than 50 or 60 priests, is one of the 3 chief towns of the canton Tessin, and becomes the seat of government alternately with Lugano and Locarno, for 6 years together. The view of it in approaching is very striking, owing to the 3 *old castles* which rise above it, and still seem to bar all passage. Within, it has all the character of an Italian town in its narrow and dirty streets, and in the arcades which run under its houses. It stretches across the valley to the river, so that

M 3

the only passage up or down lies through its gates. It is still a place of commercial importance as an entrepôt for the merchandise of Germany and Italy—situated as it is at the union of 4 roads—from the St. Gothard, the Bernardin, from Lugano, and from Locarno, on the Lago Maggiore. In ancient times, however, it was of still greater military consequence, as the key of the passage from Lombardy into Germany, and a place of great strength. It became the fruitful cause of intrigue, contest, and bloodshed, between the crafty Italians and the encroaching Swiss. The latter first obtained possession of it, and of the Val Levantina, by a nominal bargain of 2400 florins paid to the lord of Misox, and they obtained from the Empr. Sigismond a confirmation of their title. The Duke of Milan, Philip Maria Visconti, whose ancestors had lost this territory, by no means acquiesced in this transfer, and, seizing a favourable opportunity, surprised the Swiss garrison of Bellinzona by a Milanese force under Della Pergola, and took possession of the town and valley. It was this event which led to the battle of Arbedo, in which the Swiss received so severe a check. They afterwards twice gained possession of Bellinzona and its subject valleys by hard fighting, "by the help of God and their halberts," as they boastingly proclaimed, first from the Duke of Milan, and next from the French, who, in the reign of Louis XII., obtained temporary possession of these valleys.

From the beginning of the 16th to the end of the 18th century, the Swiss maintained uninterrupted possession of Bellinzona, governing its territory as a state subject to the cantons, with a rule as tyrannic as that of the absolute dukes of Milan, their predecessors. Since 1814 it forms part of the canton Ticino, or Tessin.

The *three picturesque Castles* which still seem to domineer over the town, though partly in ruins, were the residence of the 3 Swiss bailiffs deputed to govern the district, and were occu-

pied by a garrison, and armed with some pieces of cannon. The largest, called *Castello Grande*, or *San Michele*, on an isolated hill to the W. of the town, belonged to canton Uri, and now serves as an arsenal and prison, and there is a fine view from it. In a tall tower are confined the prisoners who are condemned to imprisonment for life for murder. The other prisoners are in chains, but do not seem unhappy: 1 fr. will procure admission to the prison and view. Of the two castles on the E. the lower one, *Castello di Mezzo*, belonged to canton Schwytz, and the highest of all, *Castello Corbario*, to Unterwalden; they are both unoccupied.

There remains little else to particularise here. The *principal Church*, in the square, is a handsome modern building faced with white marble, and has a pulpit ornamented with historical bas-reliefs. There are several convents here. The *Ch. of S. Biaggio* (St. Blaize), in the suburb Ravecchia, outside the Lugano gate, is said to be very ancient. A few hours of Bellinzona are quite enough, and Locarno is a more pleasant place, and the inn as good.

From Bellinzona the traveller has the choice of two roads to Milan : by the Lago Maggiore (Rte. 91) or by the Lago di Lugano (Rte. 92).

ROUTE 91.

BELLINZONA TO MAGADINO OR LO-CARNO, ON THE LAGO MAGGIORE.

	Ital. miles.	Posts.	Eng. m.
a. To Magadino	8 =	1¼ =	9
b. To Locarno	11 =	1½ =	12

From Bellinzona it is a drive of about 1½ hr. (carriage 10 fr.) to Magadino ; 2 hrs. (carriage 15 fr.) to Locarno.

a. To Magadino. Omnibus to meet the steamers.

The lower part of the valley of the Ticino, between Bellinzona and the lake, is a broad plain, from which the mountains recede to a considerable distance, but still give grandeur to the landscape. The country is highly cultivated, the slopes covered with vineyards, but the bottom becomes marshy lower down, and is therefore unhealthy.

On quitting Bellinzona by the Lugano gate the dry bed of a torrent called *Dragonata* is passed. As its name would imply, it is at times a great scourge; it carried off in 1768 the Franciscan convent outside the town, and threatens similar injury.

There are many country-houses on the outskirts; and high upon the slopes of the hills are numerous buildings, now deserted, to which in ancient times the natives of Bellinzona used to resort for safety when the plague was raging in the town. At Cadenazzo, the road to Lugano, over the Monte Cenere (Rte. 92), turns to the E. out of our route.

Magadino. (*Inn:* H. Belvedere, good and clean, better than inns at Bellinzona or Locarno.) The reputation of the unhealthiness of this place has been much exaggerated, and can only apply to the months of September and October, when fevers are at times prevalent owing to the neighbouring delta of the Ticino; much has been done to remedy this, and effectually.

Magadino, since the opening of the Railway between Turin, Genoa, and Arona, and the establishment of several daily lines of steamers in correspondence with it, has become a place of considerable commercial importance. Through it is carried a large amount of agricultural produce to Piedmont and Lombardy, and of the produce of the latter, including manufactures and colonial produce, for the consumption of Switzerland. Live stock especially is shipped from it in great numbers to the plains of Lombardy and Piedmont, and to Genoa.

Four lines of Steamers leave and arrive at Magadino daily, belonging to the Sardinian and Austrian governments; the former are to be preferred, being newer and better appointed. They perform the voyage to the Borromean Islands in 2¾, to Arona in 3·50, and to Sesto Calendo in 4½ hrs., calling at different places. The most convenient for the traveller will be those that start at 4 or 6 A.M., by which he will have time to visit the Borromean Islands, and reach Milan, Genoa, or Turin afterwards, and on the same day. By Rly. from Arona, Magadino is only 6 hrs. distant from the sea at Genoa.

b. To Locarno. Carriage and 2 horses in less than 2 hrs. (15 fr.). The road hilly, but very beautiful. Rly. in contemplation. The road soon crosses the Ticino by a long bridge of 14 arches. In the autumn the river is very small, but is flooded in the spring and is kept in by a strong dyke called Tondo Ripario, constructed by the French under Francis I. The road now leaves the flat and passes under the Monte Carasso, and commands a good view of the opposite mountains, including the Monte Cenere, and up the valley over the romantic town of Bellinzona to the snowy Alps towering behind it. The road then passes through a sort of Chinese wall lately constructed by the Swiss as a fortification. At the bridge of Sementina, a torrent issuing out of a ravine on the rt. forms a pretty waterfall. According to the superstitious notions of the peasantry, the upper part of this wild gorge is haunted by the ghosts of misers, who there do penance after death for their exactions from the poor while living. The latter part of the route, after crossing the torrent Verzasca as it winds along the W. shore of the lake, is delightful, winding amongst villas and chestnut-trees, mulberry-trees, and vines, and commanding exquisite views of the lake and mountains. The road though hilly is excellent, and there is not a more beautiful drive in Switzerland.

Locarno (Germ. Luggarus). (*Inns:* Corona; Svizzero — no worse than others.) This is one of the three capitals of canton Tessin; it has 2676 Inhab., and is said to have once contained many more, but has decayed since the 15th century in population and prosperity. It is beautifully situated on the margin of the lake, on which it has a little port, at the foot of the wooded cliffs surmounted by the church of Madonna del Sasso, the most picturesque of monastic groups, and at the entrance of the converging valleys of Verzasca, Maggia, Onsernone, and Centovalle, the last a primitive district scarcely ever visited by travellers. The climate, the vegetation, and the sky are all Italian ; even the people are Italian in laziness and superstition. The groves of orange and lemon, the tall white steeples on the hill-sides, and the little white chapels peering out from among the trellised vines, and mirrored in the glassy lake, are all characteristic features of an Italian landscape, even though, as far as frontier lines are concerned, we are still in Switzerland. The deposits of the numerous torrents here flowing into the lake have encroached considerably upon it, forming a flat marshy delta, which renders Locarno not altogether healthy. The spot, however, is one of singular beauty, and greatly to be preferred to Magadino by travellers requiring to halt for the night near the head of the Lago Maggiore, previous to embarking.

The *Government House*, in the midst of a square planted with shrubberies, was built by a joint-stock company for the sittings of the grand council. In the *old castle* are some antique rooms with beautiful wood-carvings. Here are several churches and 4 *convents*. The *Madonna del Sasso*, 20 min. walk above the town, is well worth a visit. The path is formed into a Calvary, inferior to those at Domo d'Ossola and Varallo, but beautifully laid out with steps and paths cut in the rock. The portico of the church commands an exquisite view over the blue lake, and the entrance of the valley of the Ticino, whose winding course may be traced flashing in the sun. Moreover its *church* contains paintings by Luini, stuccoes, bas-reliefs, &c.

The *market* at Locarno, held once a fortnight, is frequented by the natives of the neighbouring valleys, and exhibits a singular mixture of costumes.

The traveller will be surprised to hear that in this little paltry town the distinctions of rank are more punctiliously observed than in many of the great European capitals. No less than seven grades or castes are numbered among its inhabitants. At the head stand the signors (nobili) ; next to them the borghesi, or burghers; below them the cultivators, terrieri, or old landholders : these 3 classes have the right of pasture on the common lands, an almost worthless privilege, owing to the neglect into which they have fallen. Below hese, as to privileges, rank the oriondi (settlers from the villages) and the sessini ; and the quatrini and mensualisti, foreign settlers.

The decay of the prosperity of the town is generally traced to the intolerance of its inhabitants, who, instigated by their priests, compelled those among their fellow-citizens who had adopted the Reformed faith to emigrate. In March, 1553, 116 persons, including women and children, who had refused to purchase the privilege of remaining by the sacrifice of their religion, were banished by a decree of the Swiss Diet, and quitted their homes for ever. With them went industry and prosperity; they settled at Zürich, transferring thither the manufacture of silk, which is now of such vast commercial importance to that city. The day after the sentence of exile had been pronounced, the papal nuncio arrived with two inquisitors: he indignantly objected to the mildness of the sentence, and urged the deputies of the diet, under pain of the pope's displeasure, to couple with it confiscation of the goods of the heretics, and separation of them from their children, in order that they might be educated as papists. To this demand, however, the deputies did not yield obedience. The doctrines of the Reformation were preached here first by Beccaria, a pious Milanese monk, about 1534: he was soon expelled, and took refuge in the Val Misocco.

There were 21 convents in canton Tessin, but nearly all of them are now suppressed. The criminal statistics of the district around Locarno show a large amount of crime in proportion to the number of inhabitants. The neighbouring valley of Verzasca is in evil repute for the number of assassinations committed in it. Bonstetten, who travelled through it in 1795, says that the men all wear at their girdle, behind, a knife a foot long, called *falciuolo*, to kill one another. He states that the average number of lawsuits among a population of 17,000 souls was 1000 yearly. In 1855 one of the richest men in the town, leader of one party, was deliberately murdered by two brothers, leaders of the other party. The two brothers have been sentenced to perpetual imprisonment.

There is a path up the *Centovalli* a secluded and little-visited valley, very winding and narrow, to Domo d'Ossola on the Simplon (Rte. 59 B). 10 hrs. The path is bad.

The *Val Maggia* (Germ. Mayenthal) opens out about 2 miles to the N.W. of Locarno, beyond the narrow pass of the Ponte Brolla. A tolerable cross carriage-road has been carried up to *Cevio*, the chief village, and thence to Peccia. It cost the canton nearly 18,000*l.*

From *Fusio* beyond Cevio there is a pass to Airolo.

LAGO MAGGIORE.

Steamers (see Rte. 59c).—The hours vary from year to year, but they are regulated on the rlwy. trains at Arona. The steamers start from Magadino, and call at Locarno. There are both Austrian and Sardinian steamers; the latter are best.

Row-boats may be hired at any of the ports on the lake. N.B. Ask for the tariff, or bargain beforehand with the boatmen, for they are very extortionate.

The *Lago Maggiore*, the Lacus Verbanus of the Romans (Germ. Lan-

gen See), is about 54 m. (47 Italian m.) long, and about 3 m. wide at its greatest breadth. Only a small portion at its N. extremity, which is often called Lago di Locarno, belongs to Switzerland. About 7 m. S. of Locarno, the Austrian frontier occupies the E. shore, and the Sardinian the W. The navigation of the lake is free to the three states which form its margin. The 3 chief rivers by which it is fed are the Ticino, flowing from the St. Gothard; the Tresa, which drains the Lago Lugano; and the Toccia, or Tosa, descending from the Val Formazza, by Domo d'Ossola. The scenery of its upper end is bold and mountainous, and at the same time diversified by a constant succession of striking and beautiful features; so is the bay of Baveno (to call by that name the W. arm, containing the Borromean Islands, and overhung by the snowy peaks of the Alps); but, towards the S. and E., its shores are less lofty, subsiding gradually into the Plain of Lombardy. There is a great quantity of fish: the fishery is the property of the Borromeo family, and let for a large sum.

In 1848 the notorious Garibaldi and his friends seized the only two steamers then on the lake, armed them, and for two months cruised about, levying contributions on the Austrian towns and on the Sardinian convents, and keeping the helpless residents on the shore in a state of terror. At length he was beaten off from Laveno, and soon afterwards abandoned the steamers.

The voyage down the lake is very delightful, and the scenery exquisite. The sides are so precipitous that there is scarcely a path along them. Villages and churches are however perched on the heights; and wherever a deposit has been formed in the lake by a torrent, a village will be found.

The principal places on the W. shore are

Ascona, surmounted by a castle.

Brissago, a charming spot, conspicuous with its white houses, and avenue of cypress, leading to the church. Its inhabitants are wealthy and industrious. Terrace rises above terrace against the hill side; and the vine, fig, olive, pomegranate, and myrtle flourish in the open air. Beyond this the Swiss territory ends.

Canobbio, situated at the entrance of the Piedmontese valley Canobina, contains a church designed by Bramante. The two islands off Canero, on one of which is a ruined castle of the Borromeos, were, in the 15th cent., the resort of 5 robber-brothers, named Mazzarda, who committed depredations all along the shores of the lake. Before reaching Oggebbio is the villa of the Marquis d'Azeglio, and just below it that of Prince Poniatowski. A new and excellent carriage-road is in progress to Canero, and will be continued along the shore.

Intra (*Inns:* Veau d'Or ; Lion d'Or ; Ponte di San Giovanni : all small): 4000 Inhab. A thriving town, with manufactories of glass, cotton, and silk, and a foundry. The torrent from the Val Intrasca affords abundant water-power. The new road from Gravellona through Pallanza (Rte. 59c) is completed to this place.

A small island belonging to the Prince Borromeo lies off the point before reaching

Pallanza (*Inn*, l'Univers; quite as good, and more civil than the old inn at Baveno) ; 2500 Inhab. Here the governor of the province resides. A good carriage-road runs hence to Gravellona on the Simplon road, and an *Omnibus* daily by it to Omegna, Lago d'Orta. There is a large model prison for male convicts at Pallanza, and there is a nursery garden of some celebrity close to the town.

The Borromean Islands may be visited quite as well from Pallanza as from Baveno, and many more steamers touch here.

The places on the E. side of the Lago Maggiore are St. Abbondio (Swiss) ; *Macagno* (Austrian); *Luino* (Rte. 93), whence a good road runs by Ponte Tresa to Lugano Porto.

Laveno (*Inns:* Poste, best, fair; Il Moro, fine view from it). Hence a Diligence runs daily to the railway at Como, by Varese and the Sacro Monte. Exquisite views of Monte Rosa, between Como and Laveno. The Austrian Government are fortifying the shores of the lake near Laveno with blockhouses and circular forts.

The Austrian steamers touch at Laveno twice a day, crossing to and from Pallanza, Stresa, and the Borromean Islands. It is 5 m. across.

The Borromean Islands and the S. extremity of the lake are described in Rte. 59c.

ROUTE 92.

BELLINZONA TO LUGANO AND COMO, BY THE MONTE CENERE.

To Lugano, 2⅔ Swiss posts=20 Eng. m. Although the distance is so small, it will occupy 4 hrs. Lugano to Como, 2⅓ posts = 19 Eng. m.

Diligences daily to Lugano (4 fr. 20), and Como (8 fr. 70).

This road turns out of the valley of the Tessin at Cadenazzo (Rte. 91), about 4 m. below Bellinzona, and begins to ascend the Monte Cenere, a steep mountain, whose sides, shady with walnut and chesnut wood, are scaled by numerous zigzags, commanding exquisite views of the Vale of the Tessin and head of Lago Maggiore. The top cannot be reached in less than 2 hrs. from Bellinzona (Renfort to Caserma.) Even a light carriage must take 4 post-horses to ascend. This part of the road was formerly infested by robbers, and, not long ago, the night diligence, in crossing it, was accompanied by an armed escort; but, since a guardhouse of carabineers has been established on the summit, there appears to be no danger. From the summit a fine view is obtained over the N. extremity of the Lago Maggiore. At *Rivera* the road falls in with the river Agno, which rises about 12 m. to the E., at the foot of the Monte Camoghè, and follows it through Bironico to Morone, where it turns to the l., and again ascends a slight eminence, whence an interesting prospect opens out on the opposite descent towards Lugano. In front expands its beautiful lake, backed by mountains; and, on the rt., the Monte Salvadore, with the church on its conical summit, becomes conspicuous.

Lugano (Germ. *Lauis*) (see Rte. 93) is distant about 19 m. from Como (3 hrs. posting) and 12 from Varese: the Lago di Como at Menaggio, on the E., may be reached in 3 hrs. (Rte. 93), and the Lago Maggiore at Luino in less (Rte. 93).

The road to Como runs by the water-side, under the Monte Salvatore. The limestone rocks, composing its base, exhibit a singular phenomenon, highly interesting to the geologist. About 10 minutes' walk beyond the chapel of San Martino, a compact smoke-grey limestone appears by the road-side, in beds about a foot thick. "The further we advance, the more we find the beds of limestone traversed by small veins, lined with rhombs of dolomite. As we advance, the rock appears divided by fissures, the stratification ceases to be distinct, and, where the face of the mountain becomes perpendicular, it is found to be formed entirely of dolomite, which becomes gradually purer and more white, until a little way from Melide, where it is succeeded by a dark augite porphyry." The late celebrated geologist Von Buch considered that the gas discharged from this latter igneous rock, at the time when the mountain was upheaved by volcanic forces from below, has penetrated the fissures of the limestone, and changed the part of it nearest to the porphyry into dolomite. The change in colour and substance, from a grey limestone into a white crystalline marble, like loaf-sugar, may be easily traced in its gradual transition by the road-side.

At *Melide* a promontory projects into the lake, from the point of which a long stone pier has been thrown into the middle of the lake, and connected with either shore by stone bridges—thus replacing an inconvenient ferry, to *Bissone*. It cost more than a million francs. (A small *toll* is paid.) Melide is the birthplace of Fontana, the architect, who, in 1586, transported the Egyptian obelisk from the Coliseum at Rome, and erected it on the square in front of the Vatican.

After a delightful ride along the shore of the lake, the road quits it at *Capolago*, where are 2 printing-offices, chiefly of prohibited books, and commences a long ascent by

Mendrisio, which, though a small town of 1700 Inhab., contains 3 convents and a tolerable *Inn*. It is supposed to be the cradle of the once-powerful Milanese family Delle Torre, or Torriani. The famous *tower*, from which they derived their name, was destroyed in the civil wars of the 14th century.

The inhabitants keep their wine in caves in the mountains, which form capital cellars. The Austrian custom-house and police-office is reached a little beyond Chiasso, and within 2 miles of constant descent of

Como. In HANDBOOK FOR NORTH ITALY. Railway from Camerlata 1 m. before descending to the town. Trains 4 times a day to Milan.

Monza Stat.

MILAN STAT. (H. de la Villa; Bairr's *Inn* is capital; Albergo Reale, very good.) See HANDBOOK FOR N. ITALY.

ROUTE 93.

BAVENO TO LUINO—LUINO TO BELLAG-
GIO ON THE LAKE OF COMO, ACROSS
THE LAKE OF LUGANO.

Baveno (Rte. 59 c) or Pallanza to
Luino by steamer or by row-boat; or
to Laveno (in the Austrian territories)
by row-boat (steamer every morning
at 8), and thence by land to Luino.

Luino (*Inn* : H. Beccaria, new), a
small village, on the E. shore of the
Lago Maggiore, the birthplace of the
painter Bernardino, named after it
Luini. A calèche with 2 horses to
Lugano costs 15 frs. There is a Diligence daily at 9 A.M., corresponding
with the steamers which touch here
early, returning from Lugano at 3 P.M.
A good carriage-road leads hence to
Lugano, a drive of 4 hrs., ascending,
directly from the margin of the lake,
the steep hills behind Luino, which
command a fine prospect. It then follows the rt. bank of the Tresa, upwards, at a considerable height above
that river, through a beautiful valley,
crossing the Swiss frontier about 3 m.
from Luino, and 9 from Lugano.

Ponte Tresa, a village of 365 Inhabitants, is named from an old
wooden bridge which leads across the
river into Lombardy. At the further
end stands the Austrian toll and custom-house ; and, on this side, a Swiss
toll is exacted. A proportion of the
cattle with which Lombardy is supplied by Switzerland, pass over it.
The village is prettily situated on a
bay of the Lago Lugano, so completely land-locked as to seem a distinct lake.

Another of the winding reaches of
the lake stretches N. about half a mile
on the E. of our road, as far as

Agno, a village of 600 Inhab.,
placed at the spot where the Agno,
or Bedagio, empties itself into the
lake.

One of the prettiest scenes on this
very picturesque road is that presented by the village and small lake
of Muzzano, which lies on the l. of
the road to

Lugano — *Inns :* H. du Parc, large,
good, and well situated on the site of
the Convent of the Angels; baths in
the house; a coach to Luino daily at
3 P.M.—H. du Lac (Poste), facing the
lake—Corona—Albergo Suizzero.

Lugano, one of the 3 chief towns of
the canton Tessin, and the largest,
most thriving in trade, and most extending in population, contains 3142
Inhab., and is charmingly situated on
the margin of the Lago Lugano. It is
a regular Italian town of dirty arcaded
streets, and deserves to be visited on
account of the beauty of its site ·and
the scenery of its lake. The hills and
mountains around abound in all the
productions of the luxuriant vegetation
of Italy; and numerous villas are scattered along its slopes and margin,
embowered among vineyards and gardens, and backed by the foliage of the
umbrageous walnut. The principal
Church, of San Lorenzo, is planted on
an eminence, commanding a fine view.
The façade is richly adorned with
sculpture, and is said to be from a design of *Bramante.* A small chapel,
attached to the sequestrated convent
of S. Francisco, built by Bramante,
has been pulled down. Near the cathedral is a curious bone-house.

Close to the H. du Parc is the Ch.
of *Santa Maria degli Angioli,* founded in
1499, containing remarkable paintings
in fresco by *Bernardino Luini* ; a Crucifixion of large size and many figures
covering the wall which divides the
choir from the body of the ch. It is
one of the finest works of the Lombard
school. It is flanked by figures, life-
size, of St. Sebastian and another saint:
observe the angel and the devil ex-
tracting the souls from the mouth of
the two thieves! A Madonna with the
2 children, in fresco, removed to a side-
chapel on the rt., is a work of great
beauty and refinement. These paintings were almost the last works of
Luini executed before his death, 1530.
In the Lyceum is a good fresco by
Luini.

The *Hospital* was erected previous
to the year 1200 ; the former *Bishop's*

Palace in 1346. There is a *Theatre* here.

The *Giardino Ciani*, on the margin of the lake, contains a statue by Vincenzo Vela, the celebrated Swiss sculptor, 1852, La Dezolazione.

The landlord of the Park Hotel has an English clergyman residing with Him in summer, who performs on Sundays the English church-service. *Diligence* to Luino. Steamers on the lake.

There are considerable factories for throwing silk grown in canton Tessin; and Lugano further derives activity and prosperity from being the entrepôt of goods shipped across the lake from Italy, to be transported over the Alps, and *vice versâ*. A large fair is held here on the 9th October. No less than three *newspapers* are published here, chiefly advocating very democratic principles, and not unfrequently attacking the neighbouring monarchical governments of Austria and Sardinia. There are several printing establishments, which send forth cheap editions of works prohibited in Italy.

Monte Caprino. — The mountain opposite Lugano is penetrated by natural grottoes, which have been converted into cellars, called *Cantine.* Numerous small houses are built over them ; so that at a distance they have the appearance of a village. These are much resorted to in summer by the townspeople on account of their coolness.

No one should quit Lugano without seeing the panorama* of the Alps from the top of *Monte Salvadore. Time in ascending* from the Hotel to a turning out of high road into a char-road 15 min.; sharp ascent of 20 min. to a bad mule path; 50 min. hard climbing to the summit 2682 ft. above the sea-level. The slope is covered with cyclamen and gentian. This mountain, wooded nearly to the top, forms a promontory, washed on two sides by the Lake of Lugano. The view extends over numerous other lakes, and is bounded by the snowy chain of the Alps. Monte

* A view of it by the Polish artist, Charles Saske of Lugano, may be had.

Rosa is seen in all its grandeur ; and, according to some, the white needles of the Dom of Milan are visible when the atmosphere is very clear. Far away to the W. 2 or 3 white peaks of the Mont Blanc range skirt the horizon. S. the plain of Lombardy, comes in through 2 breaks in the hills, dark with rich vegetation, and sparkling at intervals with white campaniles. Beyond this the Apennines, seen through a cloud-like haze, close the view. The L. of Lugano, multiplied by its windings, fills up the valley below, except to the N. and N.W., where the Lago Maggiore peeps through the hills, and the nearer valley is studded with little lakes and white villages among the vineyards. Lugano itself and the volcano-like hill which hangs over it are singularly beautiful. On the summit it are a little pilgrimage chapel. It takes 4 hrs. to go and return on foot; more on horseback, the path being scarcely fit for horses. The charge for a horse and man to lead it is 5 fr., and 2 zwanzigers drink-money (*mancia*).

" Monte Salvadore stands amid the intricacies of the Lake of Lugano, and is, from a hundred points of view, its principal ornament – rising to a height of 2000 ft., and, on one side, nearly perpendicular. The ascent is toilsome, but the traveller who performs it will be amply rewarded. Splendid fertility, rich woods, and dazzling waters, seclusion and confinement of view contrasted with sea-like extent of plain, fading into the sky—and this again, in an opposite quarter, with an horizon of the loftiest and boldest Alps—unite in composing a prospect more diversified by magnificence, beauty, and sublimity than perhaps any other point in Europe, of so inconsiderable an elevation, commands."— *Wordsworth.*

The *Lago Lugano* (called also *Cerisio*) is exceedingly irregular in shape, making several very acute bends, so that the conspicuous mountain Salvadore stands on a promontory, washed on two sides by its waters : its greatest length is about 20 m. Its E. and W., and one of its S. arms, terminate in the Austrian territory, and travellers must have an Austrian visa on their passports to enable them to land there.

The scenery of this lake is exceedingly beautiful, and has a character distinct from that of its two neighbours, Como and Maggiore, in being more gloomy, rugged, and uncultivated. It at the same time presents great variety; near Lugano its shores are as smiling, as frequently speckled with white villas and churches, and as richly fringed with vines, fig-trees, and walnut-groves, as the more garden-like borders of the Lago di Como; but, in penetrating its E. bay from Lugano to Porlezza, the mountains gradually assume a more wild and precipitous outline, and the darker tints of the rock and oak copse furnish the predominating colour.

Steamer from Capo di Lago to Lugano, and Lugano to Porlezza. Rowboat from Lugano to Porlezza, 3 hrs. (12 fr.)

Oria, a single house, is the station of the Austrian police and doganiers, and all boats are obliged to touch there.

Porlezza lies within the Lombard frontier. Chars may be hired here to go to Menaggio. The road traverses a very pretty valley, passing on the rt. the little lakes of Piano and Bene. It is a walk of about 2 hrs. (carriage 10 or 12 fr.) to reach

Menaggio (Inn: Corona), an unimportant village on the W. shore of the Lago di Como. Near it is the *Villa Mylius*, with some good statues. Instead of stopping here the traveller had better take boat again and proceed to Bellaggio, Varenna, or Cadenabbia, or to the good and quiet *Hotel de la Majolica*, close to which the steamers stop. A little way down the lake is

Cadenabbia (Inn, Bellevue — very good), a place of great resort with the Milanese in summer. Near Cadenabbia, is the *Villa Carlotta*, formerly *Sommariva* (belonging to Princess Charlotte of Prussia), among terraces bordered with myrtle hedges 20 ft. high, and perfumed with citron groves. This palace contains the Palamedes of *Canova*, and, above all, *Thorwaldsen's*

grand bas-relief, the triumph of Alexander, executed for Napoleon when Emperor, and designed by him to decorate the Simplon arch at Milan.

Opposite to Cadenabbia extends the promontory of Bellaggio.

Bellaggio (a good Hotel, Genazzini) is a delightful spot, commanding beautiful views over the lake, and the hotel comfortable. The only fault is that there are no walks in the neighbourhood, if, however, that is not compensated for by the facility of boating. The prospect is triple, extending upwards, as well as down towards Como and Lecco. The best points for enjoying it are the terraces and delightful gardens of the *Villa Serbelloni* above the village.

The *Villa Melzi*, another palace in this neighbourhood, is a charming mansion, elegantly fitted up, chiefly visited on account of its beautiful flower-garden.

There are other villas in the neighbourhood to which the boatmen will take visitors. They all have their state-rooms, but are principally remarkable for the luxuriance with which English green-house plants flourish in the open air.

Varenna (Inns: Albergo Reale, di Marcionni, on lake, good and clean (Posta). Visit the remarkable galleries near it, excavated in the solid rock, to allow that magnificent *Road to the Stelvio Pass* to traverse the E. shore of the lake. Pleasant walks up the mountain behind, to the Castle, to Perleda, and along the brow of the hill to the Cascade Fiume de Latte—extensive view. The road from Bellano through *Val Sassina*, presents exceedingly fine scenery. Near Como is

Cernobbio (new and good Hotel, formerly Villa d'Este, highly recommended). There are beautiful walks in the neighbourhood. The Monte Bisbino can be ascended from the hotel in 2½ hrs., and is said to command a finer view than that from Salvadore near Lugano, and to include the whole range of the great Alps, the Bernese Alps, and the Italian lakes and plains.

Steamboats start twice a day from Como, and run to Colico and back in 6 hrs., touching at all the principal places on the lake. The fare is 5 fr. 22 c. They take carriages and land them at Colico (Rte. 88), where a pier has been erected for the purpose; but Colico is a wretched place, and in exploring the lake it is not worth while to ascend beyond Gravedona.

Railway from Milan to Camerlata, near Como; omnibus from Como to the Station.

They who wish to explore the beauties of the lake at their leisure had better take a row-boat, but the charges are high. In fine weather during summer the winds are invariable: from sunrise to 10 or 11 a gentle breeze, N., or down the lake: calm for an hour or two till past 12, when a gentle breeze, S., or up the lake, rises, and continues till sunset, after which a dead calm till sunrise. Boats avail themselves of this, and wait for wind as a river barge waits for tide. As a general rule the lake is nearly smooth, but from the appearance of the little ports it seems probable that there is sometimes a good deal of sea. The boats are most picturesque, and exactly resemble those depicted by old painters. They are not so slow as their appearance would lead one to expect.

There cannot be a more delightful voyage than that along the S. W. arm of the lake to Como; the shores are literally speckled with villages and with white villas, the summer resort of the Milanese gentry, during the season of the Villeggiatura.

The Comasques emigrate all over Europe as venders of barometers and looking-glasses.

COMO.—*Inns:* Angelo, very good and moderate; Italia; but it is better to go on about 2½ m. to the hotel at Cernobbio (see HANDBOOK FOR N. ITALY). The places most worthy mention on the lake are—

Leaving Como,—on the l., *Borgo Vico*, where are the villas Salazar, Frank, and d'Adda, and a little further is *Ulmo*, belonging to Marquis Raimondi; rt. is *Geno*, Marquis Cor-

naggia. A mile further l. is the Villa of Count Cicogna; and adjoining is *Villa d'Este*, once the residence of the late Queen Caroline, now an hotel. A little further is *Pizzo*, belonging to Archduke Ranieri, once Viceroy of Lombardy; rt. is Blevio, with the Villas Mylius and Artaria; and a little further on the same side is *Belvedere*, the property of Mad. Taglioni, the opera-dancer. Half a mile further are the Villas of *Madame Pasta*, the singer, and Count Taverua; near to this is erected a monument to the memory of Captain Locke, who was drowned here in 1833; his body was never found.

l. At the picturesque village of *Torno* is *Montrasio* (Count Passalaqua); and a mile beyond is *Orio*, whence is seen at the bottom of the retired bay *la Pliniana*, now the property of Prince Belgiojoso, a square building, so called, not because Pliny lived here, but because an intermittent spring, rising behind it, is asserted to be the one minutely described by him. The Villa Lenno is supposed to stand on the site of *Pliny's Villa*, which, from its sombre situation, he called *Tragedia;* an opinion confirmed by the discovery of broken columns, &c., in the lake.

The Lake of Como, called by the ancients *Lacus Larius* (te Lari Maxume !—*Virg.*), is about 40 miles long, from N. to S. Its S. extremity is divided into two branches by the promontory of Bellaggio; at the bottom of one of these bays lies *Como* (Comum), the birthplace of Pliny and Volta; and, at the extremity of the other, on the E., *Lecco*. The chief feeder of the lake is the Adda, which enters it at the N., and flows out at Lecco. The bay of Como has no outlet, so that its waters must also find their way out by the Adda. Taken altogether, it perhaps surpasses in beauty of scenery, and in the richness of its almost tropical vegetation, every other lake in Italy. It enjoys a classical reputation, as the residence of the two Plinys, and the scene of the scientific researches of the elder Pliny, the naturalist.

Claudian describes the voyage up the lake in the following elegant lines :—

" Protinus umbrosâ quâ vestit littus olivâ
  Larius, et dulci mentitur Nerea fluctu,
  Parvâ puppe lacum prætervolat, ocius inde
  Scandit inaccessos brumali sidere montes."

Here follows the elegant description of the author of Philip van Artevelde :—

" Sublime, but neither bleak nor bare,
  Nor misty are the mountains there,
  Softly sublime – profusely fair,
  Up to their summits clothed in green,
  And fruitful as the vales between,
      They lightly rise,
      And scale the skies,
  And groves and gardens still abound ;
      For where no shoot
      Could else take root
  The peaks are shelved, and terraced round.
  Earthward appear in mingled growth
      The mulberry and maize, above
  The trellis'd vine extends to both
      The leafy shade they love.
  Looks out the white-wall'd cottage here,
  The lowly chapel rises near;
  Far down the foot must roam to reach
  The lovely lake and bending beach ;
  While chesnut green and olive gray
  Chequer the steep and winding way."

INDEX TO SWITZERLAND.

N 2

SECTION II.

THE

ALPS OF SAVOY AND PIEDMONT.

PRELIMINARY INFORMATION.—Page 271.

SKELETON TOURS.—Page 276.

SECTION II.

THE ALPS OF PIEDMONT AND SAVOY.

PRELIMINARY INFORMATION.

CONTENTS.

§ 1. PIEDMONT has on its N. and W. sides a clearly-defined frontier in the ridge of the great chain of the Alps. From the valley of the Toccia, which lies within its frontier, to the Col Ferrex, near Mont Blanc, the Pennine Alps divide it from Switzerland; from the Col Ferrex to Mont Tabor, the Graian Alps separate Piedmont from Savoy; from Mont Tabor to the Col d'Argentière, at the head of the valley of the Stura, the Cottian Alps separate it from France; and from the Argentière to the sources of the Tanaro in the Monte Gioje, the Maritime Alps divide Southern Piedmont from the county of Nice. East of the Monte Gioje the great Alpine chain passes insensibly into the Apennines.

The Southern or Maritime Alps, the eastern boundary—the frontier of Lombardy, Piacenza, and of Parma*—are not within the object of this section, which is to furnish to travellers useful information for excursions in the Alps of Piedmont.

On the side of Italy the Alps offer a striking difference in their appearance from that presented in the approaches from Switzerland, Savoy, or France. From these the intervention of secondary ranges, and the long valleys, preclude any great extent of the chain from being seen at the same time; but from the plains of Piedmont, even from Turin—not 30 miles in a direct line from the nearest point in the crest of the chain—a range of the central peaks and passes, extending through 130 miles, is clearly seen.

A day's journey is sufficient, from many parts of the crest of the Alps, for a descent into the plains of Piedmont; whilst on the other side of the chain, two or three days of approach from the plains, in deep valleys amidst the mountains, are requisite for its attainment. The *Italian* Alpine valleys, with their umbrageous chestnuts, trellised vines, campaniles, mills, and fresco-painted oratories, on commanding knolls, are full of pictures, and differ entirely from the Swiss valleys, which are simpler and more sublime.

Few travellers repair to Switzerland without the ulterior object of a visit to *Chamouni* and *Mont Blanc;* it is the crowning point of their journey, and

* See HANDBOOK FOR NORTH ITALY.

deservedly so. Those who have time and strength should not rest satisfied with seeing Mont Blanc from Chamouni, but should make the tour of that mountain, remembering that his aspect from Cormayeur, on the S. side, is even grander than from the N. The traveller in Piedmont should especially direct his attention to the *Val d'Aosta* and the valleys around the bases of the *Monte Rosa* and *Mont Cervin*, which unfold some of the sublimest scenes in nature. The *Valleys of Zermatt* (Swiss) *and of Gressoney and Anzasca especially are unrivalled* for beauty and grandeur. There are few spots (if there be any) in the whole range of the Alps better deserving of attention than ZERMATT—"Young Chamouni," as it begins to be styled. The glorious views and the unrivalled and almost numberless excursions around, will well repay a sojourn of several days, and the Inns now afford sufficient accommodation. The valleys of Anzasca, Sesia, and Tournanche, at the S. side of Monte Rosa, are also remarkable as being inhabited, at their heads, by an interesting race of German origin and language. The *Lago d'Orta* is a lovely spot, and no one within reach of it should omit to visit that extraordinary as well as picturesque place Varallo.

The Piedmontese and Subalpine valleys furnish a large emigration, and supply all Europe with workmen in particular trades. In the Engadin are pastrycooks; near Como, thermometer and barometer makers; near Orta, plasterers; Biella, masons and builders; Canavese, carpenters; Val Sesia, masons; Val Blegno, chocolate makers and chestnut roasters; Val Calanka, glaziers; Val Bregaglia, chimney-sweepers. They are usually men of great industry and frugality, and, if possible, return to their native valleys to enjoy the results.

The *Waldensian Valleys* are not less attractive for their Alpine scenery than interesting to Englishmen as the cradle and stronghold of a brave and stedfast Protestant community, who have maintained their faith in spite of persecution, fire, and sword. Milton and Wordsworth have commemorated the patient sufferings and heroic deeds of the Vaudois; and Dr. Gilly in recent times has rendered their story fascinating by the charms of an enthusiastic pen. Let us hope that the evil day is now past, and that the perfect religious liberty now established in the Sardinian territories will never be departed from. In 1852 a handsome Protestant church was finished and consecrated at·Turin, and there are 15 other churches in the valleys tributary to the Po. The traveller may approach them most readily from Turin by rail to Pinerolo. La Tour in the Val Pellice is good headquarters for excursions (see Rtes. 131, 132). The Vaudois have been established in the valleys of the Alps since the 8th century, and refer the origin of their faith and sect to the time of the Apostles, and the first ages of Christianity. Their numbers in the valleys amount to about 22,000, but they are rapidly increasing and spreading, and there are large colonies of them in Turin and Genoa. Cromwell courageously interposed to protect them in their distress, and stirred up all the powers of Europe on their behalf; he also raised a subscription for their aid, part of which was funded, and, though the sum was appropriated by Charles II., the interest has since been paid by the British Government for their support. The best season for travelling in this part of the Alpine chain seems to be July and the first part of August;

towards the end of that month the weather becomes uncertain, and often breaks up in the middle of September.

" In the Piedmontese valleys the N.W. and N.N.W. winds bring fine weather."—*Forbes.*

§ 2. *Inns.*—The *Inns* on the frontier of Italy—excepting those on the lake of Como and a few others specially mentioned in these pages—are rather cheaper, but vastly inferior in accommodation, and especially in cleanliness, to those of Switzerland and Germany. Men may tolerate the inconveniences, but they will be more seriously felt by ladies, who must be prepared at times to " rough it" after crossing the Italian border. The want of female attendance, the dirty floor seldom or never washed, scanty service, no bells, may be generally expected.

N.B.—Dishonesty is by no means uncommon in the Italian inns, and it is generally prudent—nay, necessary, in the smaller Inns—to bargain before you enter your rooms, what you are to pay for them. Likewise in ordering dinner fix your own price—say 3 frs. a head—or you may be charged for each separate item. " My general practice, *after* having seen the best rooms the landlord has to offer, is, to say *my* price is 1½ fr. per bed, and I dine at 3 frs. per head. This is invariably acquiesced in, although sometimes after some considerable demur, and I believe few people are better served than I am. I always make a point of going into the kitchen myself, and of consulting the chef as to the important matter of dinner, which usually secures the best things the larder contains."—F.

In excursions over the high Alps of Piedmont and Savoy it is generally necessary to carry some provision of wine, bread, and meat. The shepherd's fare of a mountain châlet in those parts is limited to milk, butter, and cheese, to which is added a coarse brown bread, in thin discs, baked twice a year, and kept in store in the roof of the châlet until it is as hard as stone, and requires a hammer to break it. To this may be added pollenta, a porridge or pudding of maize-meal, and scraps of dried mutton.

When the traveller in the Alps receives the hospitality of the *curés* of retired villages, or of the pastor in the Protestant Waldensian valleys, where there are no inns, it is usual to leave with the housekeeper, or for her, a donation, which it is just should at least equal the cost of such accommodation at an inn; the tax would otherwise be heavy upon the limited means of the host, and kindness and attention are thus insured to future travellers. For supper, bed, and breakfast, 5 or 6 frs. are given. The *curés* in these valleys are rarely superior in any respect to the ordinary peasants, from whom they have no doubt sprung.

§ 3. *Roads, Mules, &c.*—The *Roads* skirting the Alps, and the approaches to them from the plains of Piedmont, are generally excellent. Wherever there is intercourse there is a good road adapted to the wants of the inhabitants: if fit for *Volantins* or chars, these may always be obtained at moderate charges, usually 12 francs a day.

Mules may readily be obtained in all mountain routes accessible to them, at charges varying from 4 to 6 francs a day; and *guides* at 4 or 5 francs a day may be had in every Alpine village of Piedmont. Ladies will now find *side-*

saddles in almost every place where there are inns and horses; where these are not, ladies had better not venture. On mountain excursions a portantine, or chaise à porteur, may be procured.

If mules, horses, or a char be taken across the frontier, a *boleta*, or permission to pass the douane, is necessary; here the animal is registered, the course of the traveller stated, and money for the horse deposited as a duty upon the *entrée*, which is repaid to the owner when he leaves the place on the frontier indicated in the boleta as the point by which he is to return to his own country.

§ 4. *Guides.*—Rigid caution should be exercised in choosing and adopting *Guides* on the Italian side of the Alps. Guides by profession are rarer here than in Switzerland, and any idle person, however unqualified, may offer himself for the sake of a good day's wages. No one should be accepted without sufficient evidence both of *good character* and experience, from the innkeepers, the curé, or some respectable person of his village. Certificates from former employers should be inquired for. The value of such testimony will be appreciated when travellers are told how in some cases, in remote places, men will press themselves into your service to conduct you over dangerous passes which they have never even seen, or of others who, in the middle of an intricate pass, where their services are indispensable, will become menacing and extortionate, and even strike for higher wages. Few scruple to avow their acquaintance with places of which they really know nothing; their only use, then, to the traveller is to bear his luggage, and talk Piedmontese, a jargon which few travellers are acquainted with. In Piedmont French and Italian are often unknown; among those, however, who are accustomed to act as guides, French is generally spoken, especially in the valleys on the frontiers of Savoy and France. In most of the French Alpine valleys of the *Dépt. de l'Isère* the guide by profession is unknown, and the stranger is liable to conspiracies between innkeepers and men who call themselves guides to extort money and enhance the value of their services.

§ 5. *Posting—Distances.*—The posting regulations in the kingdom of Sardinia have been recently assimilated to those of France, the distances being reckoned in kilomètres (see p. xvii.), and the charges nearly the same, viz. 20 centimes per kil. for each horse, and 12 for postilions; on the mountain-passes of Mt. Cenis, the Simplon, and Tenda, the charge for each horse is increased one-third, or to 30 c.

The number of horses which the postmasters can put on is regulated according to the size of the carriages and the number of people, for which purpose all vehicles are arranged under three classes. The postmasters of Turin and Genoa are allowed to charge as for additional distance.

At the posthouses on the passes of the Monts Cenis, Simplon, and Col di Tenda, the masters must provide sledges during the winter season, for the hire of which they are entitled to charge 15 c. per kilomètre; and 3 and 4 francs for dismounting and placing on the sledge each carriage, according to the class to which it may be referable. On some roads *chevaux de renfort* must be taken or paid for. For fuller details the traveller is referred to 'Articles de Règlement sur les Postes aux Chevaux,' which can be purchased everywhere.

Diligence offices at Turin, Bonafous & Co., Contrada del Teatro d'Angennes, No. 37; the Messageries Impériales, equally good, near the Contrada del Po. The postilion asks a buonamano of the passengers at every stage; the smallest coin will satisfy him.

§ 6. *Frontier and Custom-house.*—As there is much smuggling on the frontier of France, the traveller is often subjected to vexatious delay, but time will always be gained by submitting to it. The French can rarely be bribed—the Piedmontese Preposés more easily—to facilitate the passage from one country to another. They are usually very civil. N.B. *Tobacco* is strictly prohibited. Travellers ought even to declare the possession of a few cigars, otherwise they may be subjected to heavy fine and detention.

§ 7. It is almost unnecessary to advise a traveller not to sleep in the plains if he can reach the mountains. His own love of that "health in the breeze and freshness in the gale," which is so exciting and invigorating in the mountains, would prompt him to seek for the pleasure of breathing it and the spirits it inspires; but the suggestion is offered to induce young travellers to avoid sleeping near the rice-grounds of Piedmont, or near the ponds, where in the summer the Piedmontese steep their hemp: these are deleterious, and may produce fever.

§ 8. The *wines* of Piedmont are generally wholesome, often fine, and sometimes of great celebrity; and there is scarcely a hut in a village on the mountains where *grissine*—a fine sort of biscuit like long pipes, and made of excellent flour—cannot be obtained. The traveller should never fail to supply his pockets with some of this bread or biscuit broken into convenient lengths; this, with a quaff from a fresh spring, will bear him, if taken at his intervals of rest, through a long day's journey.

§ 9. The *money* of Piedmont is the same as that of France; *i. e.* of the same quality, denomination, and value.

§ 10. *Maps.*—The Sardinian Government has recently published an accurate survey of its continental territories in a map of 6 sheets, 35 fr.: 2 sheets contain Savoy, 14 fr. And a map of the kingdom, in 91 sheets, on a scale of $\frac{1}{50000}$, has been undertaken by the Government; 60 sheets have been published. A portable reduction from this map has been published at Turin. General Bourcet's map of the French Alps from Nice to Pont Beauvoisin is one of the most accurate yet published. A faithful reduction of this map to two small sheets may be had. *Perrin*, at Chambéry, has published an excellent map of Savoy at 4 fr., and a smaller at 1 fr. 50 cent. A voluminous ' Dizionario Geografico, Storico,' &c., of the States of the King of Sardinia, has been recently completed. All maps of the country may be procured at Maggi's shop in the Contrada del Po, Turin, and also at Perrin's, Chambéry. Perrin has also published maps of Savoy on a large scale, and works on the ornithology and the botany of Savoy, admirably got up and executed; also a Guide to Savoy.

The best map of the country N. of Monte Rosa is Studer's, Zürich, but the paths are unaccountably omitted.

Neither Leuthold nor Keller is very accurate on the Italian side of the Alps.

Pedestrian Tours of Six Weeks or Two Months, chiefly in the Alps of Savoy and Piedmont.

** Carriage Road.   * Char Road.   † Mule Road.   § Footpath.

All names following the marks indicated are the same as the last.

** Geneva to Sallenches, or St. Martin. (115.)
* Chamouny.
† Tête Noire to Trient. (116.)
Col de Balme to Chamouny. (117.)
§ Breven.
§ Montanvert, le Jardin.
† Chamouny to Cormayeur, by the Col de Vosa, Col de Bonhomme and the Col de la Seigne. (118.)
** Cormayeur to Aosta. (107.)
* St. Remy. (108.)
† Hospice of the Great St. Bernard.
Liddes.
* Martigny.   (*See* Switzerland, Route 59.)
** Visp in Valais.
Zermatt, Riffelberg, &c.
† Pass of the Mont Cervin. (106.)
Chatillon, Val d'Aosta.
Col de Jon. (104.)
Brussone.
Col de Ranzola.
Gressoney.
Col de Val Dobbia.
Riva.
Varallo, Val Sesia. (101.)
Rocco. (102.)
Col de Colma.
Pella—Lake of Orta.

Omegna.
** Vogogna. (59 and 105.)
† Macugnaga—Monte Rosa.
§ Col de Moro.
Saas.
† Visp, in Valais.
** Pass of the Simplon. (59.)
Arona—Lago Maggiore.
Borgomanero. (101.)
Biella. (103.)
Ivrea. (107.)
Aosta.
† Cogne.
Pont—Val d'Orca.
Ceresol.
§ Col de Galèse, and return to Chapis.
† Col de la Croix de Nivolet.
Val Savaranche.
Villeneuve—Val d'Aosta.
* St. Didier—Mont Saxe.
† The Cramont, the Belvedere and Pass of the Little St. Bernard. (114.)
* Bourg St. Maurice.
Moutiers Tarentaise. (122.)
** L'Hôpital Conflans.
Ugine.
Faverges.
Annecy.
Geneva. (53.)

Six Weeks' Excursion.   If extended to Two Months, start from

* Moutiers Tarantaise. (123.)
Baths of Brida.
† Pralorgnan.
Col de Vanoise.
Lanslebourg. (127.)
** Pass of the Mont Cenis.
Susa.
† Cesanne. (131.)
† Col de Sestrières.
* Pragelas—Val Clusone.

Perouse.
† Val Germanasca. Protestant valley. (132.)
Balsille.
Col de la Fontaines.
Pralis.
Col Julian.
Bobbio.
* La Tour.
† Val Angrona.
Rora.
** Lucerne.
Barge.

Peysanne. (133.)
† Crussoles.
§ Pass of the Monte Viso.
† Abries.
Combe de Queyras.
* Embrun.
** Gap.
Grenoble.
Chambéry.
Aix.
Annecy.
Geneva.

ROUTES IN PIEDMONT AND SAVOY.

ROUTE 101.

ARONA TO VARALLO AND ALAGNA, IN
THE VAL SESIA.

Arona.	Hours.
Borgománero	1¼
Romagnano	1¼
Borgo Sesia	2
Varallo	2¼

Altogether 7½ hours' drive from
Arona (Rte. 59c) to Varallo.

Borgománero is a large well-built
town in the direct road to Vercelli and
Turin, from Arona. [From Borgománero (no post-horses) a good carriage
road lies through the village of Gozzano to Buccione, a village at the
head of the lake of Orta, which may
be reached in an hour from Borgomanero. A new road also has been made
from Arona to Orta, avoiding the détour by Borgománero. It is good;
but the streets of two villages through
which it runs are so narrow that a *large*
travelling carriage could hardly pass.
The scenery on the road, especially the
approach to the lake of Orta (Rte.
102), is scarcely to be rivalled. At
Buccione boats may be had to Omegna
at the lower end of the lake, distant 9
m.; or the new carriage-road may be
followed by Orta to Gravellona on the
route of the Simplon, 3 m. from the
Lago Maggiore.]

From *Borgománero* there is an
excellent road to the little town of
Romagnano on the Sesia (*Inn*, La
Posta), remarkable as the spot where
Bayard—*sans peur et sans reproche*—
received his death-wound while protecting the rear of the French under
Bonnivet in their retreat across the
Alps, April 20, 1524. From Romagnano the road up the course of the
Sesia is singularly beautiful; the
mountains as they are approached
offer richly wooded slopes, and the
masses are relieved by castles,

churches, and oratories. The vegetation is most luxuriant; several
villages are passed.

The principal place before arriving
at Varallo is *Borgo Sesia;* here the
valley becomes narrower, and the road
offers some striking scenes, though
the range of view is more limited in
the narrow parts of the Val Sesia. It
opens again in the neighbourhood of
Varallo. Inns: Albergo d'Italia—
good and reasonable; dinner, 3 fr.;
bed, 1¼ fr.; breakfast, 1¼ fr. La Poste,
fine view, best. Falcone Nero, an
Italian trattoria. There is need of
many inns to provide for the bodily
wants of the pilgrim visitors to the
Sacro Monte, who, especially on the
Festas of the Church, crowd here as
devotees. The situation of this town,
and the sanctuary on its celebrated
Sacro Monte—*La Nuova Gerusalemme
nel Sacro Monte di Varallo,* as the
guide-book calls this extraordinary
place of pilgrimage—present singular
and interesting scenes, which no one
who has the means should neglect to
visit.

Varallo, from every point of view,
is highly picturesque, but it is so in a
striking degree when seen from the
lofty and narrow bridge across the
Sesia. From the dry bed of the river
below the bridge across the Maste-
lone, the Sacro Monte appearing
through its arches, the old houses and
the richly wooded slopes, form a
tableau that few sketchers fail to
possess.

The *Sacro Monte is the great object of attraction and pilgrimage. It
rises immediately above the town, and
is accessible by a paved path, which
winds up the side of the hill, and
offers from every turn the most picturesque and beautiful scenes.

In the fine *Ch. of S. Francisco,* at the
foot of the S. Monte, are some admirable

works by *Gaudenzio Ferrari*, executed after his return from Rome, 1510-13. The whole wall dividing the nave from the choir (the passage from one to the other being only through a small arch) is painted by him in fresco, in 19 compartments, representing events in our Saviour's history—the central and largest being the Crucifixion. They are all most carefully executed, and are among the best works of the master, serving to illustrate his position in Italian art. In a side chapel (rt.) are also 2 frescoes by him—the Circumcision and the Dispute with the Doctors; not so good. In the cloister is a Pietà, said to be his first work in Varallo; and in the Sacristy a Virgin and saints, on wood, by Giovenone his master, much injured.

In the *Ch. of St. Gaudenzio* is a fine altarpiece on panel by G. Ferrari.

The hill of the Sacro Monte is covered with a series of 50 chapels or oratories, containing groups of figures modelled in terra-cotta, painted and clothed, placed and composed on the floors. They chiefly represent some of the principal events in the history of Christ, in the order of their occurrence. These structures are never entered; they are merely frames or cases for the subjects grouped within them, seen from 2 or 3 peep-holes in front, like those in the raree-shows. As works of art the greater number are very indifferent. A few, on the contrary, contain works of the highest merit, and to these the attention of every traveller of taste is specially invited. He will be sorry to miss them, as he might easily do, in passing rapidly along the mass of rubbish. Externally, these oratories are rich in the architectural display of façades, porticos, domes, &c.: the figures within are the size of life.

The subjects are in the order of the numbers of the chapels.

1. The Fall of Man. Adam and Eve are seen amidst animals of all sorts and sizes, from the elephant to the rabbit.
2. The Annunciation. The series which refer to Christ commences.
3. The Visitation.
4. The Angel announcing to Joseph the Miraculous Conception.
5. The Star of the East.
6. The Nativity.
7. Joseph and Mary adoring Christ.
8. The Presentation in the Temple.
9. The Angel advising Joseph to fly into Egypt.
10. The Flight.
11. The Murder of the Innocents. One of the large compositions contains above 60 figures, the size of life, besides the painted groups on the walls; so arranged as to assist the composition.
12. The Baptism in the Jordan.
13. The Temptation.
14. Christ and the Woman of Samaria.
15. Christ Curing the Paralytic.
16. Christ Raising the Widow's Son.
17. The Transfiguration. This subject, the largest of all, perhaps 100 ft. high, is represented upon an enormous scale; the group in the foreground contains the demoniac boy; on the mountain, an immense modelled mass, are the three disciples; above them Christ, with Moses and Elias; over these, painted on the walls and ceiling of the dome, are the host of heaven; and above all, the Almighty.
18. The Raising of Lazarus.
19. The Entrance into Jerusalem.
20. The Last Supper.
21. Christ in the Garden.
22. Christ finds his Disciples Sleeping.
23. Christ betrayed by Judas.
24. Christ in the House of Anna.
25. Christ in the Hands of Caiaphas.
26. The Repentance of St. Peter.
27. Christ in the House of Pilate.
28. Christ in the House of Herod.
29. Christ Reconducted to Pilate.
30. The Flagellation.
31. Christ Crowned with Thorns.
32. Christ again conducted to Pilate.
33. Christ shown to the People.
34. Pilate Washing his Hands.

35. Christ sentenced to Death.
36. Christ Bearing the Cross.
37. Christ Nailed to the Cross.
38.**The Crucifixion.
    The paintings on the walls and ceiling of this chapel are the masterpiece of Gaudenzio Ferrari. The chief subject, a splendid composition, including 60 or 70 figures, is in good preservation. Observe the soft beauty of the group of females and children.
39. Christ taken down from the Cross.
40. The Pietà—the Women around the Body of Christ.
41. The Body wrapped in Linen.
42. San Francesco.
43. Christ Lying in the Sepulchre.
44. Saint Anna.
45. An Angel announcing to the Virgin Mary her Translation to Heaven.
46. The Sepulchre of the Virgin Mary.

All the walls are painted, and many of the pictures are masterly productions, not unworthy of the reputation of *Pelegrini Tibaldi*, whose name is found in the list of those who were employed upon the works of the Sacro Monte di Varallo; together with that of *Gaudenzio Ferrari*, a pupil and companion of Raphael, *Fiammingo* the famous sculptor of children, and many other artists of eminence, as painters, sculptors, and architects. The valleys of the Novarrese, of which Val Sesia is the principal, are remarkable for the number of painters they have produced, and the names of many are preserved here as having contributed to the embellishment of this singular sanctuary.

Much effect is produced by the appropriate situation of some of the subjects. The access to the place where Christ is laid in the sepulchre is by a vault, where little light is admitted; and as it is difficult on entering from the open day to distinguish at first any object, the effect is very imposing.

Many of the figures are clothed in real drapery, and some have real hair, which appears very grotesque, yet full of character and expression; many of the heads are finely modelled. In the subject of the Visitation the head of a female is strikingly fine. The executioners conducting to Calvary, or otherwise employed in inflicting suffering on Christ, are, to increase the disgust for their characters, modelled with goîtres appended to their throats—a proof that these are not considered beauties here, in spite of the traveller's tale. The models are painted, but no offence to taste in their class of art arises from this, because, as the subjects can only be seen through peep-holes in front of the *prie-dieus* of the oratories, and not in passing from one of those to another, as much illusion is produced in seeing them as in observing a picture.

Among the objects of religious reverence here is a flight of steps, called the Scala Santa, recommended to the especial devotion of the faithful, who are informed by an inscription on a tablet at the foot of these stairs, that they have been built in *exact imitation* of the Scala Santa at St. John Lateran in Rome. Some of the numerous devotees and pilgrims may always be seen crawling up these stairs, encouraged by a concession of plenary indulgence granted by Pope Clement XII. to all who would climb these eight-and-twenty steps on their hands and knees, say an *Ave*, a *Pater*, and a *Gloria* on each step, and kiss each step devoutly.

The Sacro Monte originated in the piety of the *blessed* (*i. e.* half saint) Bernardino Caimo, a noble Milanese, who obtained in 1486, from Pope Innocent VIII., a faculty to found this sanctuary. Only 3 or 4 chapels were built in the time of the founder, but so great did its reputation for sanctity soon become, that princes and rich devotees speedily contributed to make it what it now is. St. Carlo Borromeo twice visited it, in 1578 and 1584, and the pallet *bedstead*, upon which this patron saint of Milan died, is preserved here as a holy relic for the veneration of the faithful.

The convent, where the priests reside, in a beautiful situation, commands views of Varallo and the Val Sesia below the town. At the entrance to the Oratories, booths or shops are established for the sale of *corone*, i. e. beads, crucifixes, madonnas, &c., which have acquired sanctity, and the power (*as is asserted*) of working miracles, by having touched the blessed bed of the holy St. Carlo, or other miracle-working relics. The body is, however, provided for as well as the soul; and there are two booths within the sacred precincts for the sale of liquors.

Until lately this most remarkable and picturesque place, with the adjoining valleys of Anzasca, Sesia, Mastellone, and Sermenta, was not much visited, and the accommodation was very defective. Now, however, English visitors are becoming numerous, and the Inns are much improved. Varallo is far enough in the heart of the country to be made head-quarters, whilst researches are carried on in its neighbourhood.

Near Varallo are nickel-mines worked by an English company.

The *Ponte della Gula*, about 1 hr.'s walk up the Val Mastellone, is a remarkable scene (Rte. 101A); the green river, hemmed in by vertical rocks 150 ft. high, is spanned by a lofty bridge. A carriage-road in course of construction, 1857.

Varallo to Piode . . .	12 m.	
Piode to Alagna . . .	4¼ hrs.	

From Varallo there is an excellent carriage-road to Piode, and chars might reach Mollia, above which place the ascent of the Val Sesia can be made only on mules. N.B. On market-days it is difficult to hire mules in the villages. [There is a pass over the Col di Baranca to Ponte Grande, in the Val Anzasca (Rte. 105).]

The Val Sesia offers scenes of less rugged grandeur than some of its lateral valleys ; but in its course many of great beauty are passed, chiefly rendered so by the fine wooding of the slopes, the grand forms of the trees, and the sometimes tranquil, often furious course of the Sesia. The villages of Balmuccia and Scopa (a clean *Inn*, kept by Giuseppe Topino) are passed, and the wild valley of Sermento opens on the rt.

At *Scopello* there are many smelting houses, where the copper ore, already washed and crushed, is reduced. About 50 tons are raised annually at Alagna, at the head of the Val Sesia, 4 leagues above Scopello. Chars can be obtained from Scopello to Varallo, 7½ fr. ; 2 hrs.

There is not much variation in the scenery, though the whole is pleasing. The route passes by the villages of Campertogno and

Mollia (a new *Inn*, and good) to

Riva, the chief of the high villages in the valley. The *Inn* is filthy; only 1 bed. Within the district known as the Val Sesia there are reckoned 2 bourgs and 30 villages, evidence of a thickly populated country in the valleys of the Alps. Riva is situated at the confluence of the torrents of the Dobbia and the Sesia.

The *church of Riva* will surprise the traveller by its structure, its excessive decoration, and the real talent with which it is painted within and without, chiefly by one of the numerous painters whom the Val Sesia has produced —Tanzio, or Antonio d'Enrico, a native of Alagna. The external paintings have a remarkable freshness, though they have existed more than 200 years, exposed to the weather in this high valley.

The view of Monte Rosa from Riva is very sublime ; its enormous masses, clothed in glaciers, close the head of the Val Sesia, and offer a scene of extraordinary grandeur.

About half a league above it is

Alagna, a poor place, but agreeably situated, with a grand view of Monte Rosa. The *Inn* (Paolis, H. de Monte Rosa, fair and civil people) is the best in the Val Sesia, and famed for its vino d'Asti. Here mines of copper are wrought. From Alagna, a pass to the rt. by the *Mont Turlo* leads in

6 hrs. from the Val Sesia to Pestarena or Borca in the Val Anzasca. (Rte. 103A.) Another Pass to the l. by the Col d'Ollen leads to St. Giacomo in the Val de Lys in about 6½ hours (see Rte. 103c).

ROUTE 101A.

VARALLO TO MACUGNAGA, BY VAL MASTELLONE.

	Hours.
Varallo to Fobello	4
Fobello to the Bocchetta	2
Bocchetta to Ponte Grande	3

A route of peculiar character and beauty, and at present (1856) little frequented. The *Val Mastellone* is very narrow, very winding, and very beautifully wooded. For the first hour, up to a remarkable ravine called Ponte della Gula, it is nearly level. Here the river, hemmed in by vertical rocks 150 ft. high, is spanned by a stone arch, not passable for wheels: a new bridge, however, is in construction, and a carriage-road as far as Fobello. From the old bridge the mule-road ascends rapidly, and commands one of the finest views in the valley. Pass several villages. 3 hrs. from Varallo the valley divides: the eastern branch leads to the very poor village of Rimessa, the western to Fobello. Both lead by different and easy passes to Banio. The Rimessa branch is said to be shorter, the other more beautiful: they reunite the other side of the mountain.

At Fobello there is a very fair mountain inn, good enough for sleeping quarters. Better guides will be got here than at Varallo. The path rises rapidly to the upper pastures, passes a wild waterfall, crosses the stream as it issues from a mountain-lake, and in 10 minutes, bearing to the rt., reaches the Col, here called Bocchetta di Barranca, about 2 hrs. from Fobello. The descent is immediate and rapid: the view into the depth of the Val Anzasca, backed by Monte Rosa and the Saas mountains, is magnificent. Reach the Stura (not that which runs into the Lake of Orta): the mule-road down the valley is said to be hilly and circuitous; but beware of being tempted, without good information, to take the timber-slide, which, though easy and pleasant for the most part, is (1856) much broken and very dangerous in places. Banio may probably be reached in 2½ hrs. from the Col. Ponte Grande is ½ hr. beyond Banio; the descent is very rapid, by a good char-road (Rte. 105). The *Inn* at *Ponte Grande* is now pretty good. From Ponte Grande to *Macugnaga*, see Rte. 105.

ROUTE 101B.

MACUGNAGA TO VARALLO, BY CARCOFORO.

	Hours.
Macugnaga to Carcoforo	6
Carcoforo to Balmuccia	4
Balmuccia to Varallo	2
	12
Varallo to Pella and Orta	4½

From Macugnaga follow the route to the Turlo, crossing the Anza, without descending to La Borca. Ascent to the Val Quarazza very fine. A short hour from Macugnaga turn up a depression—it is hardly a valley—called Val Quarazzola, pass a gold-washing station, a châlet, and, in about 2 hrs. more, reach a steep bed of snow. Mount this, traversing to the left, pass a smith's forge, and follow footpath to the first ridge, which overlooks Pestarena and the lower part of Val Anzasca. Pass gold-mine, and along the very steep hill-side, for 300 or 400 yds., to second ridge, called

Bocchetta di Carcoforo. 4 hrs. from Macugnaga.

The height of this pass is not stated: it appears to be equal to the Turlo, though there is less snow. The view of Monte Rosa and the Saas mountains and the Grisons is very fine; the Pennine chain is hidden by Monte Rosa. The view over the low country is extensive, but seldom clear.

The descent to Carcoforo—2 hrs.— is very steep and very constant. Three valleys meet at Carcoforo: that which we have descended; another to the E., leading by a short and steep route to the Bocchetta di Baranca and Banio, or Fobello; and a third to the W., which leads either to Rima and Alagna, or to the upper part of Val Quarazza and Macugnaga, passing near the Col di Turlo. These are all about the same length: that by Val Quarazzola is said to command the finest views.

The *Inn* at Carcoforo, though rude, is good enough to sleep at. The inns appear to be quite as good at the lower villages.

The *Val Sermenta* is on a larger scale and less tortuous than Val Mastellone, and even more lovely. The most beautiful part is about 2 hrs. down, at the large village of Rimasco, where a side valley, of similar character, falls in from the W.: there is a pass to Rima, about 3 hrs., this way. Pass Fervento, Buccialeto, the largest village, and another half hour brings us to the high road of Val Sesia, just below Balmuccia, where the *Inn* is said to be tolerable.

The trout-fishing is reported to be very good in the Vals Sermenta and Mastellone. In both the beauty is greatly increased by the brilliant aqua-marine green of the water, and the abundant chesnut woods.

The road now follows the Val Sesia to *Varallo*, as in Rte. 101.

ROUTE 102.

BAVENO TO VARALLO, BY THE LAKE OF ORTA AND THE COL DE COLMA.

	Hours.
Baveno to Orta	2¼ (drive).
Orta to Varallo	4¼ (mules).

This is a very interesting excursion, and may be recommended to all lovers of the picturesque. Immediately above *Baveno* (Rte. 59c) rises the mountain ridge of *Monte Monterone*, which divides the Lago Maggiore from the Lago d'Orta, and a mule-path leads across it to the town of Orta. It takes 3½ hours to reach the summit from Baveno or Stresa: the path is rather difficult to find on account of the thick chestnut woods. After leaving Baveno a small chapel is reached; taking the left-hand path, which leads through the woods by a small châlet to the neck of the mountain, the summit is reached by a steep climb up the grassy slope. At the base of the ascent are several dairy-farms or châlets, where the traveller can obtain refreshment in the shape of excellent cream, milk, cheese, &c. It takes 3 hrs. to descend to Orta: in fact, it requires nearly 7 hrs. to take this walk from Baveno to Orta and enjoy the view.

The *view* from the summit of the Monte Monterone (5100 ft.) is one of the most extensive on the S. declivity of the Alps. The Mont Blanc, the Combin, and the Mont Cervin, are hidden by the nearer hills of the Val Sesia and by the Monte Rosa. The line of snowy peaks to rt. of the latter, embracing Cima de Jazzi, Fletschhorn, Monte Leone, Bortelhorn, and the St. Gothard, appears to great advantage. Farther E. rise the peaks and glaciers that lie on either side of the Bernardin and Splügen passes, and in the further distance the great mass of the Bernina Alps. Almost at his feet the traveller sees 5 lakes—the Maggiore, the Lake of Orta, those of Monato, Comabbio, and Varese; and still farther to the rt. the great plain of Lombardy and of Piedmont, studded with innumerable villages, with Milan in the centre, whose cathedral is distinctly visible. The two great tributaries of the Po, the Sesia and the Ticino, appear like silver ribbons traversing the dark ground of the plain, and the distant Apennines of Coni, Genoa, and Modena close this unrivalled panorama to the S., whilst the plains of Cremona, Parma, and Mantua are lost in the E. horizon, and beneath the observer lies, in the repose of its deep locality, the beautiful *Lake of Orta.*

Those who do not choose to go by the Monte Monterone to Orta may follow the excellent carriage-road through *Gravellona* (Rte. 59c), a short distance N.W. of Baveno, up the valley of Strona, traversed by the river that carries off the waters of the Lake of Orta, issuing from it at Omegna.

It is a constant but gradual ascent of 4 m. from the Simplon road to *Omegna* (*Inn*, not good), at the N. end of Lago d'Orta. (*Omnibus* daily to Pallanza.) Here a boat may be hired with 2 rowers for 4 or 5 fr.—time, about 1 hour to Orta.

An excellent level carriage-road was finished 1850, all along the E. shore of the lake from Omegna to *Orta.* (*Inns*: Albergo San Giulio, comfortable and moderate ;—Leone d'Oro is a very good little inn, beautifully situated at the water's edge ; —La Poste, new, and prettily situated.) This town is delightfully placed on the borders of the lake, but upon the side of a steep declivity, so that the walks have the disadvantage of being always up and down hill. The facilities for shooting in the neighbouring mountains and forests, and for fishing, boating, and bathing in the lake, offer inducements for a short stay in this cool and delicious retirement. A charming *villa* has lately been built by Count Natta, with beautiful garden, above the town.

The *Monte Sacro*, on the summit of a lofty promontory projecting into the lake, is a sanctuary, dedicated to Saint Francis of Assisi, approached by 22 chapels or oratories, like those of Varallo. Some are elegant in their architecture; and they contain, as at Varallo, groups in terra-cotta, of which at least seven are good works of art. The hill is laid out like a garden, a character which peculiarly belongs to the mountain slopes which surround this lake, and whence probably its name is derived. The views from the hill of the sanctuary are of singular beauty, comprising the lake, the proximate mountains covered with wood, villages which speckle the shores of the lake and the sides of the hills, and the whole surmounted by the Alps. Aug. 2 to 9 is a grand fête.

From Orta a boat may be taken to Buccione at the S. end of the lake, 3 m. distant. (Rte. 101.) No *Inn*.

The *Isola di San Giulio* is an object of singular beauty in the lake; it lies between Orta and Pella. The church and village surmount a rock that rises out of the deep lake; the bright buildings on it contrast with the blue waters with a fairy-like effect. The *church*, chiefly modernized, but retaining some old parts, was built on a spot rendered sacred by the retreat of San Giulio, in the 4th century ; here his ashes are preserved in a vault; and the vertebra of a monstrous serpent, in reality bones of a whale, said to have been destroyed by the saint, is shown as a relic.

Obs. an old mosaic pavement and frescoes by *P. Tibaldi* ; a side chapel rudely painted by an unknown master, 1486 ; another entirely by *Gaudenzio Ferrari*, the chief subject the Virgin and Child enthroned, singularly graceful, but injured ; above, the Martyrdom of St. Stephen ; in the vault the 4 Evangelists—interesting examples of the pure Lombard style ; a curious pulpit, bas-reliefs of St. G. driving out snakes from the island. Guilla, the wife of Beranger II., king of Lombardy, took refuge on the island in 962, and defended it resolutely against Otho I., emperor of Germany, who had invaded Italy and deposed her husband. Otho restored the island to the bishops of

Novara, who had long held it before
it was seized by Beranger.

At *Pella*, the village on the shore near
to the Isola Giulio, asses may be hired
for crossing the mountain of *Colma*
to Varallo, 4½ hrs.; a ride of great
interest, from the beautiful sites and
views which it offers. A steep path
leads up the mountain side to Arola
amidst the richest vegetation; vines,
figs, gourds, and fruit-trees. The views
looking back upon the Lago d'Orta
are superb. Magnificent forest-trees
offer their shade, and the road in some
places passes amidst precipices of
granite in a state of decomposition;
here many of the specimens sold at
Baveno are obtained. Above these
granitic masses the path continues
through scenes resembling the most
beautiful park scenery of England,
and then opens upon the *Col de Colma*,
a bushy common, where wide and
pleasing views are presented of the
lakes of Orta, Maggiore, and the plains
of Lombardy, and, towards the Alps,
of Monte Rosa.

The descent on the other side is not
less beautiful. The Val Sesia is seen in
the deep distance, richly wooded and
studded with churches and villages;
the path leads down through pastoral
scenes, which sometimes recall the
most agreeable recollections of home
to an English traveller; then changes
almost suddenly to the deep gloom of
a ravine, where there are quarries,
formerly worked for the buildings of
Varallo, buried in a forest of enormous walnut and chestnut trees.
Issuing from this wild spot, the traveller shortly finds himself in the Val
Sesia at Rocco, about 1 mile from
Varallo. See Rte. 101.

A new and shorter road turns rt.
about 150 yards beyond the top of the
Col—leaving Rocco on the l., and
joins the old road about ½ m. from
Varallo.

Another mountain path leads from
Gozzano, 2 m. to the S. of the Lago
d'Orta, to Borgo Sesia, through the
village of Val Duggia, the birthplace
of Gaudenzio Ferrari, a pupil of Raphael.

ROUTE 103.

TOUR OF MONTE ROSA.

ALAGNA TO BORCA, BY THE TURLO—
ALAGNA TO GRESSONEY, BY THE COL
DE VAL DOBBIA, OR COL D'OLLEN.

The tour of Monte Rosa may be
conveniently made in 8 days as follows :—

1. Visp to *Inn* at Mattmarksee (Rtes.
106 and 105).
2. Mattmarksee to Borca, by the
Moro (Rte. 105).
3. Borca to Alagna, by the Turlo (A).
4. Alagna to Gressoney (B).
5. Gressoney to Châtillon (Rtes.
104A).
6. Châtillon to Breuil (Rte. 106A).
7. Breuil to Zermatt (Rte. 106A).
8. Zermatt to Visp (Rte. 106).

Or from Gressoney by the Betta
Furca (Rte. 104b) and Cîmes Blanches
(Rte. 106A b) to Zermatt, by which a
day might be saved, but no accommodation for sleeping would be found.

a. *Alagna to Borca by the Col de Turlo*
(9141 ft.) " is one of the steepest and
most laborious passes that I have
crossed. It appears higher than the
Col d'Ollen, took longer to mount,
and has much more snow on it.
The first stage of the ascent is
by a mule path, so steep as to seem
dangerous: this leads to a group of
châlets in about 45 minutes, after
which we kept filing laboriously up
the stony steep mountain side, generally in the mist, and turning, it
seemed easterly, round the head of a
basin, until in 2 hours 30 m. from the
bridge, I found myself, on a lift of the
fog, at some height above a large bed
of snow in the bottom. Pursuing the
same course we crossed a large bed of

snow, and came again on thin herbage, along which we passed to the last ascent, up a steep hollow filled with snow, between which and the rock we passed on the north side. Saw here a single chamois. The passage of the Col is not where one would expect, but more to the north, marked by a cross. A well-traced path winds up to it, which, however, must be covered with snow till late in the year. The Col is a mere ridge; it is worth while to mount the cluster of rocks to the S.E., from which the descent may safely be made across the snow. The scene was very grand, including part of Lago Maggiore, the plain of Lombardy, and a host of mountain peaks, though the summits of Monte Rosa are not visible. From the bridge to the Col 3 hrs. 20 min., including a slight deviation from the route in the fog: by a fresh pair of legs it might be done in 3 hrs. from the bridge, or 4 from Alagna. On the N.E. side the snow is very much more extensive, and the descent very abrupt. It is necessary to keep well to the l. in crossing the snow, then descend rocks, and traverse back to the rt. again. This is quick work, as the slopes are often steep enough for a *glissade.* After coming to the line of vegetation, the descent becomes very fatiguing, for the mountains rise round the valley like a wall, and are covered with a thick undergrowth of scrubby rhododendron and bilberries, on which the foot takes no hold. Reached the bottom in 1 hr. 10 min., thence 1 hr. 15 min. along a very gentle slope, and through beautiful scenery to the junction with the valley of Anzasca, near the small hamlet of Borca" (see Rte. 105).

b. Alagna to Gressoney, by the Col de Val Dobbia, is up the narrow ravine of the Dobbia, by a long, steep, and difficult path, in some places overhanging the torrent, in others disputing with the river the narrow course through which both must struggle. After passing the miserable hamlet of Grato, near to which there is a fine waterfall gushing out to the black ravine, the abrupt ascent of the *Col de Val Dobbia* rises through a pine forest, and thence over Alpine pasturages by a long and fatiguing path, which offers no object of particular interest to the traveller.

The distance from Riva to the Col, which is 8250 ft. above the level of the sea, requires 4 or 5 hrs. On the summit there is an humble *Hospice*—a stone house of 2 stories, affording acceptable shelter during snow-storms to travellers ; it is the successor probably of a hovel which existed in Saussure's time. It was built at the joint expense of the commune of Riva and of an individual of Gressoney, the canon Sottile. It is inhabited throughout the year, by 2 civil men who attend to travellers and their wants. An extensive and noble view is obtained of the Italian valley and parts of the Great Chain from the immediate vicinity of Mt. Blanc to the Alps of the Val Tellina. Steep slopes of snow lie near the summit unmelted throughout the year. The Monte Rosa is concealed from the traveller, but in the course of his descent the deep valley of the Lys, and the sublime masses of Monte Rosa, offer views rivalling any in the Great Chain.

From the summit to *Gressoney* (St. Jean) requires about 2 hrs. H. Delapierre is highly praised, landlord most attentive, and an excellent guide—*S. W. K.*; H. Chianale.

In all the communes at the heads of the Piedmontese valleys of Monte Rosa, the German language is spoken; at Riva and Alagna in the Val Sesia, above Pestarena in the Val Anzasca, and at St. Giacomo in the Val Challant. The manners of these communities are as distinct as their language from that of their neighbours lower down the valleys, with whom they hold little intercourse : they encourage a pride of birth and birthplace which strongly keeps up the separation. At Gressoney, in the *Val de Lys,* this is perhaps more strongly exemplified than in any other of the valleys. Here their characters are distinguished for honesty and industry, and few communities have a higher moral tone. Crime is almost unknown among them; and if disputes arise, the syndic or magistrate elected by themselves hears the complaint, and effects an amicable settlement. They possess many of those comforts which an Englishman appreciates, and which are unknown to the lower inhabitants of the valleys. Their education and attainments are of a higher order than is usually found in such a class, especially in such a place. Many of their young men have distinguished themselves by the abilities which they have displayed when they have gone abroad in the world. They have become merchants and bankers, and many from among them have become eminent for learning and science, and reflected honour on the little community located in this Alpine solitude. Among these is Herr Zumstein, better known in the Val Sesia as M. de la Pierre, inspector of the forests of the Val Sesia, who long since explored the flanks and ascended one of the summits of Monte Rosa, and gave great assistance to Col. Von Welden in his topography of Monte Rosa.

Above Gressoney St. Jean are the hamlets of Gressoney la Trinita, Naversch or Novres (where Herr Zumstein resides), San Giacomo, and St. Pietro, above which is the summer residence of Baron Peccoz.

Gressoney St. Jean is convenient as head-quarters to those who would visit the magnificent glaciers at the head of the Val de Lys, or make excursions around Monte Rosa by the Col d'Ollen (Rte. 103C), or Betta Furca (Rte. 104 b). Excellent guides and side-saddles may be found at Gressoney, and there are few valleys in proximity with the glaciers which offer so many Alpine wonders to the examination of the traveller. It is 4530 ft. above the level of the sea.

c. *Alagna to Gressoney, by the Col d'Ollen.*—The ascent begins immediately, and occupies 4 hrs.; the last hour is very steep, and in bad weather the path may easily be lost. On reaching the Col the traveller should ascend the peak on his rt., from which there is a magnificent view of desolation on the side of the Alps and richness on the side of Italy. Nothing can be imagined finer than the head of the Lys-thal. The Lys-gletscher, which descends low, is formed by the union of two magnificent branches, which sweep down from the Lys Kamm. Rock, river, rich pasturages, forests, glaciers, and mountains, and so admirably combined as to present a series of most exquisite views, both in descending and in passing along the bottom of the valley. Near the village chapel of San Giacomo, and close by the road, there is a remarkably picturesque spot on the river, which has hollowed itself a very deep channel, across which has fallen a mass of rock, forming a · natural bridge, which leads to the chapel and some adjacent houses. A sharp descent of 2½ hrs. leads to Trinita in the Lysthal, whence it is 1½ hr. to Gressoney; or if the traveller intends to cross the Betta Furca he may stop at St. Giacomo.

ROUTE 104.

GRESSONEY TO CHATILLON, BY THE COL DE RANZOLA AND COL DE JON; OR TO ZERMATT, BY THE BETTA FURCA AND CIMES BLANCHES.

a. *Gressoney to Châtillon, by the Col de Ranzola.*

	Hours.
Gressoney to Brussone	. . 4
Brussone to Châtillon	. . . 4

In continuing the route direct to Châtillon, in the Val d'Aosta, it is necessary to ascend the steep forest paths and slopes of the mountain on the side of the valley opposite to the Col de

Val Dobbia ; it is a rather fatiguing mule-path the whole way up to the *Col de Ranzola*, the summit of the ridge which divides the valleys of the Lys and Challant.

On emerging in the ascent from the pine forest, a grand view of Monte Rosa is presented, especially when taken in connexion with the beautiful *Val de Lys* or *Val de Vallaise*, which lies far below the traveller, with its quiet villages and fertile pasturages. The Lys, like a silver thread, may be traced up to its glaciers. On either side of the valley the vast mountains, belted with forests, offer, at the depression of their ridges, the paths by which the most frequent intercourse takes place with the neighbouring valleys. The scene is imperishable from the memory whilst any recollections of the Alps remain to the traveller. From a peak rising a little above the pass, called *Pointe Gombetta*, one of the finest imaginable panoramic views of Monte Rosa and the Val d'Aosta and the Val de Gressoney may be obtained. This point can be reached in 2½ or 3 hrs. from Gressoney.

After passing the Col de Ranzola (7136 ft.) the descent is gradual to the little hamlet of St. Grat, but somewhat steep to Brussone. In the descent the Val Challant may be traced in its course down to Verrex, where it joins the Val d'Aosta, in which the Doire may be distinctly seen, flashing across like a streak of light, broken by the dark mass of the Castle of Verrex, which stands at the very junction of the two valleys, while under the feet, or not far off, is perched upon the declivity the picturesque Castle of Challant. Except at the lowest part of the valley it fails in striking objects of interest, but near its termination there are some fine scenes. Above Brussone the valley ascends through several hamlets to St. Giacomo d'Ayas, whence a pass leads over the Cîmes Blanches to the head of the Val Tournanche and the pass of St. Theodule, Rte. 106A.

Brussone is a beautifully situated village, with a tolerable *Inn* (Lion d'Or).

Another mountain range must be crossed to reach Châtillon in the Val d'Aosta [or the traveller may descend to Verrex in the Val d'Aosta, which requires 5 hrs., passing through Challant and Challard].

After crossing some meadows beyond Brussone, the road winds steeply up through a forest of pines and larches, and then opens upon one of the most beautiful pasturages in the Alps—the *Col de Jon*, which is a fine greensward, broad and luxuriant.

On reaching the descent towards the Val d'Aosta, near a little chapel of St. Grat, this beautiful valley is seen in all its length, from Châtillon to the Mont Blanc ; not traced quite to the base of the latter, for its summit only is seen on the rt. peering into the Val d'Aosta, over several compact lines of mountains, which here form the termination of the horizon. The prospect of the Val d'Aosta itself is charming ; its meadows and cultivated patches margined by thick woods of walnut-trees, which creep up the water-channelled dells at the foot of the mountain — the castles of Usselle on its rock, of Finnis overlooking its sea of wood, with numerous white ch. towers and spires—Aosta and its plain, and the winding flashes of the Doire undulating or sweeping across the vale—combine to form a view striking and beautiful, which, in the descent, constantly varies. A series of steep tourniquets down a water-worn channel with grassy banks brings the traveller to the forests of chestnut and walnut trees, for which the Val d'Aosta is celebrated. These offer to him their shade, and soon the vines add their luxuriant foliage to the cool and refreshing path which leads past the mineral spring to the village and Baths of St. Vincent (2½ or 3 hrs. from Brussone). The valley of Aosta is entered at one of its finest points near

ST. VINCENT, Rte. 107 (*Inn*, Ecu de France, fair), near

CHATILLON (Rte. 107).

[From Gressoney St. Jean, the descent to St. Martin, in the Val d'Aosta, by the valley of the Lys or *Vallaise*, is a journey of about 18 miles (5 hours' walk), passing through many villages and hamlets, of which the principal are Gaby, Issima, Fontainemore, and Lillianes,—and through some scenes of wildness and beauty, which, however, become common to the traveller in the Val d'Aosta and its lateral valleys. About Trina, the valley is strewn with huge rolled blocks or boulders. As you approach the Ponte di Trinita, the scene becomes sterner, more shattered precipices and long shoots of débris and detached rocks. Below Issime an unbroken and beautiful wood of sweet chestnut stretches across the valley. The Vallaise loses much in interest to those who *ascend* it.

At St. Martin (Rte. 107) is a very tolerable *Inn*, La Rosa Rossa.]

[An excursion only to be taken by experienced cragsmen is the ascent of the Grauenhaupt (about 11000 ft), which rises on the W. side of the valley. The view from the summit is scarcely surpassed. Chamois are not uncommon.]

b. Gressoney to Zermatt, by the Betta Furca, Cîmes Blanches, and St. Théodule.

"We left Gressoney at noon: the road lies for 2½ hrs. up the valley, then turns to the l. and ascends very rapidly for 1 hr., to the chapel of St. Giacomo, whence is a beautiful view of the Lyskammer and its glacier, whence another good hour of gentle ascent and ½ hour's descent brought us to the châlets of Reagel; no accommodation could be worse. Next morning we left the valley by a sharp ascent, rounding the head of the Val Challant, and passing close to the Ayas glacier, and in 4 hrs. arrived at a small dreary lake, where my companion's mule was left: from this 20 min. brought us to the glacier, on we were 2¾ hrs., it being steep and deeply crevassed. From the Col the descent was that of the ordinary pass." See Rte. 106A.

ROUTE 105.

VOGOGNA TO SAAS, BY THE VAL ANZASCA AND THE MONTE MORO.

Vogogna.	Hrs.
Ponte Grande	2¼ (char).
Macugnaga	5 (walk).
Summit of Moro	4
Mattmarksee	2
Saas	3

There is a carriage-road from Vogogna by Pié di Mulera, as far as Ponte Grande, 2 hrs. ride in a char, which may be hired at Vogogna for 6 fr.; the road will in time be opened further. *Guides* are required only over the Pass. The best are to be found at Saas, and on the Italian side at Macugnaga, where Franz Lochmatter, host of the Hôtel Monte Rosa, is recommended; also Luigi Sattler of Borca, 1857. A guide's fee from Macugnaga to Saas is, going and back fare from Saas to Ponte Grande, or *vice versâ*, 10 frs. Bearers expect to be paid three days.

There is difficulty in obtaining *mules* in the upper part of the Val Anzasca. It is best to cross the Moro from the Swiss to the Italian side, because the ascent is easier, and the path better on the Swiss side, and because Monte Rosa is always in front on descending into Italy.

The Val Anzasca leads directly up to Monte Rosa; it combines all that is most lovely in Italian, with all that is most grand in Swiss scenery. It is a Chamouny, of which the sides are covered with vines, figs, chestnuts, and walnuts, with the sky of Italy above, and the architecture of Italy around you.

Vogogna (Rte. 59 c) is situated in the plain of the Val d'Ossola, 8½ Eng. m. below Domo d'Ossola, and on the confluence of the torrent of the **Anza** with the Toccia.

A by-path, at the back of the village of Vogogna, leads down to the Tosa at Borgo, where boats are always ready to ferry you across. Leaving on rt. the road of the Simplon, it continues up the l. bank of the Anza, across meadow and under vine trellises, to a new bridge over the Anza, a little above its junction with the Tosa, which leads into

Pié de Mulera (*Inn :* Crocé Rossa), the first village in the Val Anzasca. *Mules* may be hired here, also chars and a portantine for ladies. Here lives the receiver of the gold and other mines situated near the head of the valley. The road ascends and is carried through two short tunnels pierced in the rock similar to the Urnerloch on the St. Gothard. It is carried high up along the vine-clad slopes, and commands a noble view downward over the Val d'Ossola and upwards towards Monte Rosa which comes into sight soon after entering the valley, and which gives an indescribable finish to the distance, while the rich valley, sending out wooded hills from either side, forms a magnificent foreground. The unrivalled prospect is seen to greatest advantage just before reaching

Castiglione (*Inn :* Au Rameau). The road leaves rt. Calasca (*Inn* tolerable), near which there is a pretty waterfall bursting out of the Val Bianca, then descends to the Anza, and runs some distance along its banks.

Ponte Grande (Albergo al Ponte Grande, a new house, 1855, good—*mules* may be hired here), a considerable village with a post-office, in one of the prettiest spots of the valley, receives its name from a *bridge* of a single arch across the Anza, carried away 1856, and replaced by a wooden bridge lower down. ¼ a day's sojourn in this part of the valley will be repaid by the grand scenery.

Vanzone. (*Inns :* Sole ; Moro ; dirty, and extortionate ; don't expect to find anything beyond a slight luncheon ; Chamois, best.) This is the chief place in the Val Anzasca. The two *Churches*, one opening out of the other, are worth visiting. See the

[*Switz.*]

view from the terrace in front of the chapel, a little above the town. Here, and elsewhere in Val Anzasca, the neat dress of the women, the general cleanliness of the people, their cheerfulness and independence, and the rareness of goître, will be remarked with pleasure, as contrasting with other parts of Piedmont.

Ceppo Morelli. Inn, small and poorly provided. A little way above this is one of the finest views in the valley; the vast height of Monte Rosa may be fully appreciated from hence, as it towers upwards into the sky. The women in the upper part of the valley carry burthens like men, and adopt lower garments usually considered peculiar to male attire.

[At *Prequartero* a path branches off (rt.) into the Saas-Thal by Prebenone, nearer than that by the Moro, but without its fine views of Monte Rosa. The guides take it as a short cut in returning.]

A spur descending from the Monte della Caccia here divides the Val Anzasca from the Val Macugnaga or Pestarena. The distinction is further marked by the languages spoken by the people; above this German prevails, below it Italian. This vast mass of mountain nearly closes up the valley—leaves only a deep and savage gorge for the Anza to escape.

At *Campiolo*, where the river Anza issues out of the gorge, it is crossed to the rt. bank, and the path is carried in a very steep ascent over this rocky barrier, which is called *Morgen :* it next descends rapidly and returns to the l. bank by the Ponte del Valt. It is proposed to carry the char-road up to

Pestarena (Alb. dei Minieri), a miserable village in an upland district, whose inhabitants earn their livelihood in the mines of gold, silver, and copper. The gold occurs in very small quantities, combined with (pyrites) sulphuret of iron. The ore is pounded and ground, and the metal obtained from it by amalgamation in the proportion of 6 grammes, or at the best 10, of gold to 100 kilogrammes of ore. There are not many places in Piedmont where gold is found. Brockedon, in consequence, has conjectured that this valley was the seat of the Icty-muli mentioned by Pliny, and traces their name in that of the villages Pié and Cima de *Mul*-era.

The rough path ascends steeply, passing the adits of many mines ; it is crossed by numerous mountain-torrents, which cut it up, or cover it with stony rubbish, rendering the ascent toilsome.

In ascending the valley 35 min. above Pestarena, the traveller comes on the very magnificent view of Monte Rosa, at a village called *Bourge*, or

Borca (a tidy and very good little *Inn*, Osteria de' Cacciatori, kept by the frères Albasini, one a great hunter, the other no mean cook)—about 2 m. below Macugnaga. *Game* — chamois, marmot, black-cock, and ptarmigan—abound in the valley.

At Borca and above it German is the language of the people.

The path over the *Col de Turlo* to Alagna and the Val Sesia (Rte. 103 *a*) diverges here l.

The commune which bears the name of *Macugnaga* consists of six different hamlets, Pestarena, Borgo, in der Stapf, zum Strich, auf der Rive, and Zertannen. Borca is 1½ m., a ½ hr.'s walk from Pestarena, and as far from the rest, which lie only a few minutes' walk apart from one another. *Im Strich*, commonly called *Macugnaga*. It is the best quarter for the unrivalled view of the amphitheatrical peaks of Monte Rosa. (*Inn:* Osteria di Monte Rosa, kept by Franz Lochmatter, who is a good guide over the Moro; H. du Glacier, new 1858.

Macugnaga is 4369 ft. above the sealevel. It has a neat, if not handsome *Church*, with a noble lime-tree close beside it, and stands in a grassy plain or luxuriant meadow, studded with hamlets, some of them almost touching the glaciers. Martin is a good guide here.

Above the village, the river Anza issues out of a grand arch of ice in the glacier of Monte Rosa.

Excursion from Macugnaga. — The great object of a visit to Macugnaga is the view of MONTE ROSA, which is not surpassed by any scene in the Alps, and is equalled by very few. The excursions usually followed by the local guides are not the best that could be chosen, and the traveller is recommended to adopt the following, as affording the best facilities for enjoying the magnificent scenery of the head of the valley. A good guide is wanted, and he will know the route when he is told the general direction in which the excursion is to be made. It can only be performed on foot, but is not particularly fatiguing ; it will occupy about 8 or 9 hrs.

First.—Ascend the meadows of the valley above Macugnaga, and then, after crossing the Anza, mount the steep wooded hill called the *Belvedere*, against which the great glacier descending from Monte Rosa divides into two ice-streams. This is one of the finest points of view ; and those who are not inclined to make the whole tour may return from hence to Macugnaga. Ladies can ascend to this point on mules in 2 hrs.

Second.—Cross the north arm of the glacier to *Fillar*, a passage attended with no danger and very little difficulty, although the edges of the ice are much encumbered with moraines. From Fillar walk up the valley to the châlets of *Jazi*, situated under the Cima di Jazi, a fine peak to the northward of Monte Rosa, and near the celebrated pass called the *Weiss Thor* (see Rte. 106 *d*), leading to Zermatt.

Third.—Ascend the steep moraine enter upon the great glacier, and proceed for some distance towards the head of the valley. This is difficult, the ice being considerably crevassed, but with a guide accustomed to glaciers there is no danger. The crevasses diminish after some distance has been traversed, and the glacier becomes more even. The traveller may pursue it as far as his inclination leads him, but a convenient goal is a singular waterfall, where a considerable stream precipitates itself into a great chasm in the ice, with a roaring which may be heard at some distance. The view from this spot is exceedingly striking, the observer be-

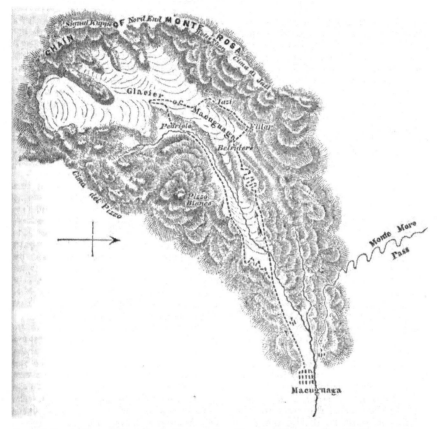

ing in the midst of the arena of a vast amphitheatre, whose snow-clad walls are formed of some of the highest mountains in Europe. Commencing on the east, are seen the Pizzo Bianco, and Cima del Pizzo, from which a snow-sheeted ridge leads to the great central group of *Monte Rosa*, whose precipitous sides descend immediately down some 7000 or 8000 feet in one almost unbroken slope to the very edge of the glacier on which the traveller stands. Avalanches of great magnitude are often seen to fall on this slope, accompanied with a noise like thunder. From the summits of Monte Rosa another ridge extends northwards to the Cima di Jazi, and then on, bending eastwards to the pass of Monte Moro, which is well seen.

Fourth.—Leave the glacier on its eastern edge, and descend the steep and high moraine to the châlets of Pedriolo, near which may be seen some enormous fragments of rock that have probably fallen from the Pizzo Bianco immediately above; one of these is 500 feet in circumference, and about 120 feet high; they are probably the largest blocks detached in this way that can be found in the Alps.

Fifth.—From Pedriolo a return track leads along the rocks on the south side of the valley, often at a great height, and commanding fine scenery; and a steep and intricate descent brings the traveller back to Macugnaga.

The whole of this excursion abounds

with the most magnificent views, presenting the most wonderful amphitheatre in every direction to the eye. It is thought by many to be a finer scene than any view of Mont Blanc at Chamouni, as no similar advantage of position for the spectator can be there obtained.

A few words on the topography of Monte Rosa may not be out of place here. It is by no means a single summit, but a *knot* or union of two ridges or chains crossing each other at right angles, E. and W., and N. and S.; so that its ground-plan may be said to resemble a +. The N.E. angle forms the head of the Val Anzasca, and encloses the glacier of Macugnaga, as the N.W. does that of Zermatt: the S.E. is the head of the Val Sesia, and the S.W. under the Lyskamm is the cradle of the glacier of the Lys, and head of the valley of Gressoney.

The four principal summits are ranged along the north ray of the cross, and are all visible from Macugnaga. Beginning at the left hand, or south end, the first is the *Signal Kuppe*; the next, a snowy pinnacle, the *Zumstein Spitze*; the third, a tremendous rocky tooth, the *Höchste Spitze*, or highest point, being 15,160 English feet above the sea; and the fourth, or most northerly, the *Nord end*. The difference in height of these four summits is little more than 200 feet, from the highest to the lowest. See also Rte. 106 *f*.

The pass of the Moro is the least difficult over the great chain between the Great St. Bernard and the Simplon: still it is not practicable for horses, though there are traces of an old paved horse-road, by which the mail was carried to Milan before the Simplon was opened. A German writer has lately maintained that it was frequented by the Saracens; and the names Moro, Allalein, Almagell, Mischabel, and others are quoted as a proof. The ascent is very abrupt, and the traveller rises rapidly above the little plain and village of Macugnaga. The path lies at first through a straggling forest, but the Alps or pasturages are soon attained, and the scene thence presented is most magnificent—all the masses of Monte Rosa are open to the view, from its peaks, still thousands of feet above you, to the basin of Macugnaga, now thousands of feet below. Such a scene cannot be conceived, and once seen can never be forgotten. From the high pasturages the path traverses a stony and barren slope to the snow which it is necessary to cross. On the summit, amidst a heap of stones, a cross is placed, and the traveller looks down on the other side of the mountain towards the Valais, and into a scene of sterility which has no relief.

Before descending towards the valley of Saas, it is desirable to walk along the crest of the Moro to the rt. about ¼ m., where, mounting some rocks, a glorious view offers itself, extending over the valleys of Anzasca and Antrona to the plains of Italy and the chain of the Alps, even to the distant Tyrol. Also from the rocks behind the wooden cross you gain a glorious view of Monte Rosa on one hand and of the whole extent of the Saas valley on the other.

[The traveller who, in going from Visp, wishes to shorten his route and avoid Macugnaga, may cross the ridge a little to the E. of the Moro and descend to Campiole in the Val Anzasca by a tolerable path, but he would lose the finest views of the Monte Rosa.]

The summit of the pass of the Monte Moro is 9640 English feet (*Forbes*) above the sea. The descent to Saas is singularly easy and pleasant. There is a steep bed of snow crossed at first, but afterwards a gentle fall leads down the whole way to Visp. On the l. rises the Saasgrat, a lofty chain of inaccessible snowy peaks, separating the valley of Saas from that of Zermatt. The path soon reaches the ancient paved road which has been cut out of the face of the precipices, and overhangs a deep hollow into which the glaciers which stream down from the surrounding peaks seem to be poured. The spot is one of the most desolate in the Alps. At length the paved road is left, and no vestige can be traced of it: it has been destroyed by the masses which have fallen from the precipices above.

The path now winds down the vast talus formed by these repeated falls of rocks, to reach the scanty herbage of the highest pasturages. From below it is impossible to trace any path, or even in what direction the path lies, by which the descent has been made.

The pass of the Moro, and another across the glaciers on the rt. into the Val Antrona, are mentioned in an old record of the date of 1440 as " fort vieux passages," and great expenses were incurred in 1724, and again in 1790, in the endeavour to restore them, in order to facilitate the conveyance of salt and other articles of commerce, but the new repairs were soon destroyed by avalanches.

The débris of fallen mountains, and the enormous glaciers which surround the traveller, give a fearful impression of desolation.

The *châlets of Distel* furnish milk, cheese, and eggs, but they are deserted early in the autumn.

[From Distel a difficult path crosses the mountains into the Val Antrona, a valley that debouches into the Val d'Ossola.]

From Distel the path continues on the rt. branch of the stream all the way to Saas. After quitting the *châlets*, the path leads down to a dreary dirty lake (½ hr.) called the *Mattmarksee*, formed by the melting of the glaciers. A convenient *Inn* was built (1856) on this dreary spot, and much facilitates the passage of the Moro by travellers. The *Allalein glacier* bounds this lake on the N., in fact, dams the valley, and these waters accumulate within it. The view over it is grand; the colossal pyramids of cleft ice rising sheer against the sky. The stream of the Visp issues out of an ice-grotto at its extremity. In 1833 this outlet closed up, so that it required to be opened by blasting the ice. From the lower end of the lake the view of the N. side of the Cima de Jazi, and

some of the peaks of the Monte Rosa, present a scene of savage sublimity. It is necessary to skirt the dam of ice and descend below it—an affair of no great difficulty; the cattle are made to ascend and traverse it to reach their pasturages. From below, this barrier of ice appears effectually to close the valley.

From this barrier the path lies down the valley, still sterile and filled with rocks and stones: the rhododendron, however, and a little brushwood, give evidence of improved vegetation.

Zurmegern or *Zurmicran.* From this village a path crosses the mountains on the E. side, and leads to Antrona; and on the W. another path leads over the Adler pass (Rte. 106 *i.*)

Allmagell. Before reaching it, larches and pines are passed, but they are stunted from their great elevation. After crossing a little plain, a rugged path leads down by a hamlet, and the traveller passes under Mont Fée, whose bright snows, rising above a forest of pines, give a singularly beautiful appearance to the mountain.

Saas, the principal commune of the valley. *Inns:* H. du Mont Rosa, very fair. A second Inn open 1858.

Saas is a good resting-place, and is now much frequented by tourists. The parish priest, Herr Imseng, has acquired an almost European reputation for his skill in difficult passes, his adventurous spirit, his incredible powers of endurance at a somewhat advanced age, and his readiness to assist travellers. He usually lives in the H. du Mont Rosa. Franz Anthamatten, Moritz Zurbrücken, and Joseph Venetz are good guides.

[*Passage of the Moro from Saas.*— Mules may be hired at Saas. You can ride as far as Telliboden, 4 hours, and about ½ an hour from the Châlets of Distel. You then ascend and cross very steep slopes of snow, and reach the summit in about 50 min. The path on the Italian side is very steep. The descent to Macugnaga takes between 3 and 4 hours. In crossing the Moro from Saas, let it be remembered that mules are not always to be had in the upper part of Val Anzasca. If ladies be of the party, either beasts must be hired by sending an express messenger ahead across the pass, or the bearers must be engaged as far as Macugnaga.]

Saas stands in a basin surrounded by an amphitheatre of mountains, which are not seen from the village, lower ranges intercepting the view. The plain of Saas is beautiful amidst the wild scenery which surrounds it: it is nearly 1 m. long, and its verdant meadows are refreshing to look upon after the sterility of the upper valley and the pass of the Moro.

An interesting excursion of a few hours, which no one should omit, may be made from Saas to the pretty *valley and hamlet of Fée*, lying nearly opposite, at a slight elevation. The head of the valley consists of an amphitheatre of glaciers, somewhat resembling the Cirques of the Pyrenees, but on a grander scale; and above these tower the peaks of the *Mischabel*, the highest of which, sometimes called Saas Grat, is 14,924 ft., or 900 ft. higher than the Finster-Aarhorn; it is the highest mountain in Switzerland proper. It was ascended in 1855 by Mr. Chapman. In the midst of the glaciers is a singular green spot, almost an island in the sea of ice, called the *Gletscher Alp*, which is used as a pasture in summer, when it is a perfect garden of wild flowers. It may usually be reached without crossing the glacier, but the path passes through a gorge between the 2 branches of the glacier with almost overhanging masses of ice on either hand, not more than 30 or 40 feet apart, and it should not be attempted without a good guide, blocks of ice frequently breaking off and falling across the path. From the head of the valley is a fine view, but the Fée glacier is reported (1855) to be so broken up as to be impassable.

There are two exceedingly difficult passes—the Adler Joch, or Col Imseng, and the Allelein, from Saas to Zermatt (Rte. 106 *i*).

East of Saas, the main chain, comprehending the Fletschorn and *Weiss-*

mies, both exceeding 13,000 ft. in height, abounds in interest. One route N. of the Fletschorn descends midway between the hospice and village of Simplon: it must command magnificent views of the Bernese Alps. The *Fletschorn* itself was ascended in 1856 by the Curé and a party of English. There is another pass up the Almagell valley over the S. flank of the Weissmies, descending by Zwischbergen to Gondo: the descent, as seen from the Simplon road, appears to be very steep and very grand; probably the Col is a difficult one. A third pass leads to the Val d'Antrona, below Domo d'Ossola, up the *Furgga-thal*, a desolate and not picturesque valley high up in the mountain-side, above Almagell: the passage of the Furgge glacier offers no difficulty, and the descent to Piedmont is free from ice, but very steep. There used to be a mule-road, of which portions still remain. North of the Col, and perhaps 1000 ft. higher, there is a point called the *Latelhorn*, which juts out like a belvedere, the main chain falling back right and left, and commands a most superb view over the entire range of the Alps from Monte Rosa to the Ortlerspitz, with the subordinate ranges of Piedmont, Tessin, and Lombardy. This point is new; it is probably not above 10,000 ft., but easy of access, and commands a splendid view. Horses can go within 1½ hr., or less, of the top; and the remainder of the ascent, except just the horn itself for some 200 ft., is easy. There are beds of snow, but no ice to cross. By a tolerable walker the excursion from Saas and back may be made in 10 hrs., allowing 1 hr. on the top, and ½ hr. for refreshment.

From Saas, by Stalden, to Visp, 6 hrs., is a good bridle-path. (Rte. 106.)

ROUTE 106.

VISP TO ZERMATT OR SAAS.

Visp.	Hours.
Stalden	2
St. Niklaus	2¼
Zermatt	4¼

The concourse of travellers to the valleys around the Monte Rosa* is every year increasing, and deservedly; and the inn accommodation has kept pace with the increased resort of strangers flowing in. The great difficulty of Zermatt or "Young Chamouni" is, that, whereas the way up to it from the Valais is easy and tempting, there is no way out except by difficult passes over the highest Alpine chain, which not every one is hardy enough to attempt. They are, however, passable in fine weather from July to the middle of September. The usual and the only easy mode of reaching Zermatt is from *Visp* or *Viége* in the Valais (R. 59 A), where horses can be obtained. Each horse costs 9 frs. a-day, and 1 fr. bonnemain to the man who leads it. Including stoppages, 11 hrs. are occupied in going up to Zermatt, and not much less in coming down. The best plan is to take horses at Visp, use them at Zermatt for the Riffelberg, &c., and return upon them, thus avoiding back fare.

Ladies not equal to a ride of 9 hrs. may stop half-way, at St. Nicholas, for the night, and resume the journey next morning. Those who are pressed for time may reach St. Niklaus in the evening, the Riffelberg next day, and ascend the Gorner-Grat and return

* The late Wm. Brockedon, author of 'Passes of the Alps,' was perhaps the first who drew the attention of English travellers to Zermatt and Monte Rosa. The fame of their unrivalled scenery has since been extended by Professor Forbes's 'Alps of Savoy,' and Sir John Forbes's 'Physician's Holiday,' a charming pocket-companion for the journey. The map of the country round Monte Rosa is principally taken from a large map by Schlagentwert.

on the third day. The scenery in the Visper Thal, or valley leading to Zermatt, is fine, but it becomes tedious in such a long ride or walk. The people in the valley seem miserably poor and afflicted with goître, and are filthily dirty in person. At every church is a well-filled charnel-house, and in the churchyards, skulls and bones are often lying about unnoticed. This valley suffered terribly from the earthquake in 1855 (Rte. 59 A); the road, which had just been made, was destroyed in many places, but it has since been restored. There is not the least occasion for a guide at any time up to Zermatt. After leaving Visp a few vines are still noticed, but the lower part of the valley is not very interesting. The snowy peak of the Balfrein is first seen, and beyond Stalden the Bruneck Horn. You cross over to the l. bank of the Visp at

Neubrücke. The trout rush down to the Rhone when the glaciers melt, and are caught here in quantities. Fine view up from this bridge of the fork of the valley, and in 2 hrs. you reach

Stalden—(Inn: Berchtold, a village at the junction of the stream descending from Zermatt, called Gorner-Visp, with that coming from Saas, called Saaser-Visp. There is a path from Stalden to the Hospice on the Simplon.

[The path to Saas (Rte. 105) here turns l. over the Kinnbrücke, a single arch 150 ft. above the Vispach torrent, and keeps on the l. bank of the Saaser-Visp for some distance, and then crosses near Boden to the rt. bank, where it attains a great height above the stream opposite to the Falls of *Schweibach,* which descend from the *Balfrein.* The road again crosses the river, amidst very wild scenery, whilst crosses in several places show where accidents have happened from avalanches or snow in spring and winter. The valley becomes contracted to a gorge, and then again opens out into the little plain of Balen, and again contracts to a very wild defile, with cataracts on each side, and in about 3 hrs. from Stalden

Saas (Rte. 105) is reached.]

The path to Zermatt ascends the W. branch, or Gorner Visp, and the *valley of St. Nicholas*, running along the edge of precipices, winding much, rising high and descending low, and twice crosses the Visp before reaching

St. Nicholas—(*Inns:* Croix Blanche, good; Soleil, tolerable)—a good place for a halt or for night quarters. This village, which is rather less miserable than the other villages, was much injured by the earthquake in 1855; it is the chief place in the valley, and is charmingly situated amidst wild Alpine scenery, tempered with forests and orchards in the foreground, on the l. bank of the Visp.

[There is a short but high cut over the shoulder of the mountain to the valley of Saas. There is also a pass accessible to mules, and leading in a long day to Gruben in the Turtman-Thal. There is not much view from the Col, but from a summit about ½ an hour higher the view is said to be unrivalled.]

After leaving St. Niklaus the path soon returns to the rt., traversing in turn meadow and forest, crossed now and then by a land-slip or glacier-stream from the snows above. Beyond Herbrüggen is

Randa, situated among extensive meadows, opposite a gap in the precipice walling in the valley on the W., through which the Bies glacier descends from the Weisshorn, which is here left behind. In 1819, Dec. 27, an avalanche discharged itself through this gap from a precipice of the Weisshorn, 1500 ft. high, behind (N. of) the village of Randa; it did not reach it in descending, but passed a little on one side of it, yet the mere draft of air produced by a fall from such a vast elevation destroyed the greater part of the houses, scattering the timbers of which they were built like straws, over the mountain side, to the distance of a mile, and hurling millstones many fathoms up hill.

About an hour higher up than Randa is a larger village, *Täsch*. [From Täsch a high path over the Adler Joch (Rte. 106 *i*) leads to Saas.]

Beyond the village of Täsch (where there is no accommodation save at the Curé's) the path ascends through a pine wood, where the river is crossed by a bridge over a ravine. On emerging from the wood, the Gorner Glacier is seen in the distance. Skirting along the l. bank, the path turns a corner where it has been excavated in the rock, and a striking view of the *Mt. Cervin*, or *Matterhorn*, distinguished from all other peaks by its slender, isolated pyramid, opens, and a view is obtained of

ZERMATT (Piedmontese Praborgne). *Inns:* H. de Monte Rosa (Seilers) very comfortable original wood house, enlarged 1856; H. du Mont Cervin (Clemenz) built of stone, good and clean, well provided with maps and guide-books, the works of Studer, &c., and with collections of plants, insects, and minerals. There is also a good Inn on the Riffelberg 2½ hrs. further, kept by the proprietors of the H. de Monte Rosa. This retired village, composed of most curious quaint old wooden houses, 5400 ft. above the sea, is placed, with its neat church, in a little plain, amidst the grandest scenery of nature, near the junction of 3 valleys, each headed by a glacier. E. is the Findelen Glacier, S. the Zermatt or Gorner Glacier and W. the Zmutt Glacier. The mineralogist, botanist, and entomologist may collect rich harvests in the neighbourhood. Here many days may be spent in excursions to the glaciers and points of view with which the neighbourhood abounds. The pasturage appears good, but the attempts to raise grain crops in this damp and shady valley are melancholy, and only serve to show the great industry of its inhabitants. The bread is not good, probably because the wheat can never ripen. In wet weather this valley must be truly miserable. It is now much frequented by travellers: 560 visited one hotel in 1854.

The grandest object in the views around Zermatt is the *Mont Cervin* (Germ. *Matterhorn*, Ital. *Monte Silvio*), which, from the village, is seen to rise in singular beauty and magnificence

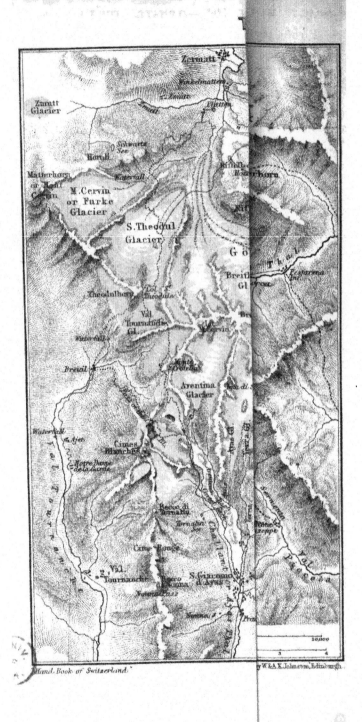

against the sky, of a pyramidal form, 14,836 Eng. feet high.

Prof. Forbes describes it " as beyond comparison the most striking natural object he had seen,— an inaccessible obelisk of rock, not 1000 ft. lower than Mont Blanc." It lifts itself from an otherwise unbroken line of glacier, which is more than 11,000 Eng. ft. above the level of the sea : this scene alone would repay the trouble of a visit to Zermatt from Visp.

Guides.—There is no difficulty in getting good guides at Zermatt, and most of them speak a little French. Jean Baptiste Brantschen, Stephen, Francis, and Joseph Biener, and Matthäus and Stephen zum Taugwald, are intelligent, trusty, and collected. Joseph Brantschen is a good chamois hunter. Those who wish to make difficult excursions find a great advantage in Zermatt over Chamouni, that the Zermatt guides are moderate in their demands, and that no rigid system of extortion prevails as at Chamouni.

Excursions.

a. Riffelberg and Gorner Grat.—The great excursion from Zermatt is up the *Riffelberg*, and to the *Gorner Grat*, and those who have time to make one expedition only usually make this. It is very comfortably accomplished by sleeping two nights at Zermatt ; but those who wish to save a day may sleep at St. Niklaus, next day to the Riffelberg Inn, and on the following day to the Gorner Grat and back to St. Niklaus. From Zermatt to the Inn on the Riffelberg is 2½ hrs. on horses, 2 hrs. good walking. From the Inn to the top of the Gorner Grat 1½ hr.

The term *Riffelberg* is properly applied to a long rocky ridge or promontory, with the *Gorner Grat* and *Riffelhorn* rising out of it, extending between the Gorner Glacier and the Findelen Glacier ; but a portion of it near the inn is sometimes so called, and apparently the rocky eminence upon it, now called the Gorner Grat, was formerly called the Riffelberg, or perhaps Riffelhorn. A good *Inn* has now been built upon a part of the Riffelberg, at an elevation of more than 7000 ft., affording fine views in the immediate neighbourhood, and about 1½ hr. from the top of the Gorner Grat, the great object of attraction.

There are several ways up the Riffelberg ; that usually followed by the mules goes past the church, then across some meadows to the l., then ascends for about an hr. by a path exceedingly steep in places, through a noble forest—first of larch, then of Arven (*pinus cembra*); it then emerges on a small alp or pasturage, and, passing some châlets, turns to the rt. and crosses the stream ; the rest of the ascent is easy, winding round the shoulder of the mountain towards the Gorner Glacier, and finally arriving at the plateau where the inn is situated. From this plateau there is a fine view of the Mont Cervin and the ranges towards the S. and W. ; and from points in the immediate neighbourhood views can be obtained over the Gorner Glacier. Leaving the inn, and keeping a little to the S., and then turning E. amongst some rocks, the path ascends, becoming very rugged, but affording magnificent views of the mountains and of the glacier below. A rugged peak is seen on the rt., now generally called the *Riffelhorn*, which it is possible, but not profitable, to ascend ; and the path continues till, in about an hr. from the inn, it reaches a little lake. The path here becomes so very rough that, though it is possible to ride to the top, it is better to dismount, and send the horses to meet you near the Guggli. The track is now over rocky masses with snow in the hollows, and vegetation becomes very scanty, until the summit of the Gorner Grat is reached, probably upwards of 9000 ft. above the sea-level. This is a round knoll, perhaps 50 yds. across, with precipices towards the Gorner Glacier and a steep slope of snow on the N., and it commands a splendid view of the Gorner Glacier, and also a complete panorama, nearly 40 m. in diameter, of snowy mountains, in which respect it exceeds anything at Chamouni, where the view is always confined to one side. The only point where there is anything to impede a complete view is a snowy eminence to the E. on a continuation of the Riffelberg ridge, and called *Hochthäligrat*. This point is about 1½ hr. from the Gorner Grat, and commands a magnificent view.

Descending from the Gorner Grat, and keeping rather towards the N. by a track not easy to find, in about ¾ hr. the eminence called *Guggli* is reached, the view from which is remarkable, though it will perhaps appear tame after that from the Gorner Grat ; but others have said, "The view from hence appeared to me extremely beautiful. The Riffel shuts out the great range to the S., but you have the double range enclosing the valley of St. Nicholas; to the E. the savage peaks of the Saas Grat, now thought to equal Monte Rosa in height; to the W. the Weisshorn, Gabelhörner, &c., in a singularly favourable point of view for estimating their magnificence. Right before you is the Bernese Oberland, of which the most conspicuous summit is that called by the Valaisans the Vietschhorn."

From Guggli there is a path by the side of the Findelen Glacier back to Zermatt, but it is usual to return in about ½ hr. over rough but level ground to the inn, whence by a circuit of ⅓ hr., or so, the foot of the Gorner-gletscher, where the river issues from it, may be visited ; and though the vault of ice at present is far inferior to those of the Glacier du Bois, or Grindelwald, the exquisite beauty of the spot well deserves a visit. There is no moraine to deform it ; and here one may literally touch the meadows with one hand, and the glacier with the other. Cornfields are seen above, at a considerable elevation, and the needles of ice which rise against the sky on the higher part of the glacier contrast with the larches which fringe the mountain side. Of near views the Alps offer few more lovely, or more remarkable. The torrent from the

vault of the glacier soon plunges into a singularly beautiful gorge of serpentine, the commencement of a romantic forest ravine, through which it leaps and struggles until it reaches the plains of Zermatt. The descent from the glacier to Zermatt is about 45 minutes.

In 1853 the Gorner Glacier was especially worth observing, owing to the alarming rapidity of its encroachments. In the course of the summer a foot-bridge, which crossed the stream just below its exit from the ice cavern, had been carried away, and the cave is now some yards beyond it. The glacier protruded into some of the richest pastures, and the turf was literally turned up and thrown back by it as by the share of an enormous plough. Several of the peasants were ruined by it. It was still advancing in 1857.

b. Schwartzsee and Zmutt Glacier.— "The ascent to the Schwartzsee occupies about 3 hours from Zermatt. Ladies can ride all the way; but the ascent, though not dangerous, is in part very steep and fatiguing. The Schwartzsee is a little lake, or rather pond, at an elevation of 8000 to 9000 feet, on a buttress of the Matterhorn, with a lone chapel beside it. There is nothing remarkable in the spot itself: but the low ridge east of it commands a superb panoramic view of the whole basin of Zermatt, with its surrounding mountains : a view decidedly finer than that from the Riffel. Here the Matterhorn, rising overhead, is the principal object; but the view also embraces the whole extent of the Gornergletscher, to the top of Monte Rosa. A still finer view is obtained by mounting the rocky peak above the lake, called the *Hörnlein*, an hour's steep ascent, in part over ice. It is so infinitely superior that no one ought to omit it. Either from this point, or from the Schwartzsee, a different route may be taken, descending westward to the foot of the great glacier of Zmutt, and through that village, following the torrent, along the W. branch of the valley to Zer-

MONTE ROSA,
highest peak.

SOUt Mt.
Lyskavin.

St.

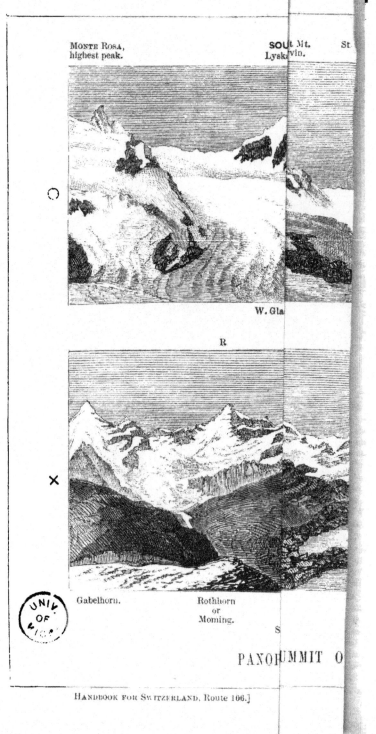

W. Gla

R

Gabelhorn.

Rothhorn
or
Moming.

S

PANOSUMMIT O

matt. This route passes through fine large forests, and abounds in most singular and beautiful pictures. It crosses the river by a wooden bridge, of large span, at an immense height above the water. The descent this way is less steep, but rather longer: it will take about 3½ hours." The Zmutt Glacier is well worth a visit on account of the magnificent views obtained from it.

Another returning route is by the side of the Gorner Glacier.

c. The *Untere Rothhorn* may be ascended in 4½ hrs. by a steep and rough path. The view is more panoramic than that from the Gorner Grat; it rises in the centre of a complete circle of snow mountains, and you see at one view the 3 chief glacier routes leading out of the valley of Zermatt, viz the Matterjoch into Val d'Aosta, the Weiss Thor into Val Anzasca, and that by Zmutt Glacier into Val d'Erin. There is a short and steep descent into the Findel-thal.

d. From Zermatt a rather difficult and dangerous path is occasionally taken by English travellers, leading directly across the glaciers of Monte Rosa to Macugnaga, by the *Arète-blanche* — German *Weiss Thor.* The distance is 12 hrs., and its highest point exceeds 12,000 Eng. ft. The distance may be shortened by sleeping at the inn on the Riffelberg. The Gorner Glacier is then ascended to the side of Cima de Jazi.

"There are two depressions on the top, one to the l. looking across the head of the vale of Saas, the other looking down the Val d'Anzasca. From the eminence between these a spur of mountain stands out at right angles to the general run of the cliff. The road lies along the ridge of this, which is exceedingly narrow for about 150 yds. In this part there is barely foot room, with a formidable slope of snow and then a precipitous fall on either side. Descending a little on the Saas side of the ridge, and after ¼ hr.'s walk in a line parallel to it, the track turns sharply across it to the rt., and begins to go down in good earnest, the descent being over rocks, and very steep. The view from the summit is magnificent, and embraces all the high points of the southern Alps from Mont Blanc in the distance to the peaks of Monte Rosa almost within reach. By a little advance the Bernese Alps are seen down the valley of Saas. On the Italian side in clear weather the Lago Maggiore is visible."

From Macugnaga the ascent of the *Weiss Thor* is best made by starting over night across the moraine and lower part of the mountain, and sleeping at the foot of the steepest part of the ascent. The traveller is then fresh for the severest climb next morning, and may pass over the snow on the N. side before the sun has softened it.

e. The Weiss-thor pass is, however, rather difficult and dangerous, and a finer view can be obtained by going part of the way and then ascending *Cima di Jazi* (13,240 ft.) This can be reached in 4 hrs. from the Riffelberg Hotel. During the greater part of the time the path is over ice and snow on easy slopes, and there is no other mountain in the Alps of that height which can be so easily ascended. The view from the top extends over the High Alps, the Bernese Alps, and the plains and lakes of Italy, and to the Oertler Spitz in the Tyrol. Two guides and a rope are sometimes necessary, but in general there is neither difficulty nor danger. The guide has usually 10 fr.

f. Monte Rosa (15,160 ft.: some surveys have made it higher than Mont Blanc). The ascent of Monte Rosa was first effected by M. Studer and Matthew Taugwald in 1849. Within the last three years it has become very common, for though it is far more difficult and dangerous than Mt. Blanc, yet, by starting from the Riffelberg, the expedition up and down again may be accomplished in about 14 hrs., and there is no necessity for sleeping out on the mountain. The summit is not one peak, but an irre-

Summit of Monte Rosa. From Schlagentwert's Stuhl.

gular assemblage of pinnacles of rock and ice, and it is difficult to ascertain which is the highest. It takes from 7 to 8 hrs.' walk over snow and glacier, passing Auf der Platte, to reach the base of the cone forming the summit. Here the real difficulty begins. It is a very steep rock, its hollows filled with ice; and, though only 500 ft. high, requires nearly an hour to ascend, and as much to descend. The best guides should be taken, and the usual charge is 50 fr. a guide.

g. Those who do not intend crossing into the Val d'Aosta from Zermatt by the St. Théodule (see below), will be gratified by ascending to the highest point of the pass. The scenery is grand in the highest degree, and the excursion neither dangerous, difficult, nor very fatiguing, unless the snow be very soft. It is possible to ride as far as the glacier in 2½ hrs.

from Zermatt: it then takes 2½ hrs.' good walking to reach the summit of the pass, the view from which is indeed magnificent. The return to Zermatt might be made in 3½ hrs.

h. *Zermatt to the Einfisch Thal* (Rte. 106D), by the glaciers of the Trift and Zinal.

"This passage had not been for many years made use of till, on the 1st Sept. 1854, accompanied by Arnold Kehrli and Ignatz Biner, of Zermatt, I effected it. We set out at 4½ o'clock. There is a good path for some way from Zermatt, by which we ascended rapidly till near the Trift glacier: we then followed sometimes this glacier, sometimes its moraine or the mountain side on its rt., till its upper plateau was reached. The scene here was very grand. The ascent was continued along the rocks on the rt. just under the Trifthorn, and before 9½ o'clock we were at the summit. Having clambered over the loose stones near the summit, we descended along the ledges of this cliff, cutting steps. The descent continued to the glacier of Zinal, which is a good deal crevassed, but is not difficult: from its l. the Grand Cornier rises in perpendicular precipices. When the glacier became steeper, and was impracticable, we left it for the moun untain marked in Professor Stüder's map of the lower Canton Valais as "Lo Besso," on its rt. I am inclined to think we were wrong in this, and that we should have continued our descent by the moraine at the foot of "Lo Besso." As it happened we had considerable difficulty and spent quite an hour in getting down to the glacier, which then was flat: we went along it for some way till Kehrli espied a track on the mountain on the left; we soon availed ourselves of this, and at ¼ before 7 o'clock reached *Ayer*, having been 14¼ hrs., including stoppages, in crossing from Zermatt: of this nearly 8 hrs. were upon the ice and the steep rocks near the summit. There is neither inn nor curé at Ayer; we called on the President of the village, and he procured us lodgings at his sister's house. Ayer is a very primitive village, and, with the exception of wine, of which the President gave us plenty, our fare was very scanty."—R.F.

i. Zermatt to Saas, by the *Adler Pass;* 14 hrs.—Starting from Saas, for the first three hours the path is the same as that of the Moro Pass. After passing the lake the road turns to the rt. and ascends to a châlet, where it is usual to sleep. After ascending for an hour the snow is reached: the path lies between the Rymphyschhorn and Alaleinhorn, and is about 12,000 feet above the level of the sea. By ascending the Strahlhorn, which adds about two hours to the time, a most magnificent view is obtained. The descent from the top of the pass, by the Findelen Glacier, is very steep and dangerous for a few hundred feet, after which it becomes easy, and Zermatt is reached. This route may be varied by an exceedingly difficult

route, taken for the first time in 1853 by Herr Imseng and Mr. Wills with guides, and said to command magnificent views.

j. The ascent of the Stockhi above the Zmutt Glacier (5 hrs.) has been strongly recommended, as also the ascent of the Mittelhorn (6 hrs., 11,300 ft.), which is represented as quite free from danger. Chamois are often seen here. Hoch-licht, opposite Zmutt, is said to contain a fine view of Mount Cervin.

k. From Zermatt it is possible for good mountaineers to reach the St. Bernard by passes along the heads of the valleys. 1. Zermatt to Evolena (Rte. 106 c) or Haudières, where Pralong, the guide, can accommodate a traveller. From Evolena there is a very difficult Pass by the side of Mt. Collon and near Mt. Combin into the Valpelline, or from Evolena there are Passes into the Val de Bagnes (Rte. 109), and thence to Martigny.

*** The Editor would feel grateful for any information as to the last-mentioned Passes, and also as to the Turtman Thal, the Einfisch Thal, and the Eringer Thal, or Val d'Heremence.

ROUTE 106 A.

PASS OF ST. THÉODULE OR MATTERJOCH. ZERMATT TO CHÂTILLON OR TO AYAS.

a. Zermatt.	Hours.
Summit of Pass	5¼
Breuil	2¼
Val Tournanche	2
Châtillon	3¼
b. Zermatt.	
Summit	5¼
St. Jean d'Ayas	5
Ayas	1¼

a. This pass is generally called *St.*

Théodule, but sometimes *Mont Cervin*, and sometimes *Matterjoch*.

Ladies not unfrequently cross this Pass. The journey is shortened if you start from the Riffel instead of from Zermatt, and may be still more shortened by sleeping at the new Inn of Breuil. A party, including a lady, crossed the Pass—1855—as follows: —Started at 2.30 A.M.; rode to the foot of the glacier in 2 hr. 30 m. Here, leaving the horses, the lady was carried in chaise-à-porteurs with 6 bearers (cost 33 francs, including pourboire) over the snow in 3 hrs. to the *summit of the Pass*. After resting ¼ hr. they descended on foot to the bottom of the glaciers in 50 min., and reached Val Tournanche, still on foot, at 12.40; rested there till 2.30; obtained a mule for the lady, and reached Châtillon in 3¾ hrs.—at 6.15 P.M. The Châtillon guides are not trustworthy. Cattle and mules are driven over this pass in fine weather.

On quitting Zermatt the torrent of Zmutt is crossed, and you wind up the steep pastures skirting the W. edge of the glacier of Gorner. There is another cluster of huts and granges called Zumsee, still further up the little plain of Zermatt; it lies close to the Gorner glacier, but is passed on the l. by the traveller who approaches the pass. It passes by some granges and up a rugged course through a pine forest, in which, however, it does not long continue. About an hour above Zumsee the path abruptly ends in a deep rift in the mountain, in the depths of which the torrents from the glaciers of the Cervin are seen to struggle and force their way into the valley of Zermatt. A path has been cut out of the overhanging rock to reach a wild Alpine bridge by which the torrent is crossed, and the ascent to the pass abruptly commences by a path which enters upon some scanty pasturages enamelled with flowers, and making a considerable *détour* to the rt., soon reaches a track of loose schist, sodden with the waters from the glaciers. Often it is necessary to traverse deep watercourses cut by the streams. This fatiguing ascent offers little variety until he reach the glaciers, which are very grand, and free from danger, though deep rifts on the l. point out the risk of deviating from the true course.

[If the traveller starts from the Riffelhaus, he leaves the Riffelhorn on the l., and descends by the steep side of the hill upon the Gorner glacier, which, however, is here impassable, so that it is necessary to ascend the moraine for 1½ hr.'s disagreeable and sometimes dangerous walking. The Gorner glacier is then crossed, and some steep rocks ascended; keeping them to the l. the snow is reached leading to the Col by a gentle ascent: about 4½ hrs. from the Riffel.]

The summit of the pass of St. Théodule is 11,185 Eng. ft. above the level of the sea. The scene around is one of extraordinary magnificence; the eye wanders over a vast intervening country to the Bernese Alps, sweeps round by the Breithorn and Monte Rosa, looks down upon a thousand peaks towards Piedmont, and rests upon that wonder of the Alps, a pinnacle of rock, the Cervin or Matterhorn, in immediate proximity, whose peak is 14,836 Eng. ft. above the sea. During the ascent, this glorious object—the motive for his journey, the reward of his exertion— is constantly before the traveller.

On the actual crest of the Col there is some bare rock, and a little space so exposed that the snow cannot rest upon it. Here Saussure remained 3 days, with his son and attendants, engaged in experiments at this elevation. Traces of the rude cabins in which they sheltered still exist, and also of a redoubt thrown up 3 centuries ago by the Valaisans, and known by the name of Fort St. Théodule: displayed to mark the Swiss frontier along the crest of the Alps.

A hut was erected on this Col, in 1854, where bread, cheese, and wine may be obtained during the summer. This is the highest habitation in Europe.

From the summit the descent towards the Val d'Aosta still lies over the glacier for the space of 1 hour, thence down the steep and loose moraines, swampy and difficult of descent, for 1 hour more, before the traveller can reach smooth pasturages enamelled with flowers, in the midst of which stand the *châlets* of Mont Jumont,— the first on the side of Piedmont.

On the plain of *Breuil* there are many granges, and a chapel, in which once a year, during the resort to the pasturages in these high regions, service is performed. Near it is a new and good inn (1857). The plain of Breuil appears to have anciently been a lake. From its lower extremity the peak of the Cervin is seen on the side opposite to Switzerland, but still towering over its enormous bed of glaciers.

Below the plain of Breuil, the route descends by a wild and deep gorge, through which a torrent rushes, and scarcely leaves space enough for a path by the side of the rock.

Val Tournanche (there is now a rough *Inn* here). This hamlet is composed of many houses, shaded with chesnuts, scattered over the slopes of an amphitheatre of rich pasturage, surrounded by mountains partly wooded.

Here the Piedmontese officers of the customs are stationed. The difficult and dangerous passes into the Valais are the surest courses for smugglers. Formerly, in defiance of Napoleon and his Berlin decrees, they passed these frightful solitudes laden with British muslins, tempted by a high reward.

[*Ascent from Val Tournanche to Zermatt.*—By sleeping at the châlets of Jumont or Breuil, and starting at 3.30, the snow may be crossed before its surface is melted by the sun, its summit reached about sunrise, and Zermatt in 7 hrs., 2 of which are over snow.]

From the village of Val Tournanche is a journey of about 3¾ hrs., through unrivalled scenery, generally deep in the ravine through which the Tournanche foams; 2 or 3 little hamlets are passed, the principal of which is Antey. About an hour below Val Tournanche some extraordinary remains of a *Roman Aqueduct* may be seen high up on the

face of the rock, on the rt., and they are continued at intervals for several miles. The finest portion consists of several arches very perfect, in front of a nearly perpendicular cliff several hundred feet above the valley, nearly opposite the village of Antey, hanging like a picture against the rock.

[About 1 hr. from Val Tournanche the traveller, in ascending, first comes in view of Mont Cervin.]

On approaching Châtillon the road rises high up on the side of the ravine, and winds amidst enormous blocks of serpentine which have fallen from the mountains whose sides and bases bound the gorge. The arid faces of the rocks, whence these have been detached, present the richest colours for the pencil of the artist, and the vast trunks and wild branches of the chestnut and walnut trees increase the picturesque character of the valley. Through a forest of these the path descends, and on emerging from it, the Val d'Aosta opens, the old and new bridges of Châtillon spanning with their single arches the deep ravine of the Tournanche ; and beyond, on the opposite side of the Val d'Aosta, the ruins of the *Castle d'Usselle* on a projecting knoll of rock, washed round its base by the torrent, present those materials of the picturesque for which the valley of Aosta is so celebrated. (Rte. 107.)

Châtillon (*Inns*: H. du Palais Royal, good; Lion d'Or.) There are superb views from this place, and several châteaux worth visiting in the neighbourhood. The walks are remarkably pretty, particularly that to the *Château d'Usselle*. The bridges deserve notice : that over which the high road now passes is a very fine single arch, thrown across a deep gulf. From it are seen, further down the torrent, the remains of a *Roman bridge*, also a single, and still an entire arch ; and immediately over it another bridge, which served its purpose for many ages, but has now been superseded by the new bridge and its improved approaches.

In the depth of the gulf, and a little up the stream, are forges, strangely placed there, for the sake of the water-power in working the tilts; a wild path leads down to them, and the view of the bridges from the bottom of the ravine forms one of the most striking scenes in the valley.

From Châtillon there is a char road to AOSTA (Rte. 107).

b. A little below the Col of St. Theodule, on the Italian side, a path turns off to the left and descends over a plateau of snow to the chain of the Cîmes Blanches (1½ hr.), whence crossing the Ayas Glacier the châlets of Aventine (1½ hr.) are reached, and in 2 hrs. more St. Giacomo d'Ayas, whence the Val d'Ayas may be descended to Brussone (Rte. 104a), or the Betta Furca may be crossed to Gressoney (Rte.104b). This is a more difficult pass than the pass to Aosta, and the accommodation for the night is bad.

ROUTE 106 B.

AOSTA TO EVOLENA, BY THE VALPELLINE AND COL DE COLLON.

An extremely interesting expedition over high and difficult passes. The natives of Valpellina are shy and inhospitable, refusing to strangers not only the shelter of their houses, but even food and refreshment. The curé should be sought for. Valpellina in the upper part is very grand.

The way follows the St. Bernard (Rte. 108) for a short distance; then turning downwards, crosses the St. Remy branch of the river Buttier, near its junction with the Valpelline branch, a very beautiful spot, and proceeds through rich fields to the village of Valpelline, 2½ hours. Here the valley narrows, and the ascent becomes rapid. Passing the village of Oyace, picturesquely situated on a high bar-

rier of rock which crosses the valley (1 hour 40 minutes), you reach in another hour Biona, and in 4 hours more the châlets of Prerayen: total from Aosta, 9 hours of rapid ascent. Cultivation extends high up the valley, which lies exposed to the afternoon sun, and is very hot. There is a good horse-road to Prerayen, where the châlets afford somewhat better quarters than most of those in Piedmont. There is no inn anywhere in the Valpelline, but the curé of Biona will receive travellers comfortably and hospitably.

The head of the valley is bounded by a very grand chain of snowy mountains, branching from the main chain at the Dent d'Erin, which separates the Valpelline and Val Tournanche. [From Prerayen to Breuil (Rte. 106 A) is a pass called Col de Val Cornère; it is said to be only 6 or 7 hours, not difficult, and not much glacier. It looks very steep, however, and none of the people in the valley seem to be personally acquainted with it. From Biona there is a high glacier pass, leading to the Val de Bagnes. On the S. side of the valley from below Prerayen there is also a pass leading by the Val St. Bartelemi to the Val d'Aosta, between Aosta and Châtillon.]

In ascending to the Col de Collon, the way lies up a steep lateral valley, which joins the main stream a little below Prerayen. It is nearly an hour's walk to the foot of the great moraine. The glacier has retreated from it a good half-mile during the last thirty years; on the side of Evolena, on the contrary, the ice has not diminished. There are two practicable routes to the upper plateau of the glacier; one over rocks, which Professor Forbes took in 1842, the other following the bottom of the valley to the foot of the glacier, which is to be mounted by climbing steep slopes of frozen snow, not without difficulty. These being surmounted, a broad plain and two or three long slopes lead to the Col. The glacier on this side does not seem dangerous.

" The height of the Col, by Professor Forbes's measurement, is 10,333 English feet. To the left is a crest of rocks, in a cleft of which is stuck a small iron cross, dated 1754. A hard varnish of rust is formed on it, which seems to protect the metal from further decay. The view from the Col is -very grand. No distance, however, is visible; nothing but spires of rock and swells of snow.

"The descent towards Evolena is more dangerous, the glacier, which on this side is called Arolla, being much more extensive, and more crevassed. Some years ago a party of villagers from Evolena being overtaken by the tourmente on the upper part of the glacier, 3 of them were lost. Professor Forbes in crossing this pass found the skeleton of one. After descending direct from the Col for some distance, it is necessary to keep to the rt. or E. side of the glacier and take to the rocks, in order to avoid a precipitous ice-fall which is quite impassable. The descent over steep rocks and snow requires caution. At the foot of this descent you return to the glacier, here free from snow, and leaning to the l., finally leave it close to its foot. In a favourable state of the glacier, it takes 4 hrs. to descend or 5 hrs. to ascend. The valley as we descend is close and winding, so that no distant views can be had; but it is of the grandest character.

"The lofty jagged ridge to the east, which divides the glacier of Arolla from that of Ferpècle, is called by Professor Forbes the Dents des Bouquetins. To the west, another very grand glacier descends from the other side of the Mont Collon, communicating with the head of the Val de Bagnes. There is a châlet at the foot of the glacier, where it is possible to pass the night. From the foot of the glacier to Evolena is about 4 hours of very grand and beautiful scenery. Total from Prerayen to Evolena, about 10 hrs.

Evolena (Rte. 106 D).

ROUTE 106 c.

EVOLENA TO ZERMATT.   COL D'ERIN.

Time 12½ hrs., excluding stoppages. It might take much more.

"An hour above Evolena the valley forks into two branches; the one leading to the glacier of Arolla and Col de Collon, the other to the glacier of Ferpècle and Col d'Erin, as Forbes has called it; the pass being apparently without a name in the country. The scenery of the latter branch is even finer than that of the former. From the hamlet of Haudières, near the junction, to the foot of the glacier, there is a rapid ascent. The termination of the glacier is remarkably fine. The ice is pure, and very high, ending on one side in a vertical section cresting a precipice; on the other sweeping grandly over it; and the effect is much increased by the near neighbourhood of fine larches.

"From hence a rapid ascent, skirting deep precipices, leads to the châlets of Abricolla, distant about 3 hours from Evolena. They are rude and more dirty than is usual in Switzerland; and the traveller who means to sleep at them should take up straw from below. The view from these heights is extremely fine.

"Started at half-past four: and by the advice of one of the Fulloniers, who accompanied us part of the way, we kept at a level, or gradually ascending, along the mountain side, instead of descending, as Forbes had done, to the glacier—a depth of several hundred feet perpendicular. In about an hour we reached the glacier, which was then a dazzling sheet of snow, hard frozen, and inclined at an angle which rendered great caution necessary in traversing it. Less than an hour brought us to the edge of a precipice, opposite to a bare rock in the middle of the ice, called Motta

Rotta. Here the sun had melted out space enough just to form a narrow, slippery, and dangerous path, along which we proceeded eastward, shouldering the ice on one side, and with the deep precipice on the other. At the end of it we dismissed Fullonier, having passed the difficulties on this side of the passage. From hence to the level of Motta Rotta is a succession of slopes, free from danger, and from that level an immense undulating snow plain extends to the Col, which lies to the right of a slightly elevated point, called by Professor Forbes the Stockhorn, the height of which he makes 11,760 feet, 600 feet higher than the Col du Géant. We reached it in 3 h. 20 m. from the châlets of Abricolla; 6¼ hrs. from Evolena, having gained an hour on Professor Forbes by the new route. His route lay at the foot of the precipice along the top of which we had passed.

" The Col is formed by a ridge extending from the Dent Blanche (which lies between the valleys of Anniviers and of Zmutt) to the main chain between the Dent d'Erin and the Mont Collon. It thus encloses the great glacier of Zmutt, which it separates from the glacier of Ferpêcle. Professor Forbes rates the view from it above any that he had seen in the higher Alps, even above that from the Col du Géant. The spectator is centrally placed between the Cervin, the Dent d'Erin, and the Dent Blanche, with the whole chain of Monte Rosa in full view. To these is to be added the Strallhorn (Cima de Jazi?) nearly of the same height, between which and Monte Rosa the pass of the Weissenthor is seen, at the same, or a higher, level on which he stands. None of these mountains is less than 14,000 feet high.

" There are two possible descents; one down the face of the cliff, a little W. of the Stockhorn, which Professor Forbes tried in 1842 ; and failed to achieve, owing to a precipice of some 30 feet, next the ice, which could not be passed. He was therefore driven to take the way which I followed, still further to the W., which, though in-

volving a considerable circuit, I should think always preferable, unless the glacier below were in a very dangerous state. The descent is shorter, and less rapid, and the rocks are masked by slopes of snow, which however are steep enough to present dangers of their own. The upper basin of the Zmutt glacier being thus reached, a black blunt point in the chain of rocks which holds up this upper glacier serves for landmark: but as the ice is much crevassed, there is many a circuit to be made ; and the passage took a good hour. The next descent is over a slope of rocks, ending, within 100 ft. of the bottom, in a precipice, down which it is possible to descend by a very steep couloir, when the glacier, which is here considerably inclined, is in too bad a state to traverse higher up. In 1843 the quantity of snow rendered it possible to reach and traverse the lower glacier to the W. of the couloir; and we struck across in the direction of Mont Cervin, and reached the lateral moraine at 12 h. 15 m., having left the Col at 8 h. 30 m. Another hour brought us off the ice; and 1¾ hour more to Zermatt (Rte. 106).

In 1853 an Englishman, Mr. Macpherson, crossed this pass from Zermatt alone. The inhabitants of Zermatt did not believe it possible, and, not hearing of him, wrote to the newspapers in order to inform his friends of his supposed loss.

ROUTE 106 D.

ST. NICHOLAS TO EVOLENA, BY THE TURTMAN THAL AND THE EINFISCH THAL.

This district was until lately seldom visited ; not many guides are acquainted with it. Joseph Brantschen of Zermatt, carpenter, is one.

A very steep ascent along the nearly precipitous rocks that rise on the W. side of the village of St. Niklaus leads to the châlets and chapel of Jung. From thence a wild and rather dreary glen leads to the crest of the ridge, which, descending from the Weisshorn, separates the valley of St. Niklaus from the Turtman Thal. There is no trace of path, and it is not easy to say which may be the least difficult course over the rugged masses of rock that close in the head of this glen. From an eminence about 200 ft. above the lowest point a wild and striking view is obtained, extending far over a wilderness of alps. This point may be about 8800 English ft. above the sea-level. A long, steep, but not very difficult descent over slopes of snow, débris, and alpine turf, leads down to the hamlet of Meiden, in the Turtman Thal, about 8 hrs. from St. Niklaus.

The *Turtman Thal* is a wild valley about 15 m. in length, from the point where its stream falls into the Rhone at Turtman, or Tourtemagne (Rte. 59 A), to the great glacier on the N. side of the Weisshorn, whence it takes its rise. Though, in addition to numerous châlets which are perched by the upper pastures above the valley, it contains several hamlets, these consist exclusively of *mayens*, which are inhabited for a few weeks only in the spring and autumn; so that to find even rough quarters it is necessary to make the circuit from St. Niklaus to Turtman, whence it is an easy and agreeable walk of 3 or 4 hrs. to Meiden.

From the Turtman Thal to the Einfisch Thal by the Meiden Pass.

Crossing the stream which descends from the great glacier of Turtman, now full in sight, an ill-defined path ascends the steep side of the valley opposite to Meiden. Keeping to the l. towards the upper part, it leads to a number of very poor châlets perched on the brow of the mountain, overlooking the Turtman valley, and commanding a magnificent view of the Weisshorn, with its attendant glaciers. From this point to the top of the pass, which lies immediately to the rt. of some steep pinnacles of quartz rock, there is no well-defined track; the upper part of the way is very steep. The scene which presents itself on the south side of the path descending towards Luc is very wild and striking, having the appearance of a gigantic ruin, caused by the falling down of some of the pinnacles of quartz rock which form the main ridge. Magnificent views are obtained of the Zinal glacier and the Matterhorn. At length a point is attained which overlooks the *Einfisch Thal*, or *Val d'Anniviers*, one of the least known, most interesting, and most beautiful valleys in the Alps.

There is another path of much beauty into the Einfisch Thal, from *Susten*, near Leuk, leading in 5 or 6 hrs. by the *Ill-see* to Vissoye. The Ill-see is about 5000 ft. above the sea, the Col some hundred feet higher.

A char-road is making (1857) from Sierre to Vissoye; the present bridle-path is very rough, and the path on the l. bank is said to be shorter and finer.

A Scandinavian origin has been attributed to the population of this valley, but at present they speak a very corrupt French *patois*, nearly identical with that spoken in the neighbouring Val d'Erin, and differing but little from that of the Val d'Aosta. They are more simple and also more courteous to strangers than in most of the districts which are frequently visited by tourists. Exposed but rarely to the contact of their fellow countrymen, their lives are passed between hard labour and the offices of religion, in both of which they are most diligent.

There are several populous villages in the valley, of which the chief is *Vissoye*, but there is no inn; and the only tolerable accommodation for a stranger is at the house of the worthy parish priest of that village. There is a curious old castle, with its dungeon. Above Vissoye, near the hamlet of Cremenz, the valley divides into two branches, of which the western, leading to the passes into the Val d'Erin, is called the Val de Torrent, while the eastern branch contains the stream descending from the great glacier of Zinal (Rte. 106*h*), and no one. who is favoured by fine weather should omit that excursion—at all events as far as the châlets of Arpitella.

[From a point called Bec de Bossons (11,000 ft.), between this and the Val d'Erin, there is a magnificent view from Combin to Cervin and the Bernese Alps.]

There are said to be three ways by the Zinal Glacier to Zermatt: two following the Glacier of Zinal round the foot of Lo Besso, up the Gl. du Durand, and the E. branch of the valley, called here the Mutterthal, at the top of which they diverge. As to the third—"Having slept at Arpitella (very rough), I ascended to within 1½ hr. of the top, with no difficulty, but considerable labour, the snow being deep and soft (June, 18, 1857), returning to Vissoye in the afternoon: a long and very grand day. It did not appear that, with proper care, there would have been material difficulty higher up. The glacier itself presents no very remarkable features. It was not in my plan to cross to Zermatt; but the Curé made no difficulty as to finding me trustworthy guides." ·

Vissoye to Evolena.

The main stream is crossed immediately below the latter village, and the track is well marked for some distance beyond the hamlet of Cremenz, when it becomes less distinct, being merged in cattle tracks. There are three passes from the Val de Torrent into the Val d'Erin, all of about the same height, probably about 7800 ft. In fine weather it is well worth while to choose that nearest to the Glacier de Torrent, on account of the views to the southward and westward, which must be magnificent. This course would increase the length of the day's walk by about 2 hrs. The direct way to Evolena is by the

pass known as the Pas de Torrent, and by that route it is about 7 hrs. distant from Vissoye. The pass is in no way difficult, but the track is ill marked, and in bad weather rather difficult to find without a guide.—T. B.

An inn is now building at *Evolena*, a spot which, from the beauty and grandeur of the neighbouring scenery, will not fail to attract many tourists when there is tolerable accommodation. The curé will not refuse lodging to those who require it, but he does not seem to expect visitors, as in some other remote villages of the Alps. Until the inn is completed it is better to lodge with Pralong, the guide, or in his sister's house at Haudières.

From the *Couronne de Breona* and the *Zatalani*, eminences above Evolena, fine views may be obtained.

ROUTE 107.

TURIN TO AOSTA AND COURMAYEUR, BY IVREA.—BIELLA.—THE VAL D'AOSTA.

		Kil.		Eng. m
Turin.				
Chivasso	. .	22	=	14
Caluso	. . .	12	=	7
Ivrea	. . .	20	=	12
Donas	. . .	20	=	12
Châtillon	. .	24	=	15
Aosta	. . .	24	=	15
Courmayeur	. .	41	=	25

The journey from Courmayeur to Turin may be made in 2 days, sleeping at Châtillon. Carriage to Caluso about 90 fr.

The Rly., which was constructed by English engineers and contractors, is now open to Caluso, and is in progress to Ivrea; and a continuation to Aosta and even a tunnel to Martigny are talked of.

At *Chivasso*, a town of some 8000 Inhab., the main line is left, and a branch goes to

Caluso. Omnibuses to the neighbouring towns meet the trains.

[From Caluso an excursion may be made to *Biella* (*Inns:* Corona, best; Testa), a town situated on the Cervo, one of the affluents of the Sesia, now the terminus of a branch Rly. from Turin. Population about 9000. It has some trifling manufactories of paper, common woollen goods, and hats. *Obs.* The *Ch. of St. Sebastian:* the pillars dividing nave from aisles seem to be Roman, and the vaulted roof is elegantly painted.

The sanctuary of *Notre Dame d'Oropa,* 6 m. distant, by a steep but good carriage-road, is an object of attraction, which brings crowds of pilgrims to offer their devotions to an image, one of the thousand black specimens of bad carving, which, under the name of *Our Lady,* is worshipped for its miracle-working powers: that of Oropa is said to have been carved by Saint Luke, who is made a sculptor as well as a painter, and is stated to have been brought by a St. Eusebius from Syria, and reserved by him in the then wild and desert mountain of Oropa. A series of steep tourniquets leads to the *Church dedicated to the Virgin,* which is a fine structure of the 14th and 15th centuries. Painting and sculpture have adorned and enriched it; and among the artists employed are found the names of *Gaudenzio Ferrari* and *Luino.* At the angles, in the zigzag ascent to the church, there are erected more than twenty-four chapels, dedicated to the Virgin, and named after some event in her life, as, the Chapel or Oratory of the Annunciation—of the Purification— of the Assumption, &c., or to some Romish Saint.

A Rlwy. is now open from Biella to Turin, 84 kil. (51 miles). It joins the line from Novara at Santhia; time employed 3½ h. The distance to Santhia is 19 m., and the intermediate stations, Candelo, Sandigliano, Vergnasco, and Saluzzola.] Biella is in the *Caravese,* a district devoted to the growing of hemp.

There are no post-stations beyond Ivrea, but the post-master, who is only obliged to take travellers 24 kil. beyond it, will generally make arrangements for sending them on with the same horses as far as Aosta. The road is very good as far as St. Didier, and practicable up to Courmayeur.

Ivrea (*Inns:* H. de l'Europe, tolerable, cuisine fair; but make a bargain;—Lion d'Or) is a large walled town at the entrance of the Val d'Aosta. The entrance is highly picturesque, across the deep bed of the Doire, which flows immediately below the *Porte de Turin.* It contains about 8000 Inhab. Here large markets are held, to which cheese and other pastoral produce of the Alps are brought. It is also a depôt for the iron which is obtained near Cogne, and from other mines worked in the valley. Here also some cotton-works have been recently established.

Here is a picturesque and interesting massive *old Castle,* degraded into a prison, and disfigured with modern windows, &c. The battlements and machicolations of two of its towers remain. These, and the old walls from many points of view, furnish good materials for the sketch-book. The small isolated hills scattered along the sides of the stream, as outposts of the Alps, and often crowned by some crumb of a wall of a feudal castle, are very picturesque seen over the thicket of rich vegetation, and backed by the Alps. This town, or city, as it is called — as the seat of a bishop — is the southern gate to the Val d'Aosta. It is of great antiquity, and mentioned by many ancient authors under the name of *Eporedia.* Strabo says that here the unfortunate Salassi, made prisoners by Terentius Varro, when these brave people of the Val d'Aosta were subdued, were sold as slaves by public auction to the number of 36,000. The Marquis of Ivrea was in the middle ages a powerful monarch.

On leaving Ivrea, on the rt. is a vast ridge of alluvium, the Monte Bolegno, which stretches into the plains. The road ascends on the left bank of the Doire, passes below the old Castle of Montalto, well preserved with its towers and battlements, and picturesque in its form, and continues through the rich broad valley of the Doire—broad enough to constitute a part of the plain, for at Settimo Vittone, 3¼ leagues, the ascent has been so gradual as scarcely to have been perceived. Nor is it, in fact, until the traveller reaches

Pont St. Martin (Inn: Rosa Rossa) that he may be said to have fairly entered this valley of the Alps.

The situation of this village is strikingly fine at the entrance to the Val de Lys, stretching up to the foot of the glaciers of Monte Rosa (Rte. 104), which will well repay the explorer.

The lofty arch which here spans the torrent of the Lys (about 20 yards higher than the new bridge) is one of the finest Roman works of its class in the valley : it now serves to communicate with the Val de Valaise, and is a striking object. The road to Aosta is carried over a modern bridge. Above St. Martin are ruins of a large Castle.

After crossing the Lys at a short distance from its confluence with the Doire, the road ascends to

Donas, where a Roman work—a pierced rock—is passed through, and near to it is a Roman milestone cut in the rock, noting xxxii. MP. A tolerable wine is grown at Donas.

From Donas the road ascends abruptly for a short distance, and close to the Doire, which it steeply overhangs, to

Fort Bard, celebrated for the temporary check of 8 days which it gave to the advance of the French army under Buonaparte, in 1800. It was garrisoned by only 400 Austrians, yet such was the strength of the position that Buonaparte almost despaired of carrying it, and a few days more must have starved his army into a retreat. By a gallant manœuvre, however, in the efficient placement of a single gun, above the precipices of the Mont Albaredo, which overhangs Bard, the French checked the battery which covered the approach to the town, and the army passed by night,

dragging their guns through the streets laid with straw to prevent the noise alarming the garrison, under the grenades and pots de feu thrown by the fort. Another gun was raised to a belfry which commanded the gate of the fort; and the Austrians, fearing an assault, surrendered. Upon such slight occurrences the fate of Europe turned. As the French army would have devoured all the supply of the Val d'Aosta in a few days, it must have retreated ; and the battle of Marengo, one of the most brilliant events of French history, would not have been fought. Within a few years the fort has been greatly strengthened, and it is now considered impregnable.

After passing through the steep and narrow streets of Bard, the entrance is seen, on the l., to the valley of Champorcher, whence a path leads, by the village of Pont Bosel, to the Col de Reale in 6 hrs., and by this pass and the valley of the Soanna to Ponte in the Val d'Orca. (Rte. 111.)

The view looking back upon Fort Bard is a perfect picture, not to be surpassed in its kind.

Above Bard the valley is narrow, and offers little variety in ascending by the deep and rapid course of the Doire to

Verrex (Inn: Ecu de France—extortion), 2½ leagues from Pont St. Martin, situated at the entrance to the Val Challant (Rte. 104). Here many improvements have been made, especially in the construction of a new bridge and many new houses.

Here is a large square keep of the old Castle, which overhangs the Val Challant. It is a picturesque object from below, and the scenes from it are worth a scramble to the ruins. Here is also a convent of Augustines.

Above Verrex the valley widens, and the little plain of the Doire shows the violence of the torrent in the sands and rocks left by it in the spring.

About 1½ league beyond Verrex the road enters upon one of the most remarkable scenes in the valley—a deep ravine, through which the Doire has cut its way, or found in such a gulf its natural channel. The road ascends steeply on the left of the river, and is cut out of the rock, in some places overhanging the foaming torrent. These rocks are surmounted by the ruins of the *Castle of St. Germains*, placed so as effectually to command the pass.

The road cut out in so remarkable a way was probably a Roman work, though a modern inscribed tablet denies them the credit. It was repaired by the inhabitants of Aosta. This defile is called the pass of *Mont Jovet*—the wine in its neighbourhood is celebrated. From the head of the pass the view down the valley is very striking. Immediately above it, the finest part of the Val d'Aosta extends to the *Cité*, as Aosta is called.

Nothing can exceed the beauty and richness of the scenery, and the magnificent character of the foliage; the walnut and chestnut trees are celebrated for their grandeur and picturesqueness.

Before arriving at St. Vincent, a singular bridge over a deep ravine is crossed. It is called the Pont des Sarasins, and by antiquaries is recognised as a Roman work. From its parapet one of the most beautiful scenes in the valley is presented on looking up towards Châtillon, including among its objects the Castle d'Usselle and other ruins. Not far from this bridge is the agreeable village of

St. Vincent (Inns: best, Ecu de France; Lion d'Or. Here is a *Bathhouse* supplied from a mineral spring in the Forest above. ½ an hour's walk higher up is

Châtillon. (See Rte. 106 A.)

Above Châtillon the same fine rich character of scenery prevails, only interrupted by the occasional traces of destruction left by the torrents which in the spring rush down from the lateral valleys into the Doire.

About a league above Châtillon is the village of *Chambave*, celebrated for its wine, one of the richest and most *recherché* in Piedmont. The wine of the Val d'Aosta has a great reputation, and the vine is cultivated on the mountain sides to an elevation of 3000 ft. above the level of the sea. In the valley, hemp, Indian corn, and fruit-trees fill the plain like a vast garden.

Nuz, a poor village with the ruins of a château, is nearly half-way between Châtillon and Aosta. At the entrance of the Val de St. Barthelemi is the picturesque castle of Fenis. [The pass from the head of that valley to Prerayen, in the Valpellina, is probably difficult, but would lead through very grand scenery.]

On the approach to Aosta the *Château Quart* is seen placed high on the mountain side; a path leads up to it from near Villefranche, and down on the other side of its glen towards Aosta, so that a visit to it requires no retracing of steps, and the beautiful scenes presented in the ascent and at the château, which is now a Hospital, repay the trouble of climbing thither. Little more than a league further up the valley is

AOSTA.—*Inns:* H. du Mont Blanc, opened 1857 by Jean Tairraz from Chamouni, recommended; H. d'Italie, not bad; Couronne, bad; Ecu du Valais, in the Townhall, well spoken of.—A city of 6100 Inhab.; more interesting for its antiquities and historical associations and the extreme beauty of the scenery around it, than for any claim it has to importance in trade, wealth, or population. Its situation is indeed striking, near the confluence of the *Buttier* and the *Doire*, in a deep rich valley, surrounded by lofty and snow-capped mountains, which peer down into its squares and streets. Aosta, the *Augusta Pratoria* of the Roman itineraries, claims a high antiquity. It was known under the name of Cordèle, as the chief city of the Salassi: its history earlier than its conquest by Terentius Varro, a general of Augustus, is fabulous, but the antiquary of Aosta has no difficulty in fixing the date of its foundation 406 before that of Rome, 1158 B.C.! By the army of the emperor it was taken 28 years before the Christian era, and its inhabitants reduced to miserable captivity. Augustus rebuilt the city, gave his own name to it, and established there 3000 soldiers from the Prætorian cohorts. The remains of large public buildings attest its importance at that time, and though much inferior in beauty and extent to those of the S. of France, will yet be viewed with interest.

A *Triumphal arch*, erected in honour of Augustus, in tolerable preservation, decorated with 10 Corinthian pillars, covered with a modern red-tiled roof, is one of the finest of the remains.

There is also a remarkable *Gate* or portal, having two façades, with a quadrangle between them, each façade composed of three arches—that in the centre is much the largest. Another relic of the Romans is a *bridge*, which once spanned the Buttier, though now 100 yards E. of it. It is buried to a considerable depth by soil. A conduit of water runs under it, and by its side a path; so that you can walk under the arch, which is a fine piece of masonry. There are also the ruins of a *Basilica* (not an *Amphitheatre*), of a barrack or Prætorian palace, towers, walls, and fragments of unknown former appropriation, now serving only to perplex antiquaries. The plan of Aosta, like that of other Roman cities, was a square, and the chief streets crossed in the centre. The triumphal arch stood outside of the town, in front of the chief gateway.

Aosta has been much improved within the last few years, the chief square is enlarged, and there is much new and handsome building, a *Hôtel de Ville*, &c. It is the seat of a bishop. A military commandant is also stationed here.

Anselm, the distinguished archbishop of Canterbury in the 11th century, was born at Aosta. An inscribed stone records the flight of Calvin from Aosta, 1541 (? on his return from Ferrara).

St. Bernard, whose name is immortally associated with the mountain pass from the valley of the Rhone to the valley of the Doire, was arch-deacon of Aosta; and his knowledge, from his situation, of the exposure and sufferings of those who traversed these regions, led to his establishment of the celebrated hospice, upon the permanent footing it has since held.

The *Cathedral* is deserving of a visit, though it has no high antiquity ; but attached to the *Ch. of St. Ours* there is a very curious cloister, probably of the 8th century, with sculptured capitals, of Bible subjects, and inscriptions in rhyming verse describing them.

[The *Becca de Nona*, 10,360 ft., 8470 ft. above Aosta, is a peak nearly S. of Aosta, and commands a magnificent view of the Alps fom Mont Blanc to M. Rosa. The ascent can be accomplished on mules the whole way in 6½ hrs. Provisions must be taken. A panoramic view from the top and full account has been published by M. Carrel at Aosta.]

Diligence to Turin daily ; chars may be had in all the intermediate towns.

The inhabitants of the Pays d'Aosta speak French almost universally, especially in the upper part of the valley above Aosta; this, too, is generally the case in those side valleys which lead by the passes of the Alps to the frontiers of Savoy and France. The inhabitants of these upper valleys bear a much better character than those who live near the plains of Piedmont.

The beautiful valley of Aosta is afflicted with crétinism and goître more perhaps than any other in Piedmont ; from Châtillon to Villeneuve this blight seems to have fallen most heavily. The peasantry appear a squalid and filthy race, generally stunted and diseased. Of the whole population in the neighbourhood of Aosta, 1 in 50 is a crétin ; and above half are more or less goîtred. Some of these are horrid objects. Tumours as large as their heads are appended to their throats.

On leaving Aosta to ascend the valley, the drive for about 4 m. lies across the open plain, and through scenes of its greatest richness in vegetation. At this distance from Aosta the road passes beneath the château *Sarra*, an unpicturesque structure; nearly opposite to it, on the other side of the valley, is a singular modern building, the château of *Aimaville*, triangular in plan, with a turret at each angle, situated on a knoll in a commanding position.

At *St. Pierre* there is one of the most picturesque châteaux in the valley. A fine scene is presented in the approach to Villeneuve, where the vast rock above the town is surrounded by the Châtel d'Argent, backed by the snowy Alps at the head of the Val Savaranche. About a mile from St. Pierre the road turns towards the river, which it crosses by a stone bridge to reach the little town of

Villeneuve, where there is nothing of interest, and where there is neither decent inn nor car. Near this the valleys of the Savaranche and the Rhèmes open almost together from the S. into the valley of the Doire. Above Villeneuve the valley narrows and becomes much more wooded, the walnut-trees forming in some places almost a forest, especially near

Arvier, about 4 m. above Villeneuve. Here the vineyards are celebrated, every slope being terraced and vines planted. The dirty village of

Ivrogne, once almost a barrier to the passage of carriages up the valley, from the steepness and narrowness of its principal street, is now altogether avoided.

A bridge is made over the torrent of the Grisanche, and the new road falls into the old road above it, and is continued to Pré St. Didier. The portion of it which is cut out of Fort Roc has also been widened, and is now carried through the defile, where it rises hundreds of feet above the bed of the Doire, which is seen foaming below through its restrained course. From the summit of this pass, Mont Blanc at the head of the valley closes the scene with its masses—a magnificent barrier. The view is strikingly beautiful. The road, thus carried along the precipice, crosses in some places deep rifts in the mountain side; over these chasms drawbridges are thrown,

[*Switz.*]

the removal of which would cut off all communication by this road, and oblige an army to make a considerable détour in order to descend into the Val d'Aosta. The pass is also closed by a gate, and enfiladed by a block-house above. A peep over the parapet wall, or through the platforms, into the depth below, excites a shudder.

From *Fort Roc* the road descends rapidly to the Doire, which it crosses on a wooden bridge, and thence continues on the l. bank. Hereabouts another fine view of Mont Blanc and the valley is presented, as the road passes into a deep ravine to cross a torrent near its head; thence winding round on the other side of this ravine, it rapidly descends.

The new line of road leaves on the rt.

La Salle, a dirty narrow village, in which, however, the name is preserved of the ancient people of this valley, the Salassi: many traces of its high antiquity have been found in and around. On a hill near La Salle are the ruins of an old feudal *Castle*.

[The Sardinian government has formed a good approach by the camp of Prince Thomas to La Tuille, and the pass of the Little St. Bernard—one of the most important benefits which the government could confer upon its subjects in the Val d'Aosta and the Tarentaise.]

At the distance of a league from Morgex a branch road descends to cross the Doire, and leads to the village and *Baths of St. Didier* (see Rte. 114), through which the road to the Little St. Bernard passes. For the general scenery around, and especially for the view of Mont Blanc *on the spot*, St. Didier seems preferable, as a resting-place, to Courmayeur. About a league from the branch road to St. Didier the traveller enters

Courmayeur. Inns: H. Royal, kept by Bertolini; clean, obliging landlord. L'Union. Angelo; frequented by Italians as a boarding-house. — H. Mont Blanc, ½ way between Courmayeur and Entrèves, a very nice country inn with fine view; moderate.

Courmayeur, though considered as

P

the head of the Val d'Aosta, is in reality in the Val d'Entrèves; it is a large village with many good houses, situated 4211 ft. above the sea, near the confluence of the two branches of the Doire, which descend from the Col Ferrex and the Col de la Seigne, at the foot of the S. side of Mont Blanc, to which it approximates so nearly, that the glaciers and snowy crests of the great chain appear to hang over the valley. From the village the summit of Mont Blanc is concealed by the Mont Dolina, but half an hour's walk discloses the chain from the "Monarch" to the grand Jorasse. There is a splendid view from Mont Dolina, ¾ hrs. That part of the chain seen from the village to close the valley includes the remarkable peak of the Géant, and the whole course of the path by which the passage may be made by the Col de Géant to Chamouny, is to be traced, on the side of Piedmont, from Courmayeur.

At Courmayeur there is a family of several brothers, named Proment, all highly recommended as guides; the traveller, however, must not expect to find on the S. side of the Alps such guides as those of Chamouny and the Oberland, either for general intelligence or extensive topographical knowledge of the Alpine districts.

Courmayeur is much resorted to in summer by invalids, for the sake of its mineral waters. There are different springs near it; that of La Victoire is half a league to the S.W.; its waters are impregnated with carbonic acid gas, sulphate of magnesia, and a little iron, and have a temperature of about 54. The spring of La Marguerite varies a little in the proportions of its components, but its temperature is 12 degrees higher. The Piedmontese have great reliance on the salutary effects of these mineral springs, and the resort to them brings together much agreeable society.

Excursions from Courmayeur; chars and mules are provided at prices fixed by tariff. 4 fr. to the Col de Checruit or Mont Saxe.

a. *Ascent of the Cramont.*—An ex-

cursion of 4 hrs. to the top, which no visitor to St. Didier or Cormayeur should fail to make, if the weather be favourable, for no spot in the Alps will afford him so fine a view of Mont Blanc, or a more glorious panorama.

The ascent up the forest lies for an hour amidst pines, then, emerging into fine pasturages, the path leads up through several clusters of châlets; at the last of these (2¼ hrs.) it is usual to leave the mules, if any have been employed, to await the return of the traveller. It is ½ hr. to the summit. The extreme smoothness of the sward, and the steepness of the slope, make the footing insecure. Nearer the top, thousands of marmots have burrowed and loosened the soil, and traces of these animals are found even to the summit.

The highest point of the Cramont is the outer edge of a large slab or flat mass of rock, dipping towards the Cramont about 20°; the upper end of this mass actually overhangs the rocks below, so that a stone dropped from it would fall perpendicularly hundreds of feet, and then striking the precipitous sides of the mountain, would bound into the abyss beneath, broken into fragments. In this savage hollow chamois are often seen.

Hence the whole of the enormous mass of Mont Blanc is open to the observer: midway of its height (for the height of the Cramont is 9040 ft. and that of Mont Blanc 6500 ft. above the peak of the Cramont), from the peaks which bound the Col de la Seigne to those of the Grand Jorasse, every aiguille and glacier through this vast line of nearly 30 miles is seen, within an angle of 150°, lying like a picture before the observer from the Cramont. The depths of the Allée Blanche are concealed by some low intervening mountains, which may be considered the western bases of the Cramont.

Towards the N.E. and E. the Val d'Aosta presents a beautiful portion of the panorama. The mountains which bound it sweep down to the Doire, and leave between them the channels which are the courses of its affluents. In the valley the Doire appears like a thread of silver. Looking S.E., directly down the line of ascent to the Cramont, the Camp of Prince Thomas, and the table-land above the precipices of the valley of La Tuille, appear to be immediately beneath. Above and beyond it lies the enormous glacier of the Ruitor, one of the finest objects within the view: this is connected with the glaciers at the head of the valleys of Cogne, the Savaranche, and the Grisanche.

Towards the S. is the pass and plain of the Little St. Bernard, guarded by the Belvedere, the Vallaisan, and the other mountains which bound that pass.

To the E. the summits of Monte Rosa and Mont Cervin arrest the attention.

Towards the Great St. Bernard the course may be traced of the path which leads by the pass of the Serena from the head of the valley of Aosta to St. Remy. The hospice cannot be seen, but the Mont Velan and the Combein are seen beyond it.

Saussure thus records his second visit to the Cramont:—" Nous passâmes trois heures sur ce sommet ; j'y en avois aussi passé trois dans mon premier voyage; et ces six heures sont certainement celles de ma vie dans lesquelles j'ai goûté les plus grands plaisirs que puissent donner la contemplation et l'étude de la nature."

The descent requires more care than the ascent, at least to guard against slipping: the guides usually sit down, and slide with great speed over the dry grass.

The traveller who proposes to make a visit to the Cramont a part of his day's journey to St. Maurice, should start very early, and direct that the mules, if he take any, should, from where he left them, be sent across the pasturages, to châlets which lie in his way to the village of La Balme. He will thus gain time in ascending the valley, though the descent to the hamlet of Evolina, down a steep and rugged path over loose stones, is very fatiguing.

La Balme is in the valley, about an hour's walk above where the path up through the forest leads to the Cramont; and there is no object of interest missed between the two places.

b. to the *Col de Checruit*, highly to be recommended on account of the splendid and uninterrupted view of the chain of Mt. Blanc and the Allée Blanche. It may be made on a mule (2 hrs. to the Col). From Courmayeur you cross the Doire, through the village of Dolina, and along the S. side of the Mt. Dolina, till you reach the Col de Checruit, 2000 ft. (?) above the Allée Blanche. [A footpath, about ½ hr. below the Col, leads in 1½ hr. to the *Mt. Chetif*, the view from which is said to be finer than that from the Cramont.] Instead of descending at once through the pine forest into the Allée Blanche, it will well repay you to keep along the slope of the mountains until you arrive above the Lac de Combal (Rte. 118) before descending. By this means you completely overlook the valley and the Glacier of Miage which impedes the view of Mt. Blanc, when you are in the Allée Blanche. From Lac de Combal you can return to Courmayeur in 2½ hrs.

c. The *Mont Saxe*, 2½ hrs. from Courmayeur, round which the path to the Col Ferrex winds, is said to command the finest near view of Mont Blanc, finer than that from the Cramont, though, being lower, it is less panoramic.

d. The *Glacier of la Brenva*, approaching the great precipices which descend from the very summit of Mont Blanc.

e. A more arduous, but not dangerous undertaking, is to ascend to the Col du Géant and return, thereby making a very interesting excursion of some 12 hrs. without incurring the difficulties and dangers of the descent over the glaciers to Chamouni. An hotel is talked of (1857) on the Mont Frety, by sleeping at which the distance will be shortened some 3 hrs. (See Rte. 115 M.)

5 routes diverge from this : 1, to Aosta (Rte. 107); 2, to the Great St. Bernard (Rte. 108); 3, the Little St. Bernard (Rte. 114) ; 4, the Col de la Seigne' to Chamouny (Rte. 118); 5, the Col Ferrex to Martigny (R. 110).

ROUTE 108.

MARTIGNY TO AOSTA. — PASS OF THE GREAT ST. BERNARD.

Martigny.	H.	M.
Bourg	0	30
St. Branchier . . .	2	0
Orsières	1	30
Liddes	1	30
St. Pierre	1	0
Hospice	3	30
St. Remy	1	30
St. Oyen	2	0
Aosta	2	30

Distance 8 or 9 hours' walk to the Hospice ; about 6 h. thence to Aosta. This pass is more remarkable in an historic and romantic point of view— on account of its Hospice, monks, and dogs—than for its scenery, which is inferior to that on most of the other great passes. Guides, mules, and chars may be hired at Martigny, Orsières, or Liddes: the *charges*, fixed by tariff, are high— 30 fr. for a char from Martigny to Liddes, and a mule thence to the hospice, including return. As far as Proz, beyond Liddes, a practicable char-road was completed by the spirited Valaisans in 1850. Thence the ascent to the hospice is made on mules, the road beyond being impracticable, at present, for any sort of carriage. There is also a char-road on the Sardinian side from St. Remy to Aosta : the intervening space is only a mule-path, but, as there are great facilities for completing the road between the

Hospice and St. Remy, it is by no means improbable that the road may be made practicable for chars in a few years.

From *Martigny* (Rte. 59) the road passes through Bourg-Martigny, and shortly after crosses the Dranse to its l. bank. The bed of this river still exhibits, in the rocks and stones with which it is strewn, evidence of the devastation occasioned in 1818, by the bursting of a lake in the valley of Bagnes. See Rte. 109.

Here the road leaves the path to Chamouny on the rt., and continues up the course of the Dranse to the miserable villages of Valette and Bouvernier. Soon after the river is recrossed, and the road continues on its rt. bank in the deep valley of the Dranse. In one part the defile is so narrow that it was found necessary to cut a *Tunnel* 200 ft. long through the rock. Emerging from it, see l. the ruins of a Convent overwhelmed with rubbish brought down by the bursting of the lake, 1818. Bouvernier was saved from the same fate by a projecting mass of rock. Beyond it the road soon after recrosses the river, and ascends on the l. bank to

St. Branchier, another dirty village situated at the confluence of the two branches of the Dranse, one coming from the Val de Bagne, the other from the Val Entremont and St. Bernard, at the foot of Mt. Catogne. (*Inn :* Croix, cheap.)

Above St. Branchier there are some fine scenes in the Val d'Entremont, but none strikingly grand ; it has the general character of an Alpine valley, and nothing that deserves to be particularly remembered. The Dranse is twice crossed before reaching

Orsières. Inn : H. des Alpes, very good and moderate. Here Val Ferrex opens into the Val Entremont, and the path which leads to the Val Ferrex turns off on the rt. (Rte. 110).

Beyond Orsières there is a fine view, and the scenery becomes rather more wild. The torrent can seldom be seen in the deep gorge which it has made its course, but there is nothing striking in the scenery until the traveller arrives in the forest of St. Pierre.

Liddes (Inn : l'Union).

The charge for a char to or from Liddes and Martigny is generally 12 francs, and for each mule from Liddes to the hospice 6 francs, and a *douceur* to the boy who returns with the mule. Beyond Liddes the char-road has now been carried to a small inn on the plain of Proz.

St. Pierre is a dirty, wretched village, but it has inscriptions enough to support some claims to antiquity. A military column, dedicated to the younger Constantine, is placed here. The *Church* dates from the 11th century.

On leaving St. Pierre the road crosses a deep abyss, through which the Dranse forces its way into the valley below. The road to the hospice leaves on the l. a torrent which descends from the Val Orsey, in which there is, not far from St. Pierre, a magnificent cascade.

The road formerly led through the forest of St. Pierre, by a path among the rocks and roots of pines, so steep and tortuous that Napoleon's difficulties in transporting his artillery were here, perhaps, the greatest that he encountered from natural obstacles during his extraordinary expedition in 1800 across these Alps. The Valaisans have cut an excellent road along the precipices which overhang the deep course of the Dranse, avoiding the steep rises and falls of the old road, and leading the traveller by a safe path through a savage defile.

Beyond the forest, where the pines and the larches are stunted from their elevation above the level of the sea, the traveller arrives at some pasturages where there are many châlets. The enormous mass of the Mont Velan appears to forbid further progress: some of its fine glaciers, particularly that of Menou, stream down into the plain of | *Proz,* where, amidst the shelter of surrounding mountains, numerous herds gather the rich herbage of this Alpine pasturage. The road ceases about 2 hours below the Hospice at the little *Inn* called the Cantine de Proz.

[From this the ascent and descent of *Mont Velan* can be made in 12 hrs. André Dorsat, who keeps the *Cantine.* is a good guide. It was first ascended in 1825, since which up to 1856 only 11 ascents have been made.

The first part of the ascent is up the pastures of the Montagne de Prou : these passed, a little rock-work follows ; then a glacier, name unknown, which runs down in the direction of the St. Bernard, is traversed, and in about 3½ hrs. from the Cantine, the main body of the Velan is reached, which rises in a wall of rock, perhaps 2000 ft. high. It is difficult and laborious, hardly dangerous; but there is only one accessible point, and it is necessary to have a guide who knows it. Hitherto every ascent has been made with the Dorsats, father or son: the young man is a first-rate guide, his charge is 20 frs. for the day. The top of the mountain is a saddle-shaped plain of snow, perhaps ½ m. in length. The entire ascent, including a halt for breakfast, will take a good walker 6 hrs. Three hrs. is enough for the descent to the Cantine; but it is much better to descend by the glacier and valley of Valsorsey to St. Pierre. This will take from 4 to 5 hrs., and, for the exquisite beauty of the glacier itself, and grandeur of the near scenery—it does not command distant views—the route is not surpassed by anything that I know in the Alps. It lies between Mont Velan and Mont Combin. The descent is along the crest of rocks which bounds the glacier on the side of Italy, and very steep; and there is some rough climbing down the rocks or over the ice.]

On rising above this basin, the path enters another defile, and beyond it another summer pasturage, steep and rugged; the scenes become more sterile and dreary, another ravine is passed, and the summit is approached. At length, after crossing some beds of snow, the solitary walls of the HOSPICE appear, and the traveller reaches, on the very crest of the pass, this dwelling in the clouds, 8200 English feet above the sea-level.

Here, in the practice of the most disinterested benevolence, lives this community of *Religieux*, who devote the best time of their life, when man is most susceptible of his powers for its enjoyment, to the service of their fellow-men; those whose pursuits oblige them to traverse these dreary fields in seasons of danger, when, without such aid and protection, hundreds must perish.

The Hospice is a massive stone building, well adapted to its perilous situation, which is on the very highest point of the pass, where it is exposed to tremendous storms from the N.E. and S.W. On the N.W. it is sheltered by the *Mont Chennelletaz*, and in an opposite direction by the *Mont Mort*. There is no mountain which bears the name of the St. Bernard. Like that of the St. Gothard, the name is only given to the pass. The chief building is capable of accommodating 70 or 80 travellers with beds; 300 may be sheltered; and between 500 and 600 have received assistance in one day. Besides this, there is a house, called Hôtel St. Louis, on the other side of the way, built as a place of refuge in case of fire—an event which has twice happened here since the foundation of the establishment.

The ground-floor of the main building consists of stabling, store-room for wood, fodder, &c. A flight of steps leads up to the principal entrance in the first floor of the building, where a long corridor connects the offices, &c., with the chapel. Another corridor on the floor above leads to the dormitories, the refectory, the gallery of the chapel, &c. The *Drawing-room*, appropriated to the reception of strangers, especially ladies, is entered from the stairs between the two corridors. Here brethren do the honours to their visitors.

The *Clavandier* (or Bursar), the commissary of the establishment, is the brother who usually presides at the hours of 12 and 6, dinner and supper. Gentlemen dine or sup with all the monks in their refectory.

The room appropriated to visitors is large and convenient; it is hung with many drawings and prints, presents sent by travellers in acknowledgment of the kind attentions which they had received from the brethren. A piano was among the presents thus sent by a lady. Attached to this room is a cabinet, in which a day, unfavourable for out-door enjoyment, may be passed with interest and pleasure. It contains collections of the plants, insects, and minerals of the Alps, and many relics of the Temple dedicated to Jupiter, which formerly stood on this pass, near to the site of the hospice. These antiquities consist of votive tablets, and figures, in bronze, and other metals, and materials, arms, coins, &c., and are curiously illustrative of the early worship on this mountain, and the intercourse established over this pass. No trace whatever now remains of the temple, though these relics are found upon what is known to have been its site. Steps cut in the rock may yet be seen, which led up to the spot upon which the temple stood.

The system of purveyance for the hospital seems to be well regulated. Supplies come from Aosta and the neighbouring villages. Their winter store of hay for their cows is so valuable that the mules which ascend from either side with travellers generally bring their own hay, or supply themselves from a vender established in the convent, at a higher rate than below. Wood for firing is one of the most important necessaries to them. Not a stick grows within 2 leagues, and all the fuel supplied to the convent is brought from the forest which belongs to it in the Val Ferrex, a distance of nearly 4 leagues. The consumption of wood at the convent is considerable, for, at the great elevation of the hospice, water boils at about 190 degrees, which is so much less favourable for the cooking of meat than at 212 degrees, that it requires 5 hrs. to effect that which, at a less elevation, may be done in 3 hrs. They have adopted stoves for warming the convent with hot air.

The *Chapel* of the hospice is generally well attended on Sundays and Festas, when the weather is not unfavourable, by the peasants from the neighbouring valleys and Alp pastures. It contains a monument to General Dessaix, who fell at Marengo, after having contributed mainly to that victory: it was erected to his memory by Napoleon.

In the chapel there is a box, where donations in aid of the funds of the establishment are put, and travellers who receive its hospitalities offer their acknowledgments in a sum not less than they would have paid for such accommodation at an inn. The payment thus made by those who can afford it ought to be in a more liberal degree, because that excess aids the monks to extend their assistance to poor and destitute travellers, a very numerous class of claimants upon them, from the great intercourse which exists by this pass between Switzerland and Italy.

Visitors universally acknowledge the kind and courteous attention which they receive from those excellent men. They are freely communicative about their establishment, and conversation has no restraint, but in the respect which their characters demand. The language used by them is French, though there are Italians and Germans among them. They are well informed upon most subjects, and intelligent upon those in which their situation has been favourable to their acquiring information. The periodical works of some academic bodies and institutions are sent to them, and they have a small library, which is chiefly theological. During their short summers, their intercourse with well-informed travellers is extensive, which is shown in the names and notices left by travellers in the albums preserved carefully by the brethren at the hospice.

There are usually 10 or 12 brethren of the Augustine order, and a number of assistant lay brethren (marronniers), here. They are all young men, who enter upon this devoted service at 18. The severities of the weather in the winter, at this height, often impair their health, and they are driven to retire to a lower and more genial clime, with broken constitutions and ruined health. Even in the summer it has happened that the ice has never melted in the lake on the summit, and in some years (1816) not a week has passed without snow falling. It always freezes early in the morning, even in the height of summer, and the hospice is rarely four months clear of deep snow. Around the building it averages 7 or 8 feet, and the drifts sometimes rest against it, and accumulate to the height of 40 feet. The severest cold recorded is 29° below zero of Fahrenheit: it has often been observed at 18° and 20° below. The greatest heat has been 68° in the height of summer.

" The monks have a deep cellar where they keep their wine, &c. unfrozen, although the thermometer often descends to 20° of Réaumur, or −13° of our scale. Fresh meat is easily procured in the summer from the valleys, but for winter they lay up a store of salted and pressed meat. They also keep a number of cows to supply them with milk, butter, and cheese. One only is kept up at the hospice during the winter: the rest are sent to Martigny, and their produce carried up in the solid form. The monks are also obliged to keep 45 horses all the year, in order to bring wood from a forest 3 leagues off. This employment lasts for 2 months during summer, hence the wood must be by far the most expensive article. Travellers are passing every day during the winter, notwithstanding the perils of such a pass at such times. These persons, when they arrive at a certain house not far from the summit, are desired to wait till the following morning, when a servant and a dog descend from the top to this kind of refuge, and take up all the persons assembled, the servant being conducted by the dog, who, it appears, never misses his way, but, entirely hidden, except his tail, in the snow, directs the march of the whole cavalcade. The stories about the monks going out searching for lost travellers, and the dogs carrying wine, are false in toto, and the proof is, that such proceeding is impossible, for as great difficulty exists to the monks roaming about as to the travellers. This labour of the dogs is so great, that their life never exceeds 9 years, owing to attacks of rheumatism, which is the bane of both dog and man up here. The infirm dogs are generally killed. If the feet of the persons are found frozen, they are immediately rubbed strongly with snow or with a stimulating ointment. If neither succeed, the mortified part is immediately amputated by one of the monks, who studies medicine a little. If necessary, stockings, &c., are given to the poor. No dead body has been left unclaimed for two years past, so that there was no addition to the morgue. The snow is generally 30 ft. deep in winter. There are generally 5 or 6 dogs at the hospice. Tradition reports that they are a cross between the Newfoundland and the Pyrenean. In the year 1825 all the dogs and 3 servants (sent on this occasion together—an unusual occurrence) were destroyed by an avalanche. Luckily the monks had recently given away a couple of dogs, which were returned to them, or the breed would have been lost. 10 servants are kept in winter, and 8 in summer, of whom 2 descend daily to the refuges to bring up travellers, from the month of October to the end of April, the time of course varying according to the season. Few of the monks are able to stand the climate for more than 15 years ; but there is no stated time for which they devote themselves ; each stays as long as he is able, being allowed 30 days' recreation—15 at a time—at a *subsidiary* house at Martigny, where also they descend when no longer able to live at the St. Bernard, or else they go to the hospice on the Simplon. We breakfasted with 9 monks. Service is performed in the chapel at 4½ A.M. in summer, and 5 in winter, and at 8 P.M. all the year round.

"The times at which the poor travellers pass in greatest numbers during the winter, are in November, February, March, and April. As many as 2000 per month will pass in February and March, because the poor inhabitants of the valleys are then going out to seek work ; in November they come home with money in their pockets." In the course of 1844, 19,000 travellers passed over the mountain.

"The scene from the W. end of the hospice looking towards Italy is sterile and dreary ; patches of snow are seen on the sides of the mountains, which sweep down to the lake ; and the *Pain de Sucre*, a pinnacled mountain on the other side of the Vacherie, with its rocks and snows, adds to its wildness and desolation.

"A column opposite to the middle of the water marks the boundary of Piedmont and the Valais ; above and beyond it, is the little plain of Jupiter, where a temple formerly stood, and from which a Roman road led down on the Piedmontese side of the pass. This road may be easily traced in the hewn rock, and the remains of a massive pavement ; but not a vestige of the temple is left above the surface.

"From the fragments which have been found it appears to have been a Roman work of a time probably not earlier than that of Augustus. The period of the substitution of a military column for the statue of Jupiter, under the younger Constantine, in the year 339, was probably not that of the destruction of the temple; for medals of the children of Theodosius, 50 years later, have been found there.

"The first foundation of the hospice has been attributed by some to Louis le Débonnaire, by others to Charlemagne. There is historical evidence that a monastery existed on the Great St. Bernard before the year 851.

"The present hospice was founded in 962, by Bernard, who was born of a noble family of Savoy, at the château of Menthon, on the lake of Annecy. A determination at an early age to devote himself to an ecclesiastical life induced him to desert his home and go to Aosta, of which city he afterwards became archdeacon. While residing there, his frequent intercourse with pilgrims and travellers probably suggested to him as a work of mercy the restoration of the convent of the Mont Joux, and the establishment of another similar. He became the founder of both houses, gave to them the name, and placed them under the protection, of his favourite saint, Nicolas de Myra, as tutelary patron of these establishments. By degrees, and after the canonization of Bernard, his name superseded that of all others, and has continued attached to the hospice since 1123. The attempt of Constantine to destroy the worship of Jupiter had not entirely succeeded; but St. Bernard rooted out the remains of paganism, and founded an establishment for active benevolence, to which thousands have been indebted. He died in 1008, after having governed the convent upwards of 40 years. For some time after the death of St. Bernard the hospice was exposed to frequent outrages from barbarians who traversed the mountains; and its records of the 11th century present a succession of calamities.

" In the contests of the emperor Frederic Barbarossa with pope Alexander III. and Humbert count of Maurienne, diplomas of protection were given by them for the security of persons and property belonging to the monastery. It was one of the very few objects in which emperors, sovereign pontiffs, and other distinguished persons, disputed the glory of fostering and protecting a foundation so important to humanity. It soon acquired great celebrity and opulence. As early as 1177, it had, in various dioceses, 88 benefices, in priories, cures, châteaux, and farms; it had lands in Sicily, in Flanders, and in England. Its climax of riches and importance was in 1480, when it possessed 98 cures alone. Subsequently, however, the Reformation, political changes in the states, loss of distant property, disputes with the popes, with the neighbouring states, and with each other, drove the monks of St. Bernard to seek even eleemosynary assistance. The very land upon which their noble duties are performed has been the subject of disputes between the neigh-

bouring states. Sardinia claimed it as within a frontier extending to the bridge of Nudri, on the northern side; but the Valaisans established a claim to it as within the diocese of Sion, by bulls of the popes from Leo IX. to Benoît XIV. The hospice, therefore, stands within the canton of the Valais; but its authority extends only to the middle of the lake, on the borders of which a column is fixed as a line of demarcation; and the excellent brethren of St. Bernard had not only all their property within the state of Sardinia taken from them, but they were actually taxed by this state for the use which they made of the summer pasturage of the Vacherie. Very little property in land still belongs to the hospice; a vineyard at Clarens, and a farm at Roche, in the Pays de Vaud, are the principal: their resources are small, and in aid of them collections are regularly made in the Swiss cantons; but this has been sometimes abused by impostors, who have collected as the agents of the hospice."—*Brockedon's Passes of the Alps.*

Buonaparte rather impoverished than enriched the monks. It was true that he had assisted them with donations, but his claims upon their funds had exceeded his benefits ; that they had had 40 men quartered upon them for months together, and 60,000 had passed in one season, and all these had been assisted.

The duties of the Brotherhood of St. Bernard and their servants sometimes lead them into fatal danger. On the 17th of Dec. 1825, a party of 3 domestics of the convent, or Marronniers—one of them was Victor, a worthy man, well remembered by Alpine travellers—went out with 2 dogs, on the side of the Vacherie, to search at a dangerous time for travellers. They met one, with whom they were returning to the convent, when an avalanche overwhelmed them, and all perished, except one of the dogs, whose prodigious strength and activity enabled it to escape. The bodies of poor Victor and his companions were found only after the

P 3

melting of the snow in the following summer. Nov. 12, 1845, the Clavandier and 3 servants were buried beneath an enormous avalanche from the Mont Mort, which covered them 15 ft. deep, and all perished.

" There is one scene of melancholy interest usually visited on the St. Bernard—the *Morgue*, or receptacle for the dead. It is a low building a few yards from the E. extremity of the convent, where the bodies of the unfortunate victims to storms and avalanches in these mountains have been placed. They have generally been found frozen, and put into this horrid receptacle in the posture in which they perished. Here many have ' dried up and withered,' and on some even the clothes have remained after 18 years; others present a horrid aspect, some of the bones of the head being blanched and exposed, whilst black integuments still attach to parts of the face. Among the victims were a mother and child. From the rapid evaporation at this height, the bodies had dried without the usual decay. In a walled enclosure on one side of the morgue was a great accumulation of bones, white, broken, and apparently the gathering of centuries. Upon this rocky and frozen soil they could not bury the dead, and, probably, as they dry up without offence, they are placed here for the chance of recognition."— *Passes of the Alps.*

On leaving the hospice to descend to the Val d'Aosta, the path skirts the lake, and passes between it and the Plain de Jupiter. A little beyond the end of the lake, after passing through a short defile, the scene opens towards Italy, into the basin of the

Vacherie, where the cows of the convent are pastured. The road turns abruptly to the right, and sweeps round the basin to descend gradually to the plain below.

The view on first looking out upon the Vacherie, from the gorge in the Mont Mort, is very fine, the mountains on the opposite side being sublime in form and elevation: the most striking in the scene is the *Pain de Sucre,* celebrated by Saussure.

At the lower end of the Vacherie the path winds down by a series of zigzags, and thence the descent is rapid to

St. Remy, a dreary little village ; *Inn* very fair. Here return chars to Aosta may generally be obtained for 10 francs. Travellers who leave Aosta to visit the hospice, in a char for St. Remy, and intend to return, cause it to wait for them there for four or six hours, and pay 20 francs for the char for the day, with a buona-mano to the postilion. But it generally happens that the traveller crosses the mountain, in which case he pays from 12 to 14 francs for the char, and the postilions wait till the evening for customers descending from the Great St. Bernard, and it is seldom that they are disappointed in a fare.

Here the passports are examined, and the Piedmontese custom-house is placed. From St. Remy the road descends, with little interest in the scenery, to

St. Oyen.

At *Etroubles,* the St. Bernard branch of the Buttier is crossed, and the road descends to the village of *Gignod,* where the vegetation begins to luxuriate, and the Italian side of the mountain is felt and seen. Here there is a fine peep into the Val Pellina. From Gignod to the city of Aosta, the richness of the scenery is constantly increasing. Trellised vines and Indian corn mark the approach to the Val d'Aosta; and the first view of the city and the valley, in the descent from the St. Bernard, where the background is filled with the magnificent forms and snowy summits of the mountains above the Val de Cogne, is very fine indeed.

AOSTA (Rte. 107).

ROUTE 108 A.

GREAT ST. BERNARD TO COURMAYEUR,
BY THE COL DE SERENA.

9 or 10 hours on foot. This is by far the shortest way of getting from the St. B. hospice to Courmayeur for those who do not wish to visit Aosta. It is an uninteresting pass. On leaving St. Remy (Rte. 108), take the road to the rt. to the village of Bosses, then through fields for ½ an hour, and you arrive at the foot of the Col. Half an hour's ascent through a pine-forest brings you to the last châlet, where milk and cheese may be obtained as long as the cows are on the mountain. Here, instead of following a road to the rt., go up the mountain by a zigzag path, immediately *behind* the châlet, and 1½ hour's good walking will land you on the top of the Col. This part of the road is exceedingly steep, but the view from the summit well rewards the traveller for his labour. The scenery is very wild, especially towards the N. and N.W., offering a great contrast to the beautifully cultivated valley of Aosta, which shortly afterwards (just above the village of Morges) you see extended at your feet. From Morges to Morgex, on the high road between Aosta and Courmayeur (Rte. 107), is a walk down a stony path of about ½ an hour. The Serena abounds with ptarmigan and chamois. There are two other routes from the St. Bernard to Courmayeur ;—1, by the Col des Fenêtres (over which the monks bring their wood from the Val Ferrex) and the Col Ferrex (Rte. 110); and 2, by the Col de St. Remy, turning off to the rt., close to the Vacherie of the convent, and getting into the Pass of the Serena at the châlet near the foot of the Col. This last is the shortest route of the three, but is very fatiguing, and requires a local guide. A good walker may easily get to Courmayeur this way in 7 hrs. There is said to be a third route up the Val Ferrex, then over the Col de St. Remy, descending near a châlet in the highest part of the Vacherie.

ROUTE 109.

MARTIGNY TO AOSTA, BY THE VAL DE BAGNES, THE COL DES FENÊTRES, AND THE VAL PELLINA.

Martigny.	Hours.
St. Branchier	2¼
Champsec	2
Torembec	5¼
Valpellina	8
Aosta	3 (char).

Martigny to *St. Branchier* (Rte. 108). From St. Branchier a good muletrack leads up the valley of Bagnes, which is very fertile, to Lourtier, passing through many villages, especially those of Chable and Morgnes. The valley is narrow, abounding in gorges, and offering many fine scenes to the pencil of the traveller. Above Lourtier, the last village in the valley, this character becomes more striking, and the pass increases in difficulty to Pont de Mauvoisin, a lofty stone-arched bridge, by which you pass from the rt. to the l. bank of the Drance, adjoining a small hamlet, not far below the glaciers of Getroz. The descent of these glaciers from the Mont Pleureur was the cause of the interruption of the waters of the Drance, which formed a lake and burst its bounds in 1595, carrying off in its destructive course more than 140 persons from the valley, besides houses and cattle. A more recent inundation, that of 1818, from a similar cause, has left fearful traces of its overwhelming power. Among the boulders brought down by that event, is one which contains above 1400 cubic ft.; and the height which the waters then attained is yet distinctly marked where the land, then covered, is even now desolate.

" Vast blocks of stone," says Brockedon, in his ' Excursions in the Alps,' " which were driven and deposited there by the force of the waters, now strew the valley; and sand and pebbles present an arid surface where rich pasturages were seen before the catastrophe. The quantity and violence of the water suddenly disengaged, and the velocity of its descent, presented a force which the mind may calculate, but cannot conceive.

" In the accounts which have been given of this event, the object of the writers has been merely to describe the catastrophe, and the extent of its injuries; but in reading the account of M. Escher de Linth, published in the *Bib. Univ. de Genève, Sci. et Arts,* tom. viii. p. 291, I was most forcibly struck with the unparalleled heroism of the brave men who endeavoured to avert the evil, by opening a channel for the waters, which had, by their accumulation, become a source of terror to the inhabitants of these valleys.

" In the spring of 1818 the people of the valley of Bagnes became alarmed on observing the low state of the waters of the Drance, at a season when the melting of the snows usually enlarged the torrent; and this alarm was increased by the records of similar appearances before the dreadful inundation of 1595, which was then occasioned by the accumulation of the waters behind the débris of a glacier that formed a dam, which remained until the pressure of the water burst the dike, and it rushed through the valley, leaving desolation in its course.

" In April, 1818, some persons went up the valley to ascertain the cause of the deficiency of water, and they discovered that vast masses of the glaciers of Getroz, and avalanches of snow, had fallen into a narrow part of the valley between Mont Pleureur and Mont Mauvoisin, and formed a dike of ice and snow 600 ft. wide and 400 ft. high, on a base of 3000 ft., behind which the waters of the Drance had accumulated, and formed

a lake above 7000 ft. long. M. Venetz, the engineer of the Vallais, was consulted, and he immediately decided upon cutting a gallery through this barrier of ice, 60 ft. above the level of the water at the time of commencing, and where the dike was 600 ft. thick. He calculated upon making a tunnel through this mass before the water should have risen 60 ft. higher in the lake. On the 10th of May the work was begun by gangs of 50 men, who relieved each other, and worked, without intermission, day and night, with inconceivable courage and perseverance, neither deterred by the daily occurring danger from the falling of fresh masses of the glacier, nor by the rapid increase of the water in the lake, which rose 62 ft. in 34 days —on an average nearly 2 ft. each day; but it once rose 5 ft. in one day, and threatened each moment to burst the dike by its increasing pressure; or, rising in a more rapid proportion than the men could proceed with their work, render their efforts abortive, by rising above them. Sometimes dreadful noises were heard, as the pressure of the water detached masses of ice from the bottom, which, floating, presented so much of their bulk above the water as led to the belief that some of them were 70 ft. thick. The men persevered in their fearful duty without any serious accident; and though suffering severely from cold and wet, and surrounded by dangers which cannot be justly described, by the 4th of June they had accomplished an opening 600 ft. long; but having begun their work on both sides of the dike at the same time, the place where they ought to have met was 20 ft. lower on one side of the lake than on the other; it was fortunate that latterly the increase of the perpendicular height of the water was less, owing to the extension of its surface. They proceeded to level the highest side of the tunnel, and completed it just before the water reached them. On the evening of the 13th the water began to flow. At first the opening was not large enough to carry off the supplies of water which the lake received, and it rose 2 ft. above the tunnel; but this soon enlarged from the action of the water, as it melted the floor of the gallery, and the torrent rushed through. In 32 hrs. the lake sunk 10 ft., and during the following 24 hrs. 20 ft. more; in a few days it would have been emptied; for the floor melting, and being driven off as the water escaped, kept itself below the level of the water within; but the cataract which issued from the gallery melted and broke up also a large portion of the base of the dike which had served as its buttress; its resistance decreased faster than the pressure of the lake lessened, and at 4 o'clock in the afternoon of the 16th of June the dike burst, and in half an hour the water escaped through the breach, and left the lake empty.

" The greatest accumulation of water had been 800,000,000 of cubic feet; the tunnel, before the disruption, had carried off nearly 330,000,000— Escher says, 270,000,000; but he neglected to add 60,000,000 which flowed into the lake in 3 days. In half an hour, 530,000,000 cubic ft. of water passed through the breach, or 300,000 ft. per second; which is 5 times greater in quantity than the waters of the Rhine at Basle, where it is 1300 English ft. wide. In one hour and a half the water reached Martigny, a distance of 8 leagues. Through the first 70,000 ft. it passed with the velocity of 33 ft. per second — four or five times faster than the most rapid river known; yet it was charged with ice, rocks, earth, trees, houses, cattle, and men; 34 persons were lost, 400 cottages swept away, and the damage done in the 2 hrs. of its desolating power exceeded a million of Swiss livres. All the people of the valley had been cautioned against the danger of a sudden irruption; yet it was fatal to so many. All the bridges in its course were swept away, and among them the bridge of Mauvoisin, which was elevated 90 feet above the ordinary height of the Drance. If the dike had remained untouched, and it could have endured the pressure until the lake had reached the level of its top, a volume of 1,700,000,000 cubic feet of water would have been accumulated there, and a devastation much more fatal and extensive must have been the consequence. From this greater danger the people of the valley of the Drance were preserved by the heroism and devotion of the brave men who effected the formation of the gallery in the dike, under the direction of M. Venetz. I know no instance on record of courage equal to this: their risk of life was not for fame or for riches—they had not the usual excitements to personal risk in a world's applause or gazetted promotion,—their devoted courage was to save the lives and property of their fellow-men, not to destroy them. They steadily and heroically persevered in their labours, amidst dangers such as a field of battle never presented, and from which some of the bravest brutes that ever lived would have shrunk in dismay. These truly brave Valaisans deserve all honour!

" But the skill of M. Venetz was not limited in its application to emptying the lake: his abilities have been properly directed to the prevention of such another catastrophe, for the liability to its recurrence was obvious. Not one-twentieth part of the ice which formed the barrier had been removed when the dike burst, and fresh masses were still falling from Mont Pleureur and Mont Mauvoisin, the mountains of which the bases formed the buttresses to the dike; in fact the dike was again accumulating so rapidly, that at the end of 1819 the barrier was almost as complete as before its bursting from the pressure of the lake.

" It became, therefore, an important object to prevent a repetition of the former catastrophe, by the adoption of such means as would prevent, or at least diminish, the increase of the barrier. Blasting by gunpowder was found impracticable, from the difficulty of firing the powder at considerable depths in the ice, and from the comparatively small masses removed by this means. After much consideration and many trials, a mode has been adopted and put in execution by M. Venetz, which promises the greatest success.

"M. Venetz had remarked that the glacier could not support itself where the river was of a certain width, but fell into it and was dissolved; whereas, where the river was comparatively narrow, the ice and snow formed a vault over it, and consequently tended to the preservation of any portion falling from the glacier above. Perceiving also the effect of the river in dissolving the part it came in contact with, he formed and executed the design of bringing the streams of the neighbouring mountains by a canal to Mauvoisin, opposite the highest part of the glacier where it touched that mountain. From hence it was conducted by wooden troughs on to the glacier in a direction parallel to the valley. The water was divided into two streams; one falling nearly on the one edge of the Drance, and the other on the other; and having been warmed by the sun in its course, soon cut very deep channels in the ice. When they reached the river the troughs were removed a few feet, and thus the stream produced the effect of a saw, which, dividing the ice, forced the portion between them to fall into the Drance.

"When the weather is fine, these streams, which are not more than 4 or 5 inches in diameter, act with extraordinary power, piercing a hole 200 feet deep and 6 feet in diameter in 24 hours. They are calculated to remove 100,000 cubical feet of ice from the barrier daily, and it is supposed that if the weather is fine the whole will be removed in three years.

"At the end of the season of 1822 the Drance remained covered only for a length of 480 feet; whereas, at the commencement of the operation, it was covered over a length of 1350 feet. M. Venetz estimates the quantity of ice removed in 1822 as between 11 and 12 millions of cubical feet."— *Bib. Univ.* xxii. 58.

"The main glacier of Getroz lies high up amidst the defiles of Mont Pleureur, and is not visible from the path along the opposite side of the valley. The glacier which did the mischief, now reduced in size, resembles a mass of unmelted snow, lying in the depths of the defile, and in reality consists of fragments which have fallen from the upper glacier over a cliff of enormous height, at whose edge it terminates. The defile is so narrow that these dirty fallen fragments still partially bar the course of the river, and must continue to choke the outlet until a tunnel be formed for the passage of the water beneath them."—See *Forbes.*

The path now lies across the bed of the glacier-lake, whose bursting did so much mischief: 4 hours' walk from Chable; 1½ hour further lie the châlets of *Torembec,* above Getroz, which can be reached in good time in one day from Martigny; and those who wish to cross the glaciers of Charmontane can sleep there, and, starting early the next morning, push on to the extremity of the valley, cross two glaciers, and attain the summit of the pass of the Col des Fenêtres in time to reach Aosta on the following day.

The ascent of the upper part of the valley, crossing to the l. bank of the Drance, presents scenes of greater grandeur than any below. As the valley turns to the S.E. several glaciers come into sight, and that of Durand, descending on the rt. from the Mont Combin, stretches over across the Drance. It requires to be traversed in order to reach the pastures, on which stand the châlets of Charmontane, on the W. of the valley, at the foot of the Mont Avril. Hence there is a magnificent view over the glacier of Charmontane, a sea of ice nearly unexplored.

[Two Englishmen are said to have ascended *Mont Combin* in 1856 from the châlets on *Mt. Corbassières,* keeping on rock the whole way.]

Professor Forbes did not descend to the châlets, but keeping high up on the flanks of Mont Avril, skirting the glacier, mounted by a tedious but not difficult ascent to the

Col des Fenêtres, 4 hrs., 9213 feet above the sea-level. Calvin fled by this pass from Aosta in 1541.

" The view towards Italy is wonderfully striking. The mountains (of Cogne) beyond Aosta, and the glaciers of Ruitor, are spread out in the distance, and beneath we have the exceeding deep valley of Ollomont, communicating with the Val Pelline, which is itself a tributary of the Val d'Aosta. It is enclosed by ridges of the most fantastic and savage grandeur, which descend from the mountains on either side of the Col on the N.E. from Mont Combin, rising to a height of 14,200 ft., and on the S.E. from Mont Gelée, 12,000 ft. high, and almost too steep to bear snow, presenting a perfect ridge of pyramidal aiguilles stretching towards Val Pellina."—*Prof. Forbes.*

The course from the Col des Fenêtres to Val Pellina is to skirt the base of the peaky ridges of *Mont Gelée,* passing a small lake by a rapid descent, and reaching the pastures. The descent is long and fatiguing to Balme, the first hamlet, and to Ollomont, where there are traces of an aqueduct built by the Romans for the supply of water to Augusta Prætoria. Thence the road descends through the village of Val Pellina, whence the path leads along the l. bank of the river to the main road, about 2 m. from AOSTA. (Rte. 107.)

ROUTE 110.

MARTIGNY TO COURMAYEUR, BY THE COL FERREX.

Martigny.	Hours.
Orsières	4
La Folie	2½
Col Ferrex	2
Courmayeur	4

A journey of 13 hrs. on foot.

This route, though shorter, is less interesting than that by the Grand St. Bernard and Aosta. The valley on the Swiss side, as well as that on the Piedmontese side, is called Val Ferrex or Ferret. The latter is a continuation of the Allée Blanche.

At *Orsières,* in the Val d'Entremont (Rte. 108), a path turns off on the rt., enters an agreeable valvey, and continues on the banks of an Alpine river, and, after pursuing a tolerable road to *Issert,* the principal village in the Val Ferrex, 3 hrs. distant from Martigny, ascends rapidly towards the higher hamlets of Pra le Fort and Branche. The mountains which bound the valley towards the W. are lofty, and crowned with the northern extremity of those vast glaciers of the chain of Mont Blanc, which, divided on the crest, descend towards the *Val Ferrex,* as the glaciers of Salena, Portalet, and Neuve; and on the other side, towards the W., form the glaciers de Trient, du Tour, and d'Argentière.

There is nothing, however, remarkable in the scenery of the Val Ferrex. The route leads up a succession of rather flat divisions of the valley, from the Issert to the *Châlets de Folie,* distant 2 hrs. On the rt., the short transversal valleys, or rather crues, in the side of the mountains, are the channels for these glaciers.

Above the Châlets de Folie the usual path to the Col Ferrex leads up through the Châlets of Ferrex, by the detritus of a mountain which fell in the year 1776, burying the pasturages of Banderai. Near to these châlets the two paths separate—that on the l. leading over the Col de la Fenêtre to the Great St. Bernard, that on the rt. to the *Col Ferrex.*

[A short path leads to another Col, close to the chain of M. Blanc, called the *Little Ferrex.* It is not a mulepath, and the distant views are inferior. The paths re-unite at Prè de Bar.]

From the ascent, the whole Val Ferrex is seen, bounded on either side by lofty mountains, and the distance is limited only by the Bernese Alps.

The woods and pasturages of part of the Val Ferrex belong to the Convent of the Great St. Bernard, and at this distance from the hospice (4 or 5 leagues) the brethren obtain all their wood and some hay, which is conveyed to them by mules over the Col des Fenêtres.

From the *crest of the Col*, the view along the S.E. side of Mont Blanc, towards Piedmont, is one of the scenes celebrated by Saussure. The eye is carried through the Val d'Entrèves and the Allée Blanche to the Col de la Seigne, an extent of 30 m. Numerous glaciers are seen on the rt., streaming down into the valley from the great glaciers of Mont Blanc; but the "Monarch" himself is not seen—the enormous masses of the Grand Jorasse and the Géant conceal him in this view.

The descent is over a soft slaty soil, in which the tracks of sheep and cattle have cut deep trenches, in which, if a man stand, he is half concealed. 10 min. below the Col a cross is placed on the edge of a precipice which the path passes. It serves to guide the course of the ascending traveller, though from below it seems to be placed on a pyramidal mass of rock which it would be impossible to attain. Far in the deep valley, the stream flowing into Italy appears like a thread of silver.

An hour and a half of fatiguing descent brings the traveller to the Châlets of *Pré de Bar*. (*Inn:* tolerable.)

Near Pré de Bar the vast glacier of Triolet sweeps down from the crest which divides this glacier from the masses, which, on the other side, form the glacier of Talèfre. Below the glacier of *Triolet*, the road descends by a fatiguing path, amidst rocks and stones and bushes, presenting a scene of Alpine desolation. The valley is very narrow, and each rift on the mountain side towards Mont Blanc has its glacier hanging down from the summit. Not less than 7 distinct glaciers are passed in the course of this valley before reaching the village of Entrèves, near to Cormayeur. These chiefly depend from the masses which form the

Grand Jorasse, and the remarkable peak of the Géant. A few miserable villages in the Val d'Entrèves are passed. The highest is Sagion; those below are Pré-sec and Plan-pansier. More than half the length of the valley is passed, on the descent, before Mont Blanc is seen. When its prodigious mass opens to the view, the effect is overwhelming. The ruggedness of the descent is increased by passing over the débris of a mountain fall beneath the Géant. This passed, the river, which descends through the Val d'Entrèves, is crossed, the village of Entrèves is left on the rt., and, winding along a path by the side of the mountain, you reach

Courmayeur (Rte. 107).

ROUTE 111.

AOSTA TO PONTE IN VAL D'ORCA, BY COGNE, FENÊTRE DE COGNE, THE COL DE REALE, AND THE VAL SOANNA.

	H.	M.
Aosta		
Cogne	3	30
Highest châlets	3	0
Col de Cogne	1	30
Campiglia	3	0
Ponte	4	0

From Aosta (Rte. 107) a road leads directly down to the river Doire, which is crossed on a wooden bridge, and a path ascends on the rt. bank through the rich plain of the valley, and through the villages of Gressau and Joveneau to *Aimaville*, where one of the most fantastical offences to good taste in building spoils one of the finest sites in the valley. A knoll jutting out into it is surmounted with a square mass of masonry, a modern antique, worse than any cockney castle. Within it is an ancient armoury of the barons of Aimaville. It is now inhabited by the Contessa di Rocca Chaland.

[Travellers from Courmayeur to Ponte can leave the high road at Villeneuve. A path, mounting at first rapidly, winds round the shoulders of a hill, and enters the valley of Cogne at a considerable height above the river. It soon crosses the Roman aqueduct.]

From Aimaville the ascent is steep to the hamlet of St. Martin. The view from the crest above it is perhaps the finest in the Val d'Aosta, in the richness of its plain, studded with villas and châteaux. The city is seen as in a glorious frame, and beyond it, towards the great chain, the peaks of the Monte Rosa close this unmatched scene of the beautiful and magnificent in nature.

On turning the brow of the mountain which forms the southern side of the entrance to the *Val de Cogne*, a path at an elevation of at least 1000 ft. above the torrent of the Cogne leads into the valley. Soon after losing sight of Aosta, deep in the valley beneath the path, the tops of the cottages of *Pont d'Ael* are seen clustered with a few trees, and near it a white line which crosses the ravine. This is well worth an examination, and a path leads down to this remarkable village, where the line crossing the gulf will be found to be an ancient aqueduct, which now serves as a road. This is one of the most remarkable of the Roman structures remaining in the Val d'Aosta, from the times of the empire. It is raised nearly 400 ft. above the torrent, which it crosses by a single arch ; immediately above the arch, and under the present road, is the ancient gallery, which is lit through slits in the wall. The gallery is 180 ft. long, 14 ft. high, and 3 ft. wide. The vault is composed of the slabs which formed the bed of the ancient watercourse. The gallery is entered by arched ports at either end; there are two, one on the upper side, at the village of Pont d'Ael, and at the other end the port opens down the valley. This singular work is in perfectly sound condition, though

built, as a still legible and even sharp inscription indicates, by Caius Aimus and his son, of Padua, in the thirteenth year of Augustus. This inscription is inaccessible ; it is placed on a tablet just over the arch on the lower side towards the valley of Aosta. Though it cannot be reached, to which fact it probably owes its preservation, yet it can be readily read from the brink of the precipice on the side of Pont d'Ael, and the following is the inscription :—

IMP. CÆSARE AUGUSTO XIII.
COS. DESIGN. C. AVILLIUS C. F. C. AIMUS
PATAVINUS PRIVATUM.

Their name is still preserved in the village and château of Aimaville.

Travellers in the Val d'Aosta should not fail to visit this interesting work of antiquity, which is placed in a situation where it is impossible to imagine that any benefit could ever have arisen commensurate with the expense of the structure. The surrounding scenery is very grand.

The distance from Aosta to Pont d'Ael by the route described is nearly 3 hours' walk. For pedestrians from Courmayeur there is a short way from Villeneuve to Pont d'Ael, winding round the slope of the hill.

In ascending the valley of Cogne it is not necessary to retrace one's steps to regain the path high upon the mountain side. A shorter cut from Pont d'Ael leads to it ; the valley for a long way above Pont d'Ael is a fearful ravine, utterly impracticable in its depth, which, except at two or three points, is equally impervious to the eye. In some places the narrow path on the edge of the precipices, wretchedly guarded by poles and trees which a child might throw over, is so obviously dangerous that none but a practised mountain traveller could pass some places without a shudder. Opposite to one spot, where the path turns suddenly into a deep rift or crue in the mountain side, is a slide, down which trees cut in the forest above are discharged, for the chance of the torrent bringing them down to the Val d'Aosta. Not one in ten escapes being broken into splinters; these, however, serve for working the iron raised in the Val de Cogne, and celebrated in Piedmont.

The difficulties of constructing a road by which the productions of the valley could be brought down, are obvious on observing its precipitous character. The valley, however, opens a little near some iron-works, and from where the river is crossed to its l. bank, a tolerable road leads to Cogne. This road was made by two brothers, iron-masters, who have recorded its formation on a tablet in a rock. It is kept in repair and has been much improved at the expense of the commune of Cogne, under the judicious administration of Dr. Grappin, a physician, a man of general information, who has acquired influence enough over his compatriots to induce them to carry out many local improvements which he has suggested. There is very little cultivation in the valley, the products of the mines giving occupation to its inhabitants; every stream drives its tilt hammer, and almost every person is employed in working, smelting, or forging the iron raised.

The hamlets of Vieille Silvenoir, Epinel, and Creta are passed before reaching the considerable *village of Cogne*, 6 hours' walk from Aosta. Here is no regular *Inn*, but accommodation may be procured on moderate terms, and there is no other place of rest or halt near at hand.

Cogne is beautifully situated at the union of three valleys, amidst charming meadows, which contrast strikingly with the barren scenes through which the traveller has passed. The valley on the l. leads to the great iron-mines, and across the mountains to the Val Soanna; that on the rt. is the Vermiana, and leads, at the distance of 3 hrs., to its vast glaciers.

A day may be spent with interest and pleasure here in visiting the iron-mines. A very steep ascent of 2½ hrs. from Cogne leads to them. The iron is worked in the face of the mountain, and seems to be of almost unlimited extent. A vast surface of pure ore yielding from 70 to 80 per cent. of metal is worked in open day. Galleries are beginning to be constructed with a view of carrying on the work during a longer part of the year than it is at present possible to do at the great elevation of the mines. The workmen live in wretched cabins during the week, but descend to spend their Sundays in the valley; they speak French, and are very civil and courteous in their manners to strangers. The mine yields at present 50,000 fr. of gross produce, and 15,000 for annual profit to the commune—a very trifling income compared to what might be drawn from this source; but the increasing scarcity of wood diminishes every year the number of forges which depend on it.

The height of the mine above the valley is at least 3000 ft., and as much as 120 rubbie, or 3000 lbs., of ore is brought down at once, upon sledges worked by men in a most extraordinary manner.

On leaving Cogne for the pass, a good road continues up to the place where the path branches off by which the iron ore is brought down from the mountain.

From all the heights round Cogne Mont Blanc is admirably seen, for the valley is a prolongation in direction of that between Villeneuve and Courmayeur. A very lofty and peaked mountain called Grivolet, between the valleys of Cogne and Savaranche, is also a conspicuous object.

Leaving the little plain of Cogne, the road to the Col ascends by a steep path on the mountain side, leaving on the rt. the valley of Vermiana, into which descends an enormous glacier from the mountain called the *Grand Paradis*. The steep path passes over what appears to be a vast dyke in the valley; the torrent flows round it to escape through a ravine at one extremity. On crossing the ridge, the traveller finds himself on a more wild and open ground, leading to the Alps and pasturages of Chavanes. Some of the lower châlets are soon reached: further up on this fine Alp, which feeds large flocks and herds during the summer, numerous châlets form the cluster known as the *Châlets of Chavanes.* Here the scene is rich in the pastoral groups and beauty of the herbage, and sublime in the magnificence of the amphitheatre of mountains and glaciers.

This pass across the glaciers is impracticable for mules. From Cogne to the crest of the path is a walk of 4 hrs.—the glacier itself may be crossed in 20 minutes. This pass is known as the *Col de l'Arietta.* Caution should be used in crossing the glaciers: the natives do not know it well, and when there is even a slight covering of snow, it is prudent to carry a rope, since the crevasses, though narrow, are very numerous. The Col is elevated and very narrow, the view from it towards the S. is magnificent; in clear weather the city of Turin is visible—seen over and far beyond the deep Val Campea, which lies at the feet of the traveller, and seemingly of perpendicular descent. Towards the N. the Monte Rosa and Mont Blanc can both be seen if the traveller can climb a rugged rock on the rt. for the enjoyment of these magnificent objects. The descent from the Col is excessively steep, but quite safe down to the valley of Campea; here, however, a commodious path leads gently down through scenes of continually increasing beauty. On looking back the Col de Cogne appears as if guarded by inaccessible precipices.

3 hrs. from the Col is *Campiglia* (no Inn), a wretched hamlet, whose male inhabitants for the most part migrate in winter into the plains of Italy to exercise their trades of coppersmith and lampmaker.

1¼ hr. Ronco. A *café* furnishes refreshments, but no beds; these can with difficulty be procured in a private house. The valley is here very narrow, with thickly wooded sides; the path continues high above the river through groves of walnut and chesnut. The distance from Campiglia to *Ponte* is only 4 hours' walk.

———

A less dangerous road, however, and one more varied and beautiful, but much longer, is found by leaving the glaciers of Cogne on the rt., and turning to the l. up a steep and difficult ascent to a narrow col, called the Fenêtre de Cogne, a mere notch in the crest of the mountain. From this place the view of the Alps, which bound the Val de Cogne on the W., is magnificent from the grandeur of their forms and the vast extent of their glaciers.

In the opposite direction, the glaciers which crest the northern side of the Val d'Orca are not less striking, and are perhaps more impressive from their greater proximity. They form a vast barrier to the rt. of the Val Champorcher, which opens into the Val d'Aosta (Rte. 107), at Fort Bard.

The descent is extremely difficult, from the steepness of the path and looseness of the soil. This difficulty ends before reaching a little chapel or oratory, built probably as an *ex voto* by some grateful Catholic for a merciful preservation here. This oratory is placed on the brink of one of several little lakes, formed by the melting of the glaciers. No spot can be more savage than this, or give a more impressive idea of dreary solitude.

The path now skirts, as it leaves it on the rt., a dark and enormous mountain mass, and descends rapidly down the valley, but nothing habitable appears. The valley deepens considerably on the l. below the path: the eye can trace its course down towards Bard, and a path across the valley is also seen, which leads from the Val Champorcher by the Châlets of Dodoney into the valley of Fenis.

After crossing the buttress of the mountains which the path skirts, and which is called the Col de Ponton, it leads to the bank of a torrent just where it issues from a great glacier; then, crossing another ridge over a beautiful pasturage, it descends to the borders of a little lake at the foot of the Col de Reale.

From this spot to *Fort Bard* down the valley of Champorcher is about 6 hrs.

Turning abruptly to the rt. the path leads to the *Col de Reale* in less than an hour, and from this crest one of the finest Alpine panoramas is presented.

From the crest the descent is rapid. Passing to the l. under a beetling mountain, the path skirts a deep ravine, leaves on the rt. some old adits of a mine worked unprofitably for silver, and, after a tortuous descent of 2 hrs., passes by some châlets. The level of the pine forests is soon reached, and deep in a little plain is seen the church and village of *Val Pra*, the highest in the Val Soanna. If the traveller arrive late at Val Pra, the worthy old peasant Giuseppe Danna will give him his best welcome.

At the opposite extremity of this little plain, the path descends by a stunted pine forest, and through the depths of the valley to the village of Peney, and by one or two little hamlets to the village of Ciampanella. There is nothing peculiar in this part of the valley, until just before reaching the hamlet of Bosco del Roco : there are the remains of a slip from the mountain, which took place in 1833, and strewed the little plain with rocks and stones.

At *Ronco* there is an *Inn*, which hunger and fatigue alone can make endurable ; below it, a bridge, in a wild and striking situation, leads across a ravine to the village of Ingria. Before reaching it, however, the opening of the valley of Campea above mentioned is passed, which leads directly to the glaciers of Cogne, shorter than the route by the Col de Reale.

The inhabitants of the valley of *Soanna* wear a singular sort of shoe or boot; it is made of coarse woollen, tied tight round the ankle, but half as broad again as the foot; its use gives an awkwardness to their gait.

———

Below *Ingria* the valley becomes a ravine of singularly wild and grand character. Vast precipices, gorges and forests, offer alternately, sometimes together, their magnificent materials for Alpine scenery. The road descends to the level of the river here so hemmed in by rocks, that it has been necessary to cut a passage through them. Enormous overhanging masses close the proximate part of the valley, hiding Ponte from view altogether, whilst beyond it the plains of Piedmont appear.

A path down through a forest, and near some quarries, leads to the Villa Nuova of Ponte, the cotton-works established by the Baron du Port, and about half a mile beyond is

Ponte, 6 hrs. from Val Pra in the mountains (*Inn :* tolerable, al Valentino) ; a singular old town ; its streets lined with arcades, under which the market is held.

The picturesque situation of this place at the confluence of the Soanna and the Orca can hardly be exceeded, rich in vineyards, enclosed by mountains, offering, in combination with the surrounding scenery, the towers and ruins of two feudal castles in the most striking situations, and the head of the valley closed by the snowy peaks of the lofty range which divides the Val d'Orca from the Tarentaise.

There are many spots about Ponte which offer views of singular beauty. Few places are so rich in the picturesque : these, too, offer a remarkable variety, for besides the views of Ponte and the valley, from the villages on the surrounding mountains' sides, both the Orca and the Soanna present retreats in their deep and retired courses, which are nowhere exceeded for picturesqueness. A walk down two or three meadows between Ponte and the Orca leads to one of these, well worth the traveller's visit, where the bright deep waters of the Orca seem hemmed in by lofty and forest-crowned precipices. The *Ch. of Sta. Maria* on an eminence, ½ hr.'s walk below the town, commands a fine view of the junction and of the valley as far as Courgne.

The establishment of the *Fabbrica*, the first cotton works known in Piedmont, has given employment to several thousands of men, women, and children, as printers, spinners, weavers, and dyers; the goods being prepared within the walls of the Fabbrica, from the raw material as imported from Genoa, to the completion of every article for the market.

Ponte is distant 6 hours from Turin, to which city a diligence goes 3 times a week. There is an excellent carriage road to the capital, which passes through

Courgne—(*Inn:* Leone d'Oro, tolerable)—a large town on the W. side of the Orca. A good walker may go from Cogne to Courgne in a day across the Col de Cogne; but the stranger should get the assistance of a guide over the Col. From Courgne the road to Turin continues through *Valperga*, celebrated for having one of the noblest campaniles in Piedmont ; Rivarolo; Lombardore, where the river Mallone is crossed; and Lemie; besides numerous villages. All those places named are towns, and some are large. They are situated in the richest part of Piedmont, amidst Indian corn, vines, mulberry and fig-trees. Those which are placed on the subsidences of the Alps, a little above the plains, are in the most beautiful situations, surrounded by vine-covered hills, and backed by lofty ranges of mountains. Little idea can be formed of the richness and beauty of Piedmont, except by those who have skirted the mountains on the borders of its rich plains. The traveller who enters it abruptly, by the usual routes, at right angles, across the chain of the Alps, sees too little of its actual and picturesque richness to estimate justly this fine country.

ROUTE 112.

PONTE TO VILLENEUVE, BY THE VAL D'ORCA (DÉTOUR TO THE COL DE GALESE), THE COL DE LA CROIX DE NIVOLET, AND THE VAL SAVA-RANCHE.

Eng. miles.

Ponte.
Locana	6
Novasca	7
Ceresol	6
Chapis	6¼
Pont	12¼
Villeneuve	16

20 hours' walk : distances approximate.

At the châlets milk, cheese, and butter may be had, but the traveller must carry bread and wine when he visits these wild valleys ; and he is especially cautioned against wandering there without a careful and well-recommended guide. At Novasca, or Ceresol, Giuseppe Bruscha, better known by the name of Muot, from the loss of one hand, may be heard of; he is a good guide, an active mountaineer, a capital chasseur, and a good-tempered, intelligent fellow.

On leaving *Ponte* to ascend the Val d'Orca, the road continues on the left bank of the river throughout its course. The scenery is very fine; the forms of the mountains vast and grand, rugged and broken, clothed with magnificent chestnut-trees, and frequently exhibiting the effects of disintegration in the enormous blocks which have fallen from the heights, in many places in such quantity that the road is carried over or around the *débris* with such sinuosity and undulation, that the variety of views they aid to present gives a peculiar character to this valley.

About 3 m. from Ponte is the village of *Sparone.* Many little hamlets lie on the road, and many usines are worked for small iron wares with tilts, and no stream is allowed to remain idle, where, at a small cost, and with simple machinery, it can be made to tilt a hammer, or move a saw.

Locana, a little town, the streets narrow and dirty. *Inns:* Leone d'Oro, tolerable ; de' Tre Pernice ('Three Partridges) is not likely to be forgotten by any traveller who has had the misfortune to enter there. In these villages many of the weavers are employed for the Fabbrica.

Above *Locana* the valley soon becomes dreary, and the road more rugged, and some smelting-houses and forges belonging to M. Binna are reached.

Thus far the road is practicable for chars. Above, there is only a mule-path, which winds up amidst the enormous masses of fallen granite and serpentine, some of which have blocked up the course of the torrent, and compelled it to find another channel—these, and the savage mountains which now domineer in the valley, give it great wildness. Yet the tortuous road rising over these *éboulemens* often leads to beautiful little plains between them.

There are several hamlets above Locana, as St. Marco, Arsone, and La Frera, but each is more and more miserable, until the climax of wretchedness is found at *Novasca*, which has pointed a proverb—

> Novasca, Novasca,
> Poco pane, lunga tasca.

Yet this spot offers to the traveller some of the most sublime horrors encountered in the Alps. Here a grand cataract bursts out from a rift in a mountain mass of granite, where all is denuded to absolute sterility. Below it, a thousand enormous masses of granite boulders are brought down and thrown together by the fall. The passage across the river, among these rocks, is unmatched in Alpine bridge-building: poles and planks are placed from rock to rock, and almost under the spray of the cataract. Beyond the passage of this torrent, the road still ascends on the left bank of the Orca.

About 1 m. above Novasca is a terrific gorge, called the Scalare de Ceresol, where enormous precipices overhang the course of the Orca, which tumbles through a succession of cataracts between these herbless precipices. The path which leads to the summit is cut out of the rocks, and a flight of steps (Scalare), practicable for mules, is carried up through the gorge; sometimes on the actual brink of the precipice which overhangs the foaming torrent; in others, cut so deep into its side, that the rocky canopy overhangs the precipice. In some places there is not room enough for the mounted traveller, and there is the danger of his head striking the rocks above him. This extraordinary path extends half a mile. In its course crosses are observed, fixed against the rock to mark the spots of fatal accidents: but as

three such accidents happened in company with an old miscreant who lived at the foot of the Scalare, suspicions were entertained of these having been murders which he had committed there. He underwent severe examinations; yet, though no doubt existed of his guilt, there was not evidence enough to convict him. It is believed that, at the spots where the crosses are placed, he pushed his victims over in an unguarded moment, where a child, unheeded, might have destroyed a giant.

The termination of this wild road is like a winding staircase, in which it is difficult for a mule to turn: near here the peep into the ravine is perfectly appalling.

On emerging from this singular path and fearful defile, the traveller finds himself on a plain, where there is barley grown, and an abundance of rich meadow land. Immediately before him is the snowy range which divides the Val Forno from the Val d'Orca, and across which a col leads to Gros Cavallo, in that valley, in a few hours.

A little way within the plain, the valley turns to the right and the Orca washes the base of a mountain, where the Comte d'Aglie has some silver-mines. The ore is smelted in the valley.

Near the works there is a spring of water slightly ferruginous, but so highly carbonated that the gas escapes from it in a sparkling state. It is almost tasteless; when drunk at the spring it is delicious.

The mountains of Levanna, seen on the left as the traveller ascends the valley, are very grand; pinnacled, glaciered, and utterly inaccessible. Three of the peaks, near together, bear the name of the *Trois Becs*. The valley widens near (30 min.) the few and scattered houses of Ceresol, the highest of its church villages, about 8 m. above the Scalare. In the solitary *Inn* near the church—a mere hovel—you may rest in what a mountaineer would call an *assez bon gite;* none but a mountaineer, however, would think it so.

To shorten the next day's journey, it will be better, however, to ascend the valley yet higher up to

The *Châlets of Chapis*, and, if mules are required, to engage them at Ceresol to come up the following morning to Chapis early enough to insure arrival, in good time, at Villeneuve, in the Val d'Aosta, 10 hrs. walk, in the evening of the same day. Fatigue only, however, is spared—no time is gained by riding.

Time walking across the pass :—

		H.	M.
From Chapis to the summit	.	2	10
„ Croix d'Arolette .	.	1	45
„ Pont . . .	.	0	30
„ Gioux . . .	.	2	0
„ Villeneuve . .	.	3	35

From *Ceresol*, the extraordinary *pass of the Galese*, at the head of the Val d'Orca, is first seen, above a perpendicular streak of snow, called the Grand Coluret, which must be climbed to cross the ridge of glaciers which surmounts it, and by which a passage may be made into the valley of the Isère in the Tarentaise.

Col de Galese.

Above the hamlet of Chapis (where the only night quarters are a hayloft) the path of the Nivolet separates from that of the Galese, which at first ascends a steep gully, and then crosses pastures to

The Châlets of Serue : here milk and cheese may be had. Beyond *Serue* the scene perhaps surpasses in sterility and savageness any other in the Alps. A narrow path leads along the steep slope of the Mont Iseran, until it stops abruptly at an inaccessible gully in the mountain called the Little Coluret. To ascend above this it is necessary to climb along the face of a fearful precipice overhanging, at a great height, a lake at the head of the valley. Having climbed round it, the *plain of Belotta* is attained. This plain is the bed of an ancient lake, now filled with an enormous glacier, which streams down from the left. The bottom of this glacier must be crossed by a very steep ascent up a vast mass of ice, and above it, up the gully of the Grand Coluret, at least 1500 ft. from the glacier. Precipices, fringed with icicles, overhang the traveller, and having climbed up close to the rocks, on the right side, it is at last necessary to cross the snow itself that lies in the hollow; this is not dangerous to a steady head, but a slip would precipitate the unlucky traveller at least 2000 ft. On the other side the footing is firm, but climbing among overhanging masses of rock requires a steady head and firm foot. Having passed these, he will reach the steep back or upper edge of a glacier, forming a precipice of ice about 40 ft. high. When this is passed, the traveller reaches

The summit of the *Galese*, about 10,000 ft. above the level of the sea, where one of the most glorious views in the Alps rewards him: he looks out over the head of the Val Isère, upon La Val and Tignes. To this valley the descent on the side of the Tarentaise is not difficult. In returning there is less danger in the descent than in the ascent, though it seems more dangerous, for the feet sink deep and firmly in the loose soil of both the Colurets. The Little Coluret can be safely descended, though, from the looseness of the soil, the ascent by it is impracticable.

The descent from the Galese on the W. is easy, as it is over snow till the upper pastures are reached. In about 1 hr. the path enters a gorge, and becomes exceedingly narrow. Emerging from this, the first châlets, S. Charles, appear. From these an easy descent over meadows to

Fornel (Rte. 122): a small *Inn*. Hence a steep ascent of 45 min. through woods leads into the direct route from Laval to Bonneval. (The course is distinctly marked by large pillars of stones placed at short intervals as far as the summit of Mont Iseran, 2 hrs. from Fornel.) The route from Fornel, by Bonneval (4 hrs.), to *Lanslebourg* (4 hrs.) is described in Rte. 122.

" The traveller to the Val d'Aosta, who has given a day to the Col de Galese, is recommended to sleep at the Châlets of Serue, or at any higher châlets which may be occupied, in preference to redescending to Chapis. It would be quite feasible to reach the Châlets of Nivolet, after ascending the Galese, whether from La Val or from Chapis: they cannot be more than 3½ to 4 hrs. from Serue—probably much less. I reached there in 3½ hrs. from Chapis."

To go to the Val Savaranche, it is not necessary to go to the pasturages of Serue. Before the abrupt ascent to the Alp of Serue commences, a torrent is seen descending from the right. Up the left bank of this torrent a difficult zigzag path ascends and at the end of 2 hrs. leads to some châlets even higher than those of Serue. The scenes presented during the ascent, of the vast ranges of the Levanna and the Iseran, are of the most sublime character. Above these châlets, the path is a series of flights of steps rudely cut in the rock. Beyond this a scene of frightful sterility is presented: numerous Alpine lakes or tarns are seen, but no prospect of escape, no path from this cul de sac seems to offer itself; yet in the most improbable of all directions there is one, which actually lies up and over the rugged and pinnacled crest of the boundary to the left, offering a path more difficult than that of the Gemmi, without the protection of its parapets. The summit attained, the scene around, viewed from this crest, known by the name of the *Col de la Croix de Nivolet,* is one without parallel in the Alps for the wild peculiarities observed on looking back into the savage valley just left. In it many lakes appear, and the brow above the last châlets cuts abruptly against the deep haze of the Val d'Orca, which is surmounted with the enormous range of the Levanna.

On looking on the other side of the col into the Plan de Nivolet, which is the head of the valley of Savaranche, many lakes are also seen at the foot of the glaciers of the Nivolet, the same mountain which, towards the Tarentaise, is known by the name of the Iseran, and directly across the head of the Plan de Nivolet is seen a still higher col than that upon which the observer stands ; it is called the *Col de Rhemes,* and leads from Laval in the valley of the Isère, through the Val de Rhemes to Villeneuve, by a shorter course than the Savaranche.

The descent towards the Plan de Nivolet is much easier than towards the Val d'Orca ; and having attained the banks of the lakes, a nearly level path leads through the fine pasturages at the head of the Plan de Nivolet ; yet not a tree or shrub grows here, and the plain is exposed to fearful storms in winter.

In about an hour from the lakes the châlets of this plain are reached. The want of other fuel than dried cow-dung gives a filthy aspect to these châlets. Below them the ground of the plain becomes boggy, and broken up into thousands of knolls. At the end of another hour, these are left, to descend by a path lying over bare and smooth granite, like that on the route of the Grimsel, above Handek. (Rte. 34.) After a considerable descent, the traveller suddenly finds himself on the brink of a vast precipice, and overlooking the village of Pont, in the deep valley, thousands of feet below him. Here, on the edge of the precipice, a cross is placed, which is seen from below ; the spot is called the Croix d'Aroletta. From it, one of those sublime scenes which occasionally bursts upon the traveller in the Alps opens upon him. The three vast peaks of the Grand Paradis, breaking through their enormous vestment of glaciers, rise before him ; and on the rt., a black mountain, that overhangs the path by which he must descend to *Pont.* Down these precipices he must wind for more than an hour to reach this village, the highest in the Val Savaranche, passing on his descent a magnificent cataract.

But here the striking and peculiar

scenery of this pass ends ; the valley below Pont is narrow, and with very little cultivation at the bottom. On the l. a path leads over the mountain of Causelles to the Val de Rhemes ; and another on the rt. crosses to the Val de Cogne. (Rte. 111.) *Gioux*, or Val Savaranche, is the principal village in the valley, and here refreshment may be obtained.

There are many little communes in this valley. Near to one of these, Pesai, an avalanche fell in 1832 ; it destroyed some cows, and three men perished. Crosses mark the spot where their bodies were found.

Before reaching Gioux there is a picturesque spot in the valley, where two villages are perched opposite each other, Tignietti and Crettom ; and here the mountains are seen which bound the valley of Aosta on the side opposite to the Val Savaranche.

In the lower part of the valley, the path continues at a vast height above the course of the river bank, on its rt. ; as it approaches the Val d'Aosta, a magnificent view of Mont Blanc, towering over all the intermediate mountains, opens to the traveller. Here the Val de Rhemes joins the Val Savaranche, and both enter the valley of Aosta. The end of the Val de Rhemes appears like a table land on the mountain side, studded with villages, rich in meadows and vines, walnut and chestnut trees.

From this elevation the descent to *Villeneuve* is rapid, fatiguing, and difficult ; and the journey from Chapis to the Val d'Aosta (Rte. 107) will be found to be quite enough for one day. At Villeneuve there is neither decent inn nor car, so you may be prepared to continue on to

Aosta, 2 h. 20 m. further.

ROUTE 113.

AOSTA TO BOURG ST. MAURICE, IN THE TARENTAISE, BY THE VAL DE GRISANCHE AND THE COL DU MONT.

Aosta (Rte. 107).

Ivrogne (Rte. 107). Hence to Bourg is about 16 hrs.

The entrance to the *Val Grisanche* by the torrent which flows into the Val d'Aosta is utterly impracticable. It is necessary to cross the torrent by the new bridge, and immediately behind the little dirty town of Ivrogne to pass a mill, and ascend through orchards and meadows that appear to lead away from the Grisanche. At the head of these the path arrives abruptly below some precipices ; thence turning and ascending along their bases, the traveller shortly finds himself in the path which is carried high above the l. bank of the Grisanche, and which leads up the valley.

For about 4 hrs. the scenes have a striking character. The river roars so deep in the gorge as scarcely to be heard ; and the rocks which bound its course are so nearly perpendicular, that the tops of lofty and enormous pines, rooted in the rifts below, can almost be touched by the hand of the traveller in passing above them. Overhanging the path, the mountains so close in, that the light of day does not half illuminate this deep and savage defile. On a sort of terrace, on the opposite banks, the ruins of a feudal castle are seen frowning over the black ravine, and fitted for tales of romance. From it, the view into the valley of Aosta must be beautiful, but what access there is to these ruins cannot be traced, or even imagined, from the opposite bank, though this is so high above the torrent, that the path seldom approaches it nearer than 200 ft.

This narrow defile continues during an ascent of more than 2 hrs. Sometimes the path is carried on terraces, rudely formed of loose stones placed across rifts in the precipices; in others, the buttresses of rock are cut away to make the road high and wide enough to pass a point of danger; this in some places has been done with a mass of rock, which, having fallen from above, and rested on the line of communication, has required boldness and skill to form a path by it; thousands of these masses have fallen into the gulf below, and only rendered the torrent more furious by the interruption.

At length, at the upper extremity of the defile, the valley opens at the *village of Seris*, a place which furnishes only the most miserable accommodation. The passage up the Grisanche to Seris is all in the valley really worth a visit from the Val d'Aosta, and it well deserves from the tourist in that valley an examination as far as Seris.

The sterility of the Val de Grisanche above Seris is striking ; it is rugged, and strewn with enormous blocks which have been detached from the mountains, often from precipices so steep that no vegetation rests upon their surfaces, where still impending masses threaten the passing traveller, and numerous crosses record the frequency of fatal accidents. Deep rifts in the sides of the precipices are channels to cataracts that pour their white foam from the dark recesses ; in some places, the black precipitous slopes of the mountain are always wet and herbless, and reeking as if from some recent avalanche.

For more than two hours up the valley from Seris, the same character of scenery prevails ; some miserable hovels and a few fields of stunted barley are found in the bottom of the valley ; on its sides there is only the dark precipice or black forest of pines. The head of the valley is bounded by the immense glaciers of Clou.

At *Fornel*, the highest village in the valley, the route to the Col du Mont leaves the Val de Grisanche, ascends a steep path on the right by a torrent, and reaches some châlets on a small but fine pasturage. Above these the path skirts the brink of precipices over a deep gorge, and enters a basin in the mountains—a scene of the most frightful disorder ; it is filled with rocks and stones constantly brought down from the surrounding mountains, the summits of which are crested with glaciers, some so precipitous that the ridge of the mountain is surmounted by one of translucent ice, which presents, when the sun shines through it, a most brilliant appearance. The ascent is very steep for nearly 3 hrs. up a trackless loose path, and up slopes of snow, steep, and many hundreds of feet across. It is fatiguing and difficult. From the Col the scene is very fine, not only of the deep valley of stones towards Piedmont, but also towards Savoy, where nature presents a gentle aspect in the mountains which bound the Val Isère ; for the Col is so narrow that both can be seen from the summit.

The *Col du Mont* was the scene of some desperate conflicts during the wars of the revolution between the French and the Piedmontese. General Moulins, who commanded the former, after many efforts succeeded in gaining the position by advancing during a snow storm, when such assailants were not expected, and retained it in spite of not less than ten efforts to repossess it. The height of the Col, from the absence of all vegetation, must exceed 8500 ft.

After passing down a steep path, leaving on the l. black precipices—the haunts of the chamois—the beautiful pasturages belonging to the commune of St. Foi appear in a deep basin, bounded below by a forest. In little more than 2 hrs. the châlets in this basin are reached, and in another hour it is traversed. Beyond it the road winds steeply down through a forest, and at length emerges to cross a torrent and enter the village of Muraille, where another bridge over a deep ravine leads to the hamlet of Massure ; thence traversing a brow on the mountain side, the road descends to the

Village of St. Foi in the *Val Isère.* The approach to it is strikingly fine, for one of the most beautiful mountains in the Alps, the Chaffe-Quarre, bounds the opposite side of the Val Isère. From its base in the torrent, far below the terrace where St. Foi stands, to its summit, which is peaked with a triangular pyramid of snow, the entire height of this stupendous mountain is seen. At St. Foi lives François Ruet, an excellent guide and sportsman, who will accommodate travellers. Chamois are not scarce ; pheasants and ptarmigan abound, and bears have been known. There are excellent trout in the Lac de Tignes.

From St. Foi the descent by a paved road is very steep to the banks of the Isère. Before reaching the river a torrent is crossed, which forms, a little way up the valley, a fine cataract. It is difficult to get a view of it. This is the stream which from above descends between the villages of Massure and Muraille.

From the bridge the path lies across meadows for some way, and on the banks of the Isère. Soon after rising, it leads to the village of *Scez*, at the foot of the Little St. Bernard. [From Scez to *Chapiu* (Rte. 118) is a walk of 3¼ hrs. up the narrow valley of the Versoie, passing Bonneval, where there is a small *Inn.*] From Scez you cross cultivated ground, to a bridge thrown over the torrent of the Reclus. Here there is abundant evidence of the destructive character of the torrent after storms, in the sand, rocks, and stones which mark its course at such times. Soon after the road passes by some coarse woollen cloth-works, and some usines for making small iron ware. Then across the winter bed of the furious Versoie, which descends from Bonneval, and below an old round tower belonging to the village of Châtelard. From this place the road to St. Maurice is wide and excellent, and ere long it is to be hoped a road of the same width and excel-

lence will lead from this valley to the Val d'Aosta by the pass of the Little St. Bernard.

Bourg St. Maurice. Inn: H. des Voyageurs, tolerable. (See Rte. 114.)

Aosta to Lanslebourg. Travellers going by the upper valley of the Isère (Rte. 122) should not take the rt. branch of the valley, which leads over the Col du Mont, but continue from Fornel to the head of the main valley, whence there is a high and wild pass by the *Col du Clou*, descending through very fine scenery to Tignes (Rte. 122). It is a very long day's journey.

ROUTE 114.

COURMAYEUR TO BOURG SAINT MAURICE, BY THE LITTLE ST. BERNARD—THE BELVEDERE.

(10 hours' walk.)

This is one of the easiest passes over the Alps, and probably one of the most ancient. These and other reasons render it probable that Hannibal made his famous passage into Italy by it.

A mule-path, much used, leads directly from *Cormayeur*, in

1 hr. to *Pré St. Didier*, a tolerably large village, having a *poste aux lettres* and a diligence to Turin. (*Inn:* Poste. St. Didier, like Courmayeur, is frequented in summer for its hot mineral springs, having a temperature of 92° of Fahrenheit in the baths, but 95° at the source.

Between the village and the springs there are some beautiful meadows, the source of its name, Pré St. Didier, sheltered by the base of the Cramont. Enormous precipices of bare rock overhang the source, and form one side of a deep gulf, through which the torrent from the glaciers of the Ruitor and the Little St. Bernard forces its way.

The hot spring lies high up this gulf, from which it is led through tubes to the baths in the meadow, where a rather elegant structure or Pavillon has been raised. There are several houses in the village, where, for very moderate charges, bed and board may be obtained.

The *view of Mont Blanc* from the meadows is a glorious scene; and, from beneath the precipices near the source, magnificent foregrounds may be obtained.

The road which leads by the valley above the gorge at the springs of St. Didier, to the Little St. Bernard, is a steep zigzag, presenting at each turn new and striking scenes of the valley below, and of Mont Blanc. On reaching the level ground above, that overhangs the deep rift in the mountain, through which the branch of the Doire from La Tuille bursts through into the plain of St. Didier, the scene is fine. It borders a pine forest, of which some vast old trunks hang over the precipices, and help to conceal the deep torrent which roars beneath.

A little above *La Balme* the torrent is crossed, and a path winds steeply up on the mountain side; it being impracticable in the depth of the valley, which is here a ravine, to form a road. This is carried on the right bank to a great height above the bed of the torrent. There are occasional peeps offered of the river, and there is one of particular interest—it is where the avalanches which descend from the Cramont fall into the ravine, sometimes in such quantity that the snow remains, under the shadow of the mountain, unmelted for the year. This is the spot, in the opinion of those who have most carefully examined into the subject, where Hannibal and his army, in their descent from the Alps, found the road, by which they could have descended into the valley, destroyed. The road

formerly lay on the l. bank of the river. Within these 60 years, the present road, to avoid this liability, has been made on the other side, high above all risk from such an accident.

Not far from this spot the road turns abruptly to the l., and the Alpine bridge and village of *La Tuille*, and the glacier of the Ruitor, open upon the traveller. The bridge is crossed, and wine and refreshment may be found in the little auberge of La Tuille.

A short way above La Tuille the stream from the glacier of the Ruitor may be crossed, and a path taken to descend into the valley of Aosta, by some beautiful pasturages, and through a forest that overhangs the precipices above St. Didier, whence the view of Mont Blanc is inferior only to that from the Cramont. After crossing the *Camp of Prince Thomas*, the path descends down the steep mountain side on the rt. bank of the Doire. It is nearly in this course that the Sardinian government contemplates the formation of a good road over the Little St. Bernard, to connect the Pays d'Aosta with the Tarentaise.

From La Tuille the road ascends rapidly to *Pont Serrant*—the last village towards the Little St. Bernard—and after crossing a very deep ravine over a wooden bridge, a striking scene, and passing the village, the road becomes more steep, but presents little interest except to the geologist. About 2 hrs. above Pont Serrant the col is reached—a fine pasturage on a plain about a league long and ⅓ a league wide, bounded on the l. by the Belvedere and the Vallaisan, and on the rt. by the Belle-face, at the foot of which mountain lies a little lake—the Vernai, which is left in its deep basin on the rt., in ascending to the Col of the *Little St. Bernard.*

After passing the ruins of some defences thrown up during the war of the Revolution, when France and Sardinia struggled for possession of these summits, the road enters upon the plain, and the traveller sees before him, at the opposite extremity of it, the hospice rebuilt.

On the plain, however, there are

objects of high antiquity. A circle of stones on the highest point of the plain bears still the name of the Cirque d'Annibal. The stones are rude masses, varying in size, none very large; they are about 10 ft. apart, and the circle measures nearly 260 yds. round. The tradition is, that Hannibal here held a council of war. That he stayed on the summit of the Alps, and waited for his stragglers, is an historical fact; and, independent of other and abundant evidence, no plain on the summit of any other of the Alpine passes is so well adapted for the encampment of his army as this.

Near to the circle there is a column standing, the *Colonne de Joux*, supposed to be of Celtic origin. It is nearly 20 ft. high, and 3 ft. in diameter. It is composed of Cipollino, a variety of marble which abounds in the Cramont. About 1½ m. from the Colonne de Joux is the

Hospice, situated at the S.W. extremity of the plain. Here some brethren of the Hospice of the Great St. Bernard administer hospitality; but at present only one ecclesiastic resides here. Some dogs of the St. Bernard breed are kept here, but the race is nearly extinct. The expenses of the hospice, which affords very tolerable accommodation, are defrayed by the commune of Aosta.

The Hospice was founded by St. Bernard, but nothing of its history is preserved. The Great St. Bernard has absorbed all the interest, though, if the veil of the obscure history of the Little St. Bernard could be removed, it would perhaps surpass in early importance that of its great rival; for Celtic remains still exist there, and the foundations of a temple constructed of Roman brick are traced on the col, near the column.

[If the traveller determine to visit the Belvedere, and has already visited the Cramont, it will be too much for one day, and he will do well to sleep at the hospice, and either ascend the *Belvedere* in the evening, or on the following morning. It is of easy accomplishment: the ascent may be made in an hour. Mont Blanc, which

is not seen from the Col of the Little St. Bernard, is from the Belvedere a magnificent object. The view is of great extent, commanding the mountains far S. of the Tarentaise, and looking down upon enormous glaciers streaming into the valleys E. of the Belvedere; but the scenes are very inferior to those discovered from the Cramont.]

[Travellers bound to the upper valley of the Isère may shorten the way to Ste. Foi (Rte. 122) by ascending, nearly due S. from the hospice, the ridge of the Traversette, to which cannon were transported during the revolutionary war. The descent to Ste. Foi is rather steep, but this path saves nearly 2 hrs.]

Descending from the hospice, the road winds down the mountain side, and in 2 hrs. the traveller reaches the village of *St. Germains*. Thence a zigzag path descends to a stream called the Reclus, which is overhung at the point of passage by an enormous bank of gypsum, bearing the name of the *Roche Blanche*. In situation it perfectly agrees with Polybius' account, in the passage of Hannibal, of such a rock, and the events which occurred there. This is one of the chief points of evidence, and, taken with the others, furnish a mass which must force conviction on the minds of unprejudiced inquirers—that by this pass of the Alps, Hannibal entered Italy. General Melville, in his examination, the basis of De Luc's treatise; Wickham and Cramer from their researches; and Brockedon from his repeated visits; all travellers in the Alps, who have examined the other passes also, in reference to this question, have come to the conclusion that on this line only can the narrative of Polybius, the only worthy authority upon the question, be borne out.

Below the Roche Blanche the ancient road by the Reclus is avoided, from its constant exposure to destruction by falls from the Mont de Scez. It now passes by cultivated fields through the hamlet of *Villars* to the village of *Scez* (Rte. 113) and thence to

Bourg St. Maurice. Inns: H. des Voyageurs; H. Royal.

Mules are kept here : there is no tariff, but the charge is 8 fr. over the Little St. Bernard to Courmayeur, and 4 fr. return for each mule, with a small pour-boire to the boy who brings it back.

Time walking from Bourg St. Maurice to Hospice, 4 hrs.; thence to Pré St. Didier, 3½ hrs.

ROUTE 115.

GENEVA TO CHAMOUNI.

86 kilom.=53½ Eng. m.

	Kil.	Eng. m.
Geneva.		
Bonneville . . .	28 =	17½
St. Martin . . .	30 =	18½
Chamouni . . .	28 =	17½

A Sardinian visé is not necessary on a F. O. passport. Diligences now book all the way to Chamouni, the travellers leaving the heavy vehicle at St. Martin and exchanging into lighter carriages better suited for the rough mountain road beyond. The journey from Geneva to St. Martin occupies about 6 hrs. ; Voituriers about the same time : from St. Martin to Chamouni 5 hrs. Pedestrians will find it as pleasant to walk from St. Martin to Chamouni, and will traverse that distance as fast as the chars, i. e. in about 4 or 5 hrs. On no account be deluded into paying back fare, by diligence or otherwise, to return to Geneva. There are several routes *from* Chamouni of great interest, by which you may avoid retracing your steps by the same road.

Travellers posting in their own carriages may send them round from St. Martin to Martigny, if they intend crossing the Tête Noire or Col de Balme.

Geneva is left for Chamouni by the Grande Place and the new quarter on the site of the levelled Porte de Rive. For some miles the road is lined with neat villas and gardens.

Chesne is a very large village on the Seime—one of the largest villages in the republic. The road offers some fine views of the l. Voirons, rt. Mont Salève, the picturesque red Château de Mornex, and the range of the Jura. Soon after leaving Chesne, the road crosses a little stream, the Foron, which has its source in the Voirons, and is the boundary between the canton of Geneva and the Sardinian frontier. A little beyond it, at Annemasse, is the station of the Sardinian douane. Here great civility is shown; and no search or trouble is given about baggage. On the first rising ground beyond, the *Môle*, a conical mountain, is seen in all its height, 5800 feet, partly concealing the only hollow in the range of mountains beyond, up which the course to Chamouni lies.

Beyond *Annemasse* the road runs up the valley of the Arve, in which the blanched stones mark by their breadth how furious the river must be after storms. A new road, well engineered, and a handsome lofty bridge, effect the passage of the Menoge, nearly on a level, avoiding the arduous descent and ascent of the old road. It next passes over an elevated plain, and soon reaches

The village of *Nangy.* A little beyond there are some ruins on the right; and, after passing Contamines, are seen those of the Château of Faucigny, that gives its name to the province of Faucigny. The road now passes so near to the Môle, that this mountain is an imposing and beautiful object. Upon it an obelisk has been built—one of the points in a trigonometrical survey of Savoy. Beyond Contamines the road declines. The mountains which bound the Arve present a bold aspect, and the entrance is striking, through an avenue of trees, to

Bonneville — (*Inns :* Couronne; Balances)—the chief place in the province of Faucigny; it is in the diocese of Annecy, and has a prefecture. Its inhabitants were formerly 3000; at present they do not exceed 1500.

The top of the Môle may be reached from this in 3½ hrs.

A road leads over the hills from this place to Annecy, and thence to Aix les Bains (Rte. 373).

At the end of the stone bridge, built 1753, over the Arve, is a Column erected in honour of Carlo Felice, and in gratitude for his having added to the security of their town by the formation of strong embankments, to restrain the furious Arve. It is surmounted by a statue of the King, and is 95 feet high.

The road now lies between the Môle and the Mont Brezon, the range that on the right bounds the valley of the Arve, which is here rich in cultivation. The road, after some time, undulates, and passes through the villages of Vaugier and Scionzier; beyond which the valley widens. Here the Arve is joined by the Giffre; a torrent that descends from the Buet, flows through the valley of Samoëns, and by the town of Tanninges. Scionzier lies at the mouth of the Valley du Réposvir.

The road continues close under the Brezon until its precipices frown over the route near Cluses. Here, crossing the Arve, on a stone bridge, it enters the town of

Cluses (Inns: Parfaite Union; Ecu de France), an old town ; was almost all burnt down in 1843, but has been rebuilt, away from the mouth of the gorge, in which it originally stood. The wind, issuing as from a furnace-blast bellows out of this gorge, used to foment any accidental fire into a general conflagration, and from this cause Cluses has suffered many times.

The population is about 2250; and many persons are employed in watch-making, for which this town was more celebrated in the last century. The Cluses artizans prepare *movements* of watches in a rough state, for the watchmakers in Geneva and in Germany.

On leaving Cluses, the road is carried through the defile on the borders of the river, and beneath grand Al-

pine precipices. The valley is very narrow, nearly all the way to Maglan, and, in some places, the road is straitened in between the river and the bases of precipices, which actually overhang the traveller. The banks of the river are well wooded, and the scenery is as beautiful as it is wild.

Before arriving at Maglan, the precipices on the left retire a little, forming an amphitheatre, which is filled, nearly half-way up, with the *débris* of the mountain. At the top of this talus, 800 feet above the valley, the *Grotto of Balme* is seen, to which a mule-path leads, which is undistinguishable below. At a little hut in the hamlet of La Balme, mules are kept for a visit to the grotto.

Those who intend to go on to Chamouni, should not waste any time here; for 2 hours are consumed in seeing the cave: but if the day's journey be only to St. Martin or Sallenches, the grotto is worth a visit. Its depth is great: it enters the mountain more than 1800 feet; but the view from it, owing to the narrowness of the valley, is limited. The peaks, however, of Mont Douron, seen on the other side of the valley, are remarkably fine in form.

A little beyond La Balme, those who are amateurs of pure water may taste from a spring which bursts out close to the road in large volume. Saussure conjectured that it might be the embouchure of the channel which empties the lake of Flaine, in the mountains above.

Maglan lies below the lofty mountains on the right bank of the Arve; the commune, which is straggling, contains nearly as many inhabitants as Cluses. About 1½ league beyond Maglan, the road passes close to one of the highest waterfalls in Savoy, that of *Nant d'Arpenaz;* the stream is small, and before it reaches half its first descent it is broken into spray, yet its shape is very graceful, and after being nearly dissipated and dispersed over the face of the precipice, it reforms after reaching the slope or talus of soil and stones which it has brought down, and rushing across the road beneath a bridge, it flows into the Arve. The rock of brown lime-stone, from which it descends, is re-markable for its tortuous stratifica-tion, forming a vast curve. The route from Geneva is so much fre-quented by strangers in the season, that it is beset by all sorts of vaga-bonds, who plant themselves in the way openly as beggars, or covertly as dealers in mineral specimens, guides to things which do not require their aid, dealers in echoes, by firing small cannon where its reverberation may be heard 2 or 3 times. These idle nuisances should be discounte-nanced.

The valley increases in width, and rich fields spread up the base of the Douron; the peaks of the Varens rise nearly 8000 ft. above the level of the sea.

St. Martin — *Inn:* Hôtel de Mont Blanc; better than any at Sallenches; beware of charges.

Within a hundred yards of the inn a bridge crosses the Arve, and leads to the town of Sallenches, half a mile from St. Martin. From this bridge *one of the noblest views in the Alps* is presented of Mont Blanc: the actual distance to the peak is more than 12 miles in a direct line, yet so sharp, and bright, and clear is every part of its stupendous mass, that the eye, unused to such magnitude with dis-tinctness, is utterly deceived, and would lead one to underrate the dis-tance. On looking up the valley over the broad winter-bed of the Arve, however, objects recede, and give the accustomed impressions of distance: above this rises the mountain of the Forclaz, its sides clothed with pines, and its summit with pasturage. Over these are seen the Aiguille du Goûté, the Dome du Goûté, and the head of the loftiest mountain in Europe, propped by ridges of aiguilles, and the intervals of these filled with glaciers.

This one view repays the journey from England.

Sallenches (*Inns:* Bellevue ; Le-man), about 36 m. from Geneva, is little town of wide, straight streets, containing about 2000 Inhab., risen out of the ashes of one which was totally destroyed by fire on Good Friday, 1840. It broke out while everybody was at church, and thus got ahead before it could be checked. Many lives were lost.

At St. Martin, or Sallenches, Gene-vese carriages are changed for local calèches, chars, mules, and guides for Chamouni, which are found in abund-ance. A *char* to Chamouni (without return) costs 12 frs.; with 2 horses 18 frs. Postilion, pourboire, 2 frs. extra. The *tariff* of the Post-book should be consulted; it is the same in both places.

The roads hence to Chamouni are practicable only for light and narrow chars; in some places they are very steep, rough, and stony, and, though the distance is only 18 Eng. m., it takes up 4 or 5 hours.

The baths of St. Gervais are scarcely worth the détour required, but the pedestrian who intends to visit Chamouni and return by Geneva is advised to go from St. Martin up the right bank of the Arve to Chêde, Servoz, and Chamouni, and return by the Col de Forclaz, and the Baths of St. Gervais. If, however, the tra-veller should not intend to return by the valley of the Arve, he can go round by the Baths of St. Gervais to Chêde.

[From Sallenches the distance along a level road to the baths of *St. Gervais* is a good league, and an agreeable drive, from the views presented of the Mont Varens, which overhangs St. Martin and the valley of Maglan. The road turns abruptly on the right into the gorge of the Bon Nant, a stream which descends from the Bon-homme. At the upper extre-mity of a little level spot, a garden in the desert, are the *Baths of St. Gervais*, with *Inns* (H. du Mont Joli), lodging and boarding houses. Most travellers used to visit St. Gervais, but until the roads destroyed by the floods of 1852 are restored, it will occupy more time than it is perhaps worth; it is a little fairy spot, in a beau-tiful valley, where excellent accom-modation may be had *en pension:* hot mineral baths for the sick, and delightful walks around for the convalescent. The waters are at 105° temperature; the heat of Bath with the qualities of Harrowgate: they contain iron and sulphur. At the back of the house, a little way up the glen, is the very fine *Cascade du Bon Nant*, which, though not large, is extremely picturesque. The views from above St. Gervais are very fine, though the higher Alps are concealed; but the limestone range of the Aiguille de Varens, above St. Martin, is singularly picturesque in its outline and detail.

The glen is a *cul-de-sac;* for chars there is no leaving it upward; it is necessary to return to the entrance, where two roads branch off—one, very steep, leads up to St. Gervais, a beautiful village in the Val Montjoie, through which the Bon Nant flows, until it falls into the gulf behind the baths, above St. Gervais. This road continues through the villages of Bionay and Tresse to Contamines, and the pass of the Bon-homme. (Rte. 118.)

The other road at the entrance of the glen of the baths of St. Gervais, after skirting a little way the mountain base below the Forclaz, leads across the valley of the Arve, and falls into the char-road by Passy to Chêde and Chamouni.

From St. Gervais to Chamouni there are 2 mule-paths over the mountains, —A, by the *Col de Voza*, a pass of great interest, on account of its noble view of the chain of Mont Blanc, 5 hrs. walk; a guide required: B, by the *Col de la Forclaz*, shorter than A, but less interesting.]

The valley of the Arve above St. Martin and Sallenches spreads out into a wide flat plain, having the appearance of a drained lake-basin. Terrible traces are still to be seen of the flood of 1852 (Rte. 56A), which in many places cut itself a broad channel through fertile fields, carrying away every particle of soil and leaving the bare rock exposed. This flood destroyed nearly all the bridges from Chamouni to St. Martin, and communication from Geneva was cut off for some days. Indescribably magnificent views open out from time to time all the way to Servoz. At the little hamlet of

Chêde, the road steeply ascends above the broad plain of the Arve. Near to Chêde there is on the left a fine cascade, which travellers, who start at 5 A.M. for Chamouni, generally visit for the sake of the beautiful iris that then plays over it.

[From Chêde there is a path over the mountains in about 8 hrs. to *Sixt*, by the Pointe de Platée and the châlets of La Sale (Rte. 115A).]

After attaining a considerable height, the road traverses the bed of a little lake, the *Lac du Chêde;* in which, as in a mirror, in former days a fine view of the summit of Mont Blanc, towering over the lower range of mountains, was reflected; this was one of the little "lions" in the excursion to Chamouni; but a *débâcle* of black mud and stones descended in 1837, and filled it, and the lake of Chêde is no more.

The road, still rising above the spot where the lake was, turns into a deep recess of the mountain side, to cross the bed of a wild torrent, which is apt to cover the road, after every severe storm, with rubbish, and to alter its direction to those who follow. From this spot there is a descent through a forest to the

Village of *Servoz* (a tolerable *Inn*). Here the horses are usually rested, and the traveller may enjoy a glorious view of the summit of Mont Blanc, which is concealed nearer to Chamouni.

Here the minerals of Mont Blanc are sold, but the collections at Chamouni are larger.

[At Servoz, guides may be had to accompany the traveller to *the Buet*, one of the panorama-commanding summits near Mont Blanc, and up to the *Col d'Anterne*, a mule-path leading over into the Valley of Sixt (Rte. 115A), a very interesting excursion. From Sixt there is a road direct to Geneva, thus varying agreeably the return route from Chamouni, instead of revisiting St. Martin and Bonneville.]

Near Servoz the road passes the adit of a copper-mine.

The mountain above Servoz abounds in tertiary fossils.

From Servoz the road, after crossing the torrent of the Dioza which descends from the Buet, lies close under the foot of the Breven, between this mountain and the Arve, which issues at Pont Pelissier from one of the finest gorges in the Alps. The valley between this bridge and Servoz was once a lake, produced, probably, by a mountain fall damming up the valley of Châtelas, by which the Arve descends to the valley of Sallenches. Near the Pont Pelissier, on a mound, are the ruins of the Castle of St. Michael.

After crossing Pont Pelissier another very steep and stony ascent opposes the traveller's course, called Les Montets: the road, an effort of nature with little aid from man, with difficulty labours up its rocky slope. The Arve on the l. rushes down it as by a staircase in constant leaps, in places plunging into ravines and chasms, whose depth makes one shudder to look down. Arrived at the top of this steep, you find yourself in an upper story of the valley of the Arve.

From the Montets, the enormous mass of Mont Blanc, now in close proximity, is magnificent; but the summit can no longer be seen; it is concealed by the vast Dome du Goûté.

The course from the Montets lies through some fine meadows to

Les Ouches, the first village in the valley of Chamouni.

[Here diverge the paths over the Col de Voza to St. Gervais, and to the Col du Bonhomme (Rte. 118).]

Even from Les Montets, the white lines of glaciers (§ 17) are seen to extend themselves into the valley. The first is that of Taconey, which is 2 m. up the valley above Les Ouches. it is, however, so mere a line compared with the vastness of other objects around, that the traveller will probably be disappointed in its apparent size. Numerous torrents are passed, descending furiously from the glaciers of Mont Blanc, and cutting deep channels, which are difficult to cross, or to keep in repair the passages over them, disrupted by every storm. The valley expands considerably.

About half a league beyond the stream from the glacier of Taconey, is the hamlet of *Bossons*, and near it the *glacier of Bossons*, which stretches further out into the valley than any other. It is a beautiful object at a distance, and deserves close examination on account of the purity of its ice and the elegant and fantastic forms of its ice pyramids. The Pavilion, at a very short walk from the high road, commands an excellent view of the glacier.

[2 m. below Chamouni is a path (rt.) by which you may visit the *Cascade du Dard* (Rte 115a).]

A little above the glacier of Bossons the Arve is crossed, and the road continues on its right bank. At the head of the valley is seen the Glacier du Bois, the largest in the valley, the terminus, in fact, of the Mer de Glace. This lies, however, a league beyond the village of Chamouni.

CHAMOUNI. *Inns:* H. de l'Union, a first-rate inn; H. Royal, beyond the river, same proprietor as the Union, the best rooms in Chamouni; H. d'Angleterre, formerly H. de Londres, rebuilt 1857; H. du Mont Blanc has baths; H. de la Couronne, good, attentive landlady.

In August and September the inns are frequently so full that travellers arriving late at night have the greatest difficulty in obtaining accommodation. The mineral warm baths, in the principal inns, offer the most refreshing and agreeable luxury after the fatigue of mountain excursions.

A Chapel for the performance of the *English Ch. Service* is built in the grounds of the H. Royal, but open to all visitors. Divine Service is performed on Sundays, alternately at the H. Royal and H. d'Angleterre.

Chamouni is now a large and important community, which displays almost the bustle of an English watering-place in the most retired, heretofore, of the Alpine valleys. With the exception, however, of the enormous hotels which appear to have

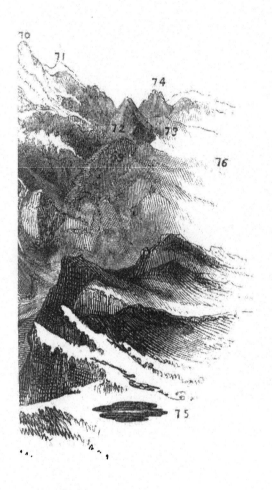

Montagne de la Gria.
Pierre-Ronde.
Mont Lacha.
Aiguille de Bionnassay.
Mont-Blanc-St.-Gervais.
Glacier de Bionnassay.
Montagne de Tricot.   [Bonhomme.
Aiguille de Bousselette au Col du
Lac du Bréven.
Pavillon de Bellevue, Col de Voza.
Village de la Molas.

time, and have a taste for such sublime scenes, he may, by sleeping at the Pavillon, enjoy these in a high degree, by exploring, after a descent from the Jardin, the upper part of the Mer de Glace and the Glacier de Lechaud: for this there will be time enough, and even to make collections of plants and minerals, which are highly interesting ; the former at the Egralets and on the Jardin, and the latter on the Moraines of the Glacier of Talèfre and on the E. side of the Mer de Glace. The next morning, therefore, instead of returning by the beaten road to Chamouni, the traveller may explore the bases of the Aiguilles between the Mer de Glace and Mont Blanc, and crossing with caution the Glacier du Pélerin, descending from the Aiguille du Midi, he will find himself on the brink of a precipice immediately overlooking the Glacier du Bossons, not far from the point where it is crossed, opposite the Grands Mulets, in the ascent of Mont Blanc. From this he will have a far better idea, than from any other point, of the real nature of the difficulties to be encountered, and the magnificence of the scenes to be enjoyed, in that daring excursion. A very steep but beautiful descent, chiefly over herbage, and parallel to the course of the Glacier du Bossons, will lead him to the valley of Chamouni, 2 miles below the village. A short day is only necessary for this interesting excursion; or he may with some difficulty pass on the N. side under the glaciers of Greppond, and Blettière to the châlets of Blettière and the Aiguille du Plan (see *k*).

d. The Flegère.—From the facility with which this mountain can be ascended, and the admirable view of Mont Blanc which it commands, it is the one most generally attained by ladies. It may be accomplished on mules the whole way, or part of the way in a char by those who are afraid of fatigue, and there is no occasion for a guide except to show the way. The point attained lies exactly opposite the Glacier du Bois, or Mer de Glace ; and from no point

is the remarkable group of Aiguilles which surround the Aiguille Verte more finely seen. The Montanvert is visited for the sake of its proximity to the Mer de Glace ; the Flegère, to enjoy a view of Mont Blanc with its attendant objects. From Chamouni to the Flegère requires only 2½ hrs., and about 2 hrs. to return. The road that leads to it lies up the valley, to the hamlet of *les Prés*, where it turns off to the l. towards the Aiguille de Chalanods, one of the Aiguilles Rouges, where a steep path up the bed of a winter torrent commences and leads up to the pasturage of Pra de Viola. Thence a good hour through a wood is required to attain the Croix de la Flegère, which commands a view of the whole range, from the Col de Balme to the furthest glacier that, below Chamouni, streams into the valley, which lies in a great part of its extent in delicious repose beneath the observer.

Within 2 minutes' walk of the Cross is the *Châlet* of Flegère, which affords shelter in unfavourable weather, and where refreshment may be had : for sight-seeing is turned to good account in every place in the neighbourhood of Chamouni, where the visitors are numerous enough to ensure a sale of the provision made. It has been enlarged, and even contains a bed or two. The height of the Croix de Flegère is 6350 ft., about 3000 feet above the valley. There is a path from the Flegère to the Breven, which the guides propose to convert into a mule-track.

If the traveller be pressed for time, and can only visit one of the spots of interest around Chamouni, it should be the Montanvert ; if two, that and the Flegère; unless he feels capable of greater things, in which case, instead of the Flegère, he should at once ascend the

e. Breven.—An excursion attended with some fatigue, yet easily practicable in 10 hrs., allowing 2 hrs. on the top. A good walker will ascend from Chamouni to the top in 3¼ hrs. and descend in 2 hrs. There is a tolerable mule-path, commencing behind the *Ch. of Chamouni*, by which you may ride in 2 hours to the Châlets of Planpra (two-thirds of the ascent), where the mules are left.

Above Planpra, either a fatiguing path may be taken, which is cut in the rocks, or one that leads directly up the pasturages, which, when dry, are very slippery ; many patches of snow are passed, and it is not uncommon to observe the red fungus upon it, such as Captain Parry noticed in the high latitudes of his northern voyages. At the end of an hour from Planpra, the path reaches the base of a steep rock, which it is necessary to climb by *La Cheminée*, a sort of open fissure or chimney, about 50 ft. high. Half a mile further on there is a convenient path by which this precipitous rock can be turned and avoided by a détour. Above it the path lies up a gentle slope, to the summit of the Breven; this has an elevation of about 8500 English feet above the level of the sea, or 5000 above Chamouni, not more than two-fifths of the height of Mont Blanc above the valley. This elevation, however, offers the finest view of the whole mass of Mont Blanc of all the numerous sites whence it can be seen. The vale of Chamouni alone separates them, and owing to this proximity every peak and glacier, and even crevices in the glaciers, can be distinguished ; every pasturage and châlet in that band on the mountain side which lies above the pine-forests and below the eternal snows.

When adventurous travellers ascend Mont Blanc, numerous visitors crowd the Flegère and the Breven to watch their progress, for the course lies like a map, from the village to the summit, and with a good glass, every step they take may be observed. From the Buet, 4000 ft. higher, there is a more extended horizon, but the Breven conceals all the lower belts of Mont Blanc, and as the Buet is double the distance from the peak of the "Monarch," he is not so distinct, nor offers a scene half so grand as the view of the entire range

from the Col de Balme to the Col de Vosa, for the cross on one and the pavillon on the other may be seen from the Breven.

The return to Chamouni may be varied by passing on the W. side of the Breven, above the valley of Dioza, near to a little lake, then descending by the châlets of Calaveiran, towards the village of Chapeau, a path leads down to les Ouches, in the valley of Chamouny, and thence up the valley to the priory, or the tourist may return by the Flegère.

The Breven and the Aiguilles Rouges form the N.W. boundary of the vale of Chamouni, nearly throughout its extent. It is strikingly distinguished, however, from its neighbour by its ridge being unbroken, and even rounded, though it offers on the side of Chamouni a vast line of precipices, apparently inaccessible.

f. Source of the Arveron.—This affluent of the Arve formerly issued from beneath a vault or cave of ice with which the Glacier du Bois and the Mer de Glace terminate; but by one of the changes to which glaciers are constantly liable, the stream now finds its way out at the side of the glacier at a spot some way higher up, forming a waterfall which is visible from Chamouni. Consequently the spot has lost much of its interest. It is a delightful walk of an hour (3 m.), along the plain of the valley, crossing beautiful meadows and a little forest, keeping on the S. side of the Arve all the way. The char-road to the Col de Balme, and up the valley, is left at *les Prés*, where that to the source of the Arveron turns off to the rt., and passes the hamlet of *Bois*, leading in about a mile from les Prés to the source. The source may very conveniently be visited on descending from the Flegère, or by a short cut from the Montanvert, or on the way to the Chapeau. The vault of ice varies greatly in different seasons, and at different times a change of from 30 to 100 ft. of height in the arch has been remarked. At times it may be entered, but with some risk, owing to the danger of blocks of ice detaching themselves from the vault. In 1797 three persons were crushed.

The scenery around the source is very grand ; the deep blackness of the depth of vault, the bright and beautiful azure where the light is transmitted through the ice, are striking. The enormous rocks brought down by the glacier from the mountains above, here tumble over and are deposited in the bed of the Arve. Here, too, the dark forest, and the broken trunks of pines, add to the wild character of the scene.

The advance and recession of the glaciers depend upon the seasons. If it be hot, a larger quantity of ice is melted, and the glacier advances, and a wet season, by depositing a greater quantity of snow, increases its weight and force. Sometimes the difference is many hundred feet. It is not more than 30 years since the Glacier du Bois reached the forests of pines, now passed through in approaching to it.

g. The Chapeau is one of the points of view over the Mer de Glace, on the side furthest from Chamouni; from it the Aiguilles of Charmoz and Blettière are seen immediately under Mont Blanc, with the vale of Chamouni, the Breven, and other vast and interesting objects; but its chief interest lies in its proximity to the Mer de Glace, where the glacier begins to break into pyramids and obelisks of ice; and here avalanches are frequently seen. A visit to the Chapeau may be accomplished either on foot or with the mules: if you go direct to it, you must continue along the valley as far as the village of Les Tines; and, after having passed this picturesque spot, ascend a narrow road on the right hand that leads to the scattered hamlet of Lavanchè, continue through this latter by a good mule-path beside the glacier, until you arrive at the foot of the ascent to the Chapeau. Here it is necessary to leave your mules in care of a boy, while the guide conducts you to a cavern, above which is the grass mound properly called the Chapeau: strangers in general are satisfied with

a visit to the cave, whence the view is unique and very astonishing, displaying the glacier split and fractured into the needles on the verge of its descent into the valley below.

On your return from the Chapeau you descend by the same path as far as Les Tines, whence there is a road on the left to the hamlet of Les Bois, situated at the source of the Arveron. This excursion may be accomplished in about 5 hrs., and will prove one of the most agreeable and least fatiguing that are made from Chamouni.

From the Chapeau it is practicable, without much difficulty, to reach the hut on the Montanvert, at first continuing to ascend on the E. side of the glacier, to a spot where a path has been cut in the face of a precipice, nearly perpendicular, called *Mauvais Pas*, which, though difficult, is no longer dangerous, and may be traversed even by ladies, provided they have a steady head. Descending by this path, the moraine and then the glacier is reached, which may be crossed to the Montanvert (see *b*).

In the month of July, when the weather permits, a large number of heifers are driven from Chamouni, each attended by its owner, to the hut on Montanvert, for the purpose of being conducted across the Mer de Glace, to pass their summer of 3 months on the slopes of the mountains that are near the Aiguille de Dru. Before they are launched upon the sea of ice, a number of peasants precede them with hatchets and other tools, in order to level such places as may thus be rendered less dangerous, although accidents generally attend this transit. At certain intervals men are stationed to point out the line of march; the operation, which requires several hours, and is truly picturesque to witness, is worthy the attention of a stranger who should happen to be at Chamouni at the time: it is a kind of *fête* or holiday, for men, women, and children attend the procession, passing the whole day on the mountain in the full enjoyment of this extraordinary and Herculean task. One man remains on the opposite side of the Mer de Glace, as guardian to the herd, that wander about in search of the rich but scanty pastures of those untenanted mountains. He carries with him sufficient bread and cheese to last one month, which is renewed at the expiration of that period, being carried to him by some one interested in his welfare, and is the contribution of those whose heifers are under his care. He is allowed one cow, which furnishes him with milk: knitting is his chief employ, and thus he passes his time of expatriation in making stockings and contemplating the wonders of nature that surround him during 3 months of the year.

h. Excursion to the *Col de Balme* and *Tête Noire* and back without going to Martigny, in about 9½ hrs., combining the chief beauties of both passes. From the inn on the summit of the Col de Balme (Rte. 116) turning l. across meadows marked with sheep and cattle tracks, and bearing away gradually to the rt. you pass a small lake, whence a rather steep descent brings you in about an hour immediately above the valley of the Tête Noire, whence there is a magnificent view of it and of the Eau Noire for a long distance. The path now turns rt., and for ½ an hour skirts the edge of the precipice until it arrives immediately above the H. de la Tête Noire, to which it descends in zigzags. This may be done on muleback. A guide is necessary to find the path.

i. The ascent of Mont Blanc is now become very common in favourable weather, especially since that of Albert Smith, in 1851, has effectually popularized the enterprise. When Saussure ascended to make experiments at that height, the motive was a worthy one; but those who are impelled by curiosity alone are hardly justified in risking the lives of the guides. The pay tempts these poor fellows to encounter the danger, but their safety, devoted as they are to their employers, is risked for a poor consideration. It is no excuse that the employer thinks his own life worthless: here he ought to think of the safety of others.

In 1838 a Mademoiselle d'Angeville

reached the summit, and when there ordered the guides to lift her over their heads, in order that she might have been higher than any one else. A Mrs. Hamilton went up in 1854. A Swiss peasant girl has also attained to the top.

It was first ascended in 1786, and up to the end of 1852, 56 persons, exclusive of guides, had ascended. The last four years have been very favourable, and 20 or 30 people have probably made the ascent in each year. In 1820 three guides were swept off by an avalanche and lost, but when Messrs. Fellowes and Hawes went up in 1827 they took a course to the left of the Roches Rouges, and this has greatly lessened the risk of the ascent by avoiding the most dangerous part of it.

In fact, though the route is long and fatiguing, Mont Blanc is not a difficult mountain, and is far easier than Monte Rosa, Mischabel, Jung Frau, Wetterhorn, &c. The expense of the ascent is not less than 25*l.*, as those who attempt it are considered fair game for imposition. In 1855 Messrs. Kennedy and Hudson, and three other Englishmen, ascended by a new route from St. Gervais, and without any guides. For fear, however, that others should think that they can follow this example, it should be mentioned that these gentlemen had spent several seasons in mountain climbing, and were experienced icemen, and had also spent a long time in surveying and discussing Mont Blanc, so that it was tolerably well known to them. They subsequently published an account of the ascent, and also of an attempt made by them to ascend from Courmayeur.

The way from Chamouni first follows the rt. bank of the Glacier des Bossons, it then crosses the glacier, and arrives near some rocks called the *Grands Mulets.* Here it is customary to pass the night in the hut which has been built for the purpose. Starting early next morning, and ascending the Glacier of Taconay, a comparative level of snow, called the *Grand Plateau,* is reached : some time afterwards the steepest part of the ascent, called the *Mur de la Cote,* is found, up which it is generally necessary to cut steps. Having remained a short time on the top, which is a narrow ridge about 200 yards long, the descent is begun, and Chamouni is usually reached on the same evening.

The excitement of sleeping out in the mountain is part of the interest of the adventure. This may, however, be enjoyed by going to the *Grands Mulets,* an excursion in which there is little danger, and by sleeping there; choosing a moonlight night and fine weather to enjoy the extensive view, the bright sky, and the thunders of falling avalanches. Sleeping, it appears from those who have spent a night there, is not so easy, owing to the noise of the avalanches and the bites of the fleas! A hut was erected 1853, by the guides, on one of the ledges of the Grands Mulets. It measures 14 ft. by 7, and is a frame of wood, composed below at Chamouni, and carried up to the spot, with walls of the rock, and 2 glazed sliding windows. Its height is 10,000 ft. above the sea-level. It is furnished with a very simple stove, but the cold is usually intense.

j. A path is contemplated (1855) by which the *plan* of the Aiguille du Midi will be easily reached—a magnificent position.

k. Those who are fond of climbing may, by taking a steep path, ascending immediately behind the Hotel Royal, mount up through woods and pastures in 1 hr. to the châlets of Blettière dessous, thence keeping to the l., and after about ¼ hr. turning to the rt., and crossing the torrent, they will reach the châlets of Blettière dessus, and so far may be effected on mules. There is not much track after this, but keeping round a little lake, and ascending through blocks of stone and débris, an enormous moraine is reached, some 500 or 600 ft. high; by climbing up this the wild glacier of Blettière is reached (in 4 hrs. from Chamouni), across which the Aiguille of Charmoz may be ascended. Messrs. Kennedy and Blackwell attempted, in 1854, to ascend the Aiguille of Blettière by this route. Mr. Blackwell ascended to this glacier Dec. 1854, and found less snow than in the valley. By keeping to the rt. after leaving the little lake the foot of the Aiguille du Plan may be reached, whence there is a very fine view. The Montanvert may be reached by a path from the châlets of Blettière dessus.

l. The Buet. This is a fatiguing expedition, but the fatigue may be much diminished by sleeping at the châlet of the Pierre à Berard. After leaving Argentière (Rte. 116) and Treléchant you follow the Eau Noire, and in 2 hrs. from Argentière a little plain and forest is reached, and in 1½ hr. more the Pierre à Berard is found, an isolated rock, to which point mules can go. A châlet has now been built here, where beds and food can be obtained, but the charges are said to be outrageous. A new *Inn,* 1858 (?) Another curious rock, called Table au Chantre, is then passed, and the track ascends, following ridges of rocks and over beds of snow, till in 3 hrs. from the Pierre à Berard the summit (10,059 ft.) is reached, commanding a magnificent view. You may descend either to Servoz by the Châlets de Villy, or to Sixt in 6 hrs. By starting from the Pierre à Berard in the morning, Sixt may be reached in the evening. (Rte. 115 A.)

m. Another excursion may be made by crossing into Piedmont, over the *Col du Géant,* 11,146 ft. above the sea. This adventure requires 3 or 4 guides. It was performed in 1822 by 2 English ladies, Mrs. and Miss Campbell, who, with 8 guides, started at mid-day, August 18, slept out one night on the mountain, and descended the next day to Courmayeur, and a Mrs. Hamilton crossed in 1854. Saussure remained out many successive nights and days engaged in experiments on the Col du Géant; and during the prohibition of English goods by Buonaparte, smugglers crossed it from Switzerland to Italy laden with British muslins.

An hotel is talked of (1857) on the Mont Frety, on the Courmayeur side:

this would shorten the journey some 3 hrs.

n. The *Tour of Mont Blanc* may be made in 7 days. 1, 2, and 3, to Courmayeur (Rte. 118); 4, to Aosta (Rte. 107); 5, to the Great St. Bernard (Rte. 108); 6, to Martigny (Rte. 108); 7, to Chamouni. Or in 4 very long days: 1 and 2, to Courmayeur (Rte. 118); 3, to Martigny, by the Col Ferret (Rte. 110); 4, to Chamouni.

A Chamouni guide coming to Martigny is not allowed to proceed further, but a local guide must be taken thence. It is therefore best to end this tour at Martigny, whence one day's pay only need be given to a guide returning to Chamouni.

ROUTE 115 A.

SERVOZ TO GENEVA, BY SIXT.

Servoz.	
Col	4 hrs.
Sixt	5 hrs.
Geneva	37 m.

The *valley of Sixt* deserves much more attention than it has yet received. It is recommended to all lovers of the picturesque, as one of the finest in Savoy. It may be explored in going from Geneva to Chamouni (Rte. 115), turning out of the Sallenches road at Nangi.

The ascent of the *Col d'Anterne* commences at Servoz (Rte. 115). It is a mule-path, and requires about 8 hours to reach Sixt. A *guide* should be taken either from Chamouny or Servoz, who knows the way: it ought not to be attempted without. Take also provisions for the day. Near Servoz may be seen a monument to an unfortunate Dane, M. Eschen, who lost his life (1800) on the Buet, in one of the crevasses concealed beneath the snow, which render its ascent so very dangerous without an experi-

enced guide. The mountain above Servoz abounds in tertiary fossils.

It takes more than 4 hrs. to reach the Col. After leaving the upper châlets, the débris of a fallen mountain has to be crossed by a rugged path. The Col is reached through a fork-like opening, from which a magnificent view of Mont Blanc and its chain is laid open to the eye. The summit of the Col d'Anterne is 7424 ft. above the sea-level.

[To reach the top of the Buet, you turn rt. from near a small lake on the Col, by the châlets of Moide, and in 1½ hr. more, partly descending across meadows to the hamlet of Villy (the only night-quarter on the ascent), you can ride as far as Salenton, ½ hr. further. Then begins the steepest and most difficult part of the ascent, of 2 hours' toil, mostly over snow. The *summit of the Buet* is 10,050 ft. above the sea-level. It is thickly covered with snow, and on the E. N. and N. W. extend glaciers. The S. side is very precipitous. From this point Mont Blanc is seen from top to bottom in full grandeur. E. stretch the mountains of the Valais, W. the view extends over numberless rocky peaks far away into Dauphiny, and over a multitude of ridges of Savoyard mountains, you have various glimpses of the lakes of Geneva and Annecy, and the horizon is bounded by the Jura. The Buet may now be ascended more easily by Valorsine (Rte. 115 *l*). From Villy you may descend the course of the Dioza to Servoz.]

The path to Sixt skirts the E. margin of the small Lac d'Anterne. The descent on the N. side is gradual, and you arrive in about an hour at the Châlets des Sales—a cluster of filthy huts. Here you will find milk and cheese, with tolerably good water, of which there is none on the Montagnes des Fys. Near these huts are fossil shells. On quitting this spot, where women, children, and swine pig together, you continue to descend rapidly, during nearly 4 hrs., through a narrow gorge, whose beauties and luxuriant appearance are very striking after the barren and bleak pass of the mountain : cascades, rushing streams, and forests of dark and imposing feature, are amongst the varied objects worthy of attention. At

Sixt (*Inns :* H. du Fer à Cheval, very cleanly and good) ; the house was an old *Convent ;* is kept by Moccand : it is good quarters for those who desire shooting. Chamois, grouse, and partridge are to be had. Delicious trout are to be obtained in great abundance, the water of this valley not being too cold for the fish, as at Chamouni. The *guides* at Sixt are banded together, as at Chamouni, and each takes his turn. The charges are fixed: To the Buet, 10 frs. ; Fer à Cheval, 2 frs. 50 c.; Chamouni, 15 frs. Moccand the shoemaker is a good *guide* for the Buet, &c. Sixt was formerly attached to a monastery (now suppressed), founded 1144 by Ponce de Faucigny, and is beautifully situated in the valley of the Giffre, at the W. base of the Buet. Many of the inhabitants are miners, employed by an English company. The valley abounds in *waterfalls :* perhaps the one most worthy a special visit is that of *Rouget*, or *Roget*, an hour's distance from the path leading to Col d'Anterne.

Excursions.—1. To the *Fer à Cheval*, a rugged precipice, in the form of a horse-shoe, ornamented with several cascades, and thence to the Fond de la Combe, which forms the termination of the valley, 3 hrs. from Sixt. A rough char-road nearly all the way. On the way the Buet raises its snowy head (rt.) into the clouds; l. is the cascade of *la Gouille.* About ⅔ of the way, a humble monument marks the spot where the entire village of Entre Deux Nants, with 180 persons, was buried beneath a landslip. The mines near the head of the valley are difficult of access, and have external communications along the face of the precipice from adit to adit. The glacier on the top of the Fer à Cheval is remarkable for the very steep angle at which it descends to the edge of the precipice. It is said to renew itself every 7 years, its lower extremity constantly fall-

ing over into the valley down a precipice 500 ft. deep. A difficult path on the N. of it leads from Sixt into the valley of the Rhone, near St. Maurice.

2. To the *Lac de Gers*, 3 hours' walk the path crosses the valley in a S.W. direction, and then mounts by a steep ascent (passing the fine cascade of Pieu, or Gers, nearly hidden in a deep cleft) for 50 min. A ravine is then crossed, and the path mounts again on the opposite side, until the Montagne de Porte is reached—50 min. Hence there is a very fine view over Sixt—the Monts Buet and Blanc, and the Pointe de Sales. Hence to the Lac de Gers is a walk of 45 min. over ground nearly level.

A Mail Carriage, taking 2 or 3 passengers, runs three times a week to Bonneville.

There are two char-roads to Geneva, by Bonneville and by St. Jeoire; but St. Jeoire is by far the most picturesque: distance either way about 36 m.

1½ hour below Sixt is *Samoens* (*Inn*: Croix d'Or (Pellets), one of the best in Savoy), a town of 3000 Inhab.

[On the way a mule-path turns rt. near Vallon, just beyond a white stone bridge, which leads to the *Col de Coux*, and in 8 hours to Champéry, in Canton Valais (Rte. 57). It crosses 2 cols. Another path leads from Samöens over the *Col de Jour Plane* to Morsine, in the valley of the Dranse, whence it is a 7 hours' walk to *Thonon* on Lac Leman (Rte. 57).]

Tanninges, a town of 2800 Inhab., has a *castle*, now custom-house.

St. Jeoire (*Inn*: Lion d'Or can furnish a dinner but not a bed) stands at the foot of the *Môle*, a mountain very conspicuous from Geneva. Its top commands a fine view.

Nangy, on the road from Chamouni to

GENEVA, Rte. 53.

ROUTE 116.

CHAMOUNI TO MARTIGNY, BY THE
TÊTE NOIRE.

Chamouni.	Hours.
Argentière	1.45
Tête Noire	3
Forclaz	1.30
Martigny	2

7½ hours' walk: 10 with a mule, including stoppages: no guide needed. Char-road for the first 6 m. above Chamouni.

Two roads lead from Chamouni to Martigny; one by the Tête Noire, the other by the Col de Balme. Travellers are often perplexed which to choose of these two passes. The general scenery of the Tête Noire is superior; but the Col de Balme has *one view* which far surpasses any in the Tête Noire.

[Those who can spare 2½ additional hours for the journey should proceed from Chamouni to the top of the Col de Balme and enjoy the view (Rte. 117, then descending l., strike off into the Val Orsine across the pastures and through the forest, dropping down upon the village of Val Orsine. Although no path is marked for the first part of the way, this détour may be made on horseback, and is well worth the trouble, combining as it does the beauties of the two passes of the Tête Noire and Col de Balme. Another course, more direct, but not well marked, leads from the Inn on the Col de Balme to the Inn of the Tête Noire, across meadows, by the side of a small lake, and finally along the edge of the precipice above the Eau Noire, whence it descends in zigzags. (Rte. 115 *h*.)]

The road lies up the vale of Chamouni, by *Les Prés* (*Praz*), where the path to the Arveron diverges. The main route of the valley continues to the chapel and hamlet of *Tines:* here the valley narrows, and the road ascends steeply on the banks of the Arve, opposite to the bases of the Aiguilles Rouges, to some pasturages,

and the hamlet of *Les Isles ;* beyond, the Arve is crossed, and the village of *Argentière* is left on the rt. hand; this is the third and highest parish in the valley, and is two leagues from the priory; here the magnificent glacier of Argentière is seen streaming down from between the Aiguilles d'Argentière and de la Tour.

The char-road here ceases. About ½ a mile beyond the village the path divides, that to the rt. leading over the Col de Balme; taking that to the l. it rises rapidly to the miserable hamlet of Treléchant, passing what is called the Montets, a sterile gorge, and a short league from Argentière the summit of the first pass is attained; the streams on either side take different courses, that through Chamouni to the Arve, and that towards Martigny to the Rhone.

A little beyond the crest, near Poya, a savage and sterile valley opens to the left, through which the Eau Noire, the torrent of the Val Orsine, descends; and on looking up this valley, the snows of the lofty *Buet* lying behind the Aiguilles Rouges are seen. [The ascent of the Buet may be made from Couteraye or La Poya (Rte. 115 *l*) following the Eau Noire upwards.] After passing the hamlet of Couteraie, the road descends to

Val Orsine, the chief village of the valley, where it is possible to get a bed. Its church having been more than once swept away, a strong rampart of masonry and earth has been raised to defend it from similar catastrophes. There is a very beautiful waterfall on the W. side of the valley called *Cascade Barberine*, with a small *Inn* near it.

Below Val Orsine the valley narrows to a gorge, abounding in season with wild fruits: through it, the torrent forces its way into the more open valley below, acquiring in its course fresh force, from the contributions of numerous waterfalls and streams which descend from the glaciers above. In this gorge a sort of barrier or gate marks the frontier of Savoy, near to which a small redoubt has been thrown up: soon after the torrent is crossed, at a spot where a mill and some pleasant meadows contrast with the generally savage character of the deep valley.

In a wild part of the ravine the new road passes under, and quite out of sight of an overhanging rock, which bears the name of *la Barme Rousse* (Roche de Balme) : an inscription on it contains some compliments to the late Lady Guildford, which, having been nearly obliterated, has been *restored*, with mistakes " too numerous to mention," but very amusing. The Guildford stone lies off the new road, to the right.

At one place, called Maupas, a short tunnel is pierced through a rock, in a situation of singular grandeur, where it overhangs precipitously the dark valley beneath.

A short distance beyond the tunnel there is a good little *Inn*, H. de la Tête Noire, the usual halting-place between Chamouni and Martigny, (about 4½ hrs. from Chamouni). This is a very good and comfortable place for those to sleep at who are unwilling to fatigue themselves by going from Chamouni to Martigny in one day. [There is a zigzag path out of the Gorge directly from the inn, by which the summit of the Col di Balme may be reached. (Rte. 115 *h*.)]

Near this spot the road turns abruptly into the ·dark forest of Trient, passing round the shoulder of a mountain covered with dark forests : this shoulder is called the Tête Noire, beyond which the road through the forest continues for half an hour. In the depths below the forest, the torrent of the Trient is heard forcing its way into the Eau Noire, which it joins before their streams fall into the Rhone.

On leaving the forest, the valley of Trient opens, and the traveller reaches

Trient, a hamlet with a little auberge, where he may rest and refresh but the dormitory is wretched.

The little valley of Trient is deeply seated amidst pine forests, the *débris* of the surrounding mountains, and the fearful precipices from which ·these have been detached. In the plain of the valley some barley is grown, and the meadows are luxuriant.

A little way beyond the hamlet of Trient, the torrent which descends from the glacier of Trient is crossed, and a steep path leads up through the forest which clothes the mountain side of the *Forclaz* (30 min.). About half way up, the path from the Col de Balme falls in. [The traveller who is going from the Forclaz to the Great St. Bernard, and does not wish to pass by St. Branchier, may, if a pedestrian, go from the Forclaz direct to Orsières by the pretty Lac de Champè.] On the Col is a gendarme, who makes a demand of 1 fr. per passport.

From the Col de la Forclaz the view is limited, but ½ hr. walk lower down and a turn in the valley displays in perfection the course of the Rhone through the Valais, a prospect celebrated in the Alps. The descent is by fine pasturages, and 1¾ hr. are required to reach Martigny-le-Bourg. The path is much sheltered by pines and beeches, and lower in the valley by the pear and apple-trees: in the neighbourhood of these are numerous cottages, and many are passed before the path falls into the route that leads from Martigny to the Great St. Bernard, and the valley of the Drance at Martigny-le-Bourg (Rte. 106). Those who are going to St. Bernard may possibly find quarters here, but it is much better to go on 2 m. to

Martigny-la-Ville (Rte. 59). Travellers proceeding hence to Chamouni are often required to show their passports at the frontier.

It takes 2½ hrs. to ascend from Martigny to the Col de Forclaz.

From Martigny to Visp, on the road to Zermatt, is 9 hrs. posting (Rte. 59A).

[*Tête Noire to Martigny by the Gorge of the Eau Noire, Finhaut, and Vernayaz.* —The route from Tête Noire to Martigny may be varied by following the stream of the Eau Noire downwards into the valley of the Rhone, through a very beautiful gorge, instead of pursuing the usual path over the Forclaz. It is more interesting than the route over the Forclaz, and is especially preferable to it in cloudy weather, but takes a good hour longer, and is barely practicable for mules. On leaving the inn at Tête Noire, the path crosses to the l. bank of the stream, and after passing a few houses, ascends by a steep zigzag to a considerable height on the l. side of the Val de Trient, overlooking the upper part of the valley, which there makes a bend to the S., and in which Trient itself is placed. This upper part of the valley, from the height to which the path ascends, looks like a narrow black trench, and the distant view of Mont Blanc filling up the depression in the side of the valley of Chamouni, through which the road of the Tête Noire passes, is also very fine. Curious examples of "glacier markings," interesting to the geologist, may be observed on the rocks of this valley. The path continues for a long time at nearly the same elevation, affording fine views of the valley of Trient, and skirting at times fearful precipices, at others running through smiling pasturages, and passes the villages of Finhaut, Tretien, and Salvent; beyond which it leaves the inaccessible gorge through which the Trient pours into the valley of the Rhone a little to the rt., and descends by a pretty little well-wooded valley upon the village of Vernayaz, a little above the Sallenche waterfall. The scenery is very fine throughout, and the path well made; and found easily without a guide. Between Tretien and Salvent a romantic little bridge is passed, similar, and at least equal in beauty of situation, to the Pantenbrücke in the Lint-thal. The auberge at Finhaut is a miserable place, and afforded nothing but wine and *pain de seigle*; but the village itself is charmingly situated.]

ROUTE 117.

MARTIGNY TO CHAMOUNI, BY THE COL DE BALME.

	Hours.
Martigny.	
Forclaz	2½
Col de Balme	3
Argentière	2
Chamouni	1½

About 24 m., 8 hours' walk, 11 hours with a mule. No guide needed.

This road, inferior in attractions to the Tête Noire, on the whole, may be recommended to travellers who approach Chamouni from the Valais, for the sake of the magnificent perspective view of Mont Blanc and his Aiguilles from the summit of the Col de Balme. It should be taken only in very clear weather.

On leaving Martigny, the route over the Forclaz (Rte. 116), renowned for its view over the Rhone-valley, is passed; but, in descending to the valley of Trient, a path to the l. avoids the village and leads towards the valley and the dark forest, up through which lies the ascent to the Col de Balme.

The path follows the margin of the Trient upward, then crosses it and ascends to the forest of *Magnin*, which takes 40 min. to traverse. The path through it is excessively steep and fatiguing, often intercepted by the entangled roots of the pines, which form steps 2 or 3 ft. in height, and it is a subject of wonder how mules get up or down such places. At length, after climbing about 1 hr. up the mountain side, and through the forest, the traveller emerges upon the pasturages and châlets of Herbagères. Above these the ascent is gradual to the Col de Balme, where one of the finest scenes in the world bursts upon the traveller. Mont Blanc, from his summit to his base in the vale of Chamouni, lies like a model before him, surrounded by the Aiguilles of La Tour, L'Argentière, Verte, de Dru, Charmoz, Midi, &c. &c.; and each divided from its neighbour by enormous glaciers which stream into the valley. How glorious is the " Monarch," thus seen, attended by all his peaks like guards ! Below, the eye sweeps its course entirely through the vale of Chamouni, to the Col de Vosa, at its other extremity. On the rt., the Aiguilles Rouges are the nearest : beyond these, bounding the valley, lies the Breven, and more to the right the snowy summit of the Buet. It is a magnificent scene to dwell upon, and those who do not arrive at Chamouni by the Col de Balme ought to make an excursion from the Prieuré, expressly to enjoy be this most glorious view.

There is a house of refuge on the Col de Balme, where shelter and refreshment, with wine, may be had, and 5 or 6 tolerable beds are ready to receive travellers overtaken by a storm. On the descent the source of the Arve is passed, at least the highest of its springs ; the path lies down over fine pasturages, and by the châlets of Charamillan to the hamlet of La Tour, where cultivation, though scanty, is reached, and barley, oats, and flax are raised. On the banks of the torrent may be observed heaps of blackish slaty rubbish, which is brought down by the torrents, and carefully preserved by the inhabitants in small heaps. The traveller will be pleased with the sagacity of the peasants when he learns that this black slaty earth is scattered over the snow with which the fields are covered in the spring to accelerate its melting, which it really effects several weeks before it would otherwise disappear. This is owing to the warmth absorbed by the black earth from the sun's rays,—a beautiful and philosophical process which the inhabitants appear to have long known and used ; for Saussure mentions it as an old practice. Just before the valley is reached the path falls into the road to Chamouni from the Tête Noire (Rte. 116).

To go in one day from Chamouni to Trient, by the Tête Noire, and return by the Col de Balme, requires 12 or 13 hrs. When this is intended, to gain time it is desirable to take a char as far as Argentière, the road

being good enough to drive over with more despatch from Chamouni.

ROUTE 118.

CHAMOUNI TO COURMAYEUR, BY THE COL DU BONHOMME AND THE COL DE LA SEIGNE.

Chamouni.	Hours.
Col de Voza	4
Contamines	3
Nant Bourant . . .	2
Bonhomme	4
Chapiù	2
Motet	2
Seigne	1½
Courmayeur	4½

Mule-path. A journey of 3 days: 1st day to Contamines, 7 hrs.; 2nd day to Chapiù 8 hrs.; 3rd day to Courmayeur, 8 hrs. A *good* and experienced guide is essential, and the expedition should not be attempted except in fine weather. A stout walker may accomplish this route in 2 long days, sleeping at Nant Bourant or the châlets of Mont Joie. The accommodation at the châlets of Nant Bourant and Chapiù is now tolerable.

From Chamouni the road to Servoz is followed as far as

Les Ouches, where a path strikes l. up the mountain side in steep zigzags, until, within sight of the châlets de la Forclaz, it is joined (rt.) by the path from St. Gervais (Rte 115), and reaches the

Col de Voza, 7000 ft. above the sealevel. The Pavillon de Bellevue, erected on it, commands a splendid view up the vale of Chamouni, and of the Mont Blanc towards the Col de Balme. A steep descent leads down into the Val de *Montjoie*, a long valley stretching N. and S. and invaded on its E. side by the grand *glacier* of Bionnassay, sweeping down from the flank of Mont Blanc, and presenting amidst rocks and snows a wild and savage aspect. The stream issuing from it must be crossed by a wooden plank bridge, a little below the spot where the stream issues from the glacier. If you miss this bridge you will be sorely puzzled to get across. From it you traverse the meadows by a direct path, through Champel, rounding the extremity of the spur from Mt. Blanc, which bounds the S. side of the valley, and entering the Val Montjoie near the village of Tresse.

The glacier torrent of Bionnassay joins the Bon-Nant, the stream which flows through the Val Montjoie, near the village Bionnay, traversed by a mule-path from the Baths of St. Gervais (Rte. 115) to Contamines, 2½ hrs.' walk.

The views presented of Val Montjoie are very fine, extending upwards to the Bonhomme, while opposite is seen the pretty village of St. Nicholas de Veroce, at the base of the Mont Joli.

Contamines (*Inns*: H. l'Union, good; H. de Bonhomme; better accommodation than elsewhere on the road), a large village with a handsome *Church*, prettily situated on a commanding height above the valley. The traveller going on to Nant Bourant to sleep, should inquire what number of travellers are gone ahead.

The path descends from Contamines to the side of the Bon Nant, which it crosses by a bridge near the hamlet and saw-mills of Pontet; rt. runs a path to the chapel of Notre Dame de la Gorge, situated at the end of a ravine—a cul-de-sac at the base of Mont Joli. On the *Fête* of the Assumption (Aug. 15) thousands of peasants resort hither from the neighbouring valleys, on a pilgrimage to the chapel.

A very steep and rudely-paved path leads directly out of the ravine, stepwise, and through a forest: the denuded face of the granite on the path, and the large stones which fill up the interstices, make this a difficult road for mules, and a fatiguing one to men. It leads to the chalets and pasturages of

Nant Bourant, where a place for sleeping has been established, with 7 or 8 beds. Here the torrent is crossed by a stone bridge. The gulf through which it rushes has a fearful depth, and a little way down, below the bridge, the water falls into a still blacker and deeper ravine, forming the *Nant*, or cataract of the Bourant; it is difficult even from above to get a view of its furious descent.

The finest fall on the Bonnant is one seldom seen, a short ¼ hour from these châlets, on that branch of the stream which descends from the glacier of Trelatête. It is not necessary to return to the châlets in ascending the Bonhomme.

Above the châlets the valley is very narrow, the road passing through the forest, which belts and clothes the base of the Mont Joli; at length it enters upon the pasturages, which are rich, though scanty from the quantity of stones and rocks that abound. After rising above the *débris* which have fallen from the mountains, the path winds up to the châlets of *Mont Joie*, where the traveller usually rests and obtains the refreshment of bread, wine, and milk. A room has been fitted up with beds, and a traveller by sleeping here may divide the journey to Chamouni—but the room should be secured beforehand, and meat brought, as none can be got. Between Nant Bourant and these châlets huge masses of glaciers extend down the crue on the S.W. flanks of Mont Blanc; but immediately above the châlets is the vast glacier of Trelatête. This, and the black rocks which support it on one side of the valley, and the precipices and *débris* over which there is a pass to the valley of Haute Luce on the other, almost inclose these châlets as in a deep basin. Upward, the valley is closed by the Bonhomme; and, on looking back, the whole length of the Val Mont Joie is seen bounded by the peaks of the Varens above St. Martin's.

From the châlets of Mont Joie the path leads up a steep acclivity which overhangs the depths of the valley. As the mountain is ascended, it becomes more and more sterile; the pine does not grow so high as the châlets of Mont Joie, and on the next terrace above the châlets, on the *Plain des Dames*, the rhododendron is the largest shrub that flourishes. On the Plain there is a cairn, a heap of stones, which has existed from time immemorial. Tradition says, that a great lady with her suite perished here in a storm, and gave name to the fatal spot; every guide adds a stone to the cairn, and requests the traveller to do so, from some feeling of awe associated with it as a duty.

From the Plain des Dames the path leads up herbless slopes and over some patches of snow, to reach what, from below, seems to be the col. On the left, wild and abrupt precipices rise: and two of the peaked rocks there bear the name of the Bonhomme and the *Femme du Bonhomme.*

The crest, however, which lies close to these pinnacles is that of the Col de la Gauche, across which a path leads down to Maxime de Beaufort, and the whole course of the valley of Beaufort to the Bourg is seen before and below the traveller. On looking back, too, the valley of Mont Joie is seen in all its length, and these glorious scenes of Alpine valleys, with the thousand peaks which crest the chains of mountains that divide them, offer displays of scenery nowhere surpassed.

The passage of the Col du Bonhomme is at times dangerous in bad weather, owing to its exposure to the W. wind, which stirs up those fearful snow-eddies called "tourmentes" upon this outlier of the Alps.

The path of the Col du Bonhomme turns on the left from the Col de Gauche, behind the pinnacles of rock, and extends by a loose, swampy, pathless slope to the col, distant an hour from the Col de Gauche. "On the summit let the traveller beware of taking the path right before him ; it leads to Beaufort. If he be going to Courmayeur, he follows an ill-traced path on his l., over black shale (or snow during part of the season), which conducts him nearly on a level, after ¼ hour's walk, to a point some-

what higher than the last, and which is called

La Croix du Bonhomme, 8195 ft. above the sea level."—*Forbes.* From it, the beautiful mountain of the Chaffe-Quarre, one of the most elegant snow-clad peaks in the Alps, in the Val Isère (Rte. 113), is finely seen. The traveller is soon convinced here how easy it would be in fog or snow-drift to lose his way. A good guide is felt to be necessary ; for though he may reach the Col de Gauche by the posts which indicate the path, it is difficult to decide upon the direction he should take where the routes divide, and the unguided stranger may wander into courses of difficulty and danger before he is aware of either.

From the col two courses branch off ; three even are mentioned by the mountaineers : that on the l. conducts, by a wild, lofty, and difficult path, to Motet.

[A middle course, one rarely followed, leads to the Hameau du Glacier; while that on the rt. leads down, in 1½ hr., to the châlets of Chapiù, over a broken swampy ground ; and from Chapiù, in 3 hrs., the traveller can reach Bourg St. Maurice, in the Tarentaise, by the valley of Bonnaval.]

It requires 4 or 5 hrs. to go from Nant Bourant to Chapiù. The state of the weather makes an important difference in the time : the journey should never be undertaken but in fine weather, or with a good prospect of it. On the 13th of September, 1830, two English gentlemen perished in a snow-storm whilst crossing it—the Rev. Richard Braken, aged 30, and Augustus Campbell, aged 20.

Chapiù. Two poor *Inns,* H. des Voyageurs best. On the hill, to the N. E., grows a rare sweet-smelling fern. Hence a path leads in 2 hrs. up by the stream of the Versoi (which descends through Bonnaval) to the Hameau du Glacier, so called from its proximity to one of the glaciers of Mont Blanc, and, half a league further, to

The châlets of Motet. Here are 2 small inns or châlets, one containing 3, the other 4 beds, clean but rough.

B 2

Those who reach Motet direct cross the Cime du Fours, to which the path on the L, on the Col du Bonhomme, leads an hour sooner than by the *détour* to Chapiù, but the road rises 850 ft. higher, and the descent is much more fatiguing; the accommodations, too, at Motet, are much worse than those at Chapiù: it is, however, often taken, for the sake of gaining time, by those who go to Courmayeur from Nant Bourant in one day.

The ascent of the Col de la Seigne, though very tedious, is not very difficult. The summit, 1½ hr. from Motet, is 8100 ft. above the sea. It commands the whole extent of the Allée Blanche and the S. side of Mont Blanc, which, rising 11,700 ft. above the Allée Blanche, without being absolutely a precipice, is too steep to allow snow to rest long on it. The ridge of the Col de la Seigne separates the waters which run into the Rhone from those which are tributaries of the Po.

"From the *Col de la Seigne*, an Alpine view of extraordinary magnificence burst upon us. We looked upon Mont Blanc, and along the course of the valleys which divide Piedmont from the Valais, and extend nearly 30 miles on the eastern side of its enormous mass, through the Allée Blanche, the Val Veni, and the Val d'Entrèves, to the Col Ferrex. Two immense pyramids of rugged rock rear from the valley their scathed heads, and appear like guards to the 'monarch of mountains;' beyond and below them lay the little lake of Combal, whence issues one of the sources of the Doira Baltea ; and down the sides of Mont Blanc appeared to stream the glaciers of the Allée Blanche and the Miage ; whilst the distant peaks which overhang the western side of this long valley or valleys (for different portions of it, from the Col de la Seigne to the Col Ferrex, bear different names) give a peculiarly grand and severe aspect to the scene ; among these the Géant and the Grand Jorasse are distinguished. The eastern side of the valley is formed by the

Cramont, and a range of mountains which extend to the Col Ferrex, and terminate the vista in Mont Velan and the masses which surround the pass of the Great St. Bernard. The summit of Mont Blanc was occasionally enveloped in clouds, and the changes which these produced upon the scene were often strikingly beautiful. Most travellers, whose expectations have been formed upon the descriptions in guide-books, are led to believe that the E. side of Mont Blanc is one vast precipice, from the summit down to the Allée Blanche : it is certainly much more abrupt than towards the vale of Chamouny ; but no such anticipation will be realised in the magnificent view from the Col de la Seigne.

"From this col, leading across the great chain of the Alps, we began our descent over some beds of snow, which, lying on the northern side of the path, remain unmelted. After a tedious descent to the first pasturage, at the base of the two immense pyramids which formed so striking a feature from the summit, we sat down upon the short and soft grass of the pasturage of the châlets of the Allée Blanche, to rest the mules and ourselves, and took refreshment, which we had brought with us. The sward around us was 'enamelled with beautiful flowers : of these, the broad patches of the deep blue gentianella were the richest in colour ; the Alpine ranunculus, and a hundred other varieties, embellished the place where we rested; being surrounded by, and in the immediate vicinity of, the loftiest mountains in Europe.

" Soon after leaving this delightful spot, we skirted the little lake of *Combal* by a very narrow path.— After passing the lake at the lower extremity, across an embankment of great thickness and strength, the path descends on the l. side of the torrent, which struggles with horrid violence in continued cataracts down the ravine for several miles, particularly where, in passing by the glacier of Miage, our route lay amidst rocks and stones, the *débris* of the mountain, brought down by the glacier, of which it concealed the base and sides.

" The path is rough and stony here and there, and a little water from streams trickles across it.

" At length we escaped from this fatiguing part of our route, and entered the beautiful meadows of the Val Veni, which are separated from the Val d'Entrèves by a high ridge that skirts the forest of St. Nicolas. There are several granges, in which the great quantities of hay made in the meadows and slopes of this valley are stored.

" The forest of St. Nicolas, which we traversed on our way to Cormayeur, is opposite to some extensive buildings at the foot of the Glacier de Brenva. These were formerly occupied by miners, who prepared the lead and copper ores raised near this place ; but the expenses having exceeded the profits, these buildings are now falling to decay. Across the valley we saw the beautiful glacier of Brenva appearing through the enormous larches and pines of the forest, presenting to us a scene deservedly esteemed one of the finest in the Alps. We now rapidly descended by a narrow road which fearfully overhangs the lower range of the glacier of the Brenva whose sides were covered with masses of granite and rocks of great magnitude. The torrent which we had seen rushing through the valley passed beneath the glacier, and reappeared increased by a stream, which issued from an arch at the termination of the glacier, like that of the Arveron in the vale of Chamouny."—*Brockedon.*

" The chief glaciers of the Allée Blanche (on the N. side) are, 1. G. de l'Estellette ; 2. G. de l'Allée Blanche; 3. G. de Miage ; 4. G. de la Brenva. The 2nd and 3rd of these have formed barriers across the valley by moraines, so as to have occasioned lakes by the interruption of the river course. That formed by the Glacier de l'Allée Blanche is nearly filled up by alluvial matter ; but an extensive flat attests its former existence, together with the barricade of débris through which the river now tumbles in a foaming rapid. The moraine of the G. de Miage is perhaps the most extraordinary in the whole Alps, and has given rise to the *Lac de Combal.* Below the moraine of Miage, which occupies the valley for some space, are some châlets, and then a level fertile plain, whilst the valley widens, and becomes less savage and more romantic. Trees appear on both sides, especially on the rt., where the forest is very fine, and clothes all the N. slope of a conical summit, called *Mont Chetif,* or Pain de Sucre, which is composed of granite, though separated from the great chain by secondary rocks. The paths through these woods are most beautiful and striking. That leading to Cormayeur, after attaining some height above the torrent, proceeds nearly on a level, until, emerging from the trees, we come into full view of the magnificent Glacier de la Brenva, which, occupying a hollow to the E. of Mont Blanc, pours its mass into the valley filled up in a good measure with its moraine, forming a kind of bridge which it has pushed before it, and on which it bestrides obliquely the Allée Blanche, abutting against its opposite side at the foot of the Mont Chetif. A chapel, dedicated to Notre Dame de la Guérison, stands on the rt. of the way, exactly opposite to the ice ; and another steep descent conducts us again to the bank of the river, which here turns abruptly, after its confluence with the stream of the Val Ferrex, into a ravine, cutting the range of the Pain de Sucre. The united streams are passed by a wooden bridge at the Baths of La Saze, and 20 min. more brings the traveller to *Courmayeur.* (Rte. 107).

ROUTE 119.

SALLENCHES TO L'HÔPITAL CONFLANS
(ALBERTVILLE), BY UGINE AND
BEAUFORT.

From *Sallenches* (Rte. 115), a new
route is being constructed, which, if it
proceed with spirit, will one day open
a char or carriage communication
between the valley of the Arve and
that of the Isère, in the Tarentaise.
It is still incomplete between Flumet
and Ugine.

The road which has been made or
improved to *Megève* rises directly
up the steep side of one of the slopes
of Mont Foron to the village of
Comblou, about an hour's ascent.
Its gay spire is seen from the road to
Chamouni, near Passy, and also from
the valley of Maglans in approaching
to it. From Comblou there is a most
beautiful prospect, well worthy the
traveller's walk from Sallenches or
St. Martin's. It commands the valley
of Maglans on one side, and the
Varens and the upper valley of the
Arve on the other. The Aiguilles de
Varens rise in great grandeur directly
en face of the spectator; and on the
rt. of the upper Arve, all the peaks
and glaciers of Mont Blanc, and its
extreme summit, are as distinctly
seen as in a model. Few spots for
such prospects can vie with the village of Comblou.

A little beyond Comblou the highest part of the road is passed. Thence
the distance is a league, over a road
nearly level, to Megève. Here are
two miserable inns. From Megève
a road leads over the Pas Sion, a col
which divides the valley of Haute Luce
from the valley of the Arly, by the
shortest course to Beaufort.

" From Megève to the Baths of St.
Gervais is a delightful walk through
fields and woods, commanding a
splendid view of the valley of the
Arve the whole way. The path turns
off from the road to Comblou about
½ a mile from Megève."—F.

From Megève the road descends
the valley of the *Arly* in

2 hrs. to *Flumet*, a little town of
Upper Faucigny, containing about
1000 Inhab., near the confluence of the
Flon and the Arly. On a rock are
the ruins of a castle, in which the first
baron of Faucigny resided.

Beyond Flumet the road is only
practicable for mules: it is excessively hilly and wild. The valley of
the Arly is a gorge, deeply seated,
and bears the name of the Combe of
Savoie. In 2 hrs. from Flumet it leads
to *Heri*, a village situated in a most
agreeable spot, surrounded by high
mountains covered with pine forests.

Below Heri, the path, in many
places cut out in the mountain side,
overhangs the deep bed of the Arly,
and alternate spots of savageness and
beauty are found throughout this valley. Its richness in walnut-trees is
celebrated, and the oil which the nuts
furnish is an important article of
commerce.

Ugine (*Inn:* H. de la Grande Maison)
is a large ill-built town, containing
3000 Inhab., famous for its fairs of
cattle and mules. To the N., on a
steep limestone rock, there are the
remains of a lofty square tower,
flanked by other towers, which defended the *Castle* attacked in the 9th
century by the Saracens. The *Castle*
was destroyed in the 13th century
by Humbert, first dauphin of Vienne.
It is situated on the rt. bank of the
Arly, on the road between Faverges
and Annecy (Rte. 120).

From Ugine an excellent carriage
road continues down the Arly to
l'Hôpital Conflans, through a deep
and rich valley. Before arriving at
l'Hôpital, one sees on the other side
of the Arly the valley of Beaufort,
where the Doron, which flows through
it, falls into the Arly.

[A hilly and rough road leads in
12 m. from Albertville, ascending
the course of the Doron into the wild
and secluded *Valley of Beaufort* to St.
Maxime de Beaufort, its chief town,
situated at the junction of 5 valleys,
accessible only by mountain-paths and
surmounted by cols more or less difficult, averaging 6500 ft. in height: they
are the Vals—de Haute Luce, traversed

by the Dorinet N.E. ; la Gite, E. by the Doron ; Pontcelamot, S. by the Argentine ; Trecols and Roselein from the S. The chief passes are—La Bâtia into Val d'Isère ; 2. The Louse and Grand Cormet (fine view) on the S. into the Isère en Tarentaise ; 3. On the N.E. Col de Fenêtre and Col Joly lead to Chamouni by the Val de Mont-Joie ; 4. E. La Platte, or Col de Biollay from La Gite to the Val de Chapieu.

Between the Doron and Dorinet rise the *Rocks of Enclaves*—a curious granite group arranged round an oval basin, so shut in by a granitic ridge that the waters from it are discharged only through subterranean channels, or over numerous fine falls into the valley of La Gite, the finest of all in scenery. In the centre of the basin stand the châlets of Putray. The *Inn* kept by Henri Martin at St. Maxime is the best in the district.]

L'Hôpital is divided from *Conflans* only by the Arly; the former being situated on its right bank, the latter on the rocky slopes on the other side.

Conflans is an ancient town, with about 1300 Inhab. It was formerly surrounded by walls, and defended by 2 very strong forts. It resisted the troops of Francis I. in the war of 1536, when it was partly burnt, and its two forts demolished. It has one or two curious old buildings; a glorious view from its Promenade over the valleys of the Isère and Arly, towards the Grande Chartreuse mountains. A little below Conflans, near the banks of the river, there is a royal smelting-house, *Fonderie Royale,* where the silver, from the ore raised in some mines in the neighbourhood, is reduced: it is seldom used.

Albertville (a name given, 1835, in compliment to the late king of Sardinia, Charles Albert ;) previously called *L'Hôpital.* (*Inns:* H. des Balances, kept by Donet, good; Etoile du Nord). L'Hôpital, with its wide streets and clean appearance, is one of the nicest little towns in Savoy; it has about 1500 Inhab., and lying in the high road, by which communi-cation is held with Ugine, Annecy, and Sallenches, with Chambéry, and with Moutiers Tarentaise, it has, since the establishment of good roads, been daily increasing in importance. *Diligences* by Faverges to Annecy—to Moutiers and Chambéry.

ROUTE 120.

GENEVA TO CHAMBÉRY, BY AIX. :

Geneva to Culoz (Rly.), 41 m.
Culoz to St. Innocent (Steamer), 1 hr.
St. Innocent to Chambéry (Rly.), 12 m.

The Lyons and Geneva Rly. now takes travellers to Culoz, whence the branch to St. Innocent on the road to Chambéry is not completed.

The high road to Aix passed through Annecy (Rte. 121), 56 m. At present travellers go from Geneva to Culoz by Rly. (Rte. 53). At Culoz an omnibus takes them to the Rhone, where they embark in a small steamer.

[Formerly steamers plied between Aix and Lyons and as high as Seyssel. The Rhône is here very rapid, though navigable for 12 m. above Chanaz, and proceeds through rather fine and wild scenery, in which the country-house of the Prince de Brignes is situated, to *Pierre Châtel.* Here the Rhône passes through an exceedingly narrow ravine with precipitous sides, having at the narrowest point a light suspension bridge thrown over it, and high over head the French fort of Pierre Châtel. Nothing on the Rhine is finer than this part of the Rhône, and the scenery is good for the next 2 hrs., when the

Sault du Rhône is reached, consisting of two rocky rapids, much talked of, but dangerous only to small boats. The river after this proceeds for another hour and a half through hills varying about 1000 ft. high, with several ruined castles on the heights. The country afterwards becomes flat, and the last 3 hrs. are dull and uninteresting. There is now a Rly. from Lyons through Culoz to Geneva. See HANDBOOK FOR FRANCE. Rtes. 155, 156.]

The steamer after descending a short distance down the Rhone, which is here very rapid, at Chanaz, the Sardinian custom-house, turns sharp round and enters a very tortuous natural canal, called Canal de Savières, by which the waters of the lake reach the Rhône. The steamer passing through the meadows, the canal being scarcely wide enough for the passage, is twisted skilfully round the sharp corners, and in about ¼ hr. reaches the Lake du Bourget described below : and in about ½ an hr. more lands at St. Innocent, a station on the Rly., or carries the passengers directly on to *Port au Puer*, whence about 1½ m. through shady lanes to

Aix les Bains (Inns : Poste, good;. —H. Venat, well situated, dear; charge 11 fr. a-day for bed, breakfast, and table-d'hôte ; H. Guillard ; H. Jeandet ; H. de l'Univers. There are numerous boarding-houses and lodgings. Maison Arc Romain is a good pension (1857).

This watering-place, situated at a little distance to the E. of the pretty Lac du Bourget, and containing 4000 Inhab., was known to the Romans under the name of Aquæ Gratianæ, and it is still resorted to on account of its mineral springs, and of the attractions of the beautiful country round it, by more than 3000 visitors yearly, many of them from Lyons, and coming more for amusement than for the baths.

Its *Mineral Springs* are warm and sulphureous; they have a temperature varying between 100° and 117° Fahr. The *Alum Spring* (incorrectly so called, as it contains no alum) issues from beneath an antique arch; it is partly employed in douching horses. The *Sulphur Spring* is exceedingly copious; it is drunk at the source, and is good for correcting derangement of the digestive organs. These waters, how-

ever, are chiefly employed for baths, and above all for douche baths. A handsome bath-house has been built by a former king of Sardinia, into the apartments of which the hot water is introduced in streams, which descend from a height of 8 or 10 ft. upon the patient. After undergoing the douching process, which consists in having the water applied to various parts of the body, while they are at the same time subjected to brisk friction by the hands of two attendants, the patient is wrapped up, dripping wet, in a blanket, carried home in a sedan-chair, and put into a warm bed. A brisk perspiration succeeds. The appearance of the baths is not tempting. There is a regular medical staff presided over by M. le Baron Despine, who has studied in England and speaks English; a code of laws as to the baths, &c.; and every conceivable complaint is curable by one or other of the springs.

Balls are given twice a week during the season in the room at the *Casino,* where there is also a reading-room. Rouge et noir and roulette were carried on to a great extent, but were stopped in 1855.

There are several very interesting *Roman Remains,* a *Triumphal Arch,* in debased Doric style, probably of the 3rd or 4th centuries, raised by T. Pompeius Campanus; a portion of an Ionic *Temple of Diana,* of which the cella is quite perfect ; it can be best examined from the garden of the cure, upon which it abuts. Other portions of Roman buildings are incorporated in the remains of the *Château* of the Marquises of Aix, a building of the 16th century. The *Roman Baths* are entered from Madame Chabert's garden. The principal portion visible is an hypocaust. The arch is a most perfect piece of construction, well worth the architect's consideration.

The caverns of St. Paul (tickets, 50 c.) are curious, and contain huge stalactites.

A portion of the time not occupied in the bathing process may be agreeably employed in rides and walks in the neighbourhood, whose varied and beautiful scenery cannot fail to afford pleasure and amusement. One excursion is to the waterfall of *Grezy*, in a picturesque ravine about 3 m. from Aix. The watercourse is covered over by vines on trellisses, and the water falls among rocks surmounted with crazy old sawing mills. There is no danger in the place, yet a French lady was drowned here before the face of the Empress Hortense in 1813. Not far from the waterfall are the ruins of an old castle. Another favourite excursion is to *Haute Combe*, on the opposite or N.W. shore of the *Lac du Bourget* (Borghetto). This monastery, beautifully situated close to the lake, and at the foot of the Mont du Chat, was founded in 1225. Its Gothic chapels were the burial-places of the princes of Savoy, canons of Citeaux, &c. Among them is Boniface archbishop of Canterbury, son of Count Thomas of Savoy, who died in 1270; Amadeus V., VI., and VII.; Jeanne de Montfort and her husband; Peter of Savoy; Anne of Zähringen, &c. The existing convent, erected 1743, was pillaged and desecrated at the French revolution; in the ch. the coffins were opened and rifled, and the monuments, paintings, and stained glass destroyed. It was, however, entirely rebuilt in a peculiar florid Gothic style about the year 1824 by Charles Felix, king of Sardinia, and contains many magnificent monuments, all however either modern or so restored as not to leave much of the original. The convent is once more occupied by Cistercian monks.

Near Haute Combe is a tower called *Phare de Gessens*, the view from which is described by Rousseau. About ½ m. beyond the abbey is an intermittent spring, called *Fontaine des Merveilles.*

The Lac du Bourget is full of fish, and forms a great addition to the charms of Aix.

The W. shore of the lake consists of a tall precipice of limestone, rising almost perpendicularly from the water's edge, and extending from Haute Combe to the castle of Bordeau. Behind Bordeau is the Mont du Chat (Rte. 125).

At the S. extremity of the lake are the ruins of the castle of Bourget, the residence of the ancient counts of Savoy, down to the time of Amedeus V. or the Great, who was born in it in 1249. He sent for the painter Giorgio di Aquila, a pupil of Giotto, to decorate its interior ; and some fragments of fresco, now nearly effaced, in a cabinet formed in the thickness of the wall of one of the towers, are probably a part of his work.

An agreeable way of visiting the scenery of the lake is to take a boat from Aix to Haute Combe, and then send it to wait at the little village of Bordeau, at the foot of the ascent to the Mont du Chat; and after visiting the chapel and fountain, walk by agreeable by-paths along the heights which skirt the S. side of the lake, and descend by the great road from the Mont du Chat (Rte. 125). The boats, both on this lake and on the lake of Annecy, are far superior to those on the Swiss or Italian lakes. The men row well and understand something of sailing, but their charges are high.

[Those who enter Switzerland by Aix, and do not wish to go round by Geneva, may at once cross from Annecy to Bonneville and thence to St. Martin, and so on to Chamouni. The road is excellent, but there are (1854) no diligences or posting arrangements beyond Annecy. A voiturier will go from Aix in one day to Bonneville, and next morning to St. Martin, so as to allow ample time for reaching Chamouni on the second day.]

The route from Aix is very beautiful as it passes below the finely wooded slopes of the Mont d'Azi and Dent de Nivolet, its undulations often presenting views of the lake of Bourget, and the fine range of the Mont du Chat. The approach to CHAMBÉRY (Rte. 127) is highly picturesque, and offers some beautiful views.

Rly. from Chambéry (Rte. 127 A).

ROUTE 121.

GENEVA BY ANNECY TO AIGUEBELLE,
ON THE MONT CENIS ROAD.

112 kil. = 70 Eng. m.

Geneva.	Kil.	Eng. m.
St. Julien . . .	10	= 6
Cruseilles . . .	16	= 10
Annecy	17	= 11
Faverges . . .	25	= 16
Albertville . . .	20	= 12
Aiguebelle . . .	24	= *15

This road was formerly adopted, but will no doubt be abandoned for the Rlwy. (Rtes. 120, 127 A.)

On leaving Geneva the road passes through the Plain Palais, crosses the Arve, and continues through Carouge and the richly cultivated plain of the Arve, until it rises to the village of

St. Julien, on the frontier of Savoy, where the passports of travellers are examined. The baggage is searched a little further on. An extra horse is required this stage.

The road ascends a long hill to the Mount Sion, a ridge which runs nearly at right angles with the Mont Saleve. From its height, more than 3300 ft. above the level of the sea, the views of the Lake of Geneva, the Jura, and the deep valley of the Rhone flowing into France, form a fine panorama. The course of the road is generally high, though it undulates until it rises to

Cruseilles, a little town possessing 1300 Inhab., the ruins of an old castle, and a dirty inn; opposite to which one of those crosses is placed, so common within the archbishopric of Chambéry, which invites everybody, under a promise of 40 days' indulgence, to say an ave and a pater.

The road to Annecy from Cruseilles crosses the stream of the Usses, sunk in a deep defile, by the lofty

Suspension bridge of La Caille, of iron-wire, erected by the Sardinian government to carry the road directly across and on a level, and thus avoid the lengthened detours of the old road, which may be still seen winding down the depths below. The length is 636 ft., and height of the road above the river is 656 ft. It is called the Pont Charles Albert, and was opened in Sept. 1839. A toll of 50 sous is paid for 2 horses, and 60 sous for a larger number.

It is a pleasing drive by the villages of Alonzier, Caval, Pringy, and Metz, through a hilly country, often presenting fine points of view; at length it crosses the Mont des Bornes, and descends a hill side which overlooks the plain and lake of Annecy, and the fine mountain scenery which surrounds it. There is a singular beauty in the views thus presented, and a charm in the approach to Annecy which is likely to be long remembered. At the Pont de Brogny the river Fier, which falls into the Rhone at Seissel, is crossed, and in half an hour the traveller finds himself at

Annecy. (Inn: H. de Genève, clean; excellent Mâcon wine; trout in perfection, and a fine cheese made in the mountains). This industrious city of 6000 Inhab. is situated at the extremity of a great plain, and on the sedgy borders of a lake, which is discharged by canals that cross its streets.

Annecy is a picturesque and clean old town, the shops in many of its streets are under arcades, and there is an air of respectable antiquity about it—though this, the ancient capital of the duchy of Geneva, is only the modern town. In the 12th century it was known as Anneciacum novum, to distinguish it from Anneciacum vetus, which formerly existed on the slopes of the beautiful hill of Annecy-le-vieux. Numerous medals of the Roman emperors of the two first centuries of the Christian era have been found here, and inscriptions, sepulchres, urns, and fragments of statues, and of a temple, attest the presence of this people.

In the 12th century the present Annecy was distinguished from Annecy-le-Vieux, by William I. Comte of the Genevais. When the house of Geneva became extinct, Annecy passed to that of Savoy. In 1412 it was totally burnt. To assist in restoring the inhabitants to their town, Amedeus VIII., duke of Savoy, gave them many privileges, and enabled them to establish flax-spinning works, which have continued to be its principal manufacture.

Perhaps there is no town in Europe whose history has been so long associated with manufactures as Annecy.

The linen bleacheries established in 1650, which have always sustained a high reputation, are still flourishing. Encouraged by Napoleon, when Savoy was under the French government, the late Baron Duport, of Turin, established here the first cotton works; these still flourish. He subsequently established those at Ponte, in Val d'Orca. (Rte. 111.)

Even now the manufactures of Annecy are not all enumerated; there are others of black glass—of sulphuric acid, of printed cottons, &c., and in the neighbourhood a fine vein of coal is worked, at Entreverne,— and at the village of Crans there are oil, corn, and fulling mills on the Fier, and mills for the manufacture of paper.

There are many objects of interest among the public buildings of Annecy —the ancient *Château*, the residence of the family of Genevois-Nemours— the old Bishop's palace—the *Cathedral*, with its sanctuary. In the modern *Ch. of St. François* are deposited the relics of Saint François de Sales, and the Mère (Sainte) Chantal. The translation of their relics from the Cathedral was made in 1826, with great ceremony.

"The tender friendship that long subsisted between St. Francis de Sales and La Mère Chantal, has given to their memory and relics, with pious Catholics, a degree of interest similar to that excited by the remains of Abélard and Eloïse.

"St. Francis de Sales was descended from the noble family of de Sales in Savoy; he was born in 1567. Having devoted himself to the church, and evinced great zeal and eloquence in its defence, he was ordained prince and bishop of Geneva by Pope Clement VIII., for the popes assumed the right to confer these titles long after the Reformed religion had been established at Geneva. Annecy being made a bishop's seat when the Genevese expelled the chapter from their city, St. Francis de Sales died at Lyons in 1622, and was buried at Annecy. His canonisation took place in 1665: but before that event his remains were so highly valued by the inhabitants, that, when the city was taken by the French in 1630, one of the six articles of capitulation stipulated that the body of the venerable Francis de Sales should never be removed from the city."—*Bakewell's Tour in the Tarentaise.*

Hither fled Rousseau on escaping from Geneva ; and many passages of the Confessions relate to his residence at Annecy.

At the lower extremity of the lake there is a beautiful *Avenue* and promenade, where fairs and public amusements are held. The views from it of the mountain and the lake are fine. Here a bronze statue has been erected to *Berthollet* the chemist, a native of Talloires on the E. side of the Lake of Annecy, by his fellow-citizens. There are many pleasant walks in its pretty neighbourhood; the only drawback being the swamps.

The level of the lake of Annecy is about 1400 ft. above that of the sea; it abounds in fine fish; among those least known to travellers are the lotte, and a fish peculiar to this lake, the *vairon.* Boating seems to be a favourite amusement at Annecy, as there are several respectable private pleasure-boats on the lake. A pleasant excursion may be made by the lake to Château Duing (see below); charge 4 fr., or 8 fr. to go and return. In ascending the lake, an opening in the lofty mountains, which bound its N.E. side, discloses the *Château of Menthon,* on the delicious slopes of a recess:

here St. Bernard, the "Apostle of the Alps," was born, and the place of his nativity, independent of its local beauty, cannot fail to interest the traveller. (Rte. 108.)

If the traveller have time, a short excursion may be made from Annecy to Annecy-le-Vieux; where, on the inner and S. angle of the tower, a Roman inscription will be found.

The establishment at Crans, of the hydraulic machines for the drainage of the lake, is also deserving of a visit.

[From Annecy there is an excellent road to Bonneville on the way to Chamouni. From this road, or by Menthon over the mountains, the valley of Thones may be visited; very unfrequented by strangers, but full of beautiful scenery.]

From Annecy to Aix the road passes through a rich and pleasing country, amidst cottages and trellised vines, by the villages of Vieugy and Balmont to

Alby, a village containing about 800 Inhab. It is situated on the Chéron, and one of the most remarkable objects between Annecy and Aix is its fine stone bridge—a single arch of great height and span, which is thrown across the Chéron, at Alby. This village was more important formerly when the Comtes of Geneva surrounded it with a wall and castles, of which some traces exist, which were built on both sides of the river to defend the passage of the valley. Beyond Alby the route is without particular interest, except at

Albens, a village of 1000 Inhab. Beyond Albens the road soon descends, and overlooks the plain of Aix, where that town, the lake of Bourget, and the basin of Chambéry, bounded by the Mont du Chat, the Mont d'Azi, the Mont Grenier, present a scene of singular beauty.

A good road carried along the S.W. shores of the lake of Annecy leads to Faverges. About two-thirds of the distance is the *Château Duing*, placed on a neck of land which runs out into the lake. Here many strangers come to board and lodge during the summer, and enjoy the most delightful excursions in its delicious neighbourhood.

Opposite the Château Duing is Talloires, the birthplace of the chemist Berthollet.

From the Château Duing, the road to Faverges continues up the valley of Eau Morte about 3 m.; it is so nearly level that the plain of the valley is often inundated.

Faverges (*Inn*: Poste, good) has a population of about 2000. It is beautifully situated amidst wooded slopes and mountains; it is well cultivated, and abounds in rich meadows. It was known in the 12th century as Fabricarium, a name arising from its numerous forges for copper and iron. It still possesses silk-mills, manufactories of cutlery, and tanneries; and since the completion of the road by Ugine into the Tarentaise it is daily improving. Its old castle is finely situated.

A slight elevation divides the head of the valley of the Eau Morte from that of the stream of Monthoux, which runs into the Arly at Ugine. (Rte. 119.) The valley of Monthoux is richly wooded and picturesque. A new road has been made from Faverges to Albertville (l'Hôpital) along the plain, by which the dirty town and hill of Ugine are avoided.

Albertville (L'Hôpital). (Rte. 119.)

Leaving Albertville, the road passes through Gfésy; it there leaves the Montmeillan road, and shortly after crosses the Isère by a wooden bridge, where a toll is paid (18 sous for a carriage with 2 horses and 3 persons).

Aiguebelle. (Rte. 127.)

ROUTE 122.

CHAMBÉRY TO LANSLEBOURG, BY ALBERTVILLE, MOUTIERS, TIGNES, AND THE COL D'ISERAN.

Chambéry to Lanslebourg, 122 m.

	Kil.		Eng. m.
Chambery.			
Montmelian . .	15	=	9
Grésy	22	=	13½
Albertville . . .	14	=	8½
Moutiers . . .	28	=	17½
Aime	16	=	10
Bourg St. Maurice .	14	=	8½
	Leagues.		
Ste. Foi	3	=	9¼
Tignes	3½	=	10¾
Laval	2	=	6¼
Bonneval . . .	4	=	12½
Lanslebourg . .	5	=	15½

Railway to St. Pierre d'Albigny, beyond Montmelian, and to Aiguebelle, from which public conveyances start for Albertville.

A post-road as far as Albertville, thence mule-path.

Montmelian. (Rte. 127 A.) Here the post routes to the Mont Cenis and the Val Isère divide: the latter ascends nearly up to the head of the Val Isère, and, after crossing the Col d'Iseran, descends by the valley of the Arc to Lanslebourg.

Montmelian is left, after having ascended through its steep streets to where two roads branch off: one, on the l., leads to Aix; the other, on the rt., proceeds along the mountain side, on the rt. bank of the Isère, to

St. Pierre d'Albigny, a neat little town with a good inn. The Isère flows through a portion only of its broad winter bed, leaving the blanched stones to mark its extent at that season. The slopes around Montmelian and St. Pierre are celebrated for the wine they produce. An omnibus to the St. Pierre Stat. on the Rlwy.

A little beyond St. Pierre is a fine feature in the scenery of the valley, the *Château de Miolans*. It is built on a mass of rock jutting out of the mountain side 800 or 900 ft. above the Isère, commanding extensive views up and down the valley, and across into the valley of the Arc; for it is nearly opposite to the confluence of the Arc and the Isère. The ascent is gradual to the platform, which on the top of the rock is extensive enough for the castle.

The château originally belonged to one of the most ancient families in Savoy, distinguished as early as the ninth cent; but the male line becoming extinct in 1523, the château was bought by Charles III., duke of Savoy, and converted into a state prison, which continued to be its appropriation until the events of the French revolution united Savoy to France, when the castle was dismantled.

A path on the northern side of the road leads down through the meadows and vineyards to the village of Fraterive in the road beyond Miolans; thence through the village of

Grésy, and the hamlets of St. Vial and Fronteney, to

Albertville (l'Hôpital) in Rte. 119.

At l'Hôpital the Arly is crossed in order to pursue the course to the upper valley of the Isère, a district distinguished as the *Tarentaise*. The road lies on the rt. bank of the Isère, through a succession of beautiful scenes.

Above *Conflans* the valley is much narrower; the lower ranges of the mountains are more richly wooded, the valley retired and pastoral in its character. The ruins of *Castles* are often seen, on heights that jut out on rocks in commanding situations from the rich backgrounds of forest trees.

The first village that is passed is *La Batie* (*Oblimum*), with a ruined castle, and the next of any importance is Roche-Cavins, which is about half-way between Conflans and Moutiers. About 10 miles from Conflans, near the hamlet of Petit Cœur, there is a fine cataract, which dashes down amidst immense rocks,—a spot forming a striking contrast to the general fertility and repose of the valley. About 3 m. farther the valley opens into a rich little plain, where the pretty village of Aigueblanche is situated. Here the road rises, and, having passed its crest, descends into a deep defile that leads to Moutiers, by a road terraced on the steep slope of this ravine, from which it abruptly enters the basin of the Val Isère.

Moutiers.—(*Inns*, bad: H. de la Diligence; H. de la Couronne, bad and extortionate).—Moutiers Tarentaise (*Darentasia*) is situated on the confluence of the Isère, and the Doron of Bozel. Inhab. 2000. This capital of the Tarentaise derives its present name from an old monastery, which was built in the 5th cent. at a little distance from the ancient Darentasia. The history of its church is perfect from its first archbishopric in 420 to its last in 1793, a period of 1373 years. The city now contains an hospital for the poor, which was founded in the 10th century, and an *Ecole des Mines*, with a laboratory for practical examination of the productions of the mines of Pesey.

The *Salt-works*, now the distinguishing feature of Moutiers, produce nearly 1500 tons of salt yearly, extracted from three springs rising at the base of a vast mass of limestone, in the deep ravine of the Doron, about a mile above its junction with the Isère. They are warm, and the strongest 99° Fahrenheit. During the great earthquake of Lisbon, the salines of Moutiers ceased to flow for 48 hours: when the reflux took place the quantity was increased, but the saline impregnation was weaker. The brine has scarcely half the strength of that of sea-water; yet it is worked to some profit by the simplicity of the process, and the use of water as the motive power for the pumps. There are four great evaporating-houses filled with faggots of black-thorn. The water from the springs is pumped to the top of these, and allowed to pass through perforated canals, slowly dropping through the woodstacks and spreading over the extensive surface of the branches. By this process the sulphate of lime attaches itself to the wood, and a large part of the watery particles evaporate, so that the proportion of salt, after the operation has been repeated 3 or 4 times, is increased nearly one-half: *i.e.* to 3, 12, and 22 per cent.

When the brine has acquired the strength of 20 per cent. it is conducted into the boiling pans, and the salt is crystallised in the usual manner.

By this system of evaporation by the air, only one sixteenth of the fuel is consumed which would be required for evaporating the weak brine as it comes from the springs. The faggots are changed once in 5 or 6 years: they acquire a coating of selenite which, when broken off, resembles the stems and branches of encrinites. Instead of wood stacks in some of the houses cords are suspended from the roof, 16 ft. long, placed as thickly as possible, consistent with free ventilation; the water when pumped up trickles down over them slowly until the greater part of the water is evaporated, and the cords are left incrusted with a cylinder of crystallized gypsum. These works belong to the government: they yield an annual profit of only 50,000 fr. = 2000*l*.

From Moutiers to Bourg St. Maurice the road, leaving the little basin of Moutiers to ascend the Isère, passes through a gorge which opens at the village of St. Marcel. The scenery around is very fine and picturesque. The road, which formerly passed on the left bank of the Isère, now rises high on the right bank, and is carried over a neck of rock at a great height above the torrent. The view looking down and back upon St. Marcel from the rock is very fine. This road was made by Victor Emanuel, Duke of Savoy, in 1766.

The valley opens above this defile; and immediately beyond it, below the road, is seen the village of Centron, still preserving the name of the Centrones, an Alpine people who inhabited this valley.

Aimé (Axuma), one of the chief towns of the Centrones, which, according to inscriptions found there, was evidently called Forum Claudii before the name of Axuma was given to it. On a hill above it there are the remains of Roman fortifications: some round towers of great antiquity, both in the town and on the site of the ancient fort, are still standing, the masonry having been strong enough to hold together through so many ages. There is also a subterraneous communication which traverses the town, from some ruins, supposed to have been a temple, to the fortress; the vault of this passage is supported by columns of stone, each shaft of a single piece. Here some inscriptions have been found, particularly one in honour of Trajan.

Generally, the valley of the Isère, from Aime to Bourg St. Maurice, is wild and dreary, and not picturesque. The vine grows as far as the village of Bellentres, which is nearly opposite to the village and valley of Landri, that lead to the mines of Pesey, the most celebrated in Savoy. They are situated near the foot of the glacier of the Chaffe-Quarre, and more than 5000 ft. above the level of the sea: the ore is a fine-grained sulphuret of lead; it contains about 60 ounces of silver per ton. These mines in 1785 yielded annually about 4000 marks of silver, and 40,000 quintals of lead: they are now less productive. The height of the mines is a serious obstacle to their being worked to great advantage.

As the valley is ascended, the pass of the Little St. Bernard opens to the observer a more obvious course than that of the road up the Isère, which turns again from St. Maurice to the E. and S.S.E., and continues in this direction to its source in the Iseran.

Bourg St. Maurice (Berigentrum). *Inns:* H. des Voyageurs, chez Mayat; H. Royal. (Rte. 114.)

Thus far up the Val Isère there is a diligence road, but beyond St. Maurice it is necessary, in order to explore the valley upwards, to go on horseback or on foot, until the road now in progress is complete. It requires one day to go from Bourg St. Maurice to La Val, and another across the Col d'Iseran to Lanslebourg and the Mont Cenis. The *Inns* above this are bad and extortionate.

From Bourg St. Maurice to St. Foi (see Rte. 113), 3 hrs. The approach to St. Foi from the meadows below it offers one of the most beautiful scenes in the valleys of the Alps. Having climbed the tortuous and difficult chaussée which leads to the village, the route continues for a long way by a wild and lofty path on the mountain side, high above the torrent, through the village of

La Tuille, where a good guide and sportsman, François Ruet, resides. He can accommodate two or three travellers, and can furnish trout from the Lac de Tignes. The *Inns* at La Tuille are bad, but Ruet is honest and trustworthy. Bears and chamois occur here.

[From La Tuille de Sainte Foi, or Tignes, an interesting excursion may be made to a peak called *La Croix de Feuillette,* which commands a magnificent view of the chain of Mont Blanc, and of a great portion of the Savoy Alps. It is possible on the same day to ascend to the summit of the Col du Clou, a pass communicating with the Val Grisanche and Ivrogne in the Val d'Aosta (Rte. 113). The scenery towards the summit of the Col is wild and striking, but there is no extensive view. The descent into the Val Grisanche from the highest point (which must be about 9000 ft. above the sea) lies over steep slopes of snow and débris. This would be the most direct course from Lanslebourg to Aosta. The path taken in returning from the Col to La Tuille is very interesting, lying through varied and striking scenery.]

The deep ravine is too narrow for the structure of a path lower down towards the torrent. On the opposite side the enormous glaciers that stretch from the Chaffe-Quarre along the crest of the mountains, offer a scene of grandeur scarcely to be surpassed in the Western Alps. A most magnificent view thus presented is opposite to the village of La Gure, of which the spire seems to touch the glaciers. More than once this village has been destroyed by the fall of ice and rocks; but the danger is defied for the sake of the little land which its terrace above the Isère affords. From the melting glaciers above, the white lines of many falls seem to stream down upon the village.

Soon after passing La Gure the road yet ascends to a ridge, which being crossed, the path leads steeply down to the Isère in the depth of the ravine. Here overhanging rocks darken the pass, and a fragile bridge, in a wild situation over a lateral stream, enables the traveller to ascend the valley. A little beyond this bridge the defile opens into the plain and village of

Brennieres. Here the Isère is crossed, and the path ascends on the other side through a rugged pine forest, where the path is carried very high to avoid a ravine. In passing over this ridge, there is one spot where a cleft in the mountain side can be passed only upon the trees, rocks, and stones, which the peasants have jammed into it, to form a path, which thence descending almost to the river side, continues a short way only, before another expansion of the valley forms a little well-cultivated plain, in which lies the chief village of the valley,—

Tignes. (3½ hrs. from St. Foi.) The approach to it, issuing from the defile below, is very striking. The inhabitants are robust and independent, and are great breeders of mules and cattle. Directly opposite to Tignes is a valley, where one may pass by the Col de la Leisse to Entre-deux-Eaux and Lanslebourg. (Rte. 123.)

[A rough bridle-road mounts from near the village of Tignes to the Lac de Tignes. Thence, keeping to the rt. of the lake, a faintly-marked path, after skirting its shores for some distance, ascends towards the S.W., and without much difficulty leads to the wild nearly level tract of snow-fields and débris which form the Col. Chamois are here frequent. The descent lies through a wild and dreary glen filled on either side by masses of débris, over which to the N. hang the precipices of a magnificent peak, called by Ruet the Aiguille de Vanoise. There is no path, but it will be better to keep first to the rt. side of the valley, then to cross the stream over some of the snow-bridges which sub-

sist through the summer, returning again to the northern side (though out of the direct course), if the traveller seek some rest and refreshment at Entre-deux-Eaux. Thence the route to Lanslebourg lies over the Plan du Loup, as described Rte. 123. A guide is required for this route.]

On leaving the plain of Tignes, a steep rugged path leads up the mountain side, to pass another of those ravines, which in this valley so singularly alternate with the little plains. This, the last, separates the plain of Tignes from that of Laval. The forest trees, from their greater elevation, are more stunted, the rocks more denuded, and the whole passage between the two villages is unmatched in savage wildness. In the midst, a fragile bridge crosses the torrent, and soon after the traveller finds himself in the plain of Laval; where barley is raised, and where irrigation is so well managed, that there is an appearance of luxuriant vegetation. Laval is 2 hrs. above Tignes, and is the highest church village in the Val Isère: it is surrounded by lofty mountains, which are crested with snow and glaciers. At the head of the valley, the Col de Galese, above its glaciers, can easily be seen. (Rte. 112.)

A miserable hovel called an inn is the only place of reception at *Laval.* Professor Forbes says that "at *Tignes,* 3 hours' walk from St. Foi, and 5 from Bourg St. Maurice, there is a humble and clean inn, Chez Bock, where the traveller is advised strongly to stay and pass the night instead of encountering the dirt and discomfort of the filthy inn of Laval. From Tignes to Lanslebourg is not a very long day's journey." If, however, the traveller intend to cross the Galese to the Val d'Orca or the Val de Forno in Piedmont, he cannot sleep too near the glaciers, in order to pass them at an early hour. Laval should in this case be his resting place. It is centrally placed in a noble country, and only wants a better inn. There are 3 routes from Laval. 1. A mule path to Lanslebourg, by the Roche d'Or, a very picturesque mountain, and Termignon. 2. By the Val de Rhemes to Aosta, shorter but higher than the Galese, and reputed more hazardous. These two may probably be taken as conveniently from Tignes, with a variation in the ascent. 3. Direct to Gros Cavallo between the Col d'Iseran and the Galese. The two last are difficult.

To cross the *Col d'Iseran* (from Laval to Bonneval, is a walk of 5 or 6 hrs.) the path ascends gradually from the valley, by a stunted pine forest. There is a hamlet called Forno, or *Fornel*, further up the valley on the route to the Galese, but this is avoided, and by the time the traveller arrives opposite to it he has attained a great elevation. The path to the Col requires a guide from Laval, as the course is confused by sheep tracks leading to different pasturages, and the true path is only known by bearings: the ascent is easy. Some crosses mark the loss of life in these solitudes; in one instance by murder, in another a poor soldier was found dead from cold and exhaustion. Near the summit, the soil produces myriads of flowers, and of great variety. On looking back upon the ridge of the great chain the view is grand, but not so fine as from the Col de Galese, and during the descent on the other side. Here the traveller looks over a thousand peaks, whose black and scathed precipices appear to spring out of the sea of glaciers which extends from the Levanna (Rte. 112) to the Roche Melon (Rte. 127).

From the col, the course lies down the denuded slopes to an elevated pasturage, which narrows to a valley terminating in a defile above deep precipices, where a cataract falls across the path. From this ravine the descent is very difficult and fatiguing down to the plain below, where the pasturages and châlets of St. Barthelemi, belonging to the inhabitants of Bonneval, offer abundant summer resources to the herds and flocks of the proprietors.

From these pasturages the descent is steep and wearying. The valley of the Arc is seen below, and on the left, looking up to the head of the valley, the glaciers of the Levanna seem to fill it; across these a path leads in 5 hrs. to Gros Cavallo in the Val Forno, and thence in 10 hrs. to Lanzo, in Piedmont.

The first village reached in the valley of the Arc is

Bonneval: here the inn (kept by Culets, an intelligent chasseur) is very poor and homely: so, in fact, are all in the valley, until the traveller reach Lanslebourg, distant 4 hrs. down the valley from Bonneval.

After crossing the *Arc*, the road passes on the left the valley of Averole, by which the Col de Lautaret and the valleys of Viu and Lanzo, on the side of Piedmont, may be reached —one of the wildest passes in the Alps.

At *Bessans* the Arc is again crossed, and a high ridge is passed which divides the commune of Bessans from that of

Lans le Villard, a village about a league above Lanslebourg. Its inhabitants salt their donkeys for food —a practice common in the Tarentaise. From Lans le Villard a path leads into the great route of the Mont Cenis. If the traveller have started early, he may reach the posthouse on the mountain on the day of his departure from Laval. If he be late, it will be better to proceed down the valley by the char road to

Lanslebourg (Rte. 127.)

ROUTE 123.

MOUTIERS TARENTAISE TO LANSLEBOURG, BY THE COL DE VANOISE.

A char may be taken as far as Bozel for this journey, but beyond, it is necessary to take a horse, or proceed on foot. This passage may be performed in one *long* day (14 hrs. on foot, including 2 hrs.' rest), starting from Brida, where the inns are good. It requires 2 days, if the place of rest be Pralorgnan.

The road passes by the *Salines* of Moutiers (Rte. 122), and ascending on the rt. bank of the Doron, reaches in a quarter of an hour the Rock of Salines, situated opposite to the confluence of the valley of Bozel, or the Doron, with that of St. Jean Belleville. Ascending the latter, there are two mountain passes : one leads to St. Jean Maurienne, the other to St. Michael, both in the valley of the Arc, either an easy day's journey.

The Château de Salins was anciently the residence of the archbishop of the Tarentaise. Its ruins are situated immediately above the *salt springs*, in the valley below. These are guarded with great care, to prevent the people of the country stealing any of the water, and making their own salt.

Salins is conjectured to have been the site of the ancient Darentasia. The town was destroyed about the end of the 14th century, by a fall from the mountains on the W. This fall of rocks and stones so filled the valley that the lower town was buried beneath the mass. All that remained were the parts most elevated. Subsequent falls destroyed what remained except the castle, and this has been demolished. A few miserable houses, rebuilt around the Salines, await a similar fate from the threatening appearance of the rocks above.

The castle, however, remained long after the destruction of the town in the 14th century. Books still exist which were printed by Maurice Mermillion at the château very soon after the discovery of printing. It is supposed that the first press in Savoy was established there, and that Mermillion was the Caxton of the Tarentaise.

Salins lies S. of Moutiers. From the confluence, the road into the valley of Bozel takes an easterly direction through a district rich in wood and highly cultivated, where there are many beautiful points of view.

Brida or *La Perrière*, 1 hr. from Moutiers. (*Inns:* Etablissement des Bains, best, and good; 2 tables-d'hôte daily, and a reading-room: there are others.) This village and watering-place is resorted to in summer by invalids on account of its mineral springs. The waters are so much impregnated with sulphuretted hydrogen as to be perfectly detestable to the taste. The temperature of the water is, according to Dr. Socquet, 99½°.

The views are extremely fine, and the neighbourhood abounds in beautiful walks; one of the pleasantest is by a footpath through the wood, at a considerable height above the S. bank of the stream, towards Moutiers.

At *Brida* the Doron is crossed, and a tolerable road leads to Bozel. Between the two villages the country is rich in cultivation: vines and fruit-trees in the valley, corn-fields and pasturages on the belts of the mountains, and above, pine-forests, surmounted by snows and glaciers, the valley being closed at the head by the mountains of Pesey, and, one of the most beautiful in form in the Alps, the *Chaffe-Quarre*.

At Bozel mules can be hired for continuing the journey. Above this village the valley widens, and the scenery increases in grandeur, except that in passing under the intermediate mountain of Plagny, this conceals the Chaffe-Quarre.

The ascent to the village of *Champagny* is deep in the valley, and on the banks of the Doron, of which the broad stony bed marks its wider winter course. On approaching Champagny the road is distinctly seen which leads up to the mines of Pesey. (Rte. 122.) It is a good mule-path, and leads across the col to the valley which descends to Landry in the Val Isère. The lateral valleys of the Doron abound with beautiful scenery, and most of them lead to points of view in the mountains where some of the finest Alpine scenes are presented, particularly in the valley of Allues, and at the châlets of Châtelet, near the Col de Forclaz, whence Mont Blanc can be seen, and a vast extent of the peaks of the great chain.

From Champagny the road to Pralorgnan lies up that branch of the Doron which flows from the S. After passing the village of Villard Goîtreux, thus named from the prevalence of goître among the inhabitants, the road ascends by a steep path to a narrow valley. On the rt. there is a cataract, formed by the fall of the Doron into the gorge at Bellentre, and the valley widens to the beautiful meadows and calm retirement of the valley of Pralorgnan.

The path to the Vanoise lies directly up to the rt., and the châlets in the mountains are reached in an hour. Each step becomes more and more dreary, until you arrive at the bases of the bleak and streaming glaciers of the Aiguille de la Vanoise. On reaching the *moraines* it is necessary to climb them on foot, and let the mules scramble as they may, or as the guide can assist them. At the base of these *moraines* a lake is formed in the winter. To its basin there is but one entrance: within nothing can exceed the savage solitude of the spot, surrounded by black precipices and glaciers; it seems to be impossible to get out, except by the way one gets in. Under the advice of the guide, however, the glaciers may be climbed and traversed—a most fatiguing and difficult task. Having surmounted the difficulty, the traveller, after crossing a few patches of snow, enters upon an open plain, covered with rich pasturages, but bounded by enormous glaciers and inaccessible peaks. On the plain of the col, which is now gradual to the summit, poles are placed to guide travellers when snow conceals the track. The path is long and tedious across these solitudes, from the glaciers of the *Vanoise* to the *summit*. Three little lakes are passed, the source of streams which descend on one side to the Doron, and on the other to the Arc. On the right, enormous glaciers are seen, which extend to the Roche Chevrière, the vast mountain which is seen from

the ascent to the Mont Cenis, overhanging Termignon.

From the col, the descent towards the châlets of Entre-deux-Eaux is rapid and difficult. The long sterile valley above these châlets, which leads by the Col de la Leisse to Tignes, in the Val Isère (Rte. 122), is seen below. After a long descent, the torrent is crossed, but instead of pursuing its course through its deep gorge to Termignon, a path is followed which leads up on the opposite mountain to the *Plan de Loup*, a long pasturage, not so wild or high, but about the breadth of the Col de Vanoise. The scene, looking back upon the valley of Entre-deux-Eaux, and the Col de Vanoise, is very sublime.

On the col of the Plan de Loup another small lake is passed, then a long and most fatiguing descent commences, which leads down to the hamlet of St. Marguerite. Soon after the path enters a pine-forest, through which a miserable road leads down to the valley above Termignon, into which there are some magnificent peeps. There is still, however, a long and fatiguing descent to make before that little town can be reached. There is a path which, going from the hamlet of St. Marguerite, skirts the Mont Parouffa, behind Lanslebourg, and leads directly to the latter town; but, though shorter, it is even more fatiguing than the route to Termignon, and one which it is difficult to pass with a laden mule. At Termignon the path from the Vanoise falls into the great route of the Cenis, which in an hour takes the traveller to *Lanslebourg* (Rte. 127.)

ROUTE 125.

PONT BEAUVOISIN TO AIX LES BAINS,
BY THE MONT DU CHAT.

The road to the Mont du Chat leaves Pont Beauvoisin to follow a course on the right bank of the river Guiers Vif, through the villages of Belmont and Tramonex to St. Genix, a large village near the confluence of the Guiers with the Rhone, thence turning abruptly up the latter river, it continues on its left bank for about 10 miles, through some fine scenery, until it reaches

Yenne, a little town most agreeably situated on a rising ground above the Rhone, nearly opposite to the fort Pierre Châtel. (Rte. 120.)

Yenne existed in the time of the Romans, under the name of Ejanna, and, according to some authorities, Epaona. It lies in the ancient route from France to Italy, by the Mont du Chat, which was much used before the opening of the Grotto near les E'chelles. The whole neighbourhood is very rich in cultivation. Corn, wine, and fruit-trees abound. The white wines named *Marètel,* and *Altesse,* grown on the banks of the Rhone, a little N. of Yenne, owe their excellence to plants which were brought here from Cyprus, by a duke of Savoy, or the lords of his court.

From Yenne, a road, which is not in a very praiseworthy condition in the plain, though it is the route of a daily diligence from Lyons to Aix les Bains, leads directly towards the Mont du Chat, by Chevalu, distant 4 m. from Yenne. This village is situated at the foot of the mountain. The extreme richness of the country cannot fail to draw the attention of the traveller, and when, beyond Chevalu, the road ascends and rises high enough above the surrounding country, its excessive fertility is its striking feature.

The road over the mountain is well constructed. The summit of the *Mont du Chat* rises on the rt. ; on the l.

steep slopes and precipices descend to the base, ending in rich pasturages, in which there are some little lakes or tarns. Many tourniquets in the road give a gradual ascent, and at the end of an hour the summit is attained. The scene, on looking back towards France, is one of the most fertile in the world ; studded with villages and towns, and so extensive, that where the distant mountains of Tarrare do not limit the horizon, it subsides into indistinctness. Immediately below, on the same side, are the rich pasturages of the western slopes of the Mont du Chat. Beyond these are the valley of the Rhone, and the hills and plains which extend to the Ain.

On the summit of the pass there is a level, about 300 yds. across. The road passes on the southern side of a large mass of rock which is upon it. The summit of the pass is covered with stones, rocks, and brushwood. A temple formerly stood here, of which the foundations may be traced, and many of the stones around made part of the building. The stones have been well cut, and the cornices of many are yet tolerably perfect. An inscription was found here by Dr. Cramer, which has given rise to the idea that the temple was dedicated to Mercury, "but the inscription itself hardly bears out this opinion. M. Albanis de Beaumont, in his description of the Alpes Grecques, calls this mountain the Mons Thuates, but without giving his authority. Now, Theut and Thait, in Armoric, are the names of the deity who presided over highways, and who was much worshipped by the Gauls ; hence Cæsar says, that the people principally worshipped Mercury, who had the same office among the Roman deities. The name, therefore, of Mons Thuates would argue a passage here of very high antiquity, and the temple, if really dedicated to Mercury, would tend strongly to the confirmation of this opinion."—*Dissertation on the Passage of Hannibal.*

It has been satisfactorily shown by De Luc, and by Wickham and Cramer, that the army under Hannibal here encountered its first difficulties in passing the Alps, having to fight the mountaineers, who kept watch during the day only. After having ascended the Rhone as far as Vienne, he led his army across the country of the Allobroges, by Bourgoin, les Abrets, and St. Genix d'Aoste (Augusta Allobrogum), now a village on the l. bank of the Guiers, nearly opposite to Yenne, thence, by Chevalu (Leviscum), across the Mont du Chat to Chambéry (Lemincum).

The form and character of the Mont du Chat agrees entirely with the account, by Polybius, of those events which could only in such a peculiar locality occur. From Chambéry the army passed to Montmeillan, and up the Val Isère to Conflans, Moutiers, and St. Maurice, and passed into Italy by the Little St. Bernard.

From the summit of the *Mont du Chat*, 5000 ft. above the level of the sea, the view on the eastern side is one of surpassing beauty. It appears to overhang the lake of Bourget, into whose deep blue waters it seems only a leap. Beyond is the rich valley of Chambéry, extending from Albens to the Mont Grenier ; the town of Aix seems to be at your feet across the lake : on the rt., the city of Chambéry lies like a model ; hundreds of hamlets and villages speckle the beautiful valley, which is bounded on the opposite side by the rich slopes of the Mont d'Azi, and the Dent de Nivolet; far beyond are seen the mountains which bound the Val Isère, and the snowy summits of those which extend to the Dauphiny Alps.

The descent is peculiarly exciting. The road is safely and finely made, it winds down the steep side of the mountain, but in many places the parapet is seen to cut abruptly against the deep blue lake, and suggests the idea of its being thousands of feet, *à plomb*, below.

On reaching the base, however, there are fields, rich woods, and villages on the steep slopes which rise from the lake, but this extends only to *Bordeau*. Beyond this village there is no path by the lake : its

shores are too abrupt, at least as far as Hautecombe. If the traveller would go direct to Aix, a path on the l. leads to the village of Bordeau, where a boat can be hired to cross the lake to the opposite shore, and a walk of 20 min. leads to Aix. (Rte. 120.)

The direct road passes through *Bourget*, where the plain of Chambéry commences ; this is traversed for about 7 miles to the city from Bourget through the villages of Motte and Bissy, and amidst a luxuriance of vegetation which cannot be imagined. *Aix les Bains.* (Rte. 120.)

ROUTE 126.

PONT BEAUVOISIN TO CHAMBÉRY, BY AIGUEBELLETTE.

About 1½ m. from *Pont Beauvoisin* the high road to Les Échelles is left: and at the village of Domessin a narrow road turns off to the l., and leads over a low hill well wooded, and thence through a remarkably rich plain, that extends to those limestone precipices which are a continuation of the ridge of rocks that make so formidable a barrier at Les Échelles. Avoiding the principal road to La Bridoire, and crossing the plain direct from near Pont Beauvoisin, the path abruptly approaches these precipices. Close to their base a zigzag path, very steep, leads up the talus formed during many ages by the débris ; in some places, however, the path is so narrow, that the wall of the precipice can be touched by one hand, whilst the other overhangs the steep and dangerous descents below : in some places two persons cannot pass each other. A little time is gained by this short cut, and there is some chance of adventure, and the situations are striking, but it is scarcely worth the fatigue. It leads to the same hamlet, Bridoire, which is highly picturesque in its situation, its cottages, and its water-mills. From this place the road ascends, crosses a ridge, and enters upon the basin of the lake of Aiguebellette, a rich open valley, finely wooded, and where a view of the lake is obtained ;—the whole scene is beautiful.

The road undulates amidst the magnificent walnut-trees which abound here, and passes through the village of *Lepin*, offering some very fine views. There is a singular character of tranquillity and retirement in the spot : the scenery resembles that of the most beautiful of our Cumberland lakes; but the visit of a traveller is so rare an occurrence, that instead of a crowd of visitors, and a season for visiting, a year may pass away without any other stranger being seen than a little *négociant* making a shorter cut to Chambéry than by the great road to Les Échelles.

A ridge divides the village of Lepin from that of Aiguebellette; at the extremity of the ridge on the left, overhanging the lake, is a château, in a most romantic and beautiful situation; the road on the other side of the ridge descends to Aiguebellette, and passes the ruins of the castle of its barons: it is of high antiquity; its foundation is unknown, and it is therefore attributed to the Romans: it is recorded to have been repaired in the 11th century. It was burnt and demolished by one of the dauphins of Vienne, in the 15th century.

Aiguebellette is a poor little village, in a most beautiful situation; it has a miserable little inn, which cannot furnish even decent wine and refreshment in a country so abundant—not even fish from the lake : these are taken and sent to distant markets. The lake is celebrated for the excellence and abundance of its carp trout, and other fish. The lake is about 3 m. long, and 2 wide ; its depth varies, but it is generally about 150 ft. deep. Around the lake are fields and meadows, but most of the slopes of the surrounding mountains are wooded. Oats, barley, potatoes, Indian corn, and flax are grown in the spots cultivated.

It is curious that a tradition exists here that Hannibal passed with a part of the Carthaginian army by Aiguebellette.

On proceeding from Aiguebellette the path skirts the churchyard, and enters a line of meadows beneath magnificent walnut trees. Soon, however, it begins to ascend the mountain side, and rises over the intervening trees, presenting views of the lake, the villages around it, and the distant hills which slope down and border the Rhone. The road now becomes very steep, ascending in zigzags, sometimes sunk in the crues of the mountain, at others rounding the projections, and increasing, as the observer rises above the lake, the beauty with the extent of the view. At length, after a very fatiguing ascent for an hour, the summit is attained, and a glorious view is presented over the basin of Chambéry, similar to that which is seen from the Mont du Chat; but, though not so elevated, it is, perhaps, superior; the idea of a fall into the lake of Bourget does not, as there, make the traveller shrink from the parapet. Instead of looking down into the lake, it is seen, at its nearest point, about 8 m. off, resting at the base of the steep Mont du Chat; and opposite to it are the houses of Aix.

Chambéry seems, from the Aiguebellette, to be just below the observer; and, in the road to it from Les Échelles, which may be seen, the cascade of *Coux* is distinctly observed; its bright white line forming a very small speck amidst the extended scale of the surrounding objects. The valley, too, between the Dent de Nivolet and the Mont Grenier is more opened, and the richly-wooded and cultivated scene more extended: few such glorious views are presented as that offered to the eye of the traveller from the mountain of Aiguebellette.

The descent from the summit of

.the col may be made by two routes : that on the right seems to have been the old Roman road, but it is now impracticable for horses. There are traces of its.having been a well-constructed road, in the remains of high and very thick dry walls, which supported, towards the plain, its terraces. Albanis de Beaumont says that, after half an hour's descent by this road, there are many stone coffins found at the foot of the lateral rocks, with slabs which formerly covered them, upon which some characters are seen, though they are too much effaced to be read: blocks, too, of cut stone are found, and he conjectures that they are the ruins of a chapel dedicated to St. Michel, which was attached to an hospital that existed here in the 9th century, and, probably, under some other denomination, even in the time of the Romans.

The road at present used from the summit of the Col d'Aiguebellette to Chambéry is the best, though only practicable for pedestrians or cattle: it might easily be rendered fit for the passage of chars; but, as there is little intercourse across it, there is no sufficient motive for its improvement.

The first village reached after an hour's descent is *Vimine*, ingeniously conjectured by Beaumont to be derived from *Via Minima*, because it lay on the shortest route from Lemincum (Chambéry) to Vienna Allobrogum (Vienne, on the Rhone). In going to or from Chambéry by this route, instead of that by Les Échelles, the pedestrian will gain 2 hrs.; the whole distance from Pont Beauvoisin requiring about 8 hrs.

From the village of Vimine to the hamlet of Cognin is a short hour's walk over a bad road, but through beautiful scenes : thence, in half an hour, the traveller will reach CHAMBÉRY. (Rte. 127.)

ROUTE 127.

LYONS TO CHAMBÉRY, BY VOIRON.

This route will be taken by those who wish to see the beautiful scenery of the Grande Chartreuse and of the Grésivaudan, and was the old Mont Cenis road from France.

Lyons to Voiron. Rly. See HANDBOOK FOR FRANCE.

Voiron.		Kil.		Eng. m.
Les Echelles	. .	22	=	14
St. Thibaud.	. .	13	=	8
Chambéry	. . .	10	=	6

Voiron to *St. Laurent du Pont.* Good carriage-road. [Hence the ascent to the Grande Chartreuse is made. See HANDBOOK FOR FRANCE.]

Les Echelles, a village on the Guiers. The valley beyond this village is a complete *cul-de-sac.* A wall of limestone, 800 ft. high, stretches directly across it; and from Les Échelles the eye in vain seeks at first for the means of exit. In former days the only road was a path, of the most rugged and difficult kind, partly conducted through a cavern by means of ladders placed one above the other. This was called the Chemin de la Grotte, or Les Échelles, from which the neighbouring village derived its name. The difficulty of the passage was increased at times by the mountain torrent, which, when swollen, took its course through the cavern. It was utterly impassable for beasts : travellers were sometimes carried through it, seated upon an arm-chair attached to the backs of stout Savoyard peasants, who performed the service of beasts of burden, as the South American Indians do at the present day on some of the passes of the Andes.

An improved road was made in 1670, by Duke Charles Emanuel II. of Savoy, at considerable cost, by removing vast masses of rock, so as to render it passable for carriages. Napoleon, however, struck out a new line, and boldly pierced through the mountain, forming a tunnel 1000 ft. long, 25 ft. high, and 25 ft. wide, along which two diligences fully loaded may pass abreast. A pompous inscription, written by the Abbé St. Réal, commemorating the enterprise of Charles Emanuel in forming his road—which, though steep and narrow, and very inconvenient, was a grand undertaking for the period—may still be seen on the face of the rock.

Our route is now carried through a wilderness of rocks, which gradually expand into a pretty valley.

St. Thibaud de Couz.

Not far from this a little waterfall descends from the cliff on the rt., described by Rousseau, in his usual strain of exaggeration, as " La plus belle que je vis de ma vie."

Another contracted ravine must be passed to reach

Chambéry Stat. (Ital., Ciamberi) (*Inns:* H. de l'Europe, good ; — Le Petit Paris, comfortable, clean, and moderate ; table d'hôte at 1;—Poste; —Ecu de France), the capital of Savoy, and an archbishop's see, contains about 20,000 Inhab., and is pleasantly situated within a circle of mountains. Around it are many lovely views.

The *Cathedral*, a Gothic building (14th century, finished 1430), though injured by modern paint and decoration, and not extensive, is interesting.

Several towers and other fragments exist of the ancient *Castle of the Dukes of Savoy,* built 1230. The Gothic *chapel* built within its enclosure (1415) survived the conflagration of 1798: it is passed on the left hand as you enter the town from Lyons. It has beautiful tall, narrow windows of painted glass. That valuable relic the Santo Sudario (holy napkin), now at Turin, was for a long time deposited in it. Francis I. of France made a pilgrimage on foot from Lyons to see it: another of these holy napkins is kept in St. Peter's at Rome, and shown to the populace on all great displays of the *relics.* The terrace near the castle, called du Verneez, is a charming promenade owing to the prospects it commands.

Before the French revolution there were 20 convents in Chambéry: there are still seven, four of which are nunneries.

Among the most conspicuous buildings at present are the *Three Barra*

There is a *Public* Library containing 13,000 volumes, an incipient museum, and a few pictures, none them calculated to afford the strang much gratification ; there is also *Theatre* and a *Royal College.*

St. Réal, author of the 'Conjuratic contre Venise,' was born at Chambéry, 1639 ; and the Comte Xavier Maistre, author of the ' Voyage tour de ma Chambre,' is also a nati This town boasts among her citize General de Boigne, who, having ma an immense fortune in the East I dies, in the service of the Rajah Sci dia, bestowed the greater portion of to the amount of 3,417,850 fr., in bene fiting his native place. He founde two hospitals, and set on foot man improvements. A new street has bee named after him, and a *monument,* con sisting of a fountain ornamented wit figures of elephants, has been erecte to his memory. He died 1830.[*]

Chambéry is, on the whole, a dul town, with little to interest the tra veller: it is celebrated for a peculia manufacture of silk gauzes.

About 20 minutes' walk to the sout of the town is *Les Charmettes,* the re sidence of Rousseau and of his frien Madame de Warens. There is no thing in the place at present wort notice independently of its connectio with J. Jacques: the house has th appearance of a poor farm-house, an Rousseau's room was the one over th entrance.

Those who have time on thei hands, and desire an agreeable tw hours' walk, may visit the ravin called *Le Bout du Monde.* The roa to it turns out of that to Turin at th end of the Faubourg de Montmeillai follows the left bank of the Leysse b the side of the great dyke, as far a the village of Leysse, where it crosse the stream, and, passing on the rigl the picturesque castle of Chaffardoi enters the gorge of the Doriat, whic is closed in on all sides by high cliff

[*] The life and adventures of General d Boigne are admirably told in 'A Ride o Horseback to Florence, by a Lady,' 1841.

forming the base of the Dent de Nivolet, and has no outlet. Behind a paper-mill, built by one of the Montgolfiers, the stream falls in a pretty cascade over the wall of rock here formed of remarkable regular and thin horizontal strata, through some of which the water forcing its way forms singular supplementary jets at distance from the main fall.

[A pleasant excursion of a day or two may be made from Chambéry to the baths of Aix, and the Lac de Bourget (Rte. 120.)]

The *Victor Emanuel Railroad*, towards the foot of the Cenis, is open as far as St. Jean de Maurienne (Rte. 127A); also to Geneva, with the exception of a few miles (Rte. 120), through Aix, Culoz, and Seyssel, and to Lyons, Macon, and Paris.

ROUTE 127A.

CHAMBERY TO TURIN—MONT CENIS.

	kil.	miles.	H.	M.
Chambéry (railway)				
Montmélian	10 =	6		
Aiguebelle	37 =	23	..	
St. Jean de Maurienne .	70 =	43	.. 3	0
St. Jean to St. Michel .	13 =	8	.. 1	45
St. Michel to Modane .	17 =	11	.. 2	0
Modane to Verney . .	11 =	7	.. 1	45
Verney to Lanslebourg .	12 =	7½	.. 2	0
Lanslebourg to Grande Croix	13 =	8	.. 4	30
Grande Croix to Molaret .	14 =	9	.. 1	15
Molaret to Susa . . .	10 =	6	.. 0	45
Susa to Turin (railway) .	54 =	34	.. 2	0

The Rly. to St. Jean de Maurienne takes 3 hrs. Diligence about 12 hrs. from St. Jean to Susa; Susa to Turin, 2 hrs. Total, 18 hrs. The diligences are usually so arranged as to cross the pass during the night:

those, therefore, who wish to see it will take a voiturier or post from St. Jean to Susa in 2 days. The travelling is very good, but very dear. Voiturier about 200 fr., posting 300 fr., all renforts and tolls included. The *Inns* on the road are all dear, bad, and dirty.

The Mont Cenis road may be considered as beginning at Chambéry and ending at Susa. It was constructed by the Chevalier Fabbroni, under the orders of Napoleon, at a cost of 300,000*l.*, and was commenced in 1803 and finished in 1810. It is one of the safest and most practicable of the roads over the Alps during the winter, but is at the same time the dullest and most uninteresting. The valley of the Arc, however, is in some places pretty, and in others wild and grand, and there is a fine view from the 17th Refuge, and beautiful views on the descent into Italy.

Now that the Rly. from Lyons to Chambéry (Rte. 120) has been so nearly completed, this road has become by far the easiest mode of reaching Italy.

Lyons to *Chambéry* (Railway, Rte. 120.)

Chambéry (Rte. 127).

The scenery in the valley above Chambéry is very fine, but the curves and gradients on the railway are very formidable. We pass, on the left, the castle of Bâtie, and farther on, close to the road, that of Chignin, links of a line of forts extending through the country, on whose towers watch-fires were lighted to alarm the inhabitants in time of war, in case of foreign inroads. For these rude means in the middle ages, telegraphs have been substituted. Up the valleys of the Arc and Isère, the chain of old castles continues almost without an interruption. The mountain seen on the rt. is the Mont Grenier, 5700 ft. high. The side facing Chambéry is a perpendicular escarpment, produced by an immense mass of the mountain having broken off in 1248 : it overwhelmed the country at its base with ruin, and buried 16 villages. The marks of this catas-

s

trophe are still visible in the series of hillocks, now covered with vineyards, called Les Abymes de Myans. The Mont Grenier stands in the angle between the valley of Chambéry and that of Gresivaudan, which leads to Grenoble : it is traversed by the Isère. On the l. bank of the river, a few miles down, stand the ruins of the *Château Bayard*, the cradle of the illustrious knight "sans peur et sans reproche." (See HANDBOOK OF FRANCE.)

Route de Grenoble Stat. Here the road to Grenoble branches off, following the valley of the Isère.

Montmélian Stat. (*Inn:* H. des Voyageurs, not good.) This little town stands on the rt. bank of the Isère, at the junction of four roads : that of the Mont Cenis, issuing out of the valley of the Maurienne ; that from the Tarentaise and Little St. Bernard (Rte. 122) ; that from Grenoble along the fertile and beautiful valley of Gresivaudan ; and that from Chambéry. The castle of Montmelian was long the bulwark of Savoy against France. Henry IV., while besieging it in 1600, was nearly killed by a cannon-shot from its walls, which covered him with dirt, and made the king cross himself devoutly; upon which Sully remarked, that he was happy to see that his Majesty was so good a Catholic. It was bravely and skilfully defended for 13 months against Louis XIII. by Count Geoffrey Bens de Cavour. The works were finally demolished by Louis XIV., who took the place in 1705. A few scanty fragments of wall, partly overgrown with briers and nettles, crowning the rock above the town, are the only remains of the former bulwark of Savoy, and the key of its Alps.

A good white wine is grown near Montmélian.

Public conveyances to the Baths of Alevard, near which are some iron-mines.

The bridge over the Isère, crossed in proceeding towards the Mount Cenis, commands, in clear weather, a fine view of Mont Blanc, which is seen from no other point in our route. The post-road follows the right bank of the Isère as far as the bridge ; the Rlwy. the opposite one, on an embankment of several miles, having crossed the river on a fine bridge beyond Montmélian; then, taking that river for its guide, enters the valley of the Maurienne, which extends up to the Mont Cenis.

St. Pierre d'Albigny Stat.

Aiguebelle, in a tolerably wide triangular valley (Rte. 121). (*Inn:* Poste, Parfaite Union.) The country hereabouts is unhealthy from marshes which produce malaria and its consequences, goître. The *Castle* above the town, called *La Charbonnière*, was the birthplace of several counts of Savoy.

La Grande Maison. (*Inn:* Poste.)

St. Jean de Maurienne Stat. (*Inns:* Europe, Poste, Voyageurs), capital of the province of Maurienne (3000 Inhab.), 1800 ft. above the sea, the original seat of the Dukes or Counts of Savoy. The cathedral is of the 15th centy., and contains some fine wood-carving, and a splendid stone reliquary. The town is unhealthy, and contains nothing else worthy of notice. The vineyards of St. Julien grow a wine of some repute.

The Rly. is to be continued, but in 1857 the high-road had been washed away, and was not repaired, and it was necessary to make a great détour over fields and across a torrent to

St. Michel. (*Inn:* H. de Londres.)

The road now crosses the river and enters a wild and beautiful gorge; the valley then opens out and turns to the E. At the angle near Tourneau, and about ½ m. from the road, are commenced the works for a proposed *tunnel* through the Alps: the tunnel is to be 9 m. long, without a shaft, and is to come out near Bardonnéche on the Italian side. The project is to cut the rock by machinery worked by water-power from each end, by which means it is hoped that the tunnel will be completed in less than 7 years, and will cost less than a million of money. The works were opened by the King of Sardinia in Sept. 1857, but English engineers have not much faith in the feasibility of the scheme. Between St. Michel and Modane is laid the last scene of Sterne's 'Sentimental Journey.'

Modane. (*Inn:* Lion d'Or.)

The road ascends high above the Arc, and the gorge, in whose depths it flows, serves as a natural and tremendous fosse to the Fort l'Esseillon, or Bramans, built on the opposite height, and commanding with its many-mouthed batteries, rising tier above tier, the passage to Italy. This fort has lately been much increased, and presents a magnificent appearance of impregnability; this is perhaps the most striking point of the pass. A light bridge, spanning the black gorge which separates the fort from the road, is a striking object: it is called the Pont du Diable.

Verney. Near this, Horace Walpole lost his lap-dog, which was carried off by a wolf pouncing down upon it from the forest.

At Termignon the path from the Col de Vanoise (Rte. 123) joins our road.

Lanslebourg (*Inn:* Hôtel Royal), a wretched village, full of cabarets, at the foot of the ascent of Mont Cenis, 4400 ft. above the level of the sea. From this point numerous excursions among the High Alps may be made, and, bad as the inn is, it seems excellent to those who descend from the mountains. Here in the winter the wheeled diligence is changed for one on sledges, and carriages are dismounted and put on sledges to cross the snow. 14 men are often required, and 12 mules, to conduct the diligence across.

After passing a large barrack, the road crosses the Arc, and bidding adieu to that stream, begins to ascend the mountain by easy and well-constructed zigzags. Extra horses are necessary to reach the summit; and it takes about 2½ hrs. for a carriage to mount from Lanslebourg to Refuge No. 18, at the top of the ascent. It is possible to walk up in a shorter time, avoiding the zigzag and following the old road, which debouches near the 18th *Refuge.*

Between Lanslebourg and Susa there are 23 houses of Refuge planted at intervals by the roadside, occupied by cantoniers, whose duty it is to take care of the road and assist travellers. Each house is numbered, beginning from the Piedmontese side of the mountain. Near No. 22 avalanches sometimes fall: the dangerous spot may be passed in 3 or 4 minutes. No. 18 is called La Ramasse. Here sledges are kept; and in winter, when deep snow covers the inequalities on the sides of the mountain, travellers may descend in one of them to Lanslebourg in 10 minutes! The sledge is guided by a peasant, who places himself in front; and, from the experience gained in collecting (*ramasser*) and transporting wood in this manner, they are so skilful, that there is little risk in this extraordinary mode of travelling. The perpendicular descent is 600 mètres—nearly 2000 ft.

The 17th Refuge is the barrier of Savoy: here a toll is levied, to keep the road in repair. Soon after the highest point of the pass is reached, 6825 ft. above the sea level; thence the road descends to the plain of Mont Cenis, passing near the margin of a small lake, which is generally frozen during 6 months of the year: it is famed for its delicious trout: the fishery belongs to the monks of the Hospice.

Inns: Posthouse of the *Mont Cenis* (Monte Cenisio), and the Old Posthouse, rough; where travellers may regale on the excellent trout of the lake, and sometimes on ptarmigan, for which they will, however, pay handsomely. This magnificent road, another monument of the genius of the imperial road-maker, Napoleon, was commenced by his orders in 1803, and finished in 1810, at an expense of 300,000*l.* The engineer was the Chevalier Fabbroni, a Tuscan. It is one of the safest roads over the Alps, and the most practicable in winter time. From the posthouse the ascent of the Little Mont Cenis (Rte. 128) commences.

About half a mile beyond the Post is the *Hospice,* originally founded by Charlemagne, who crossed the Mont Cenis with an army in the 9th century. The existing edifice, built by

Napoleon, is now occupied, half by a corps of carbineers who examine the *passports* of all travellers crossing the mountain; the other half by monks of the Benedictine order, who exercise gratuitous hospitality towards poor travellers. The house contains two or three neat bed-rooms for guests of the higher class. Near the Hospice is a loopholed wall, for the defence of the pass.

The road is tolerably level to *Grande Croix*, a wretched *Inn* at the lower extremity of the plain, with one or two taverns occupied by carters and muleteers; there the descent begins. The road, as originally constructed, skirted along the sides of the mountain; but owing to its fearful exposure to avalanches, this portion of it has been abandoned, and a new line, reached by winding tourniquets, descends directly through the plain of St. Nicolas, over which it is carried on a raised causeway, quite out of the reach of avalanches, except between the 3rd and 4th Refuges, where they still sometimes fall in spring. A gallery cut in the rock where the old road passed, is now abandoned: it exhibits a singular scene of confusion, the roof having partly fallen in. The barrier of Piedmont stands in the midst of the little plain of St. Nicolas. On issuing from this plain, a magnificent mountain on the l. is seen—the *Rochemelon*: on its summit is the chapel of Nôtre Dame des Neiges, which is visited on the 6th of August every year by an incredible number of pilgrims. Men, women, and children ascend on the day before, about three-quarters of the distance, sleep out on the mountain, and complete the ascent early on the following morning, so as to hear morning mass upon the glacier at the summit! The road now skirts a dreary ravine, at the bottom of which are seen the villages of Ferrière and Navalèse, deserted in the summer: the old mule-road passed through them.

Molaret, the first Piedmontese village. From one of the turns in the zigzags beyond this place fine views of the valley of the Dora towards Turin are obtained, but the sides of the mountain are unusually barren. A gallery is passed, built under a torrent, and only used when the main-road is dangerous or destroyed by the torrent. The descent is now continuous by long zigzags to

Susa. (*Inns:* La Posta; Hôtel de Savoie; H. de France, best.) This little town of 3500 Inhab., planted at the point of junction of the roads over the Mont Genèvre (Rte. 130) and the Mont Cenis, is chiefly remarkable on account of its antiquity, having been founded by a Roman colony in the reign of Augustus, under the name of Segusio. It appears, like most Italian towns, to have decayed, but it now seems reviving. There is a very curious Romanesque church and cloisters, and a gateway adjoining the church. There is also a Roman triumphal arch, of the Corinthian order, erected about 8 B.C., in honour of Augustus. It is in a sadly-neglected condition, and stands a little way outside the town, in what was formerly the governor's garden: but Susa and the rest of the route to Turin are described in the HANDBOOK FOR NORTH ITALY.

The railway is now open from Susa with trains for Turin 3 times a-day, performing the journey in 2 hrs.

TURIN *Terminus.* (*Inns:* Hôtel de l'Europe, the best; Grande Bretagne; Hôtel Feder; Hôtel de la Ligurie, near the Rlwy. Stat.—Omnibuses run to the different hotels on the arrival of each train.

For TURIN, see the HANDBOOK FOR NORTH ITALY.

[The voituriers now keep their horses, &c., at Susa, but are generally to be engaged at Turin. If engaged in due time they will send their horses on to Grande Croix, and post up to that point, thus saving much delay, and reaching Modane, or perhaps St. Jean and Chambery, from Turin in one day. Time actually occupied on the road, 1857:—Susa to Molaret, 2 hrs.; Grande Croix, 2 hrs.; 17th Refuge, 1 hr. 10 min.; Lanslebourg, 50 min.; Modane, 2 hrs. 25 min.; St. Jean, 2 hrs.

35 min. Total: Susa to St. Jean, 11 hrs., exclusive of stoppages.]

ROUTE 128.

MONT CENIS TO SUSA, BY THE LITTLE MONT CENIS AND THE COL DE CLAIRÉE.

Those who would make an excursion by the Little Mont Cenis, a singularly wild route, instead of quietly descending by the high road from the Mont Cenis to Susa, may accomplish it easily in 10 hrs. Turin may be reached the same day by a late train from Susa.

None but a practised mountaineer should attempt this very interesting route, as the path along the watercourse traversing the face of the precipices above the Val de Clairée, is not adapted for those who have weak heads. Take provisions. The posthouse of the Mont Cenis (Rte. 127) is left by a path which descends directly to the lake, then, skirting its upper border and across the meadows, it soon ascends rapidly towards the pasturages which lead to the châlets of the Little Mont Cenis, which are distant from the posthouse 2 hrs. The mountain slopes around the plain of the Mont Cenis offer some of the richest pasturages in the Alps; those which lead to the Little Mont Cenis are of great extent.

A very little way beyond the châlets of the Little Mont Cenis, the col is attained, and the valley which descends to Bramante, in the valley of the Arc, and which lies at right angles with the path across the col, is seen through a great part of its length. On the opposite side of this valley rises the peak of the Grand Vallon; and a little on the left, from a deep turn in the valley below, called the Combe d'Ambin, rises one of the finest peaks in this part of the Alps, the Mont d'Ambin: on it is the station used in the triangulation and measure of an arc of the meridian across the great chain. The entire crest of the Ambin is covered with glaciers, and every crue is traced by a white bed of snow that rests within it. At the lower extremity of the valley of Bramante the mountains of the Vanoise close the view.

To ascend this valley it is necessary to mount from the col of the Little Mont Cenis directly up some rocks, and continue for a short time on that side of the mountain; the path afterwards descends among vast rocks which strew this sterile-looking valley; and, after leaving on the right the turn in the ravine below, which forms the Combe d'Ambin, through which a stream, like a thread of silver, flows, the path ascends up a rugged and broken course until it reaches the châlets of Savines. Here there is a rich little spot of meadow land, and a scanty herbage on the slopes of the valley. On the left, a rugged path leads across from the posthouse on the Cenis by some little lakes in the mountains of Bard, to this valley, above the châlets of Savines: it is rather shorter, but more fatiguing. Wolves are not uncommon in the forest of Bramante, lower down the valley, the dogs kept at the châlets of Savines are of great power, having their necks armed with spiked collars. The wolves here are probably the successors of those ravenous rascals that gobbled up Walpole's poor little dog Toby, as his master passed with the poet Gray at the foot of this forest on his way into Italy.

Above the meadows of Savines, the path rises amidst rocks and stones, and at length reaches a little lake in an elevated plain, in which all seems desolate, solitary, and sterile. The black precipices of the mountain of Bard on the left hand and those of the Mont d'Ambin on the right, bound its sides:

from the Ambin enormous glaciers sweep down to the lake, and small cataracts, from the melting of the ice on either side, mark their courses by light lines that stream down the precipices, and make their dark masses still blacker. Amidst this apparent sterility thousands of gentianellas, ranunculus glacialis, violets of the richest fragrance, and a hundred other Alpine flowers, grow and bloom unseen, in every swampy spot, and between the stones with which the plain and col are covered.

This lake is filled by the meltings of the glaciers of the Mont d'Ambin. It is called the Lac Blanc, or Lac de Savines: it is about 1 m. long. At its upper extremity is a low ridge certainly not a hundred feet above the level of the lake. This is a crest of the great chain, the Col de Clairée: across it two paths lie—that on the rt., by a wild and difficult course, leads over the Col de Touilles to Salabertrand, in the Val d'Exilles.

The route to Susa lies on the left: by it the descent from the Col de Clairée is down a steep and rocky hollow, which terminates at the crossing of a bright stream near a pasturage. This spot, where wine may be cooled in the stream, is a delicious place of rest, and where the refreshment, which it is necessary for the traveller to take with him from the inn on the Mont Cenis, will be fully enjoyed. From this place of rest a steep slope leads down to the pasturage seen from the resting-place. It is a flat, surmounting enormous precipices, which seem to forbid any attempt to descend from them; and there will be little disposition immediately to seek a path, for from this spot one of the most glorious views in the Alps is presented. Immediately below is the deep basin and narrow valley of the Clairée, which is almost always filled with vapour that seems to boil as in a caldron: when the clouds from it rise high enough to catch the current of air, they disperse.

Beyond this valley, the mountain above Chaumont, in the Val d'Exilles,

bounds the view; but, turning towards the left, the Combe of Susa is seen over the intervening mountains, even to its termination in the plains of Piedmont, stretching away to the horizon far beyond the hill of the Superga.

On the rt. are the steep rocks, which must be climbed by those who would go from the Col de Clairée to the Col de Touilles.

So abrupt are the edges of the precipices that divide the lower valley from this pasturage, that descent seems hopeless. "We stood," says one who has travelled much in these unfrequented passes of the Alps, "on the brink of enormous precipices, their outlines at our feet cut abruptly against the clouds, into which, through occasional openings made by the wind, we could see the black, deep, and shadowed valley. The scene was most impressive. Our guide was puzzled for a short time by the clouds which obscured the point for which we should make. At length he led us down the precipice by a most extraordinary path, which it was difficult to discover. It was like winding steps which had been rudely cut in a crevice: it seemed like a descent through a chimney. Below this rift, a steep, difficult, stony, and most fatiguing path brought us to some Piedmontese châlets.

"Though the clouds seemed to sink as we descended, they sometimes in their changes enveloped us; and we were glad to hear the voice of a boy, who, having heard us, shouted to us from the châlets, to tell us what direction we should take.

"A still more difficult path led us further down to some other châlets, below which there were extensive pasturages on a steep slope. Having crossed these, we entered a wood, down through which the most abrupt and fatiguing part of our route lay, which would scarcely have been practicable but for the entangled roots. From the wood we emerged upon a rocky slope, and, after a march of 8 or 9 hrs., reached a few scattered stone huts at the head of the Val de Clairée. On looking back we appeared to have descended the face of a precipice, down which the numerous streams of the Clairée ran from the summit as if they issued from the sky, to the torrent by which we rested: the white lines were traceable through three or four thousand feet of their descent.

"The pass of the Clairée is, on the Italian side, the steepest that I have ever traversed. This was one of the many difficult passes by which the Vaudois, in 1687, under their pastor and captain, Henri Arnaud, returned to their valleys. They had, after entering Savoy, wandered by a course rather difficult to trace, until they had crossed the Col de Bonhomme, whence they descended into the Tarentaise, traversed the Mont Iseran into the valley of the Arc; thence by the Mont Cenis, the Little Mont Cenis, and the Col de Clairée, into the valley of the Clairée. Here they encountered the troops of the Grand Duke of Savoy, who prevented their entry into the valley of Exilles by the Clairée, and they were compelled to return and cross the Col de Touilles, from which the southern branch of the Clairée, called the Ciauri, flows. The account of their sufferings, before they cleared these mountain passes, and so signally defeated their enemies at the bridge of Salabertrand, forms a part of one of the most interesting narratives ever published; it was written by Henri Arnaud himself, their colonel and pastor.*

"The recollection of their perilous adventures," says the author of 'Excursions in the Alps,' "was vividly recalled whilst sitting on a spot which they also had visited, resting ourselves from a fatiguing descent which they

had encountered, and in sight of the savage mountain of Les Touilles, by which they were compelled to retreat, and encounter yet further dangers. The few miserable huts near us were uninhabited, and neither afforded shelter nor food. Continuing our route, we kept close to the torrent, from which a large stream was separated for irrigation. By the side of the channel of this stream we continued some way; then the road sank below it; afterwards we ascended rapidly by a steep path cut out at the foot of precipices, which rose in unbroken grandeur directly over us.

"Along the face of these rocks the channel for the watercourse was cut; and though, at our greatest elevation above the valley of Clairée, we were at least a thousand feet higher than the natural bed of the torrent, we were still below the head of the artificial channel whence its waters flowed rapidly towards us. It was difficult to believe the fact before our eyes; and, as we looked back into the short, deep, narrow valley that we had left, and whilst we saw the Clairée foaming down its course, the aqueduct seemed to *ascend* steeply from the valley. This water is led round the brow of the mountain to irrigate the meadows above Jaillon. From the highest point of our passage the view up the valley of the Doire to Exilles was very fine; and immediately after passing this point, the Combe of Susa opened to us from between the Roche Melon and the Col de Fenêtre, to the plains beyond Turin. We soon fell into the high road from the Mont Cenis (Rte. 127A); and about 7 o'clock reached the Hôtel de la Poste at

Susa Station (Rte. 127A)."

* It was translated by the late Hugh Dyke Acland, from a rare copy, under the title of 'The Glorious Recovery by the Vaudois of their Valleys.' An account of these interesting people, and of this their most remarkable adventure, has been given to the world by Dr. Wm. Beattie, in his History of the Waldenses, published by Virtue, which contains engraved views of the eventful scenes through which they passed.

ROUTE 129.

GRENOBLE TO BRIANÇON, BY BOURG
D'OYSANS AND THE COL DE LAUTA-
RET.

(Two days.)

63 kilo. = 39 Eng. m.

Grenoble (Gratianopolis), the chief
city in the Dépt. de l'Isère, an important place beautifully situated,
and having a population of 25,000,
is described in the HANDBOOK FOR
FRANCE. It is here only mentioned
as the starting point for an excursion
across the Col de Lautaret to the pass
of the Mont Genèvre.

Courier every night to Briançon
takes 4 or 5 passengers. Diligence
during the summer to Bourg in 5 or
6 hrs., whence to Briançon takes 8 or
10 hrs. Conveyance very dear. Grenoble to Susa 220 fr. Car from Bourg
to Briançon, a long and heavy day,
50 fr.

There is a good but very circuitous
road from Grenoble by Vizille, Gap
and Embrun to Briançon, and a diligence goes to the latter town daily
from Grenoble; but it is 50 m. further,
and through a country that is generally uninteresting, whilst that by the
Col de Lautaret abounds with some of
the finest scenes in the Alps.

To save this distance, Napoleon
commenced the construction of a new
road by this pass, and many magnificent works were completed upon it,
but after his abdication it was abandoned, and has only been lately completed. The bridges were all de-
troyed by the floods in May, 1856.

A perfectly level communication has
been made by the new road to Marseilles, up the plain, through fine avenues to the village of La Claix, where
there is a remarkable bridge over the
Drac. The road to Vizille thence continues up the banks of the Romanche
by a course nearly level.

Vizille has about 2000 Inhab. Its
inns are wretched. It is considered
as the cradle of the first French revolution, for here the parliament of

Dauphiny first made a declaration
fatal to the power of the Bourbons.
Here is the *Château* of the constable
Lesdiguières. It had, since the revolution, become the property of M.
Périer, the brother of the minister,
who had established cotton or flax
works here; but it was partly destroyed by fire in 1825.

The road ascends by the right
bank of the Romanche through a narrow, but beautiful and well-wooded
valley, which runs with nearly the
same wild character into the heart of
the mountains for 6 or 7 leagues. In
some places the valley widens enough
for the establishment of a village or a
hamlet: of these, Chichilane, Gavet,
and La Clavet are the principal. Near
Gavet there are some iron works.
The Combe de Gavet, a remarkable
ravine or Combe, which is also an
English, or rather Celtic name for a
defile, extends from the plain of
Vizille to the plain of the Bourg
d'Oysans, a fertile valley, surrounded
by lofty mountains. It is within
record that a large lake was formed
in the 11th century by the falling
of the neighbouring mountains at the
entrance of the Combe de Gavet:
this dammed the river, and the waters
accumulated in the plain above, and
formed a large lake, of which the
surface was 3 leagues long, and 1
wide, and its depth from 60 to 80 ft.
This lake existed for about 200 years.
At length, in September, 1229, it
burst its barrier, rushed into the
Combe of Gavet, swept away in
its fury everything that it touched,
rapidly passed into the Drac, and
hence into the Isère, then, flowing
over the plain below the two rivers,
submerged a great part of Grenoble.
At the lower extremity of the plain,
of Bourg d'Oysans, a path across the
mountains leads to the valley of Alle-
mont, where there are iron works, but
the readiest access to them is from
the valley of Gresivaudan, above
Grenoble. Very near Bourg d'Oysans, a gold-mine is still worked.

Bourg d'Oysans (H. de Milan, fair
but dear) is situated on the l. bank
of the river, and near the upper ex-

tremity of the plain. The vegetation of its valley is remarkably rich; the lofty mountains that surround it offer in some places precipitous faces that present extraordinary instances of tortuous stratification. On approaching the Bourg, the enormous Mont de Lens, wrapped in glaciers, closes the head of the valley, and divides the torrent which flows from the dark gorges of the Vençon, which descends from the valley of St. Christopher, from that of the Romanche, which flows through the Combe of Malval.

By starting from this betimes it is possible to reach Briançon before dark. In 5 or 6 hrs. to La Grave. Thence to Col de Lauteret is 2 hrs. walk (road good thus far), and 3 more hrs. down to Monestier (steep and bad road), and 3 short hrs. thence to Briançon. It is best to change chars at Villars d'Arène, as the day is long.

[An interesting excursion may be made from Bourg d'Oysans to La Berarde, in the upper part of the valley of St. Christophe, between 10 and 12 hours' walk from the Bourg. The only fair inn on the whole route is at the finely situated village of Venos (*Inn*, Pagnet, tolerable but exorbitant), 4 hrs. from Bourg d'Oysans, where there are tolerable quarters, but the traveller must carry fresh meat. St. Christophe is 2 hrs. above Venos, and La Berarde lies at the foot of Mont Pelvoux, the highest peak in the southern Alps. The scenery of the whole valley, and especially at and above La Berarde, may vie in grandeur with any in the Alps. The valley is little known; but a day devoted to visiting it will be remembered with gratification by the lover of sublime scenery.]

A little beyond the Bourg, the road twice crosses the Romanche, and ascends by its left bank very high above the *Infernet*, as the inaccessible Combe of Malval is called, and at least 800 ft. over the torrent. The ancient road—for this course was known from the Romans, from Briançon to Grenoble—passed much higher behind Mont Lens, where there is a village of this name, 4200 ft. above

the level of the sea. In carrying the new road along, above the torrent, where the escarpments of the mountains are bare, smooth, and nearly perpendicular, wherever it has been possible to cut away the rock in open day, the road has been terraced ; but where masses projected which could not be removed, these have been boldly cut through, and a gallery has been made in one place 200 ft. longer than that of Gondo, in the route of the Simplon. Three lateral openings were found to be necessary to light the gallery; from these a sight of the foaming course of the torrent, 800 ft. below, may be gained.

From the last gallery, the road rises up through a valley filled with rocks and blocks of enormous size that have fallen from the mountains above, and which are interspersed with a few trees and a scanty cultivation. In the midst of such a desert lies the hamlet of

Le Dauphin, 4 leagues from Bourg d'Oysans : here refreshment may be had at an auberge. Above Le Dauphin, the savage and rocky character of the valley predominates ; and the traveller enters a nearly straight ravine of almost unequalled wildness, bounded by the precipitous bases of mountains thousands of feet in height, almost everywhere inaccessible, those of Mont de Lens on the rt. absolutely so, and crowned by fields of ice and snow, which, owing to the height and abruptness of the defile, can only here and there be seen from below.

Numerous streams are crossed, which descend in falls from the glaciers that crest the precipices, and foaming over the steep talus formed on the sides of the valley by the disintegration of the mountain, cross the road, and add to the fury of the Romanche. Not far from Le Dauphin, on the l., a magnificent cataract gushes out from the top of the precipice, and falls in a large volume into the valley below ; this is called *Le Saut de la Pucelle*. The universal story of a peasant-girl leaping down unhurt, to escape the violence of a chasseur, is applied to this fall also.

s 3

So vast are some of the blocks that strew the valley, that one among others measures 50 paces in length, and against several, stone huts and châlets are raised and sheltered ; for though there appear to be little herbage here, what there is is rich enough to induce those who have herds to send them here to pasturage.

Still further up the valley, near a fine cataract, on the L, are the lead-mines of Les Freaux, belonging to M. Marat de l'Ombre, where many workmen are employed to raise the ore and smelt it. The adits are seen high upon the precipitous sides of the mountains, and ropes and machinery extend into the valley below ; these mines are said to be worked to advantage. The completion of this road to Grenoble would be to the proprietors a measure of great importance.

At the head of this savage valley the road rises to the miserable village of La Grave, where the *Inn*, though small, affords tolerable fare, but qy. as to beds.

The situation of La Grave is very fine, directly opposite to the vast glaciers of the range of Mont Pelvoux, which present a scene of the most striking grandeur. During the winter, the cold precludes the burying of the dead—the ground is too hard ; the bodies are therefore suspended in the granges until the returning spring. So wretchedly are the people off for fuel, that dried cow-dung is chiefly used.

On leaving La Grave, the path descends to pass some rocks ; then rising, it leads abruptly to a turn in the valley that overlooks a very fine fall of the Romanche, all its waters being poured into a deep abyss ; to flank this abyss, the road, making a little détour, rises above the head of the fall, and soon after the traveller reaches

Villars d'Arène, a wretched village (*Inn*, bad and dear). Here the mountain of the Lautaret commences, or rather, the mountain ridge, or barrier that divides the valley of the Romanche from that of Monestier or the Guisanne. This pass rises to the height of more than 6000 feet above the level of the sea; the col is covered with the most beautiful pasturage, and is one of the richest spots in the Dauphiny Alps for the harvest of the botanist.

On the summit, 2 leagues from Villars d'Arène, there is a *Maison Hospitalier*, one of those founded by Humbert II. in the 11th century; this is kept by a peasant appointed to the duty; but travellers are cautioned not to trust to getting fed there, though wine always, and bread and curds sometimes, may be found on the Lautaret.

The scene from the col is most sublime: immediately above it, on the rt., is the Mont d'Arcines, scathed, and pinnacled with rocks, and clothed with enormous glaciers, ending, on the side of the Romanche, in the glacier of Tabuchet, whence this river has its source; on the other side, the river Guisanne is seen tumbling down the Mont d'Arcines, from its glaciers, to flow through the valley of Monestier.

From the *Col de Lautaret* a very steep road descends into the sterile and miserable valley of the Guisanne, to the first hamlet, La Madelaine; still lower is the village of Casset, at the base of the glacier of Lasciale ; and at the end of nearly 3 hrs. from the Col de Lautaret are the

Baths of Monestier, 14 leagues from Bourg d'Oysans: here there are several inns, much frequented during the season, of which the best, Chez Armand, affords very humble quarters.

The mineral waters here have a temperature of 101°, and are both drank and employed in baths: they are so abundant that they are employed to turn a mill. Below Monestier, the valley exhibits cultivation; barley is grown, and the meadows, by irrigations, are very productive; and, after the naked and sterile route from Le Dauphin to Monestier, the appearance of trees is hailed as giving the highest charm to the scenery.

The whole course of the Guisanne can be seen to Briançon, where the forts of this frontier town are visible, piled above each other; beyond is a chain of lofty mountains, over which is seen the peak of the Monte Viso; this is a magnificent scene.

There are several villages in the Val Monestier below the baths; the principal are La Salle, Chantemerle, so named from the number of blackbirds that frequent it; and St. Chaffrey. The approach to Briançon is strikingly fine, its walls and forts rising as they do to the highest *l'Infernet*, which is placed on a peak, nearly 10,000 ft. above the level of the sea; the broad rich valley of the Durance below the town, and the mountain boundaries to the valley, make this one of the most picturesque towns and scenes in the Alps.

Briançon, 3 hours' walk from Monestier. (*Inn:* l'Ours, best ;—H. de la Paix, very dirty.) This town is a frontier fortress, with gates and regular defences, and every strong position is occupied with a fort or battery; it guards the frontier of France by the pass of the Mont Genèvre and the valley of the Durance. A diligence goes daily to and from Embrun, and a diligence to Susa.

It is a city of high antiquity. Pliny attributed its foundation to the Greeks, who were chased from the borders of the lake of Como; others have given its foundation to Bellovesus or Brennus. Ammianus Marcellinus calls it Virgantia Castellum. It held a Roman garrison. St. Ambrose was here on his way to Vienne in Dauphiny when he heard of the death of the Emperor Valens, whom he was going to baptize.

This little city is one of the smallest in France, having less than 3000 Inhab. The streets are narrow and steep, but many of the houses are well built. It boasts of a Grande Place : its church is not worth a visit.

The town itself is strong from its position and mural defences, but the seven forts which guard it render it almost impregnable. Between the city and some of these forts there is a bridge over the deep bed of the Durance, which foams beneath vast precipices. The bridge is of bold construction, a single arch of 130 English feet span, and 180 feet above the torrent. It was built in 1730, under the direction of the Maréchal d'Asfeld.

See HANDBOOK FOR FRANCE.

ROUTE 130.

BRIANÇON TO SUSA, BY THE PASS OF THE MONT GENÈVRE.

Diligence to Susa, but no post-horses.

On leaving Briançon for the Mont Genèvre, the valley of the Durance is ascended by a narrow gorge for more than a league, as far as La Vachette, a little hamlet at the foot of the Mont Genèvre. Here, on the l., opens the Val de Neuvache, a fine, large, and productive valley, a striking contrast to the valley of the Guisanne. It is also called the Val des Prés, from its rich meadows. Its mountains are clothed with forests ; through it the river Clairée flows for 10 leagues, and then loses its name in a less considerable torrent—the Durance, which has scarcely run 2 leagues from its source in the Mont Genèvre. At the foot of the Mont Genèvre is a fountain which formerly bore the name of Napoleon, and served to commemorate the construction of the new route. This was removed by the Bourbons, lest some thirsty wayfarer should bless his memory.

The ascent commences through a pine forest, and by a series of admirably constructed zigzags leads the traveller up to the col, and presents at every turn a variety in the views of Briançon and its forts, the valleys of the Durance and Neuvache, and the surrounding mountains : these so much relieve the tedium of ascent that the summit is attained before the traveller has any idea that he has accomplished a distance of nearly 2 leagues. The old road continued by the pine forests up the l. bank of the stream, and pedestrians still pusrue it, as it is much the shortest to attain the Col of the Mont Genèvre.

The plain of the Mont Genèvre is remarkable for the culture of barley on its summit, nearly 6000 ft. above the level of the sea, and there are fine pasturages on the slopes of the neighbouring mountains. On the plain there is a village called the

Bourg Mont Genèvre, 3 leagues from Briançon, which is inhabited all the year. Here is the custom-house, a troublesome place to those who enter *La belle France*.

On the plain, and almost from a common source, two rivers rise—the Durance, which flows into France and the Mediterranean, and the Doira-Susana, which flows into the Po and the Adriatic.

On the summit of the plain an obelisk was erected to commemorate the construction, in 1807, of this fine road over the Alps. It is 60 ft. high, and had on its pedestal inscriptions to record the event: these the Bourbons removed.

On leaving the Col of the Mont Genèvre, the course of the river is followed for 2 leagues down a series of tourniquets, made in the loose soil on the side of Mont Chabertan, along which the road is carried, until it reaches the bed of the river and crosses it about 2 miles from Cesanne; the road then continues to this village, where the stream from the Mont Genèvre falls into a larger branch, which descends from the lofty mountains that bound the Protestant Valleys of Piedmont.

Cesanne, where there are two miserable inns, is not more than 3½ hours' good walk from Briançon.

Below Cesanne, the course lies down the valley to Susa by a miserable road for carriages. The first important commune in the valley is

Oulx, 3 leagues, a large village at the entrance to the valley of Bar-

donnèche, whence there is a pass by the Col de la Rue to Modane, in the valley of the Arc. From Oulx, it is about 2 leagues to Salabertrand, a place memorable for the battle fought and won by the Vaudois, under Henri Arnaud, on their return to their valleys, after expatriation, in 1689, when they were opposed by 2500 regular entrenched troops, three times their numbers, and commanded by the Marquis de Larrey, who was wounded in the action : every spot around has interest in connection with that event : the mountain by which they had descended on the night of the battle ; and that by the Col de Sou, which they had crossed to go into their valleys after their victory.

Beyond Salabertrand the valley narrows considerably, and forms, a good league below, near the fort of Exilles, a deep defile; in the midst of this the fort is placed, which perfectly commands the valley; here the river is crossed, and the road thence continues on its rt. bank, beneath the heights of Chaumont—a spot rendered memorable by the fate of the Comte de Belleisle, who fell here on the 9th of July, 1747 : his desperate valour, which had been excited by the promise of a Bâton de Maréchal of France, if he succeeded in forcing the pass, was checked after he had received many severe wounds, by a *coup de grace* from a grenadier of the regiment of Monferrat.

At the village of Exilles tolerable accommodation and much civility will be found at the house of the postmaster.

The valley, in and below the defile, is richly wooded, and preserves nearly the same character for 3 leagues, from Salabertrand to

Susa (Rte. 127), 22 m. from Cesanne.

ROUTE 131.

BRIANÇON TO PIGNEROL, BY THE COL
DE SESTRIERES.

Travellers should send on horses to
Fénestrelles, and try to reach Pignerol in one day, as the intermediate
inns are very bad. As far as Cesanne,
see Rte. 130.

It is 10 hrs. hard walking from
Cesanne to Perouse.

The road made by order of Napoleon, from Cesanne, to descend into
Italy, is more direct than that by
Turin. Though at first neglected by
the Sardinian government, it is now in
good order, and furnished with post-
horses at Fenestrelles, 33 kilom. from
Pignerol.

The road from Cesanne crosses the
Doire, and the ascent to the col immediately commences, by a series of zigzags like that of the descent from the
Mont Genèvre ; a lengthened snake-
like course of each can be seen from the
other across the valley of the Doire. It
soon reaches the hamlet of Champlas;
still continuing to ascend over fine pasturages, till it reaches

2¼ hrs. The Col de Sestrieres and
châlets: the plain of the col is nearly
2 miles long. On the side towards
the Val Pragelas, the view is wild
and fine of the valley and the Mont
Albergian. Above the Fort of Fénestrelles, the road leads down by
tourniquets to the banks of the Clusone, and to the first village, Sestrieres,
4 leagues from Cesanne, and thence
to the villages of Pragelas and

1½ hr. Traverse: the road bed of
the river beneath the dark pine forests
opposite to Pragelas, the lowest in
the valley of the two villages, gives
rather an appearance of sterility to
the valley. At Traverse there is a
humble *Inn* (La Rose Rouge—clean
beds). The Clusone gives a general
name to the whole valley, but among
its inhabitants the upper part above
the fort of Fénestrelles is called the
Val Pragelas; below the fort it is often
called the Val de Perouse.

2 hrs 40 min. *Fénestrelles,* a village
of 800 Inhab., with a bad and filthy
Inn. The *fort of Fénestrelles* is a place
of great strength, which guards the
approach to Piedmont by this valley.
It rises, from the defile formed by the
base of the Mont Albergian, to the
summit of the mountain, and commands the left bank of the torrent by
its immense ranges of fortifications
rising in terraces. The highest battery
is accessible through a gallery that
contains 3600 steps. On the summit
is a basin covered with verdure, called
the Pré de Catinât, from that general
having encamped there.

These works have been in progress
of construction by the Sardinian government since 1816. They succeeded
an older fortress in 5 tiers of forts,
blown up by the army of the French
Republic. The 3 detached forts—
about a mile distant from the town,
called St. Charles, Trois Dents, and
des Vallées—command the approaches.
A 4th battery, called Charles Albert,
sweeps the high road and closes all
passage.

There are remains of old forts on
the base of the Albergian, which were
built by the French when this country
belonged to them, in order to defend
the pass in the opposite direction.
The village of Fénestrelles lies in the
middle of the defile below. The fort
of Fénestrelles is used as a state prison. It is the scene of M. Saintine's
pretty tale of " Picciola."

[From Fénestrelles there is a very
pretty Pass, by the *Col de la Fenêtre,*
in 6 hrs. to Susa in the valley of the
Doire. From the top, which is car-
petted with gentianellas, is a magnificent view over the Doire, in which
the Roche Melun mountain is a
striking object for the last hour or two
of rugged descent.]

From Fénestrelles to Pignerol
there are 8 leagues, almost entirely
through the valley of the Clusone.
There is little variety in its scenery;
it is generally narrow; but where there
is cultivation, corn and wine abound.
The mulberry for silkworms flourishes, and fruit and forest trees luxuriate, as they almost always do on the
side of Piedmont. Formerly, this
valley was filled with a Protestant

community, but their living in it was long prohibited. The Vaudois churches were not permitted out of the valleys of Rora. La Tour (known also as the valley of Lucerna and the Val Pelice), St. Martin, and Angrogna; but the more liberal policy of the Government since 1848 has removed this restriction.

Below Fénestrelles, the route passes through numerous villages and hamlets—Montole, Rouse Villaret, and Chapelle—before reaching Perosa or 3 hrs. 10 min. *Perouse Inns:* Sole) Antico; Auberge Nationale), the principal town in the valley, which is sometimes called the Valley of Perouse. It is situated directly opposite to the valley of St. Martin or the Germanasca, one of the most interesting of the Protestant valleys.

[This leads up by the torrent of the Germanasca to *Pomaret* and *Perrier* (or Pierrers), through scenes of great richness and beauty. Above Perrier two branches meet: that to the S.W. leads to *Rodoretto* and *Pralis;* that on the N.W. has, above a defile on its opposite side, amidst fruit-trees, corn, and pasturages, the commune of *Maneille.* A little beyond the road enters a deep ravine of the Germanasca, which is singularly wild and beautiful; at its upper extremity it opens into the valley below the Commune of *Marcel,* nearly opposite to the valley which leads across the Col de la Fontaine to Pralis.

Continuing up the valley of the Germanasca, the house of the M. Tron, the Syndic of Marcel, is passed; a singularly handsome structure in such a situation. About a league above this spot is the hamlet of *Balsille;* and immediately over it, the celebrated Castella, a terrace on the side of a peaked mountain, where the Vaudois entrenched themselves under Henri Arnaud. Here the little handful of brave men, not exceeding from 600 to 700, struggled for their fatherland, and fought, for three days, the united armies of France and Sardinia, amounting to 22,000 men. When the latter, however, found it necessary to bring up artillery, which was accom-

plished with excessive difficulty, the heroic Vaudois, foreseeing that against the cannon they could not hold their position, retreated during the night without losing a man; and the following day, their sovereign of Sardinia, having quarrelled with his allies, agreed to restore them to their valleys and their hearths. No history exists so replete with wonderful adventures as that of the simple peasants of these valleys, who fought and suffered, and reconquered, for liberty of conscience.

Above the Balsille, one of the grandest assemblages of materials for alpine scenery is to be found, in cataracts, ravines, and mountains: from the head of the valley there is a pass by the Col du Piz to Pragelas in the valley of Clusone. The author has crossed from Pragelas to Perouse in one day, and he knows no finer traverse in the Alps, and the panorama from the col is one of the most sublime in the great chain.

Another pass between the valleys of the Germanasca and the Clusone is that by the Col Albergian, which leads from the Balsille and the wild valley and Alps above it to Fénestrelles.

From Perouse to the Balsille, and back to Perouse, may be accomplished easily in a day.]

[There is an interesting pass from the lower part of the Val Germanasca to *Pra del Tor,* in the Val Angrogna, and thence to La Tour de Luserna.]

On the route from Perouse to Pignerol some fine quarries are passed, where stone is raised for the public works of Turin; nearly opposite to these is seen another of the Protestant churches, St. Germano, and the little valley which leads to *Pramol;* still further down is the church of *Prarustin,* nearly opposite to where the valley widens, and the road enters upon the plains, through the hamlets of Port and Abadia, to

Pignerol (Ital. Pinerolo)—(*Inns:* Corona, good; Albergo de Campagna, good—in existence?). Pignerol is a straggling town, having some manufactures and a large and rather uncivil population, 13,500. It was once for·tified.

The *Convent of St. Francis* is partly ancient, and its *Church* contains monuments to ancestors of the royal house of Savoy.

On the hill of *St. Brigide* are ruins of a chapel, and of the ancient *citadel*, in which the "Man in the Iron Mask" was shut up.

Railway 23½ m.; 3 trains a-day in 1 hr. 10 min. to Turin; the stations being Riva, Piscina, Avrasca, None, Candiolo, Nichelino, and·Sangone.

ROUTE 132.

PIGNEROL TO MONT DAUPHIN, BY THE VALLEYS OF THE VAUDOIS AND THE COL DE LA CROIX.

From *Pignerol* (Rte. 131) to La Tour a diligence daily; 10 Eng. m.: the route lies through St. Secundo to Bischerasco, 5 m., and 3 m. further to the first Protestant commune at

St. Giovanni. Here a church was built while Piedmont was under the government of Napoleon. Upon the restoration of the house of Sardinia, the Roman Catholics, whose church is on the other side of a little stream, complained that the voices of the Protestants in singing disturbed their devotions, and an order was given to shut out the abomination by a large barricade of wood, which the Vaudois were compelled to erect before the door of their church. This has now, however, dropped away bit by bit, and little remains of this evidence of intolerance. The church is of a singular form—a horse-shoe—but it is not favourable to the preacher or his congregation.

A short league beyond St. Giovanni, through a fertile country, lies

La Tour (*Inns*; L'Ours, chez Gay, opposite Gen. Beckwith's house, clean and good ; Lion d'Or, chez Rottier), the principal town of the Protestant communities, unusually clean for Italy. The valley of La Tour is known also as the valley of Luserna and the Val Pellice. A very handsome *Protestant Church* has been built here since 1848, with residences for the clergy and professors. General Beckwith contributed largely to it.

An *hospital* has been established for the sick and poor among the Protestants, by funds raised chiefly in Holland, Russia, and England. In 1837, by the aid of an anonymous gift from England, of 5000*l.* confided to the late Rev. Dr. Gilly, a *College* was established here for the education of young men for the ministry of the Vaudois churches, and they have thus removed the necessity which had hitherto existed of sending them to Geneva or Lausanne. This institution is chiefly endowed by funds raised in foreign countries, but owing in a great measure to the liberality, the exertions, and the zeal for the cause of the Vaudois, of General Beckwith and Dr. Gilly. To the latter the Vaudois are under the deepest obligations for the interest he took in them and the influence his writings excited in their favour. A large Roman Catholic church has been built here for the conversion of the Vaudois, but it has been attended by signal failure. An orphanage under English auspices has lately been instituted, also a normal school.

Within ½ m. of Luserna a cotton-mill of 4 stories, moved by water-power, has been built by a Swiss Company.

No part of the Alps for richness and beauty in the lower valleys, and for wild and magnificent scenery in the defiles and mountains, surpasses the valleys of the Vaudois. Easy of access, by Railroad from Turin to Pignerol, La Tour is reached in 3 hrs. from that city, through a country luxuriant in vegetation. There are good inns at La Tour, to make headquarters for excursions ; and the civility of all classes to strangers, especially English, ought to be a recommendation to rambles in their country. Of the Vaudois generally, but especially of the mountaineers, it has been justly said, that "they are far superior in moral character to the Roman Catholic inhabitants; they are, from ancient habit, honest, civil, and quiet; and, from their situation and necessity, simple and laborious.

[One of the most interesting excursions from La Tour is into the valley of *Angrogna*, which is surrounded by lofty mountains and pasturages. It is richly wooded down to the deep defiles of its torrent, and presents every variety of scenery. Some of its wild scenes are associated with the history of the Vaudois; as the defiles or *Barricades of Pra del Tor* (2½ hrs.' walk from La Tour), which, defended by them, gave security to their families, who sought refuge within this grand and most picturesque defile. Above it, in the recesses of these mountains, concealed from the world for many ages, their Barbes, or teachers, imparted instruction, and fitted their pupils for the ministry. Every foot of ground in this valley is sacred in the history of this extraordinary people. In the Pra del Tor there has lately been erected a Roman Catholic church, but the heart of the valley is not the heart of the people. This excursion may be varied by crossing directly over the hill from a little below the Pra del Tor to St. Marguerite, and thence to La Tour (3 hrs.' walk): the whole excursion may be made in half a day.

The excursion may be varied by following the high-road to the village of Angrogna, which offers from many beautiful points of view the plains of Piedmont. The return may be made through the defiles, or on the steep slopes that bound the river. A day given to explore the Val Angrogna will be remembered with pleasure.]

From La Tour, up the valley of the Pellice, the road, widened for carriages as far as Bobbio, but execrably rough, passes by the hamlet of St. Marguerite, near the rock of

Castelluz, where is situated a Protestant church. Beyond this hamlet the ascent of the valley is rich and picturesque. About 2½ hrs. from La Tour, passing the village of *Villar*,

Bobbio is reached. No inn. A station of Sardinian préposés, or douaniers, and a café, where Jacques Raimond, a civil and experienced guide for the mountains, may be heard of. Above Bobbio there is only a mulepath, 9 hrs.' walk to Abries.

[From Bobbio, a pass N. over the mountain by Serra le Cruel and the Col Julien, leads to *Pralis*, in 12 hrs. From La Tour this is a day's journey, and few excursions offer more striking scenes especially from the Col Julien. Near the summit, 4 hrs.' hard walk from Bobbio, surmounting all the neighbouring ridges, the Monte Viso appears so near that the path to the Col de Viso, on the side of France, can be distinctly traced, ascending nearly due S., beneath the precipices till it turns abruptly to the E. at the col. The descent towards Pralis is very long and fatiguing, 2 hrs.' hard walk. Pralis consists of 4 separate hamlets. there is no Inn, but at the 3rd of these strangers are received kindly at the pastor's house, if he has room. From Pralis down the valley to *Perosa* (Rte. 131) is 4 hrs. by a char road. Scenery not striking. Balsille to Pragelas 2½ hrs.]

On leaving Bobbio, a long wall is seen, an embankment, or Breakwater, made to guard the village from the inundations of the Pellice; it was built by a grant from Oliver Cromwell, during whose protectorate one of those fearful calamities nearly destroyed Bobbio. A little beyond, the river is crossed, and the mountain ascent begins; soon, on bending to the l., the scenery becomes wild, though the bottom is still occupied by water-meadows scattered here and there with walnut and chestnut. The last view down the valley towards Bobbio is very fine.

After a long course amidst strangely situated hamlets, where rocks and trees of the wildest character make up a rapid succession of picturesque scenes, the path reaches a dreary mass of rocks, over which is poured the torrent of the Pellice, and further progress seems forbidden. Up amidst these fallen fragments, however, a path is found, threading a deep ravine, in which are the ruins of the fort of *Mirabouc*, built against the steep escarpments of the mountain, in a gorge which is utterly impassable on the side opposite to the fort; nor is there a path on the side where the ruins of the fort stand that does not pass through its former gates. The fort was demolished after the wars of the French revolution, in 1796.

[A little before reaching Mirabouc, a valley towards the rt. leads to the village of Abries by the *Col de Malaure*, a shorter but more difficult path than that by the Col de la Croix.]

Above the fort Mirabouc, a roughly pitched path through a narrow and sterile valley enters upon the meadows of the Bergerie de Pra (3½ hrs. from Bobbio)—the highest hamlet in the valley, situated in the midst of fertile pasturages, where barley and potatoes are raised.

From the Bergerie of Pra, where the Alpine traveller may rest in a grange with more comfort than in many places of much greater pretension, he may reach the Monte Viso by the Col de Seyliere at a much earlier hour than from Abries in the valley of the Guil; having crossed it, the distance is short to the Col de Viso, and this is the easiest détour by the Viso from the Val de Pelice to the valley of the Po.

The lovers of the chase may find hunter's accommodation at the Bergerie de Pra. The abundance of chamois in the surrounding mountains, and the fine, honest character of the peasantry here, are great temptations to its enjoyment.

The ascent to the *Col de La Croix* is by a steep and difficult path, made in zigzags up the abrupt side of the col, towards Piedmont. This, however, is soon surmounted, and from the highest point (1½ hr.), which overlooks the side of Italy, the defile of

Mirabouc is a savage scene, and Monte Viso is a noble object. The col is nearly level for half an hour, and then the path, traversing the side of a hollow, gradually subsides to the valley of the Guil, within the territories of France. On the col there is a block of stone carved with the fleur-de-lis and cross of Savoy, to mark the frontier, and at La Monta, in the valley of the Guil, a station of the douane, where travellers are examined; the distance from La Tour to La Monta is 7 hrs.' walk; the descent into France is very gradual; traces of an intended road surveyed under Napoleon may be seen. On the rt., in descending, there is a den, miscalled an inn, at La Monta; thence, through the hamlet of Ristolas, you reach in 3½ hrs.

Abries (a country *Inn*, Etoile; homely, dirty beds, but good fare. If you would guard against an extortionate bill, make your bargain and fix prices beforehand). Here the torrent from Valprevaire flows into the Guil, and a path up its course leads to several mountain passes. Below Abries the road through the valley of the Guil good and passable for a light calèche, passes the valleys in which there are still Protestant communities, particularly that of St. Veran, in a valley which joins from the l. the valley of the Guil, at Ville-vielles: and the valley of Arvieux, which enters that of the Guil near Queiras. To these, and the Val Frassenières, on the other side of the Durance, the name of the *Pays de Neff* has been given, to commemorate the services rendered to these communities by the Swiss Protestant minister, who devoted his life to renovating and sustaining the religious worship of the primitive Christians that had existed in these valleys from time immemorial. Neff, like Oberlin, the good pastor of the Ban de la Roche, not only promoted the religious faith and practice of these people, but established schools, and taught them agriculture, and the elements of other useful knowledge. He died in 1829. His name throughout these valleys is remembered with the deepest reverence and affection.   2½ hrs. further is

The *Château de Queiras*, finely situated in the valley: it is garrisoned, and entirely commands the pass, and from every point of view presents a most picturesque object. There is a tolerable inn at Queiras.

Below Queiras a new road is in progress.   The old one skirts the deep bed of the river for a short way, then descending to the torrent, which it crosses, it continues for nearly 2 hrs., through a fine defile. In some places the mountains seem to close in above the traveller; and it is often necessary to cross the Guil to find a path on one side, which is forbidden on the other by projecting rocks or precipices of vast height: some hamlets are passed in this savage ravine.   At length the road emerges, winds up a steep and rugged path, crosses the torrent of Seillac, and descends upon *Guillestre* (vile *Inns*, avoid them), a little bourg, lying on the l. of the road to Mont Dauphin, which was one of the stations, during the war, for English prisoners.

A little below, the road passes beneath the *fort of Mont Dauphin*, which guards this entrance to France — a garrison singularly placed on a rock that is nearly insulated at the mouth of the Guil, at its confluence with the Durance.   This is the best starting-point to explore the valley of the Guil. The *Inn* is defective in sleeping accommodation, but clean lodgings and beds are kept for the officers of the garrison, and can be engaged by travellers. For the sake of this comfort it is well worth while to ascend the steep hill on which the fort stands, besides which, from the drawbridge you have a fine view of Mont Pelvoux, under Mont Dauphin.   The great route from Marseilles and Digne to Briançon is entered; and the course down the valley to Embrun (2 hrs.) is by an admirably formed and well-kept road. (See HANDBOOK FOR FRANCE.)

If this excursion be commenced from the side of France the diligence from Briançon to Gap will drop the traveller at Mt. Dauphin (5 or 6 hrs. walk from Briançon), where an omnibus will take him on to Guillestre. There he can hire a one-horse calèche for Abries, stopping at Queiras to rest and dine.   *Time*: Briançon to Guillestre, 4½ hrs. G. to Abries, 6 hrs., exclusive of stops.   *Avoid* making the journey between the 1st and 21st of July, that being the time allowed by the French Government for cutting wood in the forests—the horses are then all employed, and the charge for them is exorbitant: indeed they are so at all times.

ROUTE 133.

MONT DAUPHIN TO SALUZZO, BY THE COL DE VISO.

Time walking from Mont Dauphin to Queyras is 5 hrs. through a magnificent ravine, good road; thence to Abries 3 hrs., scenery tamer; and to the Col 3 hrs. more.   The char-road ceases at La Monta, where a steep path runs l. up the mountain, and after reaching some height turns round, keeping the declivity on the rt.   About 1 hr. brings you to a grassy defile, in which is the hut of the Douane.   To Pra 2 hrs.; to Bobbio 2½ hrs., bad road; to La Tour 2 hrs.

From Mont Dauphin to Abries (Rte. 132).

Whoever would pass the Col de Viso should start early enough to cross from Abries or La Monta to Paesana the same day: he should arrive on the Col de Viso before the ascent of the vapour, and avoid the filth and starvation of Crissolo.

After passing *Ristolas* and ascending the valley of the Guil to La Monta—where the path to the Col de la Croix turns off to the l.—the route to the Monte Viso continues up the valley to the highest village, La Chalpe, about a mile and a half above La Monta.   At La Chalpe guides may be obtained for excursions either across the Monte Viso to Saluzzo, or into the valleys and recesses of Monte Viso.

The valley of the *Guil* above Abries is narrow and savage : bare and precipitous escarpments descend to the torrent, and form its left boundary : the bed of the Guil is filled with enormous rocks. The path to the Col de Viso ascends above the rt. bank over steep acclivities and pasturages abounding in rare plants. Above these the head of the Monte Viso is continually presented filling the open space in the view, formed by the sides of the valley of the Guil. After a long and fatiguing ascent to the châlets and the Bergerie de Mon-viso, the pasturages are at length left and the ascent lies over a road rudely paved with large rough stones, lately repaired so that the ascent is practicable for mules. This paved road reaches to the *Gallery of the Traver-sette*, pierced through the mountain 250 feet below the crest. Its entrance, long closed by the fallen débris of the precipices which overhang the pass, has been cleared of all obstacles, and opened out so as to render this pass now easier than that by the Col de la Croix. The tunnel is 250 ft. long, 10 ft. high, and 10 ft. wide. The *Col of the Viso* is 5 hours distant from Abries.

From the col the view down the valley of the Po, and over the plains of Piedmont, is pre-eminently beautiful. This vast expanse, seen from a height of 10,150 English feet above the level of the sea, commands a view over an extent of 100 miles to the horizon. The rocks and vast precipices in the foreground and on the col, the deep subsidences of the mountains which bound the valley of the Po immediately below the observer, till they sink lower and lower into the plains, are most impressive. On the plain, bright but indistinct masses mark the positions of the towns and cities of Piedmont within the view, and this indistinctness, contrasted with the sharp and defined forms of the enormous peak of the Viso, rising yet 3000 feet higher than the spot on which the observer stands, and in close proximity, produce an indescribable effect upon his mind and feelings ; and the indistinct horizon makes this one of the most magnificent and sublime scenes in the world.

In order to gain a prospect of the range of Alps towards the north, the traveller must descend a little towards Italy, and then mount an eminence on the l. which before obscured that part of the chain : but this is only recommended to those who have time to spare, which few have who wish to gain Paesana on the side of Italy, or Abries in France, as resting-places for the night.

The traveller who would enjoy this view should leave Abries so as to be on the Col de Viso by 10 o'clock or earlier. This can only be made certain by starting soon after 4 in the morning from Abries, or better still, by sleeping at La Monta, or even in a grange at La Chalpe: before mid-day vapours rise in the plains and the valley of the Po, and obscure the prospect. A surer plan perhaps (and it is worth the inconvenience) is to sleep either at the Bergerie de Mon-viso, or in a more sheltered situation in the Châlet of La Trouchet, which lies in the bottom of the valley near where it is quitted to ascend the col ; here clean straw or hay may be had to sleep upon, and ewe's milk curd for food. The châlet is situated half way in time between Abries and the Col de Viso, 2½ hrs. from each.

The col is a mere ridge, so narrow that it is traversed in a few paces. On it are the remains of a redoubt; and here, during the wars of the Revolution, many struggles were made and battles fought for the possession of this position.

Some, with no better foundation than the fact that the plains of the Po could be seen from the col, have supposed that this was the route of Hannibal; but the same authority that records his having shown the plains to his army states that the army encamped on the summit, and waited three days for stragglers. Here, 100 men could not have encamped, and the pass must ever have been impracticable to elephants, and even horses. The gallery, which pierces the mountain 250 ft. below, to avoid the traverse of the last and steepest part of the crest, was only made in the 15th century; but this too was imputed to Hannibal, as if a mountain could be pierced more rapidly by an army than by as many men as could be brought to apply their labour efficiently upon a point so limited.

But the question who constructed this gallery has been recently settled by the discovery of documents at Saluces. It has been attributed to Hannibal—to Pompey—to the Dauphin Humbert of Vienne—to the Saracens—and to Francis I., and the advocates for each found arguments to support their opinions. It was, however, executed under the orders of Ludovico II., Marquis of Saluces; who, with a spirit beyond his age, undertook this extraordinary work for the commercial interests of his people, by making a route three days shorter than any other from Saluces to Dauphiny. By treaty with René, king of Provence, who contributed towards the expenses on his side of the mountain, this road was opened to receive from France, by laden mules, salt, drapery, and metal wares, in return for nut-oil, wine, rice, and flax from the marquisate of Saluces. By means of this gallery, and the roads constructed as approaches, this intercourse was open 6 or 8 months in the year. The gallery was begun in 1478, and was completed in 1480;—an extraordinary work to accomplish in that time, as the excavators could only labour, at that height above the sea level, about 7 or 8 months in the year.

This gallery has frequently been buried under rocks descending from above—in 1620, 1676, 1798, and 1812 —and the fallen masses were removed by the people of the communes on either side of the mountain. In 1823 again a mass fell, and entirely closed the entrance on the side of Piedmont, so as to conceal it from view; it had

some time before been buried on the side of France.

The passage across the col on either side, but particularly on that of Piedmont, is greatly facilitated by the gallery; for, though the perpendicular height saved is not 300 ft., this is the most difficult part.

Down a steep and difficult path the traveller has to proceed towards the valley of the Po, passing beneath precipices that every moment threaten to bury him,

About 1000 ft. below the col a mass of rock is turned abruptly, and on the rt. there lies a scene unsurpassed for the immensity of the objects above, below, and around the observer. On looking up to the rt., towards the Monte Viso, this mountain rises, in all its magnificence, on one side of a deep valley, in which are seen some little dark lakes, the sources of the Po, which below them is seen to trickle in a silver line down the back rocks, from the base of the Viso into the valley beyond. Nothing can exceed the impression of solitude and sublimity made by this scene. amidst glaciers, the beds of snow which must be traversed in the descent, and thousands of rocks and stones piled in wild confusion, a path must be found to reach the valley below, which is hid by projecting rocks and masses, seems dark, obscure, and doubtful, with nothing to indicate whither the steep descent will lead. At length, however, all these sublime horrors are passed, and vegetation is soon after reached, in a beautiful little plain covered with the richest herbage. This spot is called the *Piano del Re;* in it there is a delicious fountain, from which the traveller rarely fails to quaff.

A short descent from the Piano del Re leads to another little plain, the *Piano di Fiorenza,* so named from its beautiful flowers, with which it is enamelled. Nearly 2 m. below is the first hamlet, *Piana Malze,* a name derived from the forest of larches which is near it. The wretched appearance of its inhabitants is sickening: here is the station of the Sardinian douane. About 3 m. further down the valley is the highest village, *Crissolo*, which, for filth, poverty, and discomfort, is unmatched even in Piedmont. Beds, except of the filthiest description, cannot be obtained ; and for bread they depend upon a supply of *grisane* from Paesana.

Below Crissolo there are some fine wild scenes in the valley of the Po ; and after having passed the confluence of the Lenta with the Po, the village of Oncino is seen in a striking situation between the two rivers. From Oncino, the view of the valley of the Po, and the plains of Piedmont, is singularly fine. The inhabitants of Oncino have some celebrity as brigands ; at least their neighbours give them that character.

Professor Forbes made an interesting excursion round Monte Viso in 1829. Instead of descending to the pasturages on the side of Piedmont, he skirted, on the eastern side, the middle height of the Monte Viso, and passing the little dark lakes, the sources of the Po, ascended the valley under the Viso, which runs nearly parallel to the great chain ; and crossing the Col de Vallante, that divides this valley from that of Ponte, which leads down to Castel Delfin, and ascending on the rt. from the Val de Ponte, recrossed the main chain by the Col de Coulaon on the W. shoulder of the Monte Viso, and thence descended into the valley of the Guil, having made a complete circuit of the mountain ; but it was accomplished only with excessive fatigue and difficulty.

Paesana is distant from Crissolo about 3 hrs. It is a large town with 5000 Inhab. Here there is a very tolerable inn.* From Paesana a tolerable road branches off to

Barge—(*Inn:* Lion d'Or, good and cheap)—and passes through a beautiful and rich country, by Bibbiena and

* Desiderio king of the Lombards, who was defeated by Charlemagne, and kept prisoner for a long time at Vienne, in Dauphiny, was permitted at last to take up his residence at Paesana.

Additional corrections and information from eye-witnesses regarding Routes 132, 133, 134, are desired by the *Editor*.

St. Giovanni, to Lucerna and La Tour (Rte. 134).

From Paesana to Saluces is about 14 m., passing through the town of

Sanfront (Inhab. above 5000) and the villages of Gambasca and Martiniana. At the latter, the valley, which had widened to the plains from Paesana, is altogether left by the traveller, and the remaining distance of 6 or 7 m., after skirting the mountain, enters upon the plain, over a level road, to

Saluces (*Inn:* H. du Coq). Rly. hence to Turin by Savigliano in 1¼ hrs.

ROUTE 134.

ST. DALMAZIO TO EMBRUN, BY BARCELONETTE AND THE COL D'ARGENTIÈRE.

The Stura, one of the largest affluents of the Po, which the traveller to Nice crosses near Coni, issues from an open valley opposite to St. Dalmazio, where the high road to Nice is left, and the course up the valley of the Stura is by a very good road for a light carriage, which extends as far as Venadio—greatly facilitating the intercourse with this place, which is the principal bourg in the valley, and offering a temptation to invalids to visit the mineral springs in the neighbourhood, which are much frequented. The distance from Dalmazio to Venadio is nearly 8 leagues.

In ascending the valley, the first hamlet is that of St. Martino ; soon after passing it the Stura appears in its deep course in the valley ; and beyond it, rising abruptly amidst some pinnacled rocks and precipices, lies the village of Rocca Sparviera. Francis I. in his invasion of Italy (1515) despatched a column of cavalry under Bayard from Briançon by the Cols de Sestrière and Argentière, paths where a horse had seldom passed before, which, descending suddenly the rocks of Rocca Sparviera, surprised the

Papal general Prosper Colonna at table in Villa Franca, near the head-water of the Po, and made him prisoner, with a band of 700 knights, his followers, so suddenly that he asked if they had dropped from the clouds.

Soon after passing Rocca Sparviera the road winds down to the river, crosses the Stura, and continues on its left bank almost throughout the valley. The cultivated land which borders the Stura is very rich and luxuriant : the chestnut trees are of great magnitude ; and the forms of the mountains which bound the valley are highly picturesque.

About 4 leagues from St. Dalmazio the traveller reaches

Demont (*Inn:* Fleur de Lys, poor). A town formerly remarkable for its fort, which guarded the valley of the Stura and the communication with France by the Col d'Argentière ; it was built by Charles Emanuel I. in the 16th cent., upon the ruins of an old castle which had been razed by the Austrians in 1559. It has been memorable for its sieges in almost every war between France and Sardinia. In that of 1744, when the Spanish and French armies, commanded by the infant Don Philip and the Prince of Condé, invaded Piedmont, they forced the narrow pass of the Barricades, descended the valley of the Stura, and took the fort of Demont by the use of red-hot shot. Afterwards they besieged Coni, and fought a battle which they won from Charles Emanuel III., who succeeded, however, in throwing supplies into the city, which was gallantly defended. After a long and tedious investment, the storms of autumn and the want of supplies—which were cut off by the Piedmontese peasantry—compelled the allies to raise the siege and recross the Alps towards the latter end of November, when they suffered the severest privations from cold, hunger, and fatigue. Though pursued by the troops, assailed by the peasants, and exposed to storms, yet they returned to France, over frozen roads, and through deep snow, with all their artillery, and with a few guns

taken from their enemies,—the miserable trophies for which they had sacrificed thousands of lives and millions of treasure : on their way they destroyed the fort of Demont. It was again restored, but finally demolished in 1801 ; when Piedmont having become a part of France, the forts that guarded the defiles on the frontiers of Dauphiny were razed. Since the restoration of Piedmont the reconstruction of many has been contemplated, some begun, and this among them. The mound upon which the ruins stand is situated in the middle of the valley,—the river passing on one side and the road on the other. Further up the valley, and not far from the fort, is the Bourg of Demont, where there is a tolerable inn. From Demont to

Venadio, the scenery is, in many places, highly picturesque,—a charm for which it is much indebted to the magnificent old trees which form foregrounds to beautiful views of the river and the mountains; and these are heightened by the festoons of vines and gourds which decorate the branches. From the town of Venadio the scene down the valley is very fine. Here it is necessary to leave the char; but mules may be hired for continuing the journey up the valley, and across the Argentière into France. About an hour above Venadio, at a place called Plancie, a ravine, with a cascade at its entrance, joins the valley on the left. In this ravine, at an hour's walk from Plancie, are the Baths of Venadio—a very humble and sequestered establishment. The ravine which leads to them is in some places very grand, and abounds in cascades both above and below the baths.

Above Venadio the change is rapid to wild and Alpine scenery, varying from a road by the stream which ripples through quiet meadows, to narrow paths which overhang the course of the torrent—a course too narrow in the ravine for a path by the river: it is therefore carried on ledges of the precipices above, and forms, in some places, fearful mule paths for the traveller's ascent of the valley. Such scenes are observed near Zambucco. Above are the villages of Pied de Port and Pont Bernardo. At a place called the *Barricades*—a narrow defile, where defences of the valley were formerly erected, and which was often the scene of desperate conflicts—the road is carried along a shelf of rock above the river, and has been cut out of the precipices which darken and overhang the ravine, and offers an almost impregnable barrier to the passage of the valley. Above the Barricades the road, or rather path, lies amidst the *débris* of the mountains which bound the valley, and offer a scene of wild desolation. Above it lie the villages of Praynard and Bersesio ; the latter is the principal place between the Barricades and the Col d'Argentière. Here accommodation may be found, after a long day's journey from Coni, preparatory to another from Bersesio, across the mountain to Barcelonette.

Bersesio, about 4 hrs. from Venadio, has a very tolerable mountain inn. Above this village the scenery is wild and rugged, the mountains presenting a thousand pinnacles of rock, blighted and scathed. Still, in the valley, barley is cultivated, and the pastures are rich ; and the villages of Argentière and La Madelaine are found. Soon after passing the latter of these, the path leads abruptly to *the Col d'Argentière,* 7200 ft. above the level of the sea. Before arriving at the crest, the path skirts a little lake, the source of the Stura, called La Madelaine: it is about 600 or 700 ft. across. This lake is supposed to be the source also of the Ubayette, a stream on the side of France ; for, at a short distance from the col on that side, and a little below the level of the lake, a spring—the source of the Ubayette—gushes out: this spring, it is believed, communicates with the lake.

From the summit the view is very extensive, especially towards France, looking down the course of the Ubayette towards L'Arche, the frontier station of the French douane.

L'Arche is nearly 3 hours from Bersesio. At L'Arche is a very humble inn, but kept by civil people. Better accommodation, however, will be found, *chez Peneant,* at Meyronne, where there is a comfortable country inn; but provisions are, in this neighbourhood, very scarce. From L'Arche to Meyronne is an hour's walk, and thence to Barcelonette 3½ hrs. At Meyronne there is an excellent guide, named Dumas, to the neighbouring Alps. Below L'Arche there is little interest in the scenery. The road descends through the villages of Certamusa and Meyronne to the junction of the Ubayette with the Ubaye, where two roads lead into the Embrunnais,—the principal following the course of the Ubaye to Barcelonette, the other leading by the camp of Tournoux, the village of St. Paul, and the Col de Vars, to Guillestre and the valley of the Durance.

The scene is fine from where these roads separate. Châtelard, a well-cultivated little plain, is left on the rt., and the road passes on through Jausier. There is not much interest generally in the scenery, except at Pont de Cluse, near Jausier, where the rocky defile through which the Ubaye struggles offers some fine points of view.

The pass of the Argentière has an historic interest, because through it Francis I. penetrated with an army of 20,000 men (1513) into Italy to meet the Swiss and other foes at Marignan. They had got the start of the French by occupying Susa and seizing all the gorges communicating with the Monts Cenis and Genèvre, so that Francis was obliged either to make a very great détour or to find or make a passage for himself. The information of experienced hunters and shepherds obtained by the Signor Soleir, lord of Morets, induced him to select the passes leading from Barcelonette to the sources of the Stura and the country of Salure. The valleys were explored by the Marshals Lautrec and Trivulzio and by Pedro Novarro, who undertook not only to conduct the infantry, but all the artillery, consisting of 72 large pieces and 300 small. This was successfully achieved after great difficulty, the guns requiring to be swung by rope from rock to rock, where neither bridge could be built nor rocks blasted by powder; and on the third day the army encamped on the summit of the pass. The Rocher de St. Paul, near Barcelonette, which barred the passage, was blasted in a single day by P. Novarro, one of the first engineers who practised military mining. But this was the easiest part of the task ; far more arduous was it, on the edge of sloping crags smoothed with avalanches and slippery with ice, to plant and to fasten the timber props on which frail bridges could be reared to cross the torrents, and against the face of precipices and over yawning gulfs, to erecting scaffoldings of shaky planks which horses, mules, and 72 heavy cannon could venture to pass over. In some cases this was impossible, and the only alternative was to let down the gun by ropes into the gorge on one side and raise it up on the opposite. All these and many more difficulties were overcome ; on the third day the army camped on the summit of the pass, on the fourth the obstacles of the mountain Pico di Porco were surmounted, and on the fifth the French were pouring like a torrent over the plains of Saluzzo.

Barcelonette has 2200 Inhab., and a very good inn, Hôtel du Nord, chez Maurin. The town is larger and better built than one would expect to find in a valley so sequestered, and having so little communication with the rest of the world.

It is chiefly inhabited by the proprietors of the Alps and pasturages of the valley. More than 100,000 sheep are pastured in its communes, which come, during the summer, from the vast plains of La Crau, in the neighbourhood of Arles; these sheep are driven into the most difficult accessible pasturages of the Alps, often 20 days' journey. From their wool some coarse goods, consumed chiefly by the inhabitants, are made; there is much corn also grown in the valley;

but for almost everything else they are indebted to strangers, in other valleys or other countries; it is not long that the cultivation of potatoes has been practised among them.

This valley was known to the Romans, but little of its history is to be relied upon, except in connection with that of Embrun, which has been better preserved. It is known that it was subjected to irruptions by Saxons and by Saracens, who made their way from Marseilles; these were defeated by Charles Martel; under Charlemagne France had the benefit of a protecting government. In the sixth century, a convent of Benedictines established here did much to ameliorate the condition of the inhabitants of the valley; but all the wars in which Provence has been engaged have extended their horrors in this valley, and it was often liable to the irruptions of the Saracens, particularly in the 10th century. From the 14th century it was alternately subject to Savoy or France. Amadeus conquered it in 1388 ; it was re-attached to Provence by René of Anjou in 1447; it was again taken by the duke of Savoy, Charles III., in 1537. In the middle of the 16th century the inhabitants adopted the Reformed doctrines, but they were shortly after either forced to abjure them or were expelled their country.

Napoleon contemplated the construction of a new road through the valley of Barcelonette to pass the Co. d'Argentière and enter Piedmont, by the Val de Stura. Since his abdication the idea seems to have been abandoned; but its benefits to 20,000 inhab. of the valley, by the greater development of their energies and the increased prosperity of Barcelonette ought to have some weight with the government of France.

There are many communications with the neighbouring valleys, by passes in the mountains; as with Embrun by the Col de la Vacherie, and with Colmar and Alos by the valley of the Tinea and the Varo, which discharge their streams near Nice.

Soon after leaving Barcelonette,

near the village of St. Pons, the ruins of an old castle are seen in a fine situation. The roads down the valley of Barcelonette are in so wretched a state, that the want of embankments exposes the inhabitants of the valley to the frequent loss of communication, from the destructive effects of the torrents. Not far below Barcelonette, it is necessary to ford the beds of the Bachelar, the Rio Bourdon, and other torrents, for want of bridges.

The first large village below Barcelonette is La Thuiles, and the next, after crossing the Ubaye by a wooden bridge, Méolans; thence down the valley there is a tolerable char-road. Amidst dreary and wild scenes, the general character of the valley of Barcelonette, there is, however, a striking exception in a village, beautifully situated, called

La Lauzette, the Goshen of the valley. It is agreeably wooded; near it is a little lake which abounds in fine trout, and in the immediate neighbourhood are fruit-trees and a fertile soil. A little way, however, below the village the scene changes again to sterility. After crossing a ridge, a series of tourniquets leads down the pass of La Tour, or, as it is called, the *Chemin Royal*, a part of the road in the valley admirably made; but, unconnected as it is with the country above or below by any road so good, it is worthless.

Below these tourniquets the valley offers some of its most wild and grand scenes. On looking back from the path carried along the brink of the precipices high above the torrent, the Ubaye is seen in its deep course issuing from the defile of La Tour, and beyond, the grand forms of the mountain of *Cugulion des Trois Évêques*, which divides the valley of Barcelonette from that of the Var, the scene is one of savage dreariness.

The road continues on the l. bank of the river high above its bed; until, leaving the side of the hill upon which the fort of St. Vincent is placed, a very difficult path leads

[*Switz.*]

down to the river, which is crossed to arrive at the little village of Ubaye.

From this place, one road passes down by the river to its confluence with the Durance at La Brioule; and another, up the side of the mountain to the Col de Pontis, which leads to Savines on the Durance, in the high-road from Gap to Embrun, which is distant from Savines 8 m.

From the ascent to the Col de Pontis, on looking back towards the valley of the Ubaye, the hill of St. Vincent is a strikingly fine object, surmounted by forts which formerly guarded the entrance to the valley of Barcelonette, when it was under the dominion of Sardinia. By a wise arrangement it was ceded to France, in exchange for the valleys of Pragelas and Exilles, when the states of France and Sardinia prudently agreed upon the chain of the high Alps as their line of demarcation.

Embrun.

ROUTE 135.*

BARCELONETTE TO BRIANÇON, BY THE VALLEY OF THE UBAYE AND ST. VERAN.

Besides the routes from Barcelonette to Embrun by the valley of the Ubaye, the Col de Vacherie, and also by the Col de Vars and Guillestre, all mentioned in Rte. 134, there is another, by which the traveller may reach the valley of the Guil, and visit wild and sequestered scenes in the neighbourhood of the Monte Viso; but the Cuisa, though not impracticable for mules, is only fit for a pedestrian; at least this is the case with the pass of the Col de Longet.

About 2½ hrs. above Barcelonette lies the confluence of the Ubayette

* The routes from Turin to Nice by the *Col de Tende*, and from Nice to Genoa by the *Riviera*, formerly included in this volume, are now transferred to the HANDBOOK FOR NORTH ITALY, where they are fully described.

T

and the Ubaye; the former leading to the Col d'Argentière, the latter to the Embrunnais by the valley of Maurin.

The ascent of the Ubaye leads by a deep ravine below the camp of Tourneaux, where the remains of redoubts and intrenchments still mark the importance of this frontier passage: when the valley of Barcelonette belonged to Sardinia, this spot was the scene of many struggles in the early part of the 18th century. A mule path, which leads high above the rt. bank of the river, leads above the ravine and into the basin-shaped valley of *St. Paul.* Before reaching the village of St. Paul, the path which leads by the Col de Vars to Guillestre and Embrun winds up by the deep ravines of the Rioumonas, a torrent which descends from the Col de Vars, and the villages of Le Serrel and L'Entraye; this pass is an easy one, and by it the distance from St. Paul to Guillestre is little more than 5 hrs.

Above St. Paul the valley narrows again, and continues like a ravine until it expands into the communes of Maurin, a common name given to the three villages of Majasset, la Barge, and Combremont. The village of Majasset is about 4 hours' walk from the confluence of the Ubaye and the Ubayette, and 6½ hrs. from Barcelonette. At *Majasset,* as it is possible, it will be wise to sleep, and a trusty guide should be engaged (the services of the innkeeper Cressy may be obtained in this capacity) to cross the Col to St. Veran. Near Maurin they have begun to work serpentine as ornamental stone, and between this valley and that of the Guil serpentine and diallage constantly occur. Three or four passes across the great chain of the Alps lead on the right from this valley into Piedmont. 1, by the Col de Roux and the Col de Maira into the valley of the Maira to Dronero; 2, by the Col de Lautaret and the Col de Malecoste to Château Dauphin in the Val de Vraita; and 3, by the eastern Col de Longet from the head of the val-

ley of the Ubaye to La Chenel, at the head of the valley of the Vraita, and thence to Château Dauphin. Majasset is the station of the French douaniers, who have in this valley to guard an extensive frontier by these passes. A little above the last village the traveller arrives at the small *Lac de Paroi,* a piece of water which evidently owes its origin to a stupendous landslip from the western side of the valley called the Costabella, which, it is said, descended in the 13th century. On the margin of this lake rye is cultivated, though it has a very great elevation. Soon after passing the lake and a series of cascades, the valley is ascended steeply for several miles by a wild and dreary path, bounded by very lofty peaks, and terminates in the path that leads by the Eastern Col de Longet, which extends over fine pasturages, at a great elevation, to a very abrupt and magnificent descent into Piedmont. The path by the western *Col de Longet,* called sometimes the Col de Cula, is that which leads to St. Veran; it ascends to the left, and divides the valleys of Maurin and St. Veran. The ascent is quite pathless and often over patches of snow; the crest has a great elevation—10,345 English feet; it is nearly 200 feet higher than the Col de Viso. It is attained in 4 hours from Majasset: the view from it is stupendous; on one hand towards Monte Viso, which appears quite close, and on the other to the Dauphiny Alps, which are nowhere so finely seen as from this point. Scarcely a trace of vegetation is to be seen on the summit. A very steep descent leads, in 2½ hrs., to St. Veran, a very populous village, placed at the great elevation of 6693 English feet above the level of the sea, being probably the highest village, with the same amount of population, in Europe. Around it barley and rye are cultivated; the former to the elevation of nearly 7000 feet.

St. Veran is situated in a remarkably verdant and well-watered valley of the same name. Its appearance, when seen for the first time, is extra-ordinary ; for, instead of houses, it seems to be a mass of space and scaf-folding ; the houses are built entirely of wood, except that sometimes they rest on a basement of stone, which in-closes the stable, a common but dirty practice in the domestic structures of the high villages of these Alps. Around the houses they invariably construct a sort of veranda or gallery, with a roof projecting 6 or 8 feet, and fitted up with the sort of scaffolding which gives so odd an appearance, at first sight, to the village ; the purpose of this scaffolding is to enable the inhabitants to dry their ill-ripened corn under the shelter of the project-ing roofs : their harvests generally take place early in the autumn, before the frosts set in, the seed having been sown in the July of the preceding year.   St. Veran offers no accom-modation whatever to travellers, un-less the curé can be induced to afford hospitality.   The filthy habits of the people are most offensive, arising chiefly from their custom of living with the cattle in the stables, and this even among persons of property.

The Protestants are very numerous at St. Veran, consisting of twenty-four families ; a Protestant Church has lately been erected there ; but as the pastor, M. Ermann, who succeeded Felix Neff, resides at La Chalp, the service is neither frequent nor regular. Here were occasionally exercised the devoted services of Neff, "the modern Apostle of the Alps." The Protestant communities of St. Veran, Foussillarde, Frassynière, Dormeil-leuse, &c., some of these places being above 40 m. apart from others, formed the extensive district where he la-boured in his ministry with a devo-tion and energy to which his health and life were at last sacrificed.

The Roman Catholic church of St. Veran is situated near the highest part of the long straggling village. On its wall is cut, "1041 toises sur la mer."

The house of the curé adjoining is the only stone dwelling in the place.

From St. Veran an agreeable road leads down the valley to *Queyras,* a village which gives its name to the district in the valley of the Guil, and thence to *Briançon* (Rte. 132). But if the object of the traveller be to visit Abries and the upper valley of the Guil, he may attain them through scenes of grander character than those presented by the route through Queyras, and by a path 4 hrs. shorter than that through the valley of the Guil.   In either case he should not fail to notice a singular geolo-gical fact near Pra, on the opposite side of the torrent descending from St. Veran.   The slopes have been covered with extremely hard blocks of the diallage rock of the neighbour-hood.   In one place these have rested on a friable slaty limestone ; the weather and melting snow have gra-dually washed the soil from around these blocks, which have served as a protection to that immediately below them, and thus pillars, not unlike Gothic pinnacles, which, in some cases, have an elevation of 100 ft., have been left, with these boulders for their capitals, presenting an ex-traordinary appearance, with an ob-vious origin.   A similar geological phenomenon is presented in the Tyrol at Ober-Botzen, not far from Botzen, in the valley of the Adige.—F.

ROUTE 136.

DIGNE, IN THE VALLEY OF THE DU-RANCE, TO BARCELONETTE, BY COL-MAR AND ALOS.

Instead of following the high road to Gap, the route of the diligence, the traveller who, from Marseilles and Digne, would approach the Alps sooner, may reach them by an inte-resting line of route either on horse-back or on foot, and pass through scenes little known to English ram-blers.   From *Digne*, a valley of rather Alpine character, and therefore most welcome to the traveller, who is glad to escape from the parched plains of France, leads by the village of Drays to the *Col du Tour*, where there are fine pasturages, and which is reached in 4½ hrs. from Digne : thence a path leads down through parched valleys, rather resembling those of the north of Spain than of France, to the village *Château Garnier*, 7 hrs. from Digne, where there is a poor inn, the only resting-place. From Château Garnier, the traveller soon reaches the valley of the Verdon, and, in its ascent, the interest increases to *Colmar*, a very small fortified town, which commands the entrance to a gorge, and was, with Barcelonette, formerly in possession of the Piedmontese government. It is still garrisoned, and its gates are shut at 9 P.M. with as much regularity as when it was a more important station. From Château Garnier to Colmar is 3¼ hrs. A little above the town, in the valley, there is a small intermittent spring. Still higher up the valley of the Verdon, 1½ hr. above Colmar, is the little town of *Alos*, situate nearly 5000 ft. above the level of the sea, in a high Alpine valley, surrounded by lofty mountains. The accommodations for travellers are poor, but the people very obliging. The neighbourhood of Alos is scarcely known to English travellers, but it well deserves their examination, and an excursion should be made to the lake of Alos, a distance of about 4 hours. The route to it lies by the village of Champ Richard. The lake is one of the largest and most profound in the French Alps, though it is situated at the height of 7500 English feet. Its form is almost circular, and its circumference is nearly 4 miles. The Mont Pela, which rises from the side of the lake, has an elevation of 10,500

feet, more than 3000 above the lake. There is, perhaps, no spot in the Alps more wild and sequestered than the valley of this lake. The surrounding mountains are covered with snow and a few stunted pines, amidst vast precipices and deep ravines. Surrounding this retired lake are some of the grand materials of this most picturesque solitude. The lake is remarkable for its outlet, which, after a course under ground for 1500 feet, bursts into the valley, and after foaming through a succession of cascades meanders in gentleness and beauty through pasturages rich in their floral display. From Alos to Barcelonette the route lies up the valley of the *Verdon*, and after passing the village of *La Foax*, and crossing a stone bridge, the path to the Col de Peire, which divides the valley of Verdon from that of Barcelonette, this col is soon gained. It is a fine pasturage to the summit; and from it a charming view is suddenly presented on looking up the valley of the Ubaye. The descent to Barcelonette from the col is exceedingly romantic, leading down through a valley of great boldness richly wooded. There is an excellent path down to the valley of the Ubaye, but the descent is steep and fatiguing. *Barcelonette* may be reached on foot in 7 hours from Alos. The Hôtel du Nord affords good accommodation. In descending from the col, the valley of the torrent Bachelard opens on the rt., flanked by grand precipices; it leads to St. Dalmas le Sauvage, and thence by St. Etienne, in the valley of the Var, thence across the Col de Mont Penche, to the Baths of Venadio, in the valley of the Stura, in Piedmont (Rte. 134).

INDEX.

₊ In order to facilitate reference to the Routes, most of them are repeated in the Index twice : thus, GENEVA to Chamouni is also mentioned under the head Chamouni* to Geneva. Such *reversed* Routes are marked in the Index with an asterisk to distinguish them.

LONDON: PRINTED BY WILLIAM CLOWES AND SONS, STAMFORD STREET, AND CHARING CROSS.

MURRAY'S
HANDBOOK ADVERTISER,
1858.

THE great advantage of this medium of Advertising over all others for those who are desirous of communicating information to Travellers can scarcely be questioned, as it enables Steam, Railway, and other Public Companies, Landlords of Inns, Tradesmen, and others, to bring under the immediate notice of the great mass of English and American Tourists who resort to France, Belgium, Germany, Switzerland, Italy, Spain and Portugal, Sweden, Norway, Denmark, Russia, the East, and other parts of the world every Season, in the most direct way, the various merits of their Railways, Steamers, Hotels, Taverns, Articles of Merchandise, Works of Art, and such other information as they may desire to make known. Instead of being limited to the casual publicity of a Daily, Weekly, or Monthly Periodical, THE HANDBOOK ADVERTISER has the additional merit of being displayed, for the entire year, in a permanent work of interest and of perpetual reference by the very class of persons for whom it is specially intended.

Annual Circulation, 12,000.

Advertisements must be paid in advance and sent to the Publisher's *by 20th of April in each year*. The Charges are—A Page, 4*l.* Half-page, 2*l.* 2*s.* A Column, 2*l.* 2*s.* Half a Column, 1*l.* 2*s.*

INDEX TO ADVERTISEMENTS.

BRITISH CUSTOMS DUTIES.

LIST OF DUTIES

NOW PAYABLE IN LONDON UPON THE IMPORTATION OF WORKS OF ART, CURIOSITIES, ETC., FROM THE CONTINENT.

The following Articles are ALL FREE OF DUTY.

ALABASTER and MARBLE.
AMBER, Manufactures of.
ANCHOVIES.
AGATES and CORNELIANS, unset.
BOOKS, of editions printed prior to 1801.
BRONZE Works of Art (antiques and original works only).
BULLION, Coins and Medals of all kinds, and battered Plate.
CAMBRICS, Lawns, Damask and Diapers of Linen, or Linen and Cotton.
CAMEOS, *not* set.
CARRIAGES of all sorts.
CATLINGS, and Harp Strings, silvered or not.

CASTS of Busts, Statues, or Figures.
CORAL, whole, polished, unpolished, and fragments.
COTTON, Manufactures of, *not* being articles wholly or in part made up.
DIAMONDS, Emeralds, Pearls, and other Precious Stones, *not* set.
FLOWER Roots.
FRAMES for Pictures, Prints, Drawings, and Mirrors.
FURS and SKINS, and Articles thereof.
GLASS, all Plate, Cast or Rolled Glass.
——— Paintings on Glass.
——— Beads and Bugles.

McCRACKEN'S LIST OF DUTIES—continued.

GLASS Bottles, Wine Glasses, and Tumblers, and all white flint and common green-glass goods, *not* being cut or ornamented.

LINEN Manufactures, *not* being *articles* wholly or in part made up.

LAY Figures, imported by British Artists for their own use.

MAGNA GRECIA Ware, and Antique Earthen Vases.

MANUSCRIPTS.

MAPS and CHARTS, and parts thereof.

MINERAL Waters.

MODELS of Cork and Wood.

OLIVES and Olive Oil.

PAINTERS' COLOURS, Brushes, Pencils, and Crayons.

PICTURES.

PLANTS and TREES, alive.

SEEDS.

SAUSAGES.

SPECIMENS of Natural History, Minerals, Fossils, and Ores.

STONE, all Sculpture and Articles of Stone, Alabaster, and Marble.

SULPHUR Impressions, or Casts.

TELESCOPES.

TILES.

VASES, Ancient, *not* of Stone or Marble.

On the following Articles the Duty is 5 per cent. ad valorem.

CASHMERE SHAWLS, and all Articles of Goats' Hair or Wool.

COTTON Articles, wholly or in part made up.

LINEN Articles, wholly or in part made up.

WOOLLEN Articles, wholly or in part made up.

On the following Articles the Duty is 10 per cent. ad valorem.

BOXES of all sorts.

EGYPTIAN, and all other Antiquities.

EMBROIDERY and Needlework.

FURNITURE of all kinds.

JEWELLERY, and all Jewels set.

LACE made by hand.

MOSAIC, small Ornaments for Jewellery.

MUSICAL Instruments, *excepting* Musical Boxes, Brass Instruments, Pianos, and Accordions.

SCAGLIOLA Tables.

		£	s	d
ARQUEBUSADE WATER	the gallon	1	0	0
BEADS of CORAL	the lb.	0	1	6
———— Crystal, Jet, and Mock Pearl	ditto	0	0	2
BOOKS, of editions printed in and since 1801	the cwt.	1	10	0
———— imported under International Treaties of Copyright	ditto	0	15	0
(Pirated Editions of English Works, of which the Copyright exists in England, totally prohibited.)				
———— English, reimported (unless declared that no Drawback was claimed on Export)	the lb.	0	0	1½
BROCADE of GOLD and SILVER	ditto	0	5	0
BRONZE, BRASS, and COPPER, all Manufactures of	the cwt.	0	10	0
CARPETS and RUGS (woollen)	the square yard	0	0	6
CORAL NEGLIGEES	the lb.	0	1	0
CHINA, PORCELAIN, and EARTHENWARE, all	the cwt.	0	10	0
CLOCKS, not exceeding the value of 5s. each	the dozen	0	4	0
———— exceeding 5s., and not exceeding the value of 12s. 6d. each	ditto	0	8	0
———— exceeding 12s. 6d., and not exceeding the value of 3l. each	each	0	2	0
———— exceeding 3l., and not exceeding the value of 10l.	ditto	0	4	0
———— exceeding 10l. value	ditto	0	10	0
CIGARS and TOBACCO, manufactured (3 lbs. only allowed in a passenger's baggage, and 5 per cent. additional)	the lb.	0	9	0
TOBACCO, unmanufactured (with 5 per cent. additional on the Duty)	ditto	0	3	0
(N.B.—Unmanufactured Tobacco cannot be imported in less quantity than 300 lbs., or Cigars 80 lbs. in a Package; but small quantities are allowed for Private Use on declaration, and payment of a Fine of 1s. 6d. per lb. in addition to the Duty.)				
COFFEE	the lb.	0	0	4
CONFECTIONERY, Sweetmeats and Succades	ditto	0	0	2
CORDIALS and LIQUEURS	the gallon	1	0	0
CURTAINS, embroidered on Muslin or Net, called Swiss Curtains	the lb.	0	1	0
EAU DE COLOGNE, in long flasks	the flask	0	0	8
———— in any other description of bottles	the gallon	1	0	0

McCRACKEN'S LIST OF DUTIES—continued.

			£	s	d
FLOWERS, Artificial, the cubic foot as packed			£0	12	0
GLASS, Flint, Cut, Coloured, and Fancy Ornamental Glass, of whatever kind		*the cwt.*	0	10	0
GLOVES, of Leather (and 5 per cent. additional)		*the dozen pair*	0	3	6
LACQUERED and Japanned Wares		*the cwt.*	1	0	0
MACCARONI and VERMICELLI		*ditto*	0	1	0
NAPLES SOAP		*ditto*	0	0	8
PERFUMERY		*the lb.*	0	0	2
PERFUMED SPIRITS		*the gallon*	1	0	0
PAPERHANGINGS, Flock Paper, and Paper printed, painted, or stained		*the lb.*	0	0	3
PIANOFORTES, horizontal grand		*each*	3	0	0
———— upright and square		*ditto*	2	0	0
PLATE, of Gold		*the oz. troy*	1	1	0
——— of Silver, gilt or ungilt		*ditto*	0	1	8
PRINTS and DRAWINGS, single or bound, plain or coloured		*the lb.*	0	0	3
SILK, MILLINERY, Turbans or Caps		*each*	0	3	6
———— Hats or Bonnets		*ditto*	0	7	0½
———— Dresses		*ditto*	1	10	0
——— HANGINGS, and other Manufactures of Silk		*the 100l. value*	15	0	0
——— VELVETS, plain or figured		*the lb.*	0	9	0
TEA		*ditto*	0	1	5
TOYS and TURNERY		*the cubic foot*	0	0	4
WINE in Casks or Bottles (in bottles 6 to the gal., & 5 per cent. add.)		*the gal.*	0	5	6
SPIRITS in Cask or Bottle		*ditto*	0	15	0

No Cask can be imported of less contents than 24 Gallons.

THEIR PRINCIPAL CORRESPONDENTS ARE AT

CALAIS............ Messrs. CHARTIER, MORY, & VOGUE. Messrs. ISAAC VITAL & FILS.

BOULOGNE S. M... Messrs. CHARTIER, MORY, & VOGUE. Mr. H. SIRE. Mr. C. QUETTIER.
Mr. M. CHENUE, Packer, Rue Croix Petits Champs, No. 24.

PARIS .... { Mr. J. KLEINFELDER, 38, Rue Lafayette.
{ M. M. HOFMANN, 58, Rue Hauteville.

HAVRE............ Messrs. P. DEVOT & Co.

HONFLEUR .... Mr. J. WAGNER.

MARSEILLES...... { Messrs. HORACE BOUCHET & Co. Messrs. CLAUDE CLERC & Co.
{ Mr. PHILIGRET, 8, Rue Suffren.

BAGNERES DE BI-
GORRE (Hautes } Mr. LÉON GÉRUZET, Marble Works.
Pyrénées).........

PAU .... Mr. MERILLON AINÉ.

BORDEAUX .... { Mr. LÉON GÉRUZET, 44, Allées de Tourny.
{ Mr. LÉON SANSOT, FILS, Hôtel des Princes et de la Paix.

GIBRALTAR ...... Messrs. ARCHBOLD, JOHNSTON, & POWERS. Messrs. TURNER & Co.

LISBON........... Mr. ARTHUR VAN ZELLER, Penin. & Orient. St. Nav. Co.'s Offices.

SEVILLE .... { Mr. JULIAN B. WILLIAMS, British Vice-Consulate.
{ Don JUAN ANTO. BAILLY.

MALAGA.......... Mr. W. P. MARKS, British Consul.

NICE .... { Messrs. A. LACROIX & Co., British Consulate. Mr. T. W. HOW.
{ Messrs. AVIGDOR AINÉ & FILS. Mr. CH. GIORDAN.

GENOA .... { Messrs. GIBBS & Co. Sig. G. LOLEO, Croce di Malta.
{ Mr. BROWN, Jun., British Vice-Consul. GIO. VIGNOLO & FIGO.

MILAN .... { Messrs. BUFFET & BERUTO, Piazzale di S. Sepolcro, No. 3176.
{ Messrs. BRAMBILLA.

CARRARA......... Sig. F. BIENAIMÉ, Sculptor. Mr. VINCENZO LIVY, Sculptor.

LEGHORN .... { Messrs. W. MACBEAN & Co. Messrs. HENDERSON BROTHERS.
{ Messrs. THOMAS PATE & SONS. Messrs. MAQUAY, PAKENHAM,
{ & SMYTH. Messrs. GIACO. MICALI & FIGO. Sculptors in Alabaster
{ and Marble. Mr. M. RISTORI. Mr. JOSEPH GUANO. Messrs.
{ G. GALLIANI & Co. Mr. ULISSE COTREMAN.

PISA............. Messrs. HUGUET & VAN LINT, Sculptors in Alabaster and Marble.

FLORENCE .... { Messrs. EMME. FENZI & Co. Messrs. PLOWDEN & FRENCH. Messrs.
{ MAQUAY & PAKENHAM. Mr. E. GOODBAN. Mr. J. TOUGH.
{ Messrs. NESTI, CIARDI, & Co. Mr. ANTO DI LUIGI PIACENTI.
{ Mr. S. LOWE. Mr. GAETO. BIANCHINI, Mosaic Worker, opposite
{ the Capella de' Medici. P. BAZZANTI & FIG., Sculptors, Lungo
{ l'Arno. Heirs of F. L. PISANI, Sculptor, No. 1, sul Prato. Messrs.
{ FILI. PACETTI. Picture-frame Makers, Via del Palagio. Sig. CARLO
{ NOCCIOLL. Sig. LUIGI RAMACOL.

MESSRS. J. & R. McCRACKEN'S CORRESPONDENTS—*continued.*

VOLTERRA	Sig. OTTO. CALLAJ, and Messrs. G. CHERICI & FIGLI.
BOLOGNA	Mr. G. B. RENOLI. Sig. L. GALLI.
ANCONA	Messrs. MOORE, MERELLET, & Co.
ROME	Messrs. TORLONIA & Co. Messrs. FREEBORN & Co. Messrs. MAC-BEAN & Co. Messrs. PLOWDEN, CHOLMELEY, & Co. Messrs. PA-KENHAM, HOOKER, & Co. Mr. EDWARD TREBBI. Mr. LUIGI BRANCHINI, at the English College.
CIVITA VECCHIA.	Messrs. LOWE BROTHERS, British Vice-Consulate. Mr. T. ARATA.
NAPLES	Messrs. IGGULDEN & Co. Messrs. W. J. TURNER & Co.
PALERMO	Messrs. PRIOR, TURNER, & THOMAS.
MESSINA	Messrs. CAILLER & Co.
CORFU	Mr. J. W. TAYLOR.
ALEXANDRIA.....	Messrs. BRIGGS & Co.
CONSTANTINOPLE	Messrs. C. & E. GRACE. Mr. EDWARD LAFONTAINE.
MALTA	Mr. EMANUEL ZAMMIT. Messrs. Josh. DARMANIN & SONS, 45, Strada Levante, Mosaic Workers. Mr. FORTUNATO TESTA, 92, Strada Sta Lucia. Messrs. L. VED. DE CESARE & FIGLI. Mr. L. FRANCALANZA.
SMYRNA	Messrs. HANSON & Co.
BEYROUT	Mr. HENRY HEALD.
ATHENS, PIRÆUS	Mr. J. J. BUCHERER.
SYRA	Mr. WILKINSON, British Consul.
VENICE	Messrs. FRERES SCHIELIN. Messrs. S. & A. BLUMENTHAL & Co. Mr. L. BOVARDI, Campo S. Fantino, No. 2000, rosso.
TRIESTE	Messrs. MOORE & Co.
OSTEND	Messrs. BACH & Co. Mr. R. ST. AMOUR.
GHENT.............	Mr. J. DE BUYSER, Dealer in Antiquities, Marché au Beurre, 21.
BRUSSELS.........	
ANTWERP	Messrs. F. MACK & Co., Kipdorp, No. 1748. Mr. P. VAN ZEEBROECK, Picture Dealer, &c., Rue des Récollets, 2076.
ROTTERDAM.....	Messrs. PRESTON & Co. Messrs. S. A. LEVINO & Co. Messrs. BOUTMY & Co. Messrs. C HEMMANN & Co.
COLOGNE..........	Mr. J. M. FARINA, vis-à-vis la Place Juliers. Messrs. Gme. TILMES & Co. Mr. ALBERT HEIMANN, 29, Bishofsgartenstrasse.
MAYENCE	Mr. G. L. KAYSER, Expéditeur. Mr. W. KNUSSMANN, Cabinet Maker.
FRANKFORT O. M.	Mr. P. A. TACCHI'S SUCCESSOR, Glass Manufacturer, Zeil. Messrs. BING, Jun., & Co. Mr. F. BÖHLER, Zeil D, 17. Mr. G. A. ZIPF, Ross Markt.
HEIDELBERG	Mr. PH. ZIMMERMANN. Mr. M. LIEBER.
MANNHEIM	Mr. DINKELSPEIL. Messrs. EYSSEN & CLAUS.
MUNICH..........	Mr. HY. WIMMER, Printseller, Promenade St. No. 12. Messrs. MAY & WIDMAYER, Printsellers. Messrs. L. NEGRIOLI & Co. Heirs of NEB. PICHLER.
NUREMBERG......	Mr. PAOLO GALIMBERTI, at the Red Horse, Dealer in Antiquities. Mr. JOHN CONRAD CNOPF, Banker and Forwarding Agent.
FÜRTH	Mr. A. PICKERT.
BASLE	Messrs. JEAN PREISWERK & FILS. Mr. BISCHOFF DE ST. ALBAN. Messrs. SCHNEWLIN & Co. Mr. BENOIT LA ROCHE.
BERNE	Mr. ALBERT TRUMPY.
GENEVA	Messrs. AUG. SNELL & STRASSE.
LAUSANNE	Mr. L. LONGCHAMPS.
INTERLACKEN....	Mr. J. GROSSMANN. Mr. CLEMENT SESTL.
CONSTANCE....... SCHAFFHAUSEN .. WALDSHUT.......	Messrs. ZOLLIKOFFER & HOZ.
HAMBURG	Messrs. SCHAAR & CLAUSS. Mr. G. F. RODE.
PRAGUE..........	Mr. W. HOFMANN, Glass Manufacturer, Blauern Stern. Mr. P. CZERMAK, ditto. Mr. A. V. LEBEDA, Gun Maker.
CARLSBAD........	Mr. THOMAS WOLF, Glass Manufacturer. Mr. CARL KNOLL, au Lion Blanc.
MARIENBAD	Mr. J. T. ADLER, Glass Manufacturer.
VIENNA....	Mr. W. HOFMANN, Glass Manufacturer, am Lugeck, No. 768. Mr. JOS. LOBMEYR, Glass Manufacturer, 940, Kärntner Strasse.
BERLIN	Messrs. SCHICKLER, Brothers. Mr. LION M. COHN, Commre. Expéditeur. Messrs. C. HARSCH & Co., Glass Manufacturers, 67, Unter den Linden.
DRESDEN..........	Messrs. H. W. BASSENGE & Co. Mr. C. TEICHERT, Royal Porce-lain Manufactory Depôt. Mr. J. KREISS, Glass Manufacturer. Madame HELENA WOLFSOHN, Schössergasse, No. 5.
NEW YORK	Messrs. WILBUR & PRICE.

FRANKFORT O. M.

BING JUN^R. AND CO.

ZEIL, No. 31,

(OPPOSITE THE HOTEL DE RUSSIE,)

MANUFACTORY OF ARTICLES IN STAG'S HORN.

DEPOT OF DRESDEN CHINA.

COPY OF THE STATUE OF ARIADNE.

₊ ALL KINDS OF PARISIAN FANCY ARTICLES.

MESSRS. BING JUN. AND Co. beg respectfully to invite the Public to visit their Establishment, where they have always on show, and for sale, a most extensive Assortment of Articles in Stag's Horn, of their own manufacture; consisting of Brooches, Ear-rings, Bracelets, Pen and Pencil Holders, Seals, Inkstands, Watch-stands, Snuff-boxes, Cigar-boxes, Whips, Walking-sticks, Knives, Card-cases, and every description of article for the Writing and Work Table, besides Vases and other ornamental objects too various to be here enumerated.

Messrs. BING have also the finest Copies, both in Biscuit-China and Bronze, of the Statue of Ariadne, the chef-d'œuvre of the Sculptor DANNECKER, of which the original is in Bethman's Museum at Frankfort O. M.

Messrs. BING have likewise the *Sole Depôt* in FRANKFORT of the Porcelain of the Royal Manufactory of Dresden; and at their Establishment may be seen the most splendid assortment of Figures after the Ancient Models, ornamented with Lace-work of the most extraordinary fineness; likewise Dinner, Dessert, and Tea Services; Plates, Vases, Candelabras, Baskets, &c. &c., in the Antique Style, ornamented with flowers in relief, and the finest paintings.

Besides the above-named objects, they have a superb assortment of Clocks, Bronzes, Porcelain, and other Fancy Objects, the productions of Germany, France, and England.

DEPOT OF THE VERITABLE EAU DE COLOGNE OF JEAN MARIA FARINA, OF COLOGNE.

☞ Their Correspondents in London are J. and R. M'CRACKEN, 7, Old Jewry.

FRANKFORT O. M.

P. A. TACCHI'S SUCCESSOR,

(LATE FRANCIS STEIGERWALD,)

ZEIL D, No. 17,

BOHEMIAN FANCY GLASS AND CRYSTAL WAREHOUSE.

P. A. TACCHI'S SUCCESSOR begs to acquaint the Public that he has become the Purchaser of Mr. F. STEIGERWALD'S ESTABLISHMENT in this Town, for the Sale of Bohemian Fancy Cut Glass and Crystals.

He has always an extensive and choice Assortment of the Newest and most Elegant Patterns of

ORNAMENTAL CUT, ENGRAVED, GILT, & PAINTED GLASS,

BOTH WHITE AND COLOURED,

In Dessert Services, Chandeliers, Articles for the Table and Toilet, and every possible variety of objects in this beautiful branch of manufacture. He solicits, and will endeavour to merit, a continuance of the favours of the Public, which the late well-known House enjoyed in an eminent degree during a considerable number of years.

P. A. TACCHI'S SUCCESSOR has BRANCH ESTABLISHMENTS during the Season at

WIESBADEN AND EMS,

Where will always be found Selections of the newest Articles from his principal Establishment.

His Agents in England, to whom he undertakes to forward Purchases made of him, are Messrs. J. & R. M'CRACKEN, 7, Old Jewry, London.

DRESDEN.

MAGAZINE OF ANTIQUITIES AND FINE ARTS.

HELENA WOLFSOHN, née MEYER,

(SUCCESSOR OF L. MEYER AND SONS,)

5, SCHLOSSERGASSE,

BEGS respectfully to solicit the inspection of her Establishment, where she has always on show and for sale a most extensive assortment of Old Saxon China, Old Sèvres and Japan, Antique Furniture, Bronzes, Old Lace, such as Points de Bruxelles and d'Alençon, Points de Venise, Guipure, &c. &c. Venetian, Ruby, and Painted Glass, Rock Crystal, Ivory Work, Enamels, Mosaic Work, Armour, Gobelins Tapestry, Fans, and many other remarkable and curious articles.

HER CORRESPONDENTS IN ENGLAND ARE

Messrs. J. & R. M'CRACKEN, 7, Old Jewry, London.

WILLIAM HOFMANN,

BOHEMIAN GLASS MANUFACTURER,

TO HIS MAJESTY THE EMPEROR OF AUSTRIA,

RECOMMENDS his great assortment of Glass Ware, from his own Manufactories in Bohemia. The choicest Articles in every Colour, Shape, and Description, are sold, at the same moderate prices, at both his Establishments—

At Prague, Hotel Blue Star; at Vienna, 768, Lugeck.

Agents in London, Messrs. J. and R. M'CRACKEN, 7, Old Jewry.

Goods forwarded direct to England, America, &c.

LEGHORN.

HIACINTH MICALI AND SON,
Via Ferdinanda, No. 1230.

Manufactory of Marble, Alabaster, and Scagliola Tables, and Depôt of objects of Fine Arts.

Their extensive Show-rooms are always open to Visitors.

THEIR AGENTS IN ENGLAND ARE

MESSRS. J. AND R. M'CRACKEN,
7, Old Jewry, London.

CARLSBAD.

THOMAS WOLF,
MANUFACTURER OF

ORNAMENTAL GLASS WARES.

THOMAS WOLF begs to inform the Visitors to Carlsbad that at his Establishment will be found the finest and richest Assortment of the Crystal and Glass Wares of Bohemia— especially Table and Dessert Services— all at reasonable and fixed prices.

CORRESPONDENTS IN ENGLAND: Messrs. J. & R. M'CRACKEN, 7, Old Jewry

BERLIN.

C. HARSCH & CO.,

67, Unter den Linden,

FANCY GLASS WAREHOUSE,

BEG to call the attention of VISITORS to their EXTENSIVE ASSORTMENT of

BOHEMIAN, BAVARIAN, AND SILESIAN GLASS,

CONSISTING OF

ARTICLES OF EVERY DESCRIPTION,

OF THE NEWEST AND MOST ELEGANT PATTERNS.

Their Correspondents in London are Messrs. J. & R. M'CRACKEN, 7, Old Jewry.

ARGUS LIFE ASSURANCE COMPANY,

39, THROGMORTON STREET, BANK.

CHAIRMAN—THOMAS FARNCOMB, Esq., Alderman.
DEPUTY-CHAIRMAN—WILLIAM LEAF, Esq.

Rich. E. Arden, Esq.	Professor Hall, M.A.	Rupert Ingleby,Esq.	Jeremiah Pilcher,Esq.
Edward Bates, Esq.	J.Humphery,Esq.Ald.	S. W. Johnson, Esq.	Lewis Pocock, Esq.

PHYSICIAN—Dr. Jeaffreson, 2, Finsbury Square.
SURGEON—W. Coulson, Esq., 2, Frederick's Place, Old Jewry.
ACTUARY—George Clark, Esq.

ADVANTAGES OF ASSURING IN THIS COMPANY.

THE Premiums are on the lowest scale consistent with security.

The Assured are protected by a subscribed Capital of 300,000l., an Assurance Fund of 450,000l., invested on mortgage and in the Government Stocks, and an income of 85,000l. a-year.

Premiums to assure 100l.		Whole Term.	
Age.	One Year.	Seven Years.	With Profits.	Without Profits.
20	£0 17 8	£0 19 9	£1 15 10	£1 11 10
30	1 1 3	1 2 7	2 5 5	2 0 7
40	1 5 0	1 6 9	3 0 7	2 14 10
50	1 14 1	1 19 10	4 6 8	4 0 11
60	3 2 4	3 17 0	6 12 9	6 0 10

MUTUAL BRANCH.

ASSURERS on the Bonus System are entitled at the end of five years to participate in nine-tenths, or 90 per cent., of the profits.

The profit assigned to each policy can be added to the sum assured, applied in reduction of the annual premium, or be received in cash.

At the first division a return of 20 per cent. in cash on the premiums paid was declared; this will allow a reversionary increase varying, according to age, from 66 to 28 per cent. on the premiums, or from 5 to 15 per cent. on the sum assured.

One-half of the "Whole Term" Premium may remain on credit for seven years, or one-third of the Premium may remain for life as a debt upon the Policy at 5 per cent., or may be paid off at any time without notice.

Claims paid in one month after proofs have been approved.

Loans upon approved security.

No charge for Policy stamps.

Medical attendants paid for their reports.

Persons may, in time of peace, proceed to or reside in any part of Europe or British North America without extra charge.

The medical officers attend every day at a quarter before two o'clock.

E. BATES, *Resident Director.*

FRANKFORT O. M.

SILBERNE

STEMPEL,
bewilligt

vom

SENAT

der freien Stadt,

MEDAILLE

FRANKFURT.

FRIEDRICH BÖHLER,

MANUFACTORY OF STAGHORN,

Zeil No. 54 (next door to the Post-Office).

FURNITURE OF EVERY DESCRIPTION, as Sofas, Chairs, Tables, &c. &c. CHAN-
DELIERS, Table and Hand Candlesticks, Shooting-tackle, INKSTANDS, Paper-
knives, Penholders, Seals, &c. KNIVES, RIDING-WHIPS, Cigar-cases and
Holders, Pipes, Match-boxes, Porte-monnaies, Card-cases, Thermometers,
GOBLETS, Candle-screens, Figures and Groups of Animals executed after
Riedinger and others. BROOCHES, Bracelets, Earrings, Shirt-pins, Studs, and
Buttons. STAG AND DEER HEADS with Antlers attached to the Skull. Sofa-
rugs or Foot-cloths of Skins of Wild Animals with Head preserved.

Orders for a Complete Set or for any quantity of FURNITURE will be
promptly executed.

The Agents in London are Messrs. J. and R. McCRACKEN, 7, Old Jewry.

c

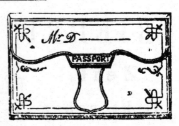

ROYAL INSURANCE COMPANY,

ROYAL INSURANCE BUILDINGS,
North John Street, and Dale Street, Liverpool,
AND
29, LOMBARD STREET, LONDON.

CAPITAL—£2,000,000 IN 100,000 SHARES OF £20 EACH.

THE City Article of the LONDON TIMES, of the 24th of July 1856, states that the transactions of the Royal Insurance Company "appear to have been of a perfectly satisfactory character." It includes the following statements confirmatory of that opinion :—

PREMIUMS.

The Premiums of Nine Offices enumerated are stated to be.. .. ..} £824,924

Of which the Royal alone amounts to   371,957

being 82 per cent. of the accumulated Premiums of the remaining eight Companies.

EXPENDITURE.

The accumulated Expenditure of 54 *Life Offices* enumerated by *The Times* of 12th August, 1856, compared with their amount of Premium and Interest, is stated to be 61 per cent.; the Expenditure of the Royal Insurance Company is only 13 per cent.

RESOURCES.

In like manner the entire Funds in hands of thirteen Offices are quoted in *The Times* at £1,238,688, including the "Royal," which alone is £372,324, and which is, therefore, equal to 43 per Cent. *of the accumulated Funds of the remaining twelve Offices,* viz. *for the year* 1855. Since increased to £600,000.

The following figures exhibit the RAPID GROWTH AND INCREASING RESOURCES OF THE COMPANY :—

Fire Premiums—1848	..	£31,346	Whilst last year, 1857, they
„ 1850	..	44,027	were.. .. ..£175,000
„ 1852	..	76,925	Total Revenue, 1857, all
„ 1854	..	128,459	sources 260,000
„ 1856	..	151,733	Increase on ONE YEAR alone 40,000

Funds in hand, to meet any claims, over £600,000.

LIFE.

LARGE BONUS DECLARED 1855,

Amounting to £2 per cent. per annum on the Sum Assured: being, on ages from Twenty to Forty, 80 per cent. on the Premium.

PERIODS OF DIVISION—EVERY FIVE YEARS.

PROGRESS OF THE LIFE BRANCH.

New Policies for the Year ending

	FIRE PREMIUMS.	SUM ASSURED.	PREMIUM.
June, 1855	396	£166,864	£4,667
„ 1856	654	288,321	8,370
„ 1857	756	391,158	11,894

Thus the New Assurers for the Year ending June, 1857, are 160 per cent. above those for the Year ending June, 1855.

PERCY M. DOVE, ACTUARY AND MANAGER.

The Company is willing to consider the propriety of establishing Agencies in Foreign places, where it has not at present any Representatives. Applications from Gentlemen of the highest position and character will alone receive attention.

CORNWALL MINING DISTRICT.

Mineralogy and Geology.

LAVIN'S MUSEUM, CHAPEL STREET, PENZANCE.

THE

LIZARD

SERPENTINE

ORNAMENTS.

VIEWS,

HANDBOOKS,

POCKET-MAPS,

ETC.

STUDENTS of Mineralogy and Geology, and Tourists to the Scenery, Antiquities, and Mines of Cornwall, will be interested by a visit to this Museum. The Collection of Cornish Minerals is unique, and contains specimens of the most interesting and rare substances, with perfect crystallizations, for which the above County has been so justly celebrated. **Selections made for Purchasers on various Scales.**

Minerals scientifically arranged in Trays containing 100, with descriptive Catalogue, from 1*l.* 5*s.* to 3*l.* Larger Specimens neatly set in a Mahogany Cabinet at 5*l.* More extensive Selections and first-rate specimens from 20*l.* to 50*l.* and upwards.

Geological Selections, comprehending Specimens of the various Rocks of the County, from 1*l.* upwards.

☞ A specimen of Carbonate of Iron, from Wheal Maudlin Mine, for which the sum of 130*l.* has been refused; as well as a great many others presumed to be unrivalled.

A LARGE ASSORTMENT OF THE LIZARD SERPENTINE ORNAMENTS.

Views of Scenery and Antiquities, Handbooks, Pocket-Maps of Cornwall and Devon.

Prompt attention given to all Orders from a distance.

ZURICH. — HOTEL BELLE VUE, By C. GUJER.

This excellent first-rate establishment, recently constructed, strongly recommended for its comfort and cleanliness, is in the best and most delightful situation on the bank of the lake opposite the landing-place of the steamers, commanding from its windows an extensive view over the lake, the Alps, and glaciers, as well as the quay and the town. It comprises upwards of 80 beds and 6 sitting-rooms, with separated breakfast and spacious dining saloons, a splendid and good restaurant à la carte, and English newspapers. Prices are moderate, a list of which will be found in each bed-room. Tables-d'hôte at 1 and 5 o'clock. Flys to meet all trains; a small boat meeting the steamers. English spoken by the servants.

From October till May a good pension (board) on reduced terms.

J. H. KEREZ,

CHEMIST AND DRUGGIST,

ZURICH,

RESPECTFULLY announces to Tourists and Visitors that he prepares and dispenses Medicines and Prescriptions according to the English Pharmacopœia with the purest and choicest Drugs and Chemicals. J. H. KEREZ, having been a principal dispensing Assistant at one of the first Houses in England, hopes that his experience and attention will merit the support and confidence of the English Nobility and Gentry.

J. H. K. keeps constantly on hand a well-selected Stock of the most popular English Patent Medicines and Perfumery.

SIR WALTER SCOTT'S WRITINGS AND LIFE.

AVERLEY NOVELS, *with the Author's ast Introductions, Notes, and Additions.*

BRARY EDITION. Illustrated by upwards of Two Hundred Engravings on Steel, after Drawings by Turner, Landseer, Wilkie, Stanfield, Roberts, &c., including Portraits of the historical personages described in the Novels. Complete in 25 volumes, demy 8vo., elegantly bound in extra cloth, 12l. 2s. 6d.

BBOTSFORD EDITION. With One Hundred and Twenty Engravings on Steel, and nearly Two Thousand on Wood. In 12 vols. super-royal 8vo. 14l. 14s.

JTHOR'S FAVOURITE EDITION, in 48 portable fcap. 8vo. vols. (96 Engravings), 7l. 4s.

ABINET EDITION, in 25 vols. fcap. 8vo. (26 Illustrations), 7s. 6d.

:OPLE'S EDITION, in 5 large vols. royal 8vo. 42s.

OETICAL WORKS—consisting of, 1st. The Metrical Romances,—THE LAY OF THE LAST MINSTREL, MARMION, THE LADY OF THE LAKE, ROKEBY, THE LORD OF THE ISLES, THE VISION OF DON RODERICK, THE BRIDAL OF TRIERMAIN, and HAROLD THE DAUNTLESS. 2nd. DRAMAS, SONGS, and BALLADS. 3rd. THE MINSTRELSY OF THE SCOTTISH BORDER.

e following are the only Copyright Editions, with the Author's last Notes & Improvements.

I. In One portable fcap. Vol. including all the Metrical Romances (except the 'Bridal of Triermain' and Harold'), the Principal Songs and Ballads, and several illustrations. Bound in cloth, gilt edges, 5s.; morocco antique, 10s.

II. In One crown 8vo. Vol. (same contents as previous edition), with numerous Engravings on Steel and Wood, after Sir David Wilkie, Stanfield, Gilbert, and Foster. Bound in cloth, gilt edges, 7s. 6d.; morocco ant. 14s.

III. In 12 Vols. fcp. 8vo. (24 Engravings), 36s. *This is the only edition which contains 'The Minstrelsy of the Scottish Border.'

IV. In 6 Vols. fcap. 8vo. (12 Engravings), 24s.

V. In One Vol. royal 8vo. (PEOPLE'S EDITION), 10s.

VI. The ABBOTSFORD EDITION, printed on Tinted Paper, with upwards of 60 Illustrations on Steel and Wood, after Turner, Gilbert, and Foster. Elegantly bound in extra cloth, gilt edges, 31s. 6d.; morocco elegant antique, 42s.

VII. TOURISTS' EDITIONS of The LAY of the LAST MINSTREL, MARMION, LADY of the LAKE, LORD of the ISLES, ROKEBY, and BRIDAL of TRIERMAIN, 1s. 3d. each; cloth, 1s. 6d.; morocco, gilt edges, 2s. 6d.

VIII. New Illustrated Editions of The LADY of the LAKE, MARMION, LAY of the LAST MINSTREL, and LORD of the ISLES, containing each from 90 to 100 Illustrations on Wood, by Birket Foster and John Gilbert. Printed in the best style on Tinted Paper, and elegantly bound in cloth, gilt edges, 18s. each; morocco elegant or antique, 25s.; enamelled tartan boards, 36s.

PROSE WORKS—consisting of, TALES OF A GRANDFATHER (History of Scotland), TALES OF A GRANDFATHER (History of France), LIFE OF JOHN DRYDEN, MEMOIRS OF JONATHAN SWIFT, MEMOIRS OF EMINENT NOVELISTS, &C., PAUL'S LETTERS TO HIS KINSFOLK, ESSAYS ON CHIVALRY, ROMANCE, AND THE DRAMA, &C., PROVINCIAL ANTIQUITIES OF SCOTLAND, LIFE OF NAPOLEON BONAPARTE, MISCELLANEOUS CRITICISMS, &C.

COMPLETE EDITIONS.

I. In 28 Vols. fcap. 8vo. with 56 Engravings from Turner, 84s.; separate volumes, 3s.

II. In 3 Vols. royal 8vo. (PEOPLE'S EDITION). Bound in cloth, 27s.; separate volumes, I. and II. 10s. each; III. (TALES of a GRANDFATHER), 6s.

Illustrated Edition of the TALES of a GRANDFATHER—(HISTORY OF SCOTLAND). With 6 Engravings after Turner, and upwards of 50 on Wood. In 3 Vols. fcap. 8vo. cloth, 12s.; extra cloth, gilt edges, 15s.

(HISTORY OF FRANCE). With 2 Engravings from Turner and upwards of 50 on Wood. 1 vol. fcap. 8vo. cloth, 4s.; extra cloth, gilt edges, 5s.

School Edition of the HISTORY of SCOTLAND, with Map. 2 vols. crown 8vo. bound, 10s.

LIFE of NAPOLEON BONAPARTE. 5 vols. fcap. 8vo. Maps, Portrait, and 9 Engravings after Turner, cloth, 20s.

Another Edition, in larger type. 9 vols. fcap. 8vo. Maps, Portraits, and Engravings, cloth, 27s.

SELECTIONS from Sir WALTER SCOTT'S WORKS—BELGIUM AND WATERLOO, FRANCE AND PARIS, TALES OF CHIVALRY, ROMANTIC NARRATIVES, CHARACTERS OF EMINENT PERSONS, THE HIGHLAND CLANS, SCOTTISH SCENES AND CHARACTERS, NARRATIVE AND DESCRIPTIVE PIECES.

Price Eighteenpence, or Two Shillings cloth.

BEAUTIES of SIR WALTER SCOTT; being Selections from his Writings and Life. 1 vol. crown 8vo., with Two Engravings, cloth gilt, 5s.; extra cloth, gilt sides and edges, 6s.

READINGS for the YOUNG, from the Works of Sir Walter Scott. 2 vols. with 26 Illustrations on Wood, 3s. 6d. each; or bound in 1 vol. cloth, gilt edges, 7s.

LIFE of SIR WALTER SCOTT. By J. G. LOCKHART, Esq. Three Editions as follows.

In Ten Vols. fcap. 8vo., uniform with the Author's Favourite Edition of the Novels. 20 Engravings on Steel, 30s.

In One Vol. royal 8vo., uniform with the Novels, PEOPLE'S EDITION. With Portrait, 10s.

The same, Large Paper, uniform with the Novels, ABBOTSFORD EDITION. With 11 Engravings from Turner, Portraits, &c., 18s.

In One Vol. crown 8vo., with 12 Engravings from Turner and others, 7s. 6d.; extra cloth, gilt edges, 8s. 6d.

Edinburgh: ADAM and CHARLES BLACK. London: HOULSTON and WRIGHT.
And all Booksellers.

THE NEW REGISTERED PORTMANTEAU,

REGISTERED AND MANUFACTURED BY

JOHN SOUTHGATE,

76, WATLING STREET,
LONDON.

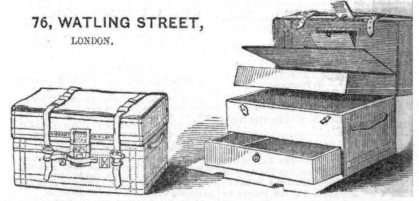

THIS Portmanteau is admitted by all who have used it to be the most PERFECT and USEFUL of an yet invented, and to combine all the advantages so long desired by those who travel.

Its peculiar conveniences consist in its containing SEPARATE COMPARTMENTS for each descriptio of Clothes, Boots, &c.; each division is kept entirely distinct, and is immediately accessible o opening the Portmanteau, without lifting or disturbing anything else; every article is packed pe fectly flat, and remains so during the whole of the journey.

SOUTHGATE'S NEW FOLDING PORTMANTEAU.

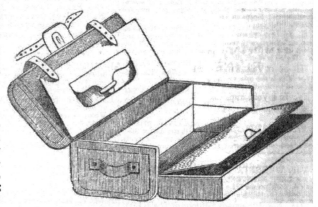

With separate divisions for Shirts, Linen, Clothes, and Boots; the whole of which are immediately accessible on opening the Portmanteau.

Both of these Portmanteaus are admirably adapted for Continental travelling, on account of the facility they offer for Customhouse examination, without disarranging the wardrobe.

JOHN SOUTHGATE'S LADIES' PORTMANTEAUS AND DRESS TRUNKS,

With Trays and Moveable Divisions for Bonnets, contain every convenience for packing separatel; Dresses, Bonnets, Linen, &c., and are made in various styles and sizes.

They may be obtained of Mr. WILKINSON, 30, Cockspur Street; of Messrs. MOORE & Co., 14, St James's Street, London; of Mr. HUNT, Above Bar, Southampton; of Mr. BAYS, Hatter, Cambridge of Mr. ELLENGER, Granger Street, Newcastle-on-Tyne; Mr. NORTHAM, Trunk Maker, opposite St Sidwell's Church, Exeter; Mr. DAMON, Weymouth; Mr. NICHOLSON, Saddler, Manchester; of anj Saddler or Outfitter throughout the kingdom; and of the Manufacturer,

JOHN SOUTHGATE, 76, WATLING STREET, LONDON.

SOUTH-EASTERN RAILWAY.

THE MAIL SHORT SEA-ROUTE TO ALL PARTS OF THE CONTINENT,
VIA FOLKESTONE AND BOULOGNE, AND DOVER AND CALAIS.

LONDON, PARIS, AND THE SOUTH OF EUROPE.

Paris in 10¼ hours. **Switzerland (Bale) 37½ hours.**
Marseilles 34 hours. **Bordeaux 38 hours.**
Sea-passage under 2 hours. **Four departures daily.**

1. By *Tidal Service via* Folkestone and Boulogne. For times of sailing
see Company's Time-book and Bradshaw's Guides.

This Service is now accelerated so as to perform the journey between
London and Paris in less than 11 hours. Small Boats are never used
in embarking or landing. The Trains are accompanied by an Inter-
preting Conductor.

OTHER SERVICES

Leave London		Arrive at Paris	Leave Paris	Arrive in London
2.	8.30 a.m. (viâ Calais)	10.20 p.m.	8. 0 a.m.	10. 0 p.m.
3.	1.30 p.m. „	5.30 a.m.	1.45 p.m.	4.30 a.m.
4.	8.30 p.m. „	9.10 a.m.	7.30 p.m.	7.45 a.m.

Baggage can be *registered* by all Through Trains.

LONDON AND PARIS.

There is a *Third Class* Service between these Cities. *Fare,* 25s.
Return Tickets are also issued, First and Second Class.

LONDON, BELGIUM, HANOVER, GERMANY, THE RHINE, AND THE NORTH OF EUROPE,

via Dover and Calais, and Dover and Ostend.

Brussels in 13 hours. **Berlin in 35 hours.**
Cologne in 19 hours. Hamburg in 36 hours.

Three departures from London daily, viz. 8.30 a.m. (the most
convenient Service), 1.30 p.m., and 8.30 p.m. Trains.

Baggage can be registered to Brussels, Cologne, &c., by which
each Passenger secures an allowance of 50 lbs. weight of Baggage *free*
on the Belgian and Rhenish Railways.

Through Tickets to nearly all the Chief Continental Cities (enabling
the passenger to stop at certain places on the journey) and all information may be obtained at the Chief Offices, London Bridge Station;
40, Regent Circus, Piccadilly. City: 147, Cheapside, and 20, Moor-
gate Street. Paris: 4, Boulevard des Italiens. Brussels: 74, Montagne de la Cour. For further particulars, see Time-book and Bills.

C. W. EBORALL, *General Manager*.

London Terminus, May, 1858.

TO TOURISTS AND TRAVELLERS.

PASSPORTS.—NEW REGULATIONS. BRITISH SUBJECTS who are preparing to visit or travel on the Continent may be saved much trouble and expense by obtaining Foreign Office Passports through EDWARD STANFORD'S Agency, 6, Charing Cross, London; whose experience and long established arrangements enable him to ensure Passports in proper form and duly *viséd*, according to the New Regulations, without personal attendance. He mounts the Passport, which is good for many years, on Muslin or Silk, in Roan, Morocco, or Russia Case, to prevent injury or loss, as well as to lessen delay in undergoing examination abroad. Residents in the country can have Passports obtained, completed, and forwarded by post.

For further particulars, including the Forms of Application, Cost of Passport, Visas, &c. &c., see Stanford's Passport Circular, which will be forwarded per post on application.

EDWARD STANFORD has on sale at all times the best English and Foreign Maps, Handbooks, and Railway Guides, Pocket Dictionaries, and Conversation Books.

THE FOLLOWING CATALOGUES,

Embracing various portions of EDWARD STANFORD'S *Stock, may be had upon application.*

1.—Ordnance Maps.—Catalogue of the ORDNANCE MAPS, published under the superintendence of LIEUT.-COLONEL JAMES, R.E., Superintendent of the Ordnance Surveys.

2.—Geological Survey Maps.—Catalogue of the GEOLOGICAL MAPS, SECTIONS and MEMOIRS of the GEOLOGICAL SURVEY of GREAT BRITAIN and IRELAND, under the superintendence of SIR RODERICK I. MURCHISON, Director-General of the Geological Surveys of the United Kingdom.

3.—Geological Maps.—Catalogues of the best GEOLOGICAL MAPS of various parts of the World.

4.—General Catalogue.—General Catalogue of Atlases, Maps, Charts, Plans &c., English and Foreign, including the Trigonometrical Surveys of various States.

5.—Useful Knowledge Maps.—Catalogue of Atlases, Maps, and Plans, engraved under the superintendence of THE SOCIETY FOR THE DIFFUSION OF USEFUL KNOWLEDGE.

6.—Admiralty Charts.—Catalogue of Charts, Plans, Views, and Sailing Directions, &c., published by order of the LORDS COMMISSIONERS OF THE ADMIRALTY, 178 pages royal 8vo., price 1s. 6d.

7.—War Department.—Catalogue of the Plans, Maps, and Drawings, issued by THE WAR DEPARTMENT, and sold by EDWARD STANFORD.

8.—Educational.—Catalogue of Educational Atlases and Maps, recently published by EDWARD STANFORD.

9.—Emigration.—A List of Publications on the British Colonies and the United States, selected from the Stock of EDWARD STANFORD.

10.—Johnston's Maps.—Johnston's List of Geographical and Educational Works, comprising Atlases, Maps, Globes, &c., sold wholesale and retail by EDWARD STANFORD.

11.—Guide-Books for Tourists.—Catalogue of Guide-Books, Maps, Plans, Dictionaries, and Conversation-Books, &c., for Tourists and Travellers.

LONDON : EDWARD STANFORD, 6, CHARING CROSS.

WORKS ON THE FINE ARTS.

The following are now Ready.

THE TREASURES OF ART: Being an Account of the Chief Collections of Paintings, Sculptures, Drawings, &c., in Great Britain. By Dr. WAAGEN. *2nd Thousand.* 4 vols. 8vo.

KUGLER'S HANDBOOK OF PAINTING: the ITALIAN SCHOOLS. Edited, with Notes, by Sir CHARLES EASTLAKE, R.A. *Third Edition.* With 150 Illustrations. 2 vols. Post 8vo. 30s.

THE EARLY FLEMISH PAINTERS: their LIVES and WORKS. By J. A. CROWE and G. B. CAVASELLE. Woodcuts. Post 8vo. 12s.

A HANDBOOK FOR YOUNG PAINTERS. By C. R. LESLIE, R.A. With Illustrations. Post 8vo. 10s. 6d.

HANDBOOK OF ARCHITECTURE: Being a Concise and Popular Account of the different Styles of Architecture prevailing in all Ages and all Countries. By JAMES FERGUSSON. *3rd Thousand.* With 850 Illustrations. 2 vols. 8vo. 36s.

A BIOGRAPHICAL DICTIONARY OF ITALIAN PAINTERS. Edited by R. N. WORNUM. With a Chart. Post 8vo. 6s. 6d.

LIFE OF THOMAS STOTHARD, R.A. By Mrs. BRAY. With 70 Illustrations. Small 4to.

MEDIÆVAL AND MODERN POTTERY. By JOSEPH MARRYAT. With Coloured Plates and 240 Woodcuts. Medium 8vo. 31s. 6d.

ANCIENT POTTERY: EGYPTIAN, ASSYRIAN, GREEK, ETRUSCAN, and ROMAN. By SAMUEL BIRCH, F.S.A. With Coloured Plates and 200 Woodcuts. 2 vols. Medium 8vo. 42s.

AN ILLUSTRATED HANDBOOK OF THE ARTS OF THE MIDDLE AGES AND RENAISSANCE. By M. J. LABARTE. With 200 Woodcuts. 8vo. 18s.

ANCIENT SPANISH BALLADS, HISTORICAL and ROMANTIC. Translated by J. G. LOCKHART. With Coloured Borders, Woodcuts, &c. 4to.

HORACE; HIS LIFE AND WORKS By DEAN MILMAN. With 300 Illustrations from the Antique. 8vo. 30s.

THE ILLUSTRATED PRAYER-BOOK. With Borders, Initial Letters, and Illustrations from the Old Masters. 8vo. 21s.

THE ANCIENT EGYPTIANS; their PRIVATE LIFE, MANNERS and CUSTOMS. By Sir J. G. WILKINSON. With 500 Woodcuts. 2 vols. Post 8vo. 12s.

JOHN MURRAY, ALBEMARLE STREET.

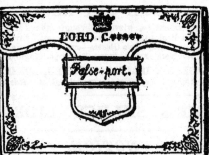

LONDON: W. CLOWES AND SONS, STAMFORD STREET, AND CHARING CROSS.

CPSIA information can be obtained
at www.ICGtesting.com
Printed in the USA
LVOW02*1458200617
538746LV00011B/245/P